HARCOURT
SOCiAL Studies

People We Know

HOUGHTON MIFFLIN HARCOURT
School Publishers

People We Know

ISBN-13: 978-0-15-385896-3
ISBN-10: 0-15-385896-6

11   0877   18 17 16 15
4500546828   BCDEFG

Contents

Program Contributors

SERIES AUTHORS

Dr. Michael J. Berson
Professor
Social Science Education
University of South Florida
Tampa, Florida

Dr. Tyrone C. Howard
Associate Professor
UCLA Graduate School of Education &
Information Studies
University of California at Los Angeles
Los Angeles, California

Dr. Cinthia Salinas
Assistant Professor
Department of Curriculum and
Instruction
College of Education
The University of Texas at Austin
Austin, Texas

SERIES CONSULTANTS

Dr. Marsha Alibrandi
Assistant Professor
Social Studies Teacher Education
Department of Curriculum and Instruction
Graduate School of Education and Allied
Professions
Fairfield University
Fairfield, Connecticut

Dr. Patricia G. Avery
Professor
College of Education and Human
Development
University of Minnesota
Minneapolis/St. Paul, Minnesota

Dr. Linda Bennett
Associate Professor
College of Education
University of Missouri–Columbia
Columbia, Missouri

Dr. Walter C. Fleming
Department Head and Professor
Native American Studies
Montana State University
Bozeman, Montana

Dr. S. G. Grant
Dean
School of Education
Binghamton University
Binghamton, New York

C. C. Herbison
Lecturer
African and African-American Studies
University of Kansas
Lawrence, Kansas

Dr. Eric Johnson
Assistant Professor
Director, Urban Education Program
School of Education
Drake University
Des Moines, Iowa

Dr. Bruce E. Larson
Professor
Social Studies Education
Secondary Education
Woodring College of Education
Western Washington University
Bellingham, Washington

Dr. Merry M. Merryfield
Professor
Social Studies and Global Education
College of Education
The Ohio State University
Columbus, Ohio

Dr. Peter Rees
Associate Professor
Department of Geography
University of Delaware
Wilmington, Delaware

Dr. Phillip J. VanFossen
James F. Ackerman Professor of Social
Studies Education
Director, James F. Ackerman Center for
Democratic Citizenship
Associate Director, Purdue Center for
Economic Education
Purdue University
West Lafayette, Indiana

Dr. Myra Zarnowski
Professor
Elementary and Early Childhood Education
Queens College
The City University of New York
Flushing, New York

CONTENT AND CLASSROOM REVIEWERS

Elaine Baggett
Teacher
Rivercrest Elementary School
Bartlett, Tennessee

Dr. Davarian L. Baldwin
Associate Professor
History Department
Boston College
Chestnut Hill, Massachusetts

Nancy Ballard
Teacher
Vandergriff Elementary School
Fayetteville, Arkansas

Deborah Batchelor
Field Consultant
Maryland Council on Economic Education
Towson University
Towson, Maryland

Melissa Bearden
Teacher
Otter Creek Elementary School
Little Rock, Arkansas

Connie Bingham
Teacher
Elm Tree Elementary
Bentonville, Arkansas

Kathy Bisol
Teacher
Bradford Elementary School
Bradford, Massachusetts

Marsha Blevins
Teacher
Earlywine Elementary School
Oklahoma City, Oklahoma

Dr. José António Brandão
Associate Professor
Department of History
Western Michigan University
Kalamazoo, Michigan

Alicia Campbell
Teacher
Oakmont Elementary School
Columbus, Ohio

Dr. Dean Antonio Cantu
Dean, Division of Education
Indiana University Kokomo
Kokomo, Indiana

Barbara Clark
Teacher
Southwind Elementary School
Memphis, Tennessee

Amy Cody
Teacher
Winds West Elementary School
Oklahoma City, Oklahoma

Dr. Steven Conn
Professor
Department of History
The Ohio State University
Columbus, Ohio

Jennifer Cook
Teacher
Walton-Verona Elementary School
Verona, Kentucky

Dr. Daniel P. Donaldson
Associate Professor of Geography
University of Central Oklahoma
Edmond, Oklahoma

Dr. Michael B. Dougan
Professor Emeritus
Department of History
Arkansas State University
Jonesboro, Arkansas

Christy Elmore
Teacher
Santa Fe Elementary School
Moore, Oklahoma

Tania Farran
Teacher
Rock Creek Elementary School
O'Fallon, Missouri

David Figurski
Teacher
Wilde Elementary School
Warren, Michigan

Dr. Maria E. Franquiz
Associate Professor
The Division of Bicultural-Bilingual
Studies
The University of Texas at San Antonio
San Antonio, Texas

Kelly Fusco
Teacher
Mackeben Elementary School
Algonquin, Illinois

Unit 1

Governing the People

I VOTED!

Unit 2

The World Around Us

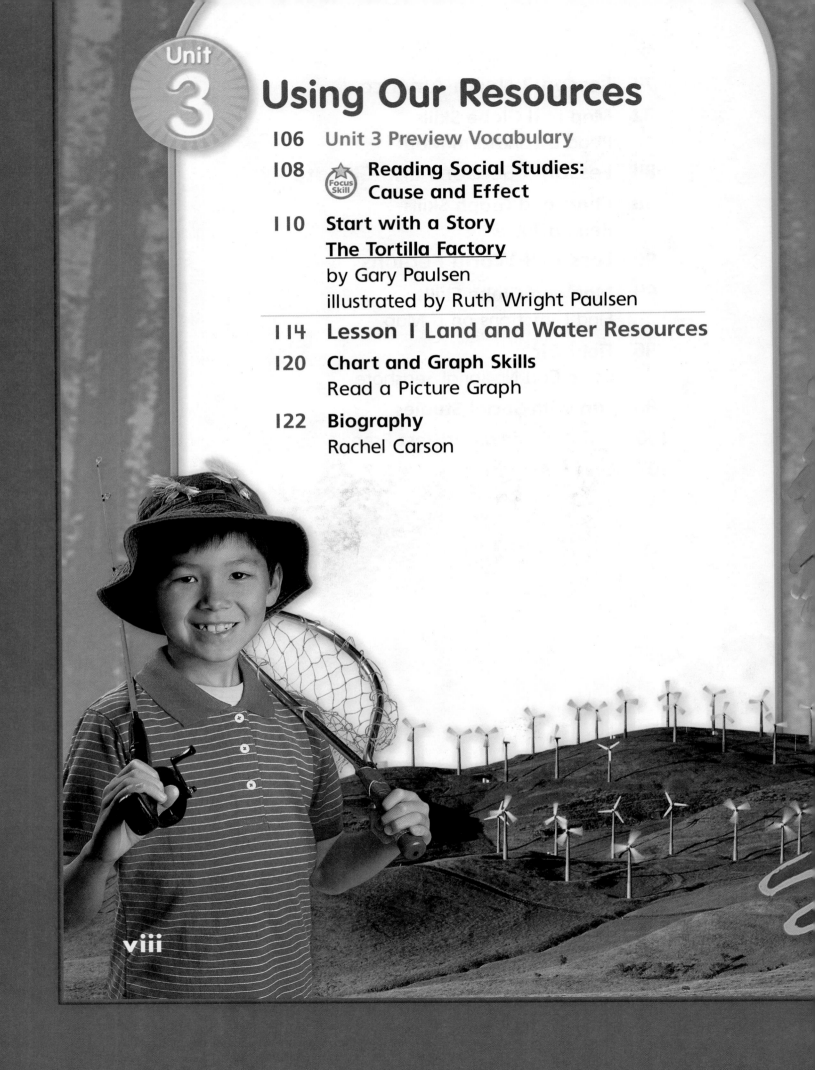

Unit 3

Using Our Resources

Unit 4 People Long Ago

xi

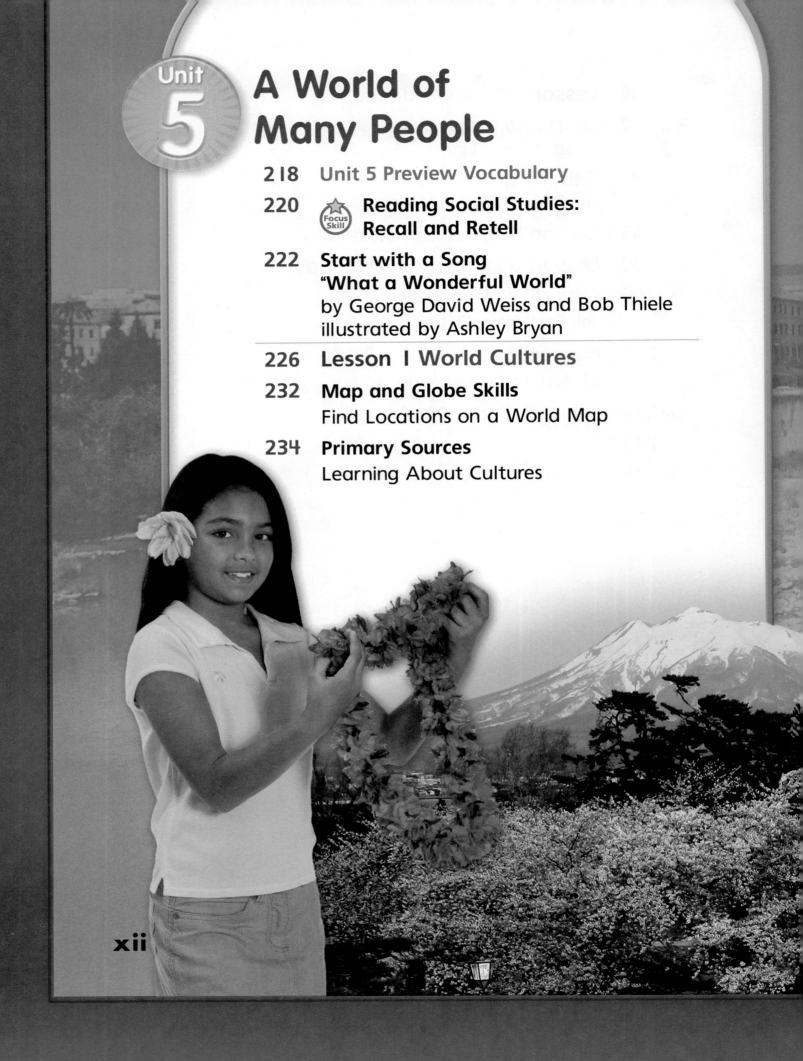

Unit 5

A World of Many People

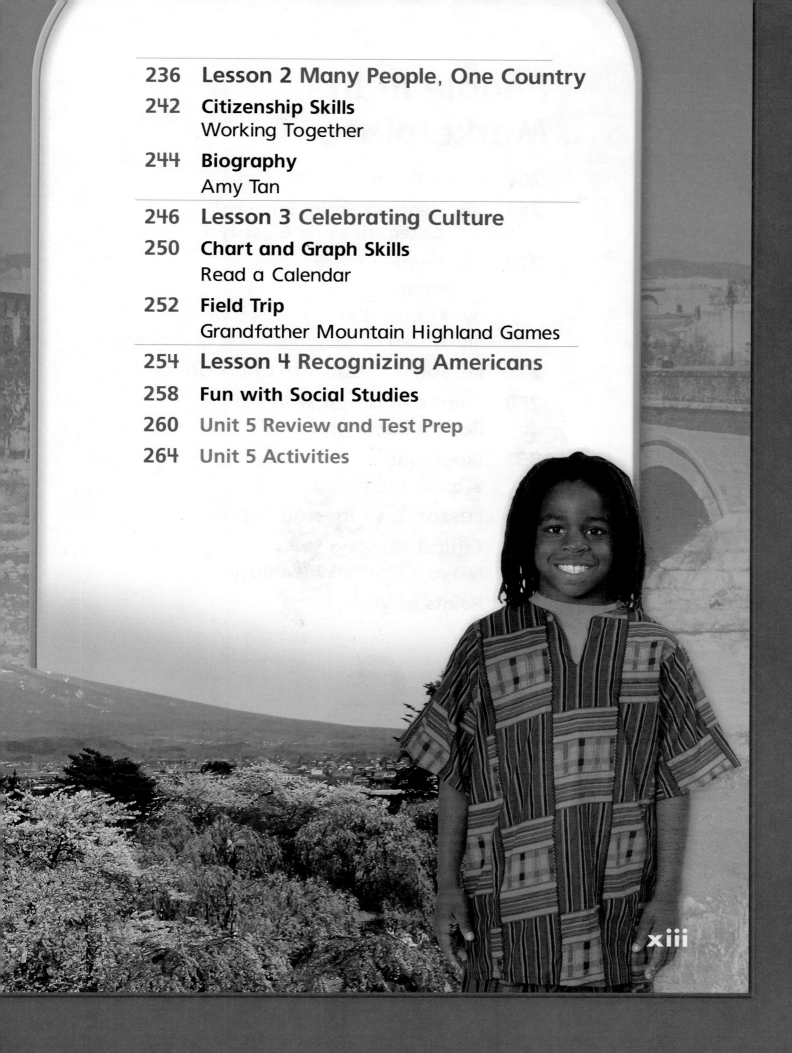

xiii

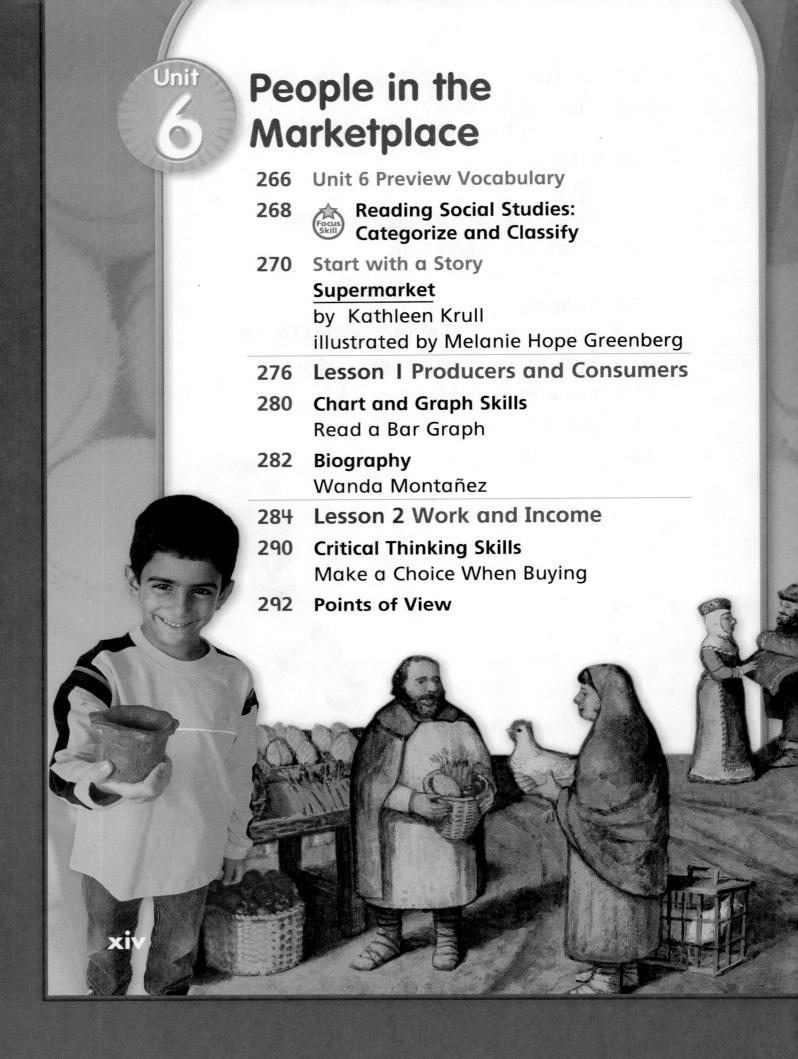

Unit 6

People in the Marketplace

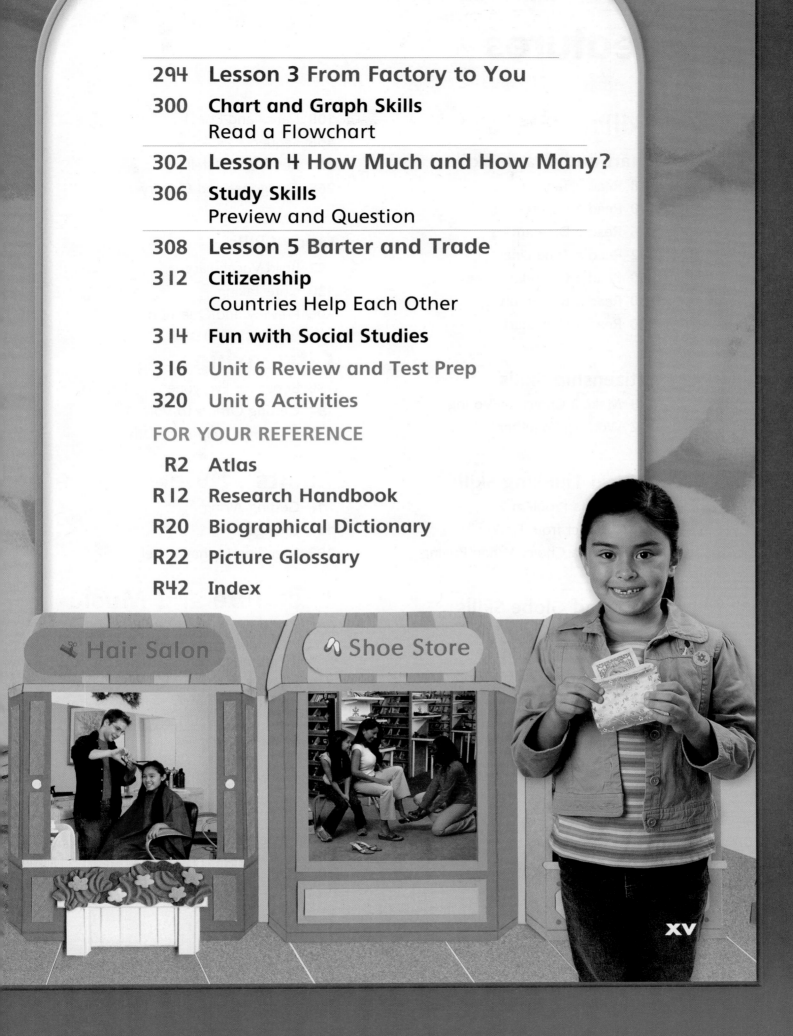

Hair Salon

Shoe Store

Features

Skills

Chart and Graph Skills

Citizenship Skills

Critical Thinking Skills

Map and Globe Skills

Reading Social Studies

Study Skills

Citizenship

Points of View

Literature and Music

Maps

Time Line

Illustrations

The Story Well Told

"I wanted children now to understand more about the beginnings of things . . . what it is that made America as they know it."
Laura Ingalls Wilder in Laura Ingalls Wilder: A Biography
by W. Anderson

Do you ever wonder about people who lived in a different time or place? This year you will be learning about how families have changed over **time**. You will meet special **people** who we remember for the important work they have done. Also, you will visit **places** near and far. You will see where people live and how they use the land around them.

People We Know

I1

You can learn how people lived long ago by reading the story of a family's past.

Important people teach us how to behave.

We get most of our resources
from the land.

13

Reading Your Textbook

GETTING STARTED

Unit title •

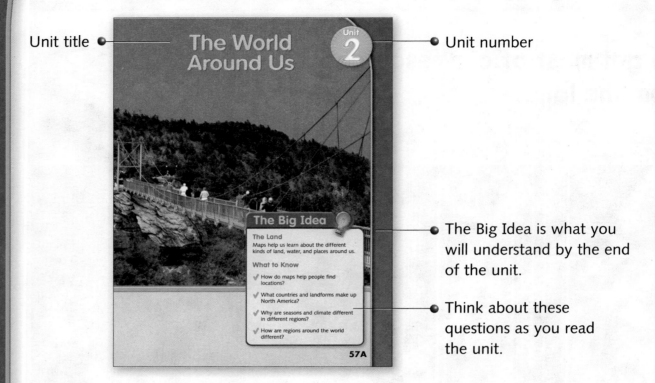

• Unit number

• The Big Idea is what you will understand by the end of the unit.

• Think about these questions as you read the unit.

PREVIEW VOCABULARY

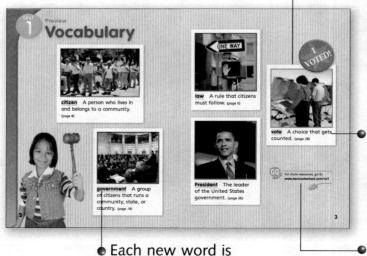

• A photograph helps you understand the meaning of the word.

• The definition tells you what the word means. The page number tells you where to find the word in this unit.

• Each new word is highlighted in yellow.

• The unit has more information and activities on the website.

READING SOCIAL STUDIES

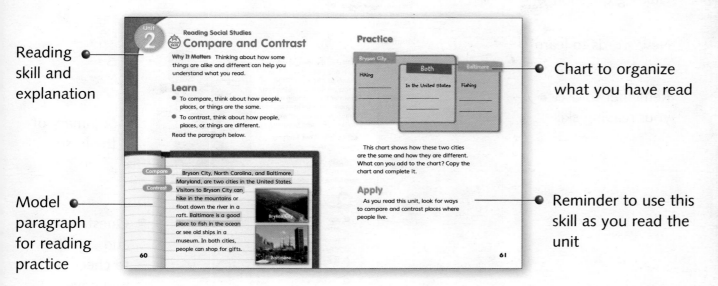

Reading skill and explanation

Model paragraph for reading practice

Chart to organize what you have read

Reminder to use this skill as you read the unit

START WITH LITERATURE

Every unit starts with a story, play, poem, song, article, or folktale.

Questions to practice the unit reading skill and to talk about personal experiences

READING A LESSON

Lesson number

Guiding question

New words to learn

Reminder to use your reading skill

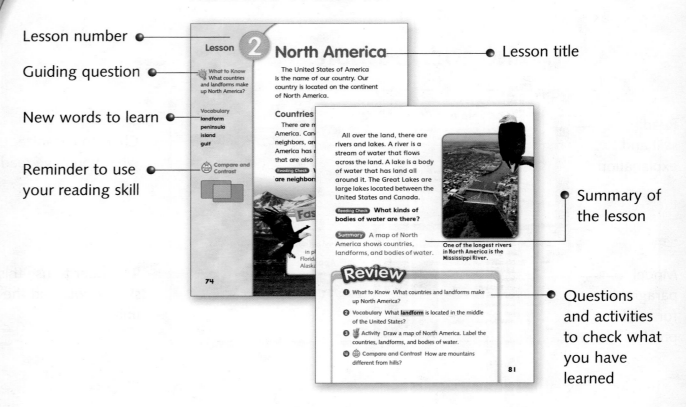

Lesson title

Summary of the lesson

Questions and activities to check what you have learned

PRACTICING SKILLS

Skill lessons help you build your map and globe, chart and graph, study, critical thinking, and citizenship skills.

Skill category
Skill lesson title

Why the skill is important

Steps to learn the skill

Skill practice questions

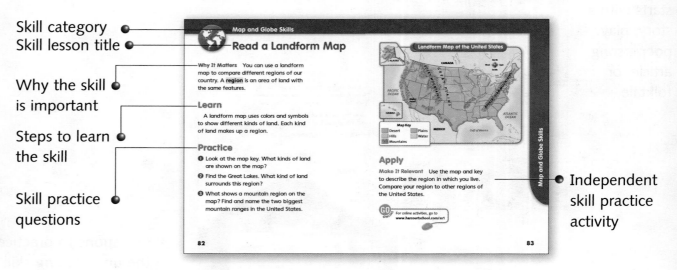

Independent skill practice activity

SPECIAL FEATURES

Name of the biography

Discussion of the person's character

Website for more information and other biographies

Important dates in the person's life

Citizenship features tell you about active citizens today.

Points of View shows how people may think differently.

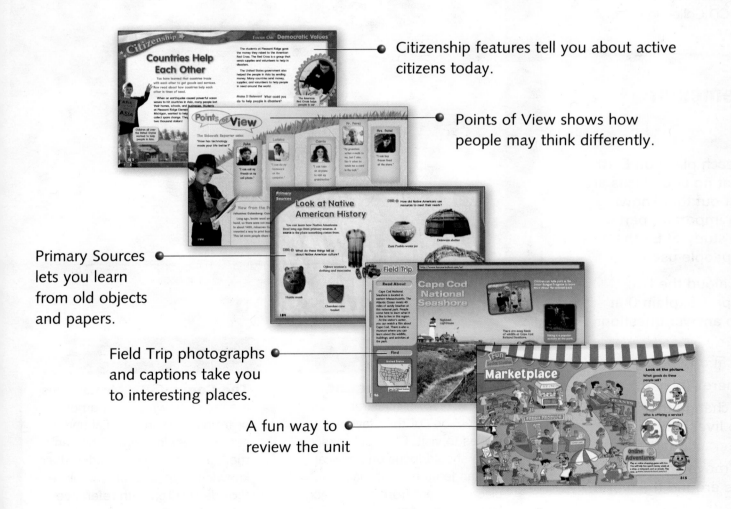

Primary Sources lets you learn from old objects and papers.

Field Trip photographs and captions take you to interesting places.

A fun way to review the unit

Go to the Reference section in the back of this book to see other special features.

17

OBJECTIVES

- Explain the five themes of geography.

- Use a globe and a map to look at Earth.

- Recognize the geography terms *continent, country, city,* and *state.*

- Explain how to read a map and use map symbols.

- Recognize different kinds of landforms and bodies of water.

RESOURCES

Primary Atlas; Interactive Atlas; Interactive Map Transparencies; Unit 1 Audiotext CD Collection; Internet Resources

The Five Themes of Geography

Tell children that each place on Earth is different and that no two places are exactly alike. Point out that knowing about places is an important part of geography, or the study of Earth's surface and the way people use it.

Geography Read aloud the five themes of geography. Explain that these themes help answer questions about a place.

- Where is it? (location)

- What is it like there? (place)

- How do people change their surroundings to live? (human-environment interactions)

- How do people move and trade goods and ideas around the world? (movement)

- How is this place like other places? How is it different? (regions)

Discuss each of the five themes.

The Five Themes of Geography

The story of people is also the story of where they live. When scientists talk about Earth, they think about five themes or main ideas.

GEOGRAPHY

Location

Everything on Earth has its own place.

Place

Every place has features that make it different from other places.

I8

Practice and Extend

INTEGRATE THE CURRICULUM

READING/LANGUAGE ARTS Ask children to write descriptions of their favorite places to visit. Children's descriptions should focus on physical and human features that make the place different from other places. **Write a Descriptive Paragraph**

MENTAL MAPPING

The Community Mental maps are maps drawn from memory or from a person's spatial understanding. By looking at children's mental maps, you can judge their knowledge of location and place. Provide children with reference materials that show where landforms and bodies of water are located in their neighborhood. Have children draw a mental map of their neighborhood, showing where these are located.

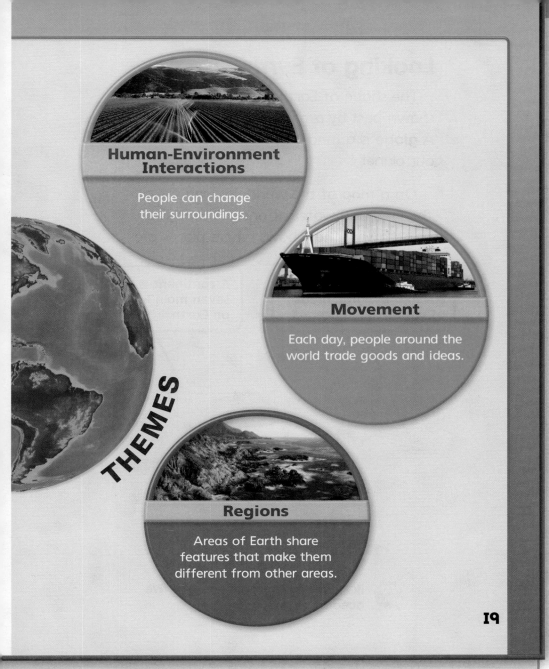

Human-Environment Interactions

People can change their surroundings.

Movement

Each day, people around the world trade goods and ideas.

THEMES

Regions

Areas of Earth share features that make them different from other areas.

I9

Location is where something can be found on Earth. Tell children that a location is described in many ways.

Q How can you describe the location of your school? your city? your state?

A Children's answers should describe the relative location of each place.

Place is made up of features made by nature or by humans. Challenge children to name examples of features in their community.

Human-Environment Interactions tell how people change their surroundings to make their lives better. Ask children to identify the ways people can change their surroundings.

Movement is how people move around the world and how they trade goods and ideas around the world.

Q How might goods and things be moved from place to place?

A Possible answers: by airplanes, by boats, by trucks, and by trains.

Regions are areas with certain features. A region can be described by its landforms, plant life, or climate. It can also be described by a common way of life, such as sharing the same language.

The Essential Elements of Geography In addition to the five themes of geography, geographers also use six other topics when they study a place. These six topics are called the six essential elements of geography.

- **The World in Spatial Terms** Geographers use maps and other kinds of information to study relationships among people and places. They want to know why things are located where they are.

- **Places and Regions** People are linked to the places and regions in which they live. Places and regions have both physical and human features.

- **Physical Systems** Physical processes, such as wind and rain, shape Earth's surface. Living things interact with physical features to create and change environments.

- **Human Systems** People's activities include where they

settle, how they earn a living, and the laws they make. All of these help shape Earth's surface.

- **Environment and Society** People's activities often affect the environment, and the environment often affects people's activities.

- **The Uses of Geography** Knowing how to use maps, globes, and other geography tools helps people in their everyday lives.

Looking at Earth

Tell children that *geography* is the name we give to all the special ways of looking at Earth. Explain that people usually look at Earth by using a map or a globe, two important tools of geography. Remind children that a *map* is a flat drawing of Earth and can show Earth's large bodies of water and continents at once.

Geography Direct children to examine a classroom globe. Have them find the equator, and explain that the equator divides Earth into a Northern Hemisphere and a Southern Hemisphere. Point out that Earth is also divided into a Western Hemisphere and an Eastern Hemisphere. Tell children they will learn more about hemispheres in Unit 2.

Visual Literacy: Map Direct children's attention to the map on page I10.

Q What do you think Earth has more of—land or water?

A water

ANSWER: Africa, Antarctica, Asia, Australia, Europe, North America, South America; Arctic, Atlantic, Indian, Pacific, Southern

Looking at Earth

The shape of Earth is shown best by a globe. A **globe** is a model of our planet.

On a map of the world you can see all the land and water at once. A **map** is a flat drawing that shows where places are.

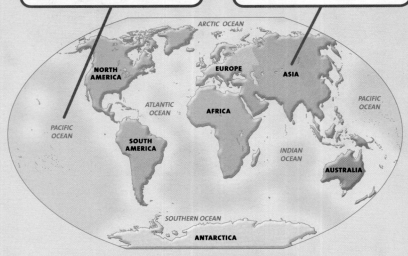

> Much of the world is covered by large areas of water called **oceans**.

> A **continent** is one of seven main land areas on Earth.

Map labels: ARCTIC OCEAN, NORTH AMERICA, EUROPE, ASIA, PACIFIC OCEAN, ATLANTIC OCEAN, AFRICA, PACIFIC OCEAN, SOUTH AMERICA, INDIAN OCEAN, AUSTRALIA, SOUTHERN OCEAN, ANTARCTICA

MAP SKILL Name the seven continents and five oceans you see on the map.

I10

Practice and Extend

MENTAL MAPPING

The Oceans of North America Have children draw the continent of North America. Ask them to point to where the Atlantic Ocean and Pacific Ocean are in relation to their map drawing. Have them label the oceans on their sketch of the continent. After children have finished their drawings, have them compare their map with an actual map of North America.

VOCABULARY POWER

Word Origin Tell children that the word *continent* is of Latin origin. It comes from *terra continens*, which means "continuous land."

Your Address

You live on the continent of North America in a **country** called the United States. Your address names the **city** and **state** in which you live.

What is your address?

I11

Your Address

Explain to children that their address is a location that tells exactly where they live. Explain that people also use the geographic terms *continent, country, state,* and *city* to tell where they live.

Visual Literacy: Pictures Direct children's attention to the illustrations on page I11. Explain that Mari Tyler lives on the continent of North America, just as they do. Then tell children that, like Mari Tyler, they live in the country called the United States, which is one country on the continent. Explain that she lives in the state of Ohio, which is in the United States, and that she lives in the city of Columbus, which is in Ohio.

Q What city and state do you live in?

A Answers will vary.

Explain to children that, generally speaking, continents contain countries, some countries contain states, states contain cities, and cities contain streets. Tell children that, by knowing this information, they can find the location of almost anyone in the world.

ANSWER: Answers will vary.

ELL ENGLISH LANGUAGE LEARNERS

Have children say and write home addresses.

(Beginning) Have children say and write their house number and street address.

(Intermediate) Have children say and write their full address including city, state, and zip code.

(Advanced) Have children write their home address on an envelope.

BACKGROUND

ZIP Codes In 1963, the United States Postal Service began using a five-digit ZIP code to expedite the delivery of mail. ZIP stands for Zone Improvement Plan, but was also meant to suggest that mail travels faster. The numbers represent specific areas of the United States. The numbers increase as you move from east to west across the country.

View from Above

Explain to children that using a map is like looking at an area or region from above. Tell children that looking at areas from above helps people find locations because they can see many things all at once, without trees or houses blocking the view.

Visual Literacy: Picture Direct children's attention to the photograph on page I12. Point out the streets, houses and different buildings in the picture. Explain to children that they probably could not see all of these things if the picture was taken from the ground level.

ANSWER: It helps to show where everything in a neighborhood is located. It helps you see what places are near a location.

View from Above

Does your neighborhood have a school, a grocery store, a library, a fire station, a park, and a bank? These are places that people share in a neighborhood. You can learn about a neighborhood by looking at a photograph.

How does a photograph taken from above help you study a neighborhood?

I12

Practice and Extend

VISUAL ARTS Arrange common objects from the classroom on the floor. Invite children to draw objects from above. Tell children to draw all of the objects and to draw them in relationship to each other, as they see them on the floor. Remind them to label objects in their drawing. **Draw an Illustration**

READING/LANGUAGE ARTS Have children work in small groups. Have each group draw a replica on construction paper, or make a copy, of the photograph on page I12. Have children cut out the picture to make a postcard. On the back side of the postcard, have children write a note of what the picture describes. Provide children the address of the school and have them address the postcard. **Write a Postcard**

You can also learn about a neighborhood by looking at a map. Mapmakers draw symbols to help you find places on the map. A **map symbol** is a small picture or shape that stands for a real thing. The **map title** tells you what the map shows.

How is this map like the photograph? How is it different?

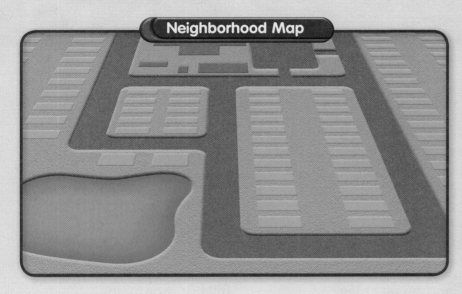

Neighborhood Map

113

Geography Remind children that a map is a drawing of a view from above. Tell children that maps help people find locations. Discuss why reading maps is an important skill. Have children brainstorm ways they might use maps in social studies. Emphasize that maps help us learn about our country and the world.

Visual Literacy: Map Direct children's attention to the map on page I13. Explain to children that map symbols are pictures or symbols that help people find specific locations on a map.

Q What are the map symbols for this neighborhood map?

A The squares stand for buildings.

Explain to children that map titles tell what the map shows. People use map titles to know what kind of map they are reading.

Q What is the map title for the map on page I13?

A Neighborhood Map

Q What would you expect to find on this map?

A buildings, streets, parks, and other features of a neighborhood

ANSWERS: The map is like the photograph because it shows the place from above. It is different because the map does not show real things like the photograph does.

BACKGROUND

Map Key Symbols Not all maps use the same symbols in the map key. However, a star is the most widely used symbol for national and state capitals. The national capital is often represented with a bigger star than state capitals. The national capital is also often set within a circle. In addition, the line for a national border is generally darker and thicker than the line for a state or county border.

Geography Terms

Direct children's attention to the illustration on page I14. Tell children that this illustration shows many of the different kinds of landforms and bodies of water found on Earth. Explain to children that a landform is a physical feature, such as a plain, hill, mountain, or valley, on Earth's surface. Tell them that they will learn more about landforms and bodies of water in Unit 2, and can use this page for reference.

Visual Literacy: Diagram Invite children to read the definition for each kind of landform and body of water and to find that feature on the diagram. Ask children if they have seen any of these features, either in their communities or in their travels to other places. Explain that people sometimes build things to help them use a landform or body of water for trade and movement.

Q Why might a bridge be important to people who need to get to the other side of a body of water?

A Possible answer: Bridges make it easier for people to cross a river or lake, rather than going around it.

Geography Tell children that water naturally goes from higher to lower ground. Because of this, a stream or river always flows from higher ground at its source, such as a mountain, to lower ground at its mouth. Explain that a stream or river may flow into another stream or river or into a large body of water, such as a lake, a gulf, or an ocean.

Geography Terms

mountain

valley

river

hill

plain

desert

forest

lake

peninsula

island

gulf

ocean

desert a large, dry area of land

forest a large area of trees

gulf a large body of ocean water that is partly surrounded by land

hill land that rises above the land around it

island a landform with water all around it

lake a body of water with land on all sides

mountain highest kind of land

ocean a body of salt water that covers a large area

peninsula a landform that is surrounded on only three sides by water

plain flat land

river a large stream of water that flows across the land

valley low land between hills or mountains

I14

Practice and Extend

MAKE IT RELEVANT

In Your Community Ask children to study a map of their community. Challenge them to use the map to locate as many examples of landforms and bodies of water that they can. Have children draw a map of their community including the landforms and bodies of water and label each feature on their map.

REACH ALL LEARNERS

Leveled Practice Have children review the illustration on page I14 and the definitions.

(**Basic**) Say a term. Have children point to the example in the diagram.

(**Proficient**) Say a term from the list, and have children identify it as a body of water or a landform.

(**Advanced**) Say a term and have children use it in a sentence.

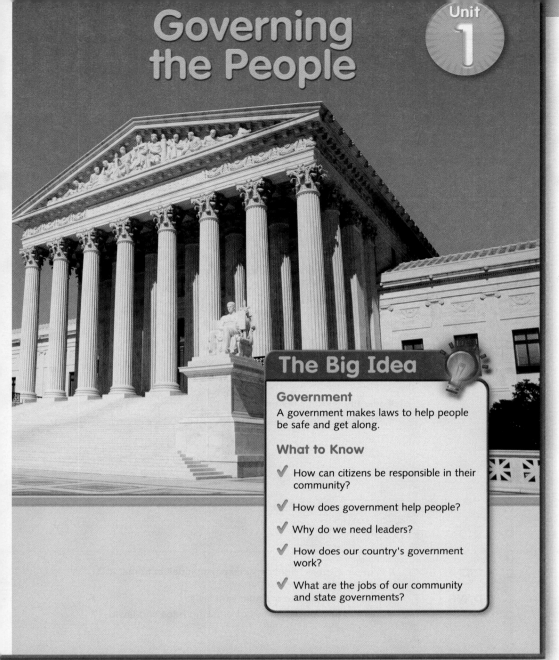

Governing the People

The Big Idea

Government
A government makes laws to help people be safe and get along.

What to Know

✔ How can citizens be responsible in their community?

✔ How does government help people?

✔ Why do we need leaders?

✔ How does our country's government work?

✔ What are the jobs of our community and state governments?

Introduce the Unit

The Big Idea

Government Read the Big Idea to children. Explain that government helps people live together in an orderly and safe way. In this unit, children will learn how Americans choose leaders and make laws. They will look at the rights and responsibilities of citizens. They will discover how the governments of a community, a state, and our country are alike and different. Remind children to refer back to the Big Idea periodically as they finish this unit.

What to Know Read What to Know to children. Explain that these five essential questions will help them focus on the Big Idea.

Assessing the Big Idea Share with children that throughout this unit they will be asked to show evidence of their understanding of the Big Idea. See Assessment Options on page 1M of this Teacher Edition.

START WITH A VIDEO DVD

To introduce the Unit Big Idea to students, show a video clip from the Start with a Video DVD.

Instructional Design

The flowchart below shows briefly how instruction was planned for Unit 1.

START WITH THE BIG IDEA	PLAN ASSESSMENT	PLAN INSTRUCTION
Lesson Objectives What to Know	Assessment Options • Option 1—Unit 1 Test • Option 2—Writing: Write a Letter • Option 3—Unit Project: Lawmaker Role-Play	Unit 1 Teacher Edition • materials • instructional strategies • activities

Governing the People

THE BIG IDEA

GOVERNMENT A government makes laws to help people be safe and get along.

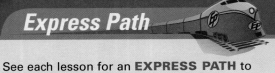

Express Path

See each lesson for an **EXPRESS PATH** to teach main ideas.

LESSON	PACING	OBJECTIVES
Preview the Unit pp. 1V–1	**4** **DAYS**	
Preview Vocabulary pp. 2–3		■ Use visuals to determine word meanings. ■ Use words and visuals to preview the content of the unit.
Reading Social Studies pp. 4–5		■ Identify the main idea of a paragraph. ■ Identify detail sentences in a paragraph. ■ Interpret information from charts.
Start with a Song "The Star-Spangled Banner" pp. 6–7		■ Identify patriotic elements in a song. ■ Understand the concepts of freedom and bravery.
① Citizens in a Community pp. 8–13 💡 **WHAT TO KNOW** How can citizens be responsible in their community?	**3** **DAYS**	■ Explain citizens' rights and responsibilities at home, at school, and in the community. ■ Recognize the need for rules and laws. ■ Identify the consequences of breaking rules and laws.
CRITICAL THINKING SKILLS **Solve a Problem** pp. 14–15	**1** **DAY**	■ Use a problem-solving process to identify a problem, gather information, and list possible solutions. ■ Describe the consequences of different solutions.
Points of View pp. 16–17	**1** **DAY**	■ Compare and contrast children's daily lives to those of others. ■ Explore different points of view about what individuals do to get along with one another.

6 WEEKS	WEEK 1	WEEK 2	WEEK 3	WEEK 4	WEEK 5	WEEK 6
	Introduce the Unit	Lesson 1	Lesson 2	Lesson 3	Lesson 4	Lesson 5	Wrap Up the Unit

READING SUPPORT VOCABULARY

Focus Skill Reading Social Studies
Main Idea and Details

Reading Social Studies
Focus Skill, pp. 4–5

Vocabulary Power:
Suffixes, p. 3

main idea p. 4
details p. 4

Focus Skill Reading Social Studies
Main Idea and Details
p. 13

Vocabulary Power:
Synonyms, p. 10

community p. 8
citizen p. 8
right p. 9
responsibility p. 10
law p. 11
consequence p. 12

problem p. 14
solution p. 14

REACH ALL LEARNERS

ENGLISH LANGUAGE LEARNERS, p. 2

Leveled Practice, pp. 5, 6

ENGLISH LANGUAGE LEARNERS, p. 11

Leveled Practice, pp. 12, 15, 17

INTEGRATE LEARNING

Reading/Language Arts
Use Prefixes, p. 1
Write a Paragraph, p. 4

Physical Education
Game Rules, p. 1

Health
Safety, p. 10

RESOURCES

Social Studies in Action:
Resources for the Classroom
Primary Source Collection
⊙ Music CD
School-to-Home Newsletter S3–S4
Interactive Map Transparencies
Interactive Desk Maps
Primary Atlas
Interactive Atlas
TimeLinks: Interactive Time Line
Picture Vocabulary Cards
Focus Skills Transparency 1
Main Idea and Details Graphic Organizer Write-On/Wipe-Off Card
Assessment Program p. 1
⊙ Unit 1 Audiotext CD Collection
Internet Resources
⊙ Start with a Video DVD

Homework and Practice Book, pp. 1–2
Reading Support and Intervention, pp. 2–5
Success for English Language Learners, pp. 2–5
Vocabulary Transparency 1-1
Focus Skills Transparency 1
Main Idea and Details Graphic Organizer Write-On/Wipe-Off Card
Activity Pattern 3
Social Studies Skills Transparency 1-1
⊙ Unit 1 Audiotext CD Collection
Internet Resources

LESSON	PACING	OBJECTIVES
2 **Government for the People** pp. 18–21 💡 **WHAT TO KNOW** How does government help people?	**3** **DAYS**	■ Identify and describe functions of government. ■ Understand how government works to help citizens through services paid for by taxes.
STUDY SKILLS **Build Vocabulary** pp. 22–23	**1** **DAY**	■ Use a word web to connect related ideas. ■ Create a word web about government based on ideas presented in the unit.
3 **Our Leaders** pp. 24–27 💡 **WHAT TO KNOW** Why do we need leaders?	**3** **DAYS**	■ Describe why we need leaders. ■ Explain how citizens choose leaders. ■ Identify local, state, and national leaders and their contributions.
CITIZENSHIP SKILLS **Make a Choice by Voting** pp. 28–29	**1** **DAY**	■ Describe the voting process ■ Explain majority rule. ■ Participate in a simulated election.
Biography: Susan B. Anthony pp. 30–31	**1** **DAY**	■ Understand the importance of the actions and character of Susan B. Anthony and explain how she made a difference in others' lives.

READING SUPPORT VOCABULARY	REACH ALL LEARNERS	INTEGRATE LEARNING	RESOURCES
Reading Social Studies (Focus Skill) **Main Ideas and Details,** p. 21 **government** p. 18 **judge** p. 19 **government service** p. 20 **tax** p. 21	**Leveled Practice,** pp. 20, 23	**Reading/Language Arts** Write a Paragraph, p. 22 **Theater** Perform a Skit, p. 21	Homework and Practice Book, pp. 3–4 Reading Support and Intervention, pp. 6–9 Success for English Language Learners, pp. 6–9 Vocabulary Transparency 1-2 Focus Skills Transparency 1 Main Idea and Details Graphic Organizer Write-On/Wipe-Off Card Social Studies Skills Transparency 1-2 Unit 1 Audiotext CD Collection Internet Resources
Reading Social Studies (Focus Skill) **Main Ideas and Details,** p. 27 **election** p. 25 **mayor** p. 26 **governor** p. 26 **President** p. 26 **vote** p. 28 **ballot** p. 28	**Leveled Practice,** pp. 26, 29, 31		Homework and Practice Book, pp. 5–6 Reading Support and Intervention, pp. 10–13 Success for English Language Learners, pp. 10–13 Vocabulary Transparency 1-3 Focus Skills Transparency 1 Main Idea and Details Graphic Organizer Write-On/Wipe-Off Card Social Studies Skills Transparency 1-3 Multimedia Biographies CD TimeLinks: Interactive Time Line Unit 1 Audiotext CD Collection Internet Resources

LESSON	PACING	OBJECTIVES
4 **Our Country's Government** pp. 32–37 💡 **WHAT TO KNOW** How does our country's government work?	**4** **DAYS**	■ Describe the three branches of government and explain their functions. ■ Identify the Constitution as the defining document for our country's government.
Citizenship: Books for Everyone pp. 38–39	**1** **DAY**	■ Understand how one person can make a difference in the community. ■ Examine ways citizens work together to solve a community problem.
5 **Community and State Governments** pp. 40–45 💡 **WHAT TO KNOW** What are the jobs of our community and state governments?	**3** **DAYS**	■ Identify the structure of local and state governments. ■ Compare and contrast the functions of local, state, and national governments.
MAP AND GLOBE SKILLS **Read a Map Key** pp. 46–47	**1** **DAY**	■ Use a map title and map key to locate information. ■ Create a map with a key and borders.
Field Trip: The White House pp. 48–49	**1** **DAY**	■ Locate and study the White House in Washington, D.C. ■ Recognize the purpose of the White House as the residence and workplace of the President of the United States.
Fun with Social Studies: It's a Match! pp. 50–51 **Unit 1 Review and Activities** pp. 52–56	**2** **DAYS**	

READING SUPPORT VOCABULARY	REACH ALL LEARNERS	INTEGRATE LEARNING	RESOURCES
Focus Skill **Reading Social Studies** **Main Ideas and Details,** pp. 34, 37 **capital** p. 33 **Congress** p. 34 **Supreme Court** p. 36 **Constitution** p. 37	**ENGLISH LANGUAGE LEARNERS,** p. 35 **Leveled Practice,** pp. 36, 39 **Special Needs,** p. 37	**Math,** Repeated Addition, p. 34 Fractions, p. 35 **Reading/Language Arts** Make a List, p. 39	Homework and Practice Book, p. 7 Reading Support and Intervention, pp. 14–17 Success for English Language Learners, pp. 14–17 Vocabulary Transparency 1-4 Focus Skills Transparency 1 Main Idea and Details Graphic Organizer Write-On/Wipe-Off Card Unit 1 Audiotext CD Collection Internet Resources
Focus Skill **Reading Social Studies** **Main Ideas and Details,** p. 45 **council** p. 42 **legislature** p. 43 **map key** p. 46 **border** p. 46	**ENGLISH LANGUAGE LEARNERS,** pp. 45, 48 **Advanced,** p. 42 **Leveled Practice,** pp. 44, 47 **Special Needs,** p. 46	**Visual Arts** Paint a Picture, p. 43 **Reading/Language Arts** Homophones, p. 43 **Theater** Role Play, p. 48	Homework and Practice Book, pp. 8–9 Reading Support and Intervention, pp. 18–21 Success for English Language Learners, pp. 18–21 Vocabulary Transparency 1-5 Focus Skills Transparency 1 Main Idea and Details Graphic Organizer Write-On/Wipe-Off Card Activity Pattern A4 Social Studies Skills Transparency 1-4 Primary Atlas Interactive Atlas Unit 1 Audiotext CD Collection Internet Resources
	Leveled Practice, p. 50	**Reading/Language Arts** Write a Speech, p. 51	Homework and Practice Book, pp. 10–11 Assessment Program, pp. 2–4 Leveled Readers Leveled Readers Teachers Guide Unit 2 Audiotext CD Collection Internet Resources

STUDENT DIGITAL LEARNING

The interactive eBook provides students with the standards-based content of Harcourt print books in addition to interactive add-ons that enhance student interest and reinforce Social Studies content. Harcourt eBooks are available in both a basic and enhanced version.

INTERACTIVE VISUALS

Students watch national landmarks and local leaders come to life through engaging interactive activities that enhance the unit content.

STREAMING VIDEO

Each Unit Opener includes video tied to the Unit Big Idea. This clip provides students with enhanced information about following rules.

SKILLS ACTIVITIES

Each Chart and Graph Skill and Map and Globe Skill is enhanced by an interactive online activity.

LIVE INK ENHANCEMENT

live ink

Live Ink provides students with reading help through a patented system that breaks sentences down into segments. The Live Ink system is proven to increase student comprehension and test scores. Live Ink is available for grades 3–6/7.

ONLINE ADVENTURES

Fun with Social Studies provides a link to our Online Adventures game. Students play a game in which they travel to the nation's capital for a parade. The game reviews important concepts from the unit.

MULTIMEDIA BIOGRAPHIES

Biographies from the student edition include additional information in an interactive Multimedia Biography. Students can find more information, view related biographies, explore maps and images, and find links to additional webpages.

THE LEARNING SITE

The eBook includes links to **www.harcourtschool.com/ss1** There students can find internal resources such as our complete Multimedia Biographies databases and our Online Adventures games. This Harcourt Social Studies site also provides students with additional research tools.

Teacher Resources

E-PLANNER

The e-Planner provides a useful tool for scheduling Social Studies lessons.

- Use it to access Teacher Edition pages and student workbook pages and to plan classroom activities.
- The calendar tool displays all your scheduled Social Studies lessons in an easy-to-use format.
- All standards are organized by grade level.

HSPOA

Harcourt School Publishers Online Assessment provides teachers with a reliable, confidential system for online delivery of Social Studies assessment. Using this system, you can track student performance correlated to standards and run prescribed reports for any missed standards. Questions are correlated to our print Assessment program.

VIDEOS AND DVDS

A comprehensive package of videos for Grades K–3 provides an entertaining overview of core social studies concepts such as government, geography, economics, culture and history. Videos in this package are available from Schlessinger Media® and are also available digitally on SAFARI Montage.

SAFARI MONTAGE™

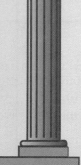

FREE AND INEXPENSIVE MATERIALS

Free and inexpensive materials are listed on the Social Studies Website at **www.harcourtschool.com/ss1**

- Addresses to write to for free and inexpensive products
- Links to unit–related materials
- Internet maps
- Internet references

COMMUNITY RESOURCES FOR THE CLASSROOM

The **National Atlas** website offers interactive, customizable maps of different areas in the United States. Use the **Map Maker** tool to zoom in on your community and view map features such as cities, roads, climate, and agriculture. **http://nationalatlas.gov/**

Educators can use the **United States Census Bureau** webpage to locate census information and facts about their local communities. **http://factfinder.census.gov/home/saff/main.html?_lang=en**

The National Park Service offers a comprehensive site with a search engine that cross-references our country's National Historic Landmarks by name, city, and state. **http://tps.cr.nps.gov/nhl/**

Museums in all 50 states are indexed on the **Virtual Library** museums pages. Use this site to find museums in and around your students' own community. **http://www.museumca.org/usa/states.html**

The **Library of Congress** site features numerous collections of primary sources, biographies, recordings, and photographs. The topic **Cities and Towns** contains photographic records of communities throughout the history of the United States. **http://memory.loc.gov/ammem/**

Additional Sites are available at www.harcourtschool.com/ss1

Lesson Plan Summaries

BELOW-LEVEL/INTERVENTION

TOPIC
Governing the People

Summary *Our Government at Work.* This Reader examines the purpose of government in our communities and explains the jobs of local, state, and national governments.

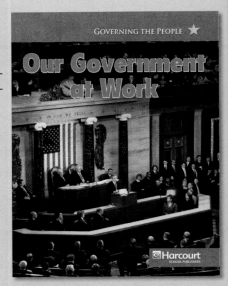

BEFORE READING

Vocabulary Power Have children define the following words. Help them write one sentence for each word as it relates to how a government works.

government   President   law   vote   capital

DURING READING

Main Idea and Details Have children complete the graphic organizer to show that they understand the main idea and details of how a government works as described in the Reader.

Main Idea

The government does many things for people.

Details

| makes laws, helps keep people safe | builds roads, schools, and parks | pays firefighters and police |

AFTER READING

Critical Thinking Lead children in a discussion about why citizens want to be able to choose their leaders.

Write a Law Have children make up and write a law that they think would be good for their community.

ON-LEVEL

TOPIC
Governing the People

Summary *The President's Helpers,* by Samuel Louis. This Reader identifies some of the 15 members of the President's Cabinet and explains their duties.

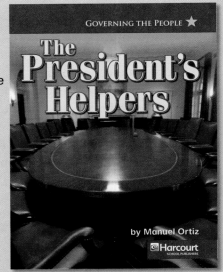

BEFORE READING

Vocabulary Power Have children define the following words. Help them write one sentence for each word as it relates to how a government works.

government   President   Cabinet   secretary   department

DURING READING

Main Idea and Details Have children complete the graphic organizer to show that they understand the main idea and details of how a government works as described in the Reader.

Main Idea

The President gets help from the members of his Cabinet.

Details

| The Secretary of State helps our government get along with other governments. | The Secretary of Defense is in charge of protecting our country. | The Secretary of the Treasury is in charge of the money in America. |

AFTER READING

Critical Thinking Lead children in a discussion about how the Cabinet helps the President do his job.

Write a Biography Have each child choose one member of the Cabinet and write a short biography of that Cabinet member.

The *Leveled Readers Teacher Guide* provides background, reading tips, fast facts, answer keys, and copying masters.

ABOVE-LEVEL

TOPIC
Governing the People

Summary *Government on the Move,* by Daniel Patterson. This Reader follows the events that led up to the establishment of the United States capital in Washington, D.C.

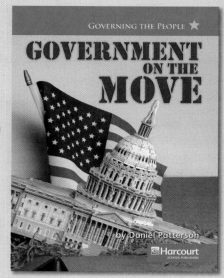

GOVERNING THE PEOPLE ★

GOVERNMENT ON THE MOVE

by Daniel Patterson

Harcourt
SCHOOL PUBLISHERS

BEFORE READING

Vocabulary Power Have children define the following words. Help them write one sentence for each word as it relates to how a government works.

> government   President   colony   congress   capital

DURING READING

Focus Skill
Main Idea and Details Have children complete the graphic organizer to show that they understand the main idea and details of how a government works as described in the Reader.

Main Idea

> The United States capital kept moving.

Details

| Philadelphia was the first capital. | York, Pennsylvania, was also a capital. | The capital finally stayed in Washington, D.C. |

AFTER READING

Critical Thinking Lead children in a discussion about why the colonists wanted to have their own government.

Write a Paragraph Have children pretend they must choose a place for the capital city. Have them write a paragraph stating where they think the capital should be located and why.

Readers' Theater
Every Student Is a Star

IT'S SHOWTIME!

Getting Started

★ Distribute the Big Idea activity sheet from your Readers' Theater.

★ Read through the script together. Make connections with unit contents.

★ Plan a performance using the **Prep ★ Practice ★ Perform** guidelines. Find ideas for props online.

Pressed for Time?

★ Perform a choral reading of the script with the whole class.

★ Assign parts for a one-time read-through.

★ Assign groups to read in your literacy center.

Read Along,

Read Aloud,

Reading Fun

BASIC

 Brown, Marc. *Arthur Meets the President.* Little Brown Children's Books, 1997. The book introduces the role of the President, how to write a letter to the President, the White House, and other sights in Washington, D.C.

 Christelow, Eileen. *Vote!* Clarion, 2004. A lively introduction to voting, this book covers every step of the process through a town's mayoral election.

 Cohen, George M. *You're a Grand Old Flag.* Picture Window Press, 2004. The spirited lyrics of this patriotic song about the American flag come alive in this colorfully illustrated book.

 Jarrie, Martin. *ABC USA.* Sterling, 2005. A patriotic alphabet book that makes history, geography, and the arts accessible to children of all ages.

 Zschock, Martha Day. *Journey Around Washington, D.C. from A to Z.* Commonwealth Editions, 2004. Take a fun tour of America's capital to see government buildings, museums, and monuments.

PROFICIENT

 Bates, Katharine Lee. *America the Beautiful.* Picture Window Press, 2004. Bates's beautiful lyrics celebrate the wonders of America in this charmingly illustrated book.

 Catrow, David. *We the Kids: The Preamble to the Constitution of the United States.* Puffin, 2005. An upbeat look at the Constitution's Preamble shows kids the role the document plays in their lives.

 Maestro, Betsy. *The Voice of the People: American Democracy in Action.* Harper Trophy, 1998. Learn what every citizen needs to know about voting and the election process.

 Quiri, Patricia Ryon. *Congress.* Scholastic, 1999. The book describes the origins, functions, and duties of the United States Congress.

 White, Linda Arms. *I Could Do That!: Esther Morris Gets Women the Vote.* Farrar, Straus, and Giroux, 2005. The book tells the story of Esther Morris, who helped gain the vote for women in Wyoming and was the first female judge and the first woman in the United States to hold political office.

ADVANCED

 Granfield, Linda. *America Votes: How Our President Is Elected.* Kids Can Press, 2005. The book teaches children about the Presidential election process.

 Keating, Frank. *Theodore.* Simon & Schuster Children's Publishing, 2006. The story of Theodore Roosevelt, who loved to learn and read, offers a strong model for hard work and the value of learning.

 Sabin, Ellen. *The Giving Book: Open the Door to a Lifetime of Giving.* Watering Can, 2005. The book inspires, teaches, and engages children to give back to the world.

 Scillian, Devin. *A Is for America: An American Alphabet.* Sleeping Bear Press, 2001. The patriotic, fact-filled book offers 26 reasons for being proud of America.

 Thomson, Sarah L. *Stars and Stripes: The Story of the American Flag.* HarperCollins, 2003. Learn about how the American flag came to be and how it has changed from colonial times to today.

Additional books also are recommended at point of use throughout the unit.
Note that information, while correct at time of publication, is subject to change.

For information about ordering these tradebooks, visit
www.harcourtschool.com/ss1

Use these activities to help differentiate instruction. Each activity has been developed to address a different level or type of learner.

ENGLISH LANGUAGE LEARNERS

20 minutes

Materials
- index cards

CONTEXT SENTENCES Have children use pairs of vocabulary words in statements about the unit content.

- Write each vocabulary word on an index card: *citizen, law, government, President, vote.* Say each word and its definition.
- Ask a child to select two cards. Guide children to use both words in a sentence, such as *A **citizen** must obey the **law***.
- Have children alternate picking cards and creating sentences.
- Repeat so that children practice various combinations of words.

SPECIAL NEEDS

20 minutes

Materials
- colored chalk or colored pencils

CONTENT CATEGORIES Have children classify unit information according to whether it relates to city, state, or country.

- Display these terms: *(your community's name), (state name), mayor, Congress, city council, governor, legislature, President.*
- Read and define each term.
- Have children circle each term that relates to a city in a designated color.
- Repeat by having children use two other colors to show terms related to the state and to the country.

Columbus
Ohio
Congress
city council
mayor
legislature

ADVANCED

40 minutes

Materials
- art materials
- posterboard

CAMPAIGN STRATEGIES Have children choose a public office and plan an election slogan.

- Organize children into pairs to choose a public office, such as President, governor, mayor, legislator, or judge.
- Have each pair plan a campaign slogan. Suggest they think about the candidate's job and how this office makes or upholds our laws.
- Invite children to use their slogan to make a poster or a bumper sticker.

Mark Lane for Mayor

He'll keep our city strong

MATHEMATICS CENTER

Capital Comparisons

Suggest that each child choose a state. Then find out the capital city and the date it became the state's capital. Have children use Internet, library, or reference resources to find information. Have each child write the name of the city and the year it became the state capital on index cards. Once several cards are made, ask children to select cards and write the cities and dates in chronological order.

Annapolis, Maryland—1788
Columbus, Ohio—1816
St. Paul, Minnesota—1858

SCIENCE CENTER

Community Critters

Have children discuss the characteristics of a community. Provide Internet and library resources about animals that live in communities, including lions, wolves, coyotes, ants, bees, dolphins, elephants, gorillas, chimpanzees, or giraffes. Have children use what they find out to make a Fact Card about the animal group that includes the name of the animal, the community name, the number of animals that usually live together, and interesting facts about how the animals interact to share work, food, and responsibilities. Encourage children to illustrate their cards.

A Pride of Lions
- Lions live in social groups.
- There can be 30 lions in a pride.
- Female lions do the hunting.

READING/LANGUAGE ARTS CENTER

Country Creation

Have children work individually or in small groups to create a country and then to write a description of it. Children should name the country, outline the duties of the President, and explain responsibilities of the citizens. Suggest that children write a set of at least five laws for citizens to follow. Have children draw a map to show where the main cities are located, indicating the capital with a star, and they can design a flag for their country.

Freelandia

Libertyville

ART CENTER

Stamp Art

Have children design a postage stamp about being a citizen of a nation. Begin by helping them brainstorm themes such as following laws, voting, and helping others, as well as specific leaders or historic places. Explain that they will make a large image of the stamp design that would be reduced to create a stamp to go on a letter. Invite children to use a variety of media to create their stamps such as pastels, paints, or paper collage. Discuss the stamp designs and then display them on a bulletin board.

Assessment Options

The Assessment Program gives all learners many opportunities to show what they know and can do. It also provides ongoing information about each student's understanding of social studies.

Online Assessment available at www.harcourtschool.com/ss1

OPTION 1

UNIT TESTS
Unit 1

- **Unit Pretest,**
  Assessment Program, p. 1
- **Unit Review and Test Prep,** pp. 52–55

- **Unit Test,**
  Assessment Program, pp. 2–4

OPTION 2

WRITING

- **Show What You Know,**
  Unit Writing Activity,
  Write a Letter, p. 56

- **Lesson Review,**
  Writing Activities, at ends of lessons

OPTION 3

UNIT PROJECT

- **Show What You Know,**
  Unit Project,
  Lawmaker Role-Play, p. 56
- **Unit Project,**
  Performance Assessment, pp. 1P–1Q

- **Lesson Review,**
  Performance Activities, at ends of lessons

INFORMAL ASSESSMENT

- **Lesson Review,** at ends of lessons
- **Skills:**
  Practice, pp. 15, 22, 29, 46
  Apply, pp. 15, 23, 29, 47

- **Reading Social Studies,**
  Main Idea and Details, pp. 4–5
- **Literature Response Corner,** p. 7
- **Points of View, It's Your Turn,** p. 17
- **Citizenship, Make It Relevant,** pp. 38–39

STUDENT SELF-EVALUATION

- **Reading Check Questions,** within lessons

- **Biography, Why Character Counts,** pp. 30–31
- **Map, Time Line, Graph, Diagram, and Illustration questions,** within lessons

OPTION 1 — PRETEST

Name _____ Date _____

Pretest

FILL IN THE BLANK (10 points each)

DIRECTIONS Write the word that completes each sentence.

President	consequences	capital	law	citizen
judge	government	rights	taxes	Congress

1. A person who belongs to a community is a __citizen__.
2. Americans have freedoms, or __rights__.
3. A rule that citizens must follow is a __law__.
4. When people break a law, they face __consequences__.
5. A group of citizens that runs a community is its __government__.
6. The person in charge of a court is the __judge__.
7. Government pays for services with __taxes__.
8. The leader of our country is the __President__.
9. The city where a state government meets and works is the __capital__.
10. The lawmaking branch of our country's government is __Congress__.

OPTION 1 — UNIT TEST

Name _____ Date _____

Test

MATCHING (5 points each)

DIRECTIONS Match the word on the right to its meaning on the left.

1. __H__ a person who belongs to a community
2. __C__ a person in charge of a court
3. __D__ the leader of a state
4. __F__ the leader of our country
5. __A__ a choice that gets counted
6. __E__ the branch of government that makes the laws for our country
7. __G__ a written set of rules that the government must follow
8. __B__ a group of citizens chosen to make decisions in a community

A. vote
B. council
C. judge
D. governor
E. Congress
F. President
G. Constitution
H. citizen

(continued)

OPTION 1 — UNIT TEST

Name _____ Date _____

FILL IN THE BLANK (5 points each)

DIRECTIONS Write the word that completes each sentence.

governor	judge	consequence	ballot
legislature	responsibility	voting	Constitution

9. A __responsibility__ is something a citizen should take care of or do.
10. Going to jail is a __consequence__ of breaking a law.
11. A __judge__ is in charge of a court.
12. People vote in elections for a __governor__ to lead their state.
13. In the United States, people choose leaders by __voting__.
14. When you vote, you mark your choice on a __ballot__.
15. The __Constitution__ is the written set of rules that our government must follow.
16. Lawmakers for a state are called the __legislature__.

OPTION 1 — UNIT TEST

Name _____ Date _____

MULTIPLE CHOICE (5 points each)

DIRECTIONS Select the letter of the best answer.

Six States

17. What is the capital of Arkansas?
    - (A) Little Rock
    - B Nashville
    - C Oklahoma City
    - D Jackson

18. Of what state is Nashville the capital?
    - A Alabama
    - (B) Tennessee
    - C Oklahoma
    - D Louisiana

19. On this map, which states share a border with Alabama?
    - A Oklahoma and Louisiana
    - B Louisiana and Arkansas
    - C Mississippi and Arkansas
    - (D) Tennessee and Mississippi

20. What is the capital city of Oklahoma?
    - A Montgomery
    - (B) Oklahoma City
    - C Baton Rouge
    - D Little Rock

OPTION 2 WRITING

RUBRIC

SCORE 4	SCORE 3	SCORE 2	SCORE 1
• clearly states and describes a community problem	• states and somewhat describes a community problem	• states a community problem but does not describe it	• states a problem unrelated to the community and offers no description
• offers clear details for a creative solution	• offers some details for a somewhat creative solution	• offers few details for a solution	• offers a solution that is unrelated to the problem
• reflects strong understanding of characteristics of good citizenship	• reflects an understanding of characteristics of good citizenship	• reflects little understanding of characteristics of good citizenship	• reflects no understanding of characteristics of good citizenship
• uses correct letter format including date, greeting, body, closing, and signature	• uses mostly correct letter format	• uses somewhat correct letter format	• does not use correct letter format
• makes no or minimal errors in grammar, punctuation, capitalization, and spelling	• makes few errors in grammar, punctuation, capitalization, and spelling	• makes some errors in grammar, punctuation, capitalization, and spelling	• makes many errors in grammar, punctuation, capitalization, and spelling

Name_____ Date_____

Unit 1 Writing Activity Guidelines

WRITE A LETTER

Writing Prompt Write a letter to the mayor about a problem in your community. Tell how you think it should be solved.

STEP 1 Think about rules and laws that keep us safe and help us get along. Make a list of problems in your community that have to do with safety or getting along.

STEP 2 Choose one of the problems. Brainstorm possible solutions to this problem. Choose the solution you think is best.

STEP 3 Be a good citizen. Write a letter to the mayor of your community. Explain the problem, and offer a solution.

STEP 4 Review your work to make sure you have used correct grammar, spelling, punctuation, and capitalization.

STEP 5 Make the changes. Then copy your letter neatly.

OPTION 3 PROJECT

RUBRIC

SCORE 4	SCORE 3	SCORE 2	SCORE 1
• shows a clear understanding of citizens' rights and the roles of lawmakers	• shows some understanding of citizens' rights and the roles of lawmakers	• shows little understanding of citizens' rights and the roles of lawmakers	• shows no understanding of citizens' rights and the roles of lawmakers
• states clearly an issue's main idea and details	• states an issue's main idea and some details	• states only an issue's main idea but no details	• cannot state an issue's main idea or any details
• offers clear solutions that emphasize fairness	• offers solutions that are mostly fair	• offers solutions that are self-serving	• offers no solutions
• speaks clearly, listens attentively, and responds appropriately	• speaks, listens, and responds appropriately	• speaks, but does not listen or respond appropriately	• does not speak, listen, or respond appropriately

Name_____ Date_____

Unit 1 Project Guidelines

LAWMAKER ROLE PLAY

Role-play how a city council makes laws.

STEP 1 Talk about the roles of people who take part in a city council meeting.
  • The mayor and council members run the meeting and vote to make decisions.
  • Citizens describe problems and offer solutions they think will be good for the community.
  • The citizens share their feelings with the council.

STEP 2 If you would like to play the mayor or a city council member, tell the group. Vote to decide who will play each role.

STEP 3 Discuss how you will run the meeting. Decide what props and costumes you will need.

STEP 4 Decide on a problem that needs to be solved. List the main idea and details of the problem. Use this list as you role-play the meeting.

STEP 5 Role-play your council meeting. Be prepared and do your part. After the vote, discuss how the meeting went.

TAKE-HOME RUBRICS Copying masters of a student *Writing Rubric* and *Project Rubric* appear in the Assessment Program, pp. 6 and 8.
GROUP PERFORMANCE RUBRIC See Assessment Program, page x.

UNIT 1 ORGANIZER ▪ 10

Lawmaker Role-Play

Getting Started

Distribute the Unit 1 Project Guidelines provided on page 7 of the Assessment Program.

Introduce the unit project as you begin Unit 1. Have children pay attention to how the three branches of government interact to make and carry out laws. Explain that in our form of government, people are encouraged to get involved. Anyone can attend a council meeting to voice opinions and concerns. At the end of the unit, children will role-play a town council meeting in which citizens raise issues and lawmakers respond.

The Big Idea

Government A government makes laws to help people be safe and get along.

Project Management

For the project, work with the entire class to vote for a mayor and six-member town council. Provide materials for balloting and props as needed. Guide the mayor and council on how to call the meeting to order. Help children who will act as citizens to determine a problem that needs to be resolved.

Materials textbook, paper, pencils, podium, gavel, name cards, art materials and poster-board, simple costumes for role-play (optional)

Organizer Provide a graphic organizer to list the main idea and details of the problem. Children can use it to develop the most important points of their argument so that they will be prepared to speak before the council.

Choosing Roles

As a class, choose the children who will play the lawmakers.

- Vote for a mayor.
- Vote for six council members.

Consider various learning styles as you involve children in the aspects of the council meeting. Ask a group of children to set up the props for the council chamber. Choose those children who will speak about the issue. Select others to listen carefully and record what is said. Work with children so that they understand how the characters they play are expected to behave at the meeting. Citizens can wear simple costumes to help the audience identify who they are playing.

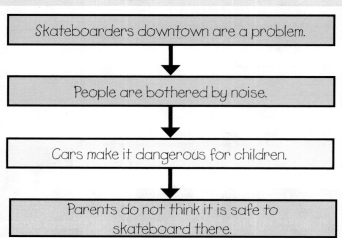

Skateboarders downtown are a problem.

↓

People are bothered by noise.

↓

Cars make it dangerous for children.

↓

Parents do not think it is safe to skateboard there.

Identify the Issue

Have the citizens' group meet to discuss the issue they want to bring before the council. For example, suggest that they are concerned about people who skateboard downtown. Point out that there are many sides to this issue.

- Some people are bothered when they are walking in town.
- Some do not like the noise.
- Parents want a safe place for kids to play.
- Skateboarders want to be able to enjoy their sport.

A group can propose that part of a parking lot near the city park be set aside for skateboard use. The discussion can touch on the following points:

- hours of use
- safety measures and etiquette
- supervision for younger kids

Citizens may want to provide a drawing of the parking lot to show its location and why it is a good place for skateboarders. Have them use art materials and posterboard to create this prop.

Holding the Meeting

Once children have practiced their parts, choose a date and time to hold the town council meeting. Encourage the audience to participate in the discussion if a point is overlooked. Lawmakers can hear all points of view, and then propose a new skateboard law and vote on it. Discuss the process with the entire class when the simulation is finished.

Lesson Review Activities

You may wish to incorporate the following lesson review activities into the unit project.

- Lesson 1: **Write About Rules**, p. 13
- Lesson 2: **Write a Thank-you Note**, p. 21
- Lesson 3: **Act as Mayor**, p. 27
- Lesson 4: **Make a Chart**, p. 37
- Lesson 5: **Make a Poster**, p. 45

Assessment

For a project rubric, see Teacher Edition, p. 1O.

What to Look For

- Children understand the rights of citizens and the role of lawmakers.
- Children state the issue's main idea.
- Children propose a solution that is fair.
- Presentations are clear, and the audience listens critically and responds appropriately.

Homework and Practice Book

LESSON 1

Name _____ Date _____

Tale of a Good Citizen

Read the story about José. Underline the things he did to be a good citizen. Then answer the questions.

   José decided to spend the day being a good citizen. First, he helped his younger brother brush his hair. His mother was so pleased that she put an extra snack in his lunch bag. At school, José was careful to follow the rules all day long. Then, after school, he saw his neighbor coming home from the grocery store. José helped carry her groceries. As his father tucked him into bed that night, José said, "I had a great day. Maybe tomorrow will be even better!"

❶ How did José act like a responsible citizen?

He helped his brother, followed the rules at school, and helped his neighbor.

❷ How do you know José likes being a good citizen?

He told his father he had a great day.

Use after reading Unit 1, Lesson 1, pages 8–13.   **Homework and Practice Book ■ 1**

SKILL PRACTICE

Name _____ Date _____

CRITICAL THINKING SKILLS
What's the Problem?

Look at the picture. Can you solve the problem? Answer the questions below.

❶ What is the problem? The boy does not have everything he needs for his sandwich.

❷ What caused the problem? All the mustard is gone.

❸ What are some solutions to the problem? He could make something else. He could use ketchup. He could eat his sandwich without mustard.

2 ■ Homework and Practice Book   Use after reading Unit 1, Skill Lesson, pages 14–15.

LESSON 2

Name _____ Date _____

Follow the Money!

What happens when people pay taxes in a community? Complete the chart by writing which government service each picture shows.

| Citizens pay taxes to the government. |

↓

| Money from the taxes is used to pay for government services. |

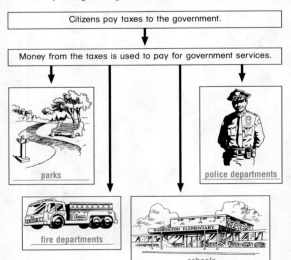

parks

police departments

fire departments

schools

Use after reading Unit 1, Lesson 2, pages 18–21.   **Homework and Practice Book ■ 3**

SKILL PRACTICE

Name _____ Date _____

Make a Word Web

What are some things that a government does for a community? Complete the word web for government services.

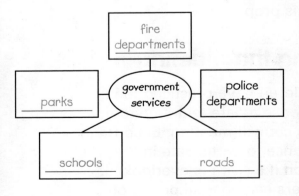

fire departments

parks — government services — police departments

schools   roads

4 ■ Homework and Practice Book   Use after reading Unit 1, Skill Lesson, pages 22–23.

1R ■ UNIT 1 ORGANIZER

LESSON 3

Name _____ Date _____

Fill in the Leader

Write a word from the Word Bank to complete each sentence.
Use each word twice.

leader	President	mayor	governor

① The _____President_____ is the person who leads our country.

② Someone who helps others to get a job done is a
_____leader_____ .

③ A _____governor_____ is elected to make sure people obey
state laws.

④ The leader of a town or a city is the _____mayor_____ .

⑤ A good _____leader_____ helps a group reach a goal.

⑥ The leader of a state is called its _____governor_____ .

⑦ In a city, the _____mayor_____ makes sure people follow
city laws.

⑧ Our country's _____President_____ talks to other world
leaders to solve problems.

SKILL PRACTICE

Name _____ Date _____

CITIZENSHIP SKILLS
Tally the Votes!

A second-grade class voted on names for the class rabbit. Look
at the results of the vote. Then answer the questions below.

Names for Our Rabbit
Herman   II
Floppy   ЖHT
Hoppy   ЖHT I
Scooter   I

① Which name got the most votes? _____Hoppy_____

② Which name got one vote? _____Scooter_____

③ How many children voted? _____14_____

LESSON 4

Name _____ Date _____

Our Country's Government

Read each sentence. Fill in the blank with a word from the
Word Bank. Use each word only once.

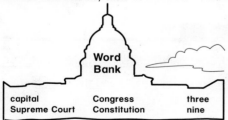

Word Bank

capital	Congress	three
Supreme Court	Constitution	nine

① Our country's government has _____three_____ branches.

② The written set of rules for our government is called the
_____Constitution_____ .

③ Washington, D.C., is the _____capital_____ of the United
States.

④ _____Congress_____ is the branch of government that makes
the laws.

⑤ The _____Supreme Court_____ makes sure all the laws are fair.

⑥ The Supreme Court has _____nine_____ judges.

LESSON 5

Name _____ Date _____

Whose Job Is It?

Write each job in the correct place in the chart below.

City parks

Highways

Mayor

Governor

EVACUATION ROUTE
Help in an emergency

Town council

Community Government Jobs	State Government Jobs
City parks	Highways
Mayor	Governor
Town council	Help in an emergency

8 ▪ Homework and Practice Book   Use after reading Unit 1, Lesson 5, pages 40–45.

SKILL PRACTICE

Name _____ Date _____

MAP AND GLOBE SKILLS
Read a Map Key

Look at the map. Then answer the questions.

Seven States

❶ What is the capital of Kentucky? _Frankfort_

❷ Which states share borders with Virginia?
Maryland, West Virginia, Kentucky, Tennessee, and North Carolina

❸ Of what state is Annapolis the capital? _Maryland_

❹ What is the capital of North Carolina? _Raleigh_

Use after reading Unit 1, Skill Lesson, pages 46–47.   Homework and Practice Book ▪ 9

STUDY GUIDE

Name _____ Date _____

Unit 1
Study Guide

Read the paragraph. Use the words in the Word Bank to fill in the blanks. Use each word only once.

responsibility	President	consequences	citizens
laws	mayor	governments	governor

A community's people, or its _citizens_, have different _laws_ they must obey. These rules help keep the people in a community safe. People have a _responsibility_ to follow the laws and to treat each other in a fair way. People who break the laws must face _consequences_. They may have to pay a fine or even go to jail. These laws are made by community, state, and national _governments_. Our leaders make sure we live in a good place. The _mayor_ is the leader of our community. The _governor_ is the leader of our state. The _President_ is the leader of our country.

10 ▪ Homework and Practice Book   Use after reading Unit 1, pages 1–56.

UNIT 1 REVIEW AND TEST PREP

Name _____ Date _____

MAIN IDEA AND DETAILS
Reading Social Studies

Fill in the chart below to show the main idea and details of this unit.

Main Idea

Each community has a government that protects all the people and their rights.

Details

A government makes laws that citizens must follow.	People who break laws face consequences.	A government is a group of citizens that runs a community.

Use after reading Unit 1, pages 1–56.   Homework and Practice Book ▪ 11

1T ▪ UNIT 1 ORGANIZER

STATE AND COMMUNITY RESOURCES

Historical Societies

Museums

Parks

Guest Speakers

Discuss the Big Idea

Government A government makes laws to help people be safe and get along.

Explain that each country has its own form of government. The government makes and carries out the laws that everyone must follow. Tell children that in this unit they will learn about how our government works for everyone.

Make It Relevant Ask the following question to help children think about how laws set by the government help people get along and stay safe.

Q What are some laws that you follow?

A Children might mention laws concerning bicycles, automobiles, and pedestrians; use of public places; or respect for the property of others.

Access Prior Knowledge

Have children brainstorm a list of school rules. Make a T-chart with the headings *Keep Order* and *Keep Us Safe*. Write each rule under the correct heading. Explain that in this unit, children will learn how the city, state, and national governments make laws for citizens to follow just as school children follow school and classroom rules.

Keep Order	Keep Us Safe
use classroom voices share supplies show respect for others	no running in hallways keep hands and feet to yourself use playground equipment properly

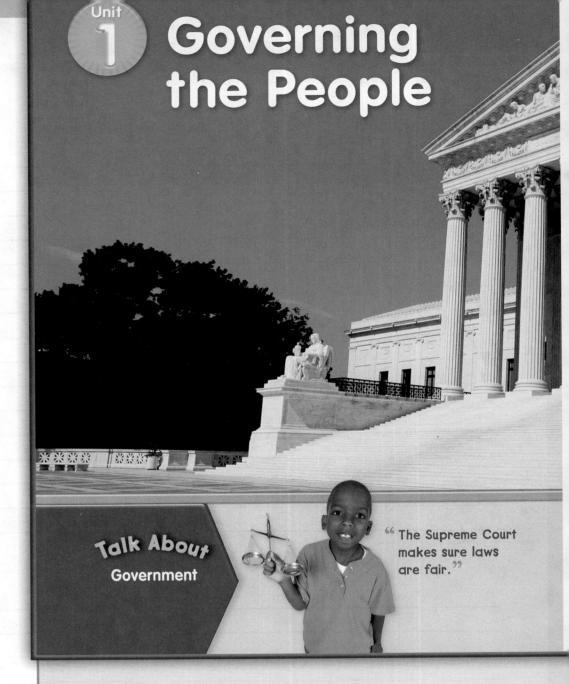

Unit 1 Governing the People

Talk About Government

" The Supreme Court makes sure laws are fair. "

Practice and Extend

BACKGROUND

The Supreme Court The Supreme Court building represents the branch of the government charged with analyzing and interpreting the law. It is located near the National Mall in Washington, D.C.

Talk About Shown in the photographs along the bottom of the unit preview pages are children holding symbols of American freedom and a postcard showing the Capitol building in Washington, D.C., the nation's capital.

> "American citizens are proud of their country."

> "People visit Washington, D.C., to see many government buildings."

Discuss the Picture

Invite children to look at the photograph and identify the Supreme Court building. Explain that in the United States, the courts make sure laws are fair for everyone. They decide when a law has been broken and the consequences a lawbreaker must face. The Supreme Court is the highest court in the land.

Q How can you tell this is an important place?

A It is located near the White House and the Capitol. The building's design makes it look important.

Discuss "Talk About"

Have a volunteer read each quotation and discuss what the children in the pictures are holding.

Q How do balance scales show fairness?

A when both sides are equal

Q Why do Americans display the flag?

A They are proud of their country.

Q Why do people visit Washington, D.C.?

A It is the capital of the United States. They want to see the government buildings.

Have children work in pairs to ask and answer questions about either the Supreme Court building photograph or Talk About.

SCHOOL TO HOME

Use the Unit 1 SCHOOL TO HOME NEWSLETTER on pages S3–S4 to introduce the unit to family members and suggest activities they can do at home.

INTEGRATE THE CURRICULUM

READING/LANGUAGE ARTS Write the words *fair* and *unfair*. Point out the prefix *un-*. Have children use the following word pairs in sentences to show how *un-* means "not": *helpful, unhelpful; safe, unsafe; lawful, unlawful.* Have children state an example of a school or home rule they think is fair and a rule that they think is unfair. **Use Prefixes**

PHYSICAL EDUCATION Discuss a playground game that children play during recess. Have children list the rules that must be followed in order for the game to be played correctly and fairly. Point out what can happen if the rules are misunderstood or ignored. Discuss how children can make sure the rules are followed. **Game Rules**

OBJECTIVES

- Use visuals to determine word meanings.
- Use words and visuals to preview the content of the unit.

RESOURCES

Picture Vocabulary Cards

Make Connections

Link Pictures with Words Have children read the word *government* and its definition. Write the following cloze paragraph on the board.

The government works for every ____. Every citizen should obey the ____. Citizens ____ to choose their leaders. The ____ leads the country.

Look at each picture and read its definition with children. Help children use the vocabulary to complete the paragraph. (citizen, law, vote, President)

1 **Visual Literacy: Pictures** Have children look at the community gathering in the picture at the top of page 2 and discuss what the people might be celebrating.

Q Who are the people shown in the picture?

A They are citizens.

2 Have children read the definition of *government* and describe what the picture shows. Elicit that the picture shows citizens in a meeting of the government.

1

citizen A person who lives in and belongs to a community.
(page 8)

2

government A group of citizens that runs a community, state, or country. (page 18)

2

Practice and Extend

ELL ENGLISH LANGUAGE LEARNERS

Frontloading Language: Government Use the following prompts to develop the academic language of government and the structures of main idea and details.

Basic Have children use the pictures to express the main idea for each vocabulary word. Use this frame: The *[subject of the picture] shows [vocabulary word].* For example: *The sign shows a law.*

Proficient Invite children to name details in the pictures that support the main idea. Have them complete this sentence frame: *A vote is ____. The President is ____.*

Advanced Have children identify the main idea in each vocabulary picture and express details that explain the picture. Use this frame: *In our country, we have [vocabulary word] because ____.*

law A rule that citizens must follow. (page 11)

President The leader of the United States government. (page 26)

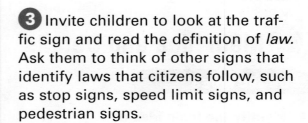

vote A choice that gets counted. (page 28)

GO ONLINE For more resources, go to **www.harcourtschool.com/ss1**

3

3 Invite children to look at the traffic sign and read the definition of *law.* Ask them to think of other signs that identify laws that citizens follow, such as stop signs, speed limit signs, and pedestrian signs.

Q Why should people follow signs and laws?

A They should follow them so they can stay safe.

4 Focus children's attention on the picture of the person above the word *President.* Read aloud the definition and ask children who this picture shows. (President Barack Obama)

Q Have you seen pictures of our President before? Where?

A Yes; in newspapers, on television, in magazines.

5 Have children look at the picture of the voters. Discuss what they are doing. Explain that citizens vote to choose their leaders. Point out that having a vote means having a say in who leads the country and makes the laws. The votes are counted, and the leaders who get the most votes win.

Q When have you voted?

A Children may respond that they have voted to make choices in the classroom.

GO ONLINE **INTERNET RESOURCES**

For more resources, go to **www.harcourtschool.com/ss1**

VOCABULARY POWER

Suffixes Create a word-building chart. Have children identify the suffixes added to make new words.

Root	Root + Suffix
citizen	citizenship
govern	government
	governor
law	lawful
	lawyer
preside	President
vote	voter

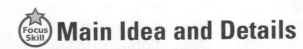

Main Idea and Details

OBJECTIVES

- **Identify the main idea of a paragraph.**

- **Identify detail sentences in a paragraph.**

- **Interpret information from charts.**

VOCABULARY

main idea p. 4   details p. 4

RESOURCES

Focus Skills Transparency 1; Main Idea and Details Graphic Organizer Write-On/Wipe-Off Card; Unit 1 Audiotext CD Collection

Introduce

1 Why It Matters Explain to children that when they look for the main idea, they are looking for the most important information in a passage. Supporting details give more information about the main idea.

Focusing on the main idea sentence will help children understand the most important information in materials they read.

1 Why It Matters When you read for information, look for the main ideas and important details.

Learn

Good paragraphs have a main idea and details.

2 ● The main idea is the most important part of what you are reading.

● The details explain the main idea.

Read the paragraph below.

Main Idea
Detail

Our town is planning a new community center. The center will be big enough for special events. It will have classes and fun activities for adults. It will also have after-school programs for children. Our new community center will have something for everyone!

4

Practice and Extend

INTEGRATE THE CURRICULUM

READING/LANGUAGE ARTS Give children the following writing prompt: *People in a community depend on one another.* Have them brainstorm detail sentences to support this main idea. For example: *People in a community depend on shopkeepers to sell food.* Then have each child write a paragraph using the writing prompt as the main idea sentence. **Write a Paragraph**

FOCUS SKILLS

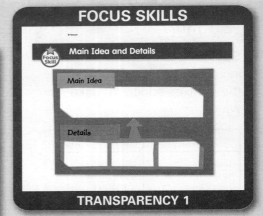

TRANSPARENCY 1

Graphic Organizer Write-On/Wipe-Off Cards available

Practice

3

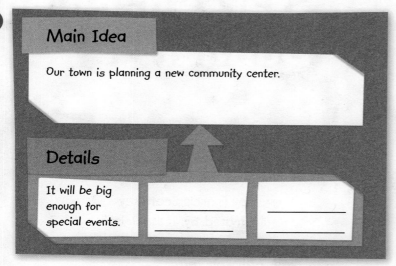

Main Idea

Our town is planning a new community center.

Details

It will be big enough for special events.

_____
_____

_____
_____

This chart shows the main idea and one detail from what you just read. Copy the chart and complete it.

Apply

As you read this unit, look for the main ideas and details about what governments do.

5

Leveled Practice Write the following paragraph on the board: _Some state governors go on to become President of the United States. Former President George W. Bush was governor of Texas. Bill Clinton was governor of Arkansas. Ronald Reagan and Jimmy Carter were also governors at one time._

Basic Have children read the first sentence in the paragraph and identify the main idea.

Proficient Ask children to read the paragraph aloud. Have a child underline the main idea. Call on other children to circle each of the supporting detail sentences.

Advanced Have children use library and Internet resources to find further examples of state governors who became President. Suggest they use the information they learn to add more details to the paragraph.

Learn

2 Discuss the definitions for _main idea_ and _details_ on page 4. Point out the following:

- In a paragraph, the main idea is often the first sentence.
- Detail sentences follow the main idea sentence.

Then read aloud and discuss the paragraph. Ask children to listen for repeating words, such as _center_ and _it,_ and words that give information, such as _classes_ and _programs._ These words signal what the paragraph is mostly about.

Practice

3 **Visual Literacy: Chart** Use Focus Skill Transparency 1 to copy the chart on page 5. Read aloud the information in the chart. Point out that the main idea is stated in the first sentence. Discuss the supporting details found in the paragraph.

Q Where does this information go in the chart?

A in the boxes labeled _Details_

ANSWERS: Details: It will have classes and fun activities for adults. It will have after-school programs for children.

Apply

Tell children that as they read each paragraph in the unit, they should ask themselves what the paragraph is mainly about. Explain that finding details to support each main idea will help them learn more about local, state, and national governments.

OBJECTIVES

- Identify patriotic elements in a song.
- Understand the concepts of freedom and bravery.

RESOURCES

Unit 1 Audiotext CD Collection

Quick Summary

"The Star-Spangled Banner" by Francis Scott Key, 1814.

Francis Scott Key was inspired to write this song about the American flag when he witnessed it flying after a British attack during the War of 1812.

Before Reading

Set the Purpose Have a volunteer read the title of the song. Ask children to predict what they think this song is about.

Invite children to tell where they have seen the United States flag on display. Ask them to describe how the flag makes them feel.

During Reading

❶ Understand the Song Tell children that most countries have a national anthem, which is a song that expresses patriotic feelings. "The Star-Spangled Banner" is America's national anthem.

Q How can you tell the songwriter is patriotic, or proud of his country?

A The songwriter uses words such as *proudly*, *free*, and *brave*.

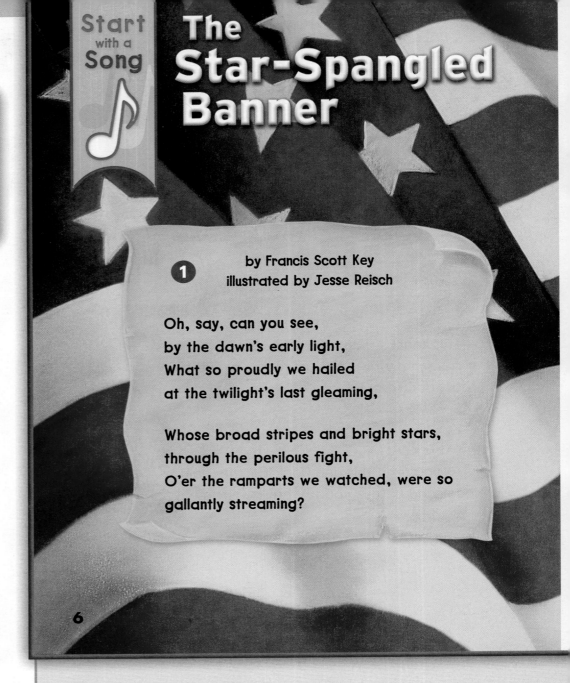

Start with a Song

The Star-Spangled Banner

❶ by Francis Scott Key
illustrated by Jesse Reisch

Oh, say, can you see,
by the dawn's early light,
What so proudly we hailed
at the twilight's last gleaming,

Whose broad stripes and bright stars,
through the perilous fight,
O'er the ramparts we watched, were so
gallantly streaming?

6

Practice and Extend

BACKGROUND

About the Author Francis Scott Key was a lawyer living in Washington, D.C., when the War of 1812 broke out. In 1814, while working to secure the release of an American prisoner, Key was aboard a British ship during the attack on Fort McHenry. In the morning, Key saw the American flag still flying and knew the United States had prevailed. Inspired, Key wrote a poem that later became our national anthem.

REACH ALL LEARNERS

Leveled Practice Explain that "The Star-Spangled Banner" is a poem set to music.
Basic Choose another patriotic song, and write the words on the board. Have children read it aloud in the manner of a poem.
Proficient Ask children to find another patriotic song and tell how it is similar to a poem.
Advanced Have children write their own patriotic poem about the flag and share it with the class.

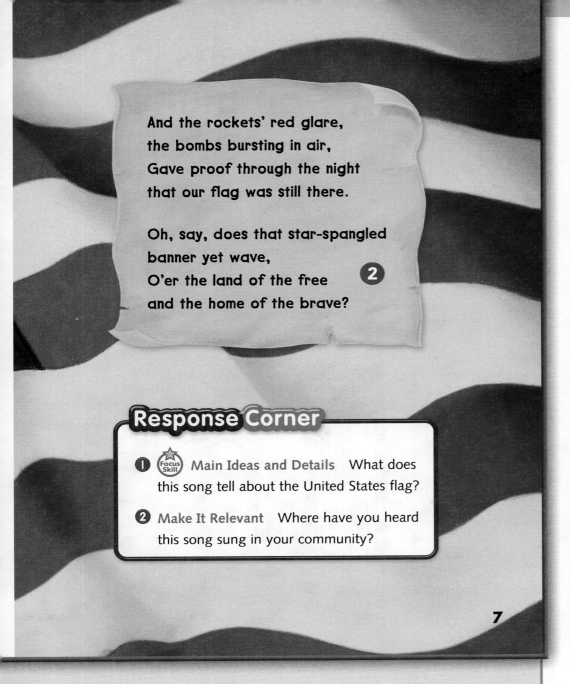

And the rockets' red glare,
the bombs bursting in air,
Gave proof through the night
that our flag was still there.

Oh, say, does that star-spangled
banner yet wave,
O'er the land of the free
and the home of the brave?

Response Corner

❶ **(Focus Skill) Main Ideas and Details** What does this song tell about the United States flag?

❷ **Make It Relevant** Where have you heard this song sung in your community?

7

❷ **Civics and Government** Ask children to discuss what the songwriter meant when he wrote "the land of the free and the home of the brave." Explain that citizens of the United States enjoy many freedoms, such as the freedom to vote and express opinions, that are protected by the Constitution. The "brave" in the song refers to Americans, many of whom serve in the military.

After Reading
Response Corner—Answers

1. **(Focus Skill) Main Idea and Details** The flag survived through a fierce battle.

2. **Make It Relevant** I have heard the song at school, at sporting events, and during parades.

✎ Write a Response

Have children pretend to be Francis Scott Key. Children can write a brief journal entry about how they felt when they saw the flag by the "dawn's early light."

For a writing response rubric, see Assessment Program, page xvi.

INDEPENDENT READING

Children may enjoy reading these books during the unit. Additional books are listed on page 1J of this Teacher Edition.

The Star-Spangled Banner by Peter Spier (Dragonfly Books, 1992). This book brings the words of the national anthem to life.

F is for Flag by Wendy Cheyette Lewison (Grosset & Dunlap, 2002). Children learn that a flag can represent many things, such as a feeling of unity, a sign of welcome, and a symbol of patriotism.

One Nation: America by the Numbers by Devin Scillian (Sleeping Bear Press, 2002). This book presents children with an illustrated look at American history, landmarks, and traditions.

For information about ordering these trade books, visit **www.harcourtschool.com/ss1**

OBJECTIVES

- Explain citizens' rights and responsibilities at home, at school, and in the community.
- Recognize the need for rules and laws.
- Identify the consequences of breaking rules and laws.

VOCABULARY

community p. 8   **responsibility** p. 10

citizen p. 8   **law** p. 11

right p. 9   **consequence** p. 12

MAIN IDEA AND DETAILS

pp. 4–5, 13

RESOURCES

Homework and Practice Book, p. 1; Reading Support and Intervention, pp. 2–5; Success for English Learners, pp. 2–5; Vocabulary Transparency 1-1; Focus Skills Transparency 1; Main Idea and Details Graphic Organizer Write-On/Wipe-Off Card; Activity Pattern A3; Unit 1 Audiotext CD Collection; Internet Resources

1 Introduce

What to Know Ask a volunteer to read the What to Know question. Explain to children that people who live in the community, including themselves, are citizens of the community. Remind children to look for answers to the question as they read.

Build Background Invite children to discuss the differences between communities, towns, and cities. Ask them to also note how these places are alike.

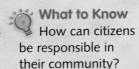

Lesson **1**

 What to Know How can citizens be responsible in their community?

Vocabulary
community
citizen
right
responsibility
law
consequence

 Main Idea and Details

Citizens in a Community

Every day, you work and play with others. People who work and play together live in a **community**. Your family and school are part of a community. The people who belong to a community are its **citizens**.

St. Louis, Missouri

8

Practice and Extend

Express Path

When minutes count, look for the **EXPRESS PATH** to focus on the lesson's main ideas.

Quick Summary

Citizens have rights. They also have different roles. Each role has different responsibilities. Citizens must follow rules and laws to keep people safe, protect their rights, and promote fairness. There are consequences for not following rules and laws.

2 Citizens Have Rights

What does it mean to be a citizen? In the United States, it means having rights. A **right** is a kind of freedom.

3

Americans have important rights. We can live and work where we want. We can follow our religious beliefs and share our ideas.

Reading Check *Focus Skill* **Main Idea and Details**

What is a community? A community is a place where people work and play together.

9

Citizens Have Rights

CONTENT FOCUS American citizens have rights that give them freedom.

Express Path

Brainstorm communities to which children belong. Ask children to answer the Reading Check question.

1 Visual Literacy: Pictures Have children look at the photograph on pages 8–9. Identify the communities a child might be a part of, such as a school, family, apartment, or neighborhood.

2 History Obtain a copy of the Bill of Rights and discuss the rights listed.

Q What rights do citizens have?

A People can live where they want, share ideas, and practice their religion.

3 Correct Misconceptions Explain that some people in the United States are not citizens. They were born in other countries. These people have some of the same rights as American citizens, and can study to become citizens.

VOCABULARY

Vocabulary Transparency 1-1

MINI-GLOSSARY Read each term, and study its definition.

community A group of people who live or work together. p. 8
citizen A person who lives in and belongs to a community. p. 8
right A freedom. p. 9
responsibility Something that a person should take care of or do. p. 10
law A rule that people in a community must follow. p. 11
consequence Something that happens because of what a person does. p. 12

WORD WORK Complete the activities below.

1. **community**
USE REFERENCE SOURCES Does *community* come before or after *citizen* in the glossary?
after

2. **citizen**
CONTEXT CLUES *Citizens* enjoy rights in their community. What context clues help you understand the meaning of *citizens*?
enjoy rights, community

3. **right**
SYNONYMS What is another word for *rights*?
freedoms

4. **responsibility**
ROOT WORDS What is the root word of *responsibility*?
responsible

5. **law**
WORD FAMILIES How are *law*, *lawyer*, *outlaw*, and *lawmaker* the same?
All four words have the root law.

6. **consequence**
USE REFERENCE SOURCES Does *consequence* come before or after *community* in the dictionary?
after

TRANSPARENCY 1-1

READING SUPPORT/ INTERVENTION

For alternate teaching strategies, use pages 2–5 of Reading Support and Intervention to:

- identify **phonemes**
- practice **phonics**
- reinforce **vocabulary**
- build **text comprehension**
- build **fluency**

Reading Support ▶ and Intervention

ELL ENGLISH LANGUAGE LEARNERS

For English Language Learners strategies to support this lesson, see Success for English Learners pages 2–5.

- English-language development activities
- background and concepts
- vocabulary extension

Success for ▶ English Learners

Citizens Have Responsibilities

CONTENT FOCUS Every person has responsibilities in the different roles he or she plays in a community.

Express Path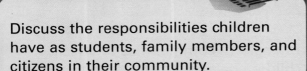

Discuss the responsibilities children have as students, family members, and citizens in their community.

4 **Civics and Government** Create a word web for children's roles and responsibilities. Have children write responsibilities that they have for each role.

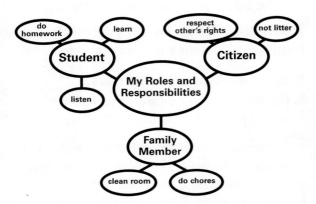

Citizens Have Responsibilities

4 Every person plays many roles, or parts, in a community. Each role has responsibilities. A **responsibility** is something you should take care of or do. A student is responsible for learning. A family member is responsible for helping. A citizen is responsible for taking care of the community and respecting people's rights.

Reading Check **What is your responsibility as a student?** My responsibility as a student is to learn.

10

Practice and Extend

VOCABULARY POWER

Synonyms List the following on the board: *duty, task, requirement, chore,* and *assignment.* Tell children that these words mean the same thing as a responsibility or something that people should do. Encourage children to use these words when they explain the responsibilities they have as students, family members, and citizens.

BACKGROUND

Groups in a Community
Although children belong to many groups, they still have their own identity. Groups influence individuals when they teach the rules for being in the group. Because of this, it is important for individuals to make good decisions about the groups in which they participate. Also explain that individuals can influence the group by modeling responsible choices.

INTEGRATE THE CURRICULUM

HEALTH Invite children to think about various signs in the community, such as *Stop, Yield, School Zone,* and speed limits. Explain how being responsible and following these laws keep citizens safe. *Stop* and *Yield* signs tell drivers whose turn it is to go. *School Zone* and speed limit signs let drivers know the safe driving speed for the area.
Safety

Rules and Laws

⑤ All communities have rules. Some rules are called laws. A **law** is a rule that citizens must follow. Rules and laws help us stay safe and protect our rights. They help us learn, work, and play together. Rules and laws also help us solve problems fairly.

⑥

Street signs show laws everyone must follow.

11

Rules and Laws

CONTENT FOCUS Rules and laws are made to keep people safe, protect our rights, and promote fairness.

Express Path

Discuss how specific examples of rules and laws help people be safe and fair.

⑤ Civics and Government Encourage children to compare rules at home and at school with laws citizens must follow.

⑥ Visual Literacy: Pictures Focus attention on the photographs on pages 10 and 11. Discuss what each sign means.

Encourage children to choose a law from one of the signs pictured or other such signs they have seen. Give each child a copy of Activity Pattern A3 and an envelope. Have children

- draw a picture of the law being followed.
- cut along the lines, and put the pieces in their envelopes.
- trade puzzles and put the pieces together.
- discuss which laws are being followed.

ELL ENGLISH LANGUAGE LEARNERS

Explain that there are different ways of saying the same thing.

Beginning Point out that when we *follow* a rule, we do not follow it the way we follow in line. We do what the law says to do. Then explain that we do not *break* a rule the way we break a pencil lead. We do not do what the law says to do. Let children find sentences with *follow* laws and *break* laws in the lesson.

Intermediate Give children a list of synonyms for *disobey* and *obey*. Then have children classify the words.

Advanced Ask children to find synonyms for *disobey* and *obey* in a thesaurus. Let them work together to make lists. Have children share their findings.

INDEPENDENT READING

Read aloud the chapter book *Marvin Redpost: Alone in His Teacher's House* by Louis Sachar (Random House, 1996). Marvin shows he can be responsible looking after his teacher's dog while she's away—even when it dies. Encourage volunteers to share opportunities they've had to show responsibility.

7 Visual Literacy: Pictures Ask children to discuss what the signs in the photograph are communicating.

Q How do these signs keep people safe?

A They keep drivers safe by telling them to go the other way. They also keep the workers safe by keeping cars away.

Q What might happen if someone does not obey the signs?

A The workers could get hurt by the car. The driver could get hurt, get a ticket, or be arrested.

8 Civics and Government Point out that consequences help people follow rules and laws.

Q What are some consequences for breaking rules at home or in school?

A Possible responses: Home: loss of TV or an activity, being grounded; School: stay in at recess, stay after school, call to parents

Q What should we do if friends ask us to do something that breaks a rule?

A We should not break the rule. If someone wants to do something dangerous, we should tell an adult.

It is our responsibility to follow rules and laws so that no one is hurt or treated unfairly. People who break rules must face consequences. A **consequence** is something that happens because of what a person does or does not do.

7

12

Practice and Extend

Leveled Practice Expand on the consequences of irresponsible behavior.

Basic Discuss behaviors that could result in injury, such as pushing in line and not stopping at a stop sign. Talk about consequences intended to encourage people to follow safety rules and laws, such as staying in from recess or getting a ticket. Have children make posters encouraging safe choices.

Proficient Ask children to discuss ways people sometimes treat others unfairly. Identify possible consequences. Have children write slogans for treating everyone fairly.

Advanced Ask children to identify rules and laws that differ for different settings. Have children write sentences that talk about laws that might help their community solve specific problems.

8 If a child breaks a rule at school, the consequence might be not being allowed to do something fun. People who break laws may have to do work for the community or pay money. People who break the most important laws must go to jail.

PARKING VIOLATION

☐ Letting the meter run out

☑ Blocking a fire hydrant

☐ Double-parking

Fine.............$65

Reading Check **Why is it important to follow rules and laws?** Rules and laws make sure that no one is hurt or treated unfairly.

Summary Citizens in a community have rights and responsibilities. They must follow rules and laws to be safe and get along.

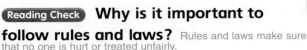

① **What to Know** How can citizens be responsible in their community?

② **Vocabulary** What can be a **consequence** of not following a rule or a law?

③ ✎ **Write** Think of a rule in your classroom or school. Explain why it is important to follow the rule.

④ ⭐ **Main Idea and Details** What is a right you have as a citizen?

13

Summary

Have children read the lesson summary and restate the main ideas.

- Citizens have rights and responsibilities.
- Rules and laws keep people safe, protect their rights, and promote fairness.
- There are consequences for breaking rules and laws.

Assess

REVIEW—Answers

1. **What to Know** They can take care of the community, respect others' rights, and follow the rules and laws.

2. **Vocabulary** A **consequence** of not following a rule or law is that someone could be hurt.

3. **Writing Assessment Guidelines** See Writing Rubric. This activity can be used with the Unit Project.

4. **Main Idea and Details** Possible responses: I can live and work where I want. I can follow my religious beliefs and share ideas with others.

Use Focus Skills Transparency 1 or Main Idea and Details Graphic Organizer Write-On/Wipe-Off Card.

HOMEWORK AND PRACTICE

Name _____ Date _____

Tale of a Good Citizen

Read the story about José. Underline the things he did to be a good citizen. Then answer the questions.

José decided to spend the day being a good citizen. First, he helped his younger brother brush his hair. His mother was so pleased that she put an extra snack in his lunch bag. At school, José was careful to follow the rules all day long. Then, after school, he saw his neighbor coming home from the grocery store. José helped carry her groceries. As his father tucked him into bed that night, José said, "I had a great day. Maybe tomorrow will be even better!"

① How did José act like a responsible citizen?
He helped his brother, followed the rules at school, and helped his neighbor.

② How do you know José likes being a good citizen?
He told his father he had a great day.

page 1

OBJECTIVES

■ Use a problem-solving process to identify a problem, gather information, and list possible solutions.

■ Describe the consequences of different solutions.

VOCABULARY

problem p. 14   **solution** p. 14

RESOURCES

Homework and Practice Book, p. 2; Social Studies Skills Transparency 1-1; Unit 1 Audiotext CD Collection

Introduce

Organize children into small groups and ask them to draw a picture of a flag. Distribute a sheet of paper for each child and one red, one white, and one blue crayon. After a few minutes, ask children how they completed the task with so few crayons. Have them share their solutions.

Why It Matters Point out that when a problem arises, figuring out how to solve it is important. Explain that being able to work with other people to solve a problem is also important. Discuss how the group had to work together to solve the problem. Explain that people have problems to solve everyday.

Solve a Problem

Why It Matters Citizens in communities work together to solve problems. A **problem** is something that makes things difficult.

Learn

1 A **solution** is a way to solve a problem. Sometimes there is more than one solution to a problem. Follow these steps.

① Name the problem.

② Gather information.

③ Think about different solutions.

④ Think about the consequences of each solution.

⑤ Try a solution.

⑥ Think about how well the solution worked.

14

Practice and Extend

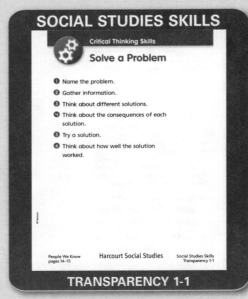

SOCIAL STUDIES SKILLS

Critical Thinking Skills

Solve a Problem

① Name the problem.
② Gather information.
③ Think about different solutions.
④ Think about the consequences of each solution.
⑤ Try a solution.
⑥ Think about how well the solution worked.

People We Know pages 14–15   Harcourt Social Studies   Social Studies Skills Transparency 1-1

TRANSPARENCY 1-1

MAKE IT RELEVANT

At School Have children think about a problem that affects the school community and follow the problem-solving steps to find a solution. Have them record every part of the process, including gathering information to identify the problem, brainstorming solutions, and anticipating the consequences before deciding on a solution.

❷ Practice

Look at the picture. Name the problem that needs to be solved. Make a list of possible solutions.

Apply

Choose the solution you think is best. Write a paragraph telling what the problem is and why you think the solution will work.

15

Learn

① Write *problem* and *solution* on the board. Read the sentences on page 14 that contain these highlighted words.

Q Which happens first, a problem or a solution?

A A problem happens first. Then you find a solution for it.

Stress that solving a problem takes several steps. Ask children to identify the steps for solving a problem.

Q When people work together to solve a problem, why do they need to listen to one another?

A Listening lets you think about many solutions. It also helps you find problems that some solutions may cause.

❷ Practice

Children should identify the problem of two groups wanting to play their sport on the same field.

Possible responses for solutions: the group plays both sports, but rotates which game to play; The two groups take turns using the field or split the field in half and both play at once; The group plays rock-paper-scissors to decide which game to play.

3 Close

Apply

Children should be able to explain why they think one solution will be more effective than others. Invite children to compare and contrast what they learned from one another's ideas.

REACH ALL LEARNERS

Leveled Practice Have children practice using the problem-solving steps.

Basic Have children state the problem.

Proficient Have children state the problem and brainstorm solutions.

Advanced Have children discuss the consequences of each solution and then vote on which one will be the most effective.

HOMEWORK AND PRACTICE

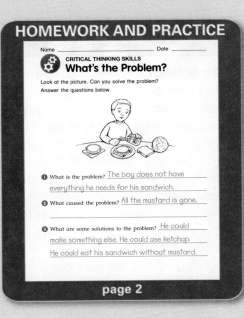

Name _____ Date _____

⚙ **CRITICAL THINKING SKILLS**
What's the Problem?

Look at the picture. Can you solve the problem?
Answer the questions below.

❶ What is the problem? The boy does not have everything he needs for his sandwich.

❷ What caused the problem? All the mustard is gone.

❸ What are some solutions to the problem? He could make something else. He could use ketchup. He could eat his sandwich without mustard.

page 2

OBJECTIVES

■ Compare and contrast children's daily lives to those of others.

■ Explore different points of view about what individuals do to get along with one another.

RESOURCES

Unit 1 Audiotext CD Collection

🔍 Link to the Big Idea

Government Point out that a government makes laws to keep people safe. People need to follow these laws so that everyone can get along. Remind children that many of these laws are based on treating others the way we want to be treated ourselves.

Vocabulary Help Explain to children that the *city council* is government that takes care of a city.

Discuss the Points of View

Civics and Government Read aloud the Sidewalk Reporter's question. Have children read aloud each answer and identify which of these actions would benefit their own neighborhood. Discuss how each person contributes to his or her neighborhood. Point out that most communities have laws about litter and speed limits. Discuss similar laws with which children are familiar.

Q Which actions provide safety or a service?

A Driving slowly and cleaning up after a dog are examples of safety. Being on the council is an example of a service.

Points of View

The Sidewalk Reporter asks:
"What do you do to get along with your neighbors?"

Amanda

"I clean up after my dog."

Mr. Kim

"I keep my home and yard neat."

View from the Past

Anyokah: Getting Along

In 1817, six-year-old Anyokah began working with her father, Sequoyah, to help the people of her community get along. By 1821, they had created an alphabet for the Cherokee people.

Practice and Extend

MAKE IT RELEVANT

At School Explain to children that a school is like a small neighborhood or a community. Everyone works together to make it a better place. Take children on a school tour. Discuss how students and staff demonstrate courtesy, safety, and service to make the school a nicer place. Then take this time to discuss the importance of treating others fairly and treating others the way we would like to be treated.

BACKGROUND

Sequoyah Sequoyah, also known as George Gist, was born in 1776 near Tuskeegee, Tennessee. Sequoyah's mother, Wut-the (or Wureth), was the daughter of a Cherokee chief who married a Virginia fur trader named Nathaniel Gist. Sequoyah was a silversmith, and his interest in writing began when he was asked to sign his work. His daughter, Anyokah, helped him demonstrate the use of his alphabet.

Josh

"I drive slowly and watch for people."

Mrs. Avila

"I work on the city council."

Elena

"I don't litter. I use trash cans in the park."

It's Your Turn

- Do you do any of the things that these citizens do? If so, which ones?
- What do you do to get along with your neighbors? What laws do you obey?

17

View from the Past

History Read aloud the information about Anyokah and her father. Explain that Sequoyah and Anyokah taught their people how to read and write Cherokee, their native language. This allowed the Cherokee to be able to communicate with others who were far away. Point out that Anyokah's story shows that children can also make a positive contribution to a community.

It's Your Turn–Answers

Have small groups discuss the questions, giving each child a chance to respond. Have groups share responses with the class. Discuss which actions are most important for maintaining a healthy neighborhood that is clean, safe, and law-abiding.

- Possible responses include cleaning up after a pet and not littering.
- Possible response: I cross the street only at crosswalks and when the light says I can walk.

18 ▪ UNIT 1

OBJECTIVES

■ **Identify and describe functions of government.**

■ **Understand how government works to help citizens through services paid for by taxes.**

VOCABULARY

government p. 18

judge p. 19

government service p. 20

tax p. 21

MAIN IDEA AND DETAILS

pp. 4–5, 21

RESOURCES

Homework and Practice Book, p. 3; Reading Support and Intervention, pp. 6–9; Success for English Learners, pp. 6–9; Vocabulary Transparency 1–2; Focus Skills Transparency 1; Main Idea and Details Graphic Organizer Write-On/Wipe-Off Card; Unit 1 Audiotext CD Collection; Internet Resources

1 Introduce

What to Know Ask children how they think government helps them. Remind children to look for answers to the What to Know question as they read.

Build Background Invite children to share examples of groups they belong to in the community. Explain that in this lesson, they will learn about a group of citizens that run a community.

Lesson 2

What to Know
How does government help people?

Vocabulary
government
judge
government service
tax

Main Idea and Details

Government for the People

In a community, people form groups to get what they need and want. Many different groups work together to help each other.

We Need Government

All communities have a **government**, or a group of citizens that runs the community. The government makes laws to keep its citizens safe. It makes sure that people get along.

❶

18

Practice and Extend

Express Path

When minutes count, look for the **EXPRESS PATH** to focus on the lesson's main ideas.

Quick Summary

Social groups help meet a community's needs. Individuals and groups need to be governed and offered services, which are paid for by taxes collected from citizens. Courts help resolve conflicts and make sure people are treated fairly.

When people do not agree, a court may decide how everyone can be treated fairly. Courts are a part of government.

The person in charge of a court is a **judge**. A judge makes sure that the court protects the rights of all citizens.

Judge Orlando Hudson, Jr., of North Carolina

Reading Check **Main Idea and Details**

What does a government do?
A government makes laws to keep its citizens safe and help them get along.

A school board, teachers, and parents work together to help schools.

We Need Government

CONTENT FOCUS A government makes laws to keep citizens safe and to help people get along. Courts protect the rights of all citizens.

Express Path

Ask children to read the title and headings. Then invite them to study the pictures and tell why they think we need government.

1 **Visual Literacy: Picture** Focus attention on a school board meeting. Point out that this is an example of how many groups or communities have some form of governance to maintain order. Explain that these school board members make decisions and solve problems for a school district.

2 **Civics and Government** Explain that the judge on page 19 works in North Carolina. Discuss the duties of a judge, such as keeping order in the courtroom, protecting citizens' rights, and making sure everyone is treated fairly.

VOCABULARY

Vocabulary Transparency [1-2]

MINI-GLOSSARY Read each term, and study its definition.

government The group of citizens that runs a community, state, or country. p. 18
judge The leader of a court. p. 19
government service A service that a government provides for citizens. p. 20
tax Money paid to the government and used to pay for services. p. 21

WORD WORK Complete the activities below.

1. **government**
WORD FAMILIES How are the words government and governor alike?
They both have the root govern.

2. **judge**
MULTIPLE MEANINGS/USE REFERENCE SOURCES Use your dictionary to find another meaning for the word judge.
Possible answer: To form an opinion about something.

3. **government service**
CONTEXT CLUES Write a sentence to show the meaning of government service.
Possible answer: My favorite government service is the library.

4. **tax**
SUFFIXES What ending do you write to make tax plural?
tax(es)

TRANSPARENCY 1-2

READING SUPPORT/ INTERVENTION

For alternate teaching strategies, use pages 6–9 of Reading Support and Intervention to:

- identify **phonemes**
- practice **phonics**
- reinforce **vocabulary**
- build **text comprehension**
- build **fluency**

Reading Support ▶ and Intervention

ELL ENGLISH LANGUAGE LEARNERS

For English Language Learners strategies to support this lesson, see Success for English Learners pages 6–9.

- English-language development activities
- background and concepts
- vocabulary extension

Success for ▶ English Learners

Government Services

CONTENT FOCUS A government offers services to citizens and uses taxes to pay for the services.

Express Path

Focus attention on the vocabulary words. Ask children to think of services the government provides. Explain that taxes pay for these services.

❸ Visual Literacy: Picture Ask children what government service the picture shows. protection from fires

Q What services does a government provide?

A roads, schools, parks, police, and fire departments

Q Why do we need these services?

A Roads help us move around our community; schools help us learn; parks give us a place to play; police and fire departments keep us safe.

❹ Economics Discuss why a government collects taxes. Explain that people pay different kinds of taxes, such as sales tax, property tax, and income tax.

Q What do taxes pay for?

A Taxes pay for government services.

Q What would happen if no taxes were collected?

A There would be no money to pay for government services. Money would have to be raised in other ways to pay for the things citizens need.

Government Services

A **government service** is something that the government of a community provides for all the citizens. Government services include roads, schools, and parks. Police and fire departments are other government services. These services help to keep citizens safe.

20

Practice and Extend

4 Government services cost money. Citizens pay for them with taxes. A **tax** is money people pay to the government. The government makes choices about how the tax money will be spent.

Reading Check **How do government services make a community better?** Government services help give citizens things they need, such as roads, schools, and protection.

Summary A government is a group of people that runs a community. It protects citizens and provides services they need.

❶ **What to Know** How does government help people?

❷ **Vocabulary** How does a **judge** help a community?

❸ **Write** Write a thank-you note for a government service. Tell how the service helps you.

❹ **Main Idea and Details** What do taxes pay for?

21

Summary

Have children read the summary and then restate the lesson ideas in their own words.

- A government is a group of people that runs a community.
- A tax is money paid to a government to be used to pay for services.

Assess

REVIEW—Answers

1. **What to Know** Government provides services that help and protect the community.

2. **Vocabulary** A **judge** makes sure the court protects the rights of all citizens.

3. **Writing Assessment Guidelines** See Writing Rubric. This activity can be used with the Unit Project.

4. **Main Idea and Details** They pay for government services, such as roads, schools, and police and fire departments.

Use Focus Skills Transparency 1 or Main Idea and Details Graphic Organizer Write-On/Wipe-Off Card.

WRITING RUBRIC

Score 4
- provides many excellent examples of how the service helps
- uses letter form with no errors

Score 3
- provides good examples of how the service helps
- uses letter form with few errors

Score 2
- provides fair examples of how the service helps
- uses letter form with many errors

Score 1
- provides few or poor examples of how the service helps
- does not use letter form

HOMEWORK AND PRACTICE

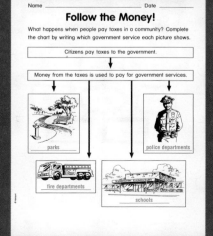

Name _____ Date _____

Follow the Money!

What happens when people pay taxes in a community? Complete the chart by writing which government service each picture shows.

Citizens pay taxes to the government.

Money from the taxes is used to pay for government services.

parks   police departments

fire departments   schools

page 3

INTEGRATE THE CURRICULUM

THEATER Ask children to act out ways that citizens can participate in government. Choose school and local issues for small groups to act out, such as:

- citizens voting.
- citizens running for office.
- citizens attending community meetings and voicing their opinions.

Perform a Skit

OBJECTIVES

- Use a word web to connect related ideas.
- Create a word web about government based on ideas presented in the unit.

RESOURCES

Homework and Practice Book, p. 4; Social Studies Skills Transparency 1-2; Unit 1 Audiotext CD Collection

Introduce

Write the word *home* on the board. Invite children to come up with words that may be related to *home*, and write them randomly. Ask children to identify how some of the words are related. Have children brainstorm different ways the words could be organized so that they would be easier to remember.

Why It Matters Explain that words help people communicate. Tell children that learning new words will help them read listen, think, talk, and write better. Point out that a word web helps people connect ideas. Explain to children they can use a word web to take notes while reading a lesson or preparing to write a report.

Study Skills

Build Vocabulary

Why It Matters Learning new words helps you understand what you read. It also helps you use the right words to talk about your ideas.

Learn

1 Making a word web is one way to show how words are connected. The main idea goes in the middle circle.

2 Practice

Copy the word web shown on the next page.

1 Add more words about a community.

2 What do the words tell you about a community?

22

Practice and Extend

SOCIAL STUDIES SKILLS

Study Skills

Build Vocabulary

offices

people — community — roads

People We Know
pages 22–23

Harcourt Social Studies

Social Studies Skills
Transparency 1-2

TRANSPARENCY 1-2

INTEGRATE THE CURRICULUM

READING/LANGUAGE ARTS Encourage children to use information recorded in the community web to write a paragraph. Point out that the middle circle can be the main idea for the paragraph's first sentence. Ideas connected to the main idea can provide supporting details for the paragraph. Let children share their completed paragraphs. **Write a Paragraph**

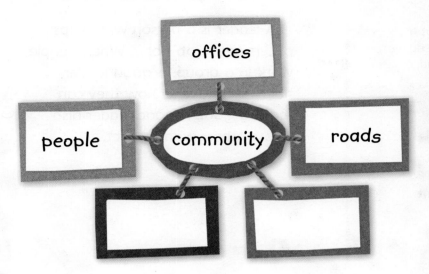

offices

people

community

roads

Apply

Make a word web for <u>government</u>. As you read more about government, add words to your web.

23

Learn

1 Demonstrate how to create a word web by writing the word *school* in a circle. Invite children to brainstorm words related to the word *school,* such as *books, teacher,* and *learn.* Point out that seeing the word web take shape can spark new ideas. For example, *books* might generate the words *library, reading,* and *dictionary.*

2 Practice

Have children read the directions on page 22. Discuss the idea of community and the things we find in a community. Have children add their ideas to the web.

Q What is the main idea? How can you tell?

A *Community* is the main idea because it is in the middle circle. All the words around the circle name things that are a part of a community.

1. Possible responses: workers, families, homes, schools, businesses, stores, parks, museums, libraries
2. Possible responses: A community is a place where people live, work, and go to school. There are many places to go and things to do in the community.

Apply

Word webs should show what children currently know about government. As they read the unit, they can add new words and ideas to the web.

REACH ALL LEARNERS

Leveled Practice Ask groups to add to the web.

Basic Have children think of two or more places to add to the web.

Proficient Help children brainstorm services that a community provides and add them to the web.

Advanced Have children go to a community website or a local newspaper to find out more about their community.

HOMEWORK AND PRACTICE

Name _____ Date _____

Make a Word Web

What are some things that a government does for a community?
Complete the word web for government services.

fire departments

parks — government services — police departments

schools   roads

page 4

OBJECTIVES

- Describe why we need leaders.
- Explain how citizens choose leaders.
- Identify local, state, and national leaders and their contributions.

VOCABULARY

election p. 25   **governor** p. 26

mayor p. 26   **President** p. 26

MAIN IDEA AND DETAILS

pp. 4–5, 27

RESOURCES

Homework and Practice Book, p. 5; Reading Support and Intervention, pp. 10–13; Success for English Learners, pp. 10–13; Vocabulary Transparency 1–3; Focus Skills Transparency 1; Main Idea and Details Graphic Organizer Write-On/Wipe-Off Card; Unit 1 Audiotext CD Collection; Internet Resources

Introduce

What to Know Invite a volunteer to read the What to Know question. Then ask children to tell who they think is a leader. Remind children to look for answers to the question as they read.

Build Background Invite children to give examples of times when they have been a leader, such as a line leader, a team captain, student of the week, or a type of helper. Have them share the responsibilities they had for each example.

Lesson **Our Leaders**

What to Know
Why do we need leaders?

Vocabulary
election
mayor
governor
President

Main Idea and Details

A leader is a person who helps others get a job done. When people work in a group, a good leader helps them decide how they can reach a goal. A good leader also treats others with respect.

24

Practice and Extend

Express Path

When minutes count, look for the **EXPRESS PATH** to focus on the lesson's main ideas.

Quick Summary

Mayors, governors, and Presidents make decisions to keep their citizens safe. They also make sure people follow laws. A mayor leads a city or town, a governor leads a state, and the President leads our country. These leaders are chosen by citizens in elections.

Choosing Leaders

2 In the United States, citizens choose leaders to run the government. Government leaders work to keep people safe and to keep order.

Citizens choose many of their government leaders at events called **elections**. People choose the leaders they think will do the best job.

Reading Check **How do citizens choose government leaders?** Citizens choose government leaders in elections.

Vote For Smith

25

Choosing Leaders

CONTENT FOCUS During elections, citizens choose leaders to run the government.

Express Path

Ask children to study the photograph and decide what the people in the picture are doing.

1 **Visual Literacy: Picture** Ask children to read the sign on the podium.

Q **Whose name do you think *Smith* is? What does Ms. Smith want everyone to do?**

A *Smith* is the name of the person behind the podium. She wants people to vote for her.

2 **Civics and Government** Explain to children that the United States is a democracy. This means that the government is run for and by the people of the country. In a democracy, citizens can run for office and choose their leaders in elections. Tell children that not all countries are democracies, and that other forms of government exist.

VOCABULARY

Vocabulary Transparency 1-3

MINI-GLOSSARY Read each term, and study its definition.

election A time when people vote for their leaders. p. 25
mayor The leader of a city or town government. p. 26
governor The leader of a state's government. p. 26
President The leader of the United States government. p. 26

WORD WORK Complete the activities below.

1. **election**
SUFFIXES What is the suffix in election?
elect(ion)

2. **mayor**
CLASSIFY/CATEGORIZE In which group would you place mayor?
place   person   thing
person

3. **governor**
ROOT WORDS Write the root word of governor.
govern

4. **President**
RELATED WORDS How are President, governor, and mayor related?
All name government leaders.

TRANSPARENCY 1-3

READING SUPPORT/ INTERVENTION

For alternate teaching strategies, use pages 10–13 of Reading Support and Intervention to:

- identify **phonemes**
- practice **phonics**
- reinforce **vocabulary**
- build **text comprehension**
- build **fluency**

Reading Support ▶
and Intervention

ELL ENGLISH LANGUAGE LEARNERS

For English Language Learners strategies to support this lesson, see Success for English Learners pages 10–13.

- English-language development activities
- background and concepts
- vocabulary extension

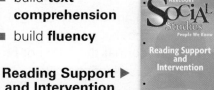

Success for ▶
English Learners

Government Leaders

CONTENT FOCUS Local, state, and national leaders work to solve problems and make sure people follow laws.

Express Path

Invite children to study the Government Leaders chart. Then have them answer the Reading Check question.

3 Civics and Government Explain that an important part of a democracy is that people can vote for the leaders they think best represent what they want and believe in. Citizens can run for office and lead the government. Provide pictures of national, state, and local leaders. Have children identify and name their community's mayor or local leader, their state's govenor, and the President of the United States.

4 Visual Literacy: Chart Ask children to compare and contrast the items of information in the chart. Explain that the President is also the Commander-in-Chief of our country's military. Discuss the President's role as our country's leader.

Children in History

Tutankhamen, Boy King

5 Tell children that King Tut did not live in a democracy and was not elected to office. He took office when his father, the king, died. Explain that in different times and places, leaders often gained power in ways that had nothing to do with what the citizens wanted. In King Tut's time, only people from one family were allowed to run the country.

Government Leaders

3 Your city, state, and country each have a government leader. A **mayor** leads a city or town. A **governor** is the leader of a state. These leaders make sure people obey community and state laws.

The **President** is the leader of our country. This person makes sure people obey our country's laws. The President also works with the leaders of other countries to solve world problems.

Reading Check **How are the jobs of the President, a governor, and a mayor alike?**
They all make sure people obey laws.

4

Government Leaders		
Mayor	Governor	President
• Leads a city or town • Makes sure community laws are obeyed	• Leads a state • Makes sure state laws are obeyed	• Leads our country • Makes sure our country's laws are obeyed • Meets with world leaders

26

Practice and Extend

Children in History

Tutankhamen, Boy King

Not all leaders are adults. Long ago, Tutankhamen became the leader of Egypt when he was only eight years old. With the help of trusted adults, he ruled his country for ten years.

Summary Government leaders work to make our communities good places to live.

Review

1. **What to Know** Why do we need leaders?

2. **Vocabulary** How does a **mayor** help a community?

3. **Activity** Imagine you are the mayor of your city. Tell how you would help your community.

4. **Main Idea and Details** How are government leaders chosen?

27

Summary

Ask children to read the summary. Have them repeat it in their own words.

- Citizens elect a mayor, governor, and President to lead their local, state, and national governments.
- Leaders make sure people follow laws and help them make decisions to reach goals.

Assess

REVIEW—Answers

1. **What to Know** Leaders help us get things done and reach goals.

2. **Vocabulary** A **mayor** makes sure that the community is a good, safe place to live.

3. **Activity Assessment Guidelines** See Performance Rubric. This activity can be used with the Unit Project.

4. **Main Idea and Details** They are chosen in elections.

Use Focus Skills Transparency 1 or Main Idea and Details Graphic Organizer Write-On/Wipe-Off Card.

PERFORMANCE RUBRIC

Score 4
- describes ideas clearly
- shows a clear understanding of a mayor's job

Score 3
- describes ideas adequately
- shows an understanding of a mayor's job

Score 2
- describes ideas inadequately
- shows little understanding of a mayor's job

Score 1
- does not describe ideas
- shows no understanding of a mayor's job

HOMEWORK AND PRACTICE

Name _____ Date _____

Fill in the Leader

Write a word from the Word Bank to complete each sentence. Use each word twice.

| leader | President | mayor | governor |

1. The _President_ is the person who leads our country.

2. Someone who helps others to get a job done is a _leader_.

3. A _governor_ is elected to make sure people obey state laws.

4. The leader of a town or a city is the _mayor_.

5. A good _leader_ helps a group reach a goal.

6. The leader of a state is called its _governor_.

7. In a city, the _mayor_ makes sure people follow city laws.

8. Our country's _President_ talks to other world leaders to solve problems.

page 5

MAKE IT RELEVANT

In Your Community Invite children to look for pictures, head-lines, and articles about their local elected and nonelected leaders. Have children use the information they find to write sentences that explain each person's contributions to the community. Ask children to identify how these leaders affect their lives. Invite children to share their findings.

OBJECTIVES

- **Describe the voting process.**
- **Explain majority rule.**
- **Participate in a simulated election.**

VOCABULARY

vote p. 28 **ballot** p. 28

RESOURCES

Homework and Practice Book, p. 6;
Social Studies Skills Transparency 1-3;
Unit 1 Audiotext CD Collection

Introduce

Write on the board several activity options for an outdoor game and explain that as a class, children must pick one that everyone will play. Discuss a fair way for the class to choose one activity. For example, suggest a show of hands and tally the results for further discussion.

Why It Matters Explain that voting is one way to let people know what you want. Review that in the United States, adult citizens have the right to vote for their leaders. Once elected, the leaders tend to do what the citizens want them to do. They represent the people who voted for them. Therefore, voting is one way people participate in the government.

Make a Choice by Voting

Why It Matters In the United States, citizens choose their leaders by voting in elections. A **vote** is a choice that gets counted.

❶ Learn

❶ Before people vote, they think about who will do the best job.

❷ People mark a ballot to vote in most elections. A **ballot** is a list of all the choices.

❸ The ballots are counted.

❹ The winner of an election is the one who gets the most votes.

28

Practice and Extend

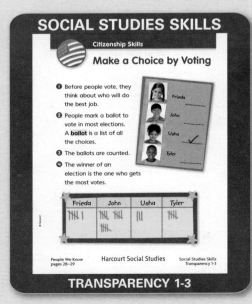

SOCIAL STUDIES SKILLS

TRANSPARENCY 1-3

BACKGROUND

Voting To be eligible to vote, you have to be a U.S. citizen and at least 18 years old on the day of the election. You cannot be in prison, be on parole for a felony, or have been ruled incompetent by a court. Each state can determine how long you have to have been a resident of the state and how long before an election you have to register. Each voting location chooses the type of ballot it will use, such as paper or electronic.

② Practice

Before Imagine that your classroom is a city that wants to choose a new mayor.

During Make ballots that list the name of each person who wants to be mayor. Give each citizen a ballot to mark.

After When everyone has voted, collect the ballots. The winner is the person who gets the most votes.

Frieda	John	Usha	Tyler
ЖЖ I	ЖЖ ЖЖ ЖЖ	III	ЖЖ

Apply

Make It Relevant Use voting as a way to make other choices in your classroom.

29

Learn

❶ Civics and Government Stress that good citizens learn about candidates and make decisions based on what they learn. If possible, display newspaper clippings and election brochures from a real election.

Write *vote* and *ballot* on the board. Demonstrate how to vote. Then tell children that voters mark their ballots in secret. They do this so that no one can see and criticize their choice. Discuss different types of ballots, such as electronic and paper.

Point out that in most elections, the winner must have a majority rule, or more than half of the votes. Let children count the tallies on page 29 to see whether anyone received a majority.

❷ Practice

Before Let children nominate four classmates to put on the ballot. Encourage candidates to tell why they would be a good leader.

During Make sure the names are written clearly and spaced adequately.

After Have children determine the winner and whether the winner received a majority.

Apply

Make It Relevant Children should present clear choices, accurately tally votes, and present results to classmates.

REACH ALL LEARNERS

Leveled Practice Practice voting to make choices.

Basic Ask children to close their eyes and raise their hands to vote for one of three choices.

Proficient Have children make a ballot with three choices, vote, then determine if there is a majority.

Advanced Invite children to give speeches for and against issues on a ballot.

HOMEWORK AND PRACTICE

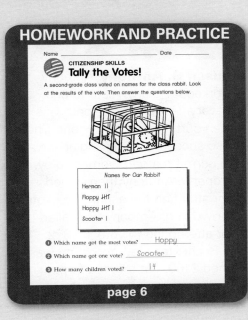

Name _____ Date _____

CITIZENSHIP SKILLS
Tally the Votes!

A second-grade class voted on names for the class rabbit. Look at the results of the vote. Then answer the questions below.

Names for Our Rabbit

Herman II
Floppy ЖЖ
Hoppy ЖЖ I
Scooter I

❶ Which name got the most votes? Hoppy

❷ Which name got one vote? Scooter

❸ How many children voted? 14

page 6

OBJECTIVES

- Understand the importance of the actions and character of Susan B. Anthony and explain how she made a difference in others' lives.

RESOURCES

Unit 1 Audiotext CD Collection; Multimedia Biographies CD; Internet Resources; TimeLinks

💡 Link to the Big Idea

Government Government Laws are made to help people get along and stay safe. Sometimes governments change laws so that everyone is treated fairly. Susan B. Anthony worked to change laws so that women could vote.

Vocabulary Help Discuss with children what it means to be a *citizen.* Remind children that citizens are people who live in a country and have rights given to them by the government.

Discuss the Biography

Primary Source: Photograph Point out that the photograph on page 31 shows women marching for the right to vote. Susan B. Anthony inspired women to take part in such marches. Explain that the law allowing women to vote was not passed until 1920, 14 years after Susan B. Anthony died.

Biography

Trustworthiness
Respect
Responsibility
Fairness
Caring
Patriotism

Susan B. Anthony

Susan B. Anthony lived at a time when women did not have the same rights as men. Most girls did not go to school. They helped their mothers cook and clean at home. Susan's family felt that both girls and boys should be given an education.

Why Character Counts

🖊 How did Susan B. Anthony show fairness to other people?

Susan B. Anthony worked for equal rights.

30

Practice and Extend

BACKGROUND

Susan B. Anthony Anthony worked for many years to end slavery. Her efforts helped pass the Fourteenth Amendment. She also succeeded in changing laws to permit married women to own property. Anthony then turned her attention to securing the vote for women. Anthony was jailed for attempting to vote in 1872, in Rochester, New York. She was fined $100, but refused to pay the fine.

INDEPENDENT READING

Have children read *Bloomers!* by Rhoda Blumberg (Bradbury, 1993), a fictional account of Elizabeth Cady Stanton, Amelia Bloomer, and Susan B. Anthony as they pioneered the women's rights movement.

Many women came together to work for women's rights.

For many years, women could not vote to help choose our country's leaders. Susan B. Anthony thought this was unfair, and she began to make speeches. She said, "It was . . . not we, the white male citizens . . . but we, the whole people, who formed the Union."

Susan B. Anthony worked hard giving speeches and writing books. Finally, 100 years after she was born, our country passed a law giving women the right to vote.

Susan B. Anthony was the first woman shown on United States money.

For more resources, go to
www.harcourtschool.com/ss1

Time

1820			1906
Born			Died

1839 Begins teaching school

1872 Arrested for voting in the Presidential election

1906 Makes her last speech for women's right to vote

31

Primary Source: Quotation Reread the quotation on page 31. Explain that Anthony is referring to the Preamble of the Constitution, which begins "We the People of the United States, in order to form a more perfect Union . . ."
Source: Susan B. Anthony, *On Women's Right to Suffrage* speech, 1873.
Source: from *U. S. Constitution*.

Q Who did Anthony feel the "we" referred to in the Constitution?

A all people, not just white male citizens

Q What does this tell you about Anthony's character?

A Possible response: She believed that all people should enjoy equal rights.

Visual Literacy: Time Line Call attention to the time line on page 31. Point out that it shows only the years in which Susan B. Anthony was born and died. Have children research the month and day of Anthony's birth and death.

Why Character Counts
Susan B. Anthony worked to change laws so that they were fair to all.

OBJECTIVES

- Describe the three branches of government and explain their functions.
- Identify the Constitution as the defining document for our country's government.

VOCABULARY

capital p. 33	**Supreme Court** p. 36
Congress p. 34	**Constitution** p. 37

MAIN IDEA AND DETAILS

pp. 4–5, 34, 37

RESOURCES

Homework and Practice Book, p. 7; Reading Support and Intervention, pp. 14–17; Success for English Learners, pp. 14–17; Vocabulary Transparency 1-4; Focus Skills Transparency 1; Main Idea and Details Graphic Organizer Write-On/Wipe-Off Card; Unit 1 Audiotext CD Collection; Internet Resources

---

I Introduce

What to Know Ask a volunteer to read the What to Know Question. Ask children to recall who leads our country's government (the President). Remind children to look for answers to the question as they read the lesson.

Build Background Discuss what children know about the work of the government. Guide children to recall that government makes laws, provides services, helps keep people safe, protects rights, and helps us get along.

Lesson 4 Our Country's Government

What to Know
How does our country's government work?

Vocabulary
capital
Congress
Supreme Court
Constitution

Main Idea and Details

① Our country's government helps the United States run smoothly. The government has three parts, or branches. The legislative branch makes the laws. The executive branch sees that the laws are obeyed. The judicial branch makes sure the laws are fair.

Washington, D.C.

White House

32

Practice and Extend

Express Path

When minutes count, look for the **EXPRESS PATH** to focus on the lesson's main ideas.

Quick Summary

The three branches of government—legislative, executive, and judicial—follow the Constitution in enforcing, making, and judging fair laws. Although each has its own role, Congress, the President, and the Supreme Court work together. Much of their work is done in the capital of our country, Washington, D.C.

The Capital

Washington, D.C., is the capital of our country. A **capital** is a city in which a state's or country's government meets and works.

The White House, which is the President's home, is in Washington, D.C. The Supreme Court and the Capitol building are also there.

Reading Check **What is the capital of the United States?** The capital of the United States is Washington, D.C.

Washington, D.C.

MARYLAND

NEW JERSEY

Potomac River

Washington, D.C.

DELAWARE

North
West • East
South

Chesapeake Bay

VIRGINIA

ATLANTIC OCEAN

MAP SKILL What river flows through our capital?

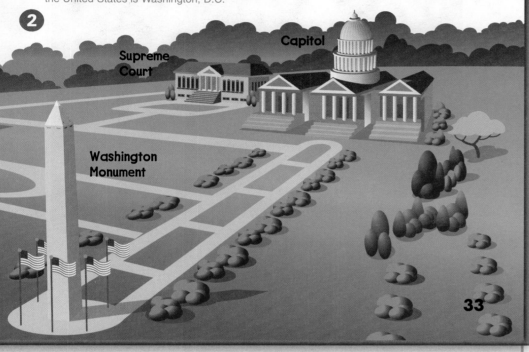

2

Supreme Court

Capitol

Washington Monument

33

2 Teach

The Capital

CONTENT FOCUS Washington, D.C., is the capital of the United States.

Express Path

Invite children to find Washington, D.C., on the map and name important buildings located in our capital city.

1 Civics and Government Draw a chart to compare the three branches of government and what they do.

Three Branches of United States Government	
Legislative Branch Executive Branch Judicial Branch	makes laws carries out laws makes sure laws are fair

2 Visual Literacy: Picture Explain that the legislative branch works at the Capitol building, the executive at the White House, and the judicial at the Supreme Court building.

Interactive in the enhanced online student eBook

CAPTION ANSWER: the Potomac River

VOCABULARY

Vocabulary Transparency 1-4

MINI-GLOSSARY Read each term, and study its definition.

capital A city in which a state's or country's government meets and works. p. 33
Congress The group of citizens chosen to make decisions for our country. p. 34
Supreme Court The court that decides on laws for the United States. p. 36
Constitution A written set of rules that the government must follow. p. 37

WORD WORK Complete the activities below.

1. **capital**
CONTEXT CLUES Use capital in a sentence to show its meaning.
Possible answer: The capital of our country is Washington, D.C.

2. **Congress**
CLASSIFY/CATEGORIZE In which group would you place Congress?
people   objects
people

3. **Supreme Court**
WORD WEB Complete the word web with related words for Supreme Court.
Possible answers:
nine justices — Supreme Court — branch of government

4. **Constitution**
RELATED WORDS How are Constitution and law related?
Many of our laws are in the Constitution.

TRANSPARENCY 1-4

READING SUPPORT/ INTERVENTION

For alternate teaching strategies, use pages 14–17 of Reading Support and Intervention to:

- identify **phonemes**
- practice **phonics**
- reinforce **vocabulary**
- build **text comprehension**
- build **fluency**

Reading Support ▶ and Intervention

HARCOURT
SOCIAL Studies
People We Know

Reading Support and Intervention

ELL ENGLISH LANGUAGE LEARNERS

For English Language Learners strategies to support this lesson, see Success for English Learners pages 14–17.

- English-language development activities
- background and concepts
- vocabulary extension

Success for ▶ English Learners

HARCOURT
SOCIAL Studies
People We Know

Success for English Learners

The Legislative Branch

CONTENT FOCUS Congress is the legislative, or lawmaking branch of our country's government. Legislators make our country's laws and decide how to spend tax money.

Express Path

Ask children to answer the Reading Check question.

3 **Civics and Government** Show children the "Three Branches of U.S. Government" chart from page 33. Ask children to identify the group who makes our country's laws (Congress). Add a third column to the chart and write *Congress* in the first row.

4 **Visual Literacy: Picture** Focus attention on the inside of the House Chamber. Explain that this is a large room where Congress meets in the Capitol building.

- Invite children to find the Capitol building in the illustration on page 33. Tell them that the Capitol building was built in 1793, and it contains 540 rooms.

- Point out on page 34 that the members of Congress are on the floor and visitors are in the balcony.

The Legislative Branch

3 **Congress** is the lawmaking branch of our country's government. The people of each state elect their own members of Congress. Besides making laws, Congress also decides on the taxes people will pay.

Reading Check **How are the members of Congress chosen?** They are elected by the people of their state.

4

34

Practice and Extend

MENTAL MAPPING

Washington, D.C. Help children find their state's location on a map of the United States. Then help them find Washington, D.C.

- Invite children to imagine that their bodies are a map of the United States. Washington, D.C., is located at their left shoulder.

- Have them figure out their state's location. For example, California would be their right leg or Florida their left leg.

INTEGRATE THE CURRICULUM

MATHEMATICS Invite children to name the number of states in the United States. Explain to them that part of Congress is made up of senators, and that there are two senators from every state. Then lead children in counting by twos for each state. Guide them to conclude that since 50 two's equals 100, there are 100 senators. **Repeated Addition**

READING SOCIAL STUDIES

Main Idea and Details Guide children to use the lesson parts to aid comprehension. Demonstrate how the lesson title and subtitles represent the main idea and details.

READING TRANSPARENCY

Use FOCUS SKILLS TRANSPARENCY 1.
Graphic Organizer Write-On/Wipe-Off Cards available

The Executive Branch

5 The President is the leader of the executive branch. The executive branch sees that everyone obeys the laws Congress makes. The President can also suggest new laws to Congress.

Reading Check **Main Idea and Details** **What is the job of the executive branch?** The executive branch makes sure that people obey the laws Congress makes.

President Obama lives and works in the White House.

35

The Executive Branch

CONTENT FOCUS The President is the leader of the executive branch. The executive branch makes sure that the laws are obeyed.

Express Path

Ask children to find the answer to the Reading Check question on the page.

5 **Civics and Government** Discuss the role of the President. Write *President* in the second row of the third column of the "Three Branches of U.S. Government" chart. Explain that the President checks the laws made by Congress when he approves or vetoes a law.

6 **Visual Literacy: Picture** Ask children to identify the person and place in the pictures. Explain that this picture shows President Obama and the White House. Invite children to share what they know about the White House.

BACKGROUND

World Events The President is responsible for foreign affairs.

- The President meets with world leaders to solve problems that affect people around the world.
- The President appoints a Secretary of State to work with leaders in other countries.
- World events affect the decisions made by the President and Congress.

INTEGRATE THE CURRICULUM

MATHEMATICS Explain that if the President does not want to sign a law, Congress can vote again, but the law can only be passed with a two-thirds majority. Majority means "the side with more votes." Set out 18 counters. Ask children to divide the counters into three equal groups. Combine two of the groups. Explain that this is $\frac{2}{3}$. The other group is $\frac{1}{3}$.
Fractions

ELL ENGLISH LANGUAGE LEARNERS

Beginning Have children name the President of the United States and point to his picture.

Intermediate Have children answer yes or no questions about the President, such as: Is the President the head of Congress? (no)

Advanced Have children identify the President by name and explain his job as head of the executive branch.

The Judicial Branch and the Constitution

CONTENT FOCUS The judicial branch makes sure laws are fair. The Constitution explains how our government needs to work.

Express Path

Have children find the answer to the Reading Check question on page 36. Then read aloud the summary on page 37. Discuss the Reading Check question on page 37.

7 **Visual Literacy: Picture** Focus on the Supreme Court judges. Tell children that they are called justices. Have children count the judges. Discuss the job of the judicial branch. Explain that this branch checks that the laws made by Congress are fair by making sure they follow the Constitution. The Supreme Court also makes sure that the President carries out the laws according to the Constitution. Add *nine justices* to the third row of the third column of the "Three Branches of U.S. Government" chart.

8 **History** Point out that the U.S. Constitution was designed to create checks and balances between the three branches of government. With three branches, no part of the government can be too powerful. One branch can correct mistakes made by another. This is how the executive, legislative, and judicial branches share power.

The Judicial Branch

The judicial branch of the government makes sure that the laws are fair. The Supreme Court is part of the judicial branch. The **Supreme Court** decides on laws for the whole country.

The Supreme Court has nine judges. Each is chosen by the President and is agreed to by Congress. These judges make sure that laws are fair to all citizens.

Reading Check **What is the job of the Supreme Court?** The Supreme Court makes sure laws for the whole country are fair.

The Supreme Court

The Constitution

36

Practice and Extend

BACKGROUND

Amendments The Constitution is considered to be the supreme law of our country. At times, people decide that the Constitution needs to be amended, or changed. Congress can propose an amendment by a two-thirds vote or Congress must call a national convention to consider an amendment. Once an amendment is proposed, it must be ratified by three-fourths of the states in order to become a part of the Constitution.

REACH ALL LEARNERS

Leveled Practice Discuss the basic concepts of American government.

Basic Invite children to describe something in school that is good for everyone, not just for a few people.

Proficient Ask children to describe their freedoms.

Advanced Challenge children to name some ways people can take part in government.

The Constitution

8 The **Constitution** is a written set of rules that the government must follow. It explains how each branch of our government needs to work. The Constitution also lists the rights of all citizens of the United States. New rights and laws are added to the Constitution when they are needed.

Reading Check **Why does our government need the Constitution?** Our government needs the Constitution because it explains how each branch of government works.

Summary The three branches of our country's government follow the Constitution and work together for our country.

Review

1 **What to Know** How does our country's government work?

2 **Vocabulary** Why is the **Constitution** important?

3 **Activity** Make a chart showing the three branches of government and what they do.

4 **Main Idea and Details** What are some things to see in our country's capital?

37

3 Close

Summary

Have children read the summary and retell the key points of the lesson.

- The government has three branches that work together to make, carry out, and judge laws.
- The Constitution is a set of rules that explains how government must work and lists the rights of citizens.

Assess

REVIEW—Answers

1. **What to Know** The three branches of government follow the Constitution and work together to make, carry out, and decide on laws.
2. **Vocabulary** The Constitution is important because it sets out the rules for the government to follow.
3. **Activity Assessment Guidelines** See Performance Rubric. This activity can be used with the Unit Project.
4. **Main Idea and Details** People can see the White House, the Capitol building, and the Supreme Court building.

Use Focus Skills Transparency 1 or Main Idea and Details Graphic Organizer Write-On/Wipe-Off Card.

PERFORMANCE RUBRIC

Score 4
- offers a clearly organized chart
- provides excellent descriptions of the three branches of government

Score 3
- offers an organized chart
- provides good descriptions of the three branches of government

Score 2
- offers a chart with little organization
- provides weak descriptions of the three branches of government

Score 1
- offers a chart with poor or no organization
- provides poor or no descriptions

HOMEWORK AND PRACTICE

Name _____ Date _____

Our Country's Government

Read each sentence. Fill in the blank with a word from the Word Bank. Use each word only once.

Word Bank

capital   Congress   three
Supreme Court   Constitution   nine

1 Our country's government has ___three___ branches.
2 The written set of rules for our government is called the ___Constitution___.
3 Washington, D.C., is the ___capital___ of the United States.
4 ___Congress___ is the branch of government that makes the laws.
5 The ___Supreme Court___ makes sure all the laws are fair.
6 The Supreme Court has ___nine___ judges.

page 7

REACH ALL LEARNERS

Special Needs Have children perform in groups of three to act as each branch of government. Invite each group to practice and perform this role play:

Child 1: I am Congress.
I write the laws.

Child 2: I am the President.
I make sure laws are carried out.

Child 3: I am the Supreme Court.
I make sure the laws are fair.

OBJECTIVES

- Understand how one person can make a difference in the community.

- Examine ways citizens work together to solve a community problem.

RESOURCES

Unit 1 Audiotext CD Collection

💡 Link to the Big Idea

Government When people help one another, a community is a better place to live. Even one person's actions can make a difference by upholding the values and principles of our Constitution.

Vocabulary Help Remind children that citizens must be responsible and work together to build a strong community. Have children recall the meaning of *responsibility*. Invite children to brainstorm ways they can show responsibility and help others in their community.

Focus On: Constitutional Principles

Primary Source: Quotation Read aloud Brandon's words on page 39.
Source: Brandon Keefe, http://myhero.com.

Q What is the "difference" that Brandon is talking about?

A Brandon made sure the children at Hollygrove had the same chance to read as other children. Being able to read means people learn about choices they need to make and chances they have to do things.

Citizenship

Books for Everyone

One responsibility people have in their community is to work together to solve problems. The Constitution says that all people must have the same chances to do things. Read about some students who believed that everyone should have books to read.

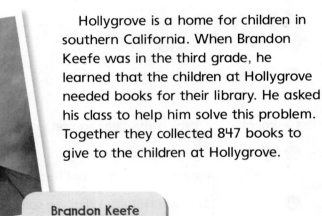

Hollygrove is a home for children in southern California. When Brandon Keefe was in the third grade, he learned that the children at Hollygrove needed books for their library. He asked his class to help him solve this problem. Together they collected 847 books to give to the children at Hollygrove.

Brandon Keefe still works for BookEnds today.

38

Practice and Extend

BACKGROUND

Brandon Keefe and BookEnds Brandon Keefe started BookEnds when he was eight years old. He now works for the American Council on Renewal Energy in Washington, D.C. He graduated from the University of California, Los Angeles in 2006. Even though he is busy working, Brandon still finds time to work with BookEnds. He serves as spokesperson for the group and sits on the board.

MAKE IT RELEVANT

At School Encourage children to hold their own book drive. Help them think of ways to collect used books. Children may donate their own books or ask family or friends for donations. Set up a donation box in the classroom. Then decide where to donate the books at the end of the book drive.

Brandon's book drive grew into an organization called BookEnds. Volunteers collect used books so that all children can have a chance to read. Brandon says, "It's great to know you've made a difference and things are going to change because of what you've done."

Make It Relevant Why is it important to your community to help others learn how to read?

These children thank BookEnds for their new books!

39

Economics Discuss why some places like Hollygrove need books. Point out that sometimes schools don't have the money to buy books.

Visual Literacy: Pictures Tell children that the photographs on page 39 show children who have been helped by Brandon's service.

Q What did BookEnds give the children at Hollygrove?

A They gave them many books to read.

Q How did this help the children?

A They had lots of books to read. They might want to read more.

Make It Relevant

Read the question aloud to children. Encourage children to tell why they think it is important to the community to help others learn to read. Explain that people who know how to read succeed at school, get jobs more easily, and are more aware of what is happening in their community.

REACH ALL LEARNERS

Leveled Practice Invite children to show ways people can help others in their community.

(Basic) Ask children to draw a picture with labels that explains how they might help a neighbor.

(Proficient) Ask children to draw a picture and write sentences that tell how to help someone else.

(Advanced) Have children make a collage and write a paragraph about people helping each other.

INTEGRATE THE CURRICULUM

READING/LANGUAGE ARTS Ask children to make a list of tips to make reading easier. For example, they can list tips such as *Read the book's title first* or *Check the meaning of words you do not know.* Then have children make a poster that includes the list of tips. Suggest that children illustrate their posters. Display the posters in the classroom or school library. **Make a List**

OBJECTIVES

- Identify the structure of local and state governments.
- Compare and contrast the functions of local, state, and national governments.

VOCABULARY

council p. 42
legislature p. 43

MAIN IDEA AND DETAILS

pp. 4–5, 45

RESOURCES

Homework and Practice Book, p. 8; Reading Support and Intervention, pp. 18–21; Success for English Learners, pp.18–21; Vocabulary Transparency 1–5; Focus Skills Transparency 1; Main Idea and Details Graphic Organizer Write-On/Wipe-Off Card; Activity Pattern A4; Unit 1 Audiotext CD Collection; Internet Resources

I Introduce

What to Know Have children read the What to Know question. Have children find their state on a U.S. map and identify it's capital city where their state government meets. Remind children to look for answers to the question as they read the lesson.

Build Background Invite children to recall the country's three branches of government and how each works. Point out that community and state governments are similar in many ways.

Lesson

Community and State Governments

 What to Know What are the jobs of our community and state governments?

Vocabulary
council
legislature

 Main Idea and Details

A community and a state both have governments. These governments do different jobs for their citizens.

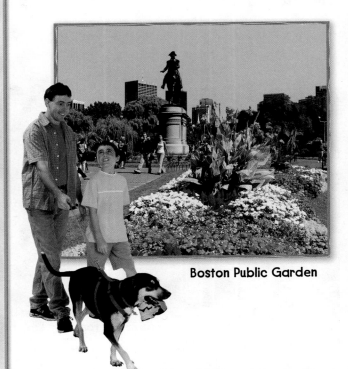

Boston Public Garden

40

Practice and Extend

 **Express Path**

When minutes count, look for the **EXPRESS PATH** to focus on the lesson's main ideas.

Quick Summary

Local governments run communities. State governments run the state. Both state and local governments have executive, legislative, and judicial branches.

Working for the People

1 Local governments work for the people of their community. They run the police and fire departments and plan buildings and parks.

2 State governments work for all the people in a state. They take care of state roads and highways. In an emergency, the state government helps people get the food and shelter they need.

Reading Check **How do community and state governments take care of citizens?**

Community governments run police and fire departments, and plan buildings and parks. State governments take care of roads and highways, and help people during emergencies.

41

Working for the People

CONTENT FOCUS Local government works for the people of a community. The state government works for all the people in the state.

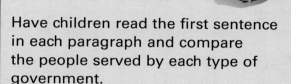

Express Path

Have children read the first sentence in each paragraph and compare the people served by each type of government.

1 Civics and Government Discuss and compare the functions of local and state governments, as described in the text. For example, local governments oversee police and fire departments and plan buildings and parks. State governments build roads and highways and plan for emergency aid.

2 Correct Misconceptions In a community, there are local (city and county) roads, as well as state roads. Who owns and takes care of the roads depends on where the roads begin and end.

VOCABULARY

Vocabulary Transparency 1-5

MINI-GLOSSARY Read each term, and study its definition.

council A group of citizens chosen to make decisions for all the people. p. 42
legislature A group of citizens chosen to make decisions for a state. p. 43

WORD WORK Complete the activities below.

1. **council**
HOMOPHONES/USE REFERENCE SOURCES Council and counsel sound the same but have different meanings. Look up counsel in a dictionary. What does it mean?
A counsel is a kind of discussion.

2. **legislature**
SUFFIXES What is the suffix in legislature?
legislat(ure)

3. **legislature**
WORD FAMILIES Are legislature and legislate in the same word family? How do you know?
Yes. They share the same root, legislate.

TRANSPARENCY 1-5

READING SUPPORT/ INTERVENTION

For alternate teaching strategies, use pages 18–21 of Reading Support and Intervention to:

- identify **phonemes**
- practice **phonics**
- reinforce **vocabulary**
- build **text comprehension**
- build **fluency**

Reading Support ▶ and Intervention

ELL ENGLISH LANGUAGE LEARNERS

For English Language Learners strategies to support this lesson, see Success for English Learners pages 18–21.

- English-language development activities
- background and concepts
- vocabulary extension

Success for ▶ English Learners

The Legislative Branch

CONTENT FOCUS State and community governments have legislative branches. The legislative branch makes laws.

Express Path

Read aloud the Reading Check question, and have children find the answer in the text.

③ Civics and Government Compare a city council with Congress. Help children conclude that both make laws and are elected by citizens. A council makes decisions for the city and Congress makes decisions for the whole country.

④ Visual Literacy: Pictures Focus attention on the picture of the city council meeting. Point out that some communities have town meetings rather than city council meetings. These meetings are less formal and have open discussions about issues.

Help children research different government leaders in their community. Distribute copies of Activity Pattern A4. Ask children to draw in the circles pictures of the people they have researched, and write their names and positions. Have children cut out the circles and tape them together to form a chain. Invite children to explain how the people in their pictures help their community.

The Legislative Branch

③ Like our country's government, state and community governments have three branches. A community's legislative branch is usually a city or town council. The **council** is a group of people chosen by citizens to make choices for them.

④ The council meets to talk about problems in the community and find solutions. In many communities, the council works with the mayor to make city laws.

Sam Bowman of the Oklahoma City City Council

42

Practice and Extend

BACKGROUND

County Governments A county government is a level of government smaller than a state but larger than a city or town. The county government administers state laws at the local level. A county is a division of a state, but in some states counties are called parishes or boroughs. Each has a county seat, where its government operates.

REACH ALL LEARNERS

Advanced Invite children to research your state's legislature to find out whether it has one house or two houses. Also ask children to find out what the state legislature is called. Challenge children to find out how many representatives each house has and who their local representatives in the state legislature are.

5 The state legislature is like a community council, but it is much larger. A state's **legislature** is a group of elected citizens who makes decisions for the state. Each member represents a community in his or her state. Members of the legislature meet in the state capital to make laws.

Reading Check In what ways are city councils and state legislatures alike?

They both make choices for the people that elected them.

6

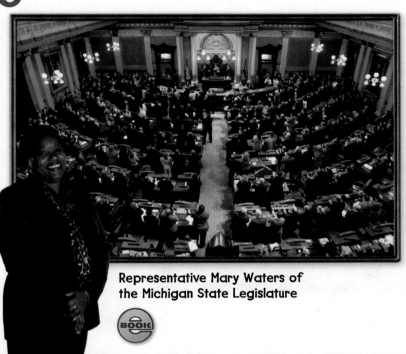

Representative Mary Waters of the Michigan State Legislature

43

5 **Civics and Government** Create a three-column chart that compares and contrasts the legislative branches at the local, state, and national level. Ask children to use what they learn to complete the chart.

The legislative branch makes laws		
National	**State**	**Local**
Congress	State Legislature	City or Town Council

6 **Visual Literacy: Pictures** Have children identify the two people on pages 42 and 43 and what their jobs are in the government.

Q How are their jobs alike and different?

A Both help make laws. The city council member works for the community government. The member of the state legislature works for the state government.

BOOK Interactive in the enhanced online student eBook

INTEGRATE THE CURRICULUM

VISUAL ARTS Display pictures of your state's capitol building, which can be found in encyclopedias and books and on the Internet. Discuss the different views, or perspectives, of the building. Then let children draw the perspective of the building that they find most interesting. Finally, invite children to create tempera or watercolor paintings of the building. **Paint a Picture**

READING/LANGUAGE ARTS Write *capital* on the board and ask children to find the word on page 43. Explain that *capital* means "a city in which a government meets." Then write *capitol*. Say both words and explain that they are homophones, or words that sound alike. Explain that a capitol is a building or group of buildings in which a government works. The U.S. Capitol is always capitalized. **Homophones**

MENTAL MAPPING

State Capital Challenge children to find your state's capital on a map of your state.

- Compare the locations of the capital and their community.
- Determine the direction of the capital from their community.
- Have children pretend that their desks are a map of your state. Ask them to find your community and the capital on their desk map.

Executive and Judicial Branches

CONTENT FOCUS The executive branch of a community government includes a mayor. A state's executive branch includes a governor. The judicial branches of these governments include courts.

Express Path

Have children find the answers to the Reading Check questions.

7 Civics and Government Create a three-column chart to fill out with children. Help them understand the structure of the executive branch.

Executive branch carries out laws		
National	**State**	**Local**
President	Governor	Mayor

8 Visual Literacy: Pictures Have children read the captions and find the leaders in the photographs.

Q What does a mayor do?

A A mayor works to helps the community's citizens.

Q What does a governor do?

A A governor sees that state laws are obeyed and suggests new laws to the state legislature.

9 Civics and Government Discuss how a court decides whether a person has broken a law and if so, what the consequences should be. Explain that a judge or a group of people called a jury may make these decisions. The local and state courts make sure that all citizens are treated fairly under the law.

Executive Branch

7 In both community and state governments, the executive branch makes sure that laws are obeyed. The executive branch of a community includes the mayor and other people who work to help the community's citizens.

Mayor Elaine Walker of Bowling Green, Kentucky

A state's executive branch includes the governor. The governor helps see that state laws are obeyed. He or she can also suggest new laws to the state legislature.

 8

Reading Check **What is the job of the executive branches?** The executive branches make sure that laws are obeyed.

Governor Mitch Daniels of Indiana

44

Practice and Extend

MAKE IT RELEVANT

In Your State Use local newspapers and other media to help children identify their state's governor, and other state leaders, by picture and name.

REACH ALL LEARNERS

Leveled Practice Show children a newspaper article about a speech by their state's governor.

Basic Invite children to make a word web that shows what the governor is discussing.

Proficient Ask children to listen to you read what the governor said and then retell it in sentences.

Advanced Have children write a paragraph about the speech.

Judicial Branch

9 The judicial branches of both community and state governments are made up of the courts. The courts and the judges make sure city and state laws are carried out fairly.

Reading Check **What is the job of the judicial branches?** The judicial branches make sure city and state laws are carried out fairly.

Summary Like our country's government, community and state governments make laws and take care of citizens.

Review

1 What to Know What are the jobs of community and state governments?

2 Vocabulary What is the job of a state **legislature**?

3 Activity Make a poster to explain to your community council a law you think your community needs.

4 Main Idea and Details What is one of the jobs of a governor?

HOMEWORK AND PRACTICE

Name _____ Date _____

Whose Job Is It?

Write each job in the correct place in the chart below.

City parks   Highways   Mayor

Governor   Help in an emergency   Town council

Community Government Jobs	State Government Jobs
City parks	Highways
Mayor	Governor
Town council	Help in an emergency

page 8

ELL ENGLISH LANGUAGE LEARNERS

Basic Have children find pictures of a city council, state legislature, mayor, and governor.

Proficient Ask questions that require children to differentiate between leaders, for example, *Does a mayor or a governor lead a state?* (governor)

Advanced Ask children to describe the work of a city council, state legislature, mayor, and governor.

---

3 Close

Summary

Have children review the summary and restate the lesson's key content.

• A community government runs a community and works for the people in the community.

• A state government runs the state and works for all the citizens of the state.

Assess

REVIEW—Answers

1. **What to Know** Community governments work for the people of their community. State governments work for all the people in a state.

2. **Vocabulary** A state **legislature** makes laws and decisions for its state.

3. **Activity Assessment Guidelines** See Performance Rubric. This activity can be used with the Unit Project.

4. **Main Idea and Details** The governor makes sure laws are carried out and suggests new laws.

Use Focus Skills Transparency 1 or Main Idea and Details Graphic Organizer Write-On/Wipe-Off Card.

Read a Map Key

OBJECTIVES

- **Use a map title and map key to locate information.**

- **Create a map with a key and borders.**

VOCABULARY

map key p. 46   **border** p. 46

RESOURCES

Homework and Practice Book, p. 9;
Social Studies Skills Transparency 1-4;
Primary Atlas; Interactive Atlas; Unit 1
Audiotext CD Collection;
Internet Resources

I Introduce

Show children a street map of your community. Ask children if they could use this map to find out what crops are grown in their state or to find the names of all fifty states. Invite children to discuss why we need different maps. Show children the map key, or legend, located on the map and discuss the pictures and symbols they see.

Why It Matters Explain that different kinds of maps show different things and are used in different ways. Point out that a road map shows the roads in a state or community. Such a map would be used to find the route for a trip. Stress that the title of the map and its key will help children know what the map is used for.

Why It Matters The title of a map helps you know what the map will show. A **map key** explains what the symbols mean.

Learn

On this map, you can use the map key to find our national capital, or our country's capital. You can also use the key to find each state capital and borders. A **border** is a line that shows where a state or country ends.

❷ Practice

❶ Find Kentucky on the map. What is the capital city?

❷ Which states are located on the borders of Oklahoma?

❸ Which states are located near our national capital?

46

Practice and Extend

SOCIAL STUDIES SKILLS

Map and Globe Skills
Read a Map Key

United States

Map Key
★ National capital
★ State capital
Border

People We Know
pages 46–47

Harcourt Social Studies

Social Studies Skills
Transparency 1-4

TRANSPARENCY 1-4

REACH ALL LEARNERS

Special Needs Provide a wooden map of the United States for children to use. You can remove their state from the map to allow children to

- easily feel the borders of the state and find its location within the United States.

- trace around the state to record it on paper.

- kinesthetically replace the state in its correct location.

United States

Map showing the United States with states and their capitals, including Canada, Mexico, the Atlantic Ocean, and the Gulf of Mexico.

Map Key
- ⊛ National capital
- ★ State capital
- — Border

Apply

Make It Relevant Make a map of your state and the states located on its borders. Include a map key.

GO ONLINE For online activities, go to www.harcourtschool.com/ss1

47

Map and Globe Skills

Leveled Practice Locate states with water borders.

Basic Name the five states that border the Gulf of Mexico.

Proficient Identify the eight states that border the Great Lakes.

Advanced Challenge children to find all the states with borders formed by bodies of water.

HOMEWORK AND PRACTICE

Name _____ Date _____

🌎 MAP AND GLOBE SKILLS
Read a Map Key
Look at the map. Then answer the questions.

Seven States

❶ What is the capital of Kentucky?   Frankfort

❷ Which states share borders with Virginia?
Maryland, West Virginia, Kentucky, Tennessee, and North Carolina

❸ Of what state is Annapolis the capital?   Maryland

❹ What is the capital of North Carolina?   Raleigh

page 9

2 ▸ Teach

Learn

❶ **Visual Literacy: Map** Write *map key* and *map legend* on the board. Explain that both names are used for the box that explains a map's symbols. Invite children to find the map key and describe each symbol in it.

Explain that the states make up our country. Remind children that each state has its own capital, in which the government meets and works. Invite children to find their state and its capital on the map.

Q How is the symbol for a state capital different from the symbol for our national capital?

A The star for the state capital does not have a circle around it.

Write *border* on the board. Read aloud the last sentence in the Learn paragraph. Invite children to use a finger to trace around the borders of their state. Challenge them to find the states that share its borders.

❷ Practice

1. Frankfort
2. Texas, New Mexico, Colorado, Kansas, Missouri, and Arkansas
3. Maryland and Virginia

3 ▸ Close

Apply

Make It Relevant Children should draw a map of their state and the states that share its borders. Their map keys should include symbols for borders and state capitals.

GO ONLINE **INTERNET RESOURCES**
For online activities, go to www.harcourtschool.com/ss1

LESSON 4 ▪ 47

Field Trip

OBJECTIVES

- **Locate and study the White House in Washington, D.C.**

- **Recognize the purpose of the White House as the residence and workplace of the President of the United States.**

RESOURCES

Unit 1 Audiotext CD Collection; Internet Resources

Link to the Big Idea

Government Remind children that the President of the United States is a part of our government. Explain that the White House is home for the President and his or her family during a term of office. They do many of the same things that families do at home, such as eating, sleeping, relaxing, and working.

Vocabulary Help Tell children that the address of a building gives the street name and number, so people can find it. Explain that some addresses, such as this one, become famous and well known.

Read About

Point out that the White House has been home for the President for over 200 years. George Washington began planning a place for the President to live in Washington, D.C., in 1790, and he helped choose the location. However, he never had the chance to live in the White House since it was not completed until 1800. John Adams was the first President to live in the White House. It was not officially called the White House until 1901.

Read About

One of the best-known addresses in the United States is 1600 Pennsylvania Avenue. This is the address of the White House, in Washington, D.C. The President of the United States lives and works here.

People can take a tour of the 132 rooms of the White House. They can see furniture, artwork, and other things used by the past Presidents.

Find

United States

Washington, D.C.

48

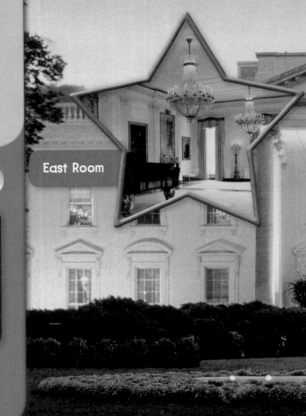

East Room

THE White House

Practice and Extend

ENGLISH LANGUAGE LEARNERS

Beginning Have children point to furniture items in each room as you identify the piece by name.

Intermediate Ask children to use words for the furnishings to answer questions about each picture.

Advanced Invite children to describe and compare each room shown in the pictures.

INTEGRATE THE CURRICULUM

THEATER Ask pairs to imagine they are giving a tour of a room in the White House. Direct partners to research a specific room online or in nonfiction books. Have them use simple props to set up an area of the classroom as the White House room. After preparing and practicing a script that includes descriptive details, allow children to take classmates on a "tour." **Role Play**

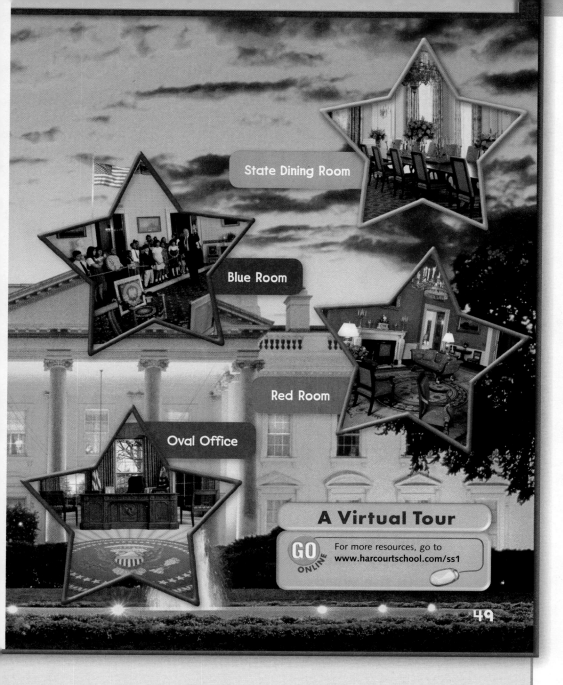

State Dining Room

Blue Room

Red Room

Oval Office

A Virtual Tour

GO ONLINE For more resources, go to www.harcourtschool.com/ss1

49

Find

Ask children to study the map and describe the location of Washington, D.C. Point out that it is not actually a state, but rather a district. Provide other maps of this area and invite volunteers to locate and name the body of water near the White House (Potomac River) and the surrounding states (Virginia, Maryland). Explain that the capital of our country was Philadelphia, Pennsylvania, before being moved to Washington, D.C.

Discuss the White House

Invite children to look closely at the rooms in the White House pictured on pages 48–49.

Q Which rooms would be used for eating meals?

A the State Dining Room

Q How do you think the President uses the other rooms? What makes you think this?

A Possible responses: Oval Office for work or interviews because of the desk; East Room for big parties because of the piano and its size

A Virtual Tour Depending on the availability of computers, have children work individually, in pairs, or in small groups to view the virtual tours. Encourage them to research the history of the White House as they explore the websites. Remind children to use what they learn on their virtual tours as background information for the Unit Project.

INTERNET RESOURCES

GO ONLINE For more resources, go to **www.harcourtschool.com/ss1**

BACKGROUND

White House by the Numbers
The White House interior currently has 35 washrooms, 147 windows, 412 doors, 28 fireplaces, 8 staircases, and 3 elevators. The kitchen is set up for 5 chefs to provide dinner for 140 guests or serve appetizers to 1,000 guests. The White House is 6 stories tall and needs 570 gallons of white paint to cover the exterior. The building has been rebuilt after 2 fires, one in 1814 and another in 1929.

MAKE IT RELEVANT

In Your State Invite children to work in pairs to research at the media center or on the Internet to learn interesting facts about the residence of the governor of their state. Have children make a diagram indicating what kinds of rooms are found there. Direct children to list the name of the residence, some of the rooms found there, and other interesting details about the place.

💡 Link to the Big Idea

Government Remind children that a government makes laws to help people be safe and get along. Help children name some of the laws and rules they know that help them get along. Rules may include those in the classroom and those at home.

Preview the Games

It's a Match! In this game, children are asked to look at four posters and find two that are exactly alike. Children will need to use their observational skills to find the matching posters. Prompt children with questions such as:

Q Which posters have the same writing?
A A, C, D

Q Which posters have the same pictures?
A A, B, C

ANSWERS: A and C are exactly the same. Poster B reads "Choose a good mayor," while the others read "Choose a good leader." Poster D shows Marla wearing a different hat than in the other posters.

Marla Manning wants to be the city's new mayor. She wants citizens to vote for her in the next election.

Find the two posters that are exactly alike. Look at the pictures and the words.

50

Practice and Extend

REACH ALL LEARNERS

Leveled Practice Have children think of a person who was elected to the government.

(Basic) Discuss with children what that person does in his or her job.

(Proficient) Ask children to draw a picture of that person doing his or her job.

(Advanced) Have children compare that job to another person's job in government.

MAKE IT RELEVANT

In Your Community Encourage children to think about the rules they follow in their community. Explain to them that the people they vote into office make the rules and laws they have to follow. Then have children write a list of rules they have to follow where they live.

C

MARLA FOR MAYOR!

CHOOSE A GOOD LEADER
VOTE FOR MARLA

D

MARLA FOR MAYOR!

CHOOSE A GOOD LEADER
VOTE FOR MARLA

Online Adventures GO ONLINE

Our country's capital is having a parade! Play an online game to help Eco find the parade and learn about government. Play now, at **www.harcourtschool.com/ss1**

51

INTERNET RESOURCES

GO ONLINE

For more resources, go to
www.harcourtschool.com/ss1

Share the Fun

At School Have children work in small groups to create their own It's a Match! game. Help them create a game similar to this activity based on what they know about government. When children are finished, ask them to share their games with their classmates.

At Home Encourage children to have their parents or guardians explain to them why it is important to vote in elections. Ask children to make a list that includes the reasons they discussed. Ask children to share their results with classmates.

The Big Idea

Government Ask a volunteer to read aloud the Big Idea. Invite children to share something they learned in this unit about the role of government.

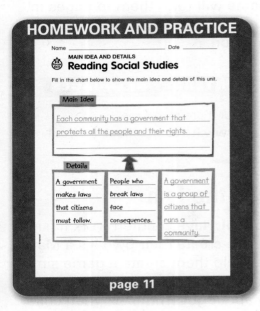

HOMEWORK AND PRACTICE

Name _____ Date _____

MAIN IDEA AND DETAILS
Reading Social Studies

Fill in the chart below to show the main idea and details of this unit.

Main Idea

Each community has a government that protects all the people and their rights.

Details

| A government makes laws that citizens must follow. | People who break laws face consequences. | A government is a group of citizens that runs a community. |

page 11

Reading Social Studies

 Main Idea and Details Remind children of the Main Idea and Details chart from Reading Social Studies at the beginning of the unit. The chart should focus on the most important information presented in the unit and the facts that support it.

 Review and Test Prep

 The Big Idea
Government A government makes laws to help people be safe and get along.

Main Idea and Details

Copy and fill in the chart to show what you learned about what a government does.

Main Idea

_____
_____

Details

| A government makes laws that citizens must follow. | People who break laws face consequences. | _____ |

52

Vocabulary

Fill in the blanks with the correct words.

My neighbor, Mrs. Arnold, likes to ❶ _____ in elections. By voting, she helps choose the people who run our community. This group of people, called a ❷ _____, helps everyone get along. Mrs. Arnold is a good ❸ _____ in our community. She follows every ❹ _____, or rule. I think she could someday be our country's ❺ _____.

Word Bank

citizen
(p. 8)

law
(p. 11)

government
(p. 18)

President
(p. 26)

vote
(p. 28)

Facts and Main Ideas

❻ What kinds of rights do Americans have?

❼ What is the job of a judge?

❽ Why do citizens pay taxes?

❾ What is the leader of a state called?
  A mayor   C judge
  B governor   D legislature

❿ What is the lawmaking branch of our country's government called?
  A Supreme Court   C Congress
  B council   D President

53

Vocabulary

1. vote
2. government
3. citizen
4. law
5. President

Facts and Main Ideas

6. We can live and work where we want. We can follow our religious beliefs and share our ideas.

7. A judge is in charge of a court and makes sure that the court protects the rights of all citizens.

8. People pay taxes so the government can pay for government services for its citizens.

9. B, governor

10. C, Congress

TEST-TAKING STRATEGIES

Review these tips with children:

- Read the directions before reading the questions.

- Read each question twice, focusing the second time on all the possible answers.

- Take time to think about all the possible answers before deciding on an answer.

- Move past questions that give you trouble, and answer the ones you know. Then return to concentrate on the difficult items.

Critical Thinking

11. Possible answer: Communities change over time and we need new laws to protect people and keep them safe.

12. **Make It Relevant** Possible answer: Some people would not follow the laws. People would not be safe.

Skills

13. Reed
14. six votes
15. nine votes
16. Arturo

---

⑪ Why do you think new laws have been added to the Constitution?

⑫ **Make It Relevant** What would happen if there were not consequences for breaking laws in your community?

✓ Skills

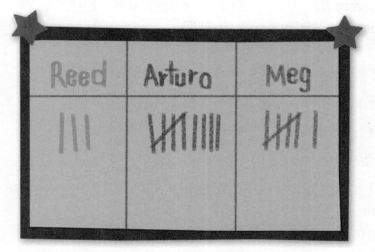

⑬ Who has the fewest votes?

⑭ How many votes does Meg have?

⑮ How many votes does Arturo have?

⑯ Who has the most votes?

54

States in the South

ⓘ⑰ What is the capital city of Arkansas?

⑱ Which states share a border with North Carolina?

⑲ What state's capital is Frankfort?

⑳ What is the capital city of Tennessee?

Skills

17. Little Rock

18. South Carolina, Virginia, Tennessee, Georgia

19. Kentucky

20. Nashville

ASSESSMENT

Use the UNIT 1 Test on pages 2–4 of the Assessment Program.

Show What You Know

Unit Writing Activity

Speak Out! Discuss rules that help citizens stay safe, such as traffic and property laws. Then talk about rules and laws that help people get along, such as protecting freedom of speech or rules for using a local park. List children's responses in two columns labeled *Keep Safe* and *Keep the Peace*.

Write a Letter Have children use their ideas to identify a problem in their community. Invite children to state the problem and propose a solution in a letter to the mayor. Review letter writing conventions, such as including a date, greeting, and closing.

You may wish to distribute the Unit 1 Writing Activity Guidelines on page 5 of the Assessment Program.

For a scoring rubric, see this Teacher Edition, page 10.

Unit Project

Role-Play Consider having children view a local council meeting on video so they can better understand the props and procedures they will need. Have children choose roles as citizens, mayor, council members, or audience. Ask children to brainstorm simple props and costumes. After practicing several times, have children role-play the council meeting.

You may wish to distribute the Unit 1 Project Guidelines on page 7 of the Assessment Program.

For a scoring rubric, see this Teacher Edition, page 10.

LEVELED READERS

Use the LEVELED READERS for Unit 1.

Activities

Show What You Know

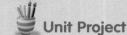

Unit Writing Activity

Speak Out! What would help the citizens of your community stay safe?

Write a Letter Write a letter to the mayor about a problem. Tell how you think it should be solved.

Unit Project

Role-Play Role-play how a city council makes laws.
- Practice presenting opinions.
- Use props and costumes.
- Role-play a council meeting and write a new law.

Read More

The U.S. Supreme Court by Muriel L. Dubois

What Presidents Are Made Of by Hanoch Piven

D is for Democracy: A Citizen's Alphabet by Elissa Grodin

GO ONLINE For more resources, go to **www.harcourtschool.com/ss1**

56

Read More

After the children's study of government, encourage independent reading with these books or books of your choice. Additional books are listed on page 1J of this Teacher Edition.

Basic *The U. S. Supreme Court* by Muriel L. Dubois (Capstone Press, 2004). Learn about the Supreme Court, its justices, and how it selects and decides cases.

Proficient *What Presidents Are Made Of* by Hanoch Piven (Atheneum, 2004). Portraits of U.S. Presidents characterize aspects of their personalities or interests.

Advanced *D is for Democracy: A Citizen's Alphabet* by Elissa Grodin (Sleeping Bear Press, 2004). Children learn about the democratic process through this alphabet book.

The World Around Us

The Big Idea

The Land

Maps help us learn about the different kinds of land, water, and places around us.

What to Know

✓ How do maps help people find locations?

✓ What countries and landforms make up North America?

✓ Why are seasons and climate different in different regions?

✓ How are regions around the world different?

Introduce the Unit

 The Big Idea

The Land Read the Big Idea to children. Explain that locating on maps where people live helps us understand how they live. In this unit, children will learn about the geography of the land, how the climate and seasons affect how we live, and how the regions in the United States compare to other regions around the world. Remind children to refer back to the Big Idea periodically as they finish this unit.

What to Know Read What to Know to children. Explain that these four essential questions will help them focus on the Big Idea.

Assessing the Big Idea Share with children that throughout this unit they will be asked to show evidence of their understanding of the Big Idea. See Assessment Options on page 57M of this Teacher Edition.

START WITH A VIDEO DVD

To introduce the Unit Big Idea to students, show a video clip from the Start with a Video DVD.

Instructional Design

The flowchart below shows briefly how instruction was planned for Unit 2.

START WITH THE BIG IDEA

Lesson Objectives
What to Know

→

PLAN ASSESSMENT

Assessment Options
• Option 1—Unit 2 Test
• Option 2—Writing: Write a Friendly Letter
• Option 3—Unit Project: Geography Bulletin Board

→

PLAN INSTRUCTION

Unit 2 Teacher Edition
• materials
• instructional strategies
• activities

Express Path

See each lesson for an **EXPRESS PATH** to teach main ideas.

The World Around Us

THE BIG IDEA

THE LAND Maps help us learn about the different kinds of land, water and places around us.

LESSON	PACING	OBJECTIVES
Preview the Unit pp. 57V–57	**5 DAYS**	
Preview Vocabulary pp. 58–59		■ Use visuals to determine word meanings. ■ Use words and visuals to preview the content of the unit.
Reading Social Studies pp. 60–61		■ Compare and contrast information. ■ Interpret information from charts.
Start with a Legend "How the Prairie Became Ocean" pp. 62–65		■ Identify the purpose of a legend. ■ Recognize how a legend relates to the location of a place.
① Maps and Locations pp. 66–69 💡 **WHAT TO KNOW** How do maps help people find locations?	**3 DAYS**	■ Compare and contrast absolute and relative location. ■ Define and describe a place by its absolute and relative location. ■ Locate children's school, community, state, and country on a map or globe.
MAP AND GLOBE SKILLS **Use a Map Grid** pp. 70–71	**1 DAY**	■ Recognize that a map grid is a tool to find the absolute location of a place on a map. ■ Use a map grid to locate places on a map.
Biography: Benjamin Banneker pp. 72–73	**1 DAY**	■ Understand the importance of the actions and character of Benjamin Banneker and explain how he made a difference in others' lives.

6 WEEKS	**WEEK 1** Introduce the Unit	**WEEK 2** Lesson 1	**WEEK 3** Lesson 2	**WEEK 4** Lesson 3	**WEEK 5** Lesson 4	**WEEK 6** Wrap Up the Unit

READING SUPPORT VOCABULARY

Focus Skill Reading Social Studies
Compare and Contrast p. 63

Reading Social Studies
Focus Skill, pp. 60–61

Vocabulary Power:
Use Reference Sources, p. 59

compare p. 60
contrast p. 60

Focus Skill Reading Social Studies
Compare and Contrast, p. 69

Vocabulary Power:
Capital Letters, p. 73

location p. 66
relative location p. 66
absolute location p. 67

map grid p. 70

REACH ALL LEARNERS

ENGLISH LANGUAGE LEARNERS, pp. 58, 64

Leveled Practice, pp. 61, 64

Advanced, p. 62

Leveled Practice, pp. 68, 71

Advanced, p. 73

INTEGRATE LEARNING

Science
Land Features, p. 57

Visual Arts
Painting, p. 57

Reading/Language Arts
Write a Paragraph, p. 60

Theater
Dramatic Reading, p. 63

RESOURCES

Social Studies in Action:
  Resources for the
  Classroom
Primary Source Collection
⊙ Music CD
School-to-Home Newsletter
  S5–S6
Interactive Map
  Transparencies
Interactive Desk Maps
Primary Atlas
Interactive Atlas
TimeLinks: Interactive
  Time Line
Picture Vocabulary Cards
Focus Skills Transparency 2
Compare and Contrast
  Graphic Organizer
  Write-On/Wipe-Off Card
Assessment Program p. 9
⊙ Unit 2 Audiotext CD
  Collection
💻 Internet Resources
⊙ Start with a Video DVD

Homework and Practice
  Book, pp. 12–13
Reading Support and
  Intervention, pp. 22–25
Success for English
  Language Learners,
  pp. 23–26
Vocabulary Transparency 2-1
Focus Skills Transparency 2
Compare and Contrast
  Graphic Organizer
  Write-On/Wipe-Off Card
Activity Pattern A5
Social Studies Skills
  Transparency 2-1
Primary Atlas
Interactive Atlas
⊙ Multimedia Biography CD
TimeLinks: Interactive Time
  Line
⊙ Unit 2 Audiotext CD
  Collection
💻 Internet Resources

LESSON	PACING	OBJECTIVES
2 **North America** pp. 74–81 ![light bulb] **WHAT TO KNOW** What countries and landforms make up North America?	**5** **DAYS**	■ Identify the countries of North America. ■ Identify landforms and bodies of water in North America.
MAP AND GLOBE SKILLS **Read a Landform Map** pp. 82–83	**1** **DAY**	■ Define *region*. ■ Use a map key and symbols to identify landforms and bodies of water on a map.
3 **Seasons and Climate** pp. 84–87 ![light bulb] **WHAT TO KNOW** Why are seasons and climate different in different regions?	**4** **DAYS**	■ Compare and contrast climate and weather. ■ Recognize that climate and seasons vary depending on location and time of year. ■ Describe the climate of a place.
CHART AND GRAPH SKILLS **Read a Table** pp. 88–89	**1** **DAY**	■ Understand how information is organized on a table or chart. ■ Interpret information from a table or chart.

READING SUPPORT VOCABULARY	REACH ALL LEARNERS	INTEGRATE LEARNING	RESOURCES
Reading Social Studies (Focus Skill) **Compare and Contrast,** pp. 78, 81 **Vocabulary Power:** Compound Words, p. 76 Plurals, p. 81 **landform** p. 76 **island** p. 79 **peninsula** p. 79 **gulf** p. 80 **region** p. 82	**ENGLISH LANGUAGE LEARNERS,** p. 79 **Leveled Practice,** pp. 80, 83 **Advanced,** p. 77 **Special Needs,** p. 77	**Music** Song Lyrics, p. 76 **Visual Arts** Clay Models, p. 80 Textured Map, p. 82	Homework and Practice Book, pp. 14–15 Reading Support and Intervention, pp. 26–29 Success for English Language Learners, pp. 27–30 Vocabulary Transparency 2-2 Focus Skills Transparency 2 Compare and Contrast Graphic Organizer Write-On/Wipe-Off Card Activity Pattern A6 Social Studies Skills Transparency 2-2 Primary Atlas Interactive Atlas Unit 2 Audiotext CD Collection Internet Resources
Reading Social Studies (Focus Skill) **Compare and Contrast,** p. 87 **climate** p. 86 **table** p. 88	**Leveled Practice,** pp. 86, 89 **Advanced,** p. 88		Homework and Practice Book, pp. 16–17 Reading Support and Intervention, pp. 30–33 Success for English Language Learners, pp. 31–34 Vocabulary Transparency 2-3 Focus Skills Transparency 2 Compare and Contrast Graphic Organizer Write-On/Wipe-Off Card Social Studies Skills Transparency 2-3 Unit 2 Audiotext CD Collection Internet Resources

LESSON	PACING	OBJECTIVES
4 **World Regions** pp. 90–93 ◾ **WHAT TO KNOW** How are regions around the world different?	**4** **DAYS**	■ Identify the cardinal directions. ■ Recognize hemispheres, the equator, and poles on a map or globe. ■ Identify and compare the characteristics of world regions.
MAP AND GLOBE SKILLS **Find Directions on a Map** pp. 94–95	**1** **DAY**	■ Identify intermediate directions. ■ Describe one place relative to another using cardinal and intermediate directions.
Field Trip: Cape Cod National Seashore pp. 96–97	**1** **DAY**	■ Identify the landforms and bodies of water of a region. ■ Recognize the unique features of a region, including wildlife, structures, and activities.
Fun with Social Studies: Weather Tic-Tac-Toe pp. 98–99 **Unit 2 Review and Activities** pp. 100–104	**3** **DAYS**	

READING SUPPORT VOCABULARY	REACH ALL LEARNERS	INTEGRATE LEARNING	RESOURCES

READING SUPPORT VOCABULARY

(Focus Skill) **Reading Social Studies**
Compare and Contrast
p. 93

cardinal directions p. 90
equator p. 90
hemisphere p. 91
pole p. 91

compass rose p. 94
intermediate directions p. 94

REACH ALL LEARNERS

ENGLISH LANGUAGE LEARNERS, p. 94

Leveled Practice, pp. 92, 95

Advanced, pp. 93, 96

Special Needs, p. 96

INTEGRATE LEARNING

Mathematics
Differences, p. 92

RESOURCES

Homework and Practice
Book, pp. 18–19
Reading Support and
Intervention,
pp. 34–37
Success for English
Language Learners,
pp. 35–38
Vocabulary
Transparency 2-4
Focus Skills
Transparency 2
Compare and Contrast
Graphic Organizer
Write-On/Wipe-Off
Card
Social Studies Skills
Transparency 2-4
Primary Atlas
Interactive Atlas
Unit 2 Audiotext CD
Collection
Internet Resources

ENGLISH LANGUAGE LEARNERS, p. 99

Leveled Practice, p. 98

Reading/Language Arts
Record Weather,
p. 98

Homework and Practice
Book, pp. 20–21
Assessment Program,
pp. 10–12
Leveled Readers
Leveled Readers Teacher
Guide
Unit 2 Audiotext CD
Collection
Internet Resources

STUDENT DIGITAL LEARNING

The interactive eBook provides students with the standards-based content of Harcourt print books in addition to interactive add-ons that enhance student interest and reinforce Social Studies content. Harcourt eBooks are available in both a basic and enhanced version.

INTERACTIVE VISUALS

Students watch the world around them come to life through engaging interactive activities that enhance the unit content.

STREAMING VIDEO

Each Unit Opener includes video tied to the Unit Big Idea. This clip provides students with enhanced information about types of landforms.

SKILLS ACTIVITIES

Each Chart and Graph Skill and Map and Globe Skill is enhanced by an interactive online activity.

LIVE INK ENHANCEMENT

Live Ink provides students with reading help through a patented system that breaks sentences down into segments. The Live Ink system is proven to increase student comprehension and test scores. Live Ink is available for grades 3–6/7.

ONLINE ADVENTURES

Fun with Social Studies provides a link to our Online Adventures game. Students play a game in which they go on a fishing trip. The game reviews important concepts from the unit.

MULTIMEDIA BIOGRAPHIES

Biographies from the student edition include additional information in an interactive Multimedia Biography. Students can find more information, view related biographies, explore maps and images, and find links to additional webpages.

THE LEARNING SITE

The eBook includes links to **www.harcourtschool.com/ss1** There students can find internal resources such as our complete Multimedia Biographies databases and our Online Adventures games. This Harcourt Social Studies site also provides students with additional research tools.

Back   Forward   Reload   Home

Teacher Resources

E-PLANNER

The e-Planner provides a useful tool for scheduling Social Studies lessons.

- Use it to access Teacher Edition pages and student workbook pages and to plan classroom activities.
- The calendar tool displays all your scheduled Social Studies lessons in an easy-to-use format.
- All standards are organized by grade level.

HSPOA

Harcourt School Publishers Online Assessment provides teachers with a reliable, confidential system for online delivery of Social Studies assessment. Using this system, you can track student performance correlated to standards and run prescribed reports for any missed standards. Questions are correlated to our print Assessment program.

VIDEOS AND DVDS

A comprehensive package of videos for Grades K–3 provides an entertaining overview of core social studies concepts such as government, geography, economics, culture and history. Videos in this package are available from Schlessinger Media® and are also available digitally on SAFARI Montage.

SAFARI MONTAGE™

For more information, see pages TEI13–TEI18.

FREE AND INEXPENSIVE MATERIALS

Free and inexpensive materials are listed on the Social Studies Website at **www.harcourtschool.com/ss1**

- Addresses to write to for free and inexpensive products
- Links to unit–related materials
- Internet maps
- Internet references

COMMUNITY RESOURCES FOR THE CLASSROOM

The **National Atlas** website offers interactive, customizable maps of different areas in the United States. Use the **Map Maker** tool to zoom in on your community and view map features such as cities, roads, climate, and agriculture. **http://nationalatlas.gov/**

Educators can use the **United States Census Bureau** webpage to locate census information and facts about their local communities. **http://factfinder.census.gov/home/saff/main.html?_lang=en**

The **National Park Service** offers a comprehensive site with a search engine that cross-references our country's National Historic Landmarks by name, city, and state. **http://tps.cr.nps.gov/nhl/**

Museums in all 50 states are indexed on the **Virtual Library** museums pages. Use this site to find museums in and around your students' own community. **http://www.museumca.org/usa/states.html**

The **Library of Congress** site features numerous collections of primary sources, biographies, recordings, and photographs. The topic **Cities and Towns** contains photographic records of communities throughout the history of the United States. **http://memory.loc.gov/ammem/**

Additional Sites are available at www.harcourtschool.com/ss1

Leveled Readers

Lesson Plan Summaries

TOPIC
The World Around Us

Summary *North, South, East, West.* This Reader identifies and explains important ideas in geography, including location, landforms, climate, and regions.

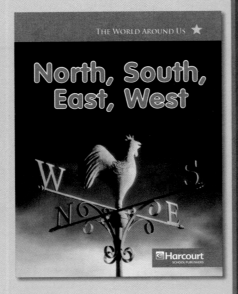

BEFORE READING

Vocabulary Power Have children define the following words. Help them write one sentence for each word as it relates to the world around us.

location   climate   landform   region   hemisphere

DURING READING

Compare and Contrast Have children complete the graphic organizer to show that they understand how to compare and contrast landforms as described in the Reader.

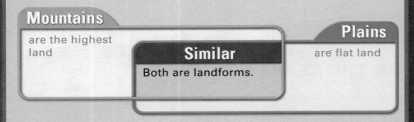

Mountains — are the highest land

Similar — Both are landforms.

Plains — are flat land

AFTER READING

Critical Thinking Lead children in a discussion about the region where they live. Ask children to describe their region's landforms, climate, plants, and animals.

Write a Travel Guide Have children choose a town or city near their community. Have children write a brief travel guide for tourists describing the area's landforms and climate.

TOPIC
The World Around Us

Summary *Different Kinds of Deserts,* by Conseulo Perez. This Reader explains what a desert is and gives examples of different kinds of deserts.

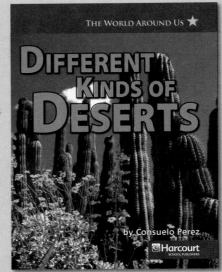

BEFORE READING

Vocabulary Power Have children define the following words. Help them write one sentence for each word as it relates to the world around us.

location   climate   desert   well   canal

DURING READING

Compare and Contrast Have children complete the graphic organizer to show that they understand how to compare and contrast deserts in the world around us, as described in the Reader.

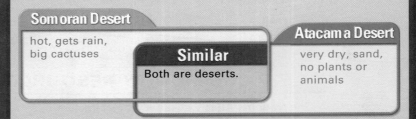

Sonoran Desert — hot, gets rain, big cactuses

Similar — Both are deserts.

Atacama Desert — very dry, sand, no plants or animals

AFTER READING

Critical Thinking Lead children in a discussion about how deserts can be the same and different.

Write a Report Have children write reports about an animal that lives in the Sonoran Desert. Invite them to draw pictures of their animals.

The *Leveled Readers Teacher Guide* provides background, reading tips, fast facts, answer keys, and copying masters.

ABOVE-LEVEL

TOPIC
The World Around Us

Summary *At the Bottom of the World,* by Sharon Fear. This Reader explains how people live and work at the South Pole.

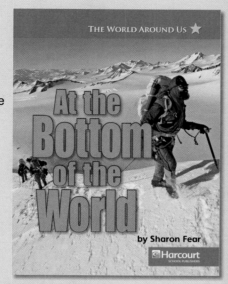

THE WORLD AROUND US ★

At the Bottom of the World

by Sharon Fear

Harcourt
SCHOOL PUBLISHERS

BEFORE READING

Vocabulary Power Have children define the following words. Help them write one sentence for each word as it relates to the world around us.

location   climate   temperature   scientist   ozone

DURING READING

Focus Skill

Compare and Contrast Have children complete the graphic organizer to show that they understand how to compare and contrast places in the world, as described in the Reader.

Living in My Community

many people live here; they live in houses or apartments; they work in office buildings, at home, and outside; we have four seasons	**Similar** Both live and work.	**Living at the South Pole** about 200 scientists live here; they live and work in a dome building; it's always cold outside

AFTER READING

Critical Thinking Lead children in a discussion about why Antarctica is a difficult place to live.

Write a Journal Entry Have children pretend they are scientists living at the South Pole. Have them write a journal entry about a typical day there. Children's journal entries should be based on facts from the Reader.

Readers' Theater
Every Student Is a Star

IT'S SHOWTIME!

Getting Started

★ Distribute the Big Idea activity sheet from your Readers' Theater.

★ Read through the script together. Make connections with unit contents.

★ Plan a performance using the **Prep ★ Practice ★ Perform** guidelines. Find ideas for props online.

Pressed for Time?

★ Perform a choral reading of the script with the whole class.

★ Assign parts for a one-time read-through.

★ Assign groups to read in your literacy center.

Read Along,

Read Aloud,

Reading Fun

Independent Reading

BASIC

DePaola, Tomie. **Four Stories for Four Seasons.** Simon and Schuster Children's Publishing, 1994. Dog, Cat, Frog, and Pig celebrate the four seasons together in these stories about the delights of each season.

Hall, Kirsten. **Buried Treasure: All About Using a Map.** Scholastic, 2004. The creatures of Beastieville follow a map to what they hope is a buried treasure.

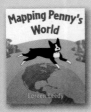

Leedy, Loreen. **Mapping Penny's World.** Holt, Henry Books for Young Readers, 2003. After learning about maps in school, Lisa maps all the favorite places of her dog Penny.

Sweeney, Joan. **Me on the Map.** Random House Children's Books, 1998. A young girl explains what maps are, from a personal to a global level.

Younger, Barbara. **Purple Mountain Majesties.** Penguin, 2002. This beautifully illustrated book tells how the western landscape inspired Katherine Lee Bates to write "America the Beautiful."

PROFICIENT

Chancellor, Deborah. **Maps and Mapping.** Houghton Mifflin, 2004. Different kinds of maps and their parts help readers understand maps and gather information from them.

Knowlton, Jack. **Geography from A to Z.** HarperCollins, 1998. This picture glossary defines and describes geographic terms about Earth's features.

Loomis, Christine. **Across America, I Love You.** Hyperion, 2000. Descriptions of landscapes and seasons relate America's geography to the relationship between a mother and her child.

Marx, David F. **Earth Day.** Scholastic, 2001. Read about Earth Day to learn how and why to celebrate this special day.

Singer, Marilyn. **On the Same Day in March: A Tour of the World's Weather.** HarperCollins, 2002. Take a trip around the world to see the different types of weather different climates have on the same day in March.

ADVANCED

Aberg, Rebecca. **Map Keys.** Scholastic, 2003. Learn how to use a map key and how to create a map and key of one's own bedroom.

Holling, Holling Clancy. **Paddle-to-the-Sea.** Houghton Mifflin, 1941. This classic tells the story of a Native American boy who carves a canoe which travels through the Great Lakes to the Atlantic Ocean.

Lewis, J. Patrick. **Earth & You: A Closer View: Nature's Features.** Dawn Publications, 2004. In this poetic look at Earth's features, the reader can experience the natural world through words and pictures.

Willis, Shirley. **The Watts Picture Atlas.** Scholastic, 2002. The atlas features photographs, pictorial maps, and fun facts to send readers on a hunt around the world.

Wolfe, Frances. **Where I Live.** Tundra Books, 2001. Visit the seaside with this poetic book about a special place where the sun winks off the waves, breezes cool the evening, and treasures wait to be discovered.

Additional books also are recommended at point of use throughout the unit.
Note that information, while correct at time of publication, is subject to change.

For information about ordering these tradebooks, visit
www.harcourtschool.com/ss1

Use these activities to help differentiate instruction. Each activity has been developed to address a different level or type of learner.

 ELL ENGLISH LANGUAGE LEARNERS

 30 minutes

Materials
- word lists
- colored chalk or colored pencils

DRAWING GAME **Play a game to help children recognize names of landforms and bodies of water.**

- Provide children with a list of landform and bodies of water, including *island, peninsula, plains, mountain, gulf, river,* and *ocean.* Discuss the meaning of each term with children.
- Organize children into small groups.
- Invite one group to choose a word and illustrate it on the board. Have the other groups identify the illustrated word.
- Alternate teams until all words have been correctly identified.

peninsula
gulf
river

SPECIAL NEEDS

 20 minutes

Materials
- crumpled paper balls
- baskets or trashcans
- index cards

BASKET GAME **Play a ball toss game to familiarize children with cardinal and intermediate direction words.**

- Place baskets or trashcans around the classroom each with the correct direction label: *N, S, E, W, NE, NW, SE, SW.*
- Shuffle a set of cards labeled *north, south, east, west, northeast, northwest, southeast,* and *southwest.*
- Practice naming a direction and indicating the matching label.
- Ask children to say a direction word and toss a paper ball into the corresponding basket as they repeat the direction word.

ADVANCED

 20 minutes

Materials
- blank index cards
- colored pencils or crayons

LANDFORMS CARD GAME **Ask children to create a matching card game about landforms.**

- Direct partners to make a set of cards with landform names and brief definitions and a set with corresponding pictures.
- Have children shuffle cards and spread them out face down on a table.
- Invite partners to take turns turning over two cards at a time until they find a match. They keep the matched cards and continue play until all matched sets have been made.

MATHEMATICS CENTER

Classroom Grid

Invite partners to create a classroom map that features a simple letter-number grid. Encourage them to draw in symbols for features such as the teacher's desk, windows, doors, centers, and bookshelves. Remind partners to create a map key to define the symbols they used. Have partners write direction riddles on index cards that others can follow to find specific locations on the map, such as: *Trace column 1. Trace row B. What do you find?* Invite children to write the answers to each on the back of the card.

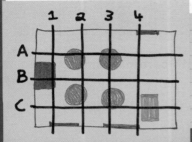

Trace column 1;
Trace row B.
What do you find?

SCIENCE CENTER

Where in the World?

Ask partners to use art materials to create a poster about a type of region found on Earth. Provide children with reference materials about different regions, such as polar, tropical, desert, forest, marine, aquatic, and wetland. Ask them to choose one region. Then have children draw or cut out pictures that show the plants, animals, geography, and climate found in the region and arrange the pictures to create a poster. Encourage children to draw a simple map that shows the location of the region on a world or continent map.

READING/LANGUAGE ARTS CENTER

Stories Maps Tell

Invite children to make treasure maps of an imaginary island. Have children research various landforms found on islands around the world. Invite children to create their own islands, assigning different colors to each landform they show. Then have children draw a large *X* on the spot where their "treasure" is buried and a dotted line that leads from some point on the edge of the island to the *X*. Ask children to write directions to find the treasure identifying landforms the treasure seeker must cross to find the *X*.

ART CENTER

Crayon Rubbings Map

Have children make rubbings of various textures to create a labeled map of North America. Provide children with an outline of North America. Ask them to think about textures that could represent various landforms and bodies of water. Explain that they will make rubbings in a variety of colors and textures, cut out shapes, and paste them to the map to represent land features. Remind children to include mountains, hills, plains, rivers, lakes, and oceans. Suggest children label well-known locations. Have them display their maps in the classroom.

The Assessment Program gives all learners many opportunities to show what they know and can do. It also provides ongoing information about each student's understanding of social studies.

 Online Assessment available at www.harcourtschool.com/ss1

OPTION 1 — UNIT TESTS
Unit 2

- **Unit Pretest,**
  Assessment Program, p. 9
- **Unit Review and Test Prep,** pp. 100–103

- **Unit Test,**
  Assessment Program, pp. 10–12

OPTION 2 — WRITING

- **Show What You Know,**
  Unit Writing Activity,
  Write a Friendly Letter, p. 104

- **Lesson Review,**
  Writing Activities, at ends of lessons

OPTION 3 — UNIT PROJECT

- **Show What You Know,**
  Unit Project,
  Geography Bulletin Board, p. 104
- **Unit Project,**
  Performance Assessment, pp. 57P–57Q

- **Lesson Review,**
  Performance Activities, at ends of lessons

INFORMAL ASSESSMENT

- **Lesson Review,** at ends of lessons
- **Skills:**
  Practice, pp. 70, 82, 88, 94
  Apply, pp. 71, 83, 89, 95

- **Reading Social Studies,**
  Compare and Contrast, pp. 60–61
- **Literature Response Corner,** p. 65

STUDENT SELF-EVALUATION

- **Reading Check Questions,** within lessons

- **Biography, Why Character Counts,** pp. 72–73
- **Map, Time Line, Graph, Diagram, and Illustration questions,** within lessons

OPTION 1 — PRETEST

Unit 2

Pretest
ANTICIPATION GUIDE (10 points each)

DIRECTIONS Read each statement, and circle Yes or No.

Name _____ Date _____

1. Maps help people find locations. **(Yes)** No

2. A map grid divides a map into squares. **(Yes)** No

3. Mexico is a neighbor of Canada. Yes **(No)**

4. North America has only one landform. Yes **(No)**

5. An island is a landform with water on only two sides. Yes **(No)**

6. A city's location affects its climate. **(Yes)** No

7. All regions have the same climate. Yes **(No)**

8. Left, right, up, and down are cardinal directions. Yes **(No)**

9. The equator is a real line that divides Earth in half. Yes **(No)**

10. Regions near the equator are very hot. **(Yes)** No

OPTION 1 — UNIT TEST

Unit 2

Test
MULTIPLE CHOICE (6 points each)

DIRECTIONS Select the letter of the best answer.

Name _____ Date _____

1. Which of these is an example of absolute location?
   A a compass rose   C a landform map
   (B) an address   D a table

2. Which continent is the United States a part of?
   A Africa   C Antarctica
   B South America   **(D) North America**

3. Which of these is NOT a landform?
   A mountain range   C plain
   (B) equator   D island

4. Which of these help you find places on a map?
   A seasons   **(C) cardinal directions**
   B landforms and regions   D climate table

5. Which of these is a point on Earth farthest from the equator?
   (A) pole   C desert
   B hemisphere   D mountain

(continued)

OPTION 1 — UNIT TEST

Name _____ Date _____

TRUE/FALSE (5 points each)

DIRECTIONS Use the table to answer the questions. Write T next to the statements that are True and F next to the statements that are False.

United States Rivers		
River	**State Where It Begins**	**Total Length**
Mississippi River	Minnesota	2,340 miles
Missouri River	Montana	2,466 miles
Ohio River	Pennsylvania	975 miles
Red River	Texas	1,018 miles

6. __F__ The table tells about rivers in Canada.

7. __T__ The Red River is longer than the Ohio River.

8. __T__ The shortest river in the table begins in Pennsylvania.

9. __T__ The Mississippi River is 2,340 miles long.

10. __F__ Two rivers begin in Montana.

11. __F__ The second column in the chart tells the river names.

12. __T__ The Ohio River is 975 miles long. *(continued)*

OPTION 1 — UNIT TEST

Name _____ Date _____

SHORT ANSWER (6 points each)

DIRECTIONS Use the map to answer the questions.

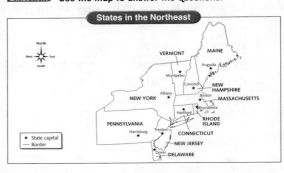

States in the Northeast

14. What does this map show? _States in the Northeast_

15. Which state is west of Massachusetts? _New York_

16. Which state capital on this map is south of Trenton, New Jersey? _Dover_

17. In what direction would you go to get from Massachusetts to Pennsylvania? _southwest_

18. Which state on this map is the farthest north? _Maine_

OPTION 2 — WRITING

RUBRIC

Name_____ **Date**_____

Unit 2 Writing Activity Guidelines

WRITE A FRIENDLY LETTER

Writing Prompt Write a letter to a pen pal telling about a place. Include a map that will help him or her get around.

▶ **STEP 1** Make a list of places in or near your community. Choose one you think your pen pal would enjoy. Think about directions, landforms, and locations that might help the person find the place.

▶ **STEP 2** Are you writing your letter to a child or an adult? Think about how the letter would need to be different for each choice.

▶ **STEP 3** Write a friendly letter to your pen pal. Explain how to get to the place from your home. On the map, show the best routes.

▶ **STEP 4** Review your work to make sure you have used correct grammar, spelling, punctuation, and capitalization.

▶ **STEP 5** Make the changes. Then copy your letter neatly.

SCORE 4
- includes clear details about important community locations
- uses language clearly appropriate for audience
- clearly describes cardinal directions, landforms, and locations
- follows conventions of correct letter form: date, greeting, body, closing, and signature
- makes no or minimal errors in grammar, punctuation, capitalization, and spelling

SCORE 3
- includes details about important community locations
- uses language mostly appropriate for chosen audience
- describes cardinal directions, landforms, and locations
- follows most conventions of correct letter form
- makes some errors in grammar, punctuation, capitalization, and spelling

SCORE 2
- includes some details about important community locations
- uses language somewhat appropriate for chosen audience
- somewhat describes cardinal directions, landforms, and locations
- follows few conventions of correct letter form
- makes several errors in grammar, punctuation, capitalization, and spelling

SCORE 1
- includes vague details about locations in the community
- uses language inappropriate for chosen audience
- does not describe cardinal directions, landforms, or locations
- does not follow correct letter form
- makes many errors in grammar, punctuation, capitalization, and spelling

OPTION 3 — PROJECT

RUBRIC

Name_____ **Date**_____

Unit 2 Project Guidelines

GEOGRAPHY BULLETIN BOARD

Design a geography bulletin board that tells about the land and how we use it.

▶ **STEP 1** Work with your group to brainstorm ideas for your bulletin board. You may want to use some of these things.
- Maps and map parts
- Pictures, drawings, or photographs
- Captions and vocabulary words
- Newspaper and magazine clippings

▶ **STEP 2** Make a plan for your bulletin board space. Gather materials your group will need.

▶ **STEP 3** Decide which part of the display you will work on. Use interesting items, and add details in captions that explain them.

▶ **STEP 4** Arrange your part of the bulletin board. Make any changes that are needed.

▶ **STEP 5** Invite others to look at your bulletin board. Be ready to explain what your part of the board shows and to answer questions.

SCORE 4
- shows clear understanding of map concepts and vocabulary
- uses pictures and words that clearly relate to topic
- is highly creative and well-organized
- works cooperatively and clearly contributes to group

SCORE 3
- shows understanding of map concepts and vocabulary
- uses pictures and words that mostly relate to topic
- is mostly creative and organized
- works cooperatively and contributes to group

SCORE 2
- shows some understanding of map concepts and vocabulary
- uses pictures and words that somewhat relate to topic
- shows little creativity or organization
- shows some difficulty with cooperation and contribution

SCORE 1
- shows little understanding of map concepts and vocabulary
- uses pictures and words that do not relate to topic
- shows no creativity or organization
- shows much difficulty with cooperation and contribution

TAKE-HOME RUBRICS Copying masters of a student *Writing Rubric* and *Project Rubric* appear in the Assessment Program, pp. 14 and 16.
GROUP PERFORMANCE RUBRIC See Assessment Program, page x.

A Geography Bulletin Board

Getting Started

Distribute the Unit 2 Project Guidelines provided on page 15 of the Assessment Program.

Introduce the unit project as you begin Unit 2. Have children create the bulletin board as they learn about the land by using maps. Explain that the completed bulletin board will include sections where children will be able to see landforms, bodies of water, how land is used, map elements, and locations of cities and landmarks.

The Big Idea

The Land Maps help us learn about the different kinds of land, water, and places around us.

Project Management

Organize the class into small groups of three or four children. As children work, meet with each group to provide instructional support for the design of each section of the bulletin board. Periodically have groups share their progress and ideas with the class.

Materials textbook, construction paper, scissors, art scraps and recyclables, small toy figures such as people or houses, paste, posterboard, books, maps and globes, travel magazines

Design the Board

As a class, scan the unit for key words and pictures. Choose topics for each section of the bulletin board, such as

- landforms or bodies of water
- North America or your state
- weather and climate
- map elements: key, compass rose

Assign a topic to each group. Have each group design a display to explain details about their topic within a section of the board. Displays can include maps and their elements, small objects, cutout pictures, captions, and brief descriptive sentences. Topics can be modified as the class progresses through the unit.

You Are Invited!

Room 20 presents our great state

California

WHERE: Jackson Elementary School, Rm. 20

WHEN: Thursday, October 4 at 2:00 p.m.

Come see what we have learned about the geography of California.

Assemble the Board

Have each group gather materials for their display. Divide the board into random, irregular-shaped sections, like a puzzle. Ask each group to attach their display to the board within their section in an attractive and interesting way. Remind children that their display will be more visible if it is colorful and lettering is large. Have groups plan how they will explain their topic to others.

Open for Viewing

Have children invite other classrooms to view the board when it is complete. Direct each group to present a short explanation of their topic beginning with how it relates to the Big Idea. Encourage group members to take turns answering questions from visitors about their display.

Lesson Review Activities

You may wish to incorporate the following lesson review activities into the unit project.

- Lesson 1: **Make a Map**, p. 69
- Lesson 2: **Draw a Map**, p. 81
- Lesson 3: **Write Sentences**, p. 87
- Lesson 4: **Draw a Picture**, p. 93

Assessment

For a project rubric, see Teacher Edition, p. 57O.

What to Look For

- Children understand map vocabulary and concepts.

- Displays relate to each topic and are clearly represented.

- Displays are creative and well-organized.

LESSON 1

Name _____ Date _____

Where Is That Place?

Look at the map and the map key. Then follow the directions.

Map Key

bus station | house | library | post office

courthouse | hospital | park | school

Mall

❶ Draw a flag on the flagpole next to the school.

❷ Color the lake in the park blue.

❸ Add another symbol to the empty block on the map. Put your symbol in the map key, and label your symbol.

SKILL PRACTICE

Name _____ Date _____

 MAP AND GLOBE SKILLS
Riddle Puzzle

Use the grid to fill in the letters of the answer to the riddle.

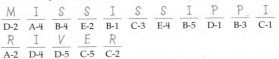

	1	2	3	4	5
A	A	R	L	I	B
B	I	J	P	S	I
C	I	R	S	Z	E
D	P	M	C	I	V
E	O	S	H	S	Z

Riddle: What runs all the way from Minnesota to Louisiana and never gets tired?

M I S S I S S I P P I
D-2 A-4 B-4 E-2 B-1 C-3 E-4 B-5 D-1 B-3 C-1

R I V E R
A-2 D-4 D-5 C-5 C-2

LESSON 2

Name _____ Date _____

Identify Land and Water

Use a word from the Word Bank to label each picture.
Then color the bodies of water blue.

lake	plain	ocean	mountain

mountain

lake

ocean

plain

SKILL PRACTICE

Name _____ Date _____

 MAP AND GLOBE SKILLS
Color a Landform Map

Find the map key. Use a different crayon to color each symbol.
Then follow the map key to color the land and water on the map.

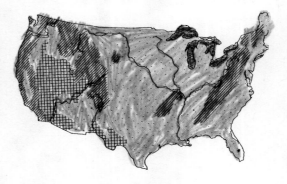

Map Key

Desert | Plain

Lake | River

Mountains

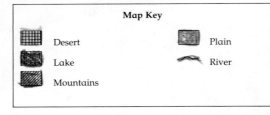

A Weather Tale

Read the story. Underline the sentences that tell about seasons. Then answer the questions.

Jenny and Alison are best friends who live in Phoenix, Arizona. In this desert region, the climate is hot and dry. Most people's favorite season in Phoenix is winter because the weather is a little cooler.

Alison just found out that her family is moving to the Rocky Mountains in Colorado. In this region, each season is very different. Summers are hot and dry, but winters are cold and snowy. Spring is warmer with lots of rain. In this climate, people wear different clothes in each season.

❶ Which region in the story has about the same climate all year long?

the desert

❷ Which region has different weather in each season?

Rocky Mountains

❸ Would you rather live in Arizona or Colorado? Why?

Answers will vary.

CHART AND GRAPH SKILLS
Fun All Year Long

Look at the table, and answer the questions.

Activities for Every Season

Season	Activity		
Spring			
Summer			
Fall			
Winter			

❶ Draw a line under the title of this table.

❷ What are the three activities shown for fall? picking pumpkins, raking leaves, playing football

❸ Name one spring activity. Possible answers: watching birds, flying a kite, picking flowers

❹ Which winter activity could also happen in spring or fall?

hiking

Parts of a Globe

Label the parts of the globe. Write a word from the Word Bank on each blank.

North Pole	Southern	Northern	equator
South Pole	Hemisphere	Hemisphere	

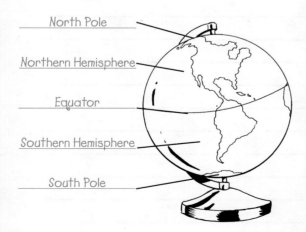

North Pole

Northern Hemisphere

Equator

Southern Hemisphere

South Pole

MAP AND GLOBE SKILLS
Using Directions

Answer the questions about the states shown on the map. Use the compass rose to help you.

❶ Which state is north of Ohio? Michigan

❷ Which state is Indiana's neighbor to the west? Illinois

❸ Which state is farthest east on the map? Ohio

❹ In which direction is Chicago from Cleveland? west

❺ In which direction is Missouri from Iowa? north

STUDY GUIDE

Name _____ Date _____

2 Study Guide

Read the paragraphs. Use the words in the Word Bank to fill in the blanks.

regions	cardinal directions	equator	Pole
location	landforms	climate	

Earth has many different ____regions____, or areas of land with the same features. A coast might have sand dunes and beaches next to an ocean. A mountain range might have hills, valleys, and rivers. Valleys, mountains, and plains are some of the ____landforms____ in our country.

The _cardinal directions_ are north, south, east, and west. Each ____location____, or place, on Earth can be found by using these terms. The United States is in North America. This continent is north of the ____equator____. Canada is north of the United States, and farther north is the North ____Pole____. The ____climate____ there is very cold. Animals and plants in this region have special ways to survive its long winters.

UNIT 2 REVIEW AND TEST PREP

Name _____ Date _____

COMPARE AND CONTRAST

Reading Social Studies

Fill in the chart to show what you have learned about geography.

Desert region	Both	Mountain region
Warm climate		Cool climate
People may need to protect themselves from the sun. Land may be flat and dry.	People live there. Land has plants and animals.	People may wear warm clothes. Land may be rocky.

NOTES

Historical Societies

_____
_____
_____
_____
_____
_____
_____
_____
_____
_____

Museums

_____
_____
_____
_____
_____
_____
_____
_____
_____
_____

Parks

_____
_____
_____
_____
_____
_____
_____
_____
_____
_____

Guest Speakers

_____
_____
_____
_____
_____
_____
_____
_____
_____
_____

Discuss the Big Idea

The Land Maps help us learn about the different kinds of land, water, and places around us.

Explain that maps can give information that is useful in many ways. Tell children that in this unit they will learn about different landforms, bodies of water, and regions of Earth. They will also learn how these locations are shown on different kinds of maps.

Make It Relevant Ask the following question to help children think about how maps are useful for finding locations.

Q What kinds of maps have you used?

A Children might mention an emergency route map of the school, floor plan maps of museums or stores, and road maps.

Access Prior Knowledge

Use a graphic organizer to help children organize their knowledge about maps. Ask questions such as How can maps help you find your location in a building? What features might be shown on a city, state, or country map? Add children's responses to the graphic organizer. Point out that in this unit they will learn how to use different kinds of maps that show many kinds of locations.

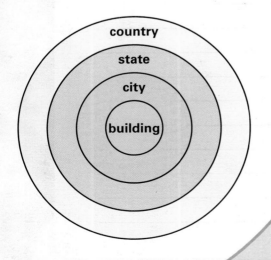

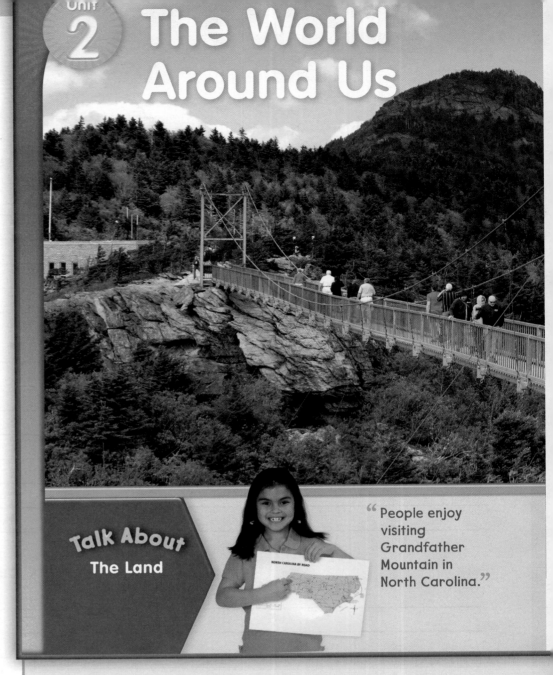

Unit 2 The World Around Us

Talk About
The Land

" People enjoy visiting Grandfather Mountain in North Carolina. "

Practice and Extend

BACKGROUND

Grandfather Mountain Swinging Bridge Located in the Blue Ridge Mountains of North Carolina, Grandfather Mountain rises as much as 4000 feet above the surrounding region. The Swinging Bridge is America's highest suspension footbridge, spanning a chasm at more than one mile in elevation. Visitors consider the trip across the bridge the highlight of a visit to Grandfather Mountain.

Talk About The photographs across the bottom of the unit preview pages show children holding a map, a compass, and binoculars, tools useful in finding and exploring locations such as Grandfather Mountain in North Carolina.

"My compass helps me use a map to find a location."

"It's fun to explore different landforms."

Discuss the Picture

Have children examine the photograph and identify it as the Swinging Bridge at Grandfather Mountain. Ask children to identify features of the land shown in the photograph.

Q What interesting details do you see?

A a bridge, a path, a mountain peak, a deep valley or chasm, plants, people

Q Why is it interesting for Americans to be able to visit the Swinging Bridge at Grandfather Mountain?

A They can see the landforms and vistas of the Blue Ridge Mountains. They can see how people build bridges to make it safer to get from one place to another.

Discuss "Talk About"

Point out the props the children are holding.

Q Why are the children holding these objects?

A They all show things that help us find locations.

Q Why do you think the girl is pointing to a feature on the map?

A She is showing where Grandfather Mountain is located in North Carolina.

Have children work in pairs to ask and answer additional questions about either the Grandfather Mountain photograph or Talk About feature.

SCHOOL TO HOME

Use the Unit 2 SCHOOL TO HOME NEWSLETTER on pages S5–S6 to introduce the unit to family members and suggest activities they can do at home.

INTEGRATE THE CURRICULUM

SCIENCE Have children work in groups to find information about the land and natural resources of the Blue Ridge Mountains. Invite the group to make a poster to share what they discovered. Ask children to present their posters to the class.
Land Features

VISUAL ARTS Provide photographs of vistas of the Blue Ridge Mountains. Encourage children to use watercolors or tempera paints to portray one of these vistas. Point out how they can show perspective by making the ridges in the background smaller and closer together than those in the foreground. Display the artworks and have children compare the techniques used in each painting.
Painting

Make Connections

Link Pictures with Words Have children read the words *location, landform, region, cardinal directions,* and *climate*. Display a world map and define these words by using parts of the map as examples. Ask children to read the words *cardinal directions*. Elicit that these directions can be used to find *locations* on the map.

1 Visual Literacy: Pictures Discuss with children if they have seen a directory map like this before. Ask why people use maps like this or others. (to find places, to find locations)

Q What other locations do maps show?

A Possible responses include cities, buildings, exits, parks, landforms, streets, and restrooms.

2 Have a child read the definition of *landform*. Ask children what type of landform this picture shows. (hills) Ask them to describe the shape. Have children describe the shapes of other landforms they have seen. Point out that these landforms are shown on various types of maps.

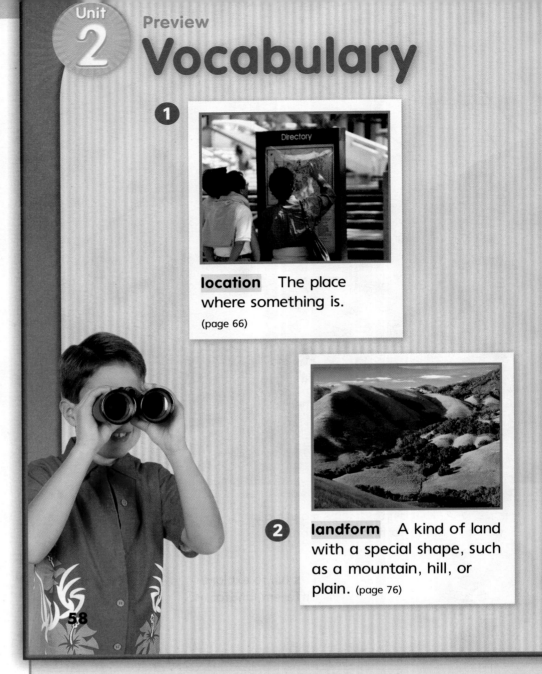

Unit 2 Preview

Vocabulary

1 **location** The place where something is. (page 66)

2 **landform** A kind of land with a special shape, such as a mountain, hill, or plain. (page 76)

58

ELL ENGLISH LANGUAGE LEARNERS

Frontloading Language: The Land Use the following prompts to develop the academic language about land and the skill of comparing and contrasting.

Beginning Have children compare landforms: *Mountains and plains are both _____.* (landforms) *Mountains are tall, but a plain is _____.* (flat)

Intermediate Have children examine a map of North America. Invite them to use cardinal directions to compare locations: *Canada and Mexico are both _____.* (locations on a map) *They are different because _____.* (one is north and one is south)

Advanced Ask children to compare and contrast the pictures for *location* and *region*: *Location and region are alike because _____. They are different because _____.*

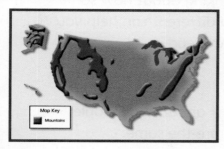

3 **region** An area of land with the same features. (page 82)

5 **climate** The kind of weather a place has over a long time. (page 86)

4 **cardinal directions** The main directions of north, south, east, and west. (page 90)

For more resources, go to **www.harcourtschool.com/ss1**

59

VOCABULARY POWER

Use Reference Sources Have children use a dictionary as a resource to help them understand the word parts of new vocabulary. Point out to children that the vocabulary word *landform* is made up of two base words. Ask children to locate the words *land* and *form* and read each definition. Discuss how each meaning relates to the whole word. Have them use the same procedure for *cardinal direction*.

3 Invite children to look at the picture of *region* and read the definition. Ask them to point to a region along a coast and trace a circle around the region of the Great Lakes. Invite children to share what they know about regions near a coast or a lake.

4 Point out the four letters N, S, E, W on the weather vane. Explain that they stand for directions. Read aloud the definition. Have children point to the appropriate letter on the weather vane as you say each direction word.

Q What is a weather vane used for?

A It shows if the wind is coming from the north, south, east, or west.

5 Ask children to look at the picture of *climate* and tell what they see. Read aloud the definition of *climate*. Have children suggest what type of weather the place in the picture might have over time.

Q How is the weather where you live the same as this region? How is it different?

A Children should compare and contrast their own climate with the sunny, dry place shown in the picture.

INTERNET RESOURCES

For more resources, go to **www.harcourtschool.com/ss1**

Compare and Contrast

Introduce

1 Why It Matters Explain to children that when they compare, they think about how items are alike or similar. When they contrast, they think about how items are different. Point out that children compare and contrast every day. Provide the following examples:

- comparing books they have read
- contrasting the tastes of different foods
- comparing one computer game with another
- contrasting two television shows

Have children suggest other examples.

Unit 2

Reading Social Studies
Compare and Contrast

1 Why It Matters Thinking about how some things are alike and different can help you understand what you read.

Learn

- To compare, think about how people, places, or things are the same.
- **2** To contrast, think about how people, places, or things are different.

Read the paragraph below.

Compare Bryson City, North Carolina, and Baltimore, Maryland, are two cities in the United States. **Contrast** Visitors to Bryson City can hike in the mountains or float down the river in a raft. Baltimore is a good place to fish in the ocean or see old ships in a museum. In both cities, people can shop for gifts.

Bryson City

Baltimore

60

Practice and Extend

INTEGRATE THE CURRICULUM

READING/LANGUAGE ARTS Ask children to write sentences that compare and contrast their own community with one of the cities described on page 60. Remind children to include sufficient details about each city. Invite children to read their sentences aloud to the class.
Write a Paragraph

FOCUS SKILLS

Compare and Contrast

Topic 1   Both   Topic 2

TRANSPARENCY 2

Graphic Organizer Write-On/Wipe-Off Cards available

Practice

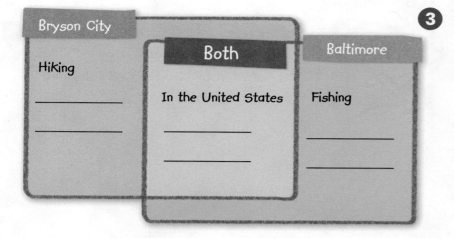

Bryson City

Hiking

_____

_____

Both

In the United States

_____

_____

Baltimore

Fishing

_____

_____

This chart shows how these two cities are the same and how they are different. What can you add to the chart? Copy the chart and complete it.

Apply

As you read this unit, look for ways to compare and contrast places where people live.

61

Leveled Practice Have children compare and contrast sets of items.

Basic Ask children to choose several kinds of lunch foods to compare and contrast. Invite them to write words and phrases that describe appearance and taste.

Proficient Have children make a Venn diagram to show likenesses and differences among two common house pets. Remind them to consider such details as appearance, size, and where the pets live.

Advanced Have children choose two characters from a favorite movie. Invite them to write sentences that compare and contrast how these characters look and act.

2 Teach

Learn

2 Discuss the definitions for *compare* and *contrast* on page 60. Then read aloud and discuss the paragraph. Invite children to locate each city on a United States map. Have them use the map key to find nearby landforms and bodies of water. Suggest words to use when comparing (*and, both, each*) and contrasting (*but, however*).

Practice

3 **Visual Literacy: Graphic Organizer** Have children read the chart on page 61. Discuss how the two cities compare and contrast. Use Focus Skills Transparency 2 to copy the chart. Ask children to share ideas to add to the chart.

Q **What is one activity that people can do in both cities?**

A shop for gifts

ANSWERS: Bryson City: river rafting; Baltimore: looking at ships in a museum; Both: shop for gifts

3 Close

Apply

Tell children that as they read the unit, they should compare and contrast people, places, things, and ideas. Have children look for what is different and alike about the communities where people live.

PAGES 62–65

OBJECTIVES

- Identify the purpose of a legend.
- Recognize how a legend relates to the location of a place.

RESOURCES

Unit 2 Audiotext CD Collection

Quick Summary

"How the Prairie Became Ocean" from *Four Ancestors: Stories, Songs, and Poems from Native North America* by Joseph Bruchac (BridgeWater Books, 1996).

Legends, such as this Yurok legend, were told to explain events in nature before people had scientific knowledge of their origin.

Before Reading

Set the Purpose Have children read the legend title. Explain that a title gives an idea of what the story is about. Invite children to predict what types of landforms might be mentioned in the legend.

Tell children that many cultures have legends to explain things in nature. Point out that the idea of the "man in the moon" helped explain the shadows on the moon's surface.

During Reading

1 Understand the Legend Point out that this legend gives an explanation of how the ocean was formed.

- People long ago wanted to understand the power of nature.
- This legend gave an answer to people's questions about how the ocean was formed.

Start with a Legend

How the Prairie Became Ocean

by Joseph Bruchac
illustrated by David McCall Johnston

2

1 This story is a Native American legend. Legends are stories that teach a lesson or help explain something.

62

Practice and Extend

BACKGROUND

About the Author Joseph Bruchac is an author of children's books, poems, and novels. He grew up in New York near the Adirondack Mountains and still lives there. Much of his work tells of his Abenaki Native American ancestry. Bruchac travels around the world as a storyteller. He has received many awards, including the 2004 Virginia Hamilton Literary Award.

REACH ALL LEARNERS

Advanced Provide children with resources so they can research information about the coastal areas of the United States. Have children work together in small groups to share information about landforms, animals, plants, and sea creatures that are found in these regions. Invite children to present their information to classmates.

3 Long ago, when there were no people, the ocean was a treeless plain. Thunder stood and looked over the land. He knew that soon people would be there.

"How will the people be able to live?" Thunder turned to his companion, Earthquake. "What do you think?" Thunder asked. "Should we place water here?"

Earthquake thought. "I believe we should do that," he said. "Far from here, at the end of the land, there is water. Salmon are swimming there."

63

2 **Geography** Invite children to read the title on page 62. Define *prairie* as land that is mostly flat and *ocean* as a large body of water. Display a map of North America, and point out oceans and prairies.

Q **What ocean is found near the west coast?**
A the Pacific Ocean

3 **Understand the Legend** Remind children that legends can explain a problem that needs to be solved. Have them identify the problem in the legend. (People would be coming soon, and they would need water.)

Q **Why would people need water?**
A to drink, to catch fish, to wash, to grow crops, to swim

Have children describe thunder and earthquakes. Point out that in legends, natural events such as these are given human qualities.

Q **How do Thunder and Earthquake act like humans in the legend?**
A They talk; they think; they look around.

Geography Explain that this legend is from the Yurok people, who lived in the area that is now northern California. Have children locate this area on a map of North America. Ask them to picture the Pacific Ocean as a treeless plain on the map.

Q **Where might Earthquake and Water Panther have found water?**

A Arctic Ocean; Atlantic Ocean

4 **Understand the Legend** Ask children to identify *Panther, abalone,* and *gullies* on page 64. Help children use context clues to predict the meaning of each word. Then have them compare their predictions to the actual meaning of the words by locating each in a dictionary.

Understand the Legend Remind children of the problem they discussed on page 63. Ask volunteers to explain how this problem was solved in the legend. (Salt water carried in abalone shells filled the treeless plain.)

So Earthquake and Water Panther went to the end of the land, where there was ocean. They picked up two big abalone shells and filled the shells with salt water. Then they carried the shells back to Thunder.

Earthquake began to walk around. As he walked, the ground sank beneath him. Water Panther filled the sunken ground with the salt water.

4

Now there was ocean where there had only been a treeless plain. Thunder rolled over the mountains and bent the trees down so they would grow on the land. Seals and salmon and whales swam through gullies made by the sinking land.

5

64

Practice and Extend

Beside the ocean, the land rose up into hills and animals came down from the mountains—deer, elk, foxes, and rabbits.

"Now this will be a good place for the people to live," Thunder said.

"This is a good place," Earthquake agreed. "Let us live here, too."

And so, to this day, Thunder and Earthquake live there, near the place they made the land into ocean for the people.

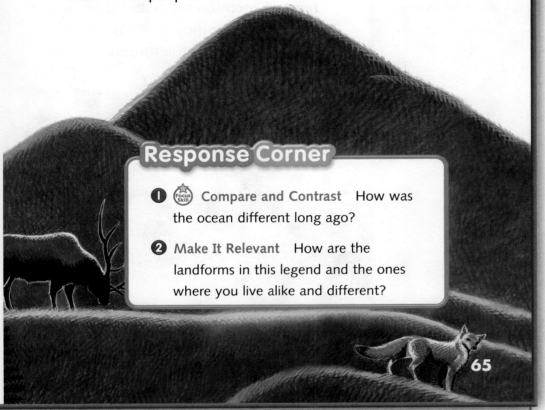

Response Corner

❶ **Compare and Contrast** How was the ocean different long ago?

❷ **Make It Relevant** How are the landforms in this legend and the ones where you live alike and different?

65

⑤ Visual Literacy: Illustration Have children read aloud the last paragraph on page 64. As they read each sentence, ask volunteers to point to each part of the illustration as it is described, such as the mountains, trees, and whales. Discuss how the illustration helps them better understand what they are reading.

After Reading
Response Corner—Answers

1. **Compare and Contrast** Long ago, the ocean was a treeless plain.

2. **Make It Relevant** Children should tell how the landforms in the legend and in their community are alike and different.

✏ Write a Response

Have children imagine they are the first people to come to this new ocean area. Ask them to write several sentences to describe what they think they would see.

For a writing response rubric, see Assessment Program, page. xvi.

INDEPENDENT READING

Children may enjoy reading these books during the unit. Additional books are listed on page 57J of this Teacher Edition.

Before & After: A Book of Nature Timescapes
by Jan Thornhill (National Geographic, 1997). Illustrations show how nature changes over time.

The Seashore Book by Charlotte Zolotow (HarperCollins, 1994). A mother describes the seashore to her son.

Back in the Beforetime
by Jane Louise Curry (Simon & Schuster Children's, 1991). This book recounts California Indian legends about the natural world.

For information about ordering these trade books, visit **www.harcourtschool.com/ss1**

OBJECTIVES

- **Compare and contrast absolute and relative location.**
- **Define and describe a place by its absolute and relative location.**
- **Locate children's school, community, state, and country on a map or globe.**

VOCABULARY

location p. 66

relative location p. 66

absolute location p. 67

 Focus Skill

COMPARE AND CONTRAST

pp. 60–61, 69

RESOURCES

Homework and Practice Book, p. 12; Reading Support and Intervention, pp. 22–25; Success for English Learners, pp. 23–26; Vocabulary Transparency 2-1; Focus Skills Transparency 2; Compare and Contrast Graphic Organizer Write-On/Wipe-Off Card; Activity Pattern A5; Unit 2 Audiotext CD Collection; Internet Resources

Introduce

What to Know Invite children to think of places shown on maps. Ask a volunteer to read aloud the What to Know question. Remind children to look for ways maps help people as they read the lesson.

Build Background Ask children to share their experiences with maps. Help them realize they use many kinds of maps. Ask them to describe places they found by using a map.

 What to Know How do maps help people find locations?

Vocabulary
location
relative location
absolute location

 **Compare and Contrast**

Lesson 1

Maps and Locations

There are many kinds of maps.

1 Maps show **location**, or the place where something is.

You can use maps to find the relative location of a place. The **relative location** tells what a place is near. On the map of Knoxville, the school is near the museum.

66

Practice and Extend

Express Path

When minutes count, look for the **EXPRESS PATH** to focus on the lesson's main ideas.

Quick Summary

This lesson discusses the different uses and purposes of maps. It explains how maps allow people to find places and demonstrates the relative and absolute locations of places on a map.

You can also use maps to find the absolute location of a place. The **absolute location** is the exact location. Your address is an absolute location. The absolute location of the library on this map is 500 West Church Avenue.

MAP SKILL Which building on this map is closest to the river?

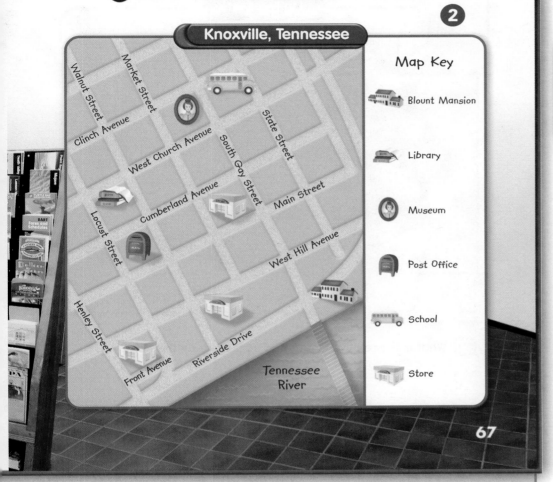

Knoxville, Tennessee

Walnut Street
Market Street
Clinch Avenue
West Church Avenue
South Gay Street
State Street
Cumberland Avenue
Main Street
Locust Street
West Hill Avenue
Henley Street
Front Avenue
Riverside Drive
Tennessee River

Map Key

Blount Mansion

Library

Museum

Post Office

School

Store

67

2 Teach

Maps and Locations

CONTENT FOCUS Maps show where places are located.

Express Path

Have children study the maps on pages 67 and 68. Invite them to compare and contrast the places shown on the two maps.

1 Geography Encourage children to list maps they have seen, such as road maps, world maps, or amusement park maps. Have volunteers point out maps in the classroom. Ask children to describe locations they find on these maps.

2 Visual Literacy: Map Offer examples of relative and absolute locations in the classroom, such as *The bookcase is next to the windows* (relative) or *This desk is the third desk in the fourth row* (absolute). Discuss the features on the map on page 67, such as street names and buildings, and the relative and absolute locations of these features.

CAPTION ANSWER: Blount Mansion

VOCABULARY

Vocabulary Transparency [2-1]

MINI-GLOSSARY Read each term, and study its definition.

location The place where something is. p. 66
relative location A description of a place that tells what it is near. p. 66
absolute location The exact location of a place. p. 67

WORD WORK Complete the activities below.

1. **location**
SYNONYMS Which of these words mean about the same thing as location?
place   spot   symbol
place, spot

2. **relative location**
CONTEXT CLUES Use relative location in a sentence to show its meaning.
Possible answer: The relative location of the library is near the school.

3. **absolute location**
USE REFERENCE SOURCES Look up the word absolute in the dictionary. Does the definition help you understand the meaning of absolute location?
Yes, because the word absolute means complete or total.

TRANSPARENCY 2-1

READING SUPPORT/ INTERVENTION

For alternate teaching strategies, use pages 22–25 of Reading Support and Intervention to:

■ identify **phonemes**

■ practice **phonics**

■ reinforce **vocabulary**

■ build **text comprehension**

■ build **fluency**

Reading Support ▶ and Intervention

ELL ENGLISH LANGUAGE LEARNERS

For English Language Learners strategies to support this lesson, see Success for English Learners pages 23–26.

■ English-language development activities

■ background and concepts

■ vocabulary extension

Success for ▶ English Learners

LESSON 1 ■ 67

3 Geography Explain to children that a map shows a place much smaller than it really is. Invite children to turn to pages R6 and R7 in the Atlas at the back of their books. Point out the map scale of this map of the United States. Explain that a map scale is a part of a map that helps you find real distance. Have them use a strip of paper to mark two cities on the map. Then have them place the paper along the map scale with one of the marks at zero. They will be able to find the real distance by seeing how far it is to the second mark.

Point out that the maps on pages 67 and 68 show areas of different sizes. Explain that because of this, they have different map scales. Help children find the map scales on other maps and globes in the classroom to see how they are different.

4 Visual Literacy: Maps Provide children with maps of their community and state. Invite children to use these maps and the map on page 68 to determine the relative and absolute locations of

- their home and school.
- their neighborhood.
- their state and cities in their state.
- their country (United States).

Ask children to pick a place to draw a map of, such as their home, school, community, state, or country. Then provide each child with a copy of Activity Pattern A5. Explain that they are to draw their map on the shirt pattern. Remind them to give their map a title. Invite children to share their t-shirt designs with the class.

3 Different maps can show different kinds of information. Some maps show small areas, such as parks or neighborhoods. Other maps show large areas, such as cities, states, and countries.

4

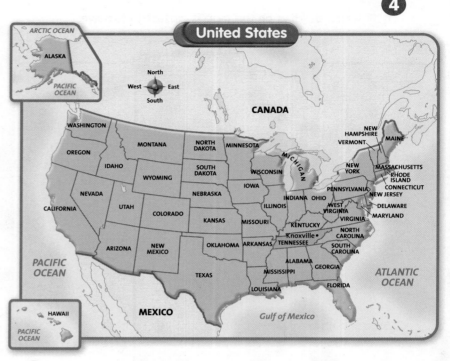

MAP SKILL What is the relative location of your state on this map?

68

Practice and Extend

REACH ALL LEARNERS

Leveled Practice Have children locate their state on a map of the United States.

Basic Ask children to point to all states that border their state. As they point to each one, ask them to complete the sentence *A state that borders my state is ____*.

Proficient Direct children to find and list the states that border their state. Encourage them to also list other features that border their state, such as rivers or mountain ranges.

Advanced Invite children to create short clues for each state that borders their state, including some description of the relative or absolute location, such as *This border state is very near our capital city.*

The map shows that the city of Knoxville is in the state of Tennessee, in the country of the United States. The map also shows all of the states in our country.

Reading Check (Focus Skill) **Compare and Contrast**

How are the absolute location and the relative location of a place different? The absolute location tells the exact location of a place. The relative location tells what a place is near.

Summary People use maps to help them find relative and absolute locations.

World's Fair Park in Knoxville, Tennessee

Review

❶ **What to Know** How do maps help people find locations?

❷ **Vocabulary** What is the **absolute location** of your home?

❸ ✎ **Write** Make a map of your school. Write how to get from your house to your school.

❹ (Focus Skill) **Compare and Contrast** How is the absolute location of your school different from its relative location?

69

3 Close

Summary

Ask children to read the summary statement and then restate it in their own words.

- Maps are used to find places.
- Maps help people know the relative and absolute location of places.

Assess

REVIEW—Answers

1. **What to Know** Maps can show people exactly where places are located. Maps can also show what can be found near a location.

2. **Vocabulary** The **absolute location** of my home is my address.

3. ✎ **Writing Assessment Guidelines** See Writing Rubric. This activity can be used with the Unit Project.

4. (Focus Skill) **Compare and Contrast** The absolute location tells exactly where the school is located. The relative location tells what is near or around the school.

Use Focus Skills Transparency 2 or Compare and Contrast Graphic Organizer Write-On/ Wipe-Off Card.

✎ WRITING RUBRIC

Score 4
- clearly maps location of school
- includes accurate directions

Score 3
- adequately maps location of school
- includes fairly accurate directions

Score 2
- somewhat maps location of school
- includes partially accurate directions

Score 1
- does not map location of school
- does not include accurate directions

HOMEWORK AND PRACTICE

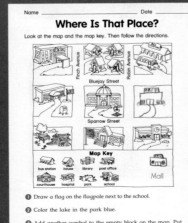

Name _____ Date _____

Where Is That Place?

Look at the map and the map key. Then follow the directions.

Map Key
bus station house library post office
courthouse hospital park school

❶ Draw a flag on the flagpole next to the school.

❷ Color the lake in the park blue.

❸ Add another symbol to the empty block on the map. Put your symbol in the map key, and label your symbol.

page 12

MENTAL MAPPING

Name the State Help children name the relative location of states from memory. Encourage children to study a United States map. Organize the class into two groups. One group names a state and covers the map. The other group names as many border states from memory as possible. Have the groups take turns. Encourage children to name other bordering features, such as water bodies or mountain ranges.

Map and Globe Skills

Use a Map Grid

OBJECTIVES

- Recognize that a map grid is a tool to find the absolute location of a place on a map.

- Use a map grid to locate places on a map.

VOCABULARY

map grid p. 70

RESOURCES

Homework and Practice Book, p. 13; Social Studies Skills Transparency 2-1; Primary Atlas; Interactive Atlas; Unit 2 Audiotext CD Collection; Internet Resources

I | Introduce

Display a large city or state map. Choose a place on the map that is not obvious, and ask children to find it. If they have difficulty, tell them that they will learn an easier way to find locations on a map.

Why It Matters Ask children to read the information on page 70. Point out that a map grid is a shortcut to find the absolute locations of places on maps. Help children understand that rows are always horizontal; they go left and right. Columns are always vertical; they go up and down.

Why It Matters   A good way to find locations on a map is to use a map grid. A **map grid** is a set of lines that divide a map into columns and rows of squares.

Learn

1. Put your finger on the gold square. Slide your finger left and right. This is row B.

2. Put your finger on the gold square again. Slide your finger up and down. This is column 2.

3. The gold square is at B-2 on the grid.

2 Practice

Look at the map grid of a park in Knoxville.

1. In which square is Fort Kid?

2. What place is in A-3?

70

Practice and Extend

SOCIAL STUDIES SKILLS

Map and Globe Skills
Use a Map Grid

World's Fair Park

People We Know
pages 70-71

Harcourt Social Studies

Social Studies Skills
Transparency 2-1

TRANSPARENCY 2-1

MAKE IT RELEVANT

In Your Community Have children use blocks, boxes, or construction-paper cutouts to make a tabletop model of their community. Then direct them to make a map and a map grid of their model. Ask children to use the map to practice identifying places and to plan routes from one place to another. Have children ask partners to locate places and give locations using the map grid.

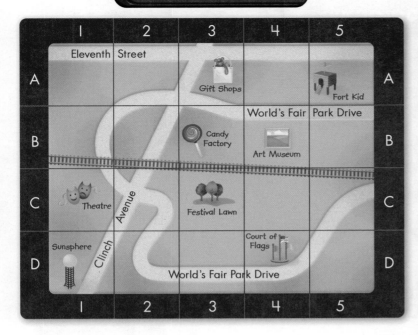

World's Fair Park

Eleventh Street

A — Gift Shops — Fort Kid
B — Candy Factory — World's Fair Park Drive — Art Museum
C — Theatre — Clinch Avenue — Festival Lawn
D — Sunsphere — World's Fair Park Drive — Court of Flags

Apply

Use this grid map to find the absolute location of places in World's Fair Park. Have a classmate tell you the row and column of the square in which a place is located.

GO ONLINE For online activities, go to **www.harcourtschool.com/ss1**

71

2 Teach

❶ Learn

Guide children to notice that on a map grid the rows are identified by the letters *A, B, C,* and *D* that appear on both sides of the grid. The columns are identified by the numbers 1 through 5 that appear at the top and bottom.

- Point out that children should slide their fingers straight across or straight up and down to locate the names of rows or columns.
- Have children practice finding squares as volunteers suggest combinations of letters and numbers.
- Discuss how map grid letters and numbers allow a person to find an absolute location on a map.

Q **Why does the grid have numbers for the columns and letters for the rows?**

A It would be confusing if both were the same.

❷ Practice

1. Fort Kid is in square A-5.
2. The gift shops are in square A-3.

3 Close

Apply

Make It Relevant Children should be able to accurately locate places on this map by using the map grid. Children should correctly identify the letter and number for the square in which places are located.

GO ONLINE **INTERNET RESOURCES**

For online activities, go to **www.harcourtschool.com/ss1**

REACH ALL LEARNERS

Leveled Practice Have children practice using a city map grid.

Basic Guide children to touch the matching left and right grid letters. Repeat with the numbers at the top and bottom.

Proficient Have partners locate places on the map, using grid coordinates.

Advanced Direct children to write map grid riddles to share.

HOMEWORK AND PRACTICE

Name _____ Date _____

MAP AND GLOBE SKILLS
Riddle Puzzle

Use the grid to fill in the letters of the answer to the riddle.

	1	2	3	4	5
A	A	R	L	I	B
B	I	J	P	S	I
C	I	R	S	Z	E
D	P	M	C	I	V
E	O	S	H	S	Z

Riddle: What runs all the way from Minnesota to Louisiana and never gets tired?

M I S S I S S I P P I
D-2 A-4 B-4 E-2 B-1 C-3 E-4 B-5 D-1 B-3 C-1

R I V E R
A-2 D-4 D-5 C-5 C-2

page 13

OBJECTIVES

■ **Understand the importance of the actions and character of Benjamin Banneker and explain how he made a difference in others' lives.**

RESOURCES

Unit 2 Audiotext CD Collection; Multimedia Biographies CD; Internet Resources; TimeLinks

Link to the Big Idea

The Land Maps help us learn about the land, water, and places around us. Benjamin Banneker helped map the land for the new city of Washington, D.C.

Vocabulary Help Discuss with children why someone might *survey* land. Point out that people survey the land before they construct buildings or roads, to find boundaries, and to make maps.

Discuss the Biography

Primary Sources: Artifact Explain that the map on page 73 shows what the city looked like at the time the map was drawn. Display a current map of the same area.

Q Which map is a primary source?

A Both maps are primary sources. One shows Washington, D.C., in the past. The other shows the present.

Biography

Benjamin Banneker

Trustworthiness
Respect
Responsibility
Fairness
Caring
Patriotism

Why Character Counts

How did Benjamin Banneker show patriotism?

When Benjamin Banneker was a young boy, he taught himself many things. He read books to learn about math. He studied the sky at night to learn about the stars. He even copied the parts of a watch and made a clock of his own. When he grew up, Benjamin Banneker became a writer and a scientist.

Benjamin Banneker helped measure the land for Washington, D.C.

72

Practice and Extend

BACKGROUND

Benjamin Banneker Benjamin Banneker, a descendant of African slaves, was born in 1731. With little formal education, Banneker accomplished many things on his own. He designed systems to improve irrigation on his family's farm, made calculations about celestial bodies, published farmer's almanacs, and corresponded with Thomas Jefferson about the end of slavery.

INDEPENDENT READING

Encourage children to read the biography *Benjamin Banneker: Pioneering Scientist* by Ginger Wadsworth (Lerner Publishing Group, 2002). The book traces Banneker's life from his childhood on the family farm through his careers as a clockmaker, surveyor, astronomer, and writer.

This is an early map of Washington, D.C.

Banneker wrote almanacs that gave weather information and other useful facts.

In 1791, Benjamin Banneker was asked to help survey, or measure, a piece of land. On this land, the new capital of the United States government would be built.

President George Washington hired Benjamin Banneker to help map out the new city, Washington, D.C. His work helped build a grand city for the new American government.

For more resources, go to **www.harcourtschool.com/ss1**

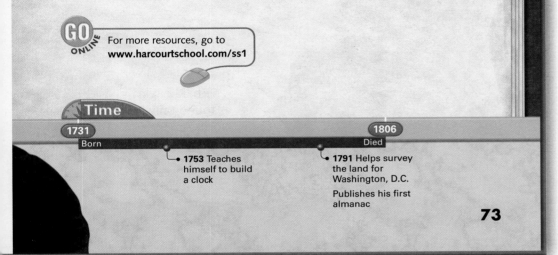

Time

1731 Born

1806 Died

1753 Teaches himself to build a clock

1791 Helps survey the land for Washington, D.C.

Publishes his first almanac

73

History Point out that Banneker did not have the opportunity to go to school or attend college. Many of the things he learned he had to teach himself.

Q Benjamin Banneker taught himself most of the things he knew. What does this show about him?

A It shows that he was eager to learn, and his interests in math and science led to his many accomplishments.

Visual Literacy: Time Line Call children's attention to the time line on page 73. Point out that it shows the years in which Benjamin Banneker was born and died, but not the months or days. Have children research the dates of Banneker's birth and death.

TIMELINKS: Interactive Time Line

Have children add the dates of Benjamin Banneker's birth and death to the one-year TimeLinks: Interactive Time Line.

Why Character Counts

Point out that patriotism is the feeling of pride people have for their country. Benjamin Banneker showed his patriotism by helping to plan the city where the country's government is located.

GO ONLINE   INTERNET RESOURCES

For more resources, go to **www.harcourtschool.com/ss1**

OBJECTIVES

- Identify the countries of North America.
- Identify landforms and bodies of water in North America.

VOCABULARY

landform p. 76   **peninsula** p. 79

island p. 79   **gulf** p. 80

COMPARE AND CONTRAST

pp. 60–61, 78, 81

RESOURCES

Homework and Practice Book, p. 14; Reading Support and Intervention, pp. 26–29; Success for English Learners, pp. 27–30; Vocabulary Transparency 2-2; Focus Skills Transparency 2; Compare and Contrast Graphic Organizer Write-On/Wipe-Off Card; Activity Pattern A6; Unit 2 Audiotext CD Collection; Internet Resources

1 | Introduce

What to Know Invite children to read aloud the What to Know question. Explain that a continent can have many countries. Ask children to name the continent where they live. Remind children to look for answers to the question as they read the lesson.

Build Background Show photographs of people using different kinds of land. For example, display pictures of horseback riders in a desert or people skiing down a mountain. Invite children to describe each picture and make comparisons about the kinds of land that are near where they live.

Lesson 2 North America

 What to Know
What countries and landforms make up North America?

Vocabulary
landform
peninsula
island
gulf

 **Compare and Contrast**

1 The United States of America is the name of our country. Our country is located on the continent of North America.

Countries in North America

There are many countries in North America. Canada and Mexico, our neighbors, are big countries. Central America has many smaller countries that are also part of North America.

Reading Check **Which two countries are neighbors of the United States?**
Canada and Mexico are neighbors of the United States.

Fast Fact

The bald eagle is found only in North America, in places from Florida and Mexico to Alaska and Canada.

74

Practice and Extend

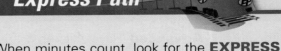
Express Path

When minutes count, look for the **EXPRESS PATH** to focus on the lesson's main ideas.

Quick Summary

This lesson describes the geography of North America. It demonstrates that a continent can have many countries, landforms, and bodies of water.

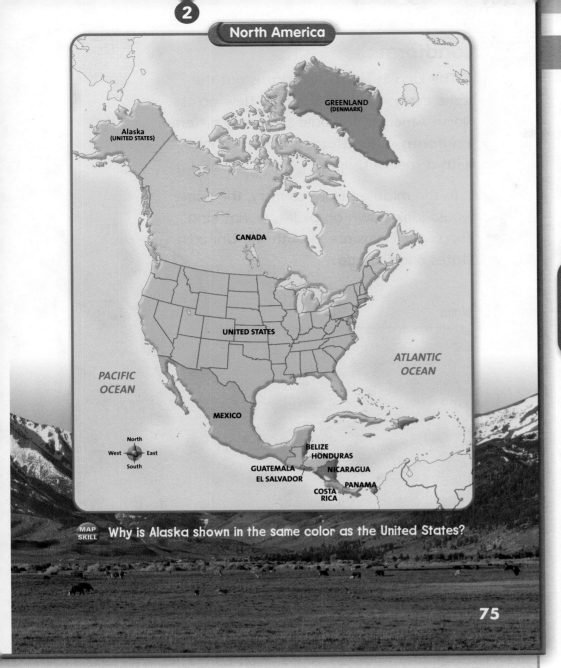

North America

GREENLAND (DENMARK)

Alaska (UNITED STATES)

CANADA

UNITED STATES

PACIFIC OCEAN

ATLANTIC OCEAN

MEXICO

North
West — East
South

BELIZE
HONDURAS
GUATEMALA
EL SALVADOR
NICARAGUA
COSTA RICA
PANAMA

MAP SKILL Why is Alaska shown in the same color as the United States?

75

2 Teach

Countries in North America

CONTENT FOCUS The United States is one of many countries in North America.

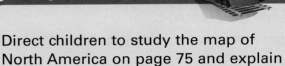
Express Path

Direct children to study the map of North America on page 75 and explain what it tells about the countries.

1 Geography Review the meaning of *country* and *continent*. Point out that a continent might have many countries, but it might also have only one country, as Australia does. Display a world map and invite children to locate other continents.

2 Visual Literacy: Map Invite children to point out and name the countries of North America.

Q What country in North America would you like to visit? Why?

A Possible answer: Canada, to see the cold, snowy mountains.

CAPTION ANSWER: Because it is a part of the United States.

VOCABULARY

Vocabulary Transparency 2-2

MINI-GLOSSARY Read each term, and study its definition.

landform A kind of land with a special shape, such as a mountain, hill, or plain. p. 76
peninsula A landform that has water on only three sides. p. 79
island A landform with water all around it. p. 79
gulf A large body of ocean water that is partly surrounded by land. p. 80

WORD WORK Complete the activities below.

1. **landform**
STRUCTURAL CLUES What two words make up the compound word landform?
land and form

2. **island**
CLASSIFY/CATEGORIZE List at least two islands.
Possible answers: Hawaii, Cuba

3. **peninsula**
USE REFERENCE SOURCES Does peninsula come before or after pole in the dictionary?
before

4. **gulf**
CONTEXT CLUES Use gulf in a sentence to show its meaning.
Possible answer: The Gulf of Mexico is partly surrounded by the United States and Mexico.

TRANSPARENCY 2-2

READING SUPPORT/ INTERVENTION

For alternate teaching strategies, use pages 26–29 of Reading Support and Intervention to:

- identify **phonemes**
- practice **phonics**
- reinforce **vocabulary**
- build **text comprehension**
- build **fluency**

Reading Support ▶ and Intervention

ELL ENGLISH LANGUAGE LEARNERS

For English Language Learners strategies to support this lesson, see Success for English Learners pages 27–30.

- English-language development activities
- background and concepts
- vocabulary extension

Success for ▶ English Learners

Landforms

CONTENT FOCUS There are many types of landforms in North America.

Express Path

Organize the class into three groups. Direct each group to study a paragraph. Solicit a volunteer from each group to share a summary of what they learned.

3 **Geography** Have children turn to page 78, and direct them to look at the map. Invite them to locate the Great Plains. Ask a volunteer to trace the outline of the plains area.

4 **Visual Literacy: Picture** Direct children to study the land in the photograph on page 76. Explain that plains are flat land areas. These wide, grassy areas are often used for ranching. If land is used for farming, as shown in the photograph, water is piped in for the crops.

Q How do you think the Great Plains look different from high above than from the ground?

A From high up, more land is visible and it looks like a pattern of squares. From the ground, the view is of a much smaller section, and more details of the plants and animals can be seen.

Landforms

The land in North America is not the same everywhere. If an eagle flew across North America, it would see many different landforms. A **landform** is a kind of land with a special shape.

3 In the middle of our country, the eagle would look down on plains, or flat land. The Great Plains are in both the United States and Canada.

plains **4**

wheat

76

Practice and Extend

✦ VOCABULARY POWER

Compound Words Remind children that two small words are sometimes combined to make a compound word. Write *grassland, hillside, seashore,* and *farmland* on the board. Ask children to draw lines between the two small words in each. Discuss the meaning of each compound word. Then direct children to look for the compound word on page 76 (landform) and tell its meaning.

INTEGRATE THE CURRICULUM

 MUSIC Have children listen as you play the song "America the Beautiful." Discuss the images of plains and mountains in the song and the meaning behind the song as an expression of love of country. Finally, help children work in small groups to make up another verse to the song, encouraging them to use images of America that inspire them. **Song Lyrics**

hills

mountains

⑤ The eagle would also see land with many hills. A hill is land that rises above the land around it. A mountain is a very high hill. A group of mountains is called a mountain range. Many mountain ranges stretch across parts of North America.

Reading Check **Focus Skill** Compare and Contrast

How are plains different from hills? Plains are flat land. Hills rise above the land around them.

77

⑤ Geography Turn children's attention to the landforms on page 77. Point out that hills are gently rolling, with rounded tops. In contrast, most mountains rise sharply from the land to great heights.

⑥ Link Geography and Economics Direct children to compare the landforms in the photographs on pages 76 and 77.

Q Which landform appears to be used for growing crops such as wheat?

A The plains are used for growing crops.

Q Do you think farmers prefer to grow crops and raise animals on the plains, hills, or mountains? Why?

A They probably prefer plains, because the flat land makes it easier for farmers to use farm machinery and to water crops, and for the animals to move around.

REACH ALL LEARNERS

Advanced Invite small groups to choose a country from the map of North America and research information about the landforms of that country. Suggest that they make several illustrations that show the landforms and ways the land is used. Encourage children to include labels, captions, and descriptive sentences to enhance their pictures. Invite groups to share their illustrations with classmates.

Special Needs Help children distinguish between mountains and hills. Display pictures of these landforms. As you say the name of each landform, ask children to trace around the example in the picture with their fingers. Invite children to draw a picture of each landform and to label it with the appropriate name.

MAKE IT RELEVANT

In Your State Have groups create a landforms display. Ask groups to divide a large poster into three parts. Have them label each part *Plains, Hills,* or *Mountains* and include the following:

• a drawing of a landform

• a landform picture cut from a magazine or newspaper

• a descriptive sentence

• an example from their state

Land and Water

CONTENT FOCUS There are many bodies of water in North America.

Express Path

Have children scan the section to find the meaning of the vocabulary words. Ask them to use the words in sentences to show what they learned.

7 **Geography** Remind children that they can find five oceans on a globe. Explain that oceans cover more of Earth's surface than does the land.

CAPTION ANSWER: Pacific Ocean, Atlantic Ocean

8 **Visual Literacy: Map** Have children look at the map on page 78. Remind children that maps can show different kinds of information. This map shows the kinds of land and water in North America. Explain that other maps could show things besides landforms, such as vegetation, land use, or climate.

 Interactive in the enhanced online student eBook

Land and Water

Besides land, the eagle would fly over many kinds of bodies of water. The biggest are oceans. North America lies between two oceans.

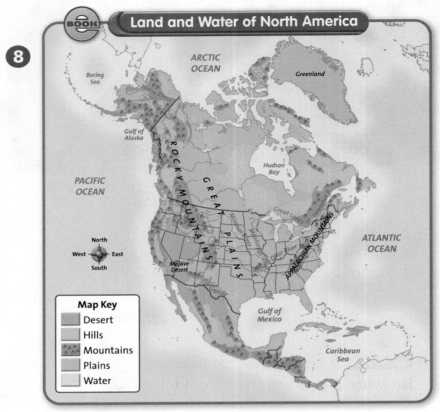

Land and Water of North America

Map Key
- Desert
- Hills
- Mountains
- Plains
- Water

MAP SKILL Between which two oceans is North America located?

78

Practice and Extend

READING SOCIAL STUDIES

Compare and Contrast
Have children use the map on page 78 to compare the Great Lakes and the Mississippi River regions. Ask children to look at other maps of these regions and to make a chart comparing locations, landforms, and water types.

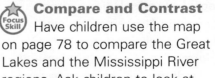 **READING TRANSPARENCY**

Use FOCUS SKILLS TRANSPARENCY 2.
Graphic Organizer Write-On/Wipe-Off Cards available

INDEPENDENT READING

Invite children to read *The Atlantic Ocean* by David Petersen and Christine Petersen (Scholastic Library Publishing, 2001). This book about the Atlantic Ocean includes interesting facts, details of ocean life, and a brief history of ocean exploration. It contains pictures, diagrams, maps, an index, and a glossary.

9 The eagle might fly over land that has water around it on only three sides. This landform is called a **peninsula**. The state of Michigan has many peninsulas.

An **island** is a landform with water all around it. Michigan also has many islands.

Michigan peninsula
in Lake Huron

10

Mackinac Island in Lake Huron

79

11 Geography Discuss differences between a *river*, a *gulf*, and a *bay*. If children have seen any of the places, invite them to share their experiences with the class. Have children look back to the map on page 78 and locate the Gulf of Mexico.

Q What rivers empty into the Gulf of Mexico? What other rivers do you see on this map?

A The Mississippi River and the Rio Grande empty into the Gulf; the Ohio and Missouri are also on the map.

12 Link Geography and Economics Remind children that there are five Great Lakes (Superior, Michigan, Huron, Erie, Ontario). Point out that they are among the largest lakes in the world in both size and volume of water. Discuss ways that the United States and Canada might work together to use and take care of these lakes. For example, we could

* make laws and agreements about clean water.
* share waters for fishing and shipping.
* cooperate to allow boating and use of beaches.

Geography Brainstorm a list of kinds of land and water in North America. Give a copy of Activity Pattern A6 to each child. Have children choose six items from the list and write one item on each face of the cube. Then help children assemble their cubes. They should read aloud the word facing up and then find an example of that land or water on a map of North America.

---

11 Sometimes a large body of water is partly surrounded by land. This body of water is called a **gulf**. The Gulf of Mexico is located between the United States and Mexico. A smaller body of water that is partly surrounded by land is called a bay.

Gulf of Mexico

Chesapeake Bay is surrounded by the states of Maryland and Virginia.

80

Practice and Extend

12 All over the land, there are rivers and lakes. A river is a stream of water that flows across the land. A lake is a body of water that has land all around it. The Great Lakes are large lakes located between the United States and Canada.

Reading Check **What kinds of bodies of water are there?**
There are oceans, gulfs, bays, lakes, and rivers.

Summary A map of North America shows countries, landforms, and bodies of water.

One of the longest rivers in North America is the Mississippi River.

Review

1 **What to Know** What countries and landforms make up North America?

2 **Vocabulary** What **landform** is located in the middle of the United States?

3 **Activity** Draw a map of North America. Label the countries, landforms, and bodies of water.

4 **Compare and Contrast** How are mountains different from hills?

81

3 Close

3 Close

Summary

Have children review the summary and discuss the lesson's key content.
- Many countries make up North America.
- North America has many kinds of landforms and bodies of water.

Assess

REVIEW—Answers

1. **What to Know** There are plains, hills, and mountains. Countries include the United States of America, Canada, Mexico, Guatemala, Belize, El Salvador, Honduras, Nicaragua, Costa Rica, and Panama.

2. **Vocabulary** Plains are a **landform** that can be found in the middle of the United States.

3. **Activity Assessment Guidelines** See Performance Rubric. This activity can be used with the Unit Project.

4. **Compare and Contrast** A mountain is much higher than a hill.

Use Focus Skills Transparency 2 or Compare and Contrast Graphic Organizer Write-On/Wipe-Off Card.

PERFORMANCE RUBRIC

Score 4
- clearly identifies map features
- includes clear, accurate labels

Score 3
- adequately identifies map features
- includes adequate labels

Score 2
- somewhat identifies map features
- includes some labels

Score 1
- does not identify map features
- does not include labels

HOMEWORK AND PRACTICE

Name _____ Date _____
Identify Land and Water
Use a word from the Word Bank to label each picture. Then color the bodies of water blue.

| lake | plain | ocean | mountain |

mountain   lake

ocean   plain

page 14

VOCABULARY POWER

Plurals Remind children that a word in the plural form names more than one of something. Invite volunteers to locate a word on page 81 that names more than one, such as *rivers*. Then help them find the form of the word that names just one (river). Have children list the pairs of words on the board (river/rivers, lake/lakes, body/bodies). Challenge children to locate more pairs throughout the lesson.

OBJECTIVES

- **Define *region*.**

- **Use a map key and symbols to identify landforms and bodies of water on a map.**

VOCABULARY

region p. 82

RESOURCES

Homework and Practice Book, p. 15;
Social Studies Skills Transparency 2-2;
Primary Atlas; Interactive Atlas;
Unit 2 Audiotext CD Collection;
Internet Resources

1 Introduce

Invite children to do a quick sketch or series of sketches showing at least three kinds of land and two bodies of water. Make sure children color their drawings. Then list on the board their color choices for corresponding land and water.

Why It Matters Explain to children that a landform map can help them locate and compare the different landforms in a region. This kind of map will also help them think about how people use the land in each region.

Read a Landform Map

Why It Matters You can use a landform map to compare different regions of our country. A **region** is an area of land with the same features.

Learn

1 A landform map uses colors and symbols to show different kinds of land. Each kind of land makes up a region.

3 Practice

1 Look at the map key. What kinds of land are shown on the map?

2 Find the Great Lakes. What kind of land surrounds this region?

3 What shows a mountain region on the map? Find and name the two biggest mountain ranges in the United States.

82

Practice and Extend

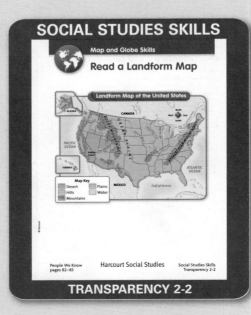

SOCIAL STUDIES SKILLS

Map and Globe Skills
Read a Landform Map

Landform Map of the United States

Map Key
Desert · Plains
Hills · Water
Mountains

People We Know
pages 82–83   Harcourt Social Studies   Social Studies Skills
Transparency 2-2

TRANSPARENCY 2-2

INTEGRATE THE CURRICULUM

VISUAL ARTS Have children make a three-dimensional, textured landform map of their state. Provide children with a large outline map of their state. Suggest that they use state maps in books or online for reference. Provide recyclable materials and art supplies for making the landforms and bodies of water. Remind children to use the same materials to assemble a map key.
Textured Map

② Landform Map of the United States

ALASKA

CANADA

North
West ⊕ East
South

ROCKY MOUNTAINS

GREAT PLAINS

APPALACHIAN MOUNTAINS

Columbia River

Lake Superior

Lake Michigan

Lake Huron

Lake Ontario

St. Lawrence River

Missouri River

Mississippi River

Lake Erie

Ohio River

PACIFIC OCEAN

Mojave Desert

Colorado River

ATLANTIC OCEAN

HAWAII

Rio Grande

MEXICO

Gulf of Mexico

Map Key
Desert	Plains
Hills	Water
Mountains	

Apply

Make It Relevant Use the map and key to describe the region in which you live. Compare your region to other regions of the United States.

GO ONLINE For online activities, go to
www.harcourtschool.com/ss1

83

Map and Globe Skills

---

② Teach

Learn

❶ Geography Point out that a region usually has a type of landform that is more common there than other landforms. Help children point to and name regions on the map on page 83, including desert, mountains, plains, and hills.

❷ Visual Literacy: Map Have children look at the map key and locate a landform region by color on the map, such as orange for the Mojave Desert or green for the Great Plains. Point out that the map key also includes a color symbol for bodies of water. Invite volunteers to name the bodies of water on the map, including oceans, gulfs, and lakes.

❸ Practice

1. Desert, plains, hills, and mountains are shown on the map.
2. Plains surround this region.
3. Purple with upside-down V's show mountain regions on this map. Rocky Mountains and Appalachian Mountains are the two biggest mountain ranges.

③ Close

Apply

Make It Relevant Children should be able to accurately identify symbols from the key and map that relate to landforms in their region. Children should be able to state several similarities between landforms in their own region and those of another region.

GO ONLINE **INTERNET RESOURCES**

For online activities, go to
www.harcourtschool.com/ss1

HOMEWORK AND PRACTICE

Name _____ Date _____

MAP AND GLOBE SKILLS
Color a Landform Map

Find the map key. Use a different crayon to color each symbol. Then follow the map key to color the land and water on the map.

Map Key
Desert	Plain
Lake	River
Mountains	

page 15

OBJECTIVES

- **Compare and contrast climate and weather.**

- **Recognize that climate and seasons vary depending on location and time of year.**

- **Describe the climate of a place.**

VOCABULARY

climate p. 86

COMPARE AND CONTRAST

pp. 60–61, 87

RESOURCES

Homework and Practice Book, p. 16; Reading Support and Intervention, pp. 30–33; Success for English Learners, pp. 31–34; Vocabulary Transparency 2-3; Focus Skills Transparency 2; Compare and Contrast Graphic Organizer Write-On/Wipe-Off Card; Unit 2 Audiotext CD Collection; Internet Resources

1 Introduce

What to Know Have a volunteer read the What to Know question. Review season names with children. Discuss the weather they associate with each season. As they read the lesson, remind them to look for reasons why regions have different climates.

Build Background Ask children to describe winter weather in their area. Have them compare this to winter weather in other places they have visited (warmer, more rain or snow, cooler, windier).

Lesson

Seasons and Climate

 What to Know
Why are seasons and climate different in different regions?

Vocabulary
climate

 **Compare and Contrast**

The United States has many kinds of regions. The location of a region affects the kind of seasons and climate it will have.

Seasons

A season is a part of the year that has a certain kind of weather. ① The four seasons are winter, spring, summer, and fall. Some regions have four very different seasons. Other regions have the same kind of weather all year long.

A warm summer day in Boston, Massachusetts

84

Practice and Extend

Express Path

When minutes count, look for the **EXPRESS PATH** to focus on the lesson's main ideas.

Quick Summary

This lesson discusses how a region's location affects its weather, seasons, and climate. Weather changes from day to day, while climate is the kind of weather a place has over a long period of time. The four seasons of a region can be very similar or very different from each other, depending on the region's location.

The season a place is having depends on how Earth is facing the sun. Earth circles the sun in a tilted position. It is summer in places that are tilted toward the sun. It is winter in places that are tilted away. As Earth travels, different parts of it are tilted toward the sun. This causes the seasons to change.

Reading Check **Why do the seasons change?**
The seasons change because a different part of Earth will be tilted toward the Sun as the Earth circles it.

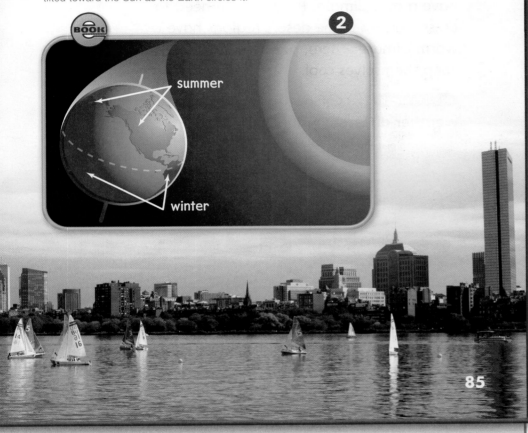

summer

winter

85

Seasons

CONTENT FOCUS Seasons are different in different regions.

Express Path

Have children read page 85 and write a main idea sentence.

1 Geography Point out that some places, such as Hawaii, have weather that changes little from season to season.

2 Visual Literacy: Diagram Explain that it is Earth's orbit that causes portions of Earth to receive more sunlight at different times. Demonstrate this by using objects, to represent the sun and Earth.

Q **Why do you think we have certain fruits and vegetables in our markets all year round?**

A Fruits and vegetables that can't be grown in cold weather can be shipped from places having warm weather.

Interactive in the enhanced online student eBook

READING SUPPORT/ INTERVENTION

For alternate teaching strategies, use pages 30–33 of Reading Support and Intervention to:

- identify **phonemes**
- practice **phonics**
- reinforce **vocabulary**
- build **text comprehension**
- build **fluency**

Reading Support ▶ and Intervention

ENGLISH LANGUAGE LEARNERS

For English Language Learners strategies to support this lesson, see Success for English Learners pages 31–34.

- English-language development activities
- background and concepts
- vocabulary extension

Success for ▶ English Learners

Weather and Climate

CONTENT FOCUS The weather in a region can vary from day to day. The climate is the overall weather of a region over time.

Express Path

Have small groups study the paragraphs in this section. Invite a volunteer from each group to explain what they learned about weather and climate.

3 **Geography** Point out that location affects climate and weather:

- Warm weather and warm water in the Gulf of Mexico lead to hurricanes.
- Dry, cool air from the Rocky Mountains meets up with warm air from the south and creates tornadoes in "Tornado Alley," parts of Nebraska, Texas, and Oklahoma.
- Locations on the western side of the Sierra Nevada get plenty of rainfall because the cooler temperatures in the mountains cause rain or snow to fall from clouds as they move over the mountains. However, the remaining clouds have little moisture in them, which means little rain or snow is left for locations on the eastern side.

Take this time to explain to children how clouds are made up of small droplets of water or ice crystals, and when clouds become too heavy, rain or snow will fall.

4 **Visual Literacy: Pictures** Have children compare the photographs on pages 86 and 87. Ask how each location affects the clothes people wear, the transportation people use, and the kinds of work people do.

Weather and Climate

In each region, the weather can change from day to day. Weather is the way the air feels outside. One day the weather might be sunny and warm. Another day it might be cloudy and cool.

Climate is the kind of weather a place has over a long time. Many mountain regions **3** have a cool climate. People there need to dress warmly. Some desert regions have a warm climate. There, people wear clothes to keep themselves cool.

Reading Check **Compare and Contrast** **How is weather different from climate?**
Weather is the way the air feels at a certain time. Climate is the kind of weather a place has over a long time.

Cleveland, Ohio, has many snowy days.

86

Practice and Extend

Smoky Mountains

Arizona desert

Summary The location of a place affects the weather, climate, and seasons it will have.

Review

① **What to Know** Why are seasons and climate different in different regions?

② **Vocabulary** What is the **climate** like where you live?

③ ✎ **Write** Write sentences that compare and contrast the weather of two different seasons where you live.

④ ⊛ **Compare and Contrast** How can a mountain climate be different from a desert climate?

87

HOMEWORK AND PRACTICE

Name _____ Date _____

A Weather Tale

Read the story. Underline the sentences that tell about seasons. Then answer the questions.

Jenny and Alison are best friends who live in Phoenix, Arizona. In this desert region, the climate is hot and dry. Most people's favorite season in Phoenix is winter because the weather is a little cooler.

Alison just found out that her family is moving to the Rocky Mountains in Colorado. In this region, each season is very different. Summers are hot and dry, but winters are cold and snowy. Spring is warmer with lots of rain. In this climate, people wear different clothes in each season.

❶ Which region in the story has about the same climate all year long?

the desert

❷ Which region has different weather in each season?

Rocky Mountains

❸ Would you rather live in Arizona or Colorado? Why?

Answers will vary.

page 16

---

3 ▸ Close

Summary

Have volunteers read the summary and then restate the main points in their own words.

• The seasons are different for different regions.

• The regions of the United States have different climates because of their location.

Assess

REVIEW—Answers

1. **What to Know** Seasons and climate are different in different regions because seasons and climate are affected by location.

2. **Vocabulary** Possible answer: The **climate** where I live is very dry.

3. ✎ **Writing Assessment Guidelines** See Writing Rubric.
   This activity can be used with the Unit Project.

4. ⊛ **Compare and Contrast** A mountain climate can be cool or cold, and a desert climate can be hot and dry.

Use Focus Skills Transparency 2 or Compare and Contrast Graphic Organizer Write-On/Wipe-Off Card.

BACKGROUND

Daylight In the Northern Hemisphere, the summer solstice, the day of the year with the most daylight hours, occurs when the North Pole is tilted greatest toward the sun. The summer solstice usually occurs around June 21st. The winter solstice is the day with the least daylight hours, around December 22nd. Twice each year, at the autumnal and vernal equinox daylight and darkness hours are equal.

OBJECTIVES

- Understand how information is organized on a table or chart.

- Interpret information from a table or chart.

VOCABULARY

table p. 88

RESOURCES

Homework and Practice Book, p. 17; Social Studies Skills Transparency 2-3; Unit 2 Audiotext CD Collection; Internet Resources

1 Introduce

Ask children to think about keeping phone numbers for all of their friends written on separate pieces of paper. Have children suggest ways to present the information so that they could easily share it with others. Write their suggestions on the board.

Why It Matters Explain to children that a table can give much information in a small space. Point out that this makes the information easy to read, understand, and compare.

Chart and Graph Skills

Read a Table

Why It Matters   A **table** is a chart that organizes information. Knowing how to read a table can help you remember information.

Learn

The title tells you what the table shows.

1 Put your finger on the first square of a row. Read the information. The column labels tell the kinds of information you see.

2 Practice

1 What does the table show?

2 What are the column labels?

3 What was the high temperature for May?

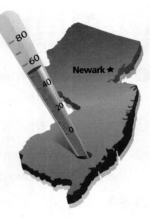

88

Practice and Extend

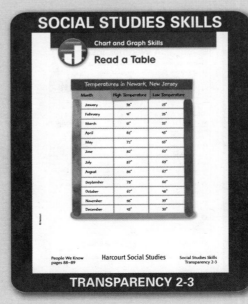

SOCIAL STUDIES SKILLS

Chart and Graph Skills

Read a Table

Temperatures in Newark, New Jersey

Month	High Temperature	Low Temperature
January	38°	23°
February	41°	25°
March	51°	33°
April	62°	43°
May	72°	53°
June	82°	63°
July	87°	69°
August	86°	67°
September	78°	60°
October	67°	48°
November	56°	39°
December	43°	30°

People We Know   Harcourt Social Studies   Social Studies Skills
pages 88–89   Transparency 2-3

TRANSPARENCY 2-3

REACH ALL LEARNERS

Advanced Have children create a table of landforms and bodies of water. Invite small groups to discuss places they have traveled and landforms and bodies of water they observed. Have groups choose column headings such as *oceans*, *mountains*, or *plains*, and row headings such as city or state names. Suggest that they consult maps to verify the location names. Remind groups to give their table a title.

Temperatures in Newark, New Jersey

Month	High Temperature	Low Temperature
January	38°	23°
February	41°	25°
March	51°	33°
April	62°	43°
May	72°	53°
June	82°	63°
July	87°	69°
August	85°	67°
September	78°	60°
October	67°	48°
November	55°	39°
December	43°	30°

Apply

Make It Relevant   Make a table that shows high and low temperatures of where you live.

For online activities, go to
www.harcourtschool.com/ss1

89

2 ▸ Teach

Learn

1 Visual Literacy: Table Discuss how the table's information is easier to see and understand than sentences about temperatures would be. Help children understand how to use a table by doing the following:

- Have children find and read the title. Ask them to predict what they will learn from this table. Explain that this chart shows the average high and low temperatures during each month of the year.

- Remind children that the columns are read from top to bottom and rows are read from left to right. Show students that headings show how the table is organized. Ask volunteers to name the heading of each column and row.

Invite children to locate specific information, such as *What was the low temperature in October? Which month has the highest temperature?*

2 Practice

1. This table shows temperatures in Newark, New Jersey.
2. The column labels are Month, High Temperature, and Low Temperature.
3. The high temperature for May is 72.

3 ▸ Close

Make It Relevant Children should create a table that has information listed in a logical and orderly way. The chart should include a title, and headings for the columns and rows.

REACH ALL LEARNERS

Leveled Practice Provide examples of tables for children.

Basic Have children name an item on a table for a partner to identify by naming the row and column headings.

Proficient Direct partners to take turns locating items by naming a row and column heading.

Advanced Ask partners to write clues to locate items or headings. Have partners find the answers.

HOMEWORK AND PRACTICE

Name _____ Date _____
CHART AND GRAPH SKILLS
Fun All Year Long
Look at the table, and answer the questions.

Activities for Every Season

Season	Activity
Spring	
Summer	
Fall	
Winter	

❶ Draw a line under the title of this table.

❷ What are the three activities shown for fall? picking pumpkins, raking leaves, playing football

❸ Name one spring activity. Possible answers: watching birds, flying a kite, picking flowers

❹ Which winter activity could also happen in spring or fall? hiking

page 17

INTERNET RESOURCES

For online activities, go to
www.harcourtschool.com/ss1

UNIT 2 ▪ 89

OBJECTIVES

- Identify the cardinal directions.
- Recognize hemispheres, the equator, and poles on a map or globe.
- Identify and compare the characteristics of world regions.

VOCABULARY

cardinal directions p. 90

equator p. 90

hemisphere p. 91

pole p. 91

COMPARE AND CONTRAST

pp. 60–61, 93

RESOURCES

Homework and Practice Book, p. 18; Reading Support and Intervention, pp. 34–37; Success for English Learners, pp. 35–38; Vocabulary Transparency 2-4; Focus Skills Transparency 2; Compare and Contrast Graphic Organizer Write-On/Wipe-Off Card; Unit 2 Audiotext CD Collection; Internet Resources

❚ Introduce

What to Know Review that a region is an area of land with similar features. Ask children to read the What to Know question. Remind them to look for ways regions are alike and different as they read the lesson.

Build Background Display pictures of world regions, such as polar, tropical, or mountain. Invite children to tell what they know about the features of each region.

Lesson 4 World Regions

💡 **What to Know**
How are regions around the world different?

Vocabulary
cardinal directions
equator
pole
hemisphere

 Compare and Contrast

A globe is a model of Earth. We can use the **cardinal directions**—

① north, south, east, and west—to find locations on a globe and on Earth.

The Equator, Poles, and Hemispheres

The **equator** is an imaginary line that divides Earth into northern and southern halves. Regions near the equator are very hot.

Equator

90

Practice and Extend

Express Path

When minutes count, look for the **EXPRESS PATH** to focus on the lesson's main ideas.

Quick Summary

This lesson discusses regions of the world. Each region is unique, with its own landforms, climate, plants, animals, and people. The location of regions can be described by where they are in relation to the hemispheres, the equator, the poles, and cardinal directions.

A **pole** is a point on Earth farthest from the equator. The farthest you can travel north from the equator is the North Pole. The farthest you can travel south is the South Pole. The regions close to each pole are very cold.

A **hemisphere** is half of Earth. The equator divides Earth into the Northern and Southern Hemispheres.

Reading Check **How would a region near a pole be different from a region near the equator?** The region near a pole would have a very cold climate. The region near the equator would have a very warm climate.

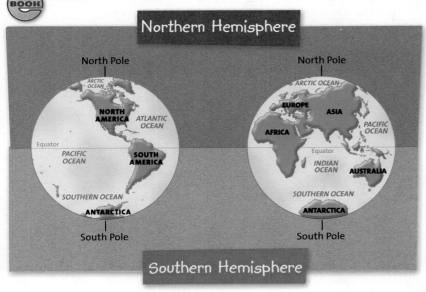

Northern Hemisphere

North Pole

ARCTIC OCEAN

NORTH AMERICA — ATLANTIC OCEAN

Equator

PACIFIC OCEAN — SOUTH AMERICA

SOUTHERN OCEAN

ANTARCTICA

South Pole

North Pole

ARCTIC OCEAN

EUROPE — ASIA

AFRICA — PACIFIC OCEAN

Equator — INDIAN OCEAN — AUSTRALIA

SOUTHERN OCEAN

ANTARCTICA

South Pole

Southern Hemisphere

91

The Equator, Poles, and Hemispheres

CONTENT FOCUS Imaginary points, lines, and areas on Earth help us locate regions.

Express Path

Have children study the maps of the world on page 91. Ask them to identify the equator, poles, and hemispheres.

1 **Geography** Point out that a globe is a model of Earth. Display a globe and help children find the equator, the poles, and the four hemispheres. Point out lines of latitude and longitude and explain that these can be used to find absolute location. Have children name and locate the continents and the hemisphere in which each is found.

Correct Misconceptions Explain that we use imaginary lines and points to find places on Earth. Point out that there is not an actual line at the equator or post-like poles at the North and South Poles.

Interactive in the enhanced online student eBook

VOCABULARY	READING SUPPORT/ INTERVENTION	ENGLISH LANGUAGE LEARNERS

VOCABULARY

Vocabulary Transparency `2-4`

MINI-GLOSSARY Read each term, and study its definition.

cardinal directions The main directions of north, south, east, and west. p. 90
equator An imaginary line that divides Earth into northern and southern halves. p. 90
pole A point on Earth farthest from the equator. p. 91
hemisphere Half of Earth. p. 91

WORD WORK Complete the activities below.

1. **cardinal directions**
CONTEXT CLUES Would you find cardinal directions on a map or in a bird book?
on a map

2. **equator**
STRUCTURAL CLUES How can knowing the definition of equal help you understand equator?
It helps me remember because the equator is a line that divides Earth into equal halves.

3. **pole**
MULTIPLE MEANINGS/USE REFERENCE SOURCES Use your dictionary to find another meaning for the word pole.
A long, smooth piece of metal, wood, or plastic.

4. **hemisphere**
STRUCTURAL CLUES How can you divide the word hemisphere into two smaller parts?
hemi-sphere

TRANSPARENCY 2-4

READING SUPPORT/ INTERVENTION

For alternate teaching strategies, use pages 34–37 of Reading Support and Intervention to:

■ identify **phonemes**

■ practice **phonics**

■ reinforce **vocabulary**

■ build **text comprehension**

■ build **fluency**

Reading Support ▶ and Intervention

ELL **ENGLISH LANGUAGE LEARNERS**

For English Language Learners strategies to support this lesson, see Success for English Learners pages 35–38.

■ English-language development activities

■ background and concepts

■ vocabulary extension

Success for ▶ English Learners

Features of World Regions

CONTENT FOCUS Each region of the world has its own features, including landforms, climate, animals, and plants.

Express Path

Have pairs of children work together to find the answer to the Reading Check question and the first Review question.

2 Geography Point out that regions have unique landforms and bodies of water. Have children use a world map or globe to locate the major mountains and ranges (Andes, Alps, Himalayas, Mt. Everest, Mt. McKinley, and Rocky Mountains) and the major world rivers (Mississippi, Amazon, Volga, Yangtze, and Nile).

Regions also have their own types of climates. Remind children that the weather or climate of a region depends on its location. Guide them to understand that locations near the equator receive more direct sunlight than places farther away. This is why regions near the equator, such as tropical regions, will be very warm. Regions farther away from the equator, such as polar regions, will be very cold.

3 Visual Literacy: Pictures Invite children to name other kinds of regions. Examples can include the Midwest and Southern United States, or regions found in their own state. Then have children study the photographs on pages 92 and 93.

Q How does your own region compare to one of the other regions in the pictures?

A Children should compare features of their region with features they see in the pictures.

Features of World Regions

The world has many different regions. Each region has its own landforms and climate. A mountain region might be cold and snowy, with rocky land. A tropical region near the equator might be warm and flat, with plenty of rain.

Each region has animals and plants that live and grow there. People use what they have in a region to help them live.

Reading Check **Compare and Constrast**

How are regions of the world the same?
All regions have their own landforms and climate. They have people, plants, and animals that use what they have to live there.

Tropical Region

Rain forest in Brazil

92

Practice and Extend

INTEGRATE THE CURRICULUM

MATHEMATICS Help children understand how a region's length of daylight varies based on its proximity to the equator or poles. Invite pairs to solve story problems such as *When a tropical region has eleven hours of sunlight on a winter day, how many hours of darkness will it have?* or *If a polar region has one hour of darkness in summer, how many daylight hours will there be?* **Differences**

REACH ALL LEARNERS

Leveled Practice Compare and contrast world regions.

Basic Ask children to name similar landforms found in different regions.

Proficient Have children draw and label an illustration of a world region. Have them include a caption describing the climate.

Advanced Have children write comparison sentences about two regions.

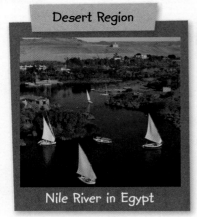

Desert Region

Nile River in Egypt

Mountain Region

Himalayas in Nepal

Summary There are many kinds of regions in different locations on Earth. Each region has its own landforms and climate.

Review

❶ What to Know How are regions around the world different?

❷ Vocabulary Where would you find the **poles** on a globe?

❸ Activity Draw a picture of a world region. Show its climate, landforms, plants, and animals.

❹ Compare and Contrast How is a mountain region like a tropical region? How are these two regions different?

93

PAGES 94–95

Find Directions on a Map

OBJECTIVES

- Identify intermediate directions.
- Describe one place relative to another using cardinal and intermediate directions.

VOCABULARY

compass rose p. 94
intermediate directions p. 94

RESOURCES

Homework and Practice Book, p. 19; Social Studies Skills Transparency 2-4; Primary Atlas; Interactive Atlas; Unit 2 Audiotext CD Collection; Internet Resources

Why It Matters   Directions help you describe where places are on a map or globe.

Learn

A **compass rose** shows directions on a map or globe. **Intermediate directions**
① are between the cardinal directions. They are northeast, northwest, southeast, and southwest.

② Practice

❶ What country is our neighbor to the north?

❷ What country is our neighbor to the south?

❸ In which direction would you travel to go from Greenland to Mexico?

94

I   Introduce

Ask children to recall how they give someone directions. Invite a volunteer to give directions to go from the classroom to the library. Discuss what phrases they might use, such as turn left, go right, and keep going straight.

Why It Matters Remind children that cardinal directions help us locate places on a map or globe. Explain that intermediate directions help us describe locations in between cardinal directions. Ask children to imagine how difficult it would be to give directions without using any direction words. Tell them that on a map, directions tell how to find the absolute locations of places and help us locate one place relative to another.

Practice and Extend

SOCIAL STUDIES SKILLS

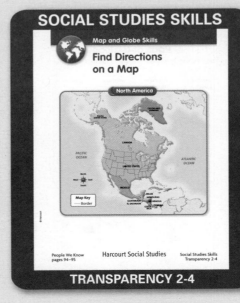

TRANSPARENCY 2-4

ELL ENGLISH LANGUAGE LEARNERS

Help children draw a large compass rose on chart paper, and place it on the floor to show directions in the classroom.

Beginning Have children point or face the direction you name.

Intermediate Point to a direction and have children identify it by name.

Advanced Ask children to take turns giving commands using direction names.

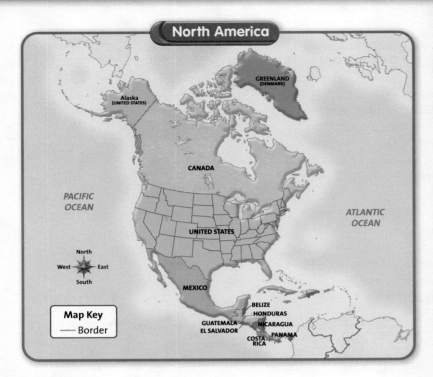

North America

PACIFIC OCEAN

GREENLAND (DENMARK)

Alaska (UNITED STATES)

CANADA

UNITED STATES

ATLANTIC OCEAN

North
West — East
South

MEXICO

BELIZE
HONDURAS
GUATEMALA NICARAGUA
EL SALVADOR
PANAMA
COSTA RICA

Map Key
— Border

Apply

Make It Relevant   Find some places on a map of your state. Use cardinal and intermediate directions to tell how to get from place to place on the map.

GO ONLINE For online activities, go to **www.harcourtschool.com/ss1**

95

Map and Globe Skills

Learn

1 Visual Literacy: Maps Explain that a compass rose shows the position of cardinal and intermediate directions on a map. Point out examples of a compass rose on maps and globes. Help children point to places on a map by naming intermediate directions.

Q What do you find is alike and different about the compass rose on various maps and globes?

A Some only have the N for north; they all point to the north direction on the maps and globes; some do not show the intermediate directions.

Use masking tape to design a compass rose on the floor. Invite children to use the compass rose to follow clues to locate things in the classroom, such as *Walk twelve steps northeast to the fishbowl* or *Skip in a southwest direction to the wall.*

2 Practice

1. Canada is our neighbor to the north.
2. Mexico is our neighbor to the south.
3. You would travel southwest to go from Greenland to Mexico.

Apply

Make It Relevant Responses should include accurate use of cardinal and intermediate directions when giving directions from one place to another.

GO ONLINE   **INTERNET RESOURCES**

For online activities, go to **www.harcourtschool.com/ss1**

REACH ALL LEARNERS

Leveled Practice Practice using a compass rose on a community map.

Basic Help children use the compass rose to name a road north and south of their homes.

Proficient Use directions to describe how to get from one park to another.

Advanced Have children write directions from one place to another.

HOMEWORK AND PRACTICE

Name _____ Date _____
MAP AND GLOBE SKILLS
Using Directions

Answer the questions about the states shown on the map. Use the compass rose to help you.

States in the Midwest

• City
— Border

NORTH DAKOTA
MINNESOTA
SOUTH DAKOTA
WISCONSIN
Minneapolis MICHIGAN
Milwaukee Detroit
NEBRASKA IOWA Chicago Cleveland
ILLINOIS INDIANA OHIO
Kansas City St. Louis Cincinnati
KANSAS MISSOURI

1 Which state is north of Ohio? _Michigan_
2 Which state is Indiana's neighbor to the west? _Illinois_
3 Which state is farthest east on the map? _Ohio_
4 In which direction is Chicago from Cleveland? _west_
5 In which direction is Missouri from Iowa? _north_

page 19

OBJECTIVES

- **Identify the landforms and bodies of water of a region.**

- **Recognize the unique features of a region, including wildlife, structures, and activities.**

RESOURCES

Unit 2 Audiotext CD Collection; Internet Resources

💡 Link to the Big Idea

The Land Tell children that the land and water of the Cape Cod National Seashore offer many recreational and educational activities. The area is cared for and protected by the National Parks System so that many people are able to visit this natural area.

Vocabulary Help Explain to children that a *national park* is an area of land that is owned by the national government. The land is preserved so that it can be used for recreation, education, and relaxation by all of the people of the country.

Read About

Explain to children that the beach area is only one part of the Cape Cod National Seashore. Besides the immediate beach area, visitors can find marshes, ponds, nature trails, wooded areas, and picnic sites. Invite children to brainstorm activities they might like to do in a park like this.

Field Trip

http://www.harcourtschool.com/ss1

Read About

Cape Cod National Seashore is located in eastern Massachusetts. The Atlantic Ocean meets 40 miles of sandy beaches at this national park. People come here to learn what it is like to live in this region.

At the visitor's center, you can watch a film about Cape Cod. There is also a museum where you can learn about the wildlife, buildings, and activities at the park.

Find

United States

Cape Cod National Seashore, Massachusetts

96

Cape Cod National Seashore

Highland Lighthouse

Practice and Extend

REACH ALL LEARNERS

Advanced Have children create a diorama to demonstrate one of the many uses of Cape Cod National Seashore. Have children research information from online sources or from books and magazines. Provide a shoebox and materials such as clay, heavy paper, art sticks, and tissue paper for children to use. Suggest children label the parts of the diorama.

Special Needs Help children read a map using cardinal directions. Display a map of Massachusetts. Remind children that north, south, east, and west refer to directions. Ask children to put a finger on a place on the map and trace it in a designated direction. Have them name places their finger crosses. For example, tracing north from the Cape Cod peninsula places their finger in the Atlantic Ocean.

Children can take part in the Junior Ranger Program to learn more about the national park.

There are many kinds of wildlife at Cape Cod National Seashore.

Biking is a popular activity at the park.

White Cedar Swamp

A Virtual Tour

GO ONLINE For more resources, go to www.harcourtschool.com/ss1

97

Find

Have children study the map and ask them to describe Cape Cod's relative location. Ask children to identify the landform name for this area (peninsula). Point out that the Atlantic Ocean is on the east side and Cape Cod Bay is on the west side.

Discuss Cape Cod National Seashore

Direct children to look at the pictures on pages 96–97.

Q What are some activities that people are enjoying?

A kayaking, exploring the water, biking, walking, going to classes or programs

Q What can people do to care for and protect this area?

A Possible responses can include: clean up litter; leave plants and animals alone; not dumping trash into the water

A Virtual Tour Depending on the availability of computers, have children work individually, in pairs, or in small groups to view the virtual tours. Encourage them to research more information about how Cape Cod National Seashore has changed over time as they explore the websites. Remind children to use what they learn on their virtual tours as background information for the Unit Project.

INTERNET RESOURCES

GO ONLINE For more resources, go to **www.harcourtschool.com/ss1**

BACKGROUND

Cape Cod National Seashore This area was designated as a National Seashore in 1966, but it has existed as a vibrant natural area since it was formed during the Ice Age. Tourists come to enjoy the activities and sites in the area, such as kettle ponds, swimming beaches, nature trails, boardwalks, paved trails, wild cranberry bogs, woodsy areas, lighthouses, and two visitor centers.

MAKE IT RELEVANT

In Your State Invite children to describe visits to national parks or nature preserves in their state. Ask children to compare and contrast each place to Cape Cod National Seashore. Encourage children to describe landforms and bodies of water they encountered. They should also explain activities that were available for people to enjoy.

Link to the Big Idea

The Land Point out to children that maps help people learn about the different places and the different kinds of land and water in the world. Show children maps of different places and explain what they represent.

Preview the Games

Weather Tic-Tac-Toe In this game, children are asked to look at the pictures in the Tic-Tac-Toe game and find the three in a row that show either summer or winter. Children will need to think about the things they see during each season. Prompt children with questions such as:

Q What things remind you of winter?

A snow, ice, icicles, snowmen, snow-covered trees

Q What things remind you of summer?

A lakes, flowers, trees with green leaves

ANSWER: the right row top to bottom; The pictures show the winter season, with a bare tree, a snowman, and icicles on a house.

Missing Letters This game asks children to read each definition and figure out to which vocabulary word it refers. Children are then asked to find the letter that is missing from every vocabulary word and use those letters to answer the riddle. Remind children that the letters that are missing are all the same letter.

ANSWER: location; island; climate; equator; The Sandwich Islands

Find the winning line.
Will the winner be Summer or Winter?

98

Practice and Extend

Leveled Practice Ask children to choose their favorite season.

(Basic) Have children list reasons why they like the season they chose.

(Proficient) Invite children to draw a picture of them doing their favorite seasonal activity. Have them write a sentence describing it.

(Advanced) Direct children to write a paragraph explaining why they like the season they chose.

READING/LANGUAGE ARTS Take children outside every day for one week at the same time each day. Have children write down the weather every day. At the end of the week, discuss the results. **Record Weather**

Missing Letters

Each word is missing the same letter. When you find it, use the letter to answer the riddle.

Clue	Word
the place where something is	loc**a**tion
a landform with water all around it	isl**a**nd
the kind of weather a place has	clim**a**te
an imaginary line that divides Earth	equ**a**tor

What islands are good to eat?

The S**a**ndwich Isl**a**nds

Online Adventures GO ONLINE

How much do you know about the world around you? In this online game you and Eco will go on a fishing trip. Play now, at www.harcourtschool.com/ss1

99

Online Adventures Before children begin playing, explain that they will need to understand how maps can be used to show locations. Review the cardinal directions: north, south, east, and west. Tell children that Help Buttons in the game will refer them to pages in their textbook if they need additional information.

GO ONLINE — INTERNET RESOURCES

For more resources, go to
www.harcourtschool.com/ss1

Share the Fun

At School Have children work in small groups to create their own Weather Tic-Tac-Toe game. Help them create a game similar to this activity based on what they know about climate. When children are finished, ask them to share their games with their classmates.

At Home Invite children to have their parents or guardians help them make their own Missing Letters game. Remind children to use vocabulary words that all have a common letter. Ask children to share their games with classmates.

ELL ENGLISH LANGUAGE LEARNERS

Assist children with difficult language and concepts.

Beginning Write the definition of the word *island* on the board and have children study it.

Intermediate Have children draw pictures of an island or group of islands.

Advanced Ask children to write a sentence about an island and what they might find there.

The Big Idea

The Land Ask a volunteer to read aloud the Big Idea. Invite children to share things they learned about land, water, and maps in this unit.

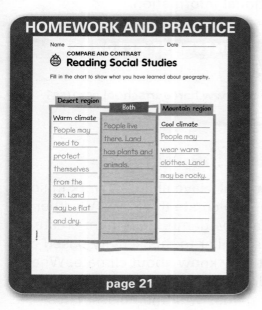

HOMEWORK AND PRACTICE

page 21

Reading Social Studies

 Compare and Contrast You may wish to have children review Reading Social Studies at the beginning of the unit. Charts should include ways the two areas are alike and different.

 The Big Idea

The Land Maps help us learn about the different kinds of land, water, and places around us.

Compare and Contrast

Copy and fill in the chart to show how a desert region and mountain region can be alike and different.

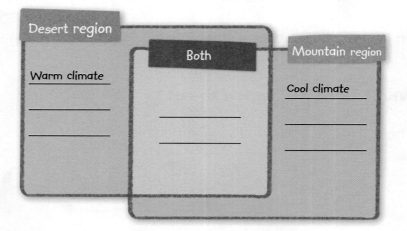

Vocabulary

Match the word to its meaning.

1 a kind of land with a special shape

2 the kind of weather a place has over a long time

3 an area of land with the same features

4 the place where something is

5 the main directions of north, south, east, and west

Facts and Main Ideas

6 What kind of location is your address?

7 Which continent is our country a part of?

8 What kind of landform has water all around it?

9 Which of these is a part of the year with its own kind of weather?

   A season   **C** hemisphere

   B climate   **D** region

10 What is the imaginary line that divides Earth into northern and southern halves?

   A pole   **C** compass rose

   B continent   **D** equator

101

Vocabulary

1. landform

2. climate

3. region

4. location

5. cardinal directions

Facts and Main Ideas

6. absolute location

7. North America

8. island

9. A, season

10. D, equator

TEST-TAKING STRATEGIES

Review these tips with children:

- Read the directions before reading the questions.

- Read each question twice, focusing the second time on all the possible answers.

- Take time to think about all the possible answers before deciding on an answer.

- Move past questions that give you trouble, and answer the ones you know. Then return to concentrate on the difficult items.

Critical Thinking

11. Possible answers: I can find a place more easily if I know the other places that are around it. Someone can tell me what to look for when I go to find the place.

12. Make It Relevant Possible answers: We would not know how to get to a place. A place might be harder to find.

Skills

13. the average winter and summer rainfall in five cities

14. City, Winter Rainfall, and Summer Rainfall

15. Louisville, Kentucky

16. Wilmington, North Carolina

✓ Critical Thinking

⑪ How does knowing the relative location help you find a place?

⑫ **Make It Relevant** How might your family trips be different if you did not have maps?

✓ Skills

Average Rainfall		
City	Winter rainfall	Summer rainfall
Little Rock, Arkansas	12 inches	10 inches
Louisville, Kentucky	20 inches	12 inches
Baltimore, Maryland	10 inches	12 inches
Wilmington, North Carolina	12 inches	20 inches
Tulsa, Oklahoma	6 inches	11 inches

⑬ What does this table show?

⑭ What are the column labels?

⑮ Which city had the most winter rainfall?

⑯ Which city had the most summer rainfall?

102

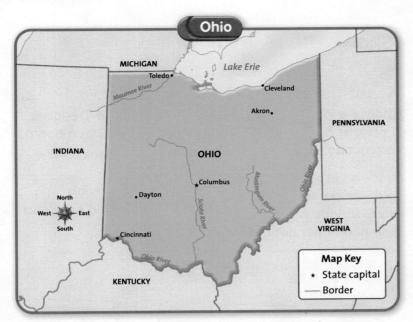

17 In which direction would you go to get from Columbus to Akron?

18 Which cities on this map are southwest of Columbus?

19 Which state is north of Ohio?

20 Which state is west of Ohio?

103

Skills
17. Northeast

18. Dayton and Cincinnati

19. Michigan

20. Indiana

ASSESSMENT

Use the UNIT 2 Test on pages 10–12 of the Assessment Program.

Show What You Know

Unit Writing Activity

Choose a Place Ask children to think about some places in or near their community that a pen pal might want to visit, such as a market, library, park, or landform. As children suggest locations, list responses on the board.

 Write a Letter Ask children to think about the things their pen pal likes to do. Suggest that these ideas will help them decide which locations to describe in the letter. Remind children that the map should include cardinal directions, street names, and descriptions of buildings and landforms so it can help the pen pal get from one place to another.

You may wish to distribute the Unit 2 Writing Activity Guidelines on page 13 of the Assessment Program.

For a scoring rubric, see this Teacher Edition, page 57O.

Unit Project

 Bulletin Board Brainstorm with children geography topics related to this unit. Invite children to review the unit for ideas. Make a list of topics on the board. Organize the class into groups, and allow each group to focus on a single topic. Discuss with children the people they should invite to view their completed bulletin board.

You may wish to distribute the Unit 2 Project Guidelines on page 15 of the Assessment Program.

For a scoring rubric, see this Teacher Edition, page 57O.

> **LEVELED READERS**
>
> Use the LEVELED READERS for Unit 2.

Unit 2 Activities

Show What You Know

 **Unit Writing Activity**

Choose a Place Think about a place in or near your community.

Write a Letter Write a letter to a pen pal telling about the place. Include a map that will help him or her get around.

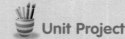 **Unit Project**

Bulletin Board Design a geography bulletin board.

- Think of ideas for the design.
- Gather materials.
- Decorate and label each section.

Read More

The Whole World in Your Hands: Looking at Maps by Melvin and Gilda Berger

The Amazing Pop-Up Geography Book by Kate Petty and Jennie Maizels

Way to Go! Finding Your Way with a Compass by Sharon Sharth

 GO ONLINE For more resources, go to www.harcourtschool.com/ss1

104

Read More

After the children's study of maps and the land, encourage independent reading with these books or books of your choice. Additional books are listed on page 57J of this Teacher Edition.

Basic *The Whole World in Your Hands: Looking at Maps* by Melvin and Gilda Berger (Ideals, 1993). This book explains what maps are and how to use them.

Proficient *The Amazing Pop-Up Geography Book* by Kate Petty and Jennie Maizels (Penguin Young Readers, 2000). Children learn about Earth's geography in this pop-up book.

Advanced *Way to Go! Finding Your Way with a Compass* by Sharon Sharth (Reader's Digest Children's, 2000). Children learn fascinating facts about how people find their way around.

Using Our Resources

The Big Idea

Resources

People use the land and its resources to help them live.

What to Know

✓ What natural resources do people use? How do they use them?

✓ What are some of the reasons people choose to live in a place?

✓ How do people change their environment?

✓ How have transportation and communication changed over time?

Introduce the Unit

The Big Idea

Resources Read the Big Idea to children. Explain that we depend on natural resources to get the things we need to live. In this unit, children will learn how people use resources and modify their environment as they build different kinds of communities. They will also learn how technology changes communities and helps us conserve resources. Remind children to refer back to the Big Idea periodically as they finish this unit.

What to Know Read What to Know to children. Explain that these four essential questions will help them focus on the Big Idea.

Assessing the Big Idea Share with children that throughout this unit they will be asked to show evidence of their understanding of the Big Idea. See Assessment Options on page 105M of this Teacher Edition.

START WITH A VIDEO DVD

To introduce the Unit Big Idea to students, show a video clip from the Start with a Video DVD.

Instruction Design

The flowchart below shows briefly how instruction was planned for Unit 3.

START WITH THE BIG IDEA

Lesson Objectives
What to Know

→

PLAN ASSESSMENT

Assessment Options
• Option 1—Unit 3 Test
• Option 2—Writing: Write a Descriptive Paragraph
• Option 3—Unit Project: Earth's Resources Flowchart

→

PLAN INSTRUCTION

Unit 3 Teacher Edition
• materials
• instructional strategies
• activities

Using Our Resources

THE BIG IDEA

RESOURCES People use the land and its resources to help them live.

Express Path

See each lesson for an **EXPRESS PATH** to teach main ideas.

LESSON	PACING	OBJECTIVES
Preview the Unit pp. 105V–105	**5** **DAYS**	
Preview Vocabulary pp. 106–107		■ Use visuals to determine word meanings. ■ Use words and visuals to preview the content of the unit.
Reading Social Studies pp. 108–109		■ Recognize cause-and-effect relationships in a text. ■ Interpret information from charts.
Start with a Story *The Tortilla Factory* pp. 110–113		■ Identify how a story can tell sequence. ■ Recognize that people depend on things from Earth to meet their food needs.
① Land and Water Resources pp. 114–119 🔆 **WHAT TO KNOW** What natural resources do people use? How do they use them?	**4** **DAYS**	■ Describe natural resources and tell how people use them. ■ Identify ways people can care for and conserve Earth's resources.
CHART AND GRAPH SKILLS **Read a Picture Graph** pp. 120–121	**1** **DAY**	■ Identify and explain the parts of a picture graph. ■ Find and compare numbers using symbols on a picture graph.
Biography: Rachel Carson pp. 122–123	**1** **DAY**	■ Understand the importance of the actions and character of Rachel Carson and explain how she made a difference in others' lives.

6 WEEKS	WEEK 1	WEEK 2	WEEK 3	WEEK 4	WEEK 5	WEEK 6
	Introduce the Unit	Lesson 1	Lesson 2	Lesson 3	Lesson 4	Wrap Up the Unit

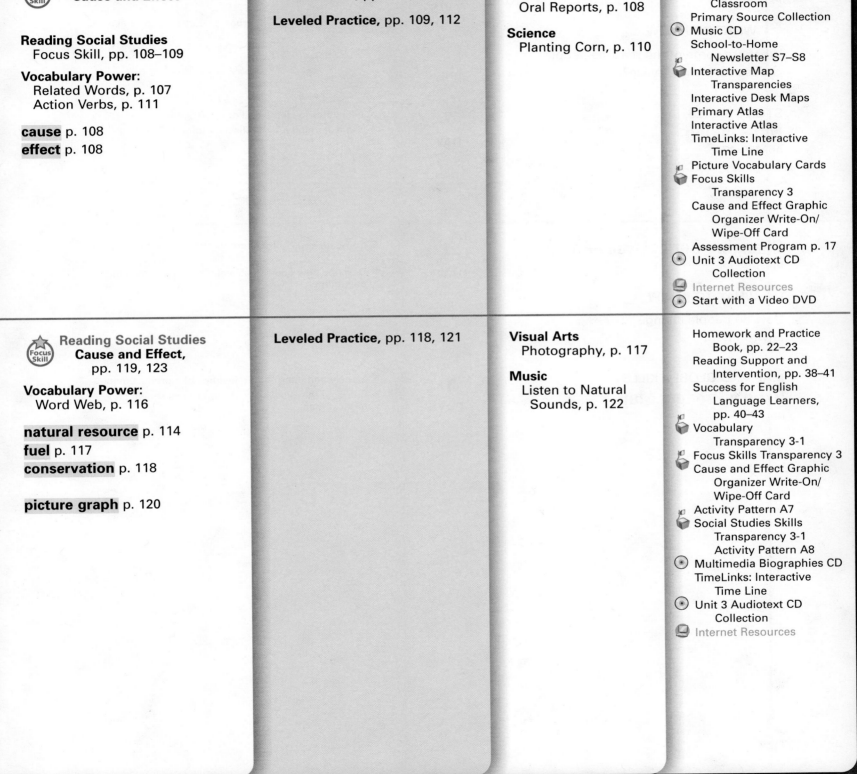

READING SUPPORT VOCABULARY	REACH ALL LEARNERS	INTEGRATE LEARNING	RESOURCES
Reading Social Studies *Focus Skill* **Cause and Effect** **Reading Social Studies** Focus Skill, pp. 108–109 **Vocabulary Power:** Related Words, p. 107 Action Verbs, p. 111 **cause** p. 108 **effect** p. 108	**ENGLISH LANGUAGE LEARNERS,** pp. 105, 106, 112 **Leveled Practice,** pp. 109, 112	**Reading/Language Arts** Oral Reports, p. 108 **Science** Planting Corn, p. 110	Social Studies in Action: Resources for the Classroom Primary Source Collection ⊙ Music CD School-to-Home Newsletter S7–S8 Interactive Map Transparencies Interactive Desk Maps Primary Atlas Interactive Atlas TimeLinks: Interactive Time Line Picture Vocabulary Cards Focus Skills Transparency 3 Cause and Effect Graphic Organizer Write-On/ Wipe-Off Card Assessment Program p. 17 ⊙ Unit 3 Audiotext CD Collection ⊟ Internet Resources ⊙ Start with a Video DVD
Reading Social Studies *Focus Skill* **Cause and Effect,** pp. 119, 123 **Vocabulary Power:** Word Web, p. 116 **natural resource** p. 114 **fuel** p. 117 **conservation** p. 118 **picture graph** p. 120	**Leveled Practice,** pp. 118, 121	**Visual Arts** Photography, p. 117 **Music** Listen to Natural Sounds, p. 122	Homework and Practice Book, pp. 22–23 Reading Support and Intervention, pp. 38–41 Success for English Language Learners, pp. 40–43 Vocabulary Transparency 3-1 Focus Skills Transparency 3 Cause and Effect Graphic Organizer Write-On/ Wipe-Off Card Activity Pattern A7 Social Studies Skills Transparency 3-1 Activity Pattern A8 ⊙ Multimedia Biographies CD TimeLinks: Interactive Time Line ⊙ Unit 3 Audiotext CD Collection ⊟ Internet Resources

LESSON	PACING	OBJECTIVES
2 **People Settle** pp. 124–129 ⚲ **WHAT TO KNOW** What are some of the reasons people choose to live in a place?	**4** **DAYS**	■ Describe the factors that influence where people live. ■ Identify how the geography of a place affects the way people live. ■ Identify and compare urban, suburban, and rural areas.
STUDY SKILLS **Note Taking** pp. 130–131	**1** **DAY**	■ Take notes to clarify and organize ideas. ■ Use a learning log to reflect on information.
3 **Changing Our Environment** pp. 132–135 ⚲ **WHAT TO KNOW** How do people change their environment?	**4** **DAYS**	■ Compare and contrast farming today with farming long ago. ■ Describe how people use technology to change the environment.
MAP AND GLOBE SKILLS **Read a Product Map** pp. 136–137	**1** **DAY**	■ Identify and interpret the features of a product map. ■ Compare the availability of products as shown on a product map.

READING SUPPORT VOCABULARY	REACH ALL LEARNERS	INTEGRATE LEARNING	RESOURCES
Reading Social Studies (Focus Skill) **Cause and Effect**, p. 129 **rural** p. 126 **urban** p. 128 **suburb** p. 128	**ENGLISH LANGUAGE LEARNERS,** p. 130 **Leveled Practice,** pp. 128, 131 **Advanced,** p. 127	**Science** Needs of Living Things, p. 126	Homework and Practice Book, pp. 24–25 Reading Support and Intervention, pp. 42–45 Success for English Language Learners, pp. 44–47 Vocabulary Transparency 3-2 Focus Skills Transparency 3 Cause and Effect Graphic Organizer Write-On/ Wipe-Off Card Social Studies Skills Transparency 3-2 Unit 3 Audiotext CD Collection Internet Resources
Reading Social Studies (Focus Skill) **Cause and Effect**, p. 135 **environment** p. 132 **technology** p. 134 **product** p. 136 **product map** p. 136	**Leveled Practice,** pp. 134, 137	**Mathematics** Story Problems, p. 135	Homework and Practice Book, pp. 26–27 Reading Support and Intervention, pp. 46–49 Success for English Language Learners, pp. 48–51 Vocabulary Transparency 3-3 Focus Skills Transparency 3 Cause and Effect Graphic Organizer Write-On/ Wipe-Off Card Social Studies Skills Transparency 3-3 Primary Atlas Interactive Atlas Unit 3 Audiotext CD Collection Internet Resources

LESSON	PACING	OBJECTIVES
④ Connecting Communities pp. 138–141 🔍 **WHAT TO KNOW** How have transportation and communication changed over time?	**4 DAYS**	▪ Identify changes in transportation and communication. ▪ Describe how new methods of transportation and communication link people, places, and ideas.
MAP AND GLOBE SKILLS **Follow a Route** pp. 142–143	**1 DAY**	▪ Interpret the features of a route map. ▪ Follow a route from one location to another on a map.
Points of View pp. 144–145	**1 DAY**	▪ Compare and contrast children's daily lives to those of others. ▪ Explore different points of view of how individuals view changes in technology.
Fun with Social Studies: What Doesn't Belong? pp. 146–147	**3 DAYS**	
Unit 3 Review and Activities pp. 148–152		

READING SUPPORT VOCABULARY	REACH ALL LEARNERS	INTEGRATE LEARNING	RESOURCES
Reading Social Studies (Focus Skill) **Cause and Effect,** p. 141 **transportation** p. 139 **communication** p. 140 **route** p. 142	**Leveled Practice,** pp. 140, 143, 145 **Advanced,** p. 141 **Special Needs,** p. 142	**Science** Inventors, p. 140 **Visual Arts** Design a Font, p. 144	Homework and Practice Book, pp. 28–29 Reading Support and Intervention, pp. 50–53 Success for English Language Learners, pp. 52–55 Vocabulary Transparency 3-4 Focus Skills Transparency 3 Cause and Effect Graphic Organizer Write-On/ Wipe-Off Card Social Studies Skills Transparency 3-4 Primary Atlas Interactive Atlas Unit 3 Audiotext CD Collection Internet Resources
Reading Social Studies (Focus Skill) **Cause and Effect,** p. 146	**Leveled Practice,** p. 147		Homework and Practice Book, pp. 30–31 Assessment Program, pp. 18–20 Leveled Readers Leveled Readers Teacher Guide Unit 3 Audiotext CD Collection Internet Resources

STUDENT DIGITAL LEARNING

The interactive eBook provides students with the standards-based content of Harcourt print books in addition to interactive add-ons that enhance student interest and reinforce Social Studies content. Harcourt eBooks are available in both a basic and enhanced version.

INTERACTIVE VISUALS

Students watch resources come to life through engaging interactive activities that enhance the unit content.

STREAMING VIDEO

Each Unit Opener includes video tied to the Unit Big Idea. This clip provides students with enhanced information about natural resources.

SKILLS ACTIVITIES

Each Chart and Graph Skill and Map and Globe Skill is enhanced by an interactive online activity.

LIVE INK ENHANCEMENT

Live Ink provides students with reading help through a patented system that breaks sentences down into segments. The Live Ink system is proven to increase student comprehension and test scores. Live Ink is available for grades 3–6/7.

ONLINE ADVENTURES

Fun with Social Studies provides a link to our Online Adventures game. Students play a game in which they help save a community park. The game reviews important concepts from the unit.

MULTIMEDIA BIOGRAPHIES

Biographies from the student edition include additional information in an interactive Multimedia Biography. Students can find more information, view related biographies, explore maps and images, and find links to additional webpages.

THE LEARNING SITE

The eBook includes links to **www.harcourtschool.com/ss1** There students can find internal resources such as our complete Multimedia Biographies databases and our Online Adventures games. This Harcourt Social Studies site also provides students with additional research tools.

Back | Forward | Reload | Home

Teacher Resources

E-PLANNER

The e-Planner provides a useful tool for scheduling Social Studies lessons.

- Use it to access Teacher Edition pages and student workbook pages and to plan classroom activities.
- The calendar tool displays all your scheduled Social Studies lessons in an easy-to-use format.
- All standards are organized by grade level.

HSPOA

Harcourt School Publishers Online Assessment provides teachers with a reliable, confidential system for online delivery of Social Studies assessment. Using this system, you can track student performance correlated to standards and run prescribed reports for any missed standards. Questions are correlated to our print Assessment program.

VIDEOS AND DVDS

A comprehensive package of videos for Grades K–3 provides an entertaining overview of core social studies concepts such as government, geography, economics, culture and history. Videos in this package are available from Schlessinger Media® and are also available digitally on SAFARI Montage.

SAFARI MONTAGE™

For more information, see pages TEI13–TEI18.

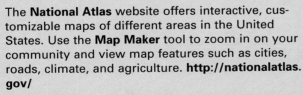

FREE AND INEXPENSIVE MATERIALS

Free and inexpensive materials are listed on the Social Studies Website at **www.harcourtschool.com/ss1**

- Addresses to write to for free and inexpensive products
- Links to unit–related materials
- Internet maps
- Internet references

COMMUNITY RESOURCES FOR THE CLASSROOM

The **National Atlas** website offers interactive, customizable maps of different areas in the United States. Use the **Map Maker** tool to zoom in on your community and view map features such as cities, roads, climate, and agriculture. **http://nationalatlas.gov/**

Educators can use the **United States Census Bureau** webpage to locate census information and facts about their local communities. **http://factfinder.census.gov/home/saff/main.html?_lang=en**

The National Park Service offers a comprehensive site with a search engine that cross-references our country's National Historic Landmarks by name, city, and state. **http://tps.cr.nps.gov/nhl/**

Museums in all 50 states are indexed on the **Virtual Library** museums pages. Use this site to find museums in and around your students' own community. **http://www.museumca.org/usa/states.html**

The **Library of Congress** site features numerous collections of primary sources, biographies, recordings, and photographs. The topic **Cities and Towns** contains photographic records of communities throughout the history of the United States. **http://memory.loc.gov/ammem/**

Additional Sites are available at www.harcourtschool.com/ss1

Lesson Plan Summaries

Leveled Readers

BELOW-LEVEL/INTERVENTION

TOPIC
Using Our Resources

Summary *Living Off the Land.* This Reader identifies our natural resources and examines how environments can shape the ways people live, work, move from place to place, and communicate.

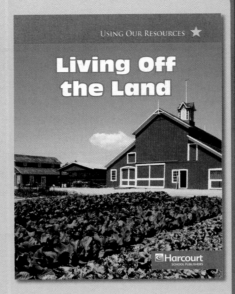

Using Our Resources ★

Living Off the Land

Harcourt
SCHOOL PUBLISHERS

BEFORE READING

Vocabulary Power Have children define the following words. Help them write one sentence for each word as it relates to our use of resources.

natural resource   technology   suburb
environment   communication

DURING READING

Cause and Effect Have children complete the graphic organizer to show that they understand causes and effects related to our use of resources, as described in the Reader.

Cause	Effect
Rachel Carson wrote a book about how nature can be hurt.	People learned about taking care of nature.

Cause	Effect
People need food, water, and a place to live.	People build homes close to natural resources.

AFTER READING

Critical Thinking Lead children in a discussion about how they use natural resources in their community.

Write a Essay Have children write short persuasive essays about why it is important to take care of our natural resources.

ON-LEVEL

TOPIC
Using Our Resources

Summary *Linking Communities,* by Christine Rowan. This Reader describes how people build bridges and tunnels to link places together and identifies some of the world's most famous bridges and tunnels.

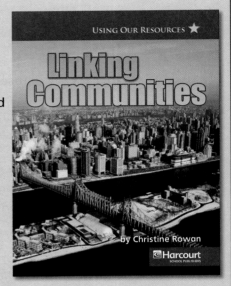

Using Our Resources ★

Linking Communities

by Christine Rowan

Harcourt
SCHOOL PUBLISHERS

BEFORE READING

Vocabulary Power Have children define the following words. Help them write one sentence for each word as it relates to our use of resources.

natural resource   technology   bridge   tunnel   tides

DURING READING

Cause and Effect Have children complete the graphic organizer to show that they understand causes and effects related to our use of resources, as described in the Reader.

Cause	Effect
People needed a safe way to cross the river.	The Brooklyn Bridge opened in 1883.

Cause	Effect
Getting from France to England was not easy.	A tunnel was built under the English Channel to link France and England.

AFTER READING

Critical Thinking Lead children in a discussion about ways communities are linked together, other than by bridges and tunnels.

Write Statistics Have children research and write down several statistics about the Golden Gate Bridge, including how many people worked on the bridge and how long the bridge took to build.

The *Leveled Readers Teacher Guide* provides background, reading tips, fast facts, answer keys, and copying masters.

ABOVE-LEVEL

TOPIC
Using Our Resources

Summary *Sticks and Stones Can Make Our Homes,* by Isabel Santiago. This Reader describes different kinds of homes and examines how people use natural resources to build their homes.

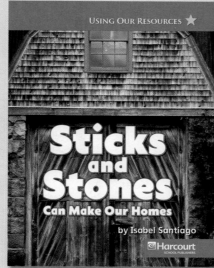

USING OUR RESOURCES ★

Sticks
and
Stones
Can Make Our Homes

by Isabel Santiago

Harcourt
SCHOOL PUBLISHERS

BEFORE READING

Vocabulary Power Have children define the following words. Help them write one sentence for each word as it relates to our use of resources.

natural resource   technology   material   adobe   prairie

DURING READING

Focus Skill **Cause and Effect** Have children complete the graphic organizer to show that they understand causes and effects related to our use of resources, as described in the Reader.

Cause		Effect
People use the natural resources where they live to build their homes.	→	In a place with many trees, a family might build a log house.

Cause		Effect
Adobe is thick.	→	Adobe keeps homes cool in the summer and warm in the winter.

AFTER READING

Critical Thinking Lead children in a discussion about the kinds of materials used in building their school.

Write a Report Have children research a new material that is used to build homes today and write a report about it.

Readers Theater
Every Student Is a Star

IT'S SHOWTIME!

Getting Started

★ Distribute the Big Idea activity sheet from your Readers' Theater.

★ Read through the script together. Make connections with unit contents.

★ Plan a performance using the **Prep ★ Practice ★ Perform** guidelines. Find ideas for props online.

Pressed for Time?

★ Perform a choral reading of the script with the whole class.

★ Assign parts for a one-time read-through.

★ Assign groups to read in your literacy center.

Read Along,

Read Aloud,

Reading Fun

Independent Reading

BASIC

Burton, Virginia Lee. **The Little House.** Houghton Mifflin, 1978. This classic tells the story of a country house that witnesses the growth of a city around it.

Geisert, Bonnie and Arthur. **Haystack.** Houghton Mifflin, 2003. This book features colored etchings and informative text to bring to life a working farm.

Gershator, David and Phyllis. **Bread Is for Eating.** Henry Holt, 1995. This bilingual story tells how bread is made, from farmer to baker.

Pluckrose, Henry Thomas. **On the Farm.** Scholastic, 1998. Photographs and text present different machines used on farms, including tractors, cultivators, balers, and combine harvesters.

Wilder, Laura Ingalls. **Summertime in the Big Woods.** Harper Trophy, 2000. A little girl and her pioneer family spend a summer in the Wisconsin woods.

PROFICIENT

Bunting, Eve. **A Day's Work.** Houghton Mifflin, 2004. A young Mexican-American boy helps his grandfather find and keep work after they arrive in California.

Egan, Robert. **From Wheat to Pasta.** Scholastic, 1997. The book describes the steps to make pasta, from growing and harvesting wheat, grinding the flour, making the dough, and shaping the final product.

Frazier, Debra. **On the Day You Were Born.** Harcourt Children's Books, 2005. A celebration of the natural world serves as a welcome to a newborn baby.

Kalman, Bobbie D. **Tools and Gadgets.** Crabtree, 2004. A presentation of tools and gadgets from the past that were found in the home, general store, doctor's office, and farm.

Millard, Anne. **A Street Through Time.** DK Publishing, 1998. Trace the development of the same street from the Stone Age to modern times.

ADVANCED

Hudson, Cheryl Willis. **Construction Zone.** Candlewick Press, 2006. Great photographs show the process of building a skyscraper.

Peterson, Chris. **Harvest Year.** Boyds Mills, 2003. The photographic essay presents foods that are harvested year-round in the United States.

Trumbauer, Lisa. **Communities.** Capstone, 2000. Learn about the various workers in a community and the services they provide.

Bial, Raymond. **Corn Belt Harvest.** Houghton Mifflin, 1991. Clear and simple text follows the growing of corn as it is planted, cultivated, and harvested.

McBrier, Page. **Beatrice's Goat.** Sagebrush Education Resources, 2004. The value of education and responsibility are stressed in this story of a girl and her income-producing goat in a small village in Uganda.

Additional books also are recommended at point of use throughout the unit.
Note that information, while correct at time of publication, is subject to change.

For information about ordering these tradebooks, visit
www.harcourtschool.com/ss1

Use these activities to help differentiate instruction. Each activity has been developed to address a different level or type of learner.

ELL ENGLISH LANGUAGE LEARNERS

30 minutes

Materials
- magazines
- cards
- paste
- scissors
- markers

CLAP, STAMP, SNAP A RESOURCE **Review lesson concepts about natural resources with sounds as responses.**

- Help pairs find or draw pictures of people using the natural resources of land, air, or water. Have children add or draw a picture to a card, marking *A* for air, *L* for land, or *W* for water on the back.
- Have pairs take turns holding up a card and identifying each by clapping for air, stamping a foot for land, and snapping for water.
- Tell children to use the letters on the back to check answers. Encourage children to describe what each picture shows.

SPECIAL NEEDS

1 hour for 3 days

Materials
- clay
- art materials
- small boxes

TECHNOLOGY MODELS **Have small groups of children create a model of how technology has changed communication.**

- Provide small groups with materials to create a model that shows an item such as a pencil, phone, radio, and computer.
- After children make models, have them add labels to explain how each item changed the way people communicate.
- Display a list of terms for children to use in labeling their models such as *Internet, e-mail, cordless, cell phone, mail,* and *letter.*
- Invite children to explain their models to the class.

ADVANCED

30 minutes

Materials
- posterboard
- crayons or markers
- game pieces, spinners, or dice

FARMERS LONG AGO BOARD GAME **Have children create a board game about farmers from long ago.**

- List experiences farmers faced long ago such as *chop trees, plow land, plant seeds, no rain, many insects,* or *good harvest.*
- Have children use posterboard to make a game board that names an experience in each space.
- Invite children to decorate the game board, decide on game pieces and rules, and give the game an interesting name.
- Allow small groups of children to play the game.

MATHEMATICS CENTER

Recycling Tally

Bring to class an assortment of aluminum cans from soft drinks. Invite children to view the containers and discuss how many cans and bottles Americans use per year. Tell children that in 2003, Americans recycled 62.6 billion aluminum cans, and if those cans were placed end-to-end, they would circle Earth 171 times. Continue to discuss the importance of recycling aluminum cans. For one week, have children keep a tally of how many aluminum cans their families use each day. At the end of the week, help children make a picture graph to show the number of cans used.

Sunday	▯
Monday	▯ ▯
Tuesday	▯ ▯ ▯ ▯
Wednesday	▯ ▯ ▯
Thursday	
Friday	▯ ▯ ▯ ▯
Saturday	▯ ▯ ▯ ▯

SCIENCE CENTER

Build a Cargo Boat

Invite children to design aluminum foil boats that will stay afloat with a cargo of pennies. Provide aluminum foil, pennies, and a tub of water to each group. Explain that shippers want to carry as much "penny cargo" as possible. Point out that the design of their boat will affect the amount of cargo it can hold, but they also need to think about how the cargo is loaded on the boat. Have children experiment with hull designs and ways of loading the penny cargo to see which group can "ship" the most cargo and keep the boat afloat. Invite them to write a summary of their findings, giving the number of pennies carried and why they think their design worked well.

READING/LANGUAGE ARTS CENTER

Farm Story Starters

Encourage children to write an imaginary story about farming. Explain that the story can be realistic or fantasy. List several story starters that children may use, such as the following:
- I drove my _____ to the field to plant the corn.
- I saw a _____ when I went to the barn to milk the cows.
- I fed my pigs _____ so they would grow strong and healthy.

Remind children to include descriptive details. Ask children to illustrate or decorate their story. Display stories in the center for others to read and enjoy.

Morning on the Farm

In the morning, I wake up to feed the cows and pigs. The rooster wakes up all the animals. The cows moo loudly.

ART CENTER

Product Prints

Provide children with a variety of interesting fruits, vegetables, and nuts that have been cut in half. Have children brush tempera paint onto the flat side and press the object onto art paper to make a design. Encourage children to think about different themes and colors before they choose which objects to use. For example, a print of summer fruits uses warm colors printed with various fruit halves or a fall food print might feature browns, reds, and oranges printed with nut shell halves and apples. Invite children to title their print and display it for others to enjoy.

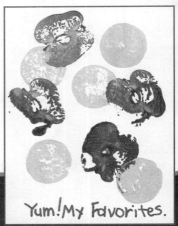

Yum! My Favorites.

Assessment Options

The Assessment Program gives all learners many opportunities to show what they know and can do. It also provides ongoing information about each student's understanding of social studies.

 Online Assessment available at www.harcourtschool.com/ss1

 OPTION 1

UNIT TESTS
Unit 3

- **Unit Pretest,**
  Assessment Program, p. 17
- **Unit Review and Test Prep,** pp. 148–151

- **Unit Test,**
  Assessment Program, pp. 18–20

 OPTION 2

WRITING

- **Show What You Know,**
  Unit Writing Activity,
  Write a Descriptive
  Paragraph, p. 152

- **Lesson Review,**
  Writing Activities, at ends of lessons

 OPTION 3

UNIT PROJECT

- **Show What You Know,**
  Unit Project,
  Earth's Resources Flowchart, p. 152
- **Unit Project,**
  Performance Assessment, pp. 105P–105Q

- **Lesson Review,**
  Performance Activities, at ends of lessons

INFORMAL ASSESSMENT

- **Lesson Review,** at ends of lessons
- **Skills:**
  Practice, pp. 120, 130, 136, 142
  Apply, pp. 121, 131, 137, 143

- **Reading Social Studies,**
  Cause and Effect, pp. 108–109
- **Literature Response Corner,** p. 113
- **Points of View, It's Your Turn,** pp. 144–145

STUDENT SELF-EVALUATION

- **Reading Check Questions,** within lessons

- **Biography, Why Character Counts,** pp. 122–123
- **Map, Time Line, Graph, Diagram, and Illustration**
  questions, within lessons

PRETEST

Name _____ Date _____

3 Pretest

TRUE/FALSE (10 points each)

DIRECTIONS Write T next to the statements that are True and F next to the statements that are False.

❶ __T__ A natural resource is something found in nature.

❷ __F__ Cars are important natural resources.

❸ __T__ People can get electricity from wind power.

❹ __F__ We cannot conserve water.

❺ __T__ You can count things on a picture graph.

❻ __F__ A suburb is a big city.

❼ __F__ Farmers use all the same tools today that farmers used long ago.

❽ __T__ Farmers can produce more food today than farmers produced long ago.

❾ __T__ You might find symbols of plants and animals on a product map.

❿ __F__ People wrote e-mails long ago.

UNIT TEST

Name _____ Date _____

3 Test

MATCHING (6 points each)

DIRECTIONS Match the word or words on the right to its meaning on the left.

❶ __D__ something found in nature that people can use, such as air, water, and land

❷ __B__ a resource that can be burned for heat and energy

❸ __A__ the saving of resources to make them last longer

❹ __C__ all of the things that people find around them

❺ __G__ the use of new objects and ideas in everyday life

❻ __F__ the moving of goods and people from place to place

❼ __E__ the sharing of ideas and information

A. conservation

B. fuel

C. environment

D. natural resource

E. communication

F. transportation

G. technology

(continued)

UNIT TEST

Name _____ Date _____

MULTIPLE CHOICE (7 points each)

DIRECTIONS Select the letter of the best answer.

❽ Which of these is a way to save our natural resources?

Ⓐ recycling newspapers
C putting garbage in the ocean
B polluting the air
D cutting down trees

❾ Which of these worried farmers long ago?

A plenty of help
C a good climate
Ⓑ bugs and mice
D rich soil

❿ How has technology helped today's farmers?

A It makes the work go slower.
Ⓒ It makes the work go faster.
B It makes the work harder.
D It makes the farmer produce fewer crops.

⓫ Which of these kinds of communication was used long ago and is still used today?

Ⓐ letters
C Internet
B e-mail
D cell phone

(continued)

UNIT TEST

Name _____ Date _____

SHORT ANSWER (6 points each)

DIRECTIONS This is a product map for a make-believe country called Waveland. Use the product map to answer the questions.

⓬ What crops are grown in Waveland?

__corn, beets__

Waveland Products

Smithville • Harbortown

• Newman

• Granger

Map Key
Fish | Corn | Sheep
Lumber | Beets | Cattle

⓭ What crop is found in the southern part of the country?

__corn__

⓮ Why is there plenty of fish around Harbortown?

__Harbortown is close to the water.__

⓯ What resource is found near Smithville?

__lumber__

⓰ Which animal is raised near Newman?

__sheep__

OPTION 2 WRITING

RUBRIC

Name _____ **Date** _____

Unit 3 Writing Activity Guidelines

WRITE A DESCRIPTIVE PARAGRAPH

Writing Prompt Write a short paragraph describing your favorite farm product. Include facts and details about your product.

▶ **STEP 1** What is your favorite farm product? To help you answer this question, you might do these things.
- Review Unit 3 for product ideas.
- Look through grocery ads for favorite foods.

▶ **STEP 2** Choose one favorite farm product to write about. Describe the way it looks, tastes, smells, and feels. Research other interesting facts about the product, for example, where it is grown and how it gets from a farm to a market.

▶ **STEP 3** Use your research to write a descriptive paragraph.

▶ **STEP 4** Review your work to make sure you have used correct grammar, spelling, punctuation, and capitalization.

▶ **STEP 5** Make the changes. Then copy your paragraph neatly.

SCORE 4
- clearly supports product choice with many sensory details
- shows a clear understanding of how products get from farm to market
- includes many details and interesting facts
- uses complete and well-structured sentences
- contains few, if any, errors in grammar and punctuation

SCORE 3
- supports product choice with some sensory details
- shows some understanding of how products get from farm to market
- includes some details and interesting facts
- uses mostly complete and well-structured sentences
- contains some errors in grammar and punctuation

SCORE 2
- partially supports product choice with few sensory details
- shows little understanding of how products get from farm to market
- includes few details
- uses some sentence fragments with little variety
- contains several errors in grammar and punctuation

SCORE 1
- does not support product choice with any sensory details
- shows no understanding of how products get from farm to market
- does not include any details
- uses mostly sentence fragments with no variety
- contains serious errors in grammar and punctuation

OPTION 3 PROJECT

RUBRIC

Name _____ **Date** _____

Unit 3 Project Guidelines

EARTH'S RESOURCES FLOWCHART

Create a flowchart about using resources to produce food.

▶ **STEP 1** Think about the steps needed to get a product from the farm to the table. Plan a flowchart that could be used to show how resources are used to do these things.

▶ **STEP 2** Choose a product for your flowchart. Research how this product is grown, harvested, transported, packaged, and sold.

▶ **STEP 3** Decide on several steps you want to show. Write out each step. Include details that the pictures for each step should show.

▶ **STEP 4** Draw a picture to show each step. Write a caption for the picture.

▶ **STEP 5** Display your finished flowchart. Share the chart with others.

SCORE 4
- shows a clear understanding of how resources are used to get food
- includes highly descriptive steps
- records steps in a logical sequence
- uses illustrations that clearly support each step

SCORE 3
- shows some understanding of how resources are used to get food
- includes somewhat descriptive steps
- records steps in a mostly logical sequence
- uses some illustrations that support each step

SCORE 2
- shows little understanding of how resources are used to get food
- includes few steps with minimal description
- records steps that are sometimes out of order
- uses illustrations that do not always support each step

SCORE 1
- shows no understanding of how resources are used to get food
- does not include descriptive steps
- does not record steps in a logical order
- does not include illustrations

TAKE-HOME RUBRICS Copying masters of a student *Writing Rubric* and *Project Rubric* appear in the Assessment Program, pp. 22 and 24.
GROUP PERFORMANCE RUBRIC See Assessment Program, page x.

An Earth's Resources Flowchart

Getting Started

Distribute the Unit 3 Project Guidelines provided on page 23 of the Assessment Program.

Introduce the unit project as you begin Unit 3. Allow time for children to work on the flowchart as they learn how people depend on the earth's resources to get food. As children read the lesson, have them note how we use resources, such as land and water, to grow the crops for food. Explain that once the food is grown, it follows a series of steps to get from the farm to our tables. Point out that a flowchart can show these steps in an easy-to-understand way.

The Big Idea

Resources People use the land and its resources to help them live.

Project Management

Organize the class into five cooperative learning groups: researchers, artists, recorders, organizers, and presenters. Allow children to choose a group based on their interests and talents. Work with each group to plan and carry out their tasks. Provide instructional support and materials as needed.

Materials textbook, research books and materials about farming, pencils, posterboard, colored paper, markers

Organizer As a class, discuss what needs to be done by each group. Record the results in a two-column chart. List each role in the left column. List jobs that each group will be responsible for in the right column, such as:

- Choose food crop for flowchart.
- Collect books and information about farming and raising the crop.
- Draw pictures for each step.
- Write captions for each picture.
- Invite guests to see finished chart.
- Decorate classroom and choose music to add to presentation.
- Set up project.
- Greet guests.
- Present display and answer questions.

Tomato Project Plan

GROUPS	JOBS
Researchers	Gather books to read about growing tomato crops. Share information with other groups. Decide on guest list.
Artists	Draw pictures to show how tomato crop gets from farm to table. Share pictures with other groups. Make invitation cover. Make welcome signs.
Recorders	Write sentences about each picture. Share sentences with other groups. Write invitation.
Organizers	Put up flowchart parts from each group. Arrange decorations and classroom for presentation. Welcome guests.
Presenters	Decide on date and time for presentation. Choose background music. Present project to guests. Answer guest questions.

Design and Prepare

Direct each group to work on their jobs for creating the flowchart. Explain that when all of their jobs are completed, the children will be presenting a flowchart about how we produce and use one of our natural resources, plants, for food. Remind children that a flowchart shows the steps in order, from first to last. Review the details of the flowchart to be sure it includes:

- growing and harvesting raw materials
- sending raw materials to a processing plant
- bringing the processed food to the market
- buying and bringing food to homes

Discuss with children how each step in their flowchart connects to the step before and after.

Have children deliver the invitations to school or family members.

Presentation Day

Direct groups to complete final preparations for their display and for the classroom before guests arrive. Have the Presenter group practice several times beforehand. Remind children to speak slowly and clearly when making their presentations or answering questions. Once guests arrive, encourage children whose jobs are completed to sit with the guests to make them feel welcome and comfortable.

Lesson Review Activities

You may wish to incorporate the following lesson review activities into the unit project.

- Lesson 1: **Write About Resources**, p. 119
- Lesson 2: **Make a Poster About Your Community**, p. 129
- Lesson 3: **Make a Poster About the Environment**, p. 135
- Lesson 4: **Make a Chart**, p. 141

Assessment

For a project rubric, see Teacher Edition, p. 105O.

What to Look For

- Children understand the arrangement and purpose of a flowchart.
- Children understand the connection between resources and the food they need.
- The flowchart display is creative, well-organized, and clearly related to topic.
- Each group completes their tasks in a cooperative and efficient manner.

LESSON 1

Name _____ Date _____

How We Use Resources

Look at the natural resources shown in the pictures.
Write at least two ways people use each resource.

❶ build houses
make paper

❷ breathe
make electricity

❸ drink
clean things

❹ grow food
grow trees
get fuel

SKILL PRACTICE

Name _____ Date _____

 CHART AND GRAPH SKILLS

Classroom Picture Graph

How many of these things are in your classroom? Use a
picture symbol to show how many of each you see.

LESSON 2

Name _____ Date _____

Urban or Rural?

Decide where you would find each thing listed in the Word Bank.
Then write it under Urban or Rural.

farm	desert	cows
apartment building	offices	field of corn
forest	many people	restaurants
traffic	museums	barn

Urban   Rural

apartment building   farm

traffic   forest

offices   desert

many people   cows

museums   field of corn

restaurants   barn

SKILL PRACTICE

Name _____ Date _____

 STUDY SKILLS

Note Taking

Read the paragraph. Then fill in the Learning Log.

Conserving natural resources is something we can all do.
Turn off the faucet while you are brushing your teeth. Take
showers, not baths. Get a recycling bin for newspapers and
containers, and use it. Instead of throwing away toys and
clothing, give them to a thrift shop. What can you do today to
conserve?

Learning Log	
Note Taking	**Note Making**
Turn off the faucet when you are brushing your teeth.	I can conserve water by doing these things.
Answers will vary. Children should write words and sentences from the paragraph here.	**Answers will vary. Children** should write their own thoughts in response to their notes here.

Name _____ Date _____

How People Change Environments

Imagine you have moved to these woods and you want to grow crops here. What will you have to do first? Make a list on the lines below the picture. Then draw what your farm will look like after you change the environment.

| cut down trees | move rocks |
| dig out stumps | plow land |

Name _____ Date _____

 MAP AND GLOBE SKILLS

Make a Product Map

Create your own state. Draw an outline of your state in the box. On the map, show the products and resources of your state. Create a symbol for each product or resource. Make a map key for the symbols on your map. Write a title for your product map.

Title: Products and Resources of Jasonland

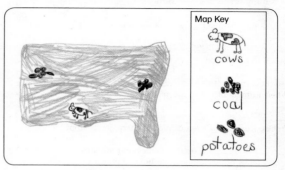

What are some jobs that people do in the state you created?

farming, coal mining, cattle ranching

_____

Name _____ Date _____

Connecting with Others

Read the paragraph. Then fill in the chart.

Long ago, transportation and communication were much slower. There were no telephones, airplanes, or paved roads. People moved goods on dirt roads by horse and wagon. They rode horses or walked instead of driving cars. When relatives and friends moved far away, they wrote letters instead of calling or e-mailing. Two things haven't changed at all, though. People still walk and talk to connect with each other!

People Connect with Each Other

Long Ago — Moved goods by horse and wagon, Rode horses, Had dirt roads

Both — Write letters, Walk, Talk

Today — Drive cars, Use telephones and e-mail, Have paved roads, Travel by airplane

---

Name _____ Date _____

 MAP AND GLOBE SKILLS

The Sheriff's Busy Day

Read the story. Draw the route on the map and answer the questions.

The sheriff of Cowtown is going to pick up some feed for his horse. First, he stops to buy a new shirt at the dry goods store. Next, he checks the railroad station to see if anyone new has just come in on the train. Then, he goes to the bank to get some more money. Finally, he arrives at the feed store.

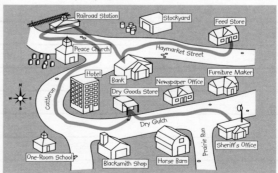

Which streets did the sheriff take to get to the feed store?

Dry Gulch, Cattlerun, Haymarket Street

STUDY GUIDE

Name _____ Date _____

3 Study Guide

Read the paragraphs. Use the words in the Word Bank to fill in the blanks.

products	technology	communication
conservation	environment	transportation
natural resources	rural	

Life has changed a lot since times long ago. Farmers still use __natural resources__, such as air, soil, and water, to grow food. Unlike farmers of long ago, however, they use modern __technology__ to raise crops and animals. When farmers of today are ready to sell their food __products__, they use modern __transportation__. Trucks, trains, and even airplanes carry goods from __rural__ areas to cities and suburbs.

As times have changed, we have changed our __environment__, not always for the better. We are learning to practice __conservation__ to save resources.

Modern forms of __communication__, such as the Internet, make it easy to learn how to save our planet.

© Harcourt

30 ■ Homework and Practice Book   Use after reading Unit 3, pages 105–152.

UNIT 3 REVIEW AND TEST PREP

Name _____ Date _____

CAUSE AND EFFECT

Reading Social Studies

Use the chart to show causes and effects about our natural resources.

Cause	Effect
Water turns big machines in dams.	The machines produce electricity.
Farmers grow trees.	Trees give us fruits and nuts.

© Harcourt

Use after reading Unit 3, pages 105–152.   Homework and Practice Book ■ 31

NOTES

STATE AND COMMUNITY RESOURCES

Historical Societies

Museums

Parks

Guest Speakers

Discuss the Big Idea

Resources **People use the land and its resources to help them live.**

Explain that our natural resources are used to give us the things we need to live. Point out that it is important that we take care of these resources. Tell children that in this unit they will learn about various kinds of natural resources and how we use the land to get the things we need.

Make It Relevant Ask the following question to help children think about the importance of land and resources in their lives.

Q What do you need in order to stay healthy?

A Children may respond that they need food, water, clothing, exercise, and a safe home.

Access Prior Knowledge

Ask children to think about the ways we use the land. Help children create a word web about land to organize their ideas. Have them include words related to natural resources, ways we take care of natural resources, land use, and farming.

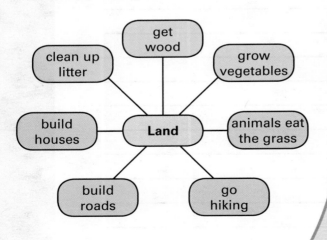

Unit 3 Using Our Resources

Talk About

Resources

" Our food is grown in Earth's rich soil. "

Practice and Extend

BACKGROUND

Resources The United States has many regions of rich farmland soil. The Great Plains region produces many of our country's grain crops, such as wheat and corn, as well as oil seed crops like sunflower and canola. Cattle, sheep, and other livestock are raised on the open grasslands. Below ground, the land provides many mineral resources, such as coal, petroleum, and natural gas.

Talk About The children in the photographs at the bottom of the unit preview pages are talking about natural resources. While some areas get enough rainfall to grow crops, other areas have a dry climate. Water needs to be redistributed from rivers and lakes to the farmlands where it is needed to irrigate the rich soil and grow crops.

> " Our neighborhood market sells fresh fruits and vegetables. "

> " Water is also an important resource. "

105

Discuss the Picture

Have children examine the photograph and identify it as farmland. Invite children to notice details in the picture. Point out tools, people, and resources in the photograph.

Q What do you see in this photograph that is familiar to you?

A grass, crops, fields, growing plants, tractor

Q How do you think a farm helps to meet your needs to live?

A Farmers grow crops or raise animals that we use for food and clothing.

Discuss "Talk About"

Have a volunteer read each quotation and discuss what the children in the pictures are holding.

Q How do you think these items show resources we get from the land?

A They are all ways we get food: by growing our own; by buying it; or by catching it.

Q What are some ways we use water to meet our needs?

A We use water to drink, to keep clean, and to water the plants we grow.

Have children work in pairs to ask and answer additional questions about either the farmland photograph or Talk About.

ELL ENGLISH LANGUAGE LEARNERS

Beginning Have children point to an item and then say a word or phrase from the quotation that relates to the picture. For example, the chili plant relates to *food*, or the grocery bag relates to *fruits and vegetables*.

Intermediate Ask children to say a sentence that explains what each child is doing, such as *The girl is holding a chili plant.* Encourage children to include describing words.

Advanced Help children read aloud each quotation. Then have them say each sentence in their own words. Explain that they need to keep the meaning of the sentence the same. For example, the sentence *Our food is grown in Earth's rich soil* can be *We grow things to eat in the our planet's healthy dirt.*

Make Connections

Link Pictures with Words Have children look at the pictures for *natural resource* and *conservation*. Help them read the definitions. Suggest that these words are related because we can run out of a natural resource if we don't practice conservation. Ask children to find other connections between words, such as *technology* and *product*. (Technology is often used to make new products.)

❶ **Visual Literacy: Pictures** Ask children what they see in the picture for the words *natural resource*. (cows, grass)

Q Why are cows a natural resource?

A Cows are animals that can be found in nature. We use them to get milk.

Q What natural resources are used to help cows grow?

A Water, air, land, and grass are resources cows need to stay healthy.

❷ Read the definition of *conservation* to children. Invite them to explain what the girl in the picture is doing that shows conservation. (She is shutting the faucet so it doesn't drip and waste water.) Invite children to name other ways they can practice water conservation. (don't let water run; use only as much as you need; don't pollute water)

Unit 3 Preview
Vocabulary

❶

natural resource Something found in nature that people can use. (page 114)

conservation The saving of resources to make them last longer. (page 118)

❷

106

Practice and Extend

ELL ENGLISH LANGUAGE LEARNERS

Frontloading Language: Resources Use the following prompts to develop the academic language of resources and the structures of cause and effect.

Beginning Ask children to look at each vocabulary word and picture to complete a sentence frame about needs. For example: *The ____ is a natural resource.* (cow) *We need the cow because it gives us ____.* (milk) *We need the machine because it milks the ____.* (cow)

Intermediate Have children use the pictures to provide responses for this sentence frame: *We need [vocabulary word] because ____.*

Advanced Have children use this frame to analyze why we need the objects in the pictures: *If we have [vocabulary word], then ____.* For example, *If we have natural resources, then we have food to eat.*

3

technology The use of new objects and ideas in everyday life. (page 134)

4

product Something that is made by nature or by people. (page 136)

GO ONLINE For more resources, go to **www.harcourtschool.com/ss1**

107

Q Why do you think a farmer would want to use this machine to milk cows?

A The machine is faster; he can milk many cows at the same time; it might keep milk cleaner.

4 Ask children to look at the picture of the milk and cheese. Have children discuss whether each item is made by nature or by people. (milk: nature; cheese: people)

Q Can you name some other food products that are made by nature? by people?

A nature: fruits, vegetables, eggs; people: bread, yogurt, cereal

GO ONLINE **INTERNET RESOURCES**

For more resources, go to **www.harcourtschool.com/ss1**

VOCABULARY POWER

Related Words Explain that the words *natural resource* and *conservation* are related. Many people want to use natural resources. Natural resources will last longer if we practice conservation. On the board, create two columns titled *natural resources* and *conservation*. Under *natural resources*, list resources such as *grass, cows, air,* and *water*. Invite children to add ways to conserve each item to write under *conservation*.

 Cause and Effect

OBJECTIVES

- Recognize cause-and-effect relationships in a text.
- Interpret information from charts.

VOCABULARY

cause p. 108   **effect** p. 108

RESOURCES

Focus Skills Transparency 3; Cause and Effect Graphic Organizer Write-On/Wipe-Off Card; Unit 3 Audiotext CD Collection

I Introduce

1 Why It Matters Explain to children that knowing what causes an event to happen can help people decide what to do and help them make plans for the future. Provide examples such as:

- If eating a whole box of cookies gives them a stomachache, then they may decide not to eat so many in the future.
- If city officials know that too many cars cause traffic jams, then they can build more roads for more cars.

Have children suggest other examples. Explain that by recognizing causes and effects, they will better understand what they read.

1 Why It Matters Knowing why things happen can help you understand what you read.

Learn

- What makes something happen is a cause.

2
- What happens is the effect.

Read the paragraph below.

Green beans come from bean plants. I grew my own beans! I filled a cup with soil. I pressed
Effect
bean seeds into the soil and waited. The seeds
Cause
did not grow because I forgot to water them. Then I watered my seeds carefully. They began to grow. When the bean plants got bigger, I planted them outside.

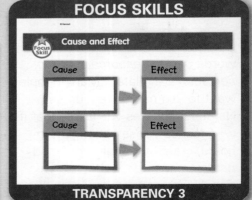

108

Practice and Extend

INTEGRATE THE CURRICULUM

READING/LANGUAGE ARTS Have children prepare a short oral report about a change at school. Ask small groups to brainstorm ideas of changes, such as a new food offered for lunch or classroom desks arranged in a different way. Encourage them to include details to explain what caused this change and what effect it has had on them. Remind children to speak clearly. **Oral Reports**

FOCUS SKILLS

Focus
Skill   Cause and Effect

Cause		Effect
	→	
Cause		Effect
	→	

TRANSPARENCY 3

Graphic Organizer Write-On/Wipe-Off Cards available

Practice

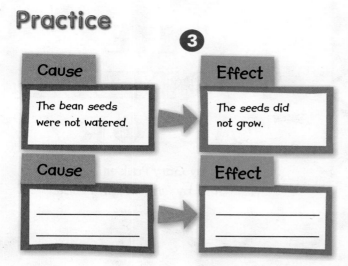

Cause

The bean seeds were not watered.

Effect

The seeds did not grow.

Cause

_____
_____

Effect

_____
_____

This chart shows what happened to the seeds and why it happened. Copy the chart and complete it.

Apply

As you read this unit, look for the ways people change the land where they live. Find out what causes these changes.

109

Learn

2 Have children read the definitions for _cause_ and _effect_ on page 108. Then read aloud and discuss the paragraph. Invite children to share their experiences planting seeds and growing plants. Point out that the clue words _because, if_, and _then_ can signal causes and effects.

Practice

3 **Visual Literacy: Graphic Organizer** Have volunteers read the chart on page 109. Use Focus Skills Transparency 3 to copy the chart. Discuss other causes and effects they could add.

Q **What happened when the bean seeds were not watered?**

A The seeds did not grow into plants.

Q **What did this person change after noticing the effect of not watering the seeds?**

A The person watered the seeds.

ANSWERS: Cause: The bean seeds were watered. Effect: The seeds began to grow.

Apply

Tell children that as they read the unit, they should look for causes that explain why people change the land around them and the effects these changes bring about.

Quick Summary

The Tortilla Factory by Gary Paulsen (Harcourt Brace, 1995).

This lyrical story describes the production of a tortilla, tracing its journey from seed to table.

Before Reading

Set the Purpose Have children look at the pictures. Point out that they show steps from start to end. Explain that many foods follow a number of steps before they are ready to be eaten.

Ask volunteers to describe foods they eat with most meals, such as bread, rice, or tortillas. Invite children to tell how they think this food gets to their table. Ask children who have helped make this food at home to describe the process.

During Reading

Understand the Story Point out that this story reads somewhat like a poem. Point out how the author uses color words and nouns (black earth, brown hands, yellow seeds) to create a sense of rhythm. Have children read aloud page 110 several times to recognize the poetic rhythm of these words.

Start with a Story

THE TORTILLA FACTORY

by Gary Paulsen

illustrated by Ruth Wright Paulsen

The black earth sleeps
in winter.
But in the spring the
black earth is worked by
brown hands that plant
yellow seeds, which become
green plants rustling in
soft wind and make golden
corn to dry in hot sun and
be ground into flour

110

Practice and Extend

for the tortilla factory,
where laughing people
and clank-clunking
machinery mix the flour
into dough,
and push the dough,
and squeeze the dough,
and flatten the dough . . .

. . . and bake the dough
into perfect disks that
come off the machine
and into a package
and onto a truck and
into a kitchen

111

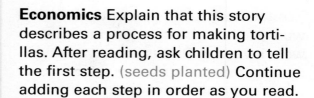

Economics Explain that this story describes a process for making tortillas. After reading, ask children to tell the first step. (seeds planted) Continue adding each step in order as you read.

Visual Literacy Ask children to read the phrase from the story that describes each illustration on pages 110 and 111.

Q What would you change or add to an illustration to fit the story? Why?

A Possible answers include: show more machines mixing the flour to seem like a noisy factory; to show more orange and yellow for sunshine.

VOCABULARY POWER

Action Verbs Explain to children that action verbs often show sequence in a story. Have children reread page 111 and list all of the action verbs they can find. (mix, push, squeeze, flatten, bake) Invite them to suggest other action verbs that could describe what happens to tortillas once they are brought home from the store. (roll, cut, slice, fill)

MAKE IT RELEVANT

In Your Community Invite someone who makes tortillas to share his or her talent with the class. If possible, ask the visitor to bring in some of the tools or ingredients to display and explain. Encourage children to prepare some questions ahead of time, such as *What do you enjoy about making tortillas?* or *Do you use machines?* Remind children to thank the visitor.

BACKGROUND

Tortillas Tortillas have been an important food source in Mexico for centuries. Recently, they have become popular in the United States. Since 1970, tortilla sales increased as national fast food chains and Mexican restaurants featured tortillas. By 2000, sales in the United States were at $4.4 billion. Some analysts predict that tortillas will soon be the top-selling bread product in the United States.

Economics Explain that tortillas were made by hand before machines were invented. Discuss reasons why machines are now used in a factory. (They can make more tortillas at once; they can make them faster; tortillas will all be the same size and shape.)

Understand the Story Ask children to read the word that describes *people*. (laughing) Repeat with *machinery* (clank-clunking) and *disks*. (perfect) Have children locate other describing words in the story. Explain that these words add details that make the story more interesting and easier to understand.

Economics Lead children to see that there are various jobs being described in the story. Have children predict the kinds of workers needed for each job. (factory worker, baker, truck driver, delivery person)

Geography Explain that many resources are needed to produce tortillas. Discuss resources mentioned throughout the story. (seeds, sun, earth)

Q Can you name other needed resources that are not in the story?

A water for plants to grow; fuel for the machinery

to be wrapped around juicy beans
and eaten by white teeth, to fill a round stomach
and give strength to the brown hands
that work the black earth
to plant yellow seeds,

112

Practice and Extend

Leveled Practice Have children show the order of events.

(Basic) As you read aloud each page, invite volunteers to pantomime the actions.

(Proficient) Ask children to list three steps in the correct sequence for making tortillas.

(Advanced) Have children complete a three-column chart, labeled *On the Farm, At the Factory*, and *In the Home*, with story details.

Have children retell the story in their own words.

(Beginning) Retell details from the story in simple sentences, leaving out one word for children to say or identify in pictures, such as *People eat (beans) in a tortilla.*

(Intermediate) Invite children to retell details of the story by using simple sentences to describe the pictures, such as *They put beans in tortillas* or *The farmer plants seeds.*

(Advanced) Have children work in pairs to retell the story aloud in their own words. Encourage them to use the illustrations as guidelines for the order of events.

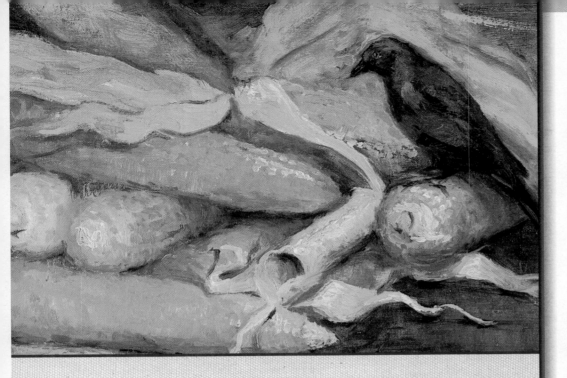

which make golden corn to be dried in hot sun and be ground into flour...

Response Corner

❶ Cause and Effect   What causes the flour to turn into dough?

❷ Make It Relevant   How do farmers help you?

113

Understand the Story Invite children to retell the beginning, middle, and end of the story. Ask them to explain how the end of the story is similar to the beginning. Help children recognize that this story is like a circle that goes around and around.

Q Why do you think Gary Paulsen wrote the story in this way?

A to tell a story about how food is made; to show food is always needed and that the work of making it is never finished

After Reading

Response Corner—Answers

1. (Focus Skill) **Cause and Effect** The people and machinery mix the flour into dough.

2. **Make It Relevant** Farmers help me by growing the plants used to make food I can eat.

✎ Write a Response

Have children write several sentences to explain how to make a favorite family food. Encourage them to use describing words and put the steps in order from beginning to end.

For a writing response rubric, see Assessment Program, page xvi.

INDEPENDENT READING

Children may enjoy reading these books during the unit. Additional books are listed on page 105J of this Teacher Edition.

Magda's Tortillas by Becky Chavarria-Chairez (Arte Publico Press, 2000). This book describes a girl's first tortilla-making adventure.

Bread, Bread, Bread by Ann Morris (William Morrow, 1993). Children will read about breads from all over the world.

Corn is Maize by Aliki (HarperCollins Children's Books, 1996). This is a simple story of how Native Americans discovered corn long ago and how important it is today.

For information about ordering these trade books, visit **www.harcourtschool.com/ss1**

OBJECTIVES

- Describe natural resources and tell how people use them.
- Identify ways people can care for and conserve Earth's resources.

VOCABULARY

natural resource p. 114
fuel p. 117
conservation p. 118

CAUSE AND EFFECT

pp. 108–109, 119

RESOURCES

Homework and Practice Book, p. 22; Reading Support and Intervention, pp. 38–41; Success for English Learners, pp. 40–43; Vocabulary Transparency 3-1; Focus Skills Transparency 3; Cause and Effect Graphic Organizer Write-On/Wipe-Off Card; Activity Pattern A7; Unit 3 Audiotext CD Collection; Internet Resources

Introduce

What to Know Invite children to read the What to Know question. Then ask children what things they use that might come from nature. Remind children to look for answers to the question as they read the lesson.

Build Background Encourage children to share how they use water, air, and land on a daily basis. For example, they play a soccer game on land and drink water after playing sports.

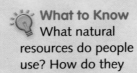

Lesson 1

 What to Know
What natural resources do people use? How do they use them?

Vocabulary
natural resource
fuel
conservation

 **Cause and Effect**

Land and Water Resources

People use natural resources to live. A **natural resource** is something found in nature that people can use.

People Use Air

People, plants, and animals need clean air to live. Some people use moving air to bring power to their homes. A wind turbine uses the wind's energy to produce electricity.

Reading Check **How do people use air?**
People use air to breathe and to produce electricity.

114

Practice and Extend

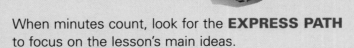
Express Path

When minutes count, look for the **EXPRESS PATH** to focus on the lesson's main ideas.

Quick Summary

People and communities depend on natural resources, including air, land, and water. It is important to take care of our resources.

People Use Water

① People use water for drinking, cooking, cleaning, and growing plants for food. Like air, water can also be used to produce electricity. In some dams, water produces electricity by flowing through and turning big machines.

Wolf Creek Dam, Kentucky

Reading Check How do people use water?

People use water for drinking, cooking, cleaning, growing plants, and to produce electricity.

Wind Turbines

115

People Use Air and Water

CONTENT FOCUS People need air and water to live. Air and water are also used to produce electricity.

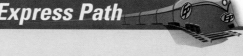

Express Path

Have pairs scan the page to find out how people use air and water.

① **Geography** Display a map of your state. Identify sources of water close to your community. Invite children to discuss other ways we use water, such as for recreation, to water plants, or to provide animal habitats.

② **Visual Literacy: Photographs** Ask children to study the photographs and captions. Let them find words from the captions that are repeated in the text. Help them connect the photos to the sentences in which the words appear.

Q How do wind turbines help people?

A Wind turbines use moving air to produce electricity.

Interactive in the enhanced online student eBook

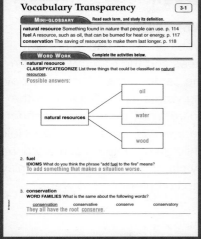
READING SUPPORT/ INTERVENTION

For alternate teaching strategies, use pages 38–41 of Reading Support and Intervention to:

- identify **phonemes**
- practice **phonics**
- reinforce **vocabulary**
- build **text comprehension**
- build **fluency**

Reading Support ▶ and Intervention

ELL ENGLISH LANGUAGE LEARNERS

For English Language Learners strategies to support this lesson, see Success for English Learners pages 40–43.

- English-language development activities
- background and concepts
- vocabulary extension

Success for ▶ English Learners

People Use Land

CONTENT FOCUS Land is a natural resource that people use to grow food and trees, build shelter, and find fuel.

Express Path

Have children scan the page, including the pictures, to answer the Reading Check question.

❸ Economics Invite children to discuss ways that land is used. Point out that land is used to grow trees and that different trees have different purposes.

Q What kinds of food come from trees?

A fruits and nuts

Q How do trees provide shelter for people?

A We use the wood to build houses. Trees give us shade from the sun.

Explain that wood from trees can also be used as fuel. It can be burned for heat.

Correct Misconceptions Help children realize that plants are a natural resource even though people grow them. Review the definition of a natural resource. Point out that plants do come from nature, but people may choose the kinds of plants to grow and the places to grow them.

People Use Land

Another natural resource is land. We grow plants and build houses on land.

❸ Trees are a very useful natural resource. Some farmers grow trees that make fruits and nuts. People use wood from trees to build furniture and ❹ homes. They also use wood to make paper.

116

Practice and Extend

BACKGROUND

Land Use Perspectives vary on how to use the land and its resources. Some people think laws should protect resources for the future. Other people believe land owners should be able to use their land freely. In the past, clearcutting of land caused problems, such as soil erosion. Presently, the need for building and mineral resources is weighed against needs for habitat and open space.

VOCABULARY POWER

Word Web Begin two word webs on chart paper, one with *trees* and the other with *fuel* in the center circles. List the following words alphabetically on the board: *coal, fruit, furniture, homes, natural gas, nuts, oil, wood.* Help children complete each word web by classifying the words. Display the completed word webs.

Under the ground, people can find other natural resources, such as coal, oil, and natural gas. People dig and drill for these resources and make them into fuel. A **fuel** is a resource that can be burned for heat or energy. **⑤**

Reading Check How do people use land?

People use land for growing plants for food and trees for wood. People also go under the ground for coal, oil, and natural gas.

117

④ History Explain that the resources available in a place directly affected the way people lived there. Land with many trees meant people built homes and fences of wood. Land with few trees meant people used rocks to build homes and fences.

Q Why do you think people in some places built homes from mud?

A Dirt and water to make mud were available resources. There probably weren't any trees or rocks to use.

⑤ Economics Discuss mineral resources people use from under the ground. Have children brainstorm and discuss other Earth products such as gold, silver, iron, and coal. Point out that aluminum and steel are made from minerals, natural resources we get from the land.

MAKE IT RELEVANT

In Your Community Invite children to talk about how the land is used in your community. Identify uses of land such as the following:

- parks
- orchards (trees)
- farms (crops and animals)
- houses and apartments
- roads
- businesses and industries

INTEGRATE THE CURRICULUM

VISUAL ARTS Invite children to study photographs of landscapes showing land being used in different ways.

- Invite children to use pictures from magazines or newspapers to make land-use collages.
- Provide digital or disposable cameras for children to use in making photo-essays of land uses in your community. **Photography**

BACKGROUND

Resource Regions The resources of a place influence the community that forms there. For example, a place with flat, fertile land might become farmland. Regions are often named for the resources that sustain them.

- America's Breadbasket
- Cornbelt
- Gold Country
- Orange State

Caring for Our Resources

CONTENT FOCUS Recycling and keeping resources clean are important.

Express Path

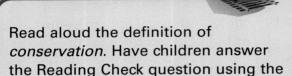

Read aloud the definition of *conservation*. Have children answer the Reading Check question using the pictures and captions.

6 Culture Point out that taking care of natural resources can become part of our day-to-day living. Discuss the conservation and recycling programs in the children's community. Have children discuss their role in protecting resources.

Q How is the woman in the picture on page 119 helping save resources?

A She is recycling food garbage. That keeps it out of landfills and makes soil healthier.

Geography Provide each child with a copy of Activity Pattern A7. Have them illustrate on the filmstrip the benefits of conserving our resources, as well as the consequences of not doing so. After children complete their drawings, have them cut around the filmstrips and tape them end to end. Invite volunteers to show their finished product to the class.

7 Economics Give examples of other sources of pollution: oil spills, litter, improper disposal of toxic chemicals, or cars that are not maintained properly. Discuss how these sources cost everyone money in terms of clean up, health risks, and destruction of other natural resources.

Caring for Our Resources

With so many people living on Earth, we must protect our resources. **Conservation** is the **6** saving of resources to make them last longer. Recycling is another way to save resources. When we recycle, we use something again in a new way.

Communities help care for resources by recycling.

118

Practice and Extend

If we do not take care of our natural resources, they can become dirty. Anything that makes the air, land, or water dirty is called pollution. Clean air, water, and land help all living things stay healthy.

Reading Check **Focus Skill** Cause and Effect

How does conservation help protect our resources?

Conservation saves resources so that we will have them for a longer time.

Summary Natural resources give us what we need to live.

Recycling food garbage can keep soil healthy.

Review

1. **What to Know** What natural resources do people use? How do they use them?

2. **Vocabulary** What are two kinds of **fuel**?

3. **Write** Think about all of the resources you use in one day. Then write a short paragraph about how you can conserve one of the resources.

4. **Cause and Effect** What would happen if we didn't take care of our natural resources?

119

---

3 Close

Summary

Let children read the summary and state the main idea in their own words.

- People use air, water, and land to meet their needs.
- People need to protect and take care of natural resources.

Assess

REVIEW—Answers

1. **What to Know** People use air to breathe and to make electricity; they use water for drinking, cooking, cleaning, growing plants, and producing electricity; they use land resources for food, houses, and fuel.

2. **Vocabulary** Possible answer: Coal and oil are two kinds of **fuel**.

3. **Writing Assessment Guidelines** See Writing Rubric. This activity can be used with the Unit Project.

4. **Cause and Effect** Our resources would run out or get dirty.

Use Focus Skills Transparency 3 or Cause and Effect Graphic Organizer Write-On/Wipe-Off Card.

WRITING RUBRIC

Score 4
- clearly identifies a resource
- conservation is very detailed

Score 3
- identifies a resource
- conservation is adequately detailed

Score 2
- vaguely identifies a resource
- conservation is somewhat detailed

Score 1
- does not identify a resource
- conservation is not detailed

HOMEWORK AND PRACTICE

Name _____ Date _____

How We Use Resources

Look at the natural resources shown in the pictures. Write at least two ways people use each resource.

1. build houses
   make paper

2. breathe
   make electricity

3. drink
   clean things

4. grow food
   grow trees
   get fuel

page 22

READING SOCIAL STUDIES

Cause and Effect Have children use the information on pages 118 and 119 to explain in their own words some causes of pollution and some effects of conservation. Encourage them to ask questions about any information that is unclear.

READING TRANSPARENCY

Use FOCUS SKILLS TRANSPARENCY 3.
Graphic Organizer Write-On/Wipe-Off Cards available

LESSON 1 ■ **119**

OBJECTIVES

- **Identify and explain the parts of a picture graph.**

- **Find and compare numbers using symbols on a picture graph.**

VOCABULARY

picture graph p. 120

RESOURCES

Homework and Practice Book, p. 23; Social Studies Skills Transparency 3-1; Activity Pattern A8; Unit 3 Audiotext CD Collection; Internet Resources

I Introduce

Write on the board in a vertical list *Soccer, Baseball, Basketball,* and *In-line skating.* Point to each item, and have children raise a hand to vote for their favorite sport. Make tallies next to each item and have a volunteer count the tallies to find out which is the class's favorite sport. Explain that in this lesson, children will compare numbers by using symbols, or pictures.

Why It Matters Point out that pictures can help children easily interpret information. Illustrate this by erasing the tallies and having children vote again. This time draw a happy face next to each choice. Have children identify the most popular sport. Point out that the longest line of happy faces indicates the sport children like best. Lead children to understand that they can see at a glance how popular each sport is.

Read a Picture Graph

Why It Matters   A **picture graph** makes information easier to understand by using pictures to show numbers of things.

Learn

1   The picture graph on the next page shows how much water Jen's family uses in one day. The key shows that each picture stands for five gallons of water.

❷ Practice

❶ How much water did Jen's family members use to brush their teeth?

❷ For what did they use the most water?

❸ Did Jen's family use more water to wash dishes or to flush the toilet?

120

Practice and Extend

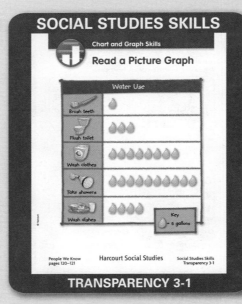

SOCIAL STUDIES SKILLS

Chart and Graph Skills

Read a Picture Graph

Water Use

People We Know pages 120–121   Harcourt Social Studies   Social Studies Skills Transparency 3-1

TRANSPARENCY 3-1

BACKGROUND

Water Usage According to the U.S. Geological Survey's calculations, the average family uses the following amounts of water in a day:

- Brush teeth: 1 gallon
- Flush toilet: 3 gallons
- Wash clothes: 10 gallons a load
- Shower: 2 gallons per minute
- Wash dishes: 20 gallons a dishwasher load or 5 gallons by hand

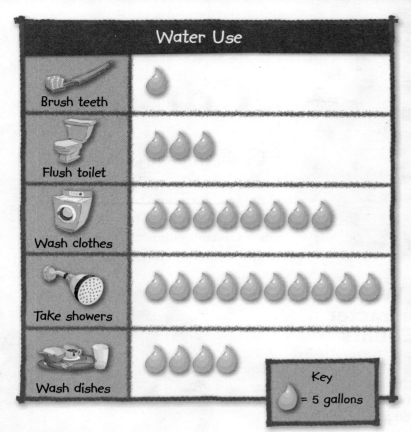

Water Use

Brush teeth	🔹
Flush toilet	🔹🔹🔹
Wash clothes	🔹🔹🔹🔹🔹🔹🔹🔹
Take showers	🔹🔹🔹🔹🔹🔹🔹🔹🔹🔹
Wash dishes	🔹🔹🔹🔹

Key
🔹 = 5 gallons

Apply

Make It Relevant Make a picture graph to show how much water your family uses in a day.

 For online activities, go to
www.harcourtschool.com/ss1

121

---

2 Teach

Learn

① Visual Literacy: Graph Have children study the Water Use graph. Point out that when comparing information on the graph, it is not necessary to count each symbol. They can get information by looking at the length of each row.

Ask children to find the key in the graph.

Q What symbol is used in the graph?

A a drop of water

Q What does each symbol represent?

A Each drop of water represents five gallons of water.

❷ Practice

1. They used five gallons.
2. They used the most water for showers.
3. They used more water to wash dishes.

3 Close

Apply

Make It Relevant You may want to distribute a copy of Activity Pattern A8 to children for their picture graphs. Remind children to include a title and a key. Ask children to work with their families to estimate how much water they use in a day. Challenge children to come up with solutions on ways their families can conserve water.

INTERNET RESOURCES

For online activities, go to
www.harcourtschool.com/ss1

REACH ALL LEARNERS

Leveled Practice Invite children to create a recycling picture graph.

(Basic) Invite children to brainstorm a symbol and a graph title.

(Proficient) Have children add the data and symbols and create a key about what kinds of materials children's families actually recycle.

(Advanced) Ask children to write questions about the completed graph.

HOMEWORK AND PRACTICE

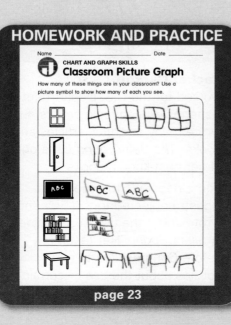

Name _____ Date _____

CHART AND GRAPH SKILLS
Classroom Picture Graph

How many of these things are in your classroom? Use a picture symbol to show how many of each you see.

page 23

OBJECTIVES

- **Understand the importance of the actions and character of Rachel Carson and explain how she made a difference in others' lives.**

RESOURCES

Unit 3 Audiotext CD Collection; Multimedia Biographies CD; Internet Resources; TimeLinks

Link to the Big Idea

Resources Explain that people depend on natural resources to help them live. Rachel Carson made people aware of the reasons why we need to protect and conserve our natural resources.

Vocabulary Help Point out the word *biologist* in the time line and explain this is a person who studies living things. Have children discuss why a biologist may be more aware than other people of the importance of protecting our natural resources.

Discuss the Biography

Primary Source: Quotation Read the quotation aloud to children. Discuss how Carson's childhood experiences might have influenced her adult life.

Source: Rachel Carson, public statement, 1954.

http://www.dep.state.pa.us

Biography

Trustworthiness
Respect
Responsibility
Fairness
Caring
Patriotism

Rachel Carson

Growing up on a farm, Rachel Carson loved the outdoors. She played in the woods around her home and drew pictures of animals. "There was no time when I wasn't interested in … the whole world of nature," Rachel Carson later said.

Why Character Counts

How did Rachel Carson show that she cared about nature?

Rachel Carson was a writer and a scientist.

122

Practice and Extend

BACKGROUND

Rachel Carson Carson first worked for the U.S. Department of Fisheries writing radio scripts. She wrote many scientific articles and books. *The Sea Around Us* is one of her best-known books.

Some people in the chemical industry objected to the way she wrote about the use of pesticides in *Silent Spring*. Her testimony before Congress led to new policies about the use of certain pesticides.

INTEGRATE THE CURRICULUM

MUSIC Obtain environmental music or natural sounds. Have children close their eyes and listen as you play various tracks. Invite them to respond to the music by describing how the music made them feel. Also have them share any mental pictures or ideas that the music sparked. After listening, tell the origin of the sounds (i.e., rain forest sounds, thunderstorm, etc.). **Listen to Natural Sounds**

Rachel Carson grew up in the country and loved to be outdoors.

Rachel Carson also liked to write about the beauty of birds, plants, and the ocean. Then she began to notice that some people were doing things that hurt nature.

In 1962, she wrote a book called <u>Silent Spring</u>. In it, she told people about the dangers of pesticides, or poisons used to kill insects. These pesticides were also killing birds and plants. Because of Rachel Carson's book, better laws were made to keep nature safe.

GO ONLINE For more resources, go to www.harcourtschool.com/ss1

Time

1907 Born			1964 Died

1918 Writes her first story, at the age of ten

1936 Works as a biologist for the United States government

1962 Writes her most famous book, <u>Silent Spring</u>

123

OBJECTIVES

Describe the factors that influence where people live.

Identify how the geography of a place affects the way people live.

Identify and compare urban, suburban, and rural areas.

VOCABULARY

rural p. 126   **suburb** p. 128
urban p. 128

CAUSE AND EFFECT

pp. 108–109, 129

RESOURCES

Homework and Practice Book, p. 24; Reading Support and Intervention, pp. 42–45; Success for English Learners, pp. 44–47; Vocabulary Transparency 3-2; Focus Skills Transparency 3; Cause and Effect Graphic Organizer Write-On/Wipe-Off Card; Unit 3 Audiotext CD Collection; Internet Resources

1 Introduce

What to Know Read aloud the What to Know question. Ask children to predict some reasons people might choose to live in a place. Remind children to look for answers to the question as they read the lesson.

Build Background Invite children to recall resources people use to live. Ask them to identify where they get these resources, such as from a faucet, bottles, a market, gardens, farm stands, and parents.

Lesson 2

People Settle

What to Know
What are some of the reasons people choose to live in a place?

Vocabulary
rural
urban
suburb

Cause and Effect

Choosing a Place to Live

All people need food, water, and shelter. In some places, these things are hard to get. It is hard to grow food on rocky mountains. Deserts do not get enough rain for drinking water. Long ago, people could not choose to live in places like these.

124

Practice and Extend

Express Path

When minutes count, look for the **EXPRESS PATH** to focus on the lesson's main ideas.

Quick Summary

People choose to live in a place for many reasons. They might choose to settle in a rural, urban, or suburban environment. The geography of a place affects how easy it is to settle.

In some places, people can find the natural resources they need. The flat, rich lands of the Great Plains are good for growing food. Rivers provide fish and water.

Once people decide to live in an area, they start to build the things they need. They build **2** roads and bridges to make it easier to get from place to place. They make homes for shelter. Communities begin to grow.

Reading Check **Why would people want to live by a river?** Rivers have water to drink and fish to eat.

125

Choosing a Place to Live

CONTENT FOCUS People get the things they need from the place they live. When people move into a place, they build some things they need.

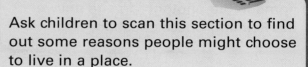

Express Path

Ask children to scan this section to find out some reasons people might choose to live in a place.

1 Geography Discuss the geographic features in the pictures. Invite children to identify the needs of people that this place meets.

Q **What must people do if they choose a place that does not have all the things they need?**

A They must get the things from another place or learn to do without.

2 History Discuss how a community develops over time. Let children share why they think people in the past chose to settle in one place over another. Point out that people used resources to build homes, roads, and bridges. They grew crops and raised animals for food.

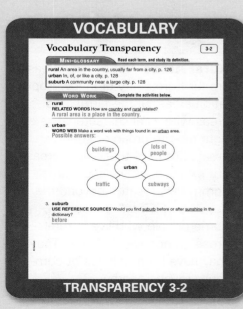

VOCABULARY

Vocabulary Transparency 3-2

MINI-GLOSSARY Read each term, and study its definition.

rural An area in the country, usually far from a city. p. 126
urban In, of, or like a city. p. 128
suburb A community near a large city. p. 128

WORD WORK Complete the activities below.

1. **rural**
   RELATED WORDS How are country and rural related?
   A rural area is a place in the country.

2. **urban**
   WORD WEB Make a word web with things found in an urban area.
   Possible answers:

   buildings — lots of people — urban — traffic — subways

3. **suburb**
   USE REFERENCE SOURCES Would you find suburb before or after sunshine in the dictionary?
   before

TRANSPARENCY 3-2

READING SUPPORT/ INTERVENTION

For alternate teaching strategies, use pages 42–45 of Reading Support and Intervention to:

   identify **phonemes**

   practice **phonics**

   reinforce **vocabulary**

   build **text comprehension**

   build **fluency**

SOCIAL Studies
People We Know
Reading Support and Intervention

Reading Support ▶ and Intervention

For English Language Learners strategies to support this lesson, see Success for English Learners pages 44–47.

   English-language development activities

   background and concepts

   vocabulary extension

SOCIAL Studies
People We Know
Success for English Learners

Success for ▶ English Learners

Rural Areas

CONTENT FOCUS Rural areas are in the country and have fewer people. The people who live there often use the land to grow food and raise animals.

Express Path

Have children describe the land and home in the photograph and answer the Reading Check question.

3 Visual Literacy: Photograph
Focus attention on the photograph of Kendra's farm. Invite children to discuss the farm's size and the number of people in the community. Discuss the different kinds of activities and types of work that people can do in a rural place.

Correct Misconceptions Children may think that the size of a community describes the amount of land it covers. Explain that a community can be described by the number of people who live there or the amount of land it takes up. A rural area usually has fewer people living in it, but may cover a large amount of land. An urban area may have less land than a rural area, but has many more people living within that area.

Rural Areas

Communities can be different sizes. Kendra lives on a soybean farm in a rural area in Indiana. **Rural** areas are usually in the country, far away from a city. People's homes may be far apart. Kendra has to travel by car to visit her neighbors.

❸

126

Practice and Extend

INTEGRATE THE CURRICULUM

 SCIENCE Ask what would happen if the plants at your school were not watered or if a pet was not fed. Explain that like all living things, people need air, water, food, and space to live. Stress that no matter where people live, they settle in places that have resources that meet their needs. **Needs of Living Things**

MAKE IT RELEVANT

In Your Community Invite children to share some of the features of your community that make it a desirable place to live. List their ideas on the board. Have children classify the features as natural or people-made. Invite them to circle the geographic features. Then discuss possible reasons people in your community might have chosen to live there. Encourage children to relate their ideas to some of the features on the list.

BACKGROUND

Rural Areas Not all rural areas are far from a city or in low population areas. Some farms and areas with rural characteristics are right next to urban or suburban areas. Some of these rural areas are *exurban*, or "having a small community located beyond the suburbs of a city." In addition, some people who live in rural areas do not live on farms. They may have home offices or commute to jobs nearby.

4 People who live in rural areas can use the natural resources there to grow food and raise animals. They use wood from the trees for building homes. Many people in rural areas also sell resources and products to people in other places. **5**

Reading Check 🔵 Cause and Effect **Why do many people in rural areas grow food and raise animals?** People in rural areas grow food and raise animals for themselves and to sell to people in other places.

Children in History **6**

Elfido Lopez

Elfido Lopez was born in Colorado in 1869. His family used the natural resources of the area to build a new home. The miles of wild grass fed their oxen. When he was older, Elfido learned how to cut down the wheat they grew. The river waters turned a millstone to crush their wheat into flour.

127

4 Geography Help children identify the resources available in rural regions that support people, including farmers.

Q What resources does Kendra's farm offer? How are they used?

A The farm has land space, water, and probably good soil. They are used to grow soybeans.

Q How do these resources help others that do not live in rural areas?

A They provide food for people that live in other places.

5 Economics Discuss the economics of farming and logging. Explain that people use rural land to grow products sold in cities and suburbs where there is not enough room to grow food or lots of trees.

Children in History

Elfido Lopez

6 Explain that like many other children born on farms in the 1800s, Lopez started working on the farm when he was very young. His family used local resources to grow food, build a home, and provide the other things they needed. Point out that his family grew wheat to grind into flour. They used the flour to make food or traded it for other things they needed.

REACH ALL LEARNERS

Advanced Lead children in a discussion of the following topics:

- How do growing communities affect resources and the environment?
- What kinds of jobs are created to get food and products from rural areas to other places where they are needed?
- Why do people in cities and suburbs need rural areas?

INDEPENDENT READING

Encourage children to read *A River Ran Wild* by Lynne Cherry (Harcourt Brace, 1992). The book tells the story of how the descendents of the Native Americans and European settlers restore a river to its natural beauty and cleanliness.

A RIVER RAN WILD

Urban Areas and Suburbs

CONTENT FOCUS Urban areas have many businesses, homes, and people. Suburbs are smaller and quieter communities near urban areas.

Express Path

Have children use the photographs to describe a city and a suburb and find both on the map.

7 Culture Invite children to compare life in urban, suburban, and rural areas. Record the following information about each area on a separate sheet of chart paper:

- the advantages of living there.
- disadvantages of living there.
- the different products and services, housing, transportation, and infrastructure such as traffic lights and sidewalks found in the area.

Guide children to conclude that people choose a place that has the things that best meet their needs.

Geography Discuss how the physical features of a place affect what people can do in an urban, a suburban, or a rural area. Focus on choices, including food, clothing, shelter, transportation, and recreation.

8 Visual Literacy: Map Invite children to read the map key. Let them find two areas with the most people. Elicit that these are large cities. Then have them find the surrounding cities in areas of most and many people. Describe these as suburbs. Explain that the surrounding areas are rural farms and natural lands.

Urban Areas and Suburbs

Michael lives in the city of Indianapolis, Indiana. A city is an **urban** area. Urban areas have many businesses, homes, and people.

Elena lives in Avon, a suburb of Indianapolis. A **suburb** is a **7** smaller community near a city. It has quieter neighborhoods, less traffic, and bigger yards.

Avon, Indiana

Indianapolis, Indiana

128

Practice and Extend

Settlement and Development
A similar process of settlement and development has occurred in many parts of the United States. First, people settle a place that is rich in natural resources. Then, people farm the land and use its resources. They sell their products to people in cities. Cities grow. A small settlement over time might become a big city. People move to the suburbs, pushing rural areas farther out.

Leveled Practice Have children use a map to find a place to live.

Basic Have children choose a place and name nearby features.

Proficient Ask children to describe how they would use the land based on features, cities, and roads.

Advanced Ask children to determine the resources they would get from the land and those they would have to bring into the area.

This map shows where people live in Indiana. The map key can help you find where rural, urban, and suburban areas are.

Reading Check **Why do some people live in suburbs?**

They want to live in a place that is less crowded and busy than an urban area.

Summary People have settled in places with good natural resources. These places can be rural, urban, or suburban areas.

People in Indiana

Map Key
- ▢ Most people
- ▢ Many people
- ▢ Fewest people

 Where do most people live in Indiana?

Review

1. **What to Know** What are some of the reasons people choose to live in a place?

2. **Vocabulary** How is a **suburb** different from a city?

3.  **Activity** Make a poster about your community. Show things that are natural and things people have made.

4. **Cause and Effect** What can cause an urban city to be a busy place to live?

HOMEWORK AND PRACTICE

Name _____ Date _____

Urban or Rural?

Decide where you would find each thing listed in the Word Bank. Then write it under Urban or Rural.

farm	desert	cows
apartment building	offices	field of corn
forest	many people	restaurants
traffic	museums	barn

Urban
- apartment building
- traffic
- offices
- many people
- museums
- restaurants

Rural
- farm
- forest
- desert
- cows
- field of corn
- barn

page 24

3 Close

Summary

Ask children to read aloud the summary and review the key concepts.

- People choose to live in a place based on its resources and the things it provides.
- People can live in urban, suburban, or rural environments.

Assess

REVIEW—Answers

1. **What to Know** People choose to live in a place because of its natural resources, because of the kind of community it is, or because it meets their needs.

2. **Vocabulary** A **suburb** is smaller and quieter, has fewer people and less traffic than a city. Its homes may have bigger yards.

3. **Activity Assessment Guidelines** See Performance Rubric. This activity can be used with the Unit Project.

4. **Cause and Effect** An urban city is full of people, cars, places to go, and things to do. People live close together and often rush from place to place.

Use Focus Skills Transparency 3 or Cause and Effect Graphic Organizer Write-On/Wipe-Off Card.

Note Taking

Why It Matters Notes are important words and sentences that help you remember what you read.

OBJECTIVES

■ **Take notes to clarify and organize ideas.**

■ **Use a learning log to reflect on information.**

RESOURCES

Homework and Practice Book, p. 25; Social Studies Skills Transparency 3–2; Unit 3 Audiotext CD Collection

Learn

Kevin used the learning log on the next page to take notes on the paragraph below.
❶ He wrote words and sentences from the paragraph under Note Taking. He wrote his own thoughts under Note Making.

❷ Practice

Read the paragraph below. Add your own notes to the learning log.

> The corn grown in Ohio is used for many things. It is used to feed animals. It can be made into cooking oil, flour, and sweeteners. Toothpaste and glue also have corn in them. Corn can even be turned into fuel for cars and machines!

130

1 Introduce

Invite children to share things people do to help them remember what they need to do. Ask children to describe ways they remember homework assignments, such as writing a list or recording assignments in a notebook.

Why It Matters Explain that listing ideas in an organized way will help children remember what they read. Point out that one way to keep notes organized is by using a learning log.

2 Teach

Learn

❶ Point out the differences between note taking and note making. Tell children that when taking notes, they write down ideas from what is read. When making notes, they include their own thoughts and ideas in what is written down.

Practice and Extend

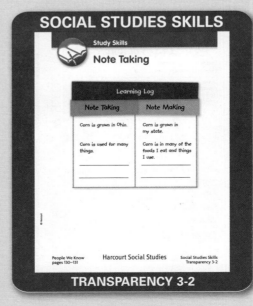

SOCIAL STUDIES SKILLS

TRANSPARENCY 3-2

ELL ENGLISH LANGUAGE LEARNERS

Have children use the paragraph to review the use of a learning log.

Beginning Ask children to name important words they might include under Note Taking.

Intermediate Read sentences from the Learning Log and ask students to tell if they belong under Note Taking or Note Making.

Advanced Ask children to name sentences that go under each column of the Learning Log.

Learning Log

Note Taking	Note Making
Corn is grown in Ohio.	Corn is grown in my state.
Corn is used for many things.	Corn is in many of the foods I eat and things I use.
_____	_____
_____	_____

Apply

Make a learning log about using our resources. As you read more about resources in this learning log.

I31

Study Skills

HOMEWORK AND PRACTICE

Name _____ Date _____

STUDY SKILLS
Note Taking

Read the paragraph. Then fill in the Learning Log.

Conserving natural resources is something we can all do. Turn off the faucet while you are brushing your teeth. Take showers, not baths. Get a recycling bin for newspapers and containers, and use it. Instead of throwing away toys and clothing, give them to a thrift shop. What can you do today to conserve?

Learning Log	
Note Taking	Note Making
Turn off the faucet when you are brushing your teeth.	I can conserve water by doing these things.
Answers will vary. Children should write words and sentences from the paragraph here.	Answers will vary. Children should write their own thoughts in response to your notes here.

page 25

❷ Practice

Have children read the paragraph under Practice. Use Social Studies Transparency 3-2 to provide children with their own copy of a learning log.

Q Which ideas are taken from the paragraph?

A the ones listed under note taking

Q Which notes are based on Kevin's thoughts?

A the ones listed under note making

Work with children to add notes to the chart's first column. Encourage children to think about each statement they write and add their own ideas and thoughts to the second column.

Possible Note Taking answers: Corn is used by people and animals; corn also has unusual uses.

Possible Note Making answers: Some pet foods contain corn; maybe fuel from corn can replace gasoline for cars someday.

3 Close

Apply

Tell children they will make a new learning log for what they will learn about resources in this unit. To assist children, point out that they should

- think about important words or ideas.
- record important ideas in the Note Taking column.
- reflect on the ideas and record their thoughts in the Note Making column.

Introduce

What to Know Read aloud the What to Know question. Invite children to identify changes to the environment that they already know about. Remind children to look for answers to the question as they read the lesson.

Build Background Ask children to recall the previous lesson and discuss how the people who first settled a place changed it with homes, roads, and bridges. Talk about other changes people may make to the land.

Lesson 3 Changing Our Environment

 What to Know
How do people change their environment?

Vocabulary
environment
technology

 Cause and Effect

The **environment** is all of the things that people find around them. People change their environment to meet their needs and make life easier.

Farming Long Ago

1 People long ago had to change the land before they could plant crops. They cut down trees, dug out stumps, and moved rocks. Then they plowed the land so they could plant seeds.

132

Practice and Extend

 Express Path

When minutes count, look for the **EXPRESS PATH** to focus on the lesson's main ideas.

Quick Summary

The physical characteristics of a place influence human activities. People also change the place to adapt its environment to meet their needs.

People faced many problems growing crops long ago. Rabbits, mice, and bugs ate the young plants. Weather was also a problem. Sometimes there would be no rain for a long time, and the plants would die. Bad storms could also kill the plants.

Reading Check **What problems did farmers face growing crops long ago?** Crops could be harmed by animals or bad weather.

133

Farming Long Ago

CONTENT FOCUS People changed the land so they could farm it. Farmers faced many problems from pests, weather, and lack of water.

Express Path

Ask children to scan the section to find out how farmers long ago changed the land.

1 History Point out that this section tells about the time when pioneers first began to settle the United States.

Q Long ago, what changes did people make so they could farm the land?

A They cut down trees, dug out stumps, moved rocks, and plowed the land.

2 Visual Literacy: Picture Have children focus on the clothing and tools the people in the picture are using.

Q What details tell you the people lived long ago?

A They are wearing clothes that people wore long ago and are using old-fashioned tools.

VOCABULARY

Vocabulary Transparency `3-3`

MINI-GLOSSARY Read each term, and study its definition.

environment All of the things around us. p. 132
technology The use of new objects and ideas in everyday life. p. 134

WORD WORK Complete the activities below.

1. environment
SUFFIXES What is the suffix in *environment*?
environ(ment)

2. technology
WORD WEB Write the word *technology* in the center of the web. Around it, list kinds of technology that have made your life better.
Possible answers:

- computer
- electric lights
- technology
- telephone
- television

TRANSPARENCY 3-3

READING SUPPORT/ INTERVENTION

For alternate teaching strategies, use pages 46–49 of Reading Support and Intervention to:

- identify **phonemes**
- practice **phonics**
- reinforce **vocabulary**
- build **text comprehension**
- build **fluency**

Reading Support ▶ and Intervention

ELL ENGLISH LANGUAGE LEARNERS

For English Language Learners strategies to support this lesson, see Success for English Learners pages 48–51.

- English-language development activities
- background and concepts
- vocabulary extension

Success for ▶ English Learners

Farming Today and in the Future

CONTENT FOCUS Today, farmers use technology to solve many problems faced by farmers in the past. We can expect more changes in the future.

 Express Path

Have children compare the photographs and describe how farming techniques have changed.

3 **Visual Literacy: Pictures** Invite children to study the three pictures on pages 134 and 135 to determine which shows farming from the past, farming today, and farming in the future.

Q How has farming changed over time?

A Farmers use technology to solve many of the problems of the past.

 Interactive in the enhanced online student eBook

Geography Explain that a change in one place affects another place. Tell children that one way to bring water to a dry area is to dam a river, which creates a lake. Point out that the water will rise and cover the land behind the dam. But below the dam, there won't be as much water flow. Discuss how these changes affect the land, animals, plants, and people.

Point out that the pictures in this lesson show how natural land is changed with human features. Help children create a community map that shows human and natural features and the roads that link them. Discuss whether and where there is room for more parks, stores, or a factory.

Farming Today

Farmers used technology to solve the problems they had growing crops. **Technology** is the use of new objects and ideas in everyday life. Better tools make planting and harvesting crops faster and easier. In dry weather, today's farmers use pipes and sprayers to bring water to crops.

Reading Check **How does new technology help farmers grow more crops?**
It helps them work faster so they can plant more crops.

3

Long ago, people planted seeds by hand. Today, machines plant many seeds at a time.

134

Practice and Extend

BACKGROUND

Farming Technology The 1900s brought huge changes in farming, including specialization, the increase in the size of farms, and the development of new plants through genetic engineering. Pests were controlled with a variety of techniques, including pesticides. Special machinery has replaced much of the work done by hand. Disadvantages of these changes are the loss of small family farms and enviromental damage.

REACH ALL LEARNERS

Leveled Practice Have children show farming in the past, present, and future.

Basic Let children refer to the illustrations in the book to create three distinct drawings.

Proficient Encourage children to create three drawings with captions about farming.

Advanced Encourage children to create a timeline to show how farming has changed over time.

Future Farming

In the future, farming may use less of one natural resource. Hydroponics is a kind of farming that does not use soil. Plants grow in water that has the minerals in it that they need. Pumps move air and water around the roots.

Hydroponics

floating plants

air line

roots

air pump

Reading Check 🔵 **Cause and Effect**

What is an effect of using hydroponics? It saves soil and land.

Summary People use technology to change their environment to meet their needs.

Review

❶ **What to Know** How do people change their environment?

❷ **Vocabulary** Name a **technology** farmers use.

❸ 🖌 **Activity** Make a poster that shows how people have changed the environment in your community.

❹ 🔵 **Cause and Effect** What effect has new technology had on farming?

135

3 Close

Summary

Have children review the summary and restate the lesson's main ideas.

- People long ago changed the land in order to farm it.
- Technology helps farmers grow more crops today and will continue to help in the future.

Assess
REVIEW—Answers

1. **What to Know** People clear the land so they can grow crops and build homes, roads, and bridges.

2. **Vocabulary** Possible answer: One kind of **technology** farmers use is pipes and sprayers to bring water to crops.

3. 🖌 **Activity Assessment Guidelines** See Performance Rubric. This activity can be used with the Unit Project.

4. 🔵 **Cause and Effect** Technology makes farming easier. Land that once could not be farmed now can be, so more food is grown and harvested.

Use Focus Skills Transparency 3 or Cause and Effect Graphic Organizer Write-On/Wipe-Off Card.

✏ WRITING RUBRIC

Score 4
- clearly reflects the community
- provides excellent examples

Score 3
- adequately reflects the community
- provides good examples

Score 2
- somewhat reflects the community
- provides fair examples

Score 1
- does not reflect the community
- provides poor or no examples

HOMEWORK AND PRACTICE

Name _____ Date _____

How People Change Environments

Imagine you have moved to these woods and you want to grow crops here. What will you have to do first? Make a list on the lines below the picture. Then draw what your farm will look like after you change the environment.

cut down trees   move rocks
dig out stumps   plow land

page 26

INTEGRATE THE CURRICULUM

MATHEMATICS Explain that although tools made the farmers' work easier, they still needed to use numbers to solve problems. Provide children with story problems to solve, such as *If a farmer used a seed planter to plant 3 rows with 2 seeds in each row, how many seeds did he need?* **Story Problems**

Read a Product Map

OBJECTIVES

- Identify and interpret the features of a product map.

- Compare the availability of products as shown on a product map.

VOCABULARY

product p. 136   product map p. 136

RESOURCES

Homework and Practice Book, p. 27; Social Studies Skills Transparency 3-3; Primary Atlas; Interactive Atlas; Unit 3 Audiotext CD Collection; Internet Resources

1 Introduce

List these products and resources on the board: *fruit, vegetables, poultry, lumber, cotton.* If necessary, define *poultry* and *lumber* for children. Invite children to suggest symbols they might use for these products on a map that shows where these products can be found. Have volunteers draw the symbols next to the product names.

Why It Matters Point out that sometimes it is easier to understand information when you can look at a picture of it. Explain that a product map uses pictures to give information about products or resources that come from an area.

Why It Matters Some maps show the resources and products of a place. A **product** is something made by nature or by people.

Learn

1　A **product map** uses symbols to show where resources and products are found or made. The map on the next page shows some of the resources and products of Arkansas.

2 Practice

1 What products are shown in the map key?

2 What animals are raised in Arkansas?

3 Where in Arkansas is oil found?

136

Practice and Extend

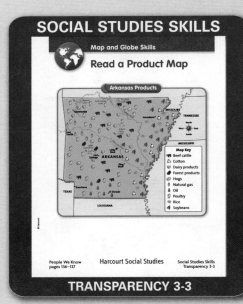

SOCIAL STUDIES SKILLS

Map and Globe Skills
Read a Product Map

People We Know pages 136–137　Harcourt Social Studies　Social Studies Skills Transparency 3-3

TRANSPARENCY 3-3

MENTAL MAPPING

Product Location Have children picture the top of their desk as a map of Arkansas. Have them trace a squiggly line down the "east" side to locate the Mississippi River on Arkansas's border. As you call out locations of products, such as "*rice is grown in the east*," have children point to the location on their "desk map."

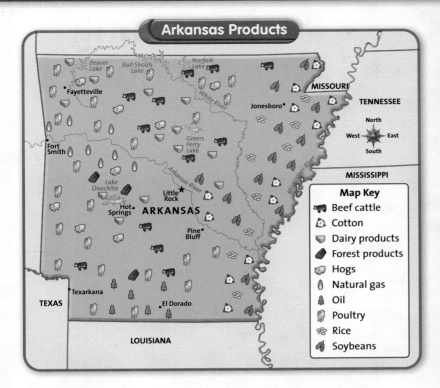

Arkansas Products

Map Key
- 🐄 Beef cattle
- Cotton
- Dairy products
- Forest products
- Hogs
- Natural gas
- Oil
- Poultry
- Rice
- Soybeans

Map labels: Beaver Lake, Bull Shoals Lake, Norfolk Lake, MISSOURI, Fayetteville, Jonesboro, TENNESSEE, White River, Greers Ferry Lake, Fort Smith, Arkansas River, MISSISSIPPI, Lake Ouachita, Little Rock ★, Hot Springs, ARKANSAS, Pine Bluff, Texarkana, El Dorado, TEXAS, LOUISIANA, Mississippi River

Compass rose: North, East, South, West

Apply

Make It Relevant Think of a product from your state. What symbol would you use for it on a product map?

For online activities, go to **www.harcourtschool.com/ss1**

137

Map and Globe Skills

HOMEWORK AND PRACTICE

Name _____ Date _____

🌐 **MAP AND GLOBE SKILLS**
Make a Product Map

Create your own state. Draw an outline of your state in the box. On the map, show the products and resources of your state. Create a symbol for each product or resource. Make a map key for the symbols on your map. Write a title for your product map.

Title: Products and Resources of Jasonland

Map Key
cows
coal
potatoes

What are some jobs that people do in the state you created?

farming, coal mining, cattle ranching

page 27

Learn

1 Geography Remind children that a product is something made by people or by nature, and a map shows where things are located.

Visual Literacy: Map Have children locate the map key. Ask them to identify each symbol in the key and tell what it represents on the map. Direct children to find each symbol from the key on the map.

Q Who might find a product map useful?

A Possible answers: people who want to start a business, people looking for a job

2 Practice

1. Beef cattle, cotton, dairy products, forest products, hogs, natural gas, oil, poultry, rice, and soybeans are products in the map key.
2. Cows, poultry, and hogs are raised in Arkansas.
3. Oil is found in the southern part of the state.

---

3 **Close**

Apply

Make It Relevant Invite children to brainstorm a list of known products from your state or look them up in an encyclopedia. Remind children that the pictures in the key most often look like the product. Encourage children to draw the symbol and name it.

GO ONLINE **INTERNET RESOURCES**

For online activities, go to **www.harcourtschool.com/ss1**

OBJECTIVES

- Identify changes in transportation and communication.
- Describe how new methods of transportation and communication link people, places, and ideas.

VOCABULARY

transportation p. 139

communication p. 140

Focus Skill CAUSE AND EFFECT

pp. 108–109, 141

RESOURCES

Homework and Practice Book, p. 28; Reading Support and Intervention, pp. 50–53; Success for English Learners, pp. 52–55; Vocabulary Transparency 3-4; Focus Skills Transparency 3; Cause and Effect Graphic Organizer Write-On/Wipe-Off Card; Unit 3 Audiotext CD Collection; Internet Resources

I Introduce

What to Know Read the What to Know question with children. Discuss the ways people get to school and how they can communicate with others who live out of town. Remind children to look for answers to the question as they read the lesson.

Build Background Invite children to think about movies they have seen that took place long ago. Ask them how the people moved from place to place and sent messages to people around town or in other locations.

Lesson **4**

 What to Know
How have transportation and communication changed over time?

Vocabulary
transportation
communication

 Focus Skill Cause and Effect

Connecting Communities

Bobby's family has lived in Missouri for a long time. Years ago, it took people a long time to travel and visit one another. They did not have telephones or e-mail. Times have changed.

1

138

Practice and Extend

 **Express Path**

When minutes count, look for the **EXPRESS PATH** to focus on the lesson's main ideas.

Quick Summary

Technology has changed how transportation moves people about and brings goods from other places. Technology has also brought new ways of communicating to link people, places, and ideas faster than ever.

Going Places

Transportation is the moving of goods and people from place to place. Long ago, Bobby's family used horses to pull wagons on dirt roads. Transportation was very slow, and it was not easy to cross certain landforms.

Technology has made transportation faster and easier. Now there are paved roads and cars. Bobby flies in a plane to visit relatives far away.

Reading Check **How is transportation today different from long ago?**
Transportation today is faster and easier.

St. Charles, Missouri

139

Going Places

CONTENT FOCUS Transportation has changed from slow and difficult to faster and easier.

Express Path

Invite children to identify and compare the forms of transportation they see in the pictures.

1 History Discuss the animal-powered carriage in the photograph Bobby is holding.

Q **How are the scene in the photograph and the scene behind Bobby alike and different?**

A Both show transportation. The photograph shows a family in a horse and buggy. The street scene shows cars and an airplane.

2 Geography Identify various landforms that would have been difficult to cross on horse or by foot. Discuss how technology makes getting past these obstacles easier. People could build bridges and boats to cross water, airplanes to cross mountains, and roads for automobiles.

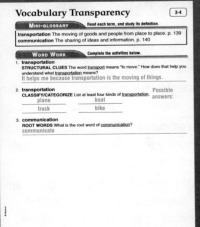

VOCABULARY

Vocabulary Transparency 3-4

MINI-GLOSSARY Read each term, and study its definition.

transportation The moving of goods and people from place to place. p. 139
communication The sharing of ideas and information. p. 140

WORD WORK Complete the activities below.

1. transportation
STRUCTURAL CLUES The word *transport* means "to move." How does that help you understand what *transportation* means?
It helps me because transportation is the moving of things.

2. transportation
CLASSIFY/CATEGORIZE List at least four kinds of transportation.   Possible answers:
plane   boat
truck   bike

3. communication
ROOT WORDS What is the root word of *communication*?
communicate

TRANSPARENCY 3-4

READING SUPPORT/ INTERVENTION

For alternate teaching strategies, use pages 50–53 of Reading Support and Intervention to:

■ identify **phonemes**

■ practice **phonics**

■ reinforce **vocabulary**

■ build **text comprehension**

■ build **fluency**

Reading Support ▶ and Intervention

ENGLISH LANGUAGE LEARNERS

For English Language Learners strategies to support this lesson, see Success for English Learners pages 52–55.

■ English-language development activities

■ background and concepts

■ vocabulary extension

Success for ▶ English Learners

LESSON 4 ■ **139**

Communication Changes

CONTENT FOCUS Technology has changed how people communicate, making it much faster than in the past.

Express Path

Have children scan the pages. Make a word web which includes these words: *letters, telephone, e-mail, television, radio, Internet.*

3 Link History and Geography Find China on a globe. Discuss how long it would take a letter to travel to China by land and ship in 1800. Compare this to the time it takes to make a phone call or send an e-mail.

4 History Tell children that long ago, transportation was powered by people and animals. People walked, rode bicycles, or had vehicles pulled by oxen, horses, or mules. Once the steam-powered engine was invented, people and things could be moved by train, boat, and ship. The invention of the gasoline-powered engine led to cars, airplanes, and other fast-moving transportation.

Q How did faster transportation affect communication?

A Information can reach people around the world in less time.

5 Culture Point out that people around the word can now learn more about each other. New forms of communication and transportation allowed communities to support each other by linking people, products, and ideas.

Communication Changes

Communication is the sharing of ideas and information. Liz's grandparents live in
3 China. Even though China is far away, Liz's family can keep in touch with them by letters, telephone, and e-mail.

Long ago, people could only write
4 letters to friends and family who lived far away. Their letters had to travel over land or by ship. This could take a long time.

140

Practice and Extend

INTEGRATE THE CURRICULUM

SCIENCE Tell children that inventors use science to create new technologies. As they develop ideas, new discoveries are often made. Discuss these inventors and inventions:

- Alexander Graham Bell, telephone, 1876
- Ray Tomlinson, e-mail, 1971
- Charles Jenkins, TV, 1922
- Vinton Cerf and Robert Kahn, Internet, 1974 **Inventors**

REACH ALL LEARNERS

Leveled Practice Have children discuss forms of communication.

Basic Invite children to compare the information we get from telephones and television.

Proficient Let children compare e-mail, radio, and Internet information.

Advanced Challenge children to investigate personal digital assistants (PDAs), cell phones, and instant messaging.

Technology has created new ways of communication that connect people. Today, television, radio, and the Internet let us know what is happening all over the world. **⑤**

Reading Check **What are some ways of communication people use today?** Today, people use letters, telephones, the Internet, television, and radio.

Summary New ways of transportation and communication connect people more easily.

Review

❶ What to Know How have transportation and communication changed over time?

❷ Vocabulary What is one tool that has made **communication** faster?

❸ Activity Make a chart to compare and contrast ways of transportation and communication of long ago and today.

❹ Cause and Effect What has caused communication to change over time?

141

---

3 Close

Summary

Have children read the summary and then restate the lesson ideas in their own words.

- Transportation and communication have changed over time.
- New technology makes moving people and products and sharing ideas easier than in the past.

Assess

REVIEW—Answers

1. **What to Know** Forms of communication and transportation have become faster and easier.

2. **Vocabulary** Possible answer: One tool that has made **communication** faster is the telephone.

3. **Activity Assessment Guidelines** See Performance Rubric. This activity can be used with the Unit Project.

4. **Cause and Effect** New technologies have caused communication to change.

Use Focus Skills Transparency 3 or Cause and Effect Graphic Organizer Write-On/Wipe-Off Card.

HOMEWORK AND PRACTICE

Name _____ Date _____
Connecting with Others

Read the paragraph. Then fill in the chart.

Long ago, transportation and communication were much slower. There were no telephones, airplanes, or paved roads. People moved goods on dirt roads by horse and wagon. They rode horses or walked instead of driving cars. When relatives and friends moved far away, they wrote letters instead of calling or e-mailing. Two things haven't changed at all, though. People still walk and talk to connect with each other!

People Connect with Each Other

Long Ago	Both	Today
Moved goods by horse and wagon	Write letters	Drive cars
Rode horses,	Walk,	Use telephones
Had dirt roads	Talk	and e-mail,
		Have paved roads, Travel by airplane

page 28

REACH ALL LEARNERS

Advanced Lead children to identify advantages and disadvantages of the different kinds of transportation and communication. Suggest they include new technologies, such as PDAs, cell phones, instant messaging, electric cars, hybrids, and airbuses. Have them consider how each affects people, the community, the environment, and the use of resources.

1 Introduce

With masking tape, create a path with several curves on the classroom floor. Give the path specific beginning and ending points, such as from the door to your desk. Invite children to walk along the path and to tell where the path begins and ends. Have them describe what they passed along the way.

Why It Matters Discuss times when children and their families have used maps to find out how to get to a new place. Tell children that people decide on a route they will take to reach a new place. Explain that some maps only show the main highways between towns and cities. Stress that taking highways is often the fastest way to get from one town to another.

Map and Globe Skills

Follow a Route

Why It Matters   A map can show you where places are and how to get to them.

Learn

   The path you follow from one place to another is called a **route**. Highways
1 are routes between towns and cities. A compass rose tells you in which direction you are going when you follow a route.

3 Practice

1 Which highway goes from Oklahoma City to Tulsa?

2 In which direction would you travel on Highway 44 to go from Oklahoma City to Lawton?

3 Which river does Highway 60 cross?

142

Practice and Extend

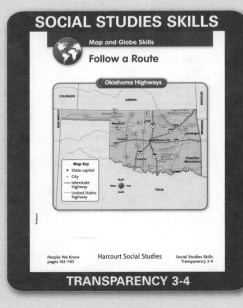

Oklahoma Highways

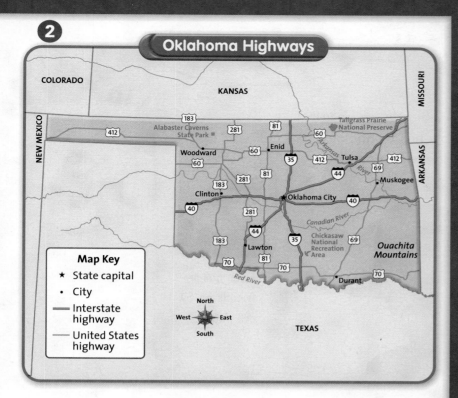

COLORADO

KANSAS

MISSOURI

NEW MEXICO

[412]

[183] Alabaster Caverns State Park ■

[281]

[281] Enid

[60] Woodward

[60]

Tallgrass Prairie National Preserve

[81]

[60]

[35] [412] Tulsa

[412]

[69]

[44]

■ Muskogee

ARKANSAS

[281] [81]

[183]

Clinton ▪

[40] ★ Oklahoma City [40]

[281]

[44] [35]

Chickasaw National Recreation Area

[69]

Ouachita Mountains

[183] Lawton ▪

[70] [81]

[70]

Durant ▪

[70]

Canadian River

Arkansas River

Red River

Map Key
★ State capital
▪ City
— Interstate highway
— United States highway

North
West ✦ East
South

TEXAS

Map and Globe Skills

Apply

Make It Relevant Draw a map to show your route to school. Add a compass rose to show directions.

For online activities, go to **www.harcourtschool.com/ss1**

143

Leveled Practice Mark a local road map with a route that passes a number of well-known places.

Basic Have children point to various locations along the route.

Proficient Ask each child to write out the route directions. Have partners trade directions and follow the route.

Advanced Have children write out two alternate routes that end at the same place.

HOMEWORK AND PRACTICE

Name _____ Date _____

🌎 MAP AND GLOBE SKILLS
The Sheriff's Busy Day

Read the story. Draw the route on the map and answer the questions.

The sheriff of Cowtown is going to pick up some feed for his horse. First, he stops to buy a new shirt at the dry goods store. Next, he checks the railroad station to see if anyone new has just come in on the train. Then, he goes to the bank to get some more money. Finally, he arrives at the feed store.

Which streets did the sheriff take to get to the feed store?

<u>Dry Gulch, Cattlerun, Haymarket Street</u>

page 29

---

2 Teach

Learn

❶ Geography Write *route* on the board. Ask children to describe a route from the classroom to the lunch area. Then use a simple school map to point out the route. Discuss how the map route could be used by a new student to find his or her way to the lunch area.

❷ Visual Literacy: Map Focus attention on the map on page 143. Ask children to find the map title and key. Then point out that each highway has a number. The symbol around the number shows what kind of highway it is.

Q What kind of routes are shown on this map?

A highways in Oklahoma

❸ Practice

1. (Interstate) Highway 44 goes from Oklahoma City to Tulsa.
2. You would be traveling southwest.
3. Highway 60 crosses the Arkansas River.

---

3 Close

Apply

Make It Relevant Maps should include a clear route from home to school, a title, symbols, a map key, and a compass rose that accurately shows cardinal directions.

INTERNET RESOURCES

For online activities, go to **www.harcourtschool.com/ss1**

OBJECTIVES

- Compare and contrast children's daily lives to those of others.
- Explore different points of view of how individuals view changes in technology.

RESOURCES

Unit 3 Audiotext CD Collection

💡 Link to the Big Idea

Resources Explain that some changes over time make life better. These changes take place because people find better, new, or different ways to use resources. Some of these changes make things easier to do. Other changes save time or provide healthier choices.

Vocabulary Help Remind children that *communication* is the sharing of ideas and information.

Discuss the Points of View

Link Geography and Economics
Read aloud the question posed by the Sidewalk Reporter. Have volunteers read aloud each person's answer. Discuss ways that each of these changes makes life better. For example, once food is harvested, it would normally keep fresh for only a few days. Freezers are a technology that preserves food for longer periods of time.

Q How might people's points of view about these changes be different?

A Someone might think a technology is helpful or better, but another person might not agree.

Points of View

The Sidewalk Reporter asks:
"How has technology made your life better?"

John
"I can call my friends on my cell phone."

Latisha
"I can do my homework on the computer."

View from the Past

Johannes Gutenberg: Communication

Long ago, books were written by hand, so there were not many of them. In about 1450, Johannes Gutenberg invented a way to print books faster. This let more people share ideas.

144

Practice and Extend

INTEGRATE THE CURRICULUM

VISUAL ARTS Explain that once Gutenberg invented the printing press, artists began designing different styles of type. Have children use classroom resources to compare alphabet style, including library books, textbooks, and word processing programs. Then have them work in small groups to design a font. Have children share their alphabet designs with the class. **Design a Font**

INDEPENDENT READING

Suggest that children read *Then and Now* by Peter Firmin (Usborne Books, 1986). Each set of facing pages forms a "then" picture and a "now" picture. Details describe the changes children can view. Invite children to find and describe the differences between things long ago and today.

Carrie

"I can take an airplane to visit my grandmother."

Mr. Perez

"My grandson writes e-mails to me, but I also like it when he sends me a card in the mail."

Mrs. Patel

"I can buy frozen food at the store."

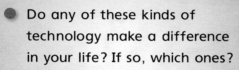

It's Your Turn

- Do any of these kinds of technology make a difference in your life? If so, which ones?
- What other kinds of technology have made your life easier or better?

145

Link History and Culture Point out that sometimes people do not like changes. Have children reread the quote from Mr. Perez. Discuss reasons that he prefers getting mail rather than e-mail. (It is more personal; it is what he is used to.) Invite children to share examples of changes or new technology that people do not always think is better.

View from the Past

History Read aloud the information about Johannes Gutenberg. Explain that many people believe that the printing press with its moveable type is the most important invention of the past 1,000 years. Gutenberg made it possible to share new ideas with large numbers of people all over the world. Have children study the picture, and encourage them to ask relevant questions about the event that is illustrated.

It's Your Turn—Answers

Read aloud the questions on page 145. Record children's ideas as they respond to the questions. Suggest children interview school workers and classmates and record their opinions as well.

- Children should describe their experiences with talking on the phone, using a computer, riding in an airplane, or eating a frozen meal.
- Possible answer: I can do research on the Internet.

Link to the Big Idea

Resources Tell children that people use the land and its resources to help them live. Point out that many of the things people use every day come from resources such as, water, oil, and coal.

Preview the Games

What Doesn't Belong? This game asks children to look at the different parts of an urban city scene. Children should look for seven things in the scene that belong in a rural scene, not in an urban scene. Prompt children with questions such as:

Q What do you normally see in an urban area?

A cars, trucks, buildings, roads, buses

Q What do you normally see in a rural area?

A mountains, trees, farm animals, woods

ANSWERS: a windmill; a man riding a tractor; a man walking a pig; a horse peeking out of a window; a cow; a barn; a person holding a fishing pole.

Fun with Social Studies

What Doesn't Belong?

Look at the picture of an urban area. Find seven things that belong in a rural area.

146

Practice and Extend

READING SOCIAL STUDIES

Cause and Effect Have children review the lesson on rural, urban, and suburban areas. Ask them to think of reasons why people would want to live in each area.

READING TRANSPARENCY

Use FOCUS SKILLS TRANSPARENCY 3.
Graphic Organizer Write-On/Wipe-Off Cards available.

MAKE IT RELEVANT

In Your Community Have children discover what type of community they live in: rural, urban, or suburban. Remind them to look at the land around them and the type of land usage. Ask children to share their findings with the class.

Online Adventures GO ONLINE

Play the online game to help Eco's class find ways to save a community park. You will need to use what you know about resources. Play now, at www.harcourtschool.com/ss1

ECO

147

Online Adventures Before children begin this game, explain that the game is set in a park where they will need to solve puzzles about natural resources such as water, trees, land, and air. Discuss different ways in which people use these resources. Tell children that Help Buttons in the game will refer them to pages in their textbook if they need additional information.

GO ONLINE — INTERNET RESOURCES

For more resources, go to
www.harcourtschool.com/ss1

Share the Fun

At School Have children work in small groups to create their own What Doesn't Belong? game. Help them create a game similar to this activity based on what they know about land use and where people settle. When children are finished, ask them to share their games with their classmates.

At Home Invite children to have their parents or guardians help them make a list of items they may find in a rural area. Have them also list ways people use the land and how they have changed it. Ask children to share their findings with classmates.

The Big Idea

Resources Ask a volunteer to read aloud the Big Idea. Invite children to share something they learned in this unit about the land and its resources.

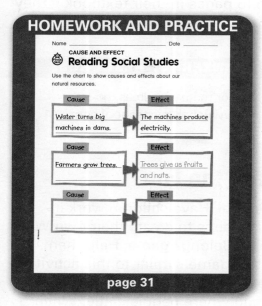

page 31

Reading Social Studies

Cause and Effect You may wish to have children review Reading Social Studies at the beginning of the unit. Charts should include information about the relationship between natural resources and how we use them.

Review and Test Prep

The Big Idea

Resources People use the land and its resources to help them live.

Cause and Effect

Copy and fill in the chart to show what you have learned about why people use natural resources.

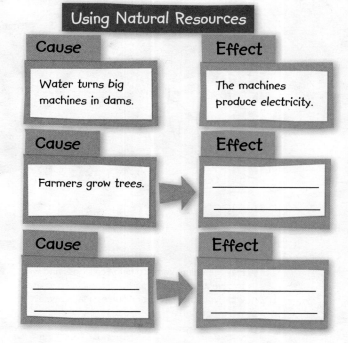

Using Natural Resources

Cause	Effect
Water turns big machines in dams.	The machines produce electricity.
Farmers grow trees.	_____
_____	_____

148

Vocabulary

Complete each sentence.

① We can protect our resources by using _____.

② New _____, such as tools and machines, helps farmers grow more crops.

③ A _____ is something made by nature or by people.

④ Water is an important _____ that people can use to make electricity.

Word Bank

natural resource
(p. 114)

conservation
(p. 118)

technology
(p. 134)

product
(p. 136)

Facts and Main Ideas

⑤ How can people use air as a natural resource?

⑥ What do we do when we recycle?

⑦ Why did few people live in the desert long ago?

⑧ What is a smaller community near a city called?

⑨ Which kind of transportation was used long ago?

    A horse and wagon   **C** car

    B plane   **D** motorcycle

⑩ What is the sharing of ideas and information?

    A pollution   **C** transportation

    B communication   **D** conservation

149

Vocabulary

1. conservation

2. technology

3. product

4. natural resource

Facts and Main Ideas

5. We use air to breathe and make electricity.

6. We use something again in a new way.

7. It was hard because there is not enough rain for drinking water.

8. A smaller community near a city is called a suburb.

9. A, horse and wagon

10. B, communication

TEST-TAKING STRATEGIES

Review these tips with children:

• Read the directions before reading the questions.

• Read each question twice, focusing the second time on all the possible answers.

• Take time to think about all the possible answers before deciding on an answer.

• Move past questions that give you trouble, and answer the ones you know. Then return to concentrate on the difficult items.

Critical Thinking

11. Possible answers: Different places need different resources. Some places have resources that other places do not have.

12. Make It Relevant Possible answers: We would have more trash if people did not recycle. We would use up resources faster if we did not conserve.

Skills

13. the amounts of money earned from recycling different things

14. cans

15. two dollars

16. glass bottles

 Critical Thinking

⑪ Why do different places use their natural resources in different ways?

⑫ **Make It Relevant** What would happen if no one recycled or conserved resources in your community?

Skills

⑬ What does this picture graph show?

⑭ Which kind of item earned the most money?

⑮ How much money was earned from recycling glass bottles?

⑯ Was more money earned from recycling paper or glass bottles?

150

Skills

Kentucky Products

Map Key
- Beef cattle
- Coal
- Corn
- Forest products
- Hogs
- Horses
- Poultry
- Soybeans

⑰ What does this map show?

⑱ What crops are grown in western Kentucky?

⑲ What kinds of animals are raised in Kentucky?

⑳ Where in Kentucky are forest products grown?

151

Skills

17. Products in Kentucky
18. Corn and Soybeans
19. Beef Cattle, Hogs, Horses, and Poultry
20. in the eastern part of Kentucky

ASSESSMENT

Use the UNIT 3 Test on pages 18–20 of the Assessment Program.

Show What You Know

Unit Writing Activity

Choose a Product Invite children to list farm products. Suggest they look through the unit for ideas and think about products at a grocery store or products that their families produce in home gardens. Discuss how these products are also used for purposes such as meals, animal feed, or decoration.

 Write a Descriptive Paragraph Ask children to identify the farm product that is their favorite. Suggest that children include sensory details in their description to explain why a product appeals to them and to support the reasons for their choice.

You may wish to distribute the Unit 3 Writing Activity Guidelines on page 21 of the Assessment Program.

For a scoring rubric, see this Teacher Edition, page 105O.

Unit Project

Earth's Resources Flowchart Before beginning, review the purpose and structure of a flowchart. Help children list possible steps for the chart. Assign groups that will work together to complete the flowchart steps. Provide materials for illustrating, such as colored paper and markers. Have children invite families or other guests to view the completed projects.

You may wish to distribute the Unit 3 Project Guidelines on page 23 of the Assessment Program.

For a scoring rubric, see this Teacher Edition, page 105O.

LEVELED READERS

Use the LEVELED READERS for Unit 3.

Unit 3 Activities

Show What You Know

 **Unit Writing Activity**

Choose a Product Think of a farm product you like.

Write a Descriptive Paragraph Write a paragraph about the product. Give facts and details.

 **Unit Project**

Earth's Resources Flowchart Create a flowchart about using resources to produce a food.

- Explain the steps and illustrate them.
- Answer any questions.

Read More

The Great Trash Bash by Loreen Leedy

Food and Farming by Pam Robson

Homes and Cities: Living for the Future by Sally Morgan

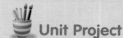 For more resources, go to **www.harcourtschool.com/ss1**

152

Read More

After the children's study of natural resources, encourage independent reading with these books or books of your choice. Additional books are listed on page 105J of this Teacher Edition.

Basic *The Great Trash Bash* by Loreen Leedy (Holiday House, 2000). Children visit a fictional town that finds better ways to recycle and control the citizens' trash.

Proficient *Food and Farming* by Pam Robson (Millbrook Press, 2001). Children learn where our food comes from through a series of projects.

Advanced *Homes and Cities: Living for the Future* by Sally Morgan (Scholastic, 1998). This book discusses settlements and the related topics of construction, waste disposal, and transportation.

SUMMATIVE TEST

Units 1-3 Summative Test

FILL IN THE BLANK (5 points each)

DIRECTIONS Write the word that completes each sentence.

climate	product	conservation
landform	laws	citizen

❶ A person who belongs to a community is called a

___citizen___.

❷ Rules that citizens must follow are ___laws___.

❸ A hill is an example of a ___landform___.

❹ The location of a place affects its ___climate___.

❺ Saving resources to make them last is called

___conservation___

❻ Something that is made by nature or by people is a

___product___.

(continued)

Units 1-3 Summative Test   Assessment Program ▪ 25

SUMMATIVE TEST

Name _____ Date _____

MULTIPLE CHOICE (5 points each)

DIRECTIONS Select the letter of the best answer.

❼ Which of these is used to solve a problem?

A Take the consequence.   (C) Think about different solutions.

B Do not cooperate.   D Ignore the problem.

❽ Which of these is the leader of a city?

A President   C governor

B judge   (D) mayor

❾ What does Congress do?

A runs elections   C leads the Supreme Court

(B) makes laws for our country   D controls city government

❿ Which of these lists the rights of all citizens?

(A) Constitution   C ballot

B government   D President

⓫ Which of these is a landform surrounded by water?

A gulf   C hill

(B) island   D plains

(continued)

26 ▪ Assessment Program   Units 1-3 Summative Test

SUMMATIVE TEST

Name _____ Date _____

MULTIPLE CHOICE (5 points each)

DIRECTIONS Select the letter of the best answer.

⓬ Which of these is a cardinal direction?

(A) north   C up

B right   D stop

⓭ Where can you look to find cardinal directions on a map?

A map title   C map grid

(B) compass rose   D map key

⓮ Which of these is not a way to conserve resources?

(A) throw trash on the ground   C recycle

B turn off the faucet   D take shorter showers

⓯ How is urban land different from rural land?

(A) It has more buildings and people.   C It is used to grow trees for lumber.

B It has more open land.   D It is used for farming.

⓰ Which of these helps farmers grow crops?

A bugs   (C) technology

B mice   D bad weather

(continued)

Units 1-3 Summative Test   Assessment Program ▪ 27

SUMMATIVE TEST

Name _____ Date _____

SHORT ANSWER (5 points each)

DIRECTIONS Use the picture graph to answer the questions.

⓱ How many books does each symbol stand for? ___1___

⓲ How many books were found about deserts? ___3___

Books About Geography	
oceans	🕮🕮🕮🕮
mountains	🕮🕮🕮🕮🕮🕮
deserts	🕮🕮🕮
lakes	🕮🕮
rivers	🕮🕮🕮

Key 🕮 = one book

⓳ About which subject were the most books found?

___mountains___

⓴ Were more books found about <u>oceans</u> or <u>lakes</u>?

___oceans___

28 ▪ Assessment Program   Units 1-3 Summative Test

NOTES

NOTES

People Long Ago

The Big Idea

History

History is the story of how people and places change over time.

What to Know

- ✓ How do people and places change over time?
- ✓ What do we know about the people who lived in North America long ago?
- ✓ How did our country get its independence?
- ✓ How do we honor our American heritage?
- ✓ How do we honor people and events in our country's history?

Introduce the Unit

The Big Idea

History Read the Big Idea to children. Explain that we can learn about history by looking at how life today is the same as, yet different from, life long ago. In this unit, children will learn how people and places change over time and how people and events become a part of our country's heritage. Remind children to refer back to the Big Idea periodically as they read the unit.

What to Know Have children read What to Know. Explain that these five essential questions will help them focus on the Big Idea.

Assessing the Big Idea Share with children that throughout this unit they will be asked to show evidence of their understanding of the Big Idea. See Assessment Options on page 153M of this Teacher Edition.

START WITH A VIDEO DVD

To introduce the Unit Big Idea to students, show a video clip from the Start with a Video DVD.

Instructional Design

The flowchart below shows briefly how instruction was planned for Unit 4.

START WITH THE BIG IDEA	PLAN ASSESSMENT	PLAN INSTRUCTION
Lesson Objectives What to Know	Assessment Options • Option 1—Unit 4 Test • Option 2—Writing: Write a Narrative Paragraph • Option 3—Unit Project: Historical Journal	Unit 4 Teacher Edition • materials • instructional strategies • activities

People Long Ago

THE BIG IDEA

HISTORY History is the story of how people and places change over time.

Express Path

See each lesson for an **EXPRESS PATH** to teach main ideas.

LESSON	PACING	OBJECTIVES
Preview the Unit pp. 153V–153	**5** DAYS	
Preview Vocabulary pp. 154–155		■ Use visuals to determine word meanings. ■ Use words and visuals to preview the content of the unit.
Reading Social Studies pp. 156–157		■ Recognize a sequence of events. ■ Interpret information from charts.
Start with a Story *When I Was Young* pp. 158–171		■ Identify *When I Was Young* as realistic fiction about family history. ■ Compare and contrast daily life with that of grandparents and great-grandparents.
① **People and Places Change** pp. 172–175 💡 **WHAT TO KNOW** How do people and places change over time?	**3** DAYS	■ Understand the concept of time in terms of past, present, and future. ■ Recognize that while some things change over time, other things stay the same.
CHART AND GRAPH SKILLS **Read a Diagram** pp. 176–177	**1** DAY	■ Identify a diagram as a chart that shows the parts of something. ■ Define and describe the relationships shown on a family tree.

6 WEEKS	WEEK 1	WEEK 2	WEEK 3	WEEK 4	WEEK 5	WEEK 6
	Introduce the Unit	Lesson 1	Lesson 2	Lesson 3	Lesson 4	Lesson 5	Wrap Up the Unit

READING SUPPORT VOCABULARY

Reading Social Studies
Focus Skill **Sequence**

Reading Social Studies
Focus Skill, pp. 156–157

Vocabulary Power:
Synonyms, p. 155
Shortened Words, p. 159
Related Words, p. 160
Word Origins, p. 161
sequence p. 156

Reading Social Studies
Focus Skill **Sequence**, p. 175

Vocabulary Power:
Antonyms, p. 174

past p. 172
present p. 173
future p. 173
change p. 174

diagram p. 176

REACH ALL LEARNERS

ENGLISH LANGUAGE LEARNERS, pp. 154, 163, 164, 168

Leveled Practice, pp. 157, 170

Advanced, p. 170

Leveled Practice, pp. 174, 177

Special Needs, p. 175

INTEGRATE LEARNING

Music
Cultural Music, p. 153
Identify Music Elements, p. 159
Mathematics
Time Intervals, p. 153
Problem Solving, p. 170
Reading/Language Arts
pp. 156, 164, 166, 167, 169
Science
Sequence of Events, p. 162
Force and Motion, p. 167
Physical Education
Childhood Games, p. 162
Theater
Classroom Skit, p. 165
Visual Arts
Creative Toymaking, p. 169

RESOURCES

Social Studies in Action: Resources for the Classroom
Primary Source Collection
Music CD
School-to-Home Newsletter S9–S10
Interactive Map Transparencies
Interactive Desk Maps
Primary Atlas
Interactive Atlas
TimeLinks: Interactive Time Line
Picture Vocabulary Cards
Focus Skills Transparency 4
Sequence Graphic Organizer Write-On/ Wipe-Off Card
Assessment Program, p. 29
Unit 4 Audiotext CD Collection
Internet Resources
Start with a Video DVD

Homework and Practice Book, pp. 32–33
Reading Support and Intervention, pp. 54–57
Success for English Language Learners, pp. 57–60
Vocabulary Transparency 4-1
Focus Skills Transparency 4
Sequence Graphic Organizer Write-On/ Wipe-Off Card
Social Studies Skills Transparency 4-1
Unit 4 Audiotext CD Collection
Internet Resources

LESSON	PACING	OBJECTIVES
② Early America pp. 178–183 💡 **WHAT TO KNOW** What do we know about the people who lived in North America long ago?	**3 DAYS**	■ Recognize Native Americans as the first groups of people to live in North America. ■ Describe the lifestyle of a Native American community. ■ Define colonies and settlers, especially European settlers and Jamestown.
Primary Sources: Look at Native American History pp. 184–185	**1 DAY**	■ Recognize that primary sources provide knowledge about people and history. ■ Understand how Native Americans met their needs.
③ Independence pp. 186–191 💡 **WHAT TO KNOW** How did our country get its independence?	**4 DAYS**	■ Understand events in early American history. ■ Identify important people related to our country's independence.
CHART AND GRAPH SKILLS **Read a Time Line** pp. 192–193	**1 DAY**	■ Read a time line. ■ Place important events on a time line and describe their order.
Citizenship: Getting Others to Vote pp. 194–195	**1 DAY**	■ Understand that voting is an important freedom. ■ Recognize how families can learn about voting together.

READING SUPPORT VOCABULARY	REACH ALL LEARNERS	INTEGRATE LEARNING	RESOURCES
Reading Social Studies (Focus Skill) **Sequence,** pp. 181, 183 **history** p. 178 **colony** p. 180 **settler** p. 180 **source** p. 184	**ENGLISH LANGUAGE LEARNERS,** p. 180 **Leveled Practice,** p. 182 **Advanced,** p. 185	**Theater** Perform a Skit, p. 182 **Visual Arts** Make a Model, p. 185	Homework and Practice Book, p. 34 Reading Support and Intervention, pp. 58–61 Success for English Language Learners, pp. 61–64 Vocabulary Transparency 4-2 Focus Skills Transparency 4 Sequence Graphic Organizer Write-On/ Wipe-Off Card Primary Source Collection Unit 4 Audiotext CD Collection Internet Resources
Reading Social Studies (Focus Skill) **Sequence,** pp. 189, 191, 193 **freedom** p. 186 **independence** p. 187 **time line** p. 192	**Leveled Practice,** pp. 190, 192, 195 **Advanced,** p. 188	**Reading/Language Arts** Proper Nouns, p. 189 Write a Poem, p. 190 **Mathematics** Tally a Vote, p. 195	Homework and Practice Book, pp. 35–36 Reading Support and Intervention, pp. 62–65 Success for English Language Learners, pp. 65–68 Vocabulary Transparency 4-3 Focus Skills Transparency 4 Sequence Graphic Organizer Write-On/ Wipe-Off Card Social Studies Skills Transparency 4-2 Activity Pattern A9 TimeLinks: Interactive Time Line Unit 4 Audiotext CD Collection Internet Resources

LESSON	PACING	OBJECTIVES
④ American Heritage pp. 196–199 **WHAT TO KNOW** How do we honor our American heritage?	**3 DAYS**	■ Identify symbols and landmarks of our country's heritage. ■ Describe how landmarks honor our country's history and ideals.
⑤ Heroes and Holidays pp. 200–205 **WHAT TO KNOW** How do we honor people and events in our country's history?	**3 DAYS**	■ Identify how the actions of individuals make a difference in our lives and for our country. ■ Identify national heroes, legends, and holidays and their significance.
CRITICAL THINKING SKILLS **Tell Fact from Fiction** pp. 206–207	**1 DAY**	■ Distinguish between fact and fiction. ■ Analyze details of factual and fictional accounts of history.
Biography: Dr. Martin Luther King, Jr. pp. 208–209	**1 DAY**	■ Understand the importance of the actions and character of Dr. Martin Luther King, Jr., and explain how he made a difference in others' lives.
Fun with Social Studies: Holiday Mix-Up pp. 210–211 **Unit 4 Review and Activities** pp. 212–216	**3 DAYS**	

READING SUPPORT VOCABULARY	REACH ALL LEARNERS	INTEGRATE LEARNING	RESOURCES
Reading Social Studies (Focus Skill) **Sequence,** p. 199 **heritage** p. 196 **landmark** p. 197 **memorial** p. 198	**Leveled Practice,** p. 198	**Visual Arts** Design a Poster, p. 199	Homework and Practice Book, p. 37 Reading Support and Intervention, pp. 66–69 Success for English Language Learners, pp. 69–72 Vocabulary Transparency 4-4 Focus Skills Transparency 4 Sequence Graphic Organizer Write-On/Wipe-Off Card Unit 4 Audiotext CD Collection Internet Resources
Reading Social Studies (Focus Skill) **Sequence,** p. 205 **Vocabulary Power:** Suffixes, p. 209 **hero** p. 200 **legend** p. 201 **fact** p. 206 **nonfiction** p. 206 **fiction** p. 206	**ENGLISH LANGUAGE LEARNERS,** p. 203 **Leveled Practice,** pp. 204, 207 **Advanced,** p. 209	**Reading/Language Arts** Recognize Legends, p. 202 **Mathematics** Use a Calendar, p. 203	Homework and Practice Book, pp. 38–39 Reading Support and Intervention, pp. 70–73 Success for English Language Learners, pp. 73–76 Vocabulary Transparency 4-5 Focus Skills Transparency 4 Sequence Graphic Organizer Write-On/Wipe-Off Card TimeLinks: Interactive Time Line Activity Pattern A10 Social Studies Skills Transparency 4-3 Multimedia Biographies CD Unit 4 Audiotext CD Collection Internet Resources
	ENGLISH LANGUAGE LEARNERS, p. 210 **Leveled Practice,** p. 211	**Reading/Language Arts** Write a Story, p. 210	Homework and Practice Book, pp. 40–41 Assessment Program, pp. 30–32 Leveled Readers Leveled Readers Teacher Guide Unit 4 Audiotext CD Collection Internet Resources

Harcourt School Online

The interactive eBook provides students with the standards-based content of Harcourt print books in addition to interactive add-ons that enhance student interest and reinforce Social Studies content. Harcourt eBooks are available in both a basic and enhanced version.

INTERACTIVE VISUALS

Students watch the history of the United States come to life through engaging interactive activities that enhance the unit content.

STREAMING VIDEO

Each Unit Opener includes video tied to the Unit Big Idea. This clip provides students with enhanced information about how communities change.

SKILLS ACTIVITIES

Each Chart and Graph Skill and Map and Globe Skill is enhanced by an interactive online activity.

LIVE INK ENHANCEMENT

live ink

Live Ink provides students with reading help through a patented system that breaks sentences down into segments. The Live Ink system is proven to increase student comprehension and test scores. Live Ink is available for grades 3–6/7.

eBOOK

ONLINE ADVENTURES

Fun with Social Studies provides a link to our Online Adventures game. Students play a game in which they visit a history museum and take a ride through the past. The game reviews important concepts from the unit.

MULTIMEDIA BIOGRAPHIES

Biographies from the student edition include additional information in an interactive Multimedia Biography. Students can find more information, view related biographies, explore maps and images, and find links to additional webpages.

THE LEARNING SITE

The eBook includes links to **www.harcourtschool.com/ss1** There students can find internal resources such as our complete Multimedia Biographies databases and our Online Adventures games. This Harcourt Social Studies site also provides students with additional research tools.

Back Forward Reload Home

Teacher Resources

E-PLANNER

The e-Planner provides a useful tool for scheduling Social Studies lessons.

- Use it to access Teacher Edition pages and student workbook pages and to plan classroom activities.
- The calendar tool displays all your scheduled Social Studies lessons in an easy-to-use format.
- All standards are organized by grade level.

HSPOA

Harcourt School Publishers Online Assessment provides teachers with a reliable, confidential system for online delivery of Social Studies assessment. Using this system, you can track student performance correlated to standards and run prescribed reports for any missed standards. Questions are correlated to our print Assessment program.

VIDEOS AND DVDS

A comprehensive package of videos for Grades K–3 provides an entertaining overview of core social studies concepts such as government, geography, economics, culture and history. Videos in this package are available from Schlessinger Media® and are also available digitally on SAFARI Montage.

SAFARI MONTAGE™

For more information, see pages TEI13–TEI18.

FREE AND INEXPENSIVE MATERIALS

Free and inexpensive materials are listed on the Social Studies Website at
www.harcourtschool.com/ss1

- Addresses to write to for free and inexpensive products
- Links to unit–related materials
- Internet maps
- Internet references

COMMUNITY RESOURCES FOR THE CLASSROOM

The **National Atlas** website offers interactive, customizable maps of different areas in the United States. Use the **Map Maker** tool to zoom in on your community and view map features such as cities, roads, climate, and agriculture. **http://nationalatlas.gov/**

Educators can use the **United States Census Bureau** webpage to locate census information and facts about their local communities. **http://factfinder.census.gov/home/saff/main.html?_lang=en**

The National Park Service offers a comprehensive site with a search engine that cross-references our country's National Historic Landmarks by name, city, and state. **http://tps.cr.nps.gov/nhl/**

Museums in all 50 states are indexed on the **Virtual Library** museums pages. Use this site to find museums in and around your students' own community. **http://www.museumca.org/usa/states.html**

The **Library of Congress** site features numerous collections of primary sources, biographies, recordings, and photographs. The topic **Cities and Towns** contains photographic records of communities throughout the history of the United States. **http://memory.loc.gov/ammem/**

Additional Sites are available at www.harcourtschool.com/ss1

Lesson Plan Summaries

BELOW-LEVEL/INTERVENTION

TOPIC
People Long Ago

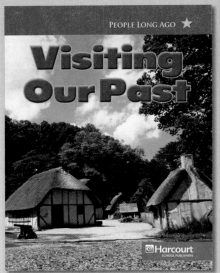

Summary *Visiting Our Past.* This Reader examines how people and communities change over time, highlights the early history of America, and explains how we remember the heroes and events of our past.

BEFORE READING

Vocabulary Power Have children define the following words. Help them write one sentence for each word as it relates to how people lived long ago.

history   change   past   independence   hero

DURING READING

Sequence Have children complete the graphic organizer to show that they understand how to sequence events described in the Reader.

First
Long ago, people lived in North America. They were Native Americans.

Next
People from Europe came to live in North America.

Last
The 13 colonies won independence. The United States was formed.

AFTER READING

Critical Thinking Lead children in a discussion about how symbols help us remember people and events. Have children name some American symbols.

 Write a Poem Have children write poems about an American symbol that is important to them.

ON-LEVEL

TOPIC
People Long Ago

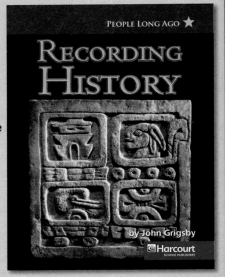

Summary *Recording History,* by John Grigsby. This Reader examines the history of written communication from paintings on cave walls to the invention of the printing press.

BEFORE READING

Vocabulary Power Have children define the following words. Help them write one sentence for each word as it relates to how people lived long ago.

history   change   sign   record   tools

DURING READING

Sequence Have children complete the graphic organizer to show that they understand how to sequence events described in the Reader.

First
People painted pictures on cave walls.

Next
People used signs and letters to record stories.

Last
Johannes Gutenberg made a machine that could print books.

AFTER READING

Critical Thinking Lead children in a discussion about the technologies we use today to record history.

 Write an Autobiography Have children write their autobiographies. Remind children that an autobiography is a history of the writer's life. Have children include where and when they were born and the place(s) they have lived.

The *Leveled Readers Teacher Guide* provides background, reading tips, fast facts, answer keys, and copying masters.

ABOVE-LEVEL

TOPIC
People Long Ago

Summary *Fact or Fiction: American Folk Heroes,* by Nancy Garhan Attebury. This Reader examines how stories about heroes can contain both facts and exaggerations and explains the true history behind one of America's folk heroes—John Chapman, or Johnny Appleseed.

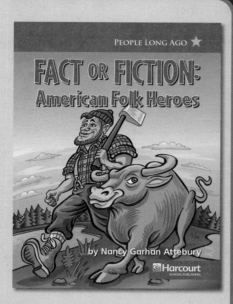

PEOPLE LONG AGO ★

FACT OR FICTION:
American Folk Heroes

by Nancy Garhan Attebury

Harcourt
SCHOOL PUBLISHERS

BEFORE READING

Vocabulary Power Have children define the following words. Help them write one sentence for each word as it relates to how people lived long ago.

history   change   hero   legend   character

DURING READING

Focus Skill **Sequence** Have children complete the graphic organizer to show that they understand how to sequence events described in the Reader.

First	Next	Last
A story is told about a hero.	The story is told over and over.	The characters become folk heroes.

AFTER READING

Critical Thinking Lead children in a discussion about how stories can change over time.

✎ **Write a Song** Read or tell children a local legend, and have them write a song retelling that legend. Encourage children to add their own changes to the legend.

Readers' Theater
Every Student Is a Star

IT'S SHOWTIME!

Getting Started

★ Distribute the Big Idea activity sheet from your Readers' Theater.

★ Read through the script together. Make connections with unit contents.

★ Plan a performance using the **Prep ★ Practice ★ Perform** guidelines. Find ideas for props online.

Pressed for Time?

★ Perform a choral reading of the script with the whole class.

★ Assign parts for a one-time read-through.

★ Assign groups to read in your literacy center.

Read Along,

Read Aloud,

Reading Fun

BASIC

Anno, Mitsumasa. **Anno's USA.** Putnam Juvenile, 2002. Go on a visual journey through American history, landscapes, and culture.

Brenner, Martha. **Abe Lincoln's Hat.** Random House Children's Books, 2005. A simple telling of events in Abraham Lincoln's daily life.

Demuth, Patricia Brennan. **Johnny Appleseed.** Sagebrush, 1996. The book goes beyond the legend by telling the true story of John Chapman, known as Johnny Appleseed.

Dooling, Michael. **The Great Horse-less Carriage Race.** Holiday House, 2002. In 1885, a Chicago newspaper sponsored the first automobile race.

Ruffin, Frances E. **Martin Luther King, Jr., and the March on Washington.** Grosset and Dunlap, 2002. On a hot summer day in Washington, D.C., Martin Luther King, Jr., made an inspiring speech about freedom and rights.

PROFICIENT

Milton, Joyce. **Pocahontas: An American Princess.** Grosset and Dunlap, 2002. Offering more than the legend, this book tells the true story of Pocahontas.

Pryor, Bonnie. **The House on Maple Street.** William Morrow & Company, 1992. This book traces the 300-year history, and the many residents, of a house at 107 Maple Street.

Sewall, Marcia. **People of the Breaking Day.** Simon & Schuster, 1997. Learn about the customs and ceremonies of the Wampanoag who lived in the area where Plymouth was built.

Waters, Kate. **Samuel Eaton's Day: A Day in the Life of a Pilgrim Boy.** Scholastic, 1996. Spend a day with Samuel Eaton as he does his chores and meets his Native American neighbors in 1627.

Waters, Kate. **Sarah Morton's Day: A Day in the Life of a Pilgrim Girl.** Scholastic, 1993. Spend a typical day on the Plymouth Plantation with Sarah Morton as she milks the goat, cooks, and learns how to write.

ADVANCED

Bruchac, Joseph. **Squanto's Journey: The Story of the First Thanksgiving.** Harcourt Children's Books, 2001. Squanto helped the Pilgrims survive by teaching them how to grow corn, beans, and squash and how to hunt and fish.

Fritz, Jean. **Just a Few Words, Mr. Lincoln: The Story of the Gettysburg Address.** Grosset and Dunlap, 2002. The true story about Abraham Lincoln and his tribute to the soldiers at the Battle of Gettysburg.

Hopkinson, Deborah. **Sweet Clara and the Freedom Quilt.** Knopf Books for Young Readers, 2003. Based on a true story, this book tells how a young slave uses a quilt map to find her way to freedom.

Krensky, Stephen. **Paul Revere's Midnight Ride.** HarperCollins, 2002. On a cold night in 1775, Paul Revere dramatically galloped into history as he warned the colonists that the British army was coming.

Additional books also are recommended at point of use throughout the unit.
Note that information, while correct at time of publication, is subject to change.

For information about ordering these tradebooks, visit
www.harcourtschool.com/ss1

Use these activities to help differentiate instruction. Each activity has been developed to address a different level or type of learner.

 ENGLISH LANGUAGE LEARNERS

 20 minutes

Materials
- index cards

VOCABULARY QUESTION AND ANSWER Use unit vocabulary words in question prompts and have children use words to respond.

- Write vocabulary words on cards and review their definitions.
- Hold up a card as you use the vocabulary word in a question prompt, such as *How will you* **change** *in ten years?*
- Encourage children to use the vocabulary word in their response, such as *I will* **change** *by growing taller.*
- Repeat the procedure with each card (history, colony, independence, landmark).

SPECIAL NEEDS

 15 minutes

Materials
- index cards

PAST & PRESENT Have children identify statements according to whether they relate to the past or to the present.

- Write *PAST* and *PRESENT* on index cards and give a pair to each child.
- Make statements that relate to the unit content such as *The Native American family made a shelter from bark. Sara's dad drove her to school in his car. James saw George Washington riding his horse.*
- After each statement, have children hold up a card to indicate whether it relates to the past or to the present.
- Encourage children to explain their answer choices.

ADVANCED

 30 minutes

Materials
- drawing paper
- art materials
- magazines
- paste
- computer with Internet clip art

PICTURE PAIRS Have children compare items that changed over time.

- Help children brainstorm examples of things that changed over time, such as vehicles, telephones, appliances, and buildings.
- Ask children to find pictures that show related items from the past and present. They can draw their own images, print out images, or cut out magazine pictures they have found.
- Have children divide a sheet of paper in half and paste the pictures side by side. For example, a crank wall phone is placed next to a cell phone or a manual cash register next to an electronic scanner register.

MATHEMATICS CENTER

Years Before Now, Years After Now

Provide cards that show an addition, subtraction, or multiplication sign and a factor, such as + *9 years*, – *4 years*, x *3 years*. Have children choose a card and use their current age with the operation and factor on the card. Invite them to use the resulting answer to describe a past event in their life or to predict an event in the future. For example, if a child is seven years old:

7 + 9 years	I will be 16. I will drive a car.
7 – 4 years	I was 3. I lived in Mexico.
7 x 3 years	I will be 21. I will be in college.

+ 3 years	x 2 years
+ 9 years	x 3 years
– 2 years	
– 4 years	

SCIENCE CENTER

Communication Station

Provide resources about different forms of communication, including radio, television, telephone, and computers. Have pairs of children work together to discover how a particular form of communication has changed over time. Have the pair share their findings in a Then & Now Report to the rest of the group. Encourage children to create charts and illustrations to support their findings.

READING/LANGUAGE ARTS CENTER

Community Time Line

Have children use Internet and print resources to find out about the history of their community. Ask children to focus on changes over time, including notable events, interesting citizens, and growth. Invite them to use the information to write captions on index cards, and then to work together to put the cards in chronological order. Attach the cards to a length of yarn or ribbon mounted on a bulletin board to create a Community Time Line. Encourage children to add illustrations to decorate the time line.

December 26, 1776
Battle of Trenton

March 18, 1837
Grover Cleveland
born

ART CENTER

Make a Journal

Have children use art supplies such as watercolors, colored pencils, or tempera paints to create a journal cover on art paper. Encourage children to create art that reflects something about their life, such as an important event or things they like to do. Help children assemble a journal by stapling writing paper inside the journal cover. Invite them to use the journal to record their impressions of important events. Remind children to date each journal entry, and encourage them to write at least a short paragraph every day.

The Assessment Program gives all learners many opportunities to show what they know and can do. It also provides ongoing information about each student's understanding of social studies.

 Online Assessment available at www.harcourtschool.com/ss1

OPTION 1
UNIT TESTS
Unit 4

- **Unit Pretest,**
  Assessment Program, p. 29
- **Unit Review and Test Prep,** pp. 212–215

- **Unit Test,**
  Assessment Program, pp. 30–32

OPTION 2
WRITING

- **Show What You Know,**
  Unit Writing Activity,
  Write a Narrative Paragraph, p. 216
- **Primary Sources, Write About It,** p. 185

- **Lesson Review,**
  Writing Activities, at ends of lessons

OPTION 3
UNIT PROJECT

- **Show What You Know,**
  Unit Project,
  Historical Journal, p. 216
- **Unit Project,**
  Performance Assessment, pp. 153P–153Q

- **Lesson Review,**
  Performance Activities, at ends of lessons

INFORMAL ASSESSMENT

- **Lesson Review,** at ends of lessons
- **Skills:**
  Practice, pp. 177, 193, 207
  Apply, pp. 177, 193, 207

- **Reading Social Studies,**
  Sequence, pp. 156–157
- **Literature Response Corner,** p. 171
- **Citizenship, Make It Relevant,** p. 195

STUDENT SELF-EVALUATION

- **Reading Check Questions,** within lessons

- **Biography, Why Character Counts,** pp. 208–209
- **Map, Time Line, Graph, Diagram, and Illustration questions,** within lessons

OPTION 1 — PRETEST

Name _____ Date _____

4 Pretest

TRUE/FALSE (10 points each)

DIRECTIONS Write T next to the statements that are True and F next to the statements that are False.

① __F__ The future is time long ago.

② __F__ Change happens when something stays the same.

③ __F__ A family tree shows events in the order that they happened.

④ __T__ History is the study of things that happened in the past.

⑤ __T__ Native Americans were the first people to live in North America.

⑥ __F__ King George signed the Declaration of Independence.

⑦ __T__ People in the colonies fought a war to be free.

⑧ __F__ Thomas Jefferson was our country's first President.

⑨ __F__ A landmark is the same as a landform.

⑩ __T__ In a fiction story, some of the information is made up.

OPTION 1 — UNIT TEST

Name _____ Date _____

4 Test

MATCHING (5 points each)

DIRECTIONS Match the word on the right to its meaning on the left.

① __D__ the time before now

② __G__ the study of things that happened in the past

③ __E__ a place that is ruled by another country

④ __C__ the freedom of people to choose their own government

⑤ __F__ a feature that makes a location special

⑥ __B__ a holiday that honors people who gave their lives for our country

⑦ __A__ a holiday that honors the Declaration of Independence

A. Fourth of July
B. Memorial Day
C. independence
D. past
E. colony
F. landmark
G. history

(continued)

OPTION 1 — UNIT TEST

Name _____ Date _____

MULTIPLE CHOICE (6 points each)

DIRECTIONS Select the letter of the best answer.

⑧ What do we call the time we live in right now?

(A) present   C future
B past   D time line

⑨ Which of these is a way that communities change over time?

A people eat in restaurants   (C) more roads and houses
B families spend time together   D families shop in stores

⑩ Who were the first people in North America?

A English settlers   C soldiers for the king
B French settlers   (D) Native Americans

⑪ Which of these leaders helped write the Declaration of Independence?

A King George   C Paul Revere
(B) Thomas Jefferson   D George Washington

⑫ Why did people in the colonies have a war with England?

A to become part of England   C to have a new king
B to grow more food   (D) to make their own laws

OPTION 1 — UNIT TEST

Name _____ Date _____

SHORT ANSWER (7 points each)

DIRECTIONS The time line tells about Jake's life. Use the time line to answer the questions.

Jake's Time Line

2000	2001	2002	2003	2004	2005
Jake is born	Jake's family moves to Indianapolis	Jake starts preschool	Jake's sister, Rose, is born		Jake's family moves to Nashville

⑬ In what year was Jake born? __2000__

⑭ Who is older—Jake or his sister, Rose? __Jake__

⑮ Did Jake's family move to Indianapolis before or after 2003? __before__

⑯ How many years did Jake's family live in Indianapolis? __3 years__

⑰ What did Jake do in 2003? __He started preschool.__

OPTION 2 — WRITING

RUBRIC

Name _____ **Date** _____

Unit 4 Writing Activity Guidelines

WRITE A NARRATIVE PARAGRAPH

Writing Prompt Write a paragraph about important events in your life. Put the events in sequence.

▶ **STEP 1** Think about your life in the past and present. What are some events that you would like to share with others? Here are some ideas to get you started:

- What is one of your earliest memories?
- What do you want people to know about you now?

▶ **STEP 2** Write down your ideas and then decide which events you want to tell about. Then decide on the order in which things happened.

▶ **STEP 3** Use your ideas to write a narrative paragraph about the events in your life. Include details and interesting facts about yourself to describe the events.

▶ **STEP 4** Review your work to make sure you have used correct grammar, spelling, punctuation, and capitalization.

▶ **STEP 5** Make the changes. Then copy your paragraph neatly.

SCORE 4
- provides rich description and many details
- clearly describes several events in order
- indicates strong understanding of sequencing from past and present
- clearly understands and uses narrative form
- uses a variety of complete sentences

SCORE 3
- provides some description and details
- describes some events
- indicates some understanding of sequencing from past and present
- understands and uses narrative form
- uses complete sentences of some variety

SCORE 2
- provides little description and few details
- describes few events or a single event
- indicates little understanding of sequencing from past and present
- shows little understanding or use of narrative form
- uses mostly complete sentences of little variety

SCORE 1
- provides no description or details
- does not describe any events
- indicates no understanding of sequencing from past and present
- does not write in narrative form
- uses incomplete sentences that show no variety

OPTION 3 — PROJECT

RUBRIC

Name _____ **Date** _____

Unit 4 Project Guidelines

HISTORICAL JOURNAL

Write a journal from the point of view of people who lived at different times in our country's history.

▶ **STEP 1** With your group, make a list of several people that are important in our country's history. Here are some ideas to get you started:

- early explorers and settlers
- Presidents and other leaders

▶ **STEP 2** Choose a person you are interested in learning more about. Be sure you are the only student who is writing about that person.

▶ **STEP 3** Write a journal entry that will help a reader understand what your person's life was like. For example, you may want to tell about a day in which that person became a hero.

▶ **STEP 4** Help your group put all the journal entries together in the correct order.

▶ **STEP 5** As a group, choose a title and design a cover for your journal.

SCORE 4
- clearly understands what the person's life was like
- gives clear details about the person's importance in history
- uses clear sequencing to place events in order
- shows strong organization and creativity

SCORE 3
- understands what the person's life was like
- gives some details about the person's importance in history
- uses sequencing to place events in order
- shows organization and creativity

SCORE 2
- somewhat understands what the person's life was like
- gives few details about the person's importance in history
- uses some sequencing to place events in order
- shows little organization and creativity

SCORE 1
- does not understand what the person's life was like
- gives no details about the person's importance in history
- does not sequence events in a logical order
- shows no organization or creativity

TAKE-HOME RUBRICS Copying masters of a student *Writing Rubric* and *Project Rubric* appear in the Assessment Program, pp. 34 and 36.
GROUP PERFORMANCE RUBRIC See Assessment Program, page x.

A Historical Journal

Getting Started

Distribute the Unit 4 Project Guidelines provided on page 35 of the Assessment Program.

Introduce the unit project as you begin Unit 4, and tell children they will learn about many people in history. Explain that some of these people may be considered heroes who are part of history long ago and the recent past. When the unit is complete, have children demonstrate their knowledge and understanding of history by writing and assembling a journal from the point of view of people who lived at different times in our country's history.

The Big Idea

History History is the story of how people and places change over time.

Project Management

Have children choose individual people for the project, but encourage them to work in small groups as they work with research books and materials. As children choose a person, maintain a class list so choices are not duplicated. Provide instructional support and additional research materials as needed.

Materials textbook, easy-to-read biographies, local newspaper, online sources for research, writing paper, pencils, crayons or markers, construction paper, stapler

Create a Questionnaire

Invite each child to choose one person from history and research information about him or her. Ask them to find out why the person is remembered, what life was like during the person's lifetime, and interesting facts about the person's life.

Remind children they will use their research to write a journal entry from the point of view of their person. Explain that a journal entry usually focuses on a single day in a person's life. Suggest that they choose an important day in the person's life, perhaps the day he or she became a hero or a day for which he or she is best remembered.

People in History

Person	Occupation
Thomas Edison	inventor
Tecumseh	leader
Betsy Ross	seamstress
Paul Revere	silversmith
Harriet Tubman	civil rights leader
Sacagawea	interpreter

Assemble the Historical Journals

Have each group assemble a historical journal. Ask each group member to share his or her journal entry with the group. Once everyone has shared, invite group members to place the entries in order from past to present. Remind them that each entry should have a date, and they can refer to the dates as they order the entries. Suggest that they collaborate on a cover design and create a catchy title, then staple their pages between the covers to form the journal.

Share the Historical Journals

Choose a date and time for groups to share their historical journals with each other. Children in each group can introduce and answer questions about their historical person for the class. Place the journals in a classroom center and encourage children to read each other's journals. Finally, discuss with children what they learned about different times in history through the people they researched.

Lesson Review Activities

You may wish to incorporate the following lesson review activities into the unit project.

- Lesson 1: **Write about Pictures,** p. 175
- Lesson 2: **Draw a Picture,** p. 183
- Lesson 3: **Write about Events,** p. 191
- Lesson 4: **Draw a Picture of a Landmark,** p. 199
- Lesson 5: **Draw a Holiday Picture,** p. 205

Assessment

For a project rubric, see Teacher Edition, p. 153O.

What to Look For

- Children determine events of importance in a person's life.
- Children understand ways various individuals have contributed to our country's history.
- Journal entries contribute to the historical context of each individual.
- Journals are well organized and creative.

LESSON 1

Name _____ Date _____

It's About Time

Look at each picture. Is it about telling time in the past, the present, or the future? Write past, present, or future on the lines.

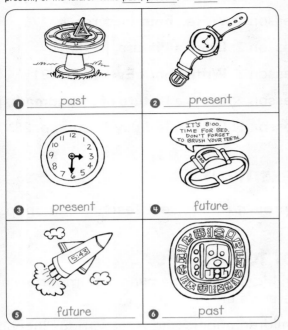

① past

② present

③ present

④ future

⑤ future

⑥ past

32 ■ Homework and Practice Book   Use after reading Unit 4, Lesson 1, pages 172–175.

SKILL PRACTICE

Name _____ Date _____

CHART AND GRAPH SKILLS
Family Tree

Look at the diagram of the family tree. Circle the correct answer for each question.

① What family is shown on this diagram?

(The Diego Family)   The Lopez Family

② What is the name of Angelo's father?

Juan   (Max)

③ Who is the youngest person?

(Ryan)   Max

④ Who is Ryan's mother?

Pilar   (Maria)

⑤ How many children do Angelo and Maria have?

(1)   2

Use after reading Unit 4, Skill Lesson, pages 176–177. **Homework and Practice Book** ■ 33

LESSON 2

Name _____ Date _____

Early America

These pictures show one place on the Atlantic coast of America long ago. Number the pictures to show the correct order.

34 ■ Homework and Practice Book   Use after reading Unit 4, Lesson 2, pages 178–183.

Name _____ Date _____

A Letter from Samuel

Read this letter from Samuel, a soldier in the American Revolution. Underline the sentences that tell why he is fighting in the war. Then answer the questions.

July, 1781

Dear Mother and Father,

I hope you are well and that this letter gets to you at the farm. You asked how the war is going. We are fighting for our freedom, and that gives me hope. It seems like a long time ago that we had to obey the King of England. His laws were so unfair! Remember how excited we were when we heard about the Declaration of Independence? Every day we fight for our new country and for our right to be free. I am hungry and tired, but I'll never give up until the colonies win their freedom from England.

Love, Samuel

❶ Why was Samuel so hungry and tired? <u>He was fighting the English in the American Revolution.</u>

❷ Why was the Declaration of Independence important to Samuel? <u>Possible answers: It gave him hope. It told the King of England that the colonists wanted to be free.</u>

Name _____ Date _____

CHART AND GRAPH SKILLS
Mark's Summer Vacation

Read the events on the time line. Then write a story about Mark's summer vacation.

Have a Great Summer!   School ends. May 30   Seventh birthday. July 24

May   June   July   August

Camp begins. June 17   School begins. August 25   Welcome to Grade 2

Possible answer:

<u>Mark got out of school on May 30. On June 17, he went to Summer Fun Camp. He turned 7 years old on July 24. Mark went back to school on August 25. Now he is in second grade.</u>

Name _____ Date _____

Honoring American Heritage

Look at the symbols of our heritage. Choose one, and write a poem or a paragraph that tells what the symbol means to you.

| Lincoln Memorial | Bald Eagle | Statue of Liberty | The Constitution |

Possible answer: <u>The bald eagle is the national bird of the United States. It is a strong bird that flies free. This symbol means a lot to me because it reminds me of our freedom.</u>

LESSON 5

Name _____ Date _____

My Hero

Complete the paragraph, and design a medal to honor the person.

    If I could choose a special person to honor, I would choose
<u>Answers will vary, but person should be a hero to the child.</u> . This

person is my ___hero___ . I would choose this person because

<u>Answer should include person's accomplishments.</u> .

We could honor this hero by <u>Answers might include having a</u>
<u>parade, putting his or her picture on a stamp or coin, or naming a</u>
<u>special day for him or her.</u> .

Design a medal for your hero.

SKILL PRACTICE

Name _____ Date _____

CRITICAL THINKING SKILLS
Nonfiction Books

Read the book titles. Write the titles of the nonfiction
books on the book covers.

Facts About the Presidents   Abe Goes to School
The Story of Paul Bunyan   The True Life of
Johnny and His Apples   George Washington
                  Harriet Tubman, A Biography

The True Life of George Washington

Harriet Tubman, A Biography

Facts About the Presidents

STUDY GUIDE

Name _____ Date _____

Unit 4 Study Guide

Read the paragraph. Use the words in the Word Bank to fill in the
blanks.

change	landmark	hero	history
colonies	settlers	Independence	freedom

    ___History___ is the study of things that happened
in the past. The first people who lived in North America were
the Native Americans. Then ___settlers___ came from
Europe. They decided to start ___colonies___ here. As
more and more people came to America, the country began to
___change___ .

    Many colonists grew tired of obeying the King of England.
They wanted the ___freedom___ to make their own laws.
On July 4, 1776, their leaders agreed to the Declaration of
___Independence___ . The colonists had to fight a long, hard
war against England. George Washington was an American
___hero___ during the war. He later became our first
President. The capital is named after him, and the Washington
Monument is a ___landmark___ there.

UNIT 4 REVIEW AND TEST PREP

Name _____ Date _____

SEQUENCE
Reading Social Studies

Fill in the chart to show the order in which events in the early
history of our country happened.

First	Next	Last
The leaders of the colonies decided to form their own country and had a meeting.	They signed the Declaration of Independence.	The people in the colonies fought and won a war with England.

First	Next	Last

Historical Societies

_____
_____
_____
_____
_____
_____
_____
_____
_____
_____
_____

Museums

_____
_____
_____
_____
_____
_____
_____
_____
_____
_____
_____

Parks

_____
_____
_____
_____
_____
_____
_____
_____
_____
_____
_____

Guest Speakers

_____
_____
_____
_____
_____
_____
_____
_____
_____
_____
_____

Discuss the Big Idea

History **History is the story of how people and places change over time.**

Explain that one way to learn about the past is to talk to family members. Family history, where people were born, moves they made from place to place, and the work they did can provide information about what life was like long ago. Tell children that in this unit they will learn how people, objects, and places help us learn about the past, understand the present, and predict the future.

Make It Relevant Ask the following question to help children think about how they can learn about their place in history.

Q **What items or activities have helped you learn about your history?**

A Children can mention family artifacts, celebrations, national holidays, and historic sites they have visited.

Access Prior Knowledge

Draw a time line model and label the ends of the span Long Ago and Today. Explain that important events in history can be marked on a time line to show when they happened. Invite children to suggest important events that have happened in the lives of themselves, their parents, and their grandparents. Record their responses on the time line. Explain that in this unit children will find ways to link events from long ago to events in our lives today.

```
├─────────────────────┤
Long                Today
Ago
```

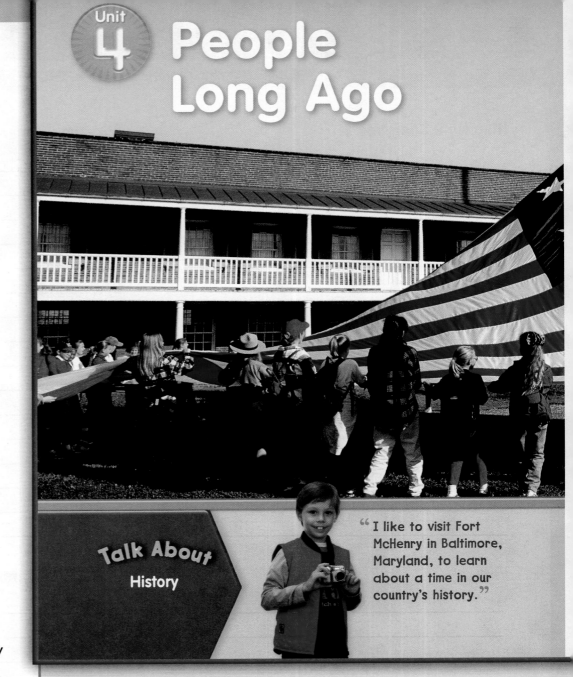

Unit 4 People Long Ago

Talk About

History

" I like to visit Fort McHenry in Baltimore, Maryland, to learn about a time in our country's history. "

Practice and Extend

BACKGROUND

Fort McHenry During the Battle of Baltimore in 1814, the valiant defense of the fort by a group of Americans against a British attack inspired Francis Scott Key to write our national anthem. Today, Fort McHenry is a National Monument and Historic Shrine. Visitors can participate in a daily flag-raising, living history events, and tours of the fort site.

Talk About Shown in the photographs along the bottom of the unit preview pages are children holding and discussing things related to our country's history. Symbols such as the bald eagle and ballot remind us of the importance of freedom and the right to vote. Point out that a camera is a useful tool for recording historical events.

"The bald eagle is a symbol of freedom."

"Voting is an important part of being a citizen in our country."

153

Discuss the Picture

Have children look at the photograph and identify it as Fort McHenry in Baltimore, Maryland. Point out that this historic site inspired Francis Scott Key to write "The Star-Spangled Banner." Ask them to describe details related to our country's heritage.

Q What are the children and adults doing in this photograph?

A They are holding an enormous U.S. flag to prevent it from touching the ground as it is raised into the air.

Q What does the photograph show about our country's heritage?

A It shows our national flag. It shows the respect we have for our flag. It shows that we have places that honor our country's history.

Discuss "Talk About"

Point out the objects the children are holding.

Q How do these objects relate to our country's history?

A Fort McHenry is a historic site, the bald eagle is our national bird, and the ballot shows voting is important to our country's history.

Q How are these things symbols of our country?

A The flag represents our 50 states and the original 13 colonies. The bald eagle is a symbol of freedom. The ballot is a symbol for our right to vote.

Have children work in pairs to ask and answer questions about either the Fort McHenry photograph or Talk About.

SCHOOL TO HOME

Use the Unit 4 SCHOOL TO HOME NEWSLETTER on pages S9–S10 to introduce the unit to family members and suggest activities they can do at home.

INTEGRATE THE CURRICULUM

MUSIC Point out that links to the past do not have to be objects. Music can provide a link to the culture of our parents and grandparents. Invite children to share favorite tunes, lullabies, or music played at family gatherings and celebrations. **Cultural Music**

MATHEMATICS Invite children to practice time order and the passage of time. On note cards, write times such as 9:00 A.M., 11:00 A.M, 1:00 P.M., 3:00 P.M., and 5:00 P.M. Invite partners to take turns selecting two cards and telling the duration of time between the two. **Time Intervals**

OBJECTIVES

- Use visuals to determine word meanings.

- Use words and visuals to preview the content of the unit.

RESOURCES

Picture Vocabulary Cards

Make Connections

Link Pictures with Words Have children read the vocabulary words *change* and *history* along with their definitions. Suggest that these words are related because over *history* people and places *change*. Invite children to describe how things *change* and become *history* by using the other vocabulary words and their pictures.

❶ Visual Literacy: Pictures Have children read the definition for *change*. Ask them to identify what they see that is changing in the picture.

Q How do buildings show change?

A New buildings go up; old buildings are torn down; buildings get bigger.

❷ Have children identify what they see in the picture for *history*. Ask them to name details that show this is a family from the past.

Q What does the picture tell us about history?

A Possible responses include that it shows clothing styles of long ago; it shows that the members of a family might be the same as those today.

❶ **change** What happens when something becomes different. (page 174)

154

history The study of things that happened in the past. (page 178)

Practice and Extend

ELL ENGLISH LANGUAGE LEARNERS

Frontloading Language: History Use the following prompts to develop the academic language of history and the structures of sequencing.

Beginning Use the pictures as examples for children to answer questions such as: *Did this family live before or after you?* (before) *Is this colony from long ago or today?* (long ago) *Does history show the past or present?* (past)

Intermediate Have children give responses to statements about a family. For example: *The child was born after the mother. The mother was born ____ the baby.* (before)

Advanced Ask children to use the following frame to suggest the changes that might occur as a landmark is built: *At first, ____. Next, ____. Last, ____.*

3

colony A place that is ruled by another country. (page 180)

5

independence The freedom of people to choose their own government. (page 187)

landmark A feature that makes a location special. (page 197)

4

For more resources, go to **www.harcourtschool.com/ss1**

155

Q Why would people choose to live in a new colony?

A Possible answers might include that they wanted more land, they wanted adventures, or perhaps they did not like the country they had left.

4 Have children look at the picture and read the definition for *landmark*. Discuss how landmarks identify important locations. Invite children to name other landmarks found in their own communities or with which they are familiar.

5 Invite children to describe what the people are doing in the picture for *independence*. Read the definition. Explain that these people are signing the Declaration of Independence, a document that is very important. This document announced that the United States of America wanted to become its own country.

Q On what holiday does our country celebrate its independence?

A the fourth of July, Independence Day

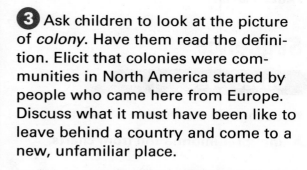

INTERNET RESOURCES

For more resources, go to **www.harcourtschool.com/ss1**

VOCABULARY POWER

Synonyms Challenge children to brainstorm synonyms for each vocabulary word. Suggest they use a thesaurus. Write the synonyms on cards and have children match the words independently.

Sequence

I Introduce

1 Why It Matters Explain to children that when they read, sequence tells them the order in which things happen. Provide the following examples:

- Some information is written in logical order: *First, I put on my T-shirt. Next, I put on my sweater. Last, I put on my jacket.*
- Some information is written in chronological order: *First, we went to the store. Next, we went to the movies, and last, we went home.*
- Some information can be sequenced using word clues: *We went to see Grandma, but first we picked up Aunt Mary. Next, we stopped for lunch.*

Have children use sequence clue words—*first, next, last*—in sentences of their own. Tell them to watch for sequence clue words as they read.

Unit 4

Reading Social Studies

Focus Skill

Sequence

Why It Matters Knowing the sequence, or
1 the order, in which events happen helps you understand what you read.

Learn

As you read, look for the words <u>first</u>,
2 <u>next</u>, and <u>last</u>. These words give sequence clues.

Read the paragraph below.

> Sequence
>
> Anna Maria's grandfather moved to Oklahoma when he was 20 years old. First, he built a small house. Next, he found a job on a ranch. Grandfather fixed fences and helped with the cattle. Last, he used the money he saved to buy his own ranch. Anna Maria now lives in the house that her grandfather built long ago.

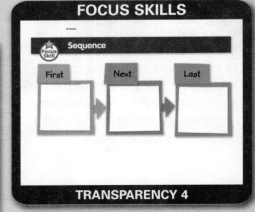

156

Practice and Extend

Practice

③

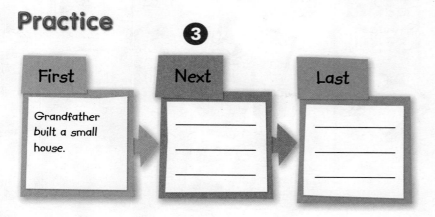

First

Grandfather built a small house.

Next

Last

This chart shows the sequence of events in Grandfather's life. What happened first? What happened next? What happened last? Copy the chart and complete it.

Apply

As you read, look for words that give sequence clues for events.

157

Leveled Practice Have children use sequence clue words to describe the order of events.

(Basic) Write the things children do in the morning. Have children add words to show sequence.

_____., I wake up.
_____., I wash my face.
_____., I take the bus to school.

(Proficient) Have children use sequence words to describe three events in their family history. For example:

First, we lived in a small farming town. Next, my sister was born. Last, we moved to an apartment in the city.

(Advanced) Have children use Internet resources to read about their community's history. Ask children to find three facts and use the sequence words to present the information in chronological order.

---

2 Teach

Learn

② Have children read the definition of *sequence* on page 156. Then read aloud and discuss the paragraph. Point out the use of sequence clue words such as *first*, *next*, and *last*. Guide children to identify that these words signal the order of events in the life of Anna Maria's grandfather.

Practice

③ Visual Literacy: Graphic Organizer Have children read the chart on page 157. Use Focus Skills Transparency 4 to copy the chart. Discuss the order of events to help children fill in the chart.

Q Look for the word *next*. What does it tell you about Grandfather?

A He found a job on the ranch.

Q What was the last thing Grandfather did?

A He bought his own ranch.

ANSWERS: First, Grandfather built a small house. Next, he found a job on a ranch. Last, he bought his own ranch.

3 Close

Apply

Tell children that as they read the unit, they should look for sequence clue words to better understand the order of events in United States history.

Quick Summary

When I Was Young by James Dunbar (Carolrhoda Books, 1999).

This realistic fiction selection connects a young boy to his ancestors and describes daily life in generations past.

Before Reading

Set the Purpose Explain that children are going to read a story about traveling back in time through memories. Ask: *What can family members tell you about the past? How can they help you understand how daily life has changed over the years?*

Discuss connections that children have to family members in past generations. Use stick figures to draw a family tree, pointing out that each generation goes back in time. Have children read to compare life in the past with daily life today. Save the drawing to use as children read.

Start with a Story

When I Was Young

by James Dunbar

illustrated by Martin Remphry

Ben   Emily   Joe   Polly

Jenny   Will

Josh   Betty

Josh likes visiting Grandma Jenny. Her apartment is full of her memories.

"What was it like when you were young, Grandma?" asks Josh.

1

58

And Grandma Jenny says—

When I was young, we lived in a new house and got our first TV. We had a kitchen with an electric stove and a fridge. Grandpa Ben used to visit us on weekends. My sister used to dress up and go dancing every Saturday night.

2

159

During Reading

Understand the Story Point out that this story is realistic fiction. It features family members who are not real but who act like real people. The events in the story could happen in real life. Ask children to identify activities that they do with their grandparents.

1 Visual Literacy: Illustration Have children look at the illustration on page 158 to identify details of Grandma Jenny's apartment.

Q What things show that this story takes place in the present?

A The coffeemaker, microwave oven, clothing styles, and furniture show that the story takes place in the present.

2 Visual Literacy: Illustrations Point out that the illustrations on page 159 show Grandma Jenny's childhood memories.

Q What things tell you that these scenes are from the past?

A The appliances, clothing styles, and furniture styles do not look modern.

 VOCABULARY POWER

Shortened Words Point out that many familiar words have shortened forms in everyday speech. The term *TV* is a shortened form of the word *television*. *Grandma* is a shortened version of *grandmother*. Have children look for more shortened words as they read, such as *photo* and *fridge*. Invite them to brainstorm other shortened words we use, such as *mom* and *ad.*

INTEGRATE THE CURRICULUM

MUSIC In the United States, the 1950s marked the beginnings of music that came to be known as rock and roll. Play songs performed by Elvis Presley, Buddy Holly, Fats Domino, and other early rock and roll icons. Invite children to identify how this type of music communicates certain ideas or moods.
Identify Music Elements

Understand the Story Point out that the little girl in the illustration is Grandma Jenny sitting on her grandfather's knee. Explain that Jenny is recalling what *her* grandfather told her about his life.

Geography Have children use a world map or globe to locate the country where Grandpa Ben grew up. (England) Point out that this is part of the area also called Great Britain.

Q What ocean do you cross when you travel from the east coast of the United States to England?

A the Atlantic

3 Understand the Story Invite children to read aloud the text that shows what Grandpa Ben said. Ask them to name details that show the action happened long ago. (polish a carriage, feed the horses, saw a car for the first time) Then have them suggest those actions or details that could happen today. (people still work in hotels)

Visual Literacy: Illustration Have children identify details from the past in the illustration on page 160, including the carriages, the early motor car, and the fashions. Point out the old-fashioned camera that the man is carrying into the building.

I remember asking Grandpa what it was like when he was young. And Grandpa Ben said—

3 When I was young, in England, my mum and dad worked in a big hotel. Dad used to polish the carriages. Sometimes he let me feed the horses. I saw a car in the street for the first time.

160

Practice and Extend

VOCABULARY POWER

Related Words Point out the author's use of the word *mum* for *mother*. Explain that in England, *mum* is used in the same way that *mom* is used in the United States. Invite children to create a class chart of the many ways they address parents and grandparents, including *mama, papa, dad, father, granddad, grandfather, gramps, gran,* and *grandmother*.

BACKGROUND

Transportation In England, the first carriages were used only by women, elderly people, or people who were ill. Men generally did not use carriages because they thought it made them look weak. The first carriages were more like farm wagons. Gradually, the designs became more comfortable, and with comfort came a wider acceptance and use, particularly among the wealthy.

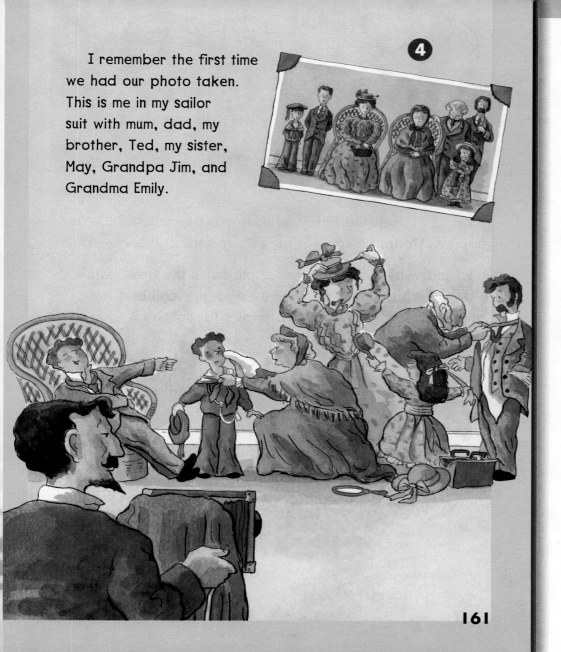

I remember the first time we had our photo taken. This is me in my sailor suit with mum, dad, my brother, Ted, my sister, May, Grandpa Jim, and Grandma Emily.

161

Understand the Story As they read page 161, remind children that this description is still from the memory of Grandma Jenny's Grandpa Ben. Show them where Grandpa Ben appears on a family tree in relation to Josh and Grandma Jenny. Have children locate Grandpa Ben in the photograph, based on his description.

4 Visual Literacy: Illustration Have children compare the people in the illustration to the people in the photograph and identify each one. Have them compare the kinds of clothes the people are wearing to the clothing styles of today.

Q What items of clothing are the same? What items are different?

A Children may say that skirts may be worn long or short now, but were only long in the past. People in the past wore hats more often and of a different style.

Point out that families still sometimes dress up for portraits just like they did long ago.

VOCABULARY POWER

Word Origins Point out that the word *photograph* comes from the root word *photo*, meaning "light," and the root word *graph*, meaning "write." Have children use a dictionary to find other words with these word parts, including *photocopy*, *photosynthesis*, *autograph*, and *telegraph*.

BACKGROUND

Photography In the past, pictures were taken only with film, and the development of different techniques for creating images and printing them spanned many decades. In the mid-1800s, the first portrait studios opened in Europe. Until the beginning of the twentieth century, it would have been unusual and expensive for ordinary people to have a family photo taken.

⑤ Understand the Story Use the illustration of the child in the sailor suit on the lap of the older woman as a clue. Guide children to understand that Grandma Jenny's Grandpa Ben is now asking *his* grandmother about her childhood. Add Grandma Emily to the family tree to help children understand how far back they are in time.

⑥ History Have children use the illustration details to ask and answer questions about life during Grandma Emily's time.

Q How did people light their houses?

A They used candles.

Q How is this different from how candles are used today?

A Candles are used today for birthdays and other celebrations, and to create light in an emergency.

I asked Grandma Emily what it was like when she was young. Grandma Emily sat me on her knee and said—

When I was young, I remember playing in the street with all the other children. At night, I used to get scrubbed in a bathtub in the kitchen. We had candles for lighting.

162

Practice and Extend

INTEGRATE THE CURRICULUM

SCIENCE Have children draw pictures that show the history of lighting, from the use of torches to modern halogen lighting. Invite children to use research materials or the Internet to find ideas for their drawings. **Sequence of Events**

PHYSICAL EDUCATION Have children play jump rope, using simple jump rope rhymes. *Anna Banana: 101 Jump-Rope Rhymes* by Joanna Cole (Morrow, 1989) and *Jump Rope Rhymes* by the Lady with the Alligator Purse (Klutz Press, 1998) are good resources for traditional and contemporary rhymes and games. **Childhood Games**

Visual Literacy: Illustration Point out that the upper right picture on page 162 shows Grandma Emily playing a game with her friends. Invite children to tell how this game is similar to or different from ones they play today.

Q What game do you recognize in the picture?

A The children are playing jump rope.

Q What does this picture tell you about where she lived?

A She lived in the city. Playing in the street was safe because there was much less traffic than today.

7 Understand the Story Add Grandfather Joe to the family tree diagram. Remind children that this is Grandma Emily's grandfather. Point out that the family tree now shows nine generations.

Visual Literacy: Illustration Point out that today huge ships carry steel containers of cargo across the ocean.

Q How was cargo packed in the past?

A Items were packed in wooden barrels.

7 We lived in a busy town. Grandfather Joe used to take me to the docks. We watched the big ships from all around the world come and go.

163

8 Visual Literacy: Illustration

Discuss the illustration of the people working on the farm.

Q What do you notice about the tools the people are using?

A They are using hand tools and animals.

Q How is this the same as or different from the farming we do today?

A Today people use machinery to do many of the jobs on the farm, even though they may use hand tools for the flower or vegetable garden.

Understand the Story Point out that most family members help with chores around the house. Relate household chores to life on a family farm today.

Q What are some of the jobs you might do if you lived on a farm?

A Possible answers include: milk the cow, gather eggs, feed livestock, plant seeds, pull weeds, or take care of horses.

I used to ask Grandfather what it was like when he was young. Grandfather Joe sat me on his knee and said—

When I was young, I lived in the country. My father and grandfather worked on a farm.

At harvesttime everybody helped, even my Grandmother Polly.

8

164

Practice and Extend

9 Two days each week, we went to the village school. The teacher was very strict.

10

165

Q **How was school for Grandfather Joe different from school today?**

A He went to school only two days a week instead of five.

Q **Why do you think farm children only went to school two days a week?**

A They were needed at home to help with the farm work.

10 **Visual Literacy: Illustration** Have children use details in the illustration to ask and answer questions about school today and long ago.

Q **What other differences do you notice between your classroom and Joe's?**

A Children write with chalk on slates, children sit at tables instead of desks, and the teacher wears a wig.

Q **What things in Joe's classroom are the same as in yours?**

A globe, books, toys

Understand the Story Ask children to describe the types of jobs that older siblings may have, such as lawn mowing, pet care, baby-sitting, working in a restaurant, or tutoring. Explain that in the past even relatively young children worked as servants. Discuss the kinds of jobs that would be required to keep up a large house without any modern things such as dishwashers and refrigerators.

11 Visual Literacy: Illustration
Discuss the details in the illustration on page 166.

Q Why would it be important to keep the fire going?

A There wasn't any other heat in the house, so fire was used to keep the house warm. One fire could be used to light other fires.

I remember asking my grandmother what it was like when she was young. Grandmother Polly sat me on her knee and said—

When I was young, I used to help my older sister, who worked at a big house. Downstairs in the kitchen, I polished candlesticks and scrubbed the tables and helped prepare the food. Upstairs in the large rooms, I dusted the furniture and helped make the fire. **11**

166

Practice and Extend

BACKGROUND

Servants In the nineteenth century, even moderately wealthy households kept at least one or two servants. Most of these were young single women. The hours were long and hard. A servant's day, often more than 12 hours of work, began long before sunrise and ended well after the household had retired for the night. Until the beginning of World War I, domestic service was the number one occupation for women.

MAKE IT RELEVANT

At Home Have children brainstorm a list of household chores that need to be done around their homes. Discuss the sequence for getting things done efficiently. For example, for a lawn, they may need to mow, rake, and water. To clean a room, they may dust, sweep, then mop. Have children use the information to make up a schedule for spring cleaning.

INTEGRATE THE CURRICULUM

READING/LANGUAGE ARTS Point out that some words have multiple meanings depending on the part of speech. For example, the words *work*, *polish*, and *dust* on page 166 have one meaning when used as nouns and another when used as verbs. Discuss the meanings, and have children use the words in sentences. **Multiple Meanings**

⑫

I remember the fair coming to town. There were games and dancing and market stalls.

167

Q **What familiar game do you see?**

A bowling

Q **How is this country fair like a fair you have attended? How is it different?**

A Answers will vary depending on their experiences with county or state fairs, Renaissance fairs, art fairs, and so on. Possible answers may include details about food, games, rides, and animals.

INTEGRATE THE CURRICULUM

READING/LANGUAGE ARTS Share with children nursery rhymes that date from the 1700s and can be related to buying and selling at market fairs, such as "As I Was Going to St. Ives," "Simple Simon," and "Old Mother Hubbard." Invite children to identify details in each that are similar to or different from our market or fair experiences today. **Nursery Rhymes**

SCIENCE Have children use a ball and "bowling pins" to explore how force and motion affect the change of an object's position. Have children use empty bottles as pins. Invite them to roll a ball at a pin, observing how changes in speeds or angles affect how the pin falls. Have them write sentences that describe their observations. **Force and Motion**

Understand the Story Guide children to understand that Grandmother Polly's grandfather is Will. Add Grandfather Will to the family tree diagram.

Economics Explain to children that, long ago, tradespeople would travel from place to place with their wares instead of having customers come to buy things at a place of business. At this time, people might have to wait until the tradesperson came through their town before they could buy certain things. Today, there are still some traveling salespeople, but very few travel door to door. Have children ask their parents and grandparents about traveling salespeople that they remember from childhood. Have children share their findings with the class.

⓭ Visual Literacy: Illustration Point out that the market was a festive, busy place. People would come from miles around to meet tradespeople, buy things, see friends, and shop for things they could not make on farms. Have children describe some of the actions they see in the illustration.

I used to ask my grandfather what it was like when he was young. Grandfather Will sat me on his knee and said—

When I was young, we traveled to all the country markets where my father and grandfather bought and sold horses.

168

Practice and Extend

I remember Grandmother Betty making dolls and small toys. They were made from wood. I used to help paint the faces. She gave one of the wooden dolls to me . . .

169

Understand the Story Ask children about the jobs that Polly's grandparents did.

Q How did Grandfather Will's father and grandfather make a living?

A They sold horses.

Q What did his grandmother do to help earn money?

A She made dolls and toys to sell.

Q How are the toys that Grandmother Betty made different from the toys you have today?

A The materials are different. Most dolls made today are not made of wood. Today's toys are usually not handmade.

Visual Literacy: Illustration Have children use the illustrations to trace the doll that Grandmother Betty made back through to the beginning of the story.

Q How can you tell the doll is an important family artifact?

A It has been passed down from generation to generation.

INDEPENDENT READING

Point out the spinning wheel in the illustration on page 169. Help children connect the role of a spinning wheel in other works of literature by reading *Sleeping Beauty* adapted by Eric Blair (Picture Window Books, 2005) to see how a spinning wheel was used in that story.

INTEGRATE THE CURRICULUM

READING/LANGUAGE ARTS Have children work together to write a dialogue between the buyer and the seller at the market. The seller can describe the horse and what makes it a great deal; the buyer can haggle over the price in order to get a bargain. Have children share their dialogues with the class. **Share a Dialogue**

VISUAL ARTS Have children use wooden spools, craft sticks, cloth, paper, and found objects to make small dolls or other toys. Challenge children to avoid using plastic parts so that the toys will look as old-fashioned as possible. Display the toys in the classroom. **Creative Toymaking**

Understand the Story Point out that this story took the children back hundreds of years in time. Explain that stories passed down through families can make history come alive. Knowing how people lived in the past, what their jobs were, and what they did for fun gives us information about what daily life was like in the past.

⑭ Visual Literacy: Illustration Have children study the captions below the portraits on pages 170 and 171.

Q Which family members were born in the 1800s?

A Emily and Ben

Q What two family members were born during the 1700s?

A Polly and Joe

History Explain to children that a century is 100 years. Have children look at the years beneath each portrait. Have them practice using the word *century* by finding the two people that were seven years old a century apart. (Will and Joe)

I remember thinking, "When I am as old as Grandmother Betty, I will tell my grandchildren what it was like when I was young."

Betty
Born in 1648

Will
7 years old in 1697

Polly
7 years old in 1744

170

Practice and Extend

Advanced Have children use the information in the captions below the portraits on pages 170 and 171 to create a time line of Josh's family from Grandmother Betty to Josh. Have children draw the portraits on a sheet of butcher paper with the dates written below each family member.

MATHEMATICS Have children look at the picture caption below the portrait of Will. Ask them how they could figure out the year Will was born. (subtract) Then model how to count backward from 1697 seven years in order to find the answer. (1697–7=1690) **Problem Solving**

Leveled Practice Have children listen to the recording of *When I Was Young.*

(Basic) Have children identify the main characters and their relationship to each other.

(Proficient) Model filling in a family tree and have children create one using the story.

(Advanced) Have children role-play the scenes from the story, using simple props.

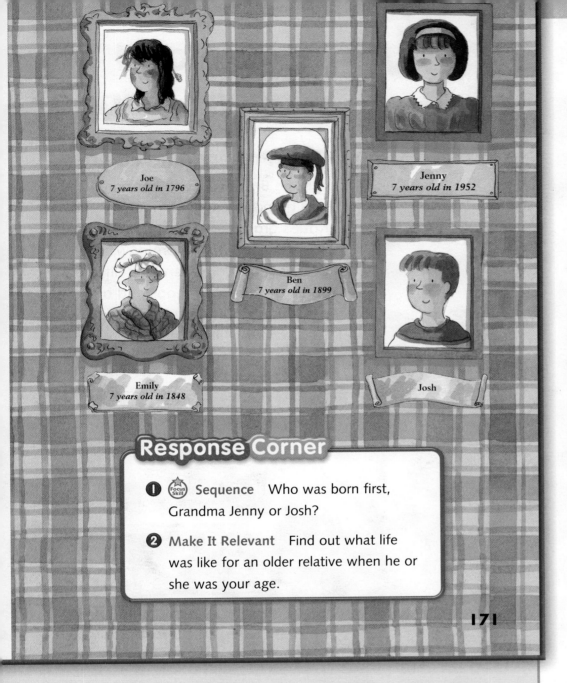

Joe
7 years old in 1796

Jenny
7 years old in 1952

Ben
7 years old in 1899

Emily
7 years old in 1848

Josh

Response Corner

1 **Sequence** Who was born first, Grandma Jenny or Josh?

2 **Make It Relevant** Find out what life was like for an older relative when he or she was your age.

171

After Reading

Response Corner—Answers

1. **Sequence** Grandma Jenny

2. **Make It Relevant** Have children interview an older relative to learn about what his or her childhood was like. Point out that they can ask questions about differences in school or work, home and clothing styles, toys and games, transportation, and ways they got food.

Write a Response

Have children write a story that they will tell their grandchildren. The story can be about family traditions, school, daily life, jobs, or community events. Begin the story with *Let me tell you what life was like when I was young.* Have children illustrate their stories to show what they think they will look like 60 years in the future.

For a writing response rubric, see Assessment Program, page xvi.

INDEPENDENT READING

Children may enjoy reading these books during the unit. Additional books are listed on page 153J of this Teacher Edition.

Love as Strong as Ginger by Lenore Look (Atheneum, 2000). A close-up of Taishanese-American life as Katie goes to work with her grandmother.

Granddaddy's Street Songs by Monalisa DeGross (Jump at the Sun, 2000). A grandfather tells about his life as a street peddler.

Century Farm: One Hundred Years on a Family Farm by Cris Peterson (Boyds Mills, 2000). The changes that take place over the years as generations tend a family farm.

For information about ordering these trade books, visit **www.harcourtschool.com/ss1**

OBJECTIVES

- **Understand the concept of time in terms of past, present, and future.**
- **Recognize that while some things change over time, other things stay the same.**

VOCABULARY

past p. 172   **future** p. 173

present p. 173   **change** p. 174

SEQUENCE

pp. 156–157, 175

RESOURCES

Homework and Practice Book, p. 32; Reading Support and Intervention, pp. 54–57; Success for English Learners, pp. 57–60; Vocabulary Transparency 4-1; Focus Skills Transparency 4; Sequence Graphic Organizer Write-On/Wipe-Off Card; Unit 4 Audiotext CD Collection; Internet Resources

1 Introduce

What to Know Choose a volunteer to read the What to Know question. Explain that change happens to everyone. Changes can be big or small, and happen slowly or quickly. Remind children to look for answers to the question as they read the lesson.

Build Background Remind children that change is when something becomes different. Have children talk about changes they have made, such as getting a hair cut or learning to play a new sport. Discuss how these specific changes made them feel.

Lesson 1

People and Places Change

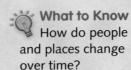 **What to Know**
How do people and places change over time?

Vocabulary
past
present
future
change

  **Sequence**

Past, Present, and Future

Katie Britt lives with her parents and grandparents in Marietta, Ohio. Katie's grandparents remember the **①** **past**, or the time before now. The clothes they wore then look different. Some of the work people did and the ways they had fun were different, too. Some are still the same.

172

Practice and Extend

 **Express Path**

When minutes count, look for the **EXPRESS PATH** to focus on the lesson's main ideas.

Quick Summary

This lesson discusses the ways that many things change from the past to the present and into the future. These changes include different styles of clothing, types of jobs, and even recreation. There are also aspects of people and places that stay the same throughout history.

Katie thinks about what her family and community are like right now in the **present**. She also likes to think about what her life will be like in the future. The **future** is the time yet to come. Katie knows she will be different but will still like to do things with her family.

Reading Check **What words name the parts of time in order?**
The words past, present, and future.

2

173

Past, Present, and Future

CONTENT FOCUS Comparing past, present, and future shows how lives change or stay the same.

Express Path

Have children scan the section to name details about a family's *past*, *present*, and *future*.

1 **History** Explain that the past is anything that has happened before today, the *present*. Using more exact words, such as *long ago*, *recent past*, or *far away*, helps us understand more precisely when something happened. Share other specific time period words, such as *decade*, *century*, *ancient times*, or *modern times*. Have children apply these time words as they describe changes in history.

2 **Visual Literacy: Pictures** Have children study the family pictures on pages 172–173, contrasting the past, present, and future. Invite children to discuss how styles, work, and recreation have changed for the members of their own families.

VOCABULARY

Vocabulary Transparency [4-1]

| MINI-GLOSSARY | Read each term, and study its definition. |

past The time before now. p. 172
present The time right now. p. 173
future The time yet to come. p. 173
change What happens when something becomes different. p. 174

| WORD WORK | Complete the activities below. |

1. **past**
   HOMOPHONES Do the words past and passed mean the same thing or sound the same?
   They sound the same but mean something different.

2. **present**
   MULTIPLE MEANINGS/USE REFERENCE SOURCES Use your dictionary to find another meaning for present.
   Something that you give someone as a gift.

3. **future**
   USE REFERENCE SOURCES Does future come before or after final in the dictionary?
   after

4. **change**
   CATEGORIZE VOCABULARY Use the word change as a verb in a sentence.
   Possible answer: The leaves change color in the fall.

TRANSPARENCY 4-1

READING SUPPORT/ INTERVENTION

For alternate teaching strategies, use pages 54–57 of Reading Support and Intervention to:

- identify **phonemes**
- practice **phonics**
- reinforce **vocabulary**
- build **text comprehension**
- build **fluency**

Reading Support ▶ **and Intervention**

ELL ENGLISH LANGUAGE LEARNERS

For English Language Learners strategies to support this lesson, see Success for English Learners pages 57–60.

- English-language development activities
- background and concepts
- vocabulary extension

Success for ▶ **English Learners**

Changes Over Time

CONTENT FOCUS Changes take place slowly over a long time, while some things in life stay the same.

Express Path

Direct children to examine the photographs. Use the photographs to discuss the main idea.

3 Economics Explain that the kinds of jobs people do change over time. Discuss how the ways people made a living in the past are different and similar today. Discuss how technology such as cell phones and computers change the way people work. Discuss how businesses, farming, and industries have changed in their region or community. Have them speculate on why those changes occurred.

4 Visual Literacy: Pictures Have children look at the pictures on page 174. Ask children to notice details such as tree height, styles of cars, and new and old buildings. Provide children with maps, photographs, and stories of their own community from past to present. Discuss changes in architecture and transportation in the community or region.

Q How will your community change in the future?

A Responses will vary, but ask children to explain why they think their suggested changes will occur.

5 Link History and Culture Explain that though things change, some things stay the same. Invite children to brainstorm things people do now for fun that are similar to the past. Invite them to identify activities that were not available to their grandparents, such as computer games. Have children predict which activities will be part of future life.

Changes Over Time

A **change** happens when something becomes different. Long ago, Marietta, Ohio, looked different. Over time, more **3** people have moved into the community. New houses and roads have been built. Technology has also changed the way people live.

Marietta, Ohio, past and present

4 Putnam Street, 1950s

Practice and Extend

VOCABULARY POWER

Antonyms Explain to children that *past* and *present* are antonyms, or words that have opposite meanings. Discuss why these words are opposites. (past is a time long ago, present is a time now) Invite children to find other antonyms in the lesson. (past/future) Have them name other opposites for changes in people or places. (old/new, tall/short, big/small, noisy/quiet)

REACH ALL LEARNERS

Leveled Practice Display pictures of the community from long ago and recent times.

Basic Ask children to identify details that show change.

Proficient Have children give details that indicate the past and present and find details that have remained constant.

Advanced Invite children to predict which details are likely to change in the future.

Places in a community may change over time, but people in the present still do some of the same things as people in the past. They still go shopping in stores and eat in restaurants. Families still enjoy playing in parks.

⑤

Reading Check **Sequence** What **changes happen after more people move into a community?** There are more houses and roads.

Summary People and places change over time.

Review

❶ What to Know How do people and places change over time?

❷ Vocabulary Describe a **change** that you have seen in your school or community.

❸ Write Look at some pictures from the past. Write about the ways things they show are different from things you see today.

❹ Sequence Which happens first, the future or the past?

175

Summary

Have volunteers read the summary and then restate the main points in their own words.

- Some things change and some things stay the same between the past, present, and future.
- The way people dress, work, play, live, and travel all change over time.

Assess

REVIEW—Answers

1. **What to Know** People look different, have different jobs and ways of having fun. Places can be changed by adding more buildings and streets.

2. **Vocabulary** Possible answer: The new library is a **change** I saw in my community.

3. **Writing Assessment Guidelines** See Writing Rubric. This activity can be used with the Unit Project.

4. **Sequence** The past happens first.

Use Focus Skills Transparency 4 or Sequence Graphic Organizer Write-On/Wipe-Off Card.

WRITING RUBRIC

Score 4
- identifies excellent examples
- presents excellent details
- has few or no errors

Score 3
- identifies adequate examples
- presents adequate details
- has few errors

Score 2
- identifies few examples
- presents few details
- has some errors

Score 1
- identifies no examples
- presents no details
- has many errors

HOMEWORK AND PRACTICE

Name _____ Date _____

It's About Time

Look at each picture. Is it about telling time in the past, the present, or the future? Write past, present, or future on the lines.

❶ past   ❷ present

❸ present   ❹ future

❺ future   ❻ past

page 32

REACH ALL LEARNERS

Special Needs Have children make figures to show how transportation has changed from the past to the present and what might be in the future. Display pictures of transportation over the years. Provide small groups with pipe cleaners to shape into types of vehicles, such as a horse and cart, car, airplane, or futuristic space vehicle. Direct them to label each with *Past, Present,* or *Future,* and arrange them in time order.

Read a Diagram

OBJECTIVES

- Identify a diagram as a chart that shows the parts of something.

- Define and describe the relationships shown on a family tree.

VOCABULARY

diagram p. 176

RESOURCES

Homework and Practice Book, p. 33;
Social Studies Skills Transparency 4-1;
Unit 4 Audiotext CD Collection;
Internet Resources

Why It Matters   A **diagram** is a picture that shows the parts of something. A family tree is a diagram that shows the parts of a family.

176

Introduce

Invite a volunteer to name the members of his or her family, including siblings, parents, and grandparents. Ask the class if they would be able to repeat all the names and relationships they just heard. Point out that getting a lot of information at one time can be hard to remember. Emphasize that a diagram can help us remember the people in a family and their relationships.

Why It Matters Point out that a diagram is a picture that shows the parts of something. Explain sometimes it is easier to understand something by looking at a diagram than by reading or hearing a detailed explanation. A family tree is a diagram that shows the parts of a family. Emphasize that this diagram helps us remember the people in a family and their relationships.

Practice and Extend

SOCIAL STUDIES SKILLS

Chart and Graph Skills

Read a Diagram

People We Know
pages 176–177   Harcourt Social Studies   Social Studies Skills
Transparency 4-1

TRANSPARENCY 4-1

MAKE IT RELEVANT

At Home Many families have records of family trees in bibles, as charts or artworks, from Internet genealogy searches, or in books. Invite a family member to bring in a family tree to share with the class. Assist children in finding their classmate on the diagram, and encourage them to ask questions. Ask the family member to share family history that children will find interesting.

Learn

This family tree gives information about Katie Britt's family. It shows Katie, her parents, and her grandparents.

❸ Practice

❶ Where can you find the youngest people on a family tree diagram?

❷ Who are the people in the middle row of Katie's family tree?

❸ What are the names of Katie's grandparents?

Apply

Make It Relevant Make a family tree that shows the members of your family.

 For online activities, go to **www.harcourtschool.com/ss1**

177

---

2 Teach

Learn

❶ Remind children that a diagram is a picture that explains the parts of something. Help children locate other examples of diagrams in books or magazines. Point out that diagrams are arranged in a clear and orderly way, and include labels for parts.

❷ **Visual Literacy: Diagram** Have children look at the family tree on page 176. Explain that each row in the family tree shows a generation in a family. Invite volunteers to tell the names of each member in a generation of Katie's family.

Q How many generations of Katie's family are shown in this diagram?

A three generations

❸ Practice

1. The youngest are at the very bottom.
2. Katie's parents are on the middle row.
3. Norma and Warren Brown, Louise and Robert Britt are the names of Katie's grandparents.

3 Close

Apply

Make It Relevant Children's family trees should correctly show their families' generations. Their diagrams should be labeled to indicate names or relationships of family members.

INTERNET RESOURCES

For online activities, go to **www.harcourtschool.com/ss1**

REACH ALL LEARNERS

Leveled Practice Have children practice making diagrams.

Basic Ask children to arrange picture cards into a family tree.

Proficient Have partners ask and answer questions about the people on their diagram.

Advanced Invite children to make picture cards of aunts, uncles, and cousins. Have children consider their places on the tree diagram.

HOMEWORK AND PRACTICE

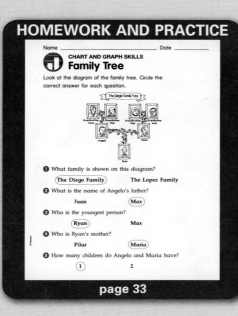

Name _____ Date _____

CHART AND GRAPH SKILLS
Family Tree

Look at the diagram of the family tree. Circle the correct answer for each question.

The Diego Family Tree

❶ What family is shown on this diagram?
   The Diego Family   The Lopez Family
❷ What is the name of Angelo's father?
   Juan   **Max**
❸ Who is the youngest person?
   Ryan   Max
❹ Who is Ryan's mother?
   Pilar   **Maria**
❺ How many children do Angelo and Maria have?
   1   2

page 33

OBJECTIVES

- **Recognize Native Americans as the first groups of people to live in North America.**

- **Describe the lifestyle of a Native American community.**

- **Define colonies and settlers, especially European settlers and Jamestown.**

VOCABULARY

history p. 178   **settler** p. 180
colony p. 180

SEQUENCE

pp. 156–157, 181, 183

RESOURCES

Homework and Practice Book, p. 34; Reading Support and Intervention, pp. 58–61; Success for English Learners, pp. 61–64; Vocabulary Transparency 4-2; Focus Skills Transparency 4; Sequence Graphic Organizer Write-On/Wipe-Off Card; Unit 4 Audiotext CD Collection; Internet Resources

Introduce

What to Know Have children read the What to Know question. Point out that there are many ways to learn about people from long ago, including artifacts, journals, and drawings. Invite children to look for answers to the question as they read the lesson.

Build Background Ask children to share stories of a relative who lived long ago. Discuss what they know about this person's life and how they learned this information.

Lesson 2

Early America

What to Know
What do we know about the people who lived in North America long ago?

Vocabulary
history
colony
settlers

Sequence

History is the study of things that happened in the past. It tells about places and people and how they have changed over time.

The First North Americans

Native Americans were the first people to live in North America. Many different groups lived all over the continent. They knew how to find and grow food. They hunted animals for food and used the skins for clothing. Some communities built shelters from wood, while others used earth.

1

Farming in fields

178

Practice and Extend

Express Path

When minutes count, look for the **EXPRESS PATH** to focus on the lesson's main ideas.

Quick Summary

This lesson describes the way of life of Native Americans, the first people to live in North America. The lesson also tells of the way of life of early settlers who came to North America from Europe.

A Native American tribe called the Powhatan used small trees to build their homes. First, they bent the trees and tied them together. Then they covered the trees with big pieces of tree bark. The people cooked on fires inside their homes.

Reading Check **Who were the first people in North America?** The Native Americans were the first people in North America.

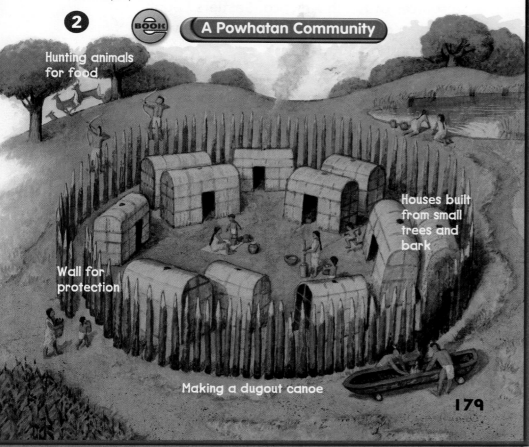

2 **BOOK** A Powhatan Community

Hunting animals for food

Houses built from small trees and bark

Wall for protection

Making a dugout canoe

179

The First North Americans

CONTENT FOCUS Native Americans were the first residents of North America.

Express Path

Have groups skim the text to find the answer to the Reading Check question.

1 **History** Tell children that many Native American groups lived in North America. Also known as American Indians, each tribe was unique. Point out that Native Americans used the resources around them to create useful everyday items. Some items were considered works of art. Each tribe had their own rich culture.

2 **Visual Literacy: Picture** Point out that the Powhatan provided food for their people by hunting, gathering, and farming. Explain that they lived in the area of what is now Virginia and New Jersey.

BOOK **Interactive in the enhanced online student eBook**

VOCABULARY

Vocabulary Transparency 4-2

MINI-GLOSSARY Read each term, and study its definition.

history The study of things that happened in the past. p. 178
colony A place that is ruled by another country. p. 180
settler One of the first people to make a home in a new place. p. 180

WORD WORK Complete the activities below.

1. **history**
STRUCTURAL CLUES You can see the word story in history. How might this help you remember the meaning of history?
It helps me remember because history is stories of things that happened in the past.

2. **colony**
CLASSIFY/CATEGORIZE Would you classify colony under people or places?
places

3. **settler**
WORD FAMILIES How are these words the same?
settle   settler   settlement
They share the same root, settle.

TRANSPARENCY 4-2

READING SUPPORT/ INTERVENTION

For alternate teaching strategies, use pages 58–61 of Reading Support and Intervention to:

■ identify **phonemes**

■ practice **phonics**

■ reinforce **vocabulary**

■ build **text comprehension**

■ build **fluency**

HARCOURT
SOCIAL Studies
People We Know
Reading Support and Intervention

Reading Support ▶ and Intervention

ELL **ENGLISH LANGUAGE LEARNERS**

For English Language Learners strategies to support this lesson, see Success for English Learners pages 61–64.

■ English-language development activities

■ background and concepts

■ vocabulary extension

HARCOURT
SOCIAL Studies
People We Know
Success for English Learners

Success for ▶ English Learners

Colonies and Settlers

CONTENT FOCUS Settlers from Europe came to North America to form colonies long ago.

Express Path

Have small groups read a paragraph. Ask volunteers to share a summary of what they learned.

3 History Discuss reasons settlers came to North America from Europe. Some reasons included better land, space to build homes, freedom, or plentiful resources. Ask children to share stories of family members who moved to a new place.

Correct Misconceptions Explain to children that all people throughout history have basic needs that need to be met. Point out that how people meet these needs is different today than it was for Native Americans and settlers long ago.

Q How was it different for Native Americans and settlers to meet their needs for food long ago than it is for families today?

A Long ago they had to grow and hunt for their own food. Today we can go to the store to buy food.

Colonies and Settlers

After a while, Native Americans were no longer the only people in North America. **3** People from Europe decided to start colonies here. A **colony** is a place that is ruled by another country.

The European countries wanted to use the resources of North America. **Settlers** began traveling across the ocean to make new homes in North America.

Coming to North America

Plymouth
Jamestown
Atlantic Ocean
England

Map Key
Route to Plymouth
Route to Jamestown

MAP SKILL Is Jamestown to the north or south of Plymouth?

180

Practice and Extend

ELL ENGLISH LANGUAGE LEARNERS

(Beginning) Ask children to point to *history*, *colony*, and *settler* in this lesson. Create cloze sentences for children to complete, such as *People traveled far to make a new home in a _____.*

(Intermediate) Ask children to give a simple definition for each of the following: *history*, colony, *settler*. Encourage them to look over the illustrations in the lesson for ideas.

(Advanced) Have children locate *history*, *colony*, and *settler* in the lesson. Invite them to read aloud a sentence containing each word. Then, ask them to explain the vocabulary in their own words.

MAKE IT RELEVANT

In Your State Guide children to create an oral presentation about a Native American tribe found in their state or region. Ask that they also explore how settlers affected the tribe as they moved into the area. Assist small groups as they research online or in nonfiction books. Have them make notes and drawings from their research. After practicing with their group, have children explain what they learned to the class.

The European country called England set up colonies along the Atlantic Ocean. The first was in what is now Virginia. A group of settlers built a colony called Jamestown. Then a group known as the Pilgrims settled in what is now Massachusetts. They began a colony called Plymouth. Soon England had thirteen colonies.

Reading Check **Sequence** **Which community was settled first, Plymouth or Jamestown?**
Jamestown was settled first.

181

4 Link History and Geography
Explain that Jamestown was settled in 1607. Plymouth was settled in 1620, thirteen years later. Point out that both groups came from England, but for different reasons. Help children locate Europe, England, and both settlements on the map on page 180.

CAPTION ANSWER: south

5 Visual Literacy: Picture As children study the painting on page 181, invite them to imagine traveling long distances by ship. Discuss problems the settlers faced, such as keeping food fresh, living in a crowded space, storms, and illnesses.

BACKGROUND

Jamestown and Plymouth
Three ships sailed from England in 1607 to find gold and a waterway to the Orient. On board were gentlemen, craftsmen, farmers, and laborers. They set up Jamestown colony, the first permanent British colony in North America, on the James River in Virginia. Despite conflicts with other tribes, they sometimes traded peacefully with and learned from the Powhatan Indians.

Plymouth was settled by English Separatists (Pilgrims) in 1620. They traveled on the Mayflower looking for a place to practice their religion freely. They wrote the Mayflower Compact, forming their own government. In 1621, a feast was held with enough food to include 90 Wampanoag Indians. Although not called Thanksgiving until much later, it did celebrate their first harvest and survival of harsh conditions.

READING SOCIAL STUDIES

Sequence Direct children to list sequence words from the lesson, such as *first* or *then*. Ask them to brainstorm other words. Invite pairs to retell what they learned in the story, using a sequence word.

READING TRANSPARENCY

Use FOCUS SKILLS TRANSPARENCY 4.
Graphic Organizer Write-On/Wipe-Off Cards available

Help from the Native Americans

CONTENT FOCUS Native Americans helped the settlers learn how to live in their new land.

Express Path

Have children examine the pictures and captions in this section and write a sentence that describes the main idea.

❻ History Remind children that life in Europe was very different from life in a colony. Many settlers were leaving behind jobs, homes, clothing, schools, and toys. Remind children that when settlers arrived, they had to make everything themselves. Because Native Americans were skilled at using the resources around them, settlers learned the skills to survive from Native Americans.

Q How do you think life was different for the children in the colonies?

A They had many chores, cared for farm animals, made food and clothes, collected firewood, and had no school to attend.

History Give brief examples of Native Americans who are part of history:

- Sacajawea, a Shoshone woman, helped explorers Lewis and Clark by talking with other Native Americans they met along the way. She was a strong, helpful, and uncomplaining member of their party.

- Tecumseh, a Shawnee chief, felt settlers should not take Native American land. He was admired for his belief that all Native Americans should unite.

Help from the Native Americans

❻ The settlers found that life was different from what they were used to. They had to build their own homes, grow their own food, and make their own furniture and clothing. Not everyone knew how to do this.

The Pilgrims and the Wampanoag had a feast together that has become known as Thanksgiving.

182

Practice and Extend

INTEGRATE THE CURRICULUM

THEATER Direct children to reenact an event from this lesson. Point out that the picture on page 182 is a reenactment with actors playing the parts. Help groups choose an event and prepare actions and dialogue. Remind them that a reenactment is a skit that is very realistic. Encourage them to use simple props, scenery, and costumes to enhance their performance. **Perform a Skit**

REACH ALL LEARNERS

Leveled Practice Have children sequence lesson events.

Basic Create sentence pairs for children to sequence.

Proficient Direct children to draw three pictures with captions showing a sequence of events.

Advanced Ask children to imagine when Native Americans first met the settlers. Have them create and label drawings to show what occurred.

The settlers learned from the Native Americans where to hunt, fish, and gather food. They also learned how to grow new kinds of crops and build shelters. Native Americans helped the settlers survive in this new place.

Reading Check **How did Native Americans help the settlers?** They helped them get food and build shelters.

Summary Native Americans were the first people to live in North America. Settlers from other countries later started colonies here.

Review

❶ **What to Know** What do we know about the people who lived in North America long ago?

❷ **Vocabulary** How are Native Americans a part of America's **history**?

❸ **Activity** Draw a picture that shows one way Native Americans helped the early North American settlers.

❹ **Sequence** What happened after settlers arrived in North America?

183

LESSON 2 ■ **183**

OBJECTIVES

- Recognize that primary sources provide knowledge about people and history.

- Understand how Native Americans met their needs.

VOCABULARY

source p. 184

RESOURCES

Unit 4 Audiotext CD Collection; Primary Source Collection; Internet Resources

💡 Link to the Big Idea

History Remind children that Native Americans lived here long before settlers came. Explain that they had the same needs that we have today for food, shelter, and clothing.

Background Explain the difference between a primary source and secondary source.

- Artifacts, historic maps, photographs, and journals are primary sources since they are from a time in history.

- Newspaper articles and books are primary sources if the author was at the event or place. If not, they are secondary sources.

- Secondary sources can use other primary sources, such as photographs and interviews, for information.

Show children examples of primary and secondary sources, and have them differentiate between them.

Vocabulary Help Invite children to look at the caption for each primary source. Explain that the first words are names for Native American groups that lived in different areas of North America.

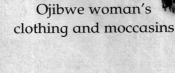

Look at Native American History

You can learn how Native Americans lived long ago from primary sources. A **source** is the place something comes from.

DBQ ❶ What do these things tell us about Native American culture?

Ojibwe woman's clothing and moccasins

Haida mask

Cherokee cane basket

184

Practice and Extend

BACKGROUND

More About Native American Moccasins The *Ojibwe* name, or *Chippewa*, is a native word meaning "to pucker." This refers to the bunched-up seam on their moccasins. Almost all Native Americans wore a form of moccasin of tanned leather sewn together like a slipper. Design variations made the moccasin distinctive for each group and appropriate to the weather, terrain, and animal resources. Cree women of Montana used caribou or moose hides rather than deer. Native Americans in the western plains or deserts made hardened rawhide soles to protect feet from sharp rocks or prickly cactus. The Inuit of the Arctic region adapted the moccasin as a boot, or *mukluk*, made of sealskin, fur, and reindeer skin. Moccasins were decorated with beads, quills, or paint, depending on available materials and their purpose.

DBQ ② How did Native Americans use resources to meet their needs?

Zuni Pueblo water jar

Delaware shelter

Chickasaw jewelry

✎ Write About It

What can primary sources tell you about history?

GO ONLINE
For more resources, go to
www.harcourtschool.com/ss1

185

Discuss the Primary Sources

Link History and Culture Invite children to look at each primary source and discuss how it was made and used. Explain that these artifacts might be thought of differently during different time periods. For example, today we might think the Delaware shelter was not strong because we are used to homes made of bricks and wood beams. After the discussion, have children answer the questions.

DBQ Document-Based Question—Answers

1. These things tell us that their culture included ceremonies. They show how the Native Americans made practical things beautiful and decorative as well.

2. They used plants, animals, and clay from the land to create these artifacts.

Write About It

Tell children that they should use the primary sources, their answers to the questions, and their knowledge of social studies to help them write their paragraphs.

Research Ask children to research additional primary sources, such as photographs or interviews, about Native Americans. Then have children select one or more of the primary sources and write a brief description telling what it is; who used it; where, when, and why it was used; and what it tells about the time period and tribe.

GO ONLINE **INTERNET RESOURCES**
For more resources, go to
www.harcourtschool.com/ss1

REACH ALL LEARNERS

Advanced Have children work in pairs to present a brief oral report about a Native American group from their region. Help children research information about artifacts and history online and in book sources. Remind children to notice primary and secondary sources. Guide them to prepare note cards to organize their information. After they have rehearsed, ask partners to share their report with the class.

INTEGRATE THE CURRICULUM

VISUAL ARTS Direct children to create a model of a particular Native American shelter. Help children research various types of dwellings such as hogans (Navajo), plank houses (Northwest tribes), pueblos (Southwest), long-houses (Northeast), or wickiups (Great Basin). Provide children with craft materials. Have children label the model and write a short description to accompany it. **Make a Model**

OBJECTIVES

- **Understand events in early American history.**
- **Identify important people related to our country's independence.**

VOCABULARY

freedom p. 186

independence p. 187

 Focus Skill

SEQUENCE

pp. 156–157, 189, 191

RESOURCES

Homework and Practice Book, p. 35; Reading Support and Intervention, pp. 62–65; Success for English Learners, pp. 65–68; Vocabulary Transparency 4-3; Focus Skills Transparency 4; Sequence Graphic Organizer Write-On/Wipe-Off Card; Unit 4 Audiotext CD Collection; Internet Resources

1 Introduce

What to Know Invite a child to read the What to Know question. Suggest that several events led to independence. As children read the lesson, have them look for answers to the question.

Build Background Have children discuss choices they make for themselves, such as choosing their clothes or games they would like to play. Invite them to share some other things they would like to do on their own when they are older.

Lesson 3 Independence

 What to Know
How did our country get its independence?

Vocabulary
freedom
independence

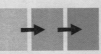 **Focus Skill** Sequence

The people living in the thirteen English colonies had to obey the laws made by England's king. They thought that some of the king's laws were unfair.

King George III

The people of the colonies wanted the freedom to make their own laws. **Freedom** is the right of people to make their own choices.

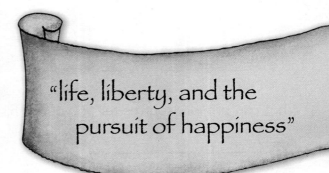

"life, liberty, and the pursuit of happiness"

186

Practice and Extend

Express Path

When minutes count, look for the **EXPRESS PATH** to focus on the lesson's main ideas.

Quick Summary

This lesson discusses the reasons and events that led to the forming of the United States of America. It describes the conflicts between England and the colonists, the signing of the Declaration of Independence, and some significant people during this time.

First Steps to Freedom

The leaders of the colonies decided to form their own country. First, they had a meeting. Then the Declaration of Independence was written. The leaders agreed to it on July 4, 1776.

Independence is the freedom of people to choose their own government. The Declaration of Independence said why the colonies should be free. It said that they were now states of a new country, the United States of America.

Reading Check **What happened on July 4, 1776?**
Leaders agreed to the Declaration of Independence.

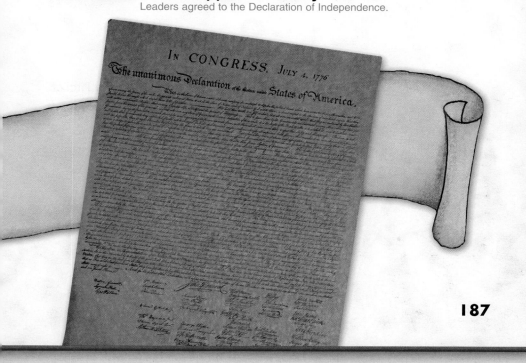

IN CONGRESS, JULY 4, 1776

The unanimous Declaration of the thirteen united States of America.

187

First Steps to Freedom

CONTENT FOCUS The Declaration of Independence gave reasons why the colonies wanted independence.

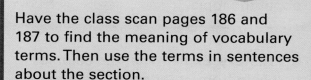
Express Path

Have the class scan pages 186 and 187 to find the meaning of vocabulary terms. Then use the terms in sentences about the section.

1 **History** Explain that some laws seemed unfair to the colonists, such as a tax on newspapers and other paper goods. The colonists could not vote on these laws. Point out that some colonists remained loyal to the King and wanted to follow his laws.

2 **Civics and Government** Point out that a country may have independence from the rule of another country, but not have the same kind of government or personal freedoms that we enjoy. Other countries around the world are independent, but do not have a democracy.

VOCABULARY

Vocabulary Transparency 4-3

MINI-GLOSSARY Read each term, and study its definition.

freedom The right of people to make their own choices. p. 186
independence The freedom of people to choose their own government. p. 187

WORD WORK Complete the activities below.

1. **freedom**
ROOT WORDS Find the root word in freedom.
free

2. **freedom**
CONTEXT CLUES Use the word freedom in a sentence that shows its meaning.
Possible answer: I have the freedom to decide which sport to play.

3. **independence**
PREFIXES/SUFFIXES What is the prefix in independence? What is the suffix?
(in)depend(ence)

TRANSPARENCY 4-3

READING SUPPORT/ INTERVENTION

For alternate teaching strategies, use pages 62–65 of Reading Support and Intervention to:

■ identify **phonemes**

■ practice **phonics**

■ reinforce **vocabulary**

■ build **text comprehension**

■ build **fluency**

Reading Support and Intervention

Reading Support ▶ and Intervention

ELL ENGLISH LANGUAGE LEARNERS

For English Language Learners strategies to support this lesson, see Success for English Learners pages 65–68.

■ English-language development activities

■ background and concepts

■ vocabulary extension

Success for English Learners

Success for ▶ English Learners

A War for Freedom

CONTENT FOCUS The colonies fought the American Revolution to gain their freedom from England.

Express Path

Have children study the illustrations and map and explain what they tell about the topic.

❸ History Explain that the colonies had help from other countries during the war, including France who provided supplies, soldiers, and money.

❹ Visual Literacy: Pictures Have children look at the pictures on page 188. Share with children that Peter Salem was an African American who had been a slave. He was freed, and then he joined the army and fought bravely to defend his new country. Explain that Molly Pitcher, whose real name was Mary Hays McCauly, brought pitchers of cool water to the men fighting. She even took over working a large gun. Point out that it was very rare for a woman to fight in a battle.

Q What are some words that describe Molly Pitcher and Peter Salem?

A brave, determined, smart, strong

A War for Freedom

❸ The king of England sent soldiers to fight against the people who wanted to be free. This war was called the American Revolution. Many brave people helped the colonies fight to become a free country.

Peter Salem helped win a battle in the war.

Women like Molly Pitcher helped win the war.

188

Practice and Extend

The war lasted for seven years. Finally, the colonies won. They were no longer ruled by England. The thirteen colonies were the first thirteen states of a free United States of America.

5

Reading Check **Sequence**

What did the king of England do after he read the Declaration of Independence? The king of England sent soldiers to fight against the people who wanted to be free.

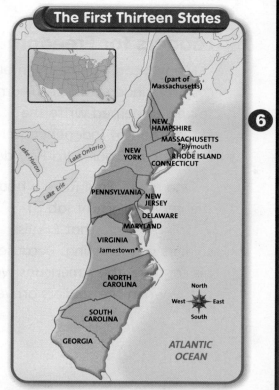

The First Thirteen States

(part of Massachusetts)

NEW HAMPSHIRE
MASSACHUSETTS
*Plymouth
NEW YORK
RHODE ISLAND
CONNECTICUT
PENNSYLVANIA
NEW JERSEY
DELAWARE
MARYLAND
VIRGINIA
Jamestown*
NORTH CAROLINA
SOUTH CAROLINA
GEORGIA

Lake Huron
Lake Ontario
Lake Erie

ATLANTIC OCEAN

North
West East
South

MAP SKILL How many states did the United States have when it became a free country?

6

5 **History** Explain that we are a result of our past, and that current events can be related to past events. Point out that wars for independence are fought today in other places around the world. Explain that it is helpful to study the American Revolution to understand current wars and conflicts.

Q **How do the events of the American Revolution affect us today?**

A We are able to live in a free United States and enjoy many rights. We can also learn from the American Revolution how to better solve problems and create change today.

6 **Visual Literacy: Map** Invite children to locate and name each of the thirteen colonies on the map. Explain that the inset map helps them understand where these colonies are located in comparison to the rest of the United States today.

CAPTION ANSWER: thirteen

Leaders for Freedom

CONTENT FOCUS Thomas Jefferson, Paul Revere, and George Washington helped our country become independent.

Express Path

Direct children to the pictures. Use the pictures as a springboard to discuss the main idea of the section.

7 Link History and Civics Invite children to compare the pictures and information about Thomas Jefferson and George Washington. Point out that both men served as President. Jefferson wrote many articles and books about freedom and democracy throughout his life. George Washington led troops in battles other than the American Revolution. We admire both men for their leadership qualities.

8 Visual Literacy: Picture Guide children to study the painting of Paul Revere's ride. Explain that this is an artist's idea of what took place. Point out that there were actually two other riders who rode with him. Revere is the best remembered because he was the subject of a famous poem. Discuss the character traits we connect with Revere. (bravery, courage)

Q What might have happened if Paul Revere and the others did not give the warning in time?

A English soldiers might have won the battle because the Americans would not have been ready to fight.

Leaders for Freedom

Many people helped win our country's independence. Thomas Jefferson helped write the Declaration of Independence. He later became our third President.

One night, Paul Revere had the very important job of warning people that English soldiers were coming. Because of his courage, the Americans were ready when the soldiers arrived.

7

Thomas Jefferson

8

Paul Revere

190

Practice and Extend

INTEGRATE THE CURRICULUM

READING/LANGUAGE ARTS Read aloud excerpts of *Paul Revere's Ride* by Henry Wadsworth Longfellow. Explain that poems are often written about famous people to tell of brave acts or special character traits. Have partners write a short poem describing a person from this lesson. Encourage them to use a variety of describing words. Invite children to share their poem to the class. **Write a Poem**

REACH ALL LEARNERS

Leveled Practice Discuss events that led to independence in our country.

Basic Ask children to describe what is happening in the pictures on pages 188 and 190.

Proficient Invite children to create a word web about *independence* from this lesson.

Advanced Invite children to write descriptive captions for each picture in the lesson.

During the American Revolution, George Washington led the army. People trusted him because they knew he was a good leader. After the war, he became our country's first President.

Reading Check **Who was the first President of the United States?**
George Washington was the first President of the United States.

Summary People in the colonies fought a war for independence from England. They won, and the colonies became a free country.

George Washington

Review

1. **What to Know** How did our country get its independence?

2. **Vocabulary** What is the Declaration of **Independence**?

3. ✎ **Write** Imagine that you are living in one of the new states. Tell about the events that led to independence in the order in which they happened.

4. **Sequence** Which came first, the Declaration of Independence or the end of the American Revolution?

191

Chart and Graph Skills

OBJECTIVES

■ Read a time line.

■ Place important events on a time line and describe their order.

VOCABULARY

time line p. 192

RESOURCES

Homework and Practice Book, p. 36;
Social Studies Skills Transparency 4-2;
Activity Pattern A9; TimeLinks;
Unit 4 Audiotext CD Collection;
Internet Resources

1 Introduce

Invite children to share important events from their lives. Provide children with a copy of Activity Pattern A9. Ask them to create a storyboard about themselves.

• Have children choose three events from their lives.

• Have them draw a picture of each event in the boxes in the order in which they happened.

• Ask children to write a date for each picture and a short sentence that describes the event.

Display the completed storyboards. Have children ask and answer questions related to the dates of the events on their storyboards.

Why It Matters Explain that a time line helps us to organize and remember information. A time line makes it easy to see the time order in which things happen. We can use a time line to compare the dates of different events and tell the amount of time that falls between two dates.

Read a Time Line

Why It Matters A **time line** shows important events in the order in which they happened.

Learn

You read a time line from left to right. The earliest events are on the left. A time line can show a long time or a short time. This one shows 15 years.

1

1775　　　　　　　　　**1780**

1776 The Declaration of Independence is written.

1781 The last big battle of the American Revolution is fought.

192

Practice and Extend

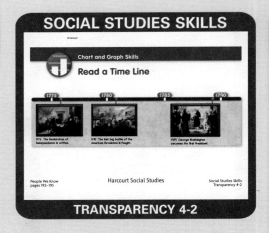

SOCIAL STUDIES SKILLS

Chart and Graph Skills
Read a Time Line

1775　　**1780**　　**1785**　　**1790**

1776 The Declaration of Independence is written.

1781 The last big battle of the American Revolution is fought.

1789 George Washington becomes the first President.

People We Know pages 192–193　　　Harcourt Social Studies　　　Social Studies Skills Transparency 4-2

TRANSPARENCY 4-2

REACH ALL LEARNERS

Leveled Practice Have children practice using a time line.

Basic Cut out and label pictures. Have children place the pictures on the time line.

Proficient Have children ask and answer questions about the events in the time line and about their order.

Advanced Ask children to research and label additional events to add to the time line.

❷ Practice

❶ When was the last big battle of the war?

❷ Did George Washington become President before or after the Declaration of Independence was written?

Apply

Make It Relevant Make a time line of important events in your life.

For online activities, go to
www.harcourtschool.com/ss1

1785   **1790**

1789 George Washington becomes the first President.

193

2 Teach

Learn

❶ **Visual Literacy: Time Line** Ask children to define *time* and *line*. Put their definitions together to explain the meaning of *time line*. Have children follow along as you read aloud the time line on pages 192 and 193. Have them find the earliest date on the left and say the years as they trace the line to the right. Invite children to look at the pictures and captions to find out what the time line is about. Point out that a time line can also be organized by months, dates, or ages.

TIMELINKS: Interactive Time Line

Have children use the one-year TimeLinks: Interactive Time Line to show events in one year of their lives.

❷ Practice

1. The last big battle was in 1781.
2. George Washington became President after the Declaration was written.

3 Close

Apply

Make It Relevant Children should create a time line that shows important events in their lives in sequential order. They can label the time line with the year or date, or they can tell what their age was at the time of each event.

INTERNET RESOURCES

For online activities, go to
www.harcourtschool.com/ss1

READING SOCIAL STUDIES

Focus Skill

Sequence Have children use information in the time line on pages 192 and 193 and retell the time line's events using sequence words such as *first*, *next*, and *last*.

READING TRANSPARENCY

Use FOCUS SKILLS Transparency 4.

Graphic Organizer Write-On/Wipe-Off Cards available

HOMEWORK AND PRACTICE

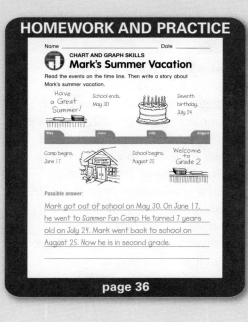

Name _____ Date _____

CHART AND GRAPH SKILLS
Mark's Summer Vacation

Read the events on the time line. Then write a story about Mark's summer vacation.

Have a Great Summer!   School ends. May 30   Seventh birthday, July 24

May   June   July   August

Camp begins, June 17   School begins, August 25   Welcome to Grade 2

Possible answer:

Mark got out of school on May 30. On June 17, he went to Summer Fun Camp. He turned 7 years old on July 24. Mark went back to school on August 25. Now he is in second grade.

page 36

Link to the Big Idea

History Point out that the struggle for the right to vote is an important part of our country's history.

Vocabulary Help Have children recall the meaning of freedom. Invite children to think of other freedoms we enjoy in our country today.

Focus On: Civic Participation

Visual Literacy: Pictures Have children describe how each photograph relates to voting.

Q Why is it helpful for children to go with their parents to vote?

A Possible answers: They can see how the voting machine works; they can ask questions and watch as their parents make choices.

Citizenship

Getting Others to Vote

Long ago, citizens of our country worked hard to get their own government and freedoms. Today, it is important to use our freedom to vote by taking part in elections.

When you turn 18 years old, you will be able to vote in elections. However, many people do not take the time to vote. A group called "Take Your Kids to Vote" wants families to learn about voting together. They think children will be more likely to vote when they are older if they see their parents vote first.

This boy watches as his father uses a voting machine.

194

Practice and Extend

Long ago, our country's leaders stood up for what they believed in. Today, people can help make changes in our country by voting. "Take Your Kids to Vote" has activities and ideas for parents and children. These help children know they can make a difference by voting when they are older.

Make It Relevant Why is it important for families to talk about voting?

Good citizens make every vote count!

195

History Point out that when American citizens long ago won their independence from Great Britain, only white male landowners over the age of 21 could vote. Over time, all qualified adult citizens were given the right to vote.

Q Why is it important to vote?

A By voting, we show our government leaders what we want them to do. Voting is an important freedom that not all citizens of other countries have.

Q Who can vote today?

A Anyone over the age of 18 has the right to vote. Citizens must register to vote before an election.

Make It Relevant

Read the question aloud to children. Encourage children to tell why they think it is important for families to talk about voting. Explain that if parents talk about voting, their children are more likely to vote when they are older.

REACH ALL LEARNERS

Leveled Practice Have children interpret the picture on page 194.

Basic Ask children to discuss what the father and son might be saying to each other.

Proficient Have children write a brief dialogue that might be occurring between the father and son.

Advanced Encourage children to work with a partner to act out a brief scene between the father and son.

INTEGRATE THE CURRICULUM

MATHEMATICS Have children poll their classmates. Have them ask: *Would you like to go with a parent to vote?* Ask children to divide a piece of paper into two columns, *Yes* and *No.* Children can record a tally mark for each classmate's response. Then ask children to add their results and share them with a partner.

Tally a Vote

Lesson 4

OBJECTIVES

- Identify symbols and landmarks of our country's heritage.

- Describe how landmarks honor our country's history and ideals.

VOCABULARY

heritage p. 196   **memorial** p. 198

landmark p. 197

SEQUENCE

pp. 156–157, 199

RESOURCES

Homework and Practice Book, p. 37; Reading Support and Intervention, pp. 66–69; Success for English Learners, pp. 69–72; Vocabulary Transparency 4-4; Focus Skills Transparency 4; Sequence Graphic Organizer Write-On/Wipe-Off Card; Unit 4 Audiotext CD Collection; Internet Resources

1 Introduce

What to Know Have a volunteer read the What to Know question. Explain that America's heritage goes back to when the country first began. Remind children to look for answers to the question as they read the lesson.

Build Background Ask children to share stories of family members who lived long ago. Talk about traditions that are handed down from one generation to the next, such as a great-grandmother's special cookie recipe or a game still played by family members today.

Lesson 4 American Heritage

 What to Know
How do we honor our American heritage?

Vocabulary
heritage
landmark
memorial

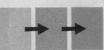 Sequence

1

Symbols of Our Country

The bald eagle is a symbol of our heritage. Heritage is the traditions and values passed on by the people who lived before us. Our national bird reminds us of our freedom.

The stars and stripes on our flag are symbols, too. They stand for the people of the colonies who worked together to form the United States.

2

196

Practice and Extend

Express Path

When minutes count, look for the **EXPRESS PATH** to focus on the lesson's main ideas.

Quick Summary

This lesson explains how symbols, landmarks, and memorials demonstrate the heritage of our country. Symbols include the bald eagle, the American flag, and the Statue of Liberty. The Washington Monument and the Jefferson Memorial are symbols as well.

The Constitution was written when our government was formed. It lists the rights of all citizens. It is a symbol that reminds us of our freedoms.

The Statue of Liberty is a symbol of freedom for people who come to our country. It is a symbol that is also a landmark. A landmark is a feature that makes a location special.

The Statue of Liberty

Visitors can see the Constitution in Washington, D.C.

Reading Check **What are some of the symbols of our heritage?** The bald eagle, our flag, the Constitution, and Statue of Liberty are symbols of our heritage.

197

2 Teach

Symbols of Our Country

CONTENT FOCUS Symbols represent the values and traditions of our country's heritage.

Express Path

Have pairs of children work together to find answers to the Reading Check question.

1 History Explain to children that a symbol can be something real that reminds us of things we cannot see, for example, a heart is a symbol for love.

Q How is the bald eagle a symbol for freedom?

A It flies free, strong, and soars high above, representing the freedoms we have as Americans.

2 Link History and Culture Point out that a flag is a patriotic symbol, and the Pledge of Allegiance is a symbol of our loyalty to our country. Have children recite the Pledge and discuss how it connects to the national flag and our country. Display the children's state flag. Share a state song, poem, or motto and discuss its meaning.

VOCABULARY

Vocabulary Transparency 4-4

MINI-GLOSSARY Read each term, and study its definition.

heritage The traditions and values passed on by the people who lived before us. p. 196
landmark A feature that makes a location special. p. 197
memorial Something people create to remember a person or an event. p. 198

WORD WORK Complete the activities below.

1. **heritage**
RELATED WORDS How are heritage and tradition related?
Traditions are part of heritage.

2. **landmark**
STRUCTURAL CLUES How can knowing the meanings of land and mark help you remember the meaning of landmark?
The two word parts help me remember that a landmark is a mark on a place, or piece of land.

3. **memorial**
ROOT WORDS What is the root word of memorial?
memory

TRANSPARENCY 4-4

READING SUPPORT/ INTERVENTION

For alternate teaching strategies, use pages 66–69 of Reading Support and Intervention to:

- identify **phonemes**
- practice **phonics**
- reinforce **vocabulary**
- build **text comprehension**
- build **fluency**

Reading Support ▶ and Intervention

ELL ENGLISH LANGUAGE LEARNERS

For English Language Learners strategies to support this lesson, see Success for English Learners pages 69–72.

- English-language development activities
- background and concepts
- vocabulary extension

Success for ▶ English Learners

Memorials and Monuments

CONTENT FOCUS Memorials and monuments honor people and events.

Express Path

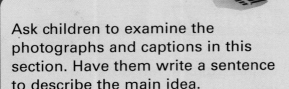

Ask children to examine the photographs and captions in this section. Have them write a sentence to describe the main idea.

3 **Civics and Government** Explain that the Declaration of Independence and the Constitution are written documents. Although both are symbols of the United States, the Constitution is a living document that is amended, or changed, to protect our rights in response to current issues.

4 **History** Play a recording of the Gettysburg Address. Explain that Lincoln gave this speech to dedicate a military cemetery, honoring soldiers who died fighting the Civil War. We remember this speech because it demonstrates Lincoln's contribution to our country during this difficult time. The speech is engraved on the south wall of the Lincoln Memorial.

History Point out that buildings, parks, streets, schools, and cities are named to honor people or events. Discuss examples of these and other memorials and landmarks found in the children's state. Help children understand how each honors an important person or event.

Q What events or individuals have you seen honored in your community?

A Answers will vary.

Memorials and Monuments

Some symbols of our country are also memorials. A memorial is something people create to remember a person or an event. When we look at the Washington Monument, we remember George Washington and all that he did for our country. The Jefferson Memorial honors Thomas Jefferson, who helped write the Declaration of Independence. **3**

The Washington Monument

The Jefferson Memorial

198

Practice and Extend

BACKGROUND

American Flag Since 1776, many flags symbolized the United States. The first official flag, in 1777, had 13 stars, one for each colony. In 1818, a law passed to set 13 red and white stripes, for the colonies, and one star for each state. The 50th star, for Hawaii, was added in 1960. The colors represent American values: hardiness and valor (red), purity (white), vigilance, perseverance, and justice (blue).

REACH ALL LEARNERS

Leveled Practice Discuss memorials and monuments that are symbols.

Basic Invite children to give examples of memorials or monuments in this country.

Proficient Help children make a chart of memorials and monuments and what each symbolizes.

Advanced Ask children to compare and contrast the symbolism of two memorials or monuments.

The Lincoln Memorial honors President Abraham Lincoln. He kept our country together during the Civil War. This was a time when Americans fought one another.

4

The Lincoln Memorial

Reading Check **What symbol honors George Washington?** The Washington Monument honors George Washington.

Summary Symbols, landmarks, and memorials remind us of our American heritage.

Review

1. **What to Know** How do we honor our American heritage?

2. **Vocabulary** Why do you think it is important to remember our **heritage**?

3. **Activity** Draw a picture of a landmark or memorial you know about. Write a sentence to tell who or what it honors and why.

4. **Sequence** What did President Lincoln do before the Lincoln Memorial was built?

199

1 Introduce

What to Know Have children read the What to Know question. Explain to children that we honor people and events from long ago and also from more recent times. Remind children to look for answers to the question as they read the lesson.

Build Background Ask children to describe how they celebrate holidays and special occasions with their families. Discuss how details such as food, games, music, and guests are a part of these celebrations.

Lesson 5 Heroes and Holidays

 What to Know
How do we honor people and events in our country's history?

Vocabulary
hero
legend

 Sequence

Heroes make a difference in people's lives with their actions. A **hero** is a person who has done something brave or important.

Heroes in History

Harriet Tubman and Sojourner Truth were heroes when African Americans had few or no rights. Both worked for equal rights for women and African Americans.

Harriet Tubman

Sojourner Truth

200

Practice and Extend

Express Path

When minutes count, look for the **EXPRESS PATH** to focus on the lesson's main ideas.

Quick Summary

This lesson discusses heroes and significant events important to our country. We have many ways in which we honor and remember them, including holiday celebrations.

Some heroes are alive today. Neil Armstrong was the first person to walk on the moon. He is a hero because he explored space for our country.

 BOOK

The Story of JOHNNY APPLESEED
Written and illustrated by Aliki

Some heroes come from legends. A legend is a story passed down through history. The people in legends are heroes, but many of their actions are made up. John Henry, Johnny Appleseed, Betsy Ross, and Paul Bunyan are heroes from legends. The stories about them are part of our country's heritage.

BETSY ROSS
written and illustrated by Alexandra Wallner

Reading Check **Who is a hero that is still alive today?** Neil Armstrong is a hero who is still alive today.

201

Heroes in History

CONTENT FOCUS Heroes can be real people or characters from legends.

Express Path

Organize the class into groups. Have each group study a different paragraph and then share a summary of what they learned.

❶ History Explain that at one time people were brought here from Africa as slaves to work without pay. They were owned like property and had no choice about where or how they would live. Slavery became illegal when the Thirteenth Amendment was added to the Constitution in 1865.

❷ Link History and Culture Explain that John Chapman (Appleseed) and Betsy Ross were real people. Chapman shared apple seeds with others. Ross made a flag at George Washington's request. John Henry and Paul Bunyan are tall tale characters. Both were extremely big and strong, much more so than one could be in real life.

 BOOK **Interactive in the enhanced online student eBook**

VOCABULARY

Vocabulary Transparency 4-5

MINI-GLOSSARY Read each term, and study its definition.

hero A person who has done something brave or important. p. 200
legend A story passed down through history. p. 201

WORD WORK Complete the activities below.

1. **hero**
CATEGORIZE VOCABULARY Give an example of a hero. Explain your choice.
Possible answer: Firefighters are heroes. They have to be brave to put out fires.

2. **legend**
MULTIPLE MEANINGS/USE REFERENCE SOURCES Use your dictionary to find another meaning for legend.
The words written beneath or beside a map to explain it.

3. **hero, legend**
COMPARE AND CONTRAST A legend is a story. A hero is a person.

TRANSPARENCY 4-5

READING SUPPORT/ INTERVENTION

For alternate teaching strategies, use pages 70–73 of Reading Support and Intervention to:

- identify **phonemes**
- practice **phonics**
- reinforce **vocabulary**
- build **text comprehension**
- build **fluency**

Reading Support ▶ and Intervention

HARCOURT SOCIAL Studies People We Know
Reading Support and Intervention

ELL ENGLISH LANGUAGE LEARNERS

For English Language Learners strategies to support this lesson, see Success for English Learners pages 73–76.

- English-language development activities
- background and concepts
- vocabulary extension

Success for ▶ English Learners

HARCOURT SOCIAL Studies People We Know
Success for English Learners

Holidays and Celebrations

CONTENT FOCUS Holidays remind us of important people and events.

Express Path

Direct children to study the pictures and use them as a springboard to discuss the main idea.

③ History Tell children that George Washington was born on February 22, 1732, and Abraham Lincoln was born on February 12, 1809. Point out that, originally, only Washington's birthday was celebrated. Lincoln's birthday was added in 1865. In 1971, Washington's birthday celebration was switched to the third Monday of the month, which then became commonly known as Presidents' Day.

TIMELINKS: Interactive Time Line

Have children add Washington's and Lincoln's birthdates to the one-year TimeLinks: Interactive Time Line.

Holidays and Celebrations

The United States has many holidays, or days on which we celebrate or remember something. Some holidays help us remember our country's heroes. Other holidays help us remember important events.

Fast Fact!

September 17 is Constitution Day. This holiday honors the signing of our Constitution and reminds us of our freedoms.

③

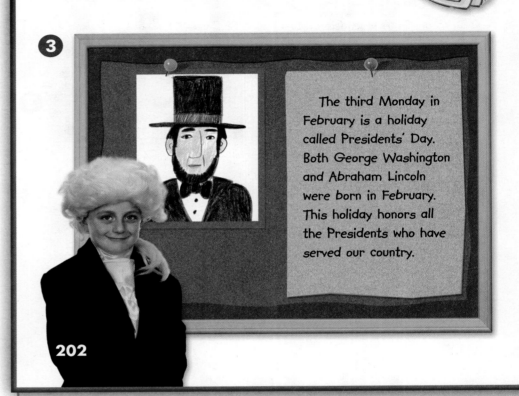

The third Monday in February is a holiday called Presidents' Day. Both George Washington and Abraham Lincoln were born in February. This holiday honors all the Presidents who have served our country.

202

Practice and Extend

INTEGRATE THE CURRICULUM

READING/LANGUAGE ARTS Have children distinguish legends (tall tales) from historical facts. Tell children the story of George Washington and the cherry tree and share factual details about his childhood. Ask them to make drawings for both stories and label each *legend* or *fact*. Explain that a legend is exaggerated and cannot be proven to be true, although a legend can be about a real person.

Provide other examples of legends for children to illustrate, such as Paul Bunyan eating forty bowls of porridge as a baby or John Henry hammering steel drills into rock faster than a machine can. **Recognize Legends**

INDEPENDENT READING

Suggest that children read *George Washington's Teeth* by Deborah Chandra and Madeleine Comora (Farrar, Straus and Giroux, 2003) and *A. Lincoln and Me* by Louise W. Borden (Scholastic, Inc., 2000). These books describe true life events based on historical fact in a poetic and artistic style.

We celebrate Memorial Day at the end of May. On this day we honor the men and women who gave their lives for our country.

The first Monday in September is Labor Day. Labor is work. On Labor Day, we honor all of the people who work in our country. Many people celebrate this day by spending time with their families.

203

Correct Misconceptions Children may be confused about different holidays that do not commemorate a national hero or a historical event. Explain that there are other types of holidays, such as religious ones (Christmas, Chanukah) and cultural ones (St. Patrick's Day, Valentine's Day). Also point out that there are local holidays and celebrations in their state, community, and school.

4 History Help children research information about a significant historical event that is celebrated in their state. Invite them to explain why this event is important. Discuss ways in which this holiday is celebrated, such as a special community program. Explain that heroes are not just people that lived long ago or are world famous.

- Share with children newspaper articles about modern-day heroes.
- Encourage children to talk about people they know who have done heroic things as well.
- Have each child choose a hero he or she knows to interview.
- Give each child a copy of Activity Pattern A10 to write his or her own front page about heroes.

5 **Link History and Culture** Provide children with pictures of patriotic holiday celebrations from sources such as the Internet, nonfiction books, and magazines. Discuss the activities shown in the pictures. Have children compare them with activities in their community during these holidays.

Children in History

The Centennial Celebration

6 Tell children that Thomas rode a train to Philadelphia for a two-day visit to the Centennial Exhibition. In his journal, he described many new and unusual sights, such as a famous living Civil War eagle named Old Abe who had witnessed 25 battles, and exhibits representing Germany, Russia, and Portugal. Frank kept a record of how much money he spent, including $5.00 for train tickets and money for ice cream he bought every day except Sunday. Point out that Frank even spent some time touring other areas of Philadelphia, including Benjamin Franklin's grave and Betsy Ross's house.

5

Independence Day is also known as the Fourth of July. On July 4, 1776, leaders of the thirteen colonies agreed to the Declaration of Independence. Communities celebrate this day with parades, speeches, and fireworks.

Reading Check **Focus Skill** **Sequence Which comes first during the year, Labor Day or Presidents' Day?** Presidents' Day comes first during the year.

204

Practice and Extend

MAKE IT RELEVANT

In Your Community Guide small groups to plan a holiday for their community. Have them research a famous person or event important to their community. Encourage them to name their holiday, and create a song, poem, or jingle to accompany it. Direct groups to plan activities, such as a ceremony, parade, or party. Allow groups to share and explain their holiday to the class.

REACH ALL LEARNERS

Leveled Practice Have children understand and explain holidays in this lesson.

Basic Ask children to name holidays related to the pictures on pages 202–204.

Proficient Invite children to explain why and how each holiday is celebrated.

Advanced Direct children to make a chart showing holidays that honor people or events.

Children in History

The Centennial Celebration

On July 4, 1876, our country was 100 years old. Seventeen-year-old Frank L. Thomas from New Jersey visited the Centennial Exhibition in Philadelphia, Pennsylvania. Frank kept a journal about what he saw. More than nine million visitors came to see what our country had done in its first hundred years.

A page from Frank's journal

Summary We honor people and events in history by having holidays to remember them.

Review

1. **What to Know** How do we honor people and events in our country's history?

2. **Vocabulary** What kind of story is a **legend**?

3. **Activity** Choose an American that you would like to honor with a special holiday. Draw a picture that shows how this holiday would be celebrated. Add a caption that explains your picture.

4. **Sequence** Which holiday do we celebrate on the first Monday in September?

205

---

3 Close

Summary

Ask children to read the summary and restate the main points in their own words.

- Heroes and legends are a part of our country's heritage.
- We remember heroes and special events in history when we celebrate holidays.

Assess

REVIEW—Answers

1. **What to Know** We remember the actions of our country's heroes. We have holidays that honor special people and events.

2. **Vocabulary** A **legend** is a story with made up people who do heroic things.

3. **Activity Assessment Guidelines** See Performance Rubric. This activity can be used with the Unit Project.

4. **Sequence** Labor Day

Use Focus Skills Transparency 4 or Sequence Graphic Organizer Write-On/Wipe-Off Card.

PERFORMANCE RUBRIC

Score 4
- clearly presents holiday information
- offers relevant details

Score 3
- presents holiday information
- offers somewhat relevant details

Score 2
- somewhat presents holiday information
- offers minimally relevant details

Score 1
- offers minimal holiday information
- includes no relevant details

HOMEWORK AND PRACTICE

Name _____ Date _____

My Hero

Complete the paragraph, and design a medal to honor the person.

If I could choose a special person to honor, I would choose
Answers will vary, but person should be a hero to the child. This

person is my ___hero___. I would choose this person because
Answer should include person's accomplishments.

We could honor this hero by _Answers might include having a parade, putting his or her picture on a stamp or coin, or naming a special day for him or her._

Design a medal for your hero.

page 38

MENTAL MAPPING

Follow a Route Ask children to plan a route that Frank's train might have traveled from New Jersey to Philadelphia, Pennsylvania. Have children study a map that includes both states. Direct them to draw an outline map, including landforms and bodies of water. Tell children to draw a path for the train on the map and write a list of geography that Frank might see as he traveled.

OBJECTIVES

- Distinguish between fact and fiction.
- Analyze details of factual and fictional accounts of history.

VOCABULARY

fact p. 206   **fiction** p. 206
nonfiction p. 206

RESOURCES

Homework and Practice Book, p. 39; Social Studies Skills Transparency 4-3; Unit 4 Audiotext CD Collection

Tell Fact from Fiction

Why It Matters   You need to be able to tell if what you read is true.

Learn

❶ A **fact** is a statement that can be proved true. **Nonfiction** books have only facts.

❷ **Fiction** stories may seem real, but some of the information is made up.

206

I Introduce

Write several simple statements on the board that describe things children have done in school. Some statements should be true facts, such as *Jan and Tom took a note to the office*. Some should be imaginary, such as *Six children rode tigers to school today*. Ask children to determine which statements are true and which could not have happened.

Why It Matters Explain that authors have many purposes for what they write. Some authors want to tell about facts that happened, so they write nonfiction. Others want to tell entertaining stories with make-believe parts, and they write fiction. Suggest that children will be better readers if they recognize what they read as fiction or nonfiction.

Practice and Extend

SOCIAL STUDIES SKILLS

Critical Thinking Skills

Tell Fact from Fiction

People We Know
pages 206–207   Harcourt Social Studies   Social Studies Skills
Transparency 4-3

TRANSPARENCY 4-3

INDEPENDENT READING

Suggest that children read the book *Betsy Ross and the Silver Thimble* by Stephanie Greene (Simon & Schuster Adult Publishing Group, 2002). In this book, stories are told of Betsy Ross' childhood. Have children identify parts of this book that make it fiction and parts that express the author's opinion.

② Practice

Look at the two books. Decide which one is fact and which one is fiction.

Apply

Make It Relevant Find a book in your library about a hero you would like to know more about. Will the book be fact or fiction?

207

HOMEWORK AND PRACTICE

page 39

2 ▸ Teach

Learn

① Visual Literacy: Pictures Have children look at the cover illustration of each book. Ask children what clues in the pictures can help them determine whether each book is nonfiction or fiction. Explain that an author's opinions may be expressed in each book. Even factual historical accounts are affected by people's perception and their view from a later time period.

② Practice

Children should look for key words, such as *biography*, *fiction*, or *tall tale* on the covers. Point out that illustrations can indicate fantasy elements in a fictional story. Detailed conversations from a person's childhood may also be fiction, made up to add to the story's excitement.

Ask children to tell if the book describes real events in a person's life. Invite them to recall any events or characters that seemed make-believe. Children should determine that *Lives and Times: Harriet Tubman* is fact and *Paul Bunyan and His Blue Ox* is fiction.

3 ▸ Close

Apply

Make It Relevant Discuss with children why a nonfiction book will give them more facts. Choosing a nonfiction book means they will not have to decide which parts are make-believe and which are real.

OBJECTIVES

■ Understand the importance of the actions and character of Dr. Martin Luther King, Jr., and explain how he made a difference in others' lives.

RESOURCES

Unit 4 Audiotext CD Collection; Multimedia Biographies CD; Internet Resources; TimeLinks

💡 Link to the Big Idea

History History teaches us how people and places change over time. Dr. Martin Luther King, Jr., has been honored with a national holiday for his efforts to get equal rights for all people. Have children explore how their state observes this day.

Discuss the Biography

Primary Source: Picture Explain that the photograph on page 209 shows Dr. King addressing people about the need for equal rights. His speeches brought some of the largest crowds in history.

Civics and Government Explain that some people have peacefully broken unfair laws in order to change those laws.

Q What are some other ways that responsible people can help change unfair laws?

A by voting; by contacting the people in government; by speaking out about the things that are unfair

Biography

Trustworthiness
Respect
Responsibility
Fairness
Caring
Patriotism

Dr. Martin Luther King, Jr.

Why Character Counts

✎ How did Dr. Martin Luther King, Jr., show responsibility?

Growing up, Martin Luther King, Jr., was not allowed to eat at certain restaurants. He also had to sit at the back of a bus. This was because of the color of his skin. Martin Luther King, Jr., took the responsibility of leading people to change these rules.

Dr. Martin Luther King, Jr., worked for equal rights.

208

Practice and Extend

BACKGROUND

Dr. Martin Luther King, Jr.
Dr. King was an ordained Baptist minister. He was a central figure in the Civil Rights movement and helped organize the bus boycott in Montgomery, Alabama. He believed in the principle of civil disobedience as a way to bring about change. The Voting Rights Act of 1965 was a result of his march from Selma to Montgomery. Dr. King was awarded the Nobel Peace Prize in 1964.

INDEPENDENT READING

Encourage children to read the biography *Happy Birthday, Martin Luther King*, written by Jean Marzullo and illustrated by J. Brian Pinckney (Scholastic, 1993). This book depicts the life of Dr. Martin Luther King, Jr., both as a young person and as an adult.

Dr. King led many people in the fight for equal rights for African Americans.

It was important to Dr. King to find peaceful ways to solve problems. He led marches to spread his message. Dr. King said, "Our lives begin to end the day we become silent about things that matter."

Dr. King was a hero whose work made a difference in our country. In 1964, a new law was made. It said that people cannot be separated or given fewer rights because of the color of their skin. Today, Dr. Martin Luther King, Jr., is honored on a national holiday in January.

GO ONLINE
For more resources, go to
www.harcourtschool.com/ss1

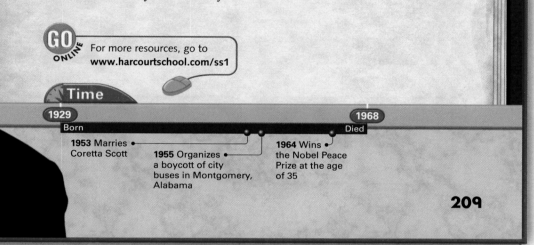

Time

1929 **Born**

1953 Marries Coretta Scott

1955 Organizes a boycott of city buses in Montgomery, Alabama

1964 Wins the Nobel Peace Prize at the age of 35

1968 **Died**

209

💡 Link to the Big Idea

History Remind children that history is the story of how people and places change over time. Tell children that every place has its own history and that each one is different.

Preview the Games

Holiday Mix-Up In this game, children are to look at each row of pictures and determine which picture does not belong. Children will need to identify the national holidays each row represents to find the picture that does not fit. Prompt children with questions such as:

Q Which holidays are being shown in each row?

A Presidents' Day; Independence Day; Labor Day

Q How do you know?

A I see government buildings and a President; I see fireworks, the United States flag, and a parade; I see people doing their jobs and relaxing and eating.

ANSWERS: Betsy Ross does not belong with Presidents' Day; The pilgrim does not belong with Independence Day; The Constitution does not belong with Labor Day

Word Fun Each question in this game is a word brainteaser in which children must use the alphabet to solve puzzles. Children should look at each word carefully to answer the questions.

ANSWERS: the letter *t*; the letter *z*; the word *leg* has to do with the legs of a table and appears in the word *legend*

RIDDLE ANSWER: in a colony

Find the picture that does not belong in each row.

1

2

3

210

Practice and Extend

INTEGRATE THE CURRICULUM

✏️ READING/LANGUAGE ARTS Have children review the riddle in the Word Fun game. Invite them to imagine what life must have been like for the colonists who came from Europe. Remind them that the colonists were coming to a new place they did not know. Ask children to write a story of what the colonists may have encountered when they arrived in the New World. **Write a Story**

ELL ENGLISH LANGUAGE LEARNERS

Help children with difficult language and concepts.

Beginning Write the definition of the word *hero* on the board and have children study it.

Intermediate Have children draw pictures of what they think of when they see the word *hero*.

Advanced Ask children to write about one of their heroes.

Word Fun

Answer the questions.

Which letter do the words past, present, and future have in common?

Which letter of the alphabet can replace the h in hero and turn it into a number?

What does a table have that is in the word legend?

Answer the riddle.

Where do both settlers and ants live?

Online Adventures

GO ONLINE

Join Eco on a trip to a history museum. You will go on a roller coaster ride through the past and the present. Play now, at www.harcourtschool.com/ss1

211

Online Adventures Before children begin playing, explain that the game is set in a museum, so they will need to know the difference between past and present. Review ways in which people and places change over time. Tell children that Help Buttons in the game will refer them to pages in their textbook if they need additional information.

GO ONLINE — INTERNET RESOURCES

For more resources, go to
www.harcourtschool.com/ss1

Share the Fun

At School Have children work in small groups to create their own Word Fun games. Help them create a game similar to this activity based on the unit vocabulary words. When children are finished, ask them to share their games with their classmates.

At Home Invite children to have their parents or guardians help them come up with other images for the Holiday Mix-Up game. Ask children to think about what those images mean and to draw some of the images. Have children share their drawings with classmates.

The Big Idea

History Ask a volunteer to read aloud the Big Idea. Invite children to share something they learned about how some things change and some things stay the same throughout history.

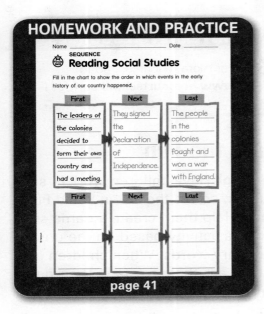

page 41

Reading Social Studies

 Sequence You may wish to have children review Reading Social Studies at the beginning of the unit. Charts should show events chronologically. Remind children that clue words such as *first*, *next*, and *last* signal the order in which things happen.

Unit 4

Review and Test Prep

 The Big Idea

History History is the story of how people and places change over time.

Sequence

Copy and fill in the chart to show what you have learned about the history of our country's independence.

First
The leaders of the colonies decided to form their own country and had a meeting.

Next
_____
_____

Last
_____
_____

✓ Vocabulary

Match the word to its meaning.

❶ the freedom of people to choose their own government

❷ a feature that makes a location special

❸ what happens when something becomes different

❹ the study of things in the past

❺ a place that is ruled by another country

Word Bank

change
(p. 174)
history
(p. 178)
colony
(p. 180)
independence
(p. 187)
landmark
(p. 197)

✓ Facts and Main Ideas

❻ How do communities change over time?

❼ Who were the first people to live in North America?

❽ How did Thomas Jefferson help our country?

❾ Which of these shows important events in the order in which they happened?

A picture graph   **C** family tree

B diagram   **D** time line

❿ Which holiday honors people who gave their lives for our country?

A Presidents' Day   **C** Memorial Day

B Labor Day   **D** Independence Day

213

Vocabulary

1. independence

2. landmark

3. change

4. history

5. colony

Facts and Main Ideas

6. New houses and roads are built; Technology changes how we live; People move into a community.

7. Native Americans were the first people to live in North America.

8. He wrote the Declaration of Independence.

9. D, time line

10. C, Memorial Day

Critical Thinking

11. Possible answers: Knowing what has happened in the past helps us make choices about the future. We can remember what works and doesn't work when we try to solve problems.

12. Make It Relevant Possible answers: I know why we have certain holidays or honor people with monuments. I can understand why people made the choices they did.

Skills

13. 2000

14. 2005

15. after

16. 2007

Critical Thinking

⓫ How does learning about the past help us in the future?

⓬ **Make It Relevant** How has learning about people in history made a difference in your life?

Skills

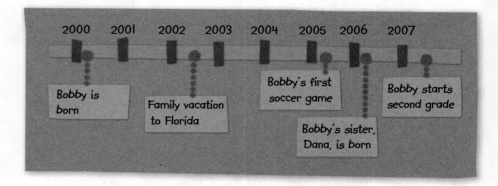

⓭ In what year was Bobby born?

⓮ When was Bobby's first soccer game?

⓯ Was Dana born before or after the family vacation?

⓰ When did Bobby start second grade?

214

⑰ Which book do you think is fiction?

⑱ What clues lead you to believe that it is fiction?

⑲ What is the title of the nonfiction book?

⑳ Which book do you think would have more facts about Rosa Parks? Why?

215

Skills

17. If a Bus Could Talk

18. Buses can't really talk; the face in the picture on the book looks make-believe.

19. Rosa Parks

20. The nonfiction book, because nonfiction has facts instead of made up parts.

ASSESSMENT

Use the UNIT 4 Test on pages 30–32 of the Assessment Program.

Show What You Know

Unit Writing Activity

 All About You Discuss with children important events in their lives such as birthdays, first days, or special vacations and list ideas on the board. Then have children think about events in their own lives from long ago to present day they would like to share.

Write a Narrative Paragraph Have children use their ideas to write a narrative paragraph about their lives. Remind them to write about the events in order. Suggest they include details that help the reader understand why each event was memorable.

You may wish to distribute the Unit 4 Writing Activity Guidelines on page 33 of the Assessment Program.

For a scoring rubric, see this Teacher Edition, page 153O.

Unit Project

Historical Journal Before children begin, help them recall events in this unit. Divide the class into groups and explain that each member will write one journal entry. Explain that they do not have to choose a famous person, but can write from the point of view of a child or adult that lived during a particular time or witnessed a certain event. Tell groups to place their completed entries in order. Display the historic journals for others to enjoy.

You may wish to distribute the Unit 4 Project Guidelines on page 35 of the Assessment Program.

For a scoring rubric, see this Teacher Edition, page 153O.

> **LEVELED READERS**
>
> Use the LEVELED READERS for Unit 4.

Show What You Know

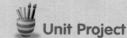

Unit Writing Activity

All About You Think about your past and present. What events do you want to share?

Write a Narrative Paragraph Write a paragraph about the events. Put them in sequence.

Unit Project

Historical Journal Create a journal with entries by people in history.

- Pick a person and write a journal entry from his or her point of view.
- Put the entries in order.

Read More

The Pledge of Allegiance: Symbols of Freedom by Lola Schaefer

If You Were at the First Thanksgiving by Anne Kamma

Judy Moody Declares Independence by Megan McDonald

 For more resources, go to www.harcourtschool.com/ss1

216

Read More

Encourage independent reading after the children's study of history with these books or books of your choice. Additional books are listed on page 153J of this Teacher Edition.

Basic *The Pledge of Allegiance: Symbols of Freedom* by Lola Schaefer (Heinemann/Raintree, 2002). Children learn details about the Pledge of Allegiance.

Proficient *If You Were at the First Thanksgiving* by Anne Kamma (Scholastic, 2001). This book answers questions about the first Thanksgiving and this land in the 1620s.

Advanced *Judy Moody Declares Independence* by Megan McDonald (Candlewick Press, 2005). Judy Moody makes her own Declaration of Independence after learning about the American Revolution during a family vacation.

A World of Many People

The Big Idea

Culture

Our country is made up of many different people and cultures.

What to Know

✓ What is culture?

✓ Why is the United States a country of many cultures?

✓ How are families different? How are they alike?

✓ Who are some Americans who have made a difference in our lives?

Introduce the Unit

The Big Idea

Culture Read the Big Idea to children. Explain that many different people and cultures are a part of our country. In this unit, children will learn about different world cultures and how groups share their traditions and customs with others. Remind children to refer back to the Big Idea periodically as they finish this unit.

What to Know Have children read What to Know. Explain that these four essential questions will help them focus on the Big Idea.

Assessing the Big Idea Share with children that throughout this unit they will be asked to show evidence of their understanding of the Big Idea. See Assessment Options on page 217M of this Teacher Edition.

START WITH A VIDEO DVD

To introduce the Unit Big Idea to students, show a video clip from the Start with a Video DVD.

Instruction Design

The flowchart below shows briefly how instruction was planned for Unit 5.

START WITH THE BIG IDEA

Lesson Objectives
What to Know

PLAN ASSESSMENT

Assessment Options
• Option 1—Unit 5 Test
• Option 2—Writing: Write a Diary Entry
• Option 3—Unit Project: Family History Storyboard

PLAN INSTRUCTION

Unit 5 Teacher Edition
• materials
• instructional strategies
• activities

A World of Many People

THE BIG IDEA

CULTURE Our country is made up of many different people and cultures.

Express Path

See each lesson for an **EXPRESS PATH** to teach main ideas.

LESSON	PACING	OBJECTIVES
Introduce the Unit pp. 217V–217 **Preview Vocabulary** pp. 218–219	**5 DAYS**	■ Use visuals to determine word meanings. ■ Use words and visuals to preview the content of the unit.
Reading Social Studies pp. 220–221		■ Recall information from a text in a logical sequence. ■ Retell information in your own words. ■ Interpret information from charts.
Start with a Song "What a Wonderful World" pp. 222–225		■ Identify selected songs related to ethnic and cultural similarities and differences. ■ Recognize the forms of diversity in the school and community.
① World Cultures pp. 226–231 🔍 **WHAT TO KNOW** What is culture?	**4 DAYS**	■ Describe cultures from around the world. ■ Identify the features of a culture, including dress, art, language, food, music, and beliefs. ■ Compare and contrast cultures.
MAP AND GLOBE SKILLS **Find Locations on a World Map** pp. 232–233	**1 DAY**	■ Find locations of countries in different hemispheres on a world map or globe. ■ Identify hemispheres, the equator, and poles.
Primary Sources: Learning About Cultures pp. 234–235	**1 DAY**	■ Understand that culture can be demonstrated through a variety of primary sources. ■ Examine cultural items from around the world.

6 WEEKS	WEEK 1	WEEK 2	WEEK 3	WEEK 4	WEEK 5	WEEK 6
	Introduce the Unit	Lesson 1	Lesson 2	Lesson 3	Lesson 4	Wrap Up the Unit

READING SUPPORT VOCABULARY

Reading Social Studies
Recall and Retell

Reading Social Studies
Focus Skill, pp. 220–221

Vocabulary Power:
Make a Vocabulary Chart, p. 219
Adjectives, p. 222

recall p. 220
retell p. 220

Reading Social Studies
Recall and Retell, p. 231

culture p. 226
language p. 227

REACH ALL LEARNERS

ENGLISH LANGUAGE LEARNERS, pp. 217, 218

Leveled Practice, pp. 221, 224

ENGLISH LANGUAGE LEARNERS, p. 235

Leveled Practice, pp. 230, 233

Special Needs, p. 229

INTEGRATE LEARNING

Theater
Pantomime, p. 220

Music
Compare Two Songs, p. 223

Visual Arts
Weaving, p. 228

Music
Music Styles, p. 229
Cultural Songs, p. 232
Make Maracas, p. 235

RESOURCES

Social Studies in Action: Resources for the Classroom
Primary Source Collection
Music CD
School-to-Home Newsletter S11–S12
Interactive Map Transparencies
Interactive Desk Maps
Primary Atlas
Interactive Atlas
TimeLinks: Interactive Time Line
Picture Vocabulary Cards
Focus Skills Transparency 5
Recall and Retell Graphic Organizer Write-On/ Wipe-Off Card
Assessment Program, p. 37
Unit 5 Audiotext CD Collection
Internet Resources
Start with a Video DVD

Homework and Practice Book, pp. 42–43
Reading Support and Intervention, pp. 74–77
Success for English Language Learners, pp. 78–81
Vocabulary Transparency 5-1
Focus Skills Transparency 5
Recall and Retell Graphic Organizer Write-On/ Wipe-Off Card
Social Studies Skills Transparency 5-1
Primary Atlas
Interactive Atlas
Primary Source Collection
Unit 5 Audiotext CD Collection
Internet Resources

LESSON	PACING	OBJECTIVES
2 **Many People, One Country** pp. 236–241 ⚡ **WHAT TO KNOW** Why is the United States a country of many cultures?	**4** **DAYS**	■ Identify the reasons immigrants come to the United States. ■ Recognize that immigrants bring a variety of cultures to the United States. ■ Describe how cultures bring diversity to our country.
CITIZENSHIP SKILLS **Working Together** pp. 242–243	**1** **DAY**	■ Recognize that people in a group have different points of view. ■ Follow steps for working together in a group.
Biography: Amy Tan pp. 244–245	**1** **DAY**	■ Understand the importance of the actions and character of Amy Tan, and explain how she made a difference in others' lives.
3 **Celebrating Culture** pp. 246–249 ⚡ **WHAT TO KNOW** How are families different? How are they alike?	**4** **DAYS**	■ Recognize that each culture has unique traditions and customs. ■ Compare the traditions and customs of different cultures.
CHART AND GRAPH SKILLS **Read a Calendar** pp. 250–251	**1** **DAY**	■ Use a calendar. ■ Determine future and past dates and events by using a calendar.
Field Trip: Grandfather Mountain Highland Games pp. 252–253	**1** **DAY**	■ Explore an event that celebrates the traditions of a culture. ■ Identify features of a culture, including clothing, games, music, dance, and food.

READING SUPPORT VOCABULARY	REACH ALL LEARNERS	INTEGRATE LEARNING	RESOURCES
(Focus Skill) Reading Social Studies **Recall and Retell,** pp. 241, 245	**ENGLISH LANGUAGE LEARNERS,** p. 238 **Leveled Practice,** pp. 240, 243 **Advanced,** p. 239	**Languages** Numbers, p. 238 **Reading/Language Arts** Poetry, p. 241 Write a Narrative, p. 245	Homework and Practice Book, pp. 44–45 Reading Support and Intervention, pp. 78–81 Success for English Language Learners, pp. 82–85 Vocabulary Transparency 5-2 Focus Skills Transparency 5 Recall and Retell Graphic Organizer Write-On/ Wipe-Off Card Activity Pattern A11 Social Studies Skills Transparency 5-2 Multimedia Biographies CD TimeLinks: Interactive Time Line Unit 5 Audiotext CD Collection Internet Resources
immigrant p. 236 **diversity** p. 240 **conflict** p. 242			
(Focus Skill) Reading Social Studies **Recall and Retell,** p. 249 **Vocabulary Power:** Related Words, p. 252 **custom** p. 246 **tradition** p. 246 **calendar** p. 250	**Leveled Practice,** pp. 248, 251		Homework and Practice Book, pp. 46–47 Reading Support and Intervention, pp. 82–85 Success for English Language Learners, pp. 86–89 Vocabulary Transparency 5-3 Focus Skills Transparency 5 Recall and Retell Graphic Organizer Write-On/ Wipe-Off Card Social Studies Skills Transparency 5-3 Activity Pattern A12 TimeLinks: Interactive Time Line Unit 5 Audiotext CD Collection Internet Resources

LESSON	PACING	OBJECTIVES
4 **Recognizing Americans** pp. 254–257 🔆 **WHAT TO KNOW** Who are some Americans who have made a difference in our lives?	**4** **DAYS**	■ Recognize that people from many cultures have contributed to American society. ■ Describe how individuals can make a difference in people's lives.
5 **Fun with Social Studies: Add Them Up** pp. 258–259 **Unit 5 Review and Activities** pp. 260–264	**3** **DAYS**	

READING SUPPORT VOCABULARY	REACH ALL LEARNERS	INTEGRATE LEARNING	RESOURCES
Reading Social Studies **Recall and Retell,** p. 257	**Leveled Practice,** p. 256	**Reading/Language Arts** Folktales, p. 256	Homework and Practice Book, p. 48 Reading Support and Intervention, pp. 86–89 Success for English Language Learners, pp. 90–93 Vocabulary Transparency 5-4 Focus Skills Transparency 5 Recall and Retell Graphic Organizer Write-On/ Wipe-Off Card Unit 5 Audiotext CD Collection Internet Resources
scientist p. 254 **invention** p. 254			
	Leveled Practice, p. 259	**Languages** Learn Spanish Terms, p. 258	Homework and Practice Book, pp. 49–50 Assessment Program, pp. 38–40 Leveled Readers Leveled Readers Teacher Guide Unit 5 Audiotext CD Collection Internet Resources

STUDENT DIGITAL LEARNING

The interactive eBook provides students with the standards-based content of Harcourt print books in addition to interactive add-ons that enhance student interest and reinforce Social Studies content. Harcourt eBooks are available in both a basic and enhanced version.

INTERACTIVE VISUALS

Students watch the cultures of the world come to life through engaging interactive activities that enhance the unit content.

STREAMING VIDEO

Each Unit Opener includes video tied to the Unit Big Idea. This clip provides students with enhanced information about different cultures.

SKILLS ACTIVITIES

Each Chart and Graph Skill and Map and Globe Skill is enhanced by an interactive online activity.

LIVE INK ENHANCEMENT

Live Ink provides students with reading help through a patented system that breaks sentences down into segments. The Live Ink system is proven to increase student comprehension and test scores. Live Ink is available for grades 3–6/7.

ONLINE ADVENTURES

Fun with Social Studies provides a link to our Online Adventures game. Students play a game in which they visit a cultural fair. The game reviews important concepts from the unit.

MULTIMEDIA BIOGRAPHIES

Biographies from the student edition include additional information in an interactive Multimedia Biography. Students can find more information, view related biographies, explore maps and images, and find links to additional webpages.

THE LEARNING SITE

The eBook includes links to **www.harcourtschool.com/ss1** There students can find internal resources such as our complete Multimedia Biographies databases and our Online Adventures games. This Harcourt Social Studies site also provides students with additional research tools.

Teacher Resources

Back Forward Reload Home

E-PLANNER

The e-Planner provides a useful tool for scheduling Social Studies lessons.

- Use it to access Teacher Edition pages and student workbook pages and to plan classroom activities.
- The calendar tool displays all your scheduled Social Studies lessons in an easy-to-use format.
- All standards are organized by grade level.

HSPOA

Harcourt School Publishers Online Assessment provides teachers with a reliable, confidential system for online delivery of Social Studies assessment. Using this system, you can track student performance correlated to standards and run prescribed reports for any missed standards. Questions are correlated to our print Assessment program.

VIDEOS AND DVDS

A comprehensive package of videos for Grades K–3 provides an entertaining overview of core social studies concepts such as government, geography, economics, culture and history. Videos in this package are available from Schlessinger Media® and are also available digitally on SAFARI Montage.

SAFARI MONTAGE™

For more information, see pages TEI13–TEI18.

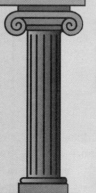

FREE AND INEXPENSIVE MATERIALS

Free and inexpensive materials are listed on the Social Studies Website at **www.harcourtschool.com/ss1**
- Addresses to write to for free and inexpensive products
- Links to unit–related materials
- Internet maps
- Internet references

COMMUNITY RESOURCES FOR THE CLASSROOM

The **National Atlas** website offers interactive, customizable maps of different areas in the United States. Use the **Map Maker** tool to zoom in on your community and view map features such as cities, roads, climate, and agriculture. **http://nationalatlas.gov/**

Educators can use the **United States Census Bureau** webpage to locate census information and facts about their local communities. **http://factfinder.census.gov/home/saff/main.html?_lang=en**

The National Park Service offers a comprehensive site with a search engine that cross-references our country's National Historic Landmarks by name, city, and state. **http://tps.cr.nps.gov/nhl/**

Museums in all 50 states are indexed on the **Virtual Library** museums pages. Use this site to find museums in and around your students' own community. **http://www.museumca.org/usa/states.html**

The **Library of Congress** site features numerous collections of primary sources, biographies, recordings, and photographs. The topic **Cities and Towns** contains photographic records of communities throughout the history of the United States. **http://memory.loc.gov/ammem/**

Additional Sites are available at www.harcourtschool.com/ss1

Lesson Plan Summaries

BELOW-LEVEL/INTERVENTION

TOPIC
A World of Many People

Summary *Many People, Many Cultures.* This Reader defines culture, explains why people adopt ways from other cultures, and describes how people celebrate their traditions.

BEFORE READING

Vocabulary Power Have children define the following words. Help them write one sentence for each word as it relates to the people of the world.

culture   language   immigrant   tradition   scientist

DURING READING

Recall and Retell Have children complete the graphic organizer to show that they understand how to recall and retell details about the people of the world, as described in the Reader.

Recall Detail
Immigrants learn a new culture.

Recall Detail
Families pass along traditions.

Retell

AFTER READING

Critical Thinking Lead children in a discussion about why we learn about different cultures.

Write a Letter Have children pretend they have a pen pal in a different country. Have children write letters to their pen pals describing what it is like to live in the United States.

ON-LEVEL

TOPIC
A World of Many People

Summary *Regional Festivals,* by Susan McCloskey. This Reader describes a festival in Oklahoma, a winter carnival in Minnesota, and a fiesta in Texas.

BEFORE READING

Vocabulary Power Have children define the following words. Help them write one sentence for each word as it relates to the people of the world.

culture   language   festival   cowboy   fiesta

DURING READING

Recall and Retell Have children complete the graphic organizer to show that they understand how to recall and retell details about the people of the world, as described in the Reader.

Recall Detail
Many festivals celebrate a culture.

Recall Detail
Festivals are a good way to think about our country's past.

Retell

AFTER READING

Critical Thinking Lead children in a discussion about why people hold festivals.

Write an Description Have children write a short description of a festival in their community.

The *Leveled Readers Teacher Guide* provides background, reading tips, fast facts, answer keys, and copying masters.

TOPIC
A World of Many People

Summary *Talk to Me,* by John Grigsby. This Reader describes how people can communicate without words by using pictures, sign language, and gestures and examines how languages other than English are spoken in the United States.

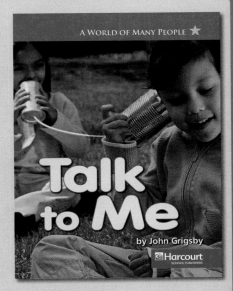

A WORLD OF MANY PEOPLE ★

Talk to Me

by John Grigsby

Harcourt
SCHOOL PUBLISHERS

BEFORE READING

Vocabulary Power Have children define the following words. Help them write one sentence for each word as it relates to the people of the world.

culture   language   communicate   tradition   translate

DURING READING

Focus Skill **Recall and Retell** Have children complete the graphic organizer to show that they understand how to recall and retell details about the people of the world, as described in the Reader.

Recall Detail	Retell
People can talk without words.	

Recall Detail	
People who move to the United States bring their cultures with them.	

AFTER READING

Critical Thinking Lead children in a discussion about why it is important for people to be able to communicate with each other.

 Write a List Have children find out what languages their classmates speak and write a list of these languages.

Readers' Theater
Every Student Is a Star

IT'S SHOWTIME!

Getting Started

★ Distribute the Big Idea activity sheet from your Readers' Theater.

★ Read through the script together. Make connections with unit contents.

★ Plan a performance using the **Prep ★ Practice ★ Perform** guidelines. Find ideas for props online.

Pressed for Time?

★ Perform a choral reading of the script with the whole class.

★ Assign parts for a one-time read-through.

★ Assign groups to read in your literacy center.

Read Along,

Read Aloud,

Reading Fun

BASIC

Ada, Alma Flor. *I Love Saturdays y domingos.* Turtleback Books, 2004. A young girl experiences the two cultures that represent her heritage by visiting her European American grandparents on Saturdays and her Mexican-American grandparents on Sundays (Domingos).

Avi. *Silent Movie.* Simon and Schuster Children's Publishing, 2003. In the early 1900s, a Swedish family faces separation and hardships to immigrate to the United States where their son is in a silent movie.

Miller, Elizabeth I. *Just Like Home/Como en mi tierra.* Albert Whitman, 2004. A girl compares her old and new homes as she learns to adjust to her new life in America (bilingual: English and Spanish).

Recorvits, Helen. *My Name Is Yoon.* Farrar, Straus and Giroux, 2003. A Korean girl learns to accept her new American self, her name written in English, and her new American friends.

PROFICIENT

Brown, Don. *Odd Boy Out: Young Albert Einstein.* Houghton Mifflin, 2004. Learn about the work and early life of the famous physicist, a scientist who looks at how the world works.

Polacco, Patricia. *The Keeping Quilt.* Aladdin, 2001. A quilt made from old clothes tells the story of a Jewish family's history.

Schraff, Anne E. *Charles Drew: Pioneer in Medicine.* Enslow Publishers, 2003. A simple biography tells the story of the doctor known for his work with storing blood.

Wahl, Jan. *Candy Shop.* Charlesbridge, 2005. An African American boy goes shopping with his aunt and faces subtle discrimination.

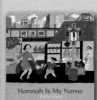

Yang, Belle. *Hannah Is My Name.* Candlewick Press, 2004. In this immigration story, a Chinese girl and her family learn to fit in while waiting for their green cards.

ADVANCED

Bruchac, Joseph. *A Boy Called Slow: The True Story of Sitting Bull.* Putnam Juvenile, 2002. This picture-book biography tells the story of the Lakota Sioux boy who overcame his childhood name to become a great leader.

Hopkins, Deborah. *A Band of Angels: A Story Inspired by the Jubilee Singers.* Aladdin, 2002. A young African American girl learns about her family's history through her aunt's stories.

Johnson, Paul Brett. *Bearhide and Crow.* Holiday House, 2000. This good-natured trickster tale centers around a foolish trade.

Say, Allen. *Grandfather's Journey.* Houghton Mifflin, 1993. Grandfather reminisces about life in America and Japan.

Denenberg, Dennis & Roscoe, Lorraine. *50 American Heroes Every Kid Should Meet.* Millbrook Press, 2002. This is a collection of short biographies of men and women from different eras, professions, and ethnic backgrounds.

Additional books also are recommended at point of use throughout the unit. Note that information, while correct at time of publication, is subject to change.

For information about ordering these tradebooks, visit www.harcourtschool.com/ss1

Use these activities to help differentiate instruction. Each activity has been developed to address a different level or type of learner.

ELL ENGLISH LANGUAGE LEARNERS

30 minutes

CULTURE COLLAGE **Have children create a collage of various cultures.**

- Display these vocabulary terms: *culture, immigrant, tradition, custom.* Talk about how these words relate to their lives.
- Invite children to draw pictures showing themselves enjoying toys, games, or fun activities that are part of their own family's cultures, such as a dreidel or piñata.
- Direct children to label their pictures.
- Encourage children to arrange their pictures as a collage on a bulletin board titled *Cultures.*

Materials
- construction paper
- crayons or colored pencils

SPECIAL NEEDS

30 minutes

VOCABULARY FILL-INS **Have children create fill-in-the-blank sentences using vocabulary related to culture.**

- Discuss the meaning of vocabulary words from this unit, such as *culture, immigrant, tradition, custom, language, diversity, invention,* and *scientist.*
- Have children use a computer to write sentences for two words, leaving blank lines for the vocabulary terms.
- Remind them to make a separate answer sheet.
- Save and print their document. Have partners trade papers and complete each other's sentences. Encourage them to use the answer sheet to check their work.

Materials
- computer with program to create document
- printer paper

ADVANCED

30 minutes for 3 days

MUSICAL RECORDING **Have children create a collection of songs from many cultures for others to enjoy.**

- Ask children to share a song that is a family tradition. This can be a traditional song of the United States or from another country.
- Invite children to teach the song to several other children. Have them practice singing it together.
- Record the children introducing and singing the song.
- Have children compile all of the songs on one recording. Provide opportunities for children to listen to the music.

Materials
- tape recorder or computer recording system

MATHEMATICS CENTER

Time Line Quiz

Display a time line showing dates of important cultural events in American history. Show children how to subtract or count years to figure out how much time has passed at each event on the time line. Provide calculators to help children check their answers.

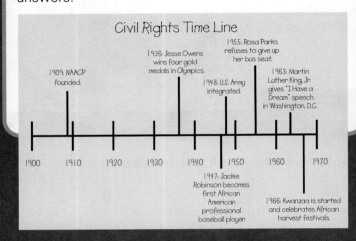

Civil Rights Time Line

1909: NAACP founded.
1936: Jesse Owens wins four gold medals in Olympics.
1948: U.S. Army integrated.
1955: Rosa Parks refuses to give up her bus seat.
1963: Martin Luther King, Jr. gives "I Have a Dream" speech in Washington, D.C.
1947: Jackie Robinson becomes first African American professional baseball player.
1966: Kwanzaa is started and celebrates African harvest festivals.

1900 1910 1920 1930 1940 1950 1960 1970

SCIENCE CENTER

Talk of the Town

Explain to children that inventors such as Thomas Edison and Alexander Graham Bell worked very hard to invent and improve products, and sometimes they made mistakes before they got things right. Invite children to work with a partner to experiment with telephones for passing messages. Provide funnels and plastic tubing they use to determine the longest length that still allows a clear message. Have children record their findings in illustrations and sentences to be posted in the center. Encourage them to describe how the tube length affects the loudness of the messages.

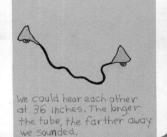

We could hear each other at 36 inches. The longer the tube, the farther away we sounded.

READING/LANGUAGE ARTS CENTER

Cultural Hall of Fame

Provide books with information about famous people from other cultures. Point out that children can focus on a person who is an artist, writer, scientist, inventor, athlete, or politician. Have children read about the person and design a medal or an award that reflects the person's accomplishments. Ask children to write a paragraph telling when the person lived and how he or she made life better for others. Display children's writings and awards in a Cultural Hall of Fame.

Charles Drew, Scientist
Made the first blood bank.

ART CENTER

Cultural Monument

Explain that communities build monuments so that they can honor historic events and remind people of what happened in the past. Some monuments are sculptures and buildings that inspire people to work for certain causes, such as equality, fairness, or peace. Provide children with modeling clay in various colors. Ask them to create a small monument or statue that honors a cultural or historic event or reminds people of a certain cause. Display the artwork in the center.

The Assessment Program gives all learners many opportunities to show what they know and can do. It also provides ongoing information about each student's understanding of social studies.

 Online Assessment available at www.harcourtschool.com/ss1

UNIT TESTS
Unit 5

- **Unit Pretest,**
  Assessment Program, p. 37
- **Unit Review and Test Prep,** pp. 260–263

- **Unit Test,**
  Assessment Program, pp. 38–40

WRITING

- **Show What You Know,**
  Unit Writing Activity,
  Write a Diary Entry, p. 264

- **Primary Sources, Write About It,** p. 235
- **Lesson Review,**
  Writing Activities, at ends of lessons

UNIT PROJECT

- **Show What You Know,**
  Unit Project,
  Family History Storyboard, p. 264
- **Unit Project,**
  Performance Assessment, pp. 217P–217Q

- **Lesson Review,**
  Performance Activities, at ends of lessons

INFORMAL ASSESSMENT

- **Lesson Review,** at ends of lessons
- **Skills:**
  Practice, pp. 232, 243, 250
  Apply, pp. 233, 243, 251

- **Reading Social Studies,**
  Recall and Retell, pp. 220–221
- **Literature Response Corner,** p. 225

STUDENT SELF-EVALUATION

- **Reading Check Questions,** within lessons

- **Biography, Why Character Counts,** pp. 244–245
- **Map, Time Line, Graph, Diagram, and Illustration questions,** within lessons

OPTION 1 — PRETEST

Name _____ Date _____

5 Pretest

FILL IN THE BLANK (10 points each)

DIRECTIONS Write the word that completes each sentence.

> languages immigrant calendar tradition cooperate
> culture conflict scientist inventions diversity

1. A group's way of life is their ___culture___.
2. People around the world speak different ___languages___.
3. Someone who comes from another place to live in a country is an ___immigrant___.
4. We see ___diversity___ in our many kinds of food, clothing, languages, and beliefs.
5. When people have different points of view on how to do something, they might have a ___conflict___.
6. When people have a conflict, they need to ___cooperate___.
7. Something passed on from older family members to children is a ___tradition___.
8. We keep track of days and months on a ___calendar___.
9. Thomas Edison is famous for his ___inventions___.
10. George Washington Carver was a ___scientist___.

OPTION 1 — UNIT TEST

Name _____ Date _____

5 Test

MULTIPLE CHOICE (6 points each)

DIRECTIONS Select the letter of the best answer.

1. Which is NOT a reason why immigrants have come to America?
   - **A** to have a better life
   - **B** to find jobs
   - **C** to escape war
   - (**D**) to meet a king

2. What is a culture's way of doing something called?
   - (**A**) a custom
   - **B** a language
   - **C** a family tree
   - **D** a party

3. Which is NOT something you might find on a calendar?
   - **A** days of the week
   - **B** holidays
   - **C** months
   - (**D**) daily rainfall

4. Who was Thomas Edison?
   - (**A**) a scientist
   - **B** a writer
   - **C** our third President
   - **D** a painter

5. Which of these people shares Cuban culture with music?
   - **A** Ieoh Ming Pei
   - **B** Thomas Edison
   - (**C**) Gloria Estefan
   - **D** George Washington Carver

(continued)

OPTION 1 — UNIT TEST

Name _____ Date _____

SHORT ANSWER (7 points each)

DIRECTIONS Use Mike's home calendar to answer the questions.

APRIL 2007

Sunday	Monday	Tuesday	Wednesday	Thursday	Friday	Saturday
1 April Fool's Day	2	3	4	5 Mom's birthday	6	7
8	9 Dentist	10	11	12	13	14
15	16	17	18	19	20	21
22 Earth Day	23	24	25	26	27 Field trip to Mack's Farm!	28
29	30					

6. How many days are in the month of April? ___30___
7. On which day does Mike go to the dentist? ___April 9___
8. What happens on April 22? ___Earth Day___
9. Does the field trip happen before or after Earth Day? ___after___
10. On what day of the week does April begin? ___Sunday___

(continued)

OPTION 1 — UNIT TEST

Name _____ Date _____

MATCHING (5 points each)

DIRECTIONS Match the word on the right to its meaning on the left.

11. ___C___ a group's way of life
12. ___F___ someone who comes from another place to live in a country
13. ___D___ many different ideas and ways of living
14. ___G___ something that is passed on from older family members to children
15. ___B___ a chart that keeps track of time and special days
16. ___E___ a person who observes things and makes discoveries
17. ___A___ a new product that has not been made before

> **A.** invention
> **B.** calendar
> **C.** culture
> **D.** diversity
> **E.** scientist
> **F.** immigrant
> **G.** tradition

OPTION 2 WRITING

RUBRIC

Name _____ **Date** _____

Unit 5 Writing Activity Guidelines

WRITE A DIARY ENTRY

Writing Prompt Write a diary entry telling about the events of a day when your family celebrates a tradition.

▶ **STEP 1** Think of traditions in your family that you do every year. Here are some ideas to get you started:
- a holiday you celebrate
- a trip you take together
- an activity you do at home as a family, such as playing a game

▶ **STEP 2** Choose one tradition to write about. Think of at least three events that happen on the day when your family celebrates the tradition.

▶ **STEP 3** Use your ideas to write a diary entry for the day. Remember to tell the date. You will probably want to tell about the events in the order in which they happened.

▶ **STEP 4** Review your work to make sure you have used correct grammar, spelling, punctuation, and capitalization.

▶ **STEP 5** Make the changes. Then copy your diary entry neatly.

SCORE 4
- provides rich description of details
- includes details that describe several events or activities
- indicates strong understanding of family traditions
- is well organized and includes correctly written date
- uses a variety of complete sentences

SCORE 3
- provides some description of details
- includes details that describe few events or activities
- indicates some understanding of family traditions
- is somewhat organized and includes correctly written date
- uses complete sentences of some variety

SCORE 2
- provides little description of details
- includes details that describe a single event or activity
- indicates little understanding of family traditions
- is poorly organized and includes an incorrectly written date
- uses mostly complete sentences of little variety

SCORE 1
- provides no description of details
- does not describe any events or activities
- indicates no understanding of family traditions
- is not organized and includes an incorrectly written date
- uses incomplete sentences that have no variety

OPTION 3 PROJECT

RUBRIC

Name _____ **Date** _____

Unit 5 Project Guidelines

FAMILY HISTORY STORYBOARD

Design a family history storyboard that shows important events from past to present.

▶ **STEP 1** Think about events that tell your family's history.
- Make a list of questions to ask family members about important events.
- Make copies of family photographs or important papers.
- Take pictures or make drawings of family artifacts.

▶ **STEP 2** Use the information you gathered to draw pictures of several important events. Try to use pictures that tell about your family's culture.

▶ **STEP 3** Put the events in order from past to present, and attach them to your storyboard.

▶ **STEP 4** Write captions to explain each event and tell the date. Attach drawings, photographs, or artifacts that will add detail to your storyboard.

▶ **STEP 5** Display your storyboard, and answer questions others may have about your family's history.

SCORE 4
- shows several important events
- shows clear understanding of sequence from past to present
- represents family culture clearly and with several details
- includes neatly written, completely correct captions

SCORE 3
- shows some important events
- shows an understanding of sequence from past to present
- represents family culture with some details
- includes neatly written, mostly correct captions

SCORE 2
- shows some events that are not important
- shows some understanding of sequence from past to present
- represents family culture with few details
- includes captions with some errors

SCORE 1
- shows few events or a single event of little importance
- shows minimal understanding of sequence from past to present
- does not correctly represent family culture with appropriate details
- includes illegible captions with many errors

TAKE-HOME RUBRICS Copying masters of a student *Writing Rubric* and *Project Rubric* appear in the Assessment Program, pp. 42 and 44.
GROUP PERFORMANCE RUBRIC See Assessment Program, page x.

A Family History Storyboard

Getting Started

Distribute the Unit 5 Project Guidelines provided on page 43 of the Assessment Program.

Introduce the unit project as you begin Unit 5, and have children create a plan for gathering information about their own family histories for a storyboard. Explain that a storyboard is an illustrated time line that highlights important events in order from first to last. When the unit is complete, have children display their family history storyboards to share with family members and classmates.

The Big Idea

Culture Our country is made up of many different people and cultures.

Project Management

Present the storyboard format to the class before children start, but have children work individually on their own projects. Offer assistance as children write captions and add details, drawings, and photographs to illustrate each panel.

Materials textbook, questionnaire, card stock, writing paper, pencils, crayons or markers, masking tape, scissors, paste, photos, postcards, magazine pictures, construction paper

Create a Questionnaire

Begin by brainstorming topics for children to discuss with family members, such as
- where and when the family immigrated
- family business
- stories and memories
- birth of family members
- how family culture is shared
- special family traditions or customs

As a class, create a questionnaire that children can use to gather information from a family member. Children should record responses on the questionnaire or draw pictures of events. Then they can cut out and arrange the events in chronological order to provide a framework for the storyboard panels.

Encourage children to
- place each panel of their storyboards on a separate sheet of card stock.
- show an important family tradition or custom and include a caption.
- illustrate panels with drawings, magazine cut-outs, or photographs.

My Family History

Where and when were you born?
My grandfather was born in Italy in 1942.

What important family event happened when you were growing up?
Grandpa and his brother moved to Napa, California with their parents.

What was your first job?
Grandpa and his brother started their own olive oil company.

What do you do now?
Now Grandpa visits all his grandchildren and takes us places like the zoo.

Assemble the Storyboards

When the individual panels are complete, have children lay them out on a flat surface. Help them double-check to be sure the panels are in chronological order. Use masking tape on the back to connect panels together. Finished storyboards can be displayed on a bulletin board or laid out on tabletops.

Share the Storyboards

Choose a date and time to invite family members to the classroom to view the family history storyboards. Children can introduce and answer questions about their storyboards during an informal storyboard gallery tour. Finally, discuss with children how families of different cultures are the same as and different from each another.

Lesson Review Activities

You may wish to incorporate the following lesson review activities into the unit project.
- Lesson 1: **Write about a Culture,** p. 231
- Lesson 2: **Interview Family Members,** p. 241
- Lesson 3: **Make a Storyboard,** p. 249

Assessment

For a project rubric, see Teacher Edition, p. 217O.

What to Look For

- Children understand sequence and chronological order.

- Children understand how culture influences family events.

- Storyboard panels use a variety of media, and events are clearly represented.

- Storyboards include captions that are legible and spelled correctly.

LESSON 1

Name _____ Date _____

About My Culture

Draw a picture of an object that tells about your culture. Choose an object that shows how your culture is special. Finish the sentence to tell why you chose this object.

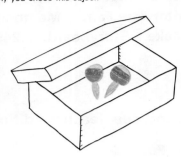

I chose _____ to tell about my culture because

Possible answer: I chose maracas to tell about my culture because my family likes to get together and play music on holidays. The maracas are my favorite instrument to play.

SKILL PRACTICE

Name _____ Date _____

 MAP AND GLOBE SKILLS
A Map of Central America

The map shows the countries south of Mexico in Central America. Use the map and the compass rose to answer the questions. Then color each country a different color.

❶ What country is north of Costa Rica? Nicaragua
❷ Find El Salvador. What country is to the east of it?
Honduras
❸ What country is farthest south? Panama
❹ What countries border Honduras? Guatemala
El Salvador, Nicaragua
❺ What country is west of Belize? Guatemala
Children should color each country a different color.

LESSON 2

Name _____ Date _____

Letter from Far Away

Pretend you are an immigrant in the United States. Write a letter home, telling about your trip and your life in the United States.

Possible answer:
Dear Misha ,
My trip to the United States was exciting. I flew in an airplane for the first time! I saw lots of ocean and mountains and land.
My family and I have moved into an apartment in Boston. I see many tall buildings from my bedroom window. I am making new friends here.

Yours truly,
Samira

SKILL PRACTICE

Name _____ Date _____

A Tale About Working Together

Read the story about children who are making costumes for a culture parade. Underline the sentences that tell how they cooperate. Then answer the questions.

Will, Julie, and Teresa are marching in a parade. They want to wear costumes that tell about cultures. First, they share ideas, and everyone has a turn to talk. Will and Julie have a conflict about which costumes they should wear. Teresa suggests they take a vote to decide fairly.

After the vote, the children plan who will do each task. Will says he will look for pictures of clothing from different cultures. Julie will ask her mom for cloth and sewing supplies. Teresa will ask her sewing club to help make the costumes. When the costumes are finished, the children talk about their project and practice marching together. The parade will be fun!

❶ How did the children settle their conflict? Possible answers: They voted. They cooperated.
❷ Think of a time you worked with someone else to get a job done. What was the most important thing you did to cooperate? Answers will vary. Children might mention listening to each other, assigning tasks, or talking about the project when it is done.

LESSON 3

Name _____ Date _____

Pass on a Tradition!

Draw a picture to show something the person on the
left might pass on to the person on the right.

Name _____ Date _____

 CHART AND GRAPH SKILLS
Read a Calendar

Use Madison's calendar to answer the questions.

June 2008						
S	**M**	**T**	**W**	**T**	**F**	**S**
1	2	3	4	5	6 Last day of school	7
8	9	10	11	12	13	14
15 Father's Day	16	17	18	19	20 Children's Theater	21
22	23	24	25	26	27	28
29	30 Mother's birthday!					

Trip to Grandmother's (written across June 9–14)

❶ What month is on the calendar? __June__

❷ How many days are in this month? __30__

❸ When is the last day of school? __June 6__

❹ How many days will Madison visit her grandmother?
__6 days__

❺ On what day of the week is Madison going to the
Children's Theater? __Friday__

LESSON 4

Name _____ Date _____

Scientists and Artists

Match the hero to his or her description. Write the letter next to
the person's name on the lines. You will write each letter twice.

a. Thomas Edison   b. Ieoh Ming Pei
c. George Washington Carver   d. Gloria Estefan

❶ __a__ He invented the lightbulb.

❷ __c__ He found many uses for growing peanuts.

❸ __d__ She holds concerts to raise money for people in
need.

❹ __b__ He is a Chinese American architect.

❺ __b__ He designs interesting buildings.

❻ __a__ He is a famous inventor.

❼ __d__ She is a singer, dancer, and songwriter.

❽ __c__ He found new ways to make medicines and glue.

STUDY GUIDE

Name _____ Date _____

Unit 5 Study Guide

Read the paragraphs. Use the words in the Word Bank to fill in the blanks.

customs	Immigrants	traditions
languages	culture	diversity

A ____culture____ is a group's way of life. ____Immigrants____ who move to the United States from other countries bring their cultures here. Every culture has its own ____customs____. The differences among cultures help create ____diversity____. The way people dress, the foods they eat, even the ____languages____ they speak are all examples of diversity.

Your family has ____traditions____ that are passed on from older family members to children. Special things you do to celebrate holidays or birthdays are family traditions.

Use after reading Unit 5, pages 217–264. Homework and Practice Book ■ 49

UNIT 5 REVIEW AND TEST PREP

Name _____ Date _____

RECALL AND RETELL
Reading Social Studies

Use the chart to recall and retell details about people who make a difference in others' lives.

Recall Detail
Scientists observe things and make discoveries.

Recall Detail
Thomas Edison invented the lightbulb.

Recall Detail
George Washington Carver helped farmers improve soil for crops.

Retell
Scientists like Edison and Carver watch how things work and invent new products.

50 ■ Homework and Practice Book   Use after reading Unit 5, pages 217–264.

NOTES

Historical Societies

_____
_____
_____
_____
_____
_____
_____
_____
_____
_____
_____

Museums

_____
_____
_____
_____
_____
_____
_____
_____
_____
_____
_____

Parks

_____
_____
_____
_____
_____
_____
_____
_____
_____
_____
_____

Guest Speakers

_____
_____
_____
_____
_____
_____
_____
_____
_____
_____
_____

Discuss the Big Idea

Culture **Our country is made up of many different people and cultures.**

Explain that our country is made up of people that have come from all over the world. Some families have arrived recently from other countries. Others have relatives that came to this country long ago. Point out that all families have special ways of doing things.

Make It Relevant Ask the following question to help children think about how culture is a part of their family life.

Q **What special ways of doing things have you learned from your parents or grandparents?**

A Children might mention crafts or skills they have been taught, celebrations they have learned, or special clothing or artifacts they have been given.

Access Prior Knowledge

Draw a concept map with the central circle marked *My Family*. Have children discuss celebrations, special events, and other activities family members do together. Add their ideas to the concept map. Point out those ideas that children's families have in common. Tell children that in this unit, they will learn how these ideas are related to different cultures that are a part of our country.

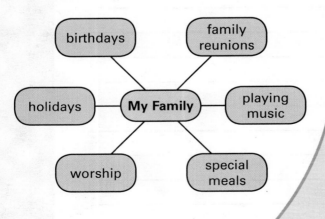

Unit 5 — A World of Many People

Talk About Culture

"My ancestors wore clothes made of colorful cloth."

Practice and Extend

BACKGROUND

Aloha Festivals The Aloha Festivals are Hawaii's largest collection of cultural festivals created to preserve the unique island traditions. It is the only state-wide cultural event in the United States. With celebrations held on six islands over a two-month period, the Aloha Festivals celebrate Pacific, Asian, and Western cultural influences in the Hawaiian Islands.

Talk About Shown in the photographs along the bottom of the unit preview pages are children discussing customs related to their cultures. The clothing styles we wear, the ways we greet people, and the languages we speak are all a part of a person's culture.

" Aloha! I welcome friends with leis. "

" Hola means hello in Spanish. "

217

Discuss the Picture

Invite children to look at the photograph and identify it as the Aloha Festivals in Hawaii. Discuss the people, decorations, and scenery they can find in the photograph.

Q What event is happening in the picture?

A It is a parade. People ride or walk beside a colorful float. Hawaiian patterns decorate the float, and people are dressed in Hawaiian clothing.

Q Why do people enjoy celebrations such as this?

A They can show pride in their culture and ways of doing things. They can show what is important to their history.

Discuss "Talk About"

Have a volunteer read each quotation. Explain that ancestors are family members who lived before us. Discuss what the children in the pictures are wearing or holding.

Q What special things are the children sharing?

A They share special ways of dress, special ways of greeting people, and words in other languages.

Have children work in pairs to ask and answer questions about either the Aloha Festivals photograph or Talk About feature.

ELL ENGLISH LANGUAGE LEARNERS

Beginning Identify an item or a detail from the quotations, such as the lei or waving hello as children point to the matching picture. Then ask children to point to and say the name for a similar example in the larger photograph.

Intermediate Ask children to say sentences that describe what people are doing or wearing in the pictures as a partner identifies the detail. Suggest they include descriptive words so the partner can locate the correct person.

Advanced Invite children to describe what they would like to be doing if they were a part of the Aloha Festivals. For example, they may say *I would want to ride on the float and wave to the people* or *I would like to welcome people with leis.*

OBJECTIVES

- Use visuals to determine word meanings.
- Use words and visuals to preview the content of the unit.

RESOURCES

Picture-Word Cards

Make Connections

Link Pictures with Words Have children read the word *immigrant* and its definition. On the board, draw a simple outline of a person with the word *immigrant* in the head. Write the words *culture*, *custom*, and *tradition* on the body. Ask children to describe how each word is related to *immigrant*. Briefly write their responses under each word.

❶ Visual Literacy: Pictures Ask children to describe what is happening in the picture for the word *culture*. Discuss why these people might be dressed in the same outfits.

Q What does special clothing tell others about culture?

A It might show others how a culture celebrates; it might show important symbols, colors, or patterns.

❷ Discuss with children how the *immigrant* family might be feeling in this picture. (scared, tired, worried) Ask children to suggest why they might be tired. (because they traveled from another country)

Unit 5 Preview

Vocabulary

❶

culture   A group's way of life.
(page 226)

❷

immigrant   Someone who comes from another place to live in a country.
(page 236)

218

Practice and Extend

ELL ENGLISH LANGUAGE LEARNERS

Frontloading Language: Culture Use the following prompts to develop the academic language of culture and the structures of recalling and retelling information.

Beginning Have children use the pictures and vocabulary to complete this sentence frame: *Immigrants bring their ____, ____, and ____ with them when they move to another country.* (culture, customs, traditions)

Intermediate Have children use this frame to recall information they learned in the definitions: *Children around the world learn [noun]. This is because the definition says ____.* (traditions; something passed on from family members to children)

Advanced Invite children to use this frame to recall and retell information about culture: *Culture is ____, and includes ____ and ____.* (a group's way of life, customs, traditions)

3

custom A group's way of doing something. (page 246)

4

tradition Something that is passed on from older family members to children. (page 246)

GO ONLINE For more resources, go to www.harcourtschool.com/ss1

219

3 Invite children to explain what the woman is doing in the picture above the word *custom*. (serving tea) Ask them to explain how this picture relates to the word *custom*. (The way she is serving might be a custom; her dress might be a custom.)

4 Focus children's attention on the picture above the word *tradition*. Read aloud the definitions and ask what this picture shows. (a father, a grandfather, and a boy are fishing together) Point out that shared activites are a way people share information about their culture and traditions.

Q What traditions have you learned from your parents, grandparents, and other older relatives?

A Possible answers include traditions about holidays, religion, and even how they spend special meals or events with the family.

GO ONLINE **INTERNET RESOURCES**

For more resources, go to **www.harcourtschool.com/ss1**

VOCABULARY POWER

Make a Vocabulary Chart
Have children make a three-column chart. Label the columns *culture*, *customs*, and *traditions*. Have children share examples of each and list them under the correct heading. Possible answers can include artwork, language, beliefs, music, poetry, folktales, habit, pattern, specific articles of clothing, toys, specific holidays such as Christmas, Hanukkah, and Kwanzaa.

Recall and Retell

Reading Social Studies

OBJECTIVES

- Recall information from a text in a logical sequence.
- Retell information in your own words.
- Interpret information from charts.

VOCABULARY

recall p. 220   **retell** p. 220

RESOURCES

Focus Skills Transparency 5; Recall and Retell Graphic Organizer Write-On/Wipe-Off Card; Unit 5 Audiotext CD Collection

Introduce

1 Why It Matters Explain to children that when they recall something, they remember what they have heard or read. When they retell something, they tell in their own words what they remember. Point out that children recall and retell stories and events every day. Share these examples:

- telling family members about a funny story they read in school
- telling their teacher about an interesting book they read

Have children add their own examples. Explain that recalling information helps them to remember it. Retelling information helps them understand it and share it with others.

Unit 5

Reading Social Studies
Recall and Retell

1 Why It Matters It is important to remember and understand what you read.

Learn

As you read, be sure to recall and retell information.

- To recall, think about what you have
2 just read.

- To retell, put that information in your own words.

Read the paragraph below.

Recall

St. Lucia Day is a Swedish holiday. It is celebrated on December 13 because it is one of the shortest days of the year. Girls dress in white robes with red or white sashes. They wear wreaths with candles on their heads. Boys carry poles with stars on the tops. Everyone eats sweet buns and pinwheel cookies.

220

Practice and Extend

INTEGRATE THE CURRICULUM

THEATER Write familiar activities, such as *sharpen a pencil*, *make a sandwich*, and *put away groceries*, on paper strips. Have children take turns selecting a strip and pantomiming a series of movements that illustrate the activity. Invite the class to recall the movements, guess the activity, and retell the movements they observed. **Pantomime**

FOCUS SKILLS

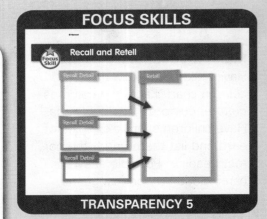

Recall and Retell

TRANSPARENCY 5

Graphic Organizer Write-On/Wipe-Off Cards available

Practice

3

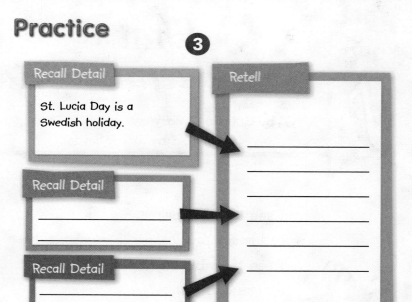

Copy the chart and complete it. Write details you recall from what you just read. Then use your own words to retell what you read.

Apply

As you read, recall and retell information about people in this unit.

221

Leveled Practice Have children recall and retell personal events.

(Basic) Ask children to recall something they did yesterday. Have them retell the event orally with sentences such as *I recall that I played ball yesterday.*

(Proficient) Have children draw a picture of an activity they have done in the last week. Ask them to write several sentences below the picture as a caption.

(Advanced) Have children recall several things they did in the last month. Ask them to write a short paragraph to retell those events.

Learn

2 Discuss the definitions for *recall* and *retell* on page 220. Then read aloud and discuss the paragraph. Point out that the first details tell where and when the holiday takes place. The next details tell how girls and boys celebrate. Explain that it is easier to recall and retell what happened if they think about the organization of details.

Practice

3 **Visual Literacy: Chart** Have children read the chart on page 221. Use Focus Skill Transparency 5 to copy the chart. Discuss the organization of details to help children fill it in.

Q How do girls celebrate St. Lucia Day?

A They wear wreaths with candles on their heads.

Q How do boys celebrate?

A They carry poles with stars on top.

ANSWERS: Recall details: Girls wear wreaths with candles on their heads. Boys carry poles with stars on top. Retell: St. Lucia is a Swedish holiday. On this day, girls wear wreaths with candles on their heads. Boys carry poles with stars on top.

3 **Close**

Apply

Tell children that as they read the unit, they should recall and retell facts about cultures around the world.

OBJECTIVES

- Identify selected songs related to ethnic and cultural similarities and differences.

- Recognize the forms of diversity in the school and community.

RESOURCES

Unit 5 Audiotext CD Collection

Quick Summary

"What a Wonderful World" by George David Weiss and Bob Thiele (Atheneum Books for Young Readers, 1995).

This song celebrates the wonderful diverse world in which we live. The lyrics are accompanied by illustrations that show the differences in color among people, plants, places, and things. The illustrations also represent different beliefs, customs ceremonies, traditions, and social practices of the varied cultures.

Before Reading

Set the Purpose Have a volunteer read the title of the song. Ask: *What do you think this song will be about?* (good things about our world)

Encourage children to scan the illustrations that accompany the song. Then have them predict things the songwriters might find wonderful. Write children's suggestions on the board. Ask their opinion about whether they also think these things are wonderful. Allow children to add their own suggestions to the list.

Start with a Song

What a Wonderful World

by George David Weiss and Bob Thiele
illustrated by Ashley Bryan

I see trees of green,
red roses too,
I see them bloom
for me and you,
and I think to myself,
"What a wonderful world!"

1

222

Practice and Extend

BACKGROUND

About the Authors George David Weiss and Bob Thiele's song "What a Wonderful World" has appeared in many movies and productions. Louis Armstrong gave the song its fame when he recorded it.

VOCABULARY POWER

Adjectives Point out that the writers of this song use many adjectives to describe things in the world. List some of the adjectives on the board: *green, red, wonderful, bright, dark*, and so on. Have children locate other adjectives in the song, and add them to the list. Talk about how these adjectives help singers and listeners get a picture in their minds of what is being described.

I see skies of blue
and clouds of white,
the bright, blessed day,
the dark, sacred night,
and I think to myself,
"What a wonderful world!"

223

During Reading

1 Visual Literacy: Illustrations

Explain to children that the people in the illustrations represent the different cultures in our schools, communities, and country. Explain that they also represent people who live in other countries all over the world. As you sing the song, have children follow along to learn how people are still very much the same despite their many differences.

Q How does the artist show in his illustrations that people are different?

A He uses color to show that people have different skin colors. He shows people in various settings and wearing different clothing styles.

Q How does the artist show that people are the same?

A They are all laughing, singing, and dancing. They all seem to have family and friends, and they seem to care about each other.

INTEGRATE THE CURRICULUM

MUSIC Lead children in singing the song "It's a Small World." Then guide children in a discussion about the meaning of the expression *It's a small world*. Encourage them to tell how this song is similar to and different from "What a Wonderful World."
Compare Two Songs

MAKE IT RELEVANT

In Your Community Ask children to think about their own community as they listen to the lyrics of the song. Then have children brainstorm what the illustrations might look like if they showed only people from their community. If time allows, children can create a mural that represents the song as it applies to where they live.

2 Understand the Song Help children recognize the writers' description of racial and cultural harmony. Discuss the imagery used on page 224.

Q What do the writers mean when they say that the colors of the rainbow are in the faces going by?

A People come in many colors, just as a rainbow has many colors. It also means that the colors of the people are beautiful, just like a rainbow.

3 Culture Ask children to tell how shaking hands might also mean that someone is saying "I care about you." Have them see that shaking hands is a sign of respect and friendship in many cultures. Ask children to share other ways people greet one another or show affection, such as hugging, holding hands, kissing, bowing, and waving.

4 Understand the Song Have children discuss what they think the writers mean by the line "They'll learn much more than I'll ever know," on page 225. Discuss how this line shows hope that new generations will continue to grow, change, and learn new things about the world.

2 The colors of the rainbow, so pretty in the sky
are also on the faces of people going by.
I see friends shaking hands, saying, "How do you do?"
They're really saying, "I love you." **3**

224

Practice and Extend

MAKE IT RELEVANT

At School Guide the class in corresponding with pen pals in another country. As a group, write to a class in another country to exchange information about school life. After children receive a response, encourage them to compare and contrast a typical school day in the other country to their school.

REACH ALL LEARNERS

Leveled Practice Have children look for song patterns.
Basic Point out that songwriters often repeat phrases. Have children read or sing the repeating lines in this song.
Proficient Ask children to find patterns in other songs. Have them read or sing the repeating lines aloud.
Advanced Encourage children to create another verse to the song, following the same pattern.

I hear babies cry, I watch them grow.

4 They'll learn much more than I'll ever know,

and I think to myself,

"What a wonderful world!"

Yes, I think to myself,

"What a wonderful world!"

Response Corner

1 Recall and Retell   What is this song telling us about the world?

2 Make It Relevant   What do you think is wonderful about the world?

225

After Reading

Response Corner—Answers

1. **Recall and Retell** The world is full of beautiful people and things that are all different but still special. This is what makes us all the same.

2. **Make It Relevant** Responses should include not just what the children find wonderful but also reasons for their answers.

Write a Response

Have children write a brief description of their school or community, telling what they think are the beautiful qualities of either one.

For a writing response rubric, see Assessment Program, page xvi.

INDEPENDENT READING

Children may enjoy reading these books during the unit.
Additional books are listed on page 217J of this Teacher Edition.

Giving Thanks: A Native American Good Morning Message by Chief Jake Swamp (Lee & Low Books, Inc., 1997). This book tells of giving thanks for beautiful things found in the world.

Whoever You Are by Mem Fox (Harcourt Brace & Company, 2001). Children learn that even though children around the world are different, they all have much in common.

The Mitten by Jan Brett (Putnam Juvenile, 1989). This book tells a story of how a child's lost mitten becomes a home for many wild animals.

For information about ordering these trade books, visit **www.harcourtschool.com/ss1**

OBJECTIVES

- **Describe cultures from around the world.**

- **Identify the features of a culture, including dress, art, language, food, music, and beliefs.**

- **Compare and contrast cultures.**

VOCABULARY

culture p. 226   **language** p. 227

CAUSE AND EFFECT

pp. 220–221, 231

RESOURCES

Homework and Practice Book, p. 42; Reading Support and Intervention, pp. 74–77; Success for English Learners, pp. 78–81; Vocabulary Transparency 5-1; Focus Skills Transparency 5; Recall and Retell Graphic Organizer Write-On/Wipe-Off Card; Unit 5 Audiotext CD Collection; Internet Resources

Introduce

What to Know Read aloud the What to Know question. Ask children to find the word *culture* on the page. Read aloud the paragraph in which it appears. Remind children to look for answers to the question as they read the lesson.

Build Background Invite children to share examples of the foods, clothes, art, and music that they know are from other parts of the world.

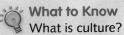

Lesson 1 World Cultures

What to Know
What is culture?

Vocabulary
culture
language

Recall and Retell

Our world is made up of many cultures. **Culture** is a group's way of life. Food, clothes, art, music, and beliefs are all parts of a group's culture.

A Community in Ghana

Abena lives in Ghana, a country in Africa. The people in her village sell fruits, vegetables, and crafts at the market.

A market in Ghana, Africa

226

Practice and Extend

Express Path

When minutes count, look for the **EXPRESS PATH** to focus on the lesson's main ideas.

Quick Summary

There are many different cultures around the world and in our own country. Clothes, art, language, food, music, and beliefs are features of a group's culture, or way of life.

Besides English, people in Abena's village speak a **language** called Twi. The children listen to folktales told in Twi. Many of the stories are about Anansi the spider. The people of Ghana say that it was Anansi who brought stories to the world.

A folktale from Ghana

Reading Check **Recall and Retell** What things are parts of Abena's culture?

Buying and selling things at a market, the Twi language, and stories about Anansi the spider are all parts of Abena's culture.

227

2 Teach

A Community in Ghana

CONTENT FOCUS In a village in Ghana, Africa, the people buy and sell at a market. They speak English and Twi. Children listen to folktales in their native language.

Express Path

Have children describe the market and folktale from Ghana and answer the Reading Check question.

1 Culture Explain that different places around the world have unique cultures, but all cultures share similar things. Create a three-column "Culture Chart" on the board. Title the columns *Ghana, Spain,* and *Japan.* As children read about Ghana, invite them to add information about its culture to the chart.

2 Geography Let partners find Africa and Ghana on a world map. Then elicit details from the class about Ghana's geography and nearby landforms.

Interactive in the enhanced online student eBook

READING SUPPORT/ INTERVENTION

For alternate teaching strategies, use pages 74–77 of Reading Support and Intervention to:

■ identify **phonemes**

■ practice **phonics**

■ reinforce **vocabulary**

■ build **text comprehension**

■ build **fluency**

Reading Support ▶ and Intervention

ELL ENGLISH LANGUAGE LEARNERS

For English Language Learners strategies to support this lesson, see Success for English Learners pages 78–81.

■ English-language development activities

■ background and concepts

■ vocabulary extension

Success for ▶ English Learners

A Community in Spain

CONTENT FOCUS Eating together is an important part of family life in Spain. Festivals are also part of Spanish culture.

Express Path

Let children scan the text to find the answer to the Reading Check question.

3 Culture Point out that belonging to a culture makes people a part of a group. Discuss the details of Spanish culture that make people who live in Spain feel like part of a group. Add these cultural details under *Spain* on the "Culture Chart."

Link Culture and Civics Explain that a culture is a kind of group in which people share different ways of living that help to meet their needs. These include food, clothing, and family. Have children give examples of these aspects of life in their own family. Point out that though the ways we live can be different, we all share the same needs.

A Community in Spain

3 Eduardo lives with his family in Cordoba, a city in Spain. Eating together is an important part of family life in Spain. The biggest meal of the day is lunch. Many businesses close then so that people can go home to eat with their families.

Paella, a rice dish, is a favorite meal in Spain.

Cordoba, Spain

228

Practice and Extend

BACKGROUND

Ghana The rich culture of Ghana meets the needs of its people. Ghana is a country along the west coast of Africa. It has many natural resources and gained independence earlier than other African countries. Folktales are an important part of Ghana's culture and traditions. Anansi the spider is a tiny trickster who cleverly defeats larger foes.

MAKE IT RELEVANT

In Your Community Invite children to look in your local newspaper to learn about different aspects of local culture. Look for cultural events. Discuss the importance of cultural unity and diversity within a community. Look for events that occur outside your community that impact its citizens. Discuss how places around the world are connected.

INTEGRATE THE CURRICULUM

VISUAL ARTS In Ghana, men weave narrow strips of cloth to make Kente cloth. The fabric shows the social status of the person wearing it. Have children make a cardboard loom. Make $\frac{1}{4}$-inch cuts at the top and bottom of a 6-inch cardboard square. Wind red yarn around the cardboard. Weave blue yarn through the red yarn. **Weaving**

Every year during the last week of May, Cordoba holds a big festival. The streets fill with people who come to see the parade of horses, the lights, and dancing to guitar music.

Reading Check **What is an important part of Spanish family life?** Eating together is an important part of Spanish family life.

4

Flamenco dancer

229

4 Culture Have children use the text and pictures to identify details about Spanish culture. Ask them to compare these details to their own culture. Elicit from children that they may also have meals with their families, go to festivals, and listen to music.

Link History and Culture Ask children to recall the languages spoken in Ghana. (English and Twi) Point out that Twi is the native language spoken in Ghana. When the English began to settle there, they brought their language to Ghana. Explain that this is an example of how cultures come in contact and exchange their ways of life. Guide children to understand that Spanish is spoken in Spain.

Q People in what other countries speak Spanish?

A People in Mexico, South American countries, and Central American countries

Point out that explorers for Spain brought Spanish to the Americas when they explored and settled in these parts of the world.

BACKGROUND

Culture of Spain Paella is a dish made with seafood, meat, tomatoes, and rice. Seafood is popular in Spain because of its proximity to the ocean. Spanish food also often includes tomatoes, which were brought to Spain after its explorations of the Americas. Cordoba is a city in southern Spain famous for its textiles, beautiful buildings, and narrow, winding streets in its old quarter.

REACH ALL LEARNERS

Special Needs Help children realize the different languages spoken in other cultures. Point out Ghana, Spain, and Japan on a world map. Invite children to use their finger to trace the outline of each country as they identify the country and its language. (Twi, Spanish, Japanese) Use the following prompt: In ___ [country], the people speak ___ [language].

INTEGRATE THE CURRICULUM

MUSIC Flamenco is a style of dancing, guitar music, and singing from southern Spain. The Our Lady of Health Festival in late May includes flamenco contests. Find a source for flamenco music from a library or downloaded from the Internet. Play the music for children. Have them clap, tap, or snap along with the rhythm of the music. **Music Styles**

A Community in Japan

CONTENT FOCUS Families in Japan eat together at low tables, using chopsticks. Japan also celebrates special festivals of its own.

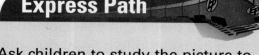

Express Path

Ask children to study the picture to answer the Reading Check question.

⑤ Culture Invite children to add details about the culture of Japan to the "Culture Chart." Discuss the chart.

Q How are Ghana, Spain, and Japan similar? How are they different?

A Help children conclude that all three have a strong cultural identity that helps people get what they need and feel part of a group. Each has different kinds of foods, clothing, languages, and places to live.

⑥ Link Culture and Geography Let partners find Japan on a world map. Ask them to identify countries that are nearby. Identify China as the largest nearby country. Explain that Japan and China have influenced each other's cultures over time. Their writing, arts, and ways of eating are similar.

Help children understand that the place where a culture develops affects what a culture is like. Explain that the natural resources in a place are important since they provide the materials that people use for food, clothing, and homes. Point out that contact with other groups also influences culture.

Q How has technology affected culture around the world?

A Because of technology, cultures around the world are becoming more alike.

A Community in Japan

Yukio lives in Aomori, Japan. Many people in Japan eat with chopsticks.
⑤ They sit on cushions on the floor at a low table. Favorite foods are rice, seaweed, vegetables with meat, and raw fish called sushi.

The Nebuta Festival in Aomori celebrates summer with a parade of colorful floats. Everyone takes part and dances to the drums and bamboo flutes.

Reading Check **What do people eat with in Japan?** Many people use chopsticks to eat in Japan.

⑥ **BOOK**

Aomori, Japan

230

Practice and Extend

REACH ALL LEARNERS

Leveled Practice Ask children to identify and share information about different cultures. Provide children with books with many pictures of cultures located around the world.

Basic Invite children to identify and share pictures that show examples of clothing, art, and activities people do in a particular culture.

Proficient Ask children to compare and contrast the food, clothing, art, and clothing of two cultures. Suggest they use a Venn diagram to share their findings.

Advanced Have children make stick puppets dressed in the clothing of a particular culture. Explain that they should make a backdrop and props to show the art, music, food, and activities of the culture. Invite children to use the puppets to act as storytellers who explain the culture to their classmates.

Aomori's Nebuta Festival

Summary People in countries around the world have different cultures.

Review

1 **What to Know** What is culture?

2 **Vocabulary** What **language** do you speak as part of your culture?

3 ✎ **Write** Choose a culture in your community. Write a short paragraph about things that are part of this culture.

4 ⭐ **Recall and Retell** Who do people in Ghana say brought stories to the world?

231

Summary

Have children read the summary and restate the main points in their own words.

- Many different cultures are found around the world.
- Culture is a group's way of life, including food, clothes, art, music, beliefs, and language.

Assess

REVIEW—Answers

1. **What to Know** Culture is the way a group of people lives, such as what they eat, what they wear, their language, art, music, and beliefs.

2. **Vocabulary** Possible answers: Spanish is a **language** I speak as part of my culture. I also speak English.

3. ✎ **Writing Assessment Guidelines** See Writing Rubric. This activity can be used with the Unit Project.

4. ⭐ **Recall and Retell** Anansi the spider brought stories to the world.

Use Focus Skills Transparency 5 or Recall and Retell Graphic Organizer Write-On/Wipe-Off Card.

✎ **WRITING RUBRIC**

Score 4
- clearly identifies a culture
- provides excellent examples
- shows clear organization

Score 3
- adequately identifies a culture
- provides good examples
- shows adequate organization

Score 2
- somewhat identifies a culture
- provides fair examples
- shows little organization

Score 1
- does not identify a culture
- does not include examples
- shows no organization

HOMEWORK AND PRACTICE

Name _____ Date _____

About My Culture

Draw a picture of an object that tells about your culture. Choose an object that shows how your culture is special. Finish the sentence to tell why you chose this object.

I chose _____ to tell about my culture because

Possible answer: I chose maracas to tell about my culture because my family likes to get together and play music on holidays. The maracas are my favorite instrument to play.

page 42

BACKGROUND

Japan Aomori is a city on a harbor in Japan. Because the people there live on an island surrounded by the ocean, the people of Aomori eat seaweed, fish, and other seafood. They use traditional chopsticks. During the Nebuta Festival, huge floats made of wood, paper, and wire are lit with hundreds of tiny lights and are pulled through the city.

OBJECTIVES

- **Find locations of countries in different hemispheres on a world map or globe.**

- **Identify hemispheres, the equator, and poles.**

RESOURCES

Homework and Practice Book, p. 43; Social Studies Skills Transparency 5-1; Primary Atlas; Interactive Atlas; Unit 5 Audiotext CD Collection; Internet Resources

1 Introduce

Show children several books that have colorful pictures of different countries. Invite them to pass the books around and discuss the pictures. Have them choose two countries that they would like to visit. Ask them what they would need to do to plan a trip to these countries. Elicit that they would have to use a map to plan such a trip.

Why It Matters Explain that as children learn about cultures and countries around the world, it is helpful to locate the countries on a map. Sometimes knowing nearby countries helps us understand the culture of a country. Point out that a country's location in relation to the poles or the equator can also give us clues about how the people there live.

Find Locations on a World Map

Why It Matters We can use a world map to find countries and their neighbors.

Learn

❶ There are more than 190 countries in the world. Russia is the largest country. China has the most people.

❷ Countries that are close together are more alike than different.

❸ Practice

❶ Which continent has more countries, South America or Africa?

❷ Which continent is Japan a part of?

❸ Which countries are Spain's neighbors?

232

Practice and Extend

SOCIAL STUDIES SKILLS

Map and Globe Skills

Find Locations on a World Map

The World

People We Know
pages 232–233

Harcourt Social Studies

Social Studies Skills Transparency 5-1

TRANSPARENCY 5-1

INTEGRATE THE CURRICULUM

♪ **MUSIC** Invite children to share songs of the countries from where their families originally came.

- Invite children to share music or a dance from their families' original country.
- Let children make posters about their families' countries.
- Teach children a song or folk dance from a country discussed in the lesson. **Cultural Songs**

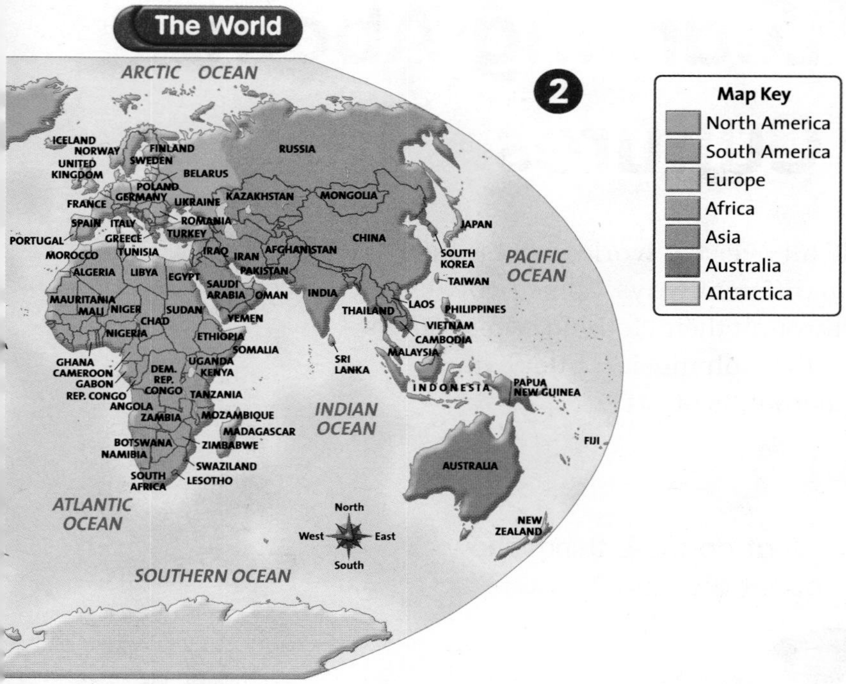

The World
ARCTIC OCEAN
2
Map Key
North America
South America
Europe
Africa
Asia
Australia
Antarctica
ICELAND
NORWAY
FINLAND
SWEDEN
UNITED KINGDOM
RUSSIA
BELARUS
POLAND
GERMANY
UKRAINE
KAZAKHSTAN
MONGOLIA
FRANCE
SPAIN
ITALY
ROMANIA
PORTUGAL
GREECE
TURKEY
JAPAN
CHINA
MOROCCO
TUNISIA
IRAQ
IRAN
AFGHANISTAN
SOUTH KOREA
PACIFIC OCEAN
ALGERIA
LIBYA
EGYPT
PAKISTAN
TAIWAN
SAUDI ARABIA
MAURITANIA
OMAN
INDIA
MALI
NIGER
SUDAN
LAOS
THAILAND
PHILIPPINES
CHAD
YEMEN
VIETNAM
NIGERIA
ETHIOPIA
CAMBODIA
SOMALIA
MALAYSIA
GHANA
CAMEROON
UGANDA
KENYA
SRI LANKA
GABON
DEM. REP. CONGO
REP. CONGO
TANZANIA
INDONESIA
PAPUA NEW GUINEA
ANGOLA
ZAMBIA
MOZAMBIQUE
INDIAN OCEAN
MADAGASCAR
FIJI
BOTSWANA
NAMIBIA
ZIMBABWE
AUSTRALIA
SWAZILAND
SOUTH AFRICA
LESOTHO
ATLANTIC OCEAN
North
West
East
South
NEW ZEALAND
SOUTHERN OCEAN

Apply

Make It Relevant Name the country or countries your family came from. Find them on a world map or a globe.

GO ONLINE For online activities, go to **www.harcourtschool.com/ss1**

233

Map and Globe Skills

2 Teach

❶ Link Culture and Geography Have children recall the countries they have learned about in Lesson 1—Ghana, Spain, and Japan. Ask children to

- locate each country on the world map on pages 232 and 233.
- identify the neighboring countries of each.
- discuss how these countries may influence each other's cultures.

❷ Visual Literacy: Map Ask children to find where the equator and North and South Poles would be on the map. Help children see how the equator divides Earth into Northern and Southern Hemispheres. Then point out where the Eastern and Western Hemispheres are on the map. Invite children to describe the location of countries by identifying which hemispheres they are in.

❸ Practice

1. Africa has more countries.
2. Japan is a part of Asia.
3. Portugal, France, Italy, and Morocco are Spain's neighbors.

3 Close

Apply

Make It Relevant Help children find their family's countries by identifying the continent on which it is located and which hemisphere. Then have children construct tally charts or picture graphs of the countries that the children's families come from.

INTERNET RESOURCES

GO ONLINE For online activities, go to **www.harcourtschool.com/ss1**

REACH ALL LEARNERS

Leveled Practice Find and name countries on different continents.

Basic Invite children to find and name the countries in North America.

Proficient Ask children to locate and name the countries in North America and South America.

Advanced Explain that Central America is part of North America. Invite children to find and name the countries of Central America.

HOMEWORK AND PRACTICE

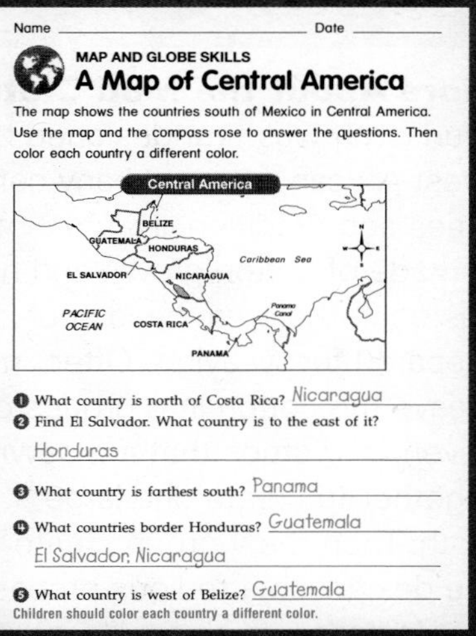
Name ______ Date ______

MAP AND GLOBE SKILLS

A Map of Central America

The map shows the countries south of Mexico in Central America. Use the map and the compass rose to answer the questions. Then color each country a different color.

Central America
BELIZE
GUATEMALA
HONDURAS
Caribbean Sea
EL SALVADOR
NICARAGUA
PACIFIC OCEAN
COSTA RICA
PANAMA

1. What country is north of Costa Rica? Nicaragua
2. Find El Salvador. What country is to the east of it? Honduras
3. What country is farthest south? Panama
4. What countries border Honduras? Guatemala, El Salvador, Nicaragua
5. What country is west of Belize? Guatemala

Children should color each country a different color.

page 43

OBJECTIVES

- **Understand that culture can be demonstrated through a variety of primary sources.**

- **Examine cultural items from around the world.**

RESOURCES

Unit 5 Audiotext CD Collection; Primary Source Collection; Internet Resources

💡 Link to the Big Idea

Culture Remind children that when people come to live in this country, they bring their culture with them. These parts of other cultures all become part of the life and culture in the United States.

Background Explain to children that learning about other cultures from primary sources helps us understand other people. Remind children that when people understand each other, they get along and have fewer conflicts.

Vocabulary Help Ask children to read aloud the label for each primary source and discuss the terms. Explain that a *kimono* is a full-length traditional robe with wide sleeves, worn most often by Japanese women, and sometimes by men and children, for special occasions. It is to be worn in specific ways, and there are required parts that go along with it, including a wide belt called an *obi* that wraps around the waist and is tied in the back.

Learning About Cultures

People all over the world express their culture in different ways. Some people show it through their clothing, while others express it through music, pottery, and many other kinds of art.

DBQ ❶ What do these things show about a culture?

Mask from Colombia

Maracas from Mexico

Kimono from Japan

234

Practice and Extend

BACKGROUND

More About the Mud Cloth
Mud cloth was first designed by West African women many centuries ago. Traditionally, the cloth is made of cotton grown and harvested in the area, hand spun, and prepared for weaving. Often, men weave the cotton into groups of seven long strips that are sewn together to create one large cloth. Then the women create the designs in a tedious process that includes washing, drying, and soaking the cloth in plant juices and teas. The mud dye is painted on from the borders to the inner area, causing a chemical reaction that creates the desired color. This process takes several weeks to complete. The various patterns that are eventually created have specific names and meanings, such as "fish bones." The most traditional colors are white designs on a black background, although other colors might also be used.

DBQ ② How can you use these things to compare cultures?

Hat from Peru

Mud cloth from Mali

Boots from Turkey

✎ Write About It

How are the things on these pages like things from your culture?

GO ONLINE For more resources, go to www.harcourtschool.com/ss1

235

Discuss the Primary Sources

Link Culture and Geography Call out each primary source, and ask volunteers to point to the corresponding picture in the lesson. Invite children to locate the origin country for each artifact on a world map. Discuss each item, and then have children answer the questions.

DBQ Document-Based Question—Answers

1. These things show ways that people dress and some types of entertainment that people enjoy in other cultures.

2. When we compare things such as traditional clothing, we learn how cultures are alike and different from each other. We also learn how the climate or natural resources of a country affect what cultures make or use.

Write About It

Tell children that they should use the primary sources, their answers to the questions, and their knowledge of social studies to help them write their paragraphs.

Research Ask children to research additional primary sources about cultures. Then have children select one or more of the primary sources and write a brief description telling what it is; who used it; where, when, and why it was used; and what it tells about the time period.

GO ONLINE **INTERNET RESOURCES** For more resources, go to **www.harcourtschool.com/ss1**

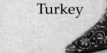

INTEGRATE THE CURRICULUM

🎵 **MUSIC** Have children use maracas to celebrate a special event while listening to Mexican music. Provide children with maracas, or invite them to make maracas by taping together two plastic cups filled with a handful of dried beans. Play music as children shake the maracas in time with the music. Have children find out what occasions and holidays in Mexico would feature maracas.
Make Maracas

ELL ENGLISH LANGUAGE LEARNERS

Beginning Have children point to the appropriate picture as you call out *clothing*, *music*, or *art*.

Intermediate Ask children to read aloud items from the lesson that show culture as shown in clothing. Repeat with music and art.

Advanced Invite children to read aloud each item shown in the lesson pictures. Have them explain which items are types of clothing, music instruments, or art.

OBJECTIVES

- Identify the reasons immigrants come to the United States.
- Recognize that immigrants bring a variety of cultures to the United States.
- Describe how cultures bring diversity to our country.

VOCABULARY

immigrant p. 236   **diversity** p. 240

RECALL AND RETELL

pp. 220–221, 241

RESOURCES

Homework and Practice Book, p. 44; Reading Support and Intervention, pp. 78–81; Success for English Learners, pp. 82–85; Vocabulary Transparency 5-2; Focus Skills Transparency 5; Recall and Retell Graphic Organizer Write-On/Wipe-Off Card; Activity Pattern A11; Unit 5 Audiotext CD Collection; Internet Resources

Introduce

What to Know Read the What to Know question aloud. Ask children to predict how the lesson might answer the question. Remind children to look for answers to the question as they read the lesson.

Build Background Ask children to recall the definition of *culture*. Invite them to describe the different ways people dress and the different languages that are spoken in their community. Point out that when people come from other countries to the United States, they bring their culture with them.

Lesson 2 Many People, One Country

What to Know Why is the United States a country of many cultures?

Vocabulary
immigrant
diversity

Recall and Retell

On a city street, you may see a Chinese, French, or Italian restaurant. You may hear people speaking Spanish, Arabic, and other languages. Immigrants have brought their cultures to the United States. An **immigrant** is someone who comes from another place to live in a country.

❷

These immigrants are taking part in a ceremony to become American citizens.

236

Practice and Extend

Express Path

When minutes count, look for the **EXPRESS PATH** to focus on the lesson's main ideas.

Quick Summary

Immigrants come to the United States for many reasons. The cultures immigrants bring have helped create United States history and heritage. The diversity of cultures in our country creates a wide variety of beliefs, causing Americans to have different points of view.

Coming to the United States

Immigrants have been coming to the United States for many years and for many different reasons. In the past, immigrants from Ireland came because they did not have enough food. Today, immigrants from some African countries come to escape war. Many immigrants come to the United States for a better life.

Reading Check **What is a reason immigrants come to the United States?** A reason immigrants come to the United States is to make a better life.

Many immigrants who came in the past arrived at Ellis Island in New York Harbor.

237

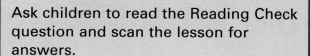

2 Teach

Coming to the United States

CONTENT FOCUS Immigrants have come to the United States for many different reasons.

Express Path

Ask children to read the Reading Check question and scan the lesson for answers.

1 Culture Help children recognize diversity in your community. Invite them to identify diverse restaurants in your neighborhood. Brainstorm a list of languages they have heard people speak. Invite them to name the cultures of their families.

2 Civics and Government Point out that the people in the photograph on pages 236 and 237 are becoming U.S. citizens. Discuss how new citizens promise to show respect for U.S. laws and to support democracy.

3 Visual Literacy: Pictures Invite children to compare and contrast the immigrants from the past and those from the present on pages 236 and 237.

VOCABULARY

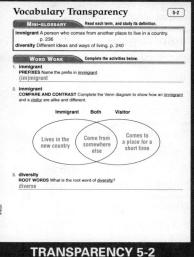

TRANSPARENCY 5-2

READING SUPPORT/ INTERVENTION

For alternate teaching strategies, use pages 78–81 of Reading Support and Intervention to:

- identify **phonemes**
- practice **phonics**
- reinforce **vocabulary**
- build **text comprehension**
- build **fluency**

Reading Support ▶ and Intervention

ELL ENGLISH LANGUAGE LEARNERS

For English Language Learners strategies to support this lesson, see Success for English Learners pages 82–85.

- English-language development activities
- background and concepts
- vocabulary extension

Success for ▶ English Learners

Cultural Differences

CONTENT FOCUS Immigrants learn new ways of doing things while keeping their own culture.

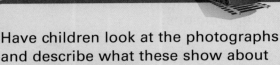

Express Path

Have children look at the photographs and describe what these show about immigrant cultures.

4 History Point out that unless we have Native American ancestors, all of us have ancestors who were once immigrants. Explain that the Native Americans were the first Americans. Later, immigrants from Europe settled in what became the United States. In time, people from all parts of the world have come to our country. Stress that these different cultures have shaped our national heritage.

5 Link Culture and Geography Have children imagine they are going to take a trip to their family's country or countries of origin. Invite them to research what they will see when they get there. Help children research the food, customs, games, and music of these places. Also have them identify important sites and events.

Point out that each person must have a passport to take a trip to another country.

- Provide children with a copy of Activity Pattern A11, and have them fill out their passports.
- Have them fold the passports like books. Inside they should include a picture of themselves.
- Have them write the names of the countries they plan to visit.

Cultural Differences

At first, life in a new country is hard. Immigrants have to find new homes and new **4** jobs. They may have to learn a new language and new ways of doing things.

As immigrants learn about the culture of their new country, they also keep their own culture. They pass on their old ways of doing things to their children and grandchildren.

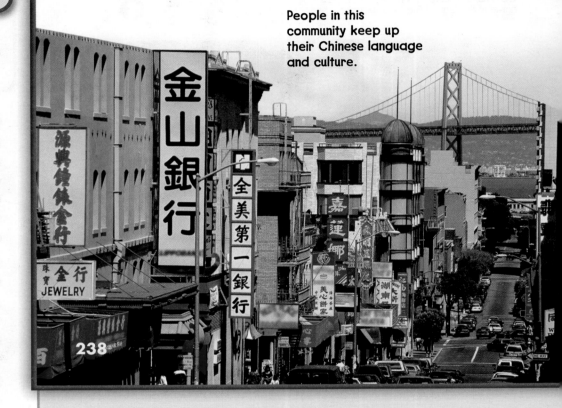

People in this community keep up their Chinese language and culture.

Practice and Extend

INTEGRATE THE CURRICULUM

LANGUAGES Have children compare words from different cultures. Make a chart to show how to count to three in different languages.

- French: *un, deux, trois*
- Italian: *uno, due, tre*
- Spanish: *uno, dos, tres*

Invite parents or school workers that speak another language to teach children how to count in their native language. **Numbers**

ELL ENGLISH LANGUAGE LEARNERS

Beginning Have children name aspects of culture they see in the pictures on pages 238 and 239, such as clothes, games, language, and music.

Intermediate Have pairs take turns stating details about a picture and identifying the picture that the description matches.

Advanced Ask children to describe what one picture shows about an immigrant culture.

Dhanya's parents are from India. Her father plays Indian songs on a sitar, a stringed instrument. For many Indian celebrations, Dhanya wears a colorful dress called a sari. **5**

Anthony's family loves to get together with neighbors to play bocce ball. Bocce ball is a game that is played in Italy. Anthony's grandfather taught him how to play.

Reading Check **Focus Skill** **Recall and Retell**

What makes life hard at first in a new country? People need to find new homes and jobs, and may have to learn a new language.

6

6 Link History and Civics and Government Ask children to describe the sari that Dhanya wears for special Indian celebrations. Then brainstorm a list of American holidays that people from all cultures in the United States celebrate, such as Independence Day, Memorial Day, and Veterans Day, and discuss the significance of these holidays. Point out that people from different cultures also study American history. Stress that this brings Americans together.

Culture Help children understand ethnic, racial, and religious diversity by helping them to identify different cultural groups in their community and state.

Q What kinds of religious groups have you seen in your community?

A Answers will vary, but may include Jewish, Muslim, and Catholic.

Help children research different kinds of cultural groups in other communities and states. Invite them to compare these groups with ones they have observed in their own community and state.

BACKGROUND

Indian Culture Intense colors, music, and flavors are predominant in Asian Indian culture. A sari is a 15- to 20-foot piece of brightly colored cloth that is wrapped around its wearer. A sitar is an instrument related to the lute and might have as many as 20 metal strings. A sitar player plucks the strings to play a raga, or pattern of melodic notes. The sound resonates through a gourd under the pegbox of the instrument.

Bocce Ball An Italian form of bowling, bocce ball is popular in the regions across Italy and in Italian communities in the United States. During a game, each player or team takes a turn rolling or tossing four balls (or bocce) toward one smaller ball (or boccino). The purpose of the game is to get one of your balls closer to the smaller ball than any of the oppositions' balls.

REACH ALL LEARNERS

Advanced Children can ask the school librarian to help them find appropriate books about different immigrant groups. Encourage children to pick a book that interests them and to take it home to read with a family member. Ask children to write a short report about the people in their book. Place the reports in a central area so other children can read them.

Diversity in America Today

CONTENT FOCUS Americans learn from each other's ideas and share different ways of living.

Express Path

Invite children to work with partners to find and list answers to the Reading Check question.

7 Culture Ask children to write a favorite food on a sticky note. Let children place their sticky notes on the board. Have them read each other's ideas. Point out the many points of view about favorite foods. Connect children's differing viewpoints with how different backgrounds and cultures contribute to different points of view.

Q How can different points of view be a good thing?

A We can learn new things from each other, such as trying new foods.

Q How might differing points of view cause problems?

A Children should recognize that problems only get solved when people share their points of view, are respectful, and work together.

8 Link Culture and Government Point out that our laws protect Americans' freedoms and rights, which is one of the reasons many immigrants come to the United States. Explain that people from many different countries come to the United States, and together we make up one American family. The United States' motto—E Pluribus Unum, or "Out of Many, One"—further emphasizes this.

Diversity in America Today

Immigrants bring **diversity**, or many different ideas and ways of living. We see this in our many kinds of food, clothing, music, dance, languages, and beliefs. Because cultures have different ideas and beliefs, people in our country have many different points of view. We learn from each other's ideas and share different ways of living.

240

Practice and Extend

REACH ALL LEARNERS

Leveled Practice Emphasize that American freedoms and rights bring many people to the United States.

Basic Invite children to talk about the right to vote. Discuss why being able to choose leaders makes people free. Talk about why someone who could not vote in his or her own country might come here.

Proficient Invite children to talk about freedom of speech. Discuss why being able to share ideas freely is important. Talk about why someone without this freedom might move here.

Advanced Discuss with children the Bill of Rights, the first ten amendments to the Constitution. Ask them to explain why the rights listed there might make someone move here.

8

We come from different cultures, but we are all Americans. We share a belief in freedom and the rights of every citizen.

Reading Check What are some kinds of diversity in the United States?

Some kinds of diversity are different kinds of food, clothing, music, dance, languages, and beliefs.

Summary Immigrants from other countries and cultures bring diversity to the United States.

❶ What to Know Why is the United States a country of many cultures?

❷ Vocabulary Name some **immigrant** groups who have come to the United States.

❸ 🖌 **Activity** Interview family members about how and why your family came to the United States.

❹ 🌟 **Recall and Retell** How do immigrants change the United States?

241

---

3 Close

Summary

Have children read the summary and restate the main points in their own words.

- Diversity brings new ideas, ways of living, and points of view to our country.
- Americans share a belief in freedom and the rights of every citizen.

Assess
REVIEW—Answers

1. **What to Know** Immigrants to the United States bring and carry on their own cultures.

2. **Vocabulary** Possible answer: Some **immigrant** groups who have come to the United States are African, Japanese, Irish, Italian, Spanish, Mexican, and Indian.

3. **Activity Assessment Guidelines** See Performance Rubric. This activity can be used with the Unit Project.

4. 🌟 **Recall and Retell** People adopt some of the immigrants' ways of living and thinking.

Use Focus Skills Transparency 5 or Recall and Retell Graphic Organizer Write-On/Wipe-Off Card.

HOMEWORK AND PRACTICE

Name _____ Date _____

Letter from Far Away

Pretend you are an immigrant in the United States. Write a letter home, telling about your trip and your life in the United States.

Possible answer:
Dear Misha ,

My trip to the United States was exciting. I flew in an airplane for the first time! I saw lots of ocean and mountains and land.

My family and I have moved into an apartment in Boston. I see many tall buildings from my bedroom window. I am making new friends here.

Yours truly,
Samira

page 44

WRITING RUBRIC

Score 4
- clearly explains reasons
- interview has many details
- child speaks clearly

Score 3
- adequately explains reasons
- interview has some details
- child speaks somewhat clearly

Score 2
- somewhat explains reasons
- interview has few details
- child speaks softly

Score 1
- gives no reasons
- interview has no details
- child does not speak clearly

INTEGRATE THE CURRICULUM

 READING/LANGUAGE ARTS Invite children to write an acrostic poem. Have them write *DIVERSITY* vertically down the side of their paper. Model how to write a word, phrase, or sentence about diversity that begins with the letter *D*. For example: *Differences make America strong.* Then brainstorm ideas for the letter *I*, such as: *Immigrants bring new ideas.* Display completed poems. **Poetry**

OBJECTIVES

- Recognize that people in a group have different points of view.
- Follow steps for working together in a group.

VOCABULARY

conflict p. 242

RESOURCES

Homework and Practice Book, p. 45; Social Studies Skills Transparency 5-2; Unit 5 Audiotext CD Collection

Introduce

Give children the following scenario: Arthur, the class rabbit, got out of his cage last night! He hopped to the art center and knocked over all the crayons. He chewed a hole in the bag of rabbit food and now it's all over the floor. Worst of all, he's not in his cage! Ask children how they can clean up the room and find Arthur before the class starts in 15 minutes. Help children realize that they should make a plan and work together.

Why It Matters Explain that it is important to get along with others for many reasons. It helps us make friends. It helps us work together to get a job done. It helps people from different cultures and points of view share ideas. Working together makes group members feel like they belong.

Citizenship Skills

Working Together

Why It Matters Sometimes when people work in a group, there is conflict. **Conflict** happens when people have different points of view on what to do or how to do it. To get a job done, people must cooperate, or work together.

Learn

Following these steps will help members of a group cooperate to get a job done.

1. Listen to each person's ideas. Plan together how to do the job.
2. Give each person a task.
3. When the job is done, talk about it.

242

Practice and Extend

SOCIAL STUDIES SKILLS

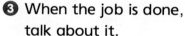

Citizenship Skills

Working Together

1. Listen to each person's ideas. Plan together how to do the job.
2. Give each person a task.
3. When the job is done, talk about it.

People We Know pages 242–243   Harcourt Social Studies   Social Studies Skills Transparency 5-2

TRANSPARENCY 5-2

INDEPENDENT READING

Invite children to read *We Can Work It Out: Conflict Resolution for Children* by Barbara Kay Polland (Tricycle Press, 2000). The book offers children the chance to think and talk about their experiences with conflict and how to resolve it.

we can work it out
CONFLICT RESOLUTION FOR CHILDREN

Our Garden of Diversity

Practice

Suppose your group wants to make a bulletin board showing different cultures in your school. Work together to list the steps. Write what to do in each step.

②

Apply

Make It Relevant Work together in a group to research a culture in your community or state.

243

Learn

① Visual Literacy and Pictures Read aloud the meaning of *conflict* in the text. Point out that conflict sometimes arises in groups of people. To get a job done, group members need to cooperate, or work together.

Q How can you tell the children in the pictures are cooperating?

A They are sharing, listening to each other, and taking turns. Each child has a job to do.

You may want to point out that stereotyping and prejudice are examples of conflict. Explain that stereotyping is thinking or believing negative things about others. Prejudice means to prejudge someone before we know them. Discuss how both behaviors show a lack of cooperation or respect.

❷ Practice

- Each group should make a list of everyone's ideas.
- Each person in the group should have a task that he or she can do.
- When they are finished, the group should look at what they did and talk about it.

3 Close

Apply

Make It Relevant As they work together, children should listen to each person's ideas about a culture to research. Then they should talk about the steps they should take. The group needs to decide who will do what job and how to later share the information. Invite children to reflect on how the job was completed.

REACH ALL LEARNERS

Leveled Practice Have children give examples of cooperation.

Basic Ask children to tell what they do and say to show they know how to work together.

Proficient Have children draw a poster with a descriptive sentence about working together.

Advanced Ask children to make a list of rules that help others work together in a certain situation.

HOMEWORK AND PRACTICE

Name _____ Date _____

A Tale About Working Together

Read the story about children who are making costumes for a culture parade. Underline the sentences that tell how they cooperate. Then answer the questions.

Will, Julie, and Teresa are marching in a parade. They want to wear costumes that tell about cultures. First, they share ideas, and everyone has a turn to talk. Will and Julie have a conflict about which costumes they should wear. Teresa suggests they take a vote to decide fairly.

After the vote, the children plan who will do each task. Will says he will look for pictures of clothing from different cultures. Julie will ask her mom for cloth and sewing supplies. Teresa will ask her sewing club to help make the costumes. When the costumes are finished, the children talk about their project and practice marching together. The parade will be fun!

❶ How did the children settle their conflict? Possible answers: They voted. They cooperated.

❷ Think of a time you worked with someone else to get a job done. What was the most important thing you did to cooperate? Answers will vary. Children might mention listening to each other, assigning tasks, or talking about the project when it is done.

page 45

OBJECTIVES

- **Understand the importance of the actions and character of Amy Tan, and explain how she made a difference in others' lives.**

RESOURCES

Unit 5 Audiotext CD Collection; Multimedia Biographies CD, Internet Resources; TimeLinks

💡 Link to the Big Idea

Culture Explain that many people in our country bring their culture and traditions from other countries. Amy Tan is a writer who uses her books to share her family's traditions with others.

Vocabulary Help Remind children that *traditions* are customs and beliefs passed from one generation to another so families will remember their past. Ask children about traditions their own families observe.

Discuss the Biography

History Explain that the photograph on page 245 shows a Chinese New Year parade in San Francisco, California. Chinese New Year parades have been held there since the 1860s. The festival begins on the first day of the first month of the Chinese calendar and ends on the fifteenth day. Chinese New Year traditions include visiting friends and relatives, wearing red clothing, giving gifts, eating special foods, and attending parades.

Geography Help children locate China and San Francisco on a map or a globe. Have children note the distance between the two places. Ask them to name ways that Tan's family could have traveled from China to the United States.

Biography

Trustworthiness

Respect

Responsibility

Fairness

Caring

Patriotism

Amy Tan

Amy Tan was born in Oakland, California, but her parents were born in China. In the 1940s, they left China to find a safer place to live. They moved to the United States.

When Amy Tan was young, she used her imagination to write. When she was eight years old, she won first prize for an essay she wrote. It was called "What the Library Means to Me."

Why Character Counts

🖊 **How does Amy Tan show respect for her culture?**

Amy Tan is an Asian American author.

244

Practice and Extend

BACKGROUND

Amy Tan When Amy Tan was in her teens, her father and brother died. Her mother then moved the family to Switzerland. Many of Tan's books explore the relationships between mothers and daughters as well as the Chinese cultural traditions that influence modern life. Tan was working as a language consultant for disabled young children when she took a writing workshop that helped launch her career as a novelist.

INDEPENDENT READING

Invite children to read *Sagwa, The Chinese Siamese* Cat by Amy Tan (Aladdin, 2001). In this original folktale, a mother cat tells her kittens the true story of their heritage.

Many Chinese Americans honor their culture with traditional celebrations.

Amy Tan now writes stories about her family. She is an American who remembers the Chinese traditions of her family's past. She uses her writing as a way to honor her family's history.

In her stories for children, Amy Tan shares her Chinese heritage.

GO ONLINE For more resources, go to www.harcourtschool.com/ss1

Time

1952 Born — Present

1969 Finishes high school in Switzerland

1985 Takes a writing class that leads to her first book

1989 Publishes her first book, The Joy Luck Club

245

Culture Explain that Amy Tan uses true stories from her life and the lives of her family members to weave fictional stories about Chinese Americans.

Q Are the stories that Amy Tan writes fact or fiction?

A They are fiction, but they are based on fact.

Visual Literacy: Time Line Call attention to the time line on page 245. Point out that it shows the year in which Amy Tan was born, but not the month or day. Have children find out the month and day of Amy Tan's birth.

TIMELINKS: Interactive Time Line

Have children add Amy Tan's birth date to the one-year TimeLinks: Interactive Time Line.

Why Character Counts

Amy Tan is a United States citizen, but she has great respect for her background and culture. She shows her respect by sharing her culture and heritage through her writing.

GO ONLINE **INTERNET RESOURCES**

For more resources, go to www.harcourtschool.com/ss1

Lesson 3

OBJECTIVES

- Recognize that each culture has unique traditions and customs.
- Compare the traditions and customs of different cultures.

VOCABULARY

custom p. 246   **tradition** p. 246

RECALL AND RETELL

pp. 220–221, 249

RESOURCES

Homework and Practice Book, p. 46; Reading Support and Intervention, pp. 82–85; Success for English Learners, pp. 86–89; Vocabulary Transparency 5-3; Focus Skills Transparency 5; Recall and Retell Graphic Organizer Write-On/Wipe-Off Card; Unit 5 Audiotext CD Collection; Internet Resources

Introduce

What to Know Read the What to Know question. Ask children to describe their routine as they get ready for school. Have them compare how their routines are alike and different. Explain that families also have traditions and customs that are alike and different. Remind children to look for answers to the question as they read the lesson.

Build Background Ask children to recall the previous lesson and describe ways that Dhanya's and Anthony's families shared their culture with their children. Invite children to predict other things families might share or pass on to their children.

Lesson # Celebrating Culture

 What to Know How are families different? How are they alike?

Vocabulary
custom
tradition

 Recall and Retell

Families in the United States celebrate their cultures. They may do different things, but families are alike in many ways.

David's Family

David and his family are Jewish. ① They have **customs**, or ways of doing things. They also have traditions. A **tradition** is something that is passed from older family members to children.

My family celebrating Shabbat

246

Practice and Extend

Express Path

When minutes count, look for the **EXPRESS PATH** to focus on the lesson's main ideas.

Quick Summary

Various cultures preserve their history through traditions, customs, and celebrations. Families pass down these traditions and customs to their children and, though cultures are different, families are alike in many ways.

Every Friday night, it is a tradition for all of David's family to share a special meal for Shabbat. They know that many Jewish families all over the world are sharing this tradition.

David's parents want their children to do well in school. David and his sister also go to a Jewish school to learn about Jewish customs and traditions. They are also learning the Hebrew language.

Reading Check **What do Jewish people all over the world share?** They share their customs and traditions.

My sister studying Hebrew

My older brother's bar mitzvah

247

2 Teach

David's Family

CONTENT FOCUS Families all over the world celebrate the customs and traditions of their cultures.

Express Path

Let children use the pictures to describe details of the Jewish culture.

1 History Explain that religion plays a large role in influencing some cultures. Tell children that David's family has a long history. The Jewish religion has many customs and traditions that have been passed from generation to generation.

Q Why do you think David's family believes it is important to honor their traditions?

A They are proud of their culture and want to remember their history.

Interactive in the enhanced online student eBook

VOCABULARY

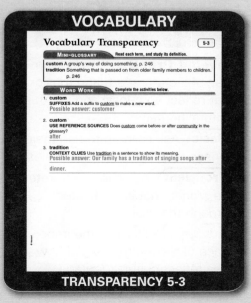

Vocabulary Transparency 5-3

MINI-GLOSSARY Read each term, and study its definition.

custom A group's way of doing something. p. 246
tradition Something that is passed on from older family members to children. p. 246

WORD WORK Complete the activities below.

1. **custom**
   SUFFIXES Add a suffix to custom to make a new word.
   Possible answer: customer

2. **custom**
   USE REFERENCE SOURCES Does custom come before or after community in the glossary?
   after

3. **tradition**
   CONTEXT CLUES Use tradition in a sentence to show its meaning.
   Possible answer: Our family has a tradition of singing songs after dinner.

TRANSPARENCY 5-3

READING SUPPORT/ INTERVENTION

For alternate teaching strategies, use pages 82–85 of Reading Support and Intervention to:

■ identify **phonemes**
■ practice **phonics**
■ reinforce **vocabulary**
■ build **text comprehension**
■ build **fluency**

Reading Support ▶ and Intervention

ELL ENGLISH LANGUAGE LEARNERS

For English Language Learners strategies to support this lesson, see Success for English Learners pages 86–89.

■ English-language development activities
■ background and concepts
■ vocabulary extension

Success for ▶ English Learners

LESSON 3 ■ 247

Luz's Family

CONTENT FOCUS Families are alike because they teach their children their customs and traditions. Since families have different cultures, their customs and traditions vary.

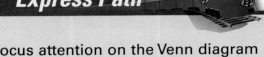

Express Path

Focus attention on the Venn diagram on page 249. Ask children to tell how the two families are alike and different.

2 **Culture** Ask children to compare how David's family and Luz's family learn about their culture's traditions.

Q What are some ways that your family learns traditions?

A Children may share that they help plan special events, attend classes to learn customs, go to special schools, or learn from an older family member.

Link Culture and Geography Help children understand cultural regions by explaining that people who share cultures and beliefs tend to live together in communities. Point out that Chinatown, from the previous lesson, is an example of such a region. Invite children to share examples of places like these in their community.

You may want to expand the discussion on cultural regions by using a map of the United States to show examples of these regions in our country, such as Amish (Pennsylvania), Mormon (Utah), and Cajun (Louisiana).

Luz's Family

Luz and her family are Mexican American. They speak both Spanish and English. It is a custom to celebrate birthdays with big parties. They also celebrate holidays, such as Easter. It is a family tradition to celebrate these holidays at Luz's grandparents' house.

Luz's parents were not able to go to college in Mexico. They want their children to study hard, go to college, and get good jobs.

Reading Check **Why do Luz's parents want their children to study hard?** They want their children to study hard so they can go to college and get good jobs.

When my sister turned fifteen years old, she had a big party called a Quinceañera.

Easter celebration at my grandmother's house

248

Practice and Extend

David's Family
Jewish American

Shares Shabbat

Children learn Hebrew

Both
Value education

Spend time together

Luz's Family
Mexican Amercian

Celebrates Easter

Speaks Spanish and English

How are the customs of these two cultures alike?

Summary Families of different cultures have special customs and traditions.

Review

1 What to Know How are families different? How are they alike?

2 Vocabulary How is a **tradition** different from other activities?

3 Activity Make a storyboard of pictures showing customs and traditions your family celebrates. Add captions to your pictures.

4 Recall and Retell What is a tradition both families had in this lesson?

249

---

3 Close

Summary

Have children read the summary and retell the main ideas.

- Families celebrate their own traditions and customs.
- Although traditions and customs may differ, families use them to teach their children about their culture.

Assess

REVIEW—Answers

1. **What to Know** Each family has its own customs and traditions, yet because of a common culture, many families share the same beliefs and ideas.

2. **Vocabulary Traditions** are passed on in families.

3. **Activity Assessment Guidelines** See Performance Rubric. This activity can be used with the Unit Project.

4. **Recall and Retell** celebrating special occasions with family

Use Focus Skills Transparency 5 or Recall and Retell Graphic Organizer Write-On/Wipe-Off Card.

WRITING RUBRIC

Score 4
- clearly illustrates traditions
- includes excellent details
- has few or no errors

Score 3
- adequately illustrates traditions
- includes adequate details
- has few errors

Score 2
- somewhat illustrates traditions
- includes few details
- has some errors

Score 1
- does not illustrate traditions
- includes no details
- has many errors

HOMEWORK AND PRACTICE

Name _____ Date _____

Pass on a Tradition!

Draw a picture to show something the person on the left might pass on to the person on the right.

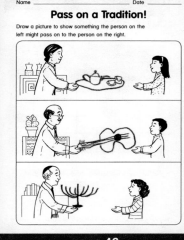

page 46

READING SOCIAL STUDIES

Recall and Retell Have small groups choose a family from this lesson. Ask groups to recall what they learned about the family and retell the facts to their classmates.

READING TRANSPARENCY

Use FOCUS SKILLS TRANSPARENCY 5.
Graphic Organizer Write-On/Wipe-Off Cards available

Read a Calendar

OBJECTIVES

- Use a calendar.
- Determine future and past dates and events by using a calendar.

VOCABULARY

calendar p. 250

RESOURCES

Homework and Practice Book, p. 47;
Social Studies Skills Transparency 5-3;
Activity Pattern A12; TimeLinks;
Unit 5 Audiotext CD Collection;
Internet Resources

I Introduce

Invite children to think of things they do that depend on knowing the date or day of the week. For example, have them name the days they have lessons, appointments, birthdays, or the days they go to school. Ask children to tell how they know when each of these days arrives. Point out that calendars are one way of keeping track of changes.

Why It Matters Explain to children that a calendar gives information about days of the week and helps us keep track of important events. Point out that knowing how to read a calendar can help children remember upcoming events. Discuss how a calendar is used at school and in their homes.

Why It Matters A **calendar** is a chart that keeps track of the days in a week, month, or year. You can use a calendar to measure time or to find special days.

Learn

❶ There are seven days in a week.

❷ There are about four weeks in a month. Most months have 30 or 31 days. February has just 28 days or, in some years, 29 days.

❸ There are 12 months in a year.

❷ Practice

❶ How many days are in this month?

❷ What special day is Sunday, March 25?

❸ When is St. Patrick's Day?

250

Practice and Extend

SOCIAL STUDIES SKILLS

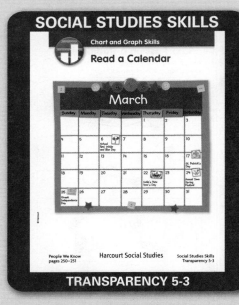

BACKGROUND

Cultural Days There are several cultural holidays in March.

- March 17 is the anniversary of the death of St. Patrick, the patron saint of Ireland.
- In India, the new year starts in a month called Caitra. The day is March 22 on a U.S. calendar.
- Greek Independence Day is celebrated on the anniversary of March 25, 1821, when Greeks fought for their independence.

March

Sunday	Monday	Tuesday	Wednesday	Thursday	Friday	Saturday
				1	2	3
4	5	6 School Red, White and Blue Day	7	8	9	10
11	12	13	14	15	16	17 St. Patrick's Day
18	19	20	21	22 India's New Year's Day	23	24 Annual Town Spring Festival
25 Greek Independence Day	26	27	28	29	30	31

Chart and Graph Skills

Apply

Make It Relevant Make a calendar page for next month. Show events that will happen at school and in your community.

For online activities, go to
www.harcourtschool.com/ss1

251

---

2 Teach

Learn

1 Visual Literacy: Calendar Have children say aloud the days of the week and the months of the year. Then direct children to the calendar on page 251.

Q The first day of next month will be on which day of the week? How do you know?

A Sunday; because the last day of this month is Saturday, and Sunday is the day after Saturday.

> **TIMELINKS: Interactive Time Line**
>
> Have children add the holidays shown on this calendar page to the one-year TimeLinks: Interactive Time Line.
>
>

2 Practice

1. There are 31 days in March.
2. Greek Independence Day is on March 25.
3. St. Patrick's Day is on Saturday, March 17.

3 Close

Apply

Make It Relevant Provide each child with a copy of Activity Pattern A12. Have them fill in the calendar with the name of the month and days of the week. They should include on the appropriate day weekly school activities, special events, and important tests.

HOMEWORK AND PRACTICE

Name _____ Date _____

CHART AND GRAPH SKILLS
Read a Calendar

Use Madison's calendar to answer the questions.

June 2008

S	M	T	W	T	F	S
1	2	3	4	5	6 Last day of school	7
8	9	10 Trip to Grandmother's	11	12	13	14
15 Father's Day	16	17	18	19	20 Children's Theater	21
22	23	24	25	26	27	28
29	30 Mother's birthday					

1 What month is on the calendar? _June_

2 How many days are in this month? _30_

3 When is the last day of school? _June 6_

4 How many days will Madison visit her grandmother?
6 days

5 On what day of the week is Madison going to the Children's Theater? _Friday_

page 47

Link to the Big Idea

Culture Tell children that many people who came here from Scotland want to remember their Scottish traditions and to pass those traditions on to their children and grandchildren. They enjoy being in a place that reminds them of their culture. Ask children to share stories of family gatherings they have attended and describe how these pass on the culture of another country.

Vocabulary Help Explain to children that a *kilt* is a woolen knee-length skirt that men in the Scottish Highlands wear. Kilts are worn for special events, such as weddings, parades, and cultural events. The Scottish word *kilt* means "to tuck up." Discuss traditional clothing from other cultures.

Read About

Explain to children that many immigrants came here from Scotland in the 1700s. They brought their culture with them, including games and competitions. These competitions include activities and games in which children participate. In this way, the competitions involve the children in the traditions as well.

Field Trip

Read About

Every July, the Grandfather Mountain Highland Games in North Carolina honor the culture of people from Scotland. At the games, you can see traditional Scottish clothing, such as kilts and tartan plaids. You can watch Scottish games and dancing, listen to music, and eat Scottish foods. You can also learn about the history of many families who came to the United States from Scotland.

Find

United States

Linville, North Carolina

252

Grandfather Mountain Highland Games

Caber toss

Practice and Extend

VOCABULARY POWER

Related Words Write the word *Scotland* on the board. Ask children to locate a related word in the lesson *(Scottish)*. Invite children to describe how these two words are related. (One names a country, the other describes people or things from that country.) Help children name other examples, such as *Spain/Spanish*, *Ireland/Irish*, or *Sweden/Swedish*.

INDEPENDENT READING

Share with children the books *Welcome to Scotland* by Graeme Cane (Gareth Stevens Audio, 2002) and *Visit to Scotland* by Anita Ganeri (Heinemann, 2003). Both books contain interesting information about the land, culture, traditions, and people who live in the Scottish Highlands. Invite children to compare the culture of Scotland with that of the United States.

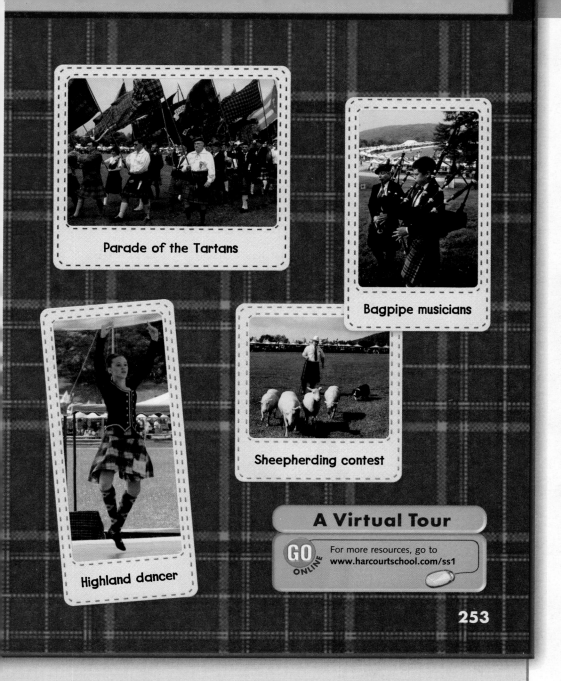

Parade of the Tartans

Bagpipe musicians

Highland dancer

Sheepherding contest

A Virtual Tour

GO ONLINE For more resources, go to www.harcourtschool.com/ss1

253

Find

Have children study the map. Ask them to identify the relative location of Linville, North Carolina. Point out that this region is very similar to a region in Scotland, including the hills and mountains, climate, and even flowers and trees. Ask children to compare maps of North Carolina and Scotland, looking at landforms and bodies of water.

Discuss Grandfather Mountain Highland Games

Ask children to focus on the photographs on pages 252–253.

Q Which of these activities would you like to try? Why?

A Possible answer: playing bagpipes, because it could be fun to see how they work.

Q Which of these events came from the work that people did to support and protect their families?

A sheepherding to supply food and wool for clothes or caber toss to build strength

A Virtual Tour Depending on the availability of computers, have children work individually, in pairs, or in small groups. Encourage them to research the history of the events at the Grandfather Mountain Highland Games as they explore the websites. Remind children to use what they learn on their virtual tours as background information for the Unit Project.

 **INTERNET RESOURCES**

GO ONLINE For more resources, go to **www.harcourtschool.com/ss1**

BACKGROUND

Grandfather Mountain Highland Games The first Games, held in 1956, were based on gatherings held in northern Scotland as early as the eleventh century. The event, founded by Agnes MacRae Morton and Donald F. MacDonald and held on Grandfather Mountain in Linville, North Carolina, includes activities such as footraces, dance competitions, shot put, tossing the caber, and sing-alongs of Gaelic songs.

MAKE IT RELEVANT

In Your Community Help children use local newspapers to find information about a cultural event in their community. Direct children to research information online or in books to learn about the event's culture. If possible, encourage children to interview a person who has attended the event. Invite children to use drawings or clip art to make a poster describing activities that might be found at this event.

OBJECTIVES

- Recognize that people from many cultures have contributed to American society.

- Describe how individuals can make a difference in people's lives.

VOCABULARY

scientist p. 254   invention p. 254

RECALL AND RETELL

pp. 220–221, 257

RESOURCES

Homework and Practice Book, p. 48; Reading Support and Intervention, pp. 86–89; Success for English Learners, pp. 90–93; Vocabulary Transparency 5-4; Focus Skills Transparency 5; Recall and Retell Graphic Organizer Write-On/Wipe-Off Card; Unit 5 Audiotext CD Collection; Internet Resources

Introduce

What to Know Read the What to Know question. Let children do a picture walk of the lesson to predict who they might read about. Remind children to look for answers to the question as they read the lesson.

Build Background Ask children to share how they have helped other people. Discuss the ways people can help one another. Explain that in this lesson, they will be learning about Americans from a variety of backgrounds who have helped make a difference in the lives of others.

Lesson 4 Recognizing Americans

 What to Know
Who are some Americans who have made a difference in our lives?

Vocabulary
scientist
invention

 Recall and Retell

Many different people live in the United States. Some Americans have done important things that have affected our lives and culture.

Famous Scientists

Thomas Edison was a **scientist**, a person who observes things and makes discoveries. His most famous invention was the lightbulb. An **invention** is a new product that has not been made before.

❶

"Genius is one percent inspiration, ninety-nine percent perspiration."

Thomas Edison

254

Practice and Extend

Express Path

When minutes count, look for the **EXPRESS PATH** to focus on the lesson's main ideas.

Quick Summary

People from a variety of backgrounds have made important contributions to American society. This lesson highlights the contributions of specific inventors, scientists, artists, and musicians.

George Washington Carver was a scientist who helped farmers. He showed that growing peanuts, soybeans, and sweet potatoes made poor soil rich again. He also found new ways to use these crops. They could be used to make medicines and even glue.

Reading Check **Focus Skill** Recall and Retell **In what ways did Edison and Carver improve people's lives?** Edison invented the lightbulb. Carver found new ways to use crops.

"Where there is no vision, there is no hope."

George Washington Carver

George Washington Carver found that more than 300 products could be made from peanuts. Some of these are peanut butter, ink, and shampoo.

255

---

2 **Teach**

Famous Scientists

CONTENT FOCUS Scientists make discoveries that improve our lives.

Express Path

Have children work in small groups. Assign one of the scientists to a group. Ask children to find the person's accomplishments.

1 **Primary Sources: Quotations**
Read aloud Edison's quotation. Discuss how his words describe how discovery and invention is hard work. Then read Carver's quotation aloud. Ask children to explain why Carver's words would be good for other scientists to remember.

Source: Thomas Alva Edison, *Harper's Magazine*, September 1932.

Source: George Washington Carver, **http://www.nps.gov/gwca**

Correct Misconceptions Point out that although Carver invented a product similar to peanut butter, it was actually invented long ago in South America. Peanut butter as we know it today was invented by a physician in 1890 as a health food for his patients.

VOCABULARY

Vocabulary Transparency 5-4

MINI-GLOSSARY Read each term, and study its definition.

scientist A person who observes things and makes discoveries. p. 254
invention A new product that has not been made before. p. 254

WORD WORK Complete the activities below.

1. **scientist**
WORD WEB Use the words scientist, experiment, inventor, and invention in a word web.

Possible answer: Center circle: scientist; Outer circles: experiment, inventor, invention

2. **invention**
ROOT WORDS What is the root word of invention?
invent

TRANSPARENCY 5-4

READING SUPPORT/ INTERVENTION

For alternate teaching strategies, use pages 86–89 of Reading Support and Intervention to:

■ identify **phonemes**
■ practice **phonics**
■ reinforce **vocabulary**
■ build **text comprehension**
■ build **fluency**

Reading Support ▶ and Intervention

ELL ENGLISH LANGUAGE LEARNERS

For English Language Learners strategies to support this lesson, see Success for English Learners pages 90–93.

■ English-language development activities
■ background and concepts
■ vocabulary extension

Success for ▶ English Learners

Famous Artists

CONTENT FOCUS Artists have contributed to American culture.

Express Path

Ask children to scan the section to find out how Ieoh Ming Pei and Gloria Estefan have made a difference in our lives.

2 Primary Source: Quotations Read aloud the quotations by Ieoh Ming Pei and Gloria Estefan, and discuss their meanings. Point out that technology, such as television, radio, the Internet, and even air travel, have made Pei and Estefan well known around the world. Point out that technology brings people and cultures from around the world closer together.

Source: Ieoh Ming Pei, *Asian-American Biographies*; *I.M. Pei*, Raintree, 2006.

Source: Gloria Estefan, comment to The Associated Press, September 10, 2005.

3 Culture Invite children to review all four featured Americans in this lesson.

Q How are these people similar and different?

A These Americans come from different backgrounds, yet they have all helped our country in some way.

Link History and Culture Discuss with children famous Americans who have influenced American culture. Possibilities include Cesar Chavez, Charles Drew, Albert Einstein, Benjamin Franklin, Helen Keller, Golda Meir, Rosa Parks, and Sally Ride. Invite children to share what they know about these Americans. Challenge children to identify men and women from different cultures and backgrounds who have given to their community, state, and country.

Famous Artists

Ieoh Ming Pei is a Chinese American architect, or a person who designs buildings. He designs interesting buildings that become landmarks in urban areas in the United States and around the world.

2 "Take your position and have faith in yourself."

Ieoh Ming Pei

Rock and Roll Hall of Fame and Museum in Cleveland, Ohio

256

Practice and Extend

INTEGRATE THE CURRICULUM

READING/LANGUAGE ARTS Invite children to think about folktales they have heard or read from different cultures. Point out that the hero of a folktale often shows qualities admired by people of a culture. Ask children to discuss how folktales help them understand a culture from around the world. Read aloud folktales for children to compare and discuss. **Folktales**

REACH ALL LEARNERS

Leveled Practice Let children share information about people in American history.

Basic Ask children to create a portrait of a famous American and include a descriptive caption.

Proficient Have children read a biography about an American and review it for the class.

Advanced Have children research a famous American on the Internet.

Gloria Estefan is a singer, dancer, and songwriter. Through her music, she shares her Cuban culture. Estefan's songs have helped make Latin music popular in the United States. She also holds concerts to raise money to help people in need.

Reading Check **How have Ieoh Ming Pei and Gloria Estefan affected American culture?** Ieoh Ming Pei creates interesting buildings in our country's cities. Gloria Estefan shares her culture through her music.

Summary Some Americans have done important things that have made a difference in our lives.

" I strongly feel that we are all connected. "

3

Gloria Estefan

Review

1 **What to Know** Who are some Americans who have made a difference in our lives?

2 **Vocabulary** What was Thomas Edison's most famous **invention**?

3 **Write** Write a paragraph about people in your community or state who have affected your life.

4 **Recall and Retell** How does Gloria Estefan help other people?

257

💡 Link to the Big Idea

Culture Tell children that the United States is made up of many different people and cultures. The languages people speak and the traditions they have are important parts of culture.

Preview the Games

Add Them Up In this game, children are asked to look at each pair of images and determine to which person they refer. Children will need to identify each person and his or her accomplishments to solve each equation. Discuss these accomplishments with children.

ANSWERS: Thomas Edison; George Washington Carver; Ieoh Ming Pei; Gloria Estefan

Missing Letters This game asks children to read each clue and figure out to which vocabulary word it refers. Children are then asked to figure out which letter is missing from the vocabulary word and use those letters to spell the answer to the riddle. Remind children that in each word, both letters that are missing are the same letter.

ANSWERS: language; invention; tradition; scientist; ANTS

Add Them Up

Match these people with the answers to the problems.

Gloria Estefan

George Washington Carver

Ieoh Ming Pei

Thomas Edison

258

Practice and Extend

🏳️ **LANGUAGES** Remind children that language is an important part of culture. Tell them that in Spanish, the word for "four" is *quatro*. Write the word on the board. Also write the Spanish word *casa* on the board, and explain that the word means "house" in English. See if children know any other Spanish words.
Learn Spanish Terms

At Home Ask children to go home and ask their family about their own traditions. Encourage them to inquire about any dress, food, music, or other elements of culture that are important to their family. Invite them to report their findings to the class.

Missing Letters

Use the missing letters to answer the riddle.

Word	Clue
l**?**ngu**?**ge	the words people use to communicate
i**?**ventio**?**	a new product that has not been made before
?radi**?**ion	something passed down from older family members to children
?cienti**?**t	a person who observes things and makes discoveries

What do uncles find at picnics?

? **?** **?** **?**

Online Adventures

A culture fair is coming to Eco's school. Visit the online fair to play games and learn about the cultures of many places. Play now, at **www.harcourtschool.com/ss1**

259

Online Adventures Before children begin this game, tell them that they will be solving puzzles at a school cultural fair. Discuss how people have different cultures, customs, and traditions. Tell children that Help Buttons in the game will refer them to pages in their textbook if they need additional information.

Share the Fun

At School Have children work in small groups to create their own Missing Letters games. Help them create a game similar to this activity based on the unit vocabulary words. When children are finished, ask them to share their games with classmates.

At Home Invite children to have their parents or guardians help them come up with other figures from the unit to use in an Add Them Up game. Ask children to find images that represent those people. Have children share their games with classmates.

REACH ALL LEARNERS

Leveled Practice Have children review the Add Them Up game.

(Basic) Discuss with children why these figures were important.

(Proficient) Invite children to go to the library to find a book about one of these figures to read.

(Advanced) Ask children to research and tell the class about one of these figures.

The Big Idea

Culture Ask a volunteer to read aloud the Big Idea. Invite children to share something they learned about cultures in this unit that supports the Big Idea.

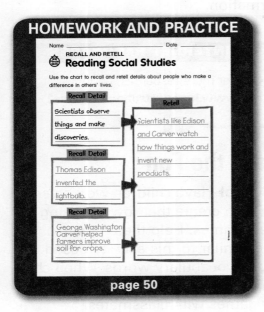

page 50

Reading Social Studies

Recall and Retell You may wish to have children review Reading Social Studies at the beginning of the unit. Charts should include information that demonstrates an understanding of details and an ability to retell information in their own words.

Unit 5

Review and Test Prep

 The Big Idea

Culture Our country is made up of many different people and cultures.

Recall and Retell

Copy and fill in the chart to recall and retell what you have learned about Americans who have done important things for our country.

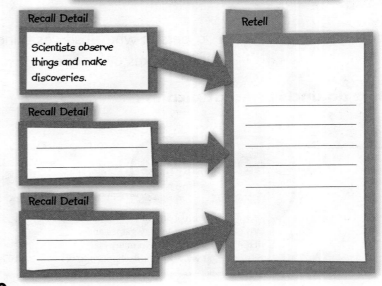

Americans Who Made a Difference

Recall Detail
Scientists observe things and make discoveries.

Retell

Recall Detail

Recall Detail

260

Vocabulary

Choose the word that matches the description.

1. Dhanya's father came here from India.

2. Anthony's family is Italian American.

3. Yukio eats with chopsticks.

4. Luz's parents pass down how their family celebrates special days.

Word Bank

culture
   (p. 226)
immigrant
   (p. 236)
tradition
   (p. 246)
custom
   (p. 246)

Facts and Main Ideas

5. What are parts of a group's culture?

6. What is an immigrant?

7. What beliefs do many Americans share?

8. What can happen when people have different points of view?

9. Which word describes the many ideas and ways of living we find in the United States?

   A immigrant   **C** diversity

   B language   **D** tradition

10. Which American helped farmers grow crops?

   A George Washington Carver   **C** Ieoh Ming Pei

   B Gloria Estefan   **D** Thomas Edison

261

Vocabulary

1. immigrant

2. culture

3. custom

4. tradition

Facts and Main Ideas

5. Food, dress, art, music, language, and beliefs are part of a group's culture.

6. An immigrant is someone who comes from another place to live in a country.

7. Americans share a belief in freedom and the rights of every citizen.

8. A conflict can happen when people have different points of view.

9. C, diversity

10. A, George Washington Carver

Critical Thinking

11. Possible answer: We would have to use candles or oil lamps to see when it is dark.

12. Make It Relevant Possible answers: They are the things my family does together. They are the ways I can learn about my family's history and culture.

Skills

13. 30 days

14. Native American Day

15. September 9

16. It is the first day of autumn.

⑪ How would life be different today if Thomas Edison had not invented the electric lightbulb?

⑫ **Make It Relevant** How do customs and traditions make your family special?

Skills

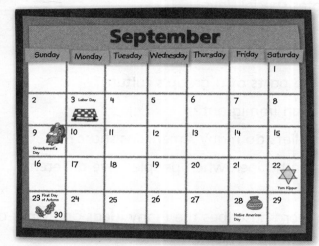

⑬ How many days are in this month?

⑭ What special day is Friday, September 28?

⑮ When is Grandparents' Day?

⑯ What happens on September 23?

262

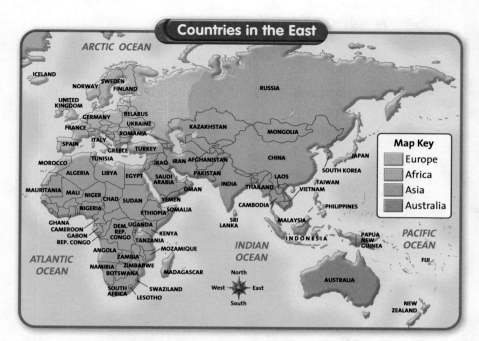

Countries in the East

ARCTIC OCEAN

ICELAND
NORWAY SWEDEN FINLAND
UNITED KINGDOM
GERMANY BELARUS
FRANCE UKRAINE
ROMANIA
SPAIN ITALY
GREECE TURKEY
MOROCCO TUNISIA
ALGERIA LIBYA EGYPT
MAURITANIA MALI NIGER
CHAD SUDAN
NIGERIA
GHANA UGANDA
CAMEROON DEM.
GABON REP.
REP. CONGO CONGO TANZANIA
ANGOLA ZAMBIA
NAMIBIA ZIMBABWE
BOTSWANA
SOUTH AFRICA MADAGASCAR
LESOTHO SWAZILAND

RUSSIA
KAZAKHSTAN
MONGOLIA
IRAQ IRAN AFGHANISTAN
SAUDI PAKISTAN CHINA
ARABIA INDIA
OMAN THAILAND LAOS
YEMEN VIETNAM
ETHIOPIA CAMBODIA
SOMALIA
KENYA SRI LANKA
MOZAMBIQUE INDONESIA

JAPAN
SOUTH KOREA
TAIWAN
PHILIPPINES
PAPUA NEW GUINEA

ATLANTIC OCEAN

INDIAN OCEAN

PACIFIC OCEAN

FIJI

AUSTRALIA

NEW ZEALAND

North
West — East
South

Map Key
- Europe
- Africa
- Asia
- Australia

⑰ Which continent has more countries, Africa or Australia?

⑱ On which continent is Pakistan located?

⑲ Which countries are Libya's neighbors?

⑳ Which ocean is north of Finland?

263

Skills

17. Africa

18. Asia

19. Egypt, Sudan, Chad, Niger, Algeria, and Tunisia

20. the Arctic Ocean

ASSESSMENT

Use the UNIT 5 Test on pages 38–40 of the Assessment Program.

Show What You Know

Unit Writing Activity

Remember Traditions Lead children in a discussion about family traditions. Record children's ideas on a word web with *Family Traditions* written in the central circle. Have children add details about who attends, what they do, when and where it takes place, and why it is a tradition.

 Write a Diary Entry Have children use their ideas to write a diary entry about a day when they celebrated a family tradition. Remind children to use several details from their word web and to include a date for their entry.

You may wish to distribute the Unit 5 Writing Activity Guidelines on page 41 of the Assessment Program.

For a scoring rubric, see this Teacher Edition, page 217O.

Unit Project

Storyboard Before children begin, help them list interview questions to ask family members. Use the questions to create a handout children can use. Point out that a storyboard looks similar to a comic strip, using pictures and words to tell a story. Remind children that their storyboard needs to show important events from past to present.

You may wish to distribute the Unit 5 Project Guidelines on page 43 of the Assessment Program.

For a scoring rubric, see this Teacher Edition, page 217O.

> **LEVELED READERS**
>
> Use the LEVELED READERS for Unit 5.

Activities

Show What You Know

 Unit Writing Activity

Remember Traditions Think about a tradition in your family. Why do you have it?

Write a Diary Entry Write a diary entry about a day you celebrate a tradition.

 Unit Project

Storyboard Design a family history storyboard.
- Interview family members.
- Collect photographs or draw pictures of events.
- Put the pictures in order.
- Share your storyboard.

Read More

Goldfish and Chrysanthemums by Michelle Cheng

The Color of Home by Mary Hoffman

How Marten Got His Spots and Other Kootenai Indian Stories by Kootenai Cultural Committee

 For more resources, go to www.harcourtschool.com/ss1

264

Read More

After the children's study of culture, encourage independent reading with these books or books of your choice. Additional books are listed on page 217J of this Teacher Edition.

Basic *Goldfish and Chrysanthemums* by Michelle Cheng (Lee & Low, 2003). A Chinese American girl helps her grandmother remember her home in China.

Proficient *The Color of Home* by Mary Hoffman (Phyllis Fogelman Books, 2002). A boy paints a picture to tell others about the home he left behind in Somalia.

Advanced *How Marten Got his Spots and Other Kootenai Indian Stories* by Kootenai Cultural Committee (Montana Historical Society, 2002). Children learn some of the folktales Native American elders share with their children.

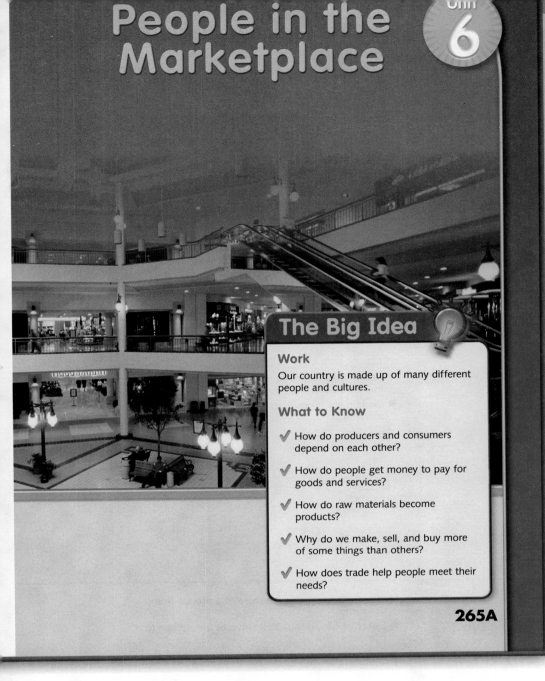

People in the Marketplace

The Big Idea

Work

Our country is made up of many different people and cultures.

What to Know

- ✓ How do producers and consumers depend on each other?
- ✓ How do people get money to pay for goods and services?
- ✓ How do raw materials become products?
- ✓ Why do we make, sell, and buy more of some things than others?
- ✓ How does trade help people meet their needs?

265A

Introduce the Unit

 The Big Idea

Work Read the Big Idea to children. Explain that we depend on many different workers to help us live. In this unit, children will learn about the jobs people do to earn money and how they choose to spend their money. Remind children to refer back to the Big Idea periodically as they finish this unit.

What to Know Have children read What to Know. Explain that these five essential questions will help them focus on the Big Idea.

Assessing the Big Idea Share with children that throughout this unit they will be asked to show evidence of their understanding of the Big Idea. See Assessment Options on page 265M of this Teacher Edition.

START WITH A VIDEO DVD

To introduce the Unit Big Idea to students, show a video clip from the Start with a Video DVD.

Instructional Design

The flowchart below shows briefly how instruction was planned for Unit 6.

START WITH THE BIG IDEA

Lesson Objectives
What to Know

→

PLAN ASSESSMENT

Assessment Options
- Option 1—Unit 6 Test
- Option 2—Writing: Write an Advertisement
- Option 3—Unit Project: Class Fair

→

PLAN INSTRUCTION

Unit 6 Teacher Edition
- materials
- instructional strategies
- activities

People in the Marketplace

THE BIG IDEA

WORK Producers and consumers depend on each other for goods and services.

Express Path

See each lesson for an **EXPRESS PATH** to teach main ideas.

LESSON	PACING	OBJECTIVES
Preview the Unit pp. 265V–265	**5 DAYS**	
Preview Vocabulary pp. 266–267		■ Use visuals to determine word meanings. ■ Use words and visuals to preview the content of the unit.
Reading Social Studies pp. 268–269		■ Use categories to classify information into groups. ■ Interpret information from charts.
Start with a Story *Supermarket* pp. 270–275		■ Recognize the importance of the supermarket to buyers in a community. ■ Explain the process by which goods are delivered to markets.
① Producers and Consumers pp. 276–279 💡 **WHAT TO KNOW** How do producers and consumers depend on each other?	**3 DAYS**	■ Identify and explain the roles of a producer and a consumer. ■ Describe how goods and services are related to a business. ■ Recognize how producers are also consumers.
CHART AND GRAPH SKILLS **Read a Bar Graph** pp. 280–281	**1 DAY**	■ Identify parts of a bar graph. ■ Use a bar graph to interpret information.
Biography: Wanda Montañez pp. 282–283	**1 DAY**	■ Understand the importance of the actions and character of Wanda Montañez, and explain how she made a difference in others' lives.

6 WEEKS	WEEK 1	WEEK 2	WEEK 3	WEEK 4	WEEK 5	WEEK 6	
	Introduce the Unit	Lesson 1	Lesson 2	Lesson 3	Lesson 4	Lesson 5	Wrap Up the Unit

READING SUPPORT VOCABULARY

(Focus Skill) **Reading Social Studies**
Categorize and Classify

Reading Social Studies,
Focus Skills, pp. 268–269

Vocabulary Power:
Word Meanings, p. 267
Figurative Language, p. 271
Compound Words, p. 272
Synonyms, p. 274

categorize p. 268
classify p. 268

(Focus Skill) **Reading Social Studies**
Categorize and Classify,
p. 278

producer p. 276
goods p. 277
services p. 277
business p. 278
consumer p. 279

bar graph p. 280

REACH ALL LEARNERS

ENGLISH LANGUAGE LEARNERS, pp. 266, 273

Leveled Practice,
pp. 269, 270, 274

ENGLISH LANGUAGE LEARNERS, p. 283

Leveled Practice, pp. 278, 281

Special Needs, p. 279

INTEGRATE LEARNING

Reading/Language Arts
Write a Story, p. 265
Make Comparisons, p. 268
Adjectives, p. 271
Sequence, p. 274

Mathematics
Money, p. 265

Health
Plan a Healthful Meal, p. 271

Science
Characteristics of Plants, p. 272

Science
Physical Attributes, p. 280
Languages
Spanish, p. 282
Visual Arts
Design a Product, p. 283

RESOURCES

Social Studies in Action: Resources for the Classroom
Primary Source Collection
⊙ Music CD
School-to-Home Newsletter S13–S14
Interactive Map Transparencies
Interactive Desk Maps
Primary Atlas
Interactive Atlas
TimeLinks: Interactive Time Line
Picture Vocabulary Cards
Focus Skills Transparency 6
Categorize and Classify Graphic Organizer Write-On/Wipe-Off Card
Assessment Program, p. 45
⊙ Unit 6 Audiotext CD Collection
Internet Resources
⊙ Start with a Video DVD

Homework and Practice Book, pp. 51–52
Reading Support and Intervention, pp. 90–93
Success for English Language Learners, pp. 95–98
Vocabulary Transparency 6-1
Focus Skills Transparency 6
Categorize and Classify Graphic Organizer Write-On/Wipe-Off Card
Social Studies Skills Transparency 6-1
⊙ Multimedia Biographies CD
TimeLinks: Interactive Time Line
⊙ Unit 6 Audiotext CD Collection
Internet Resources

LESSON	PACING	OBJECTIVES
2 **Work and Income** pp. 284–289 **WHAT TO KNOW** How do people get money to pay for goods and services?	**3** **DAYS**	■ Understand people have many occupations. ■ Recognize that people make choices about wants when spending money.
CRITICAL THINKING SKILLS **Make a Choice When Buying** pp. 290–291	**1** **DAY**	■ Recognize that people do not always have enough money to buy everything they want. ■ Understand the benefits and costs of making an economic choice.
Points of View pp. 292–293	**1** **DAY**	■ Compare and contrast children's daily lives to those of others. ■ Explore different points of view about how individuals spend their money.
3 **From Factory to You** pp. 294–299 **WHAT TO KNOW** How do raw materials become products?	**3** **DAYS**	■ Understand how raw materials and resources are used to make a product. ■ Identify the steps in a production process. ■ Recognize that products are shipped to and sold at markets.
CHART AND GRAPH SKILLS **Read a Flowchart** pp. 300–301	**1** **DAY**	■ Describe the purpose of a flowchart. ■ Interpret data on a flowchart.

READING SUPPORT VOCABULARY	REACH ALL LEARNERS	INTEGRATE LEARNING	RESOURCES

READING SUPPORT VOCABULARY

(Focus Skill) **Reading Social Studies**
Categorize and Classify, p. 289

Vocabulary Power:
Synonyms, p. 286

occupation p. 284
income p. 284
free enterprise p. 286
want p. 288

budget p. 290
bank p. 290

REACH ALL LEARNERS

ENGLISH LANGUAGE LEARNERS, p. 289

Leveled Practice, pp. 288, 291, 293

INTEGRATE LEARNING

Mathematics
Profit, p. 286

Saving Money, p. 292

Reading/Language Arts
Use Rhyme and Rhythm, p. 287

Commas, p. 288

RESOURCES

Homework and Practice Book, pp. 53–54
Reading Support and Intervention, pp. 94–97
Success for English Language Learners, pp. 99–102
Vocabulary Transparency 6-2
Focus Skills Transparency 6
Categorize and Classify Graphic Organizer Write-On/Wipe-Off Card
Social Studies Skills Transparency 6-2
Unit 6 Audiotext CD Collection
Internet Resources

(Focus Skill) **Reading Social Studies**
Categorize and Classify, p. 299

Vocabulary Power:
Word Web, p. 296

raw material p. 295
factory p. 296
human resources p. 296
capital resources p. 297

flowchart p. 300

ENGLISH LANGUAGE LEARNERS, p. 297

Leveled Practice, pp. 298, 301

Advanced, p. 296

Health
Safety, p. 298

Music
Song Patterns, p. 300

Homework and Practice Book, pp. 55–56
Reading Support and Intervention, pp. 98–101
Success for English Language Learners, pp. 103–106
Vocabulary Transparency 6-3
Focus Skills Transparency 6
Categorize and Classify Graphic Organizer Write-On/Wipe-Off Card
Social Studies Skills Transparency 6-3
Activity Pattern A13
Unit 6 Audiotext CD Collection
Internet Resources

LESSON	PACING	OBJECTIVES
④ How Much and How Many pp. 302–305 🔅 **WHAT TO KNOW** Why do we make, sell, and buy more of some things than others?	**3** DAYS	■ Understand the concept of scarcity. ■ Understand that prices go up or down based on supply and demand.
STUDY SKILLS **Preview and Question** pp. 306–307	**1** DAY	■ Use a K-W-L chart to preview a passage and set a purpose for reading. ■ Record data and information in a K-W-L chart.
⑤ Barter and Trade pp. 308–311 🔅 **WHAT TO KNOW** How does trade help people meet their needs?	**3** DAYS	■ Define and identify barter and the use of money as types of trade. ■ Understand reasons why using money is considered a more efficient means of buying and selling. ■ Understand the concept of trade with other countries.
Citizenship: Countries Help Each Other pp. 312–313	**1** DAY	■ Understand that countries help each other in times of need. ■ Recognize ways young citizens can make a difference in the lives of others.
Fun with Social Studies: Marketplace pp. 314–315 **Unit 6 Review and Activities** pp. 316–320	**3** DAYS	

READING SUPPORT VOCABULARY	REACH ALL LEARNERS	INTEGRATE LEARNING	RESOURCES
Reading Social Studies (Focus Skill) **Categorize and Classify,** p. 305 **Vocabulary Power:** Compound Words, p. 304 **scarce** p. 303 **marketplace** p. 304	**Leveled Practice,** pp. 304, 307		Homework and Practice Book, pp. 57–58 Reading Support and Intervention, pp. 102–105 Success for English Language Learners, pp. 107–110 Vocabulary Transparency 6-4 Focus Skills Transparency 6 Categorize and Classify Graphic Organizer Write-On/Wipe-Off Card Social Studies Skills Transparency 6-4 ⊙ Unit 6 Audiotext CD Collection ▭ Internet Resources
Reading Social Studies (Focus Skill) **Categorize and Classify,** p. 311 **barter** p. 308 **trade** p. 309	**Leveled Practice,** pp. 310, 313 **Advanced,** p. 311	**Mathematics** Monetary Units, p. 310 **Visual Arts** Design a Poster, p. 313	Homework and Practice Book, p. 59 Reading Support and Intervention, pp. 106–109 Success for English Language Learners, pp. 111–114 Vocabulary Transparency, 6-5 Focus Skills Transparency 6 Categorize and Classify Graphic Organizer Write-On/Wipe-Off Card Activity Pattern A14 ⊙ Unit 6 Audiotext CD Collection ▭ Internet Resources
	Leveled Practice, p. 314	**Mathematics** Making Money, p. 314	Homework and Practice Book, pp. 60–61 Assessment Program, pp. 46–48 Leveled Readers Leveled Readers Teacher Guide ⊙ Unit 6 Audiotext CD Collection ▭ Internet Resources

STUDENT DIGITAL LEARNING

The interactive eBook provides students with the standards-based content of Harcourt print books in addition to interactive add-ons that enhance student interest and reinforce Social Studies content. Harcourt eBooks are available in both a basic and enhanced version.

INTERACTIVE VISUALS

Students watch trade and the marketplace come to life through engaging interactive activities that enhance the unit content.

STREAMING VIDEO

Each Unit Opener includes video tied to the Unit Big Idea. This clip provides students with enhanced information about consumers buying goods.

SKILLS ACTIVITIES

Each Chart and Graph Skill and Map and Globe Skill is enhanced by an interactive online activity.

LIVE INK ENHANCEMENT

Live Ink provides students with reading help through a patented system that breaks sentences down into segments. The Live Ink system is proven to increase student comprehension and test scores. Live Ink is available for grades 3–6/7.

ONLINE ADVENTURES

Fun with Social Studies provides a link to our Online Adventures game. Students play a game in which they must spend their money wisely during a shopping trip. The game reviews important concepts from the unit.

THE LEARNING SITE

The eBook includes links to **www.harcourtschool.com/ss1** There students can find internal resources such as our complete Multimedia Biographies databases and our Online Adventures games. This Harcourt Social Studies site also provides students with additional research tools.

MULTIMEDIA BIOGRAPHIES

Biographies from the student edition include additional information in an interactive Multimedia Biography. Students can find more information, view related biographies, explore maps and images, and find links to additional webpages.

E-PLANNER

The e-Planner provides a useful tool for scheduling Social Studies lessons.

- Use it to access Teacher Edition pages and student workbook pages and to plan classroom activities.
- The calendar tool displays all your scheduled Social Studies lessons in an easy-to-use format.
- All standards are organized by grade level.

HSPOA

Harcourt School Publishers Online Assessment provides teachers with a reliable, confidential system for online delivery of Social Studies assessment. Using this system, you can track student performance correlated to standards and run prescribed reports for any missed standards. Questions are correlated to our print Assessment program.

VIDEOS AND DVDS

A comprehensive package of videos for Grades K–3 provides an entertaining overview of core social studies concepts such as government, geography, economics, culture and history. Videos in this package are available from Schlessinger Media® and are also available digitally on SAFARI Montage.

SAFARI MONTAGE™

For more information, see pages TEI13–TEI18.

FREE AND INEXPENSIVE MATERIALS

Free and inexpensive materials are listed on the Social Studies Website at
www.harcourtschool.com/ss1

- Addresses to write to for free and inexpensive products
- Links to unit–related materials
- Internet maps
- Internet references

COMMUNITY RESOURCES FOR THE CLASSROOM

The **National Atlas** website offers interactive, customizable maps of different areas in the United States. Use the **Map Maker** tool to zoom in on your community and view map features such as cities, roads, climate, and agriculture. **http://nationalatlas.gov/**

Educators can use the **United States Census Bureau** webpage to locate census information and facts about their local communities. **http://factfinder.census.gov/home/saff/main.html?_lang=en**

The National Park Service offers a comprehensive site with a search engine that cross-references our country's National Historic Landmarks by name, city, and state. **http://tps.cr.nps.gov/nhl/**

Museums in all 50 states are indexed on the **Virtual Library** museums pages. Use this site to find museums in and around your students' own community. **http://www.museumca.org/usa/states.html**

The **Library of Congress** site features numerous collections of primary sources, biographies, recordings, and photographs. The topic **Cities and Towns** contains photographic records of communities throughout the history of the United States. **http://memory.loc.gov/ammem/**

Additional Sites are available at www.harcourtschool.com/ss1

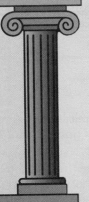

Lesson Plan Summaries

BELOW-LEVEL/INTERVENTION

TOPIC
People in the Marketplace

Summary *Buying and Selling.* This Reader identifies the difference between goods and services, explains how people earn incomes, and examines why prices change in the marketplace.

BEFORE READING

Vocabulary Power Have children define the following words. Help them write one sentence for each word as it relates to the marketplace.

goods   trade   income   services   consumer   producers

DURING READING

Categorize and Classify Have children complete the graphic organizer to show that they understand how to categorize and classify information about the marketplace, as described in the Reader.

Producers	Topic	Consumers
farmer, shop owner	Buying and Selling	a child buying new sneakers

Goods		
apples, shoes		

AFTER READING

Critical Thinking Lead children in a discussion about why prices of goods change over time.

Write a Report Have children write a report about a raw material that is produced in their community. Children should describe in their reports the goods that are made from the raw material.

ON-LEVEL

TOPIC
People in the Marketplace

Summary *Businesses Depend on Each Other,* by Lynne Hunter. This Reader describes ways many businesses buy goods and services from each other or trade with each other.

BEFORE READING

Vocabulary Power Have children define the following words. Help them write one sentence for each word as it relates to the marketplace.

goods   trade   business   owner   borrow

DURING READING

Categorize and Classify Have children complete the graphic organizer to show that they understand how to categorize and classify information about the marketplace, as described in the Reader.

Betsy's Bakery	Topic	Harry's Auto Place
makes bread and cakes	Businesses	fixes trucks

The Sandwich Shop		The Bank
makes sandwiches		keeps money safe

AFTER READING

Critical Thinking Lead children in a discussion about why it is important for businesses to help each other.

Write a Story Have children write a story about two businesses helping each other.

The *Leveled Readers Teacher Guide* provides background, reading tips, fast facts, answer keys, and copying masters.

ABOVE-LEVEL

TOPIC
People in the Marketplace

Summary *Bartering,* by B.E. Bostian. This Reader explains how people can use bartering instead of money to get the things they want.

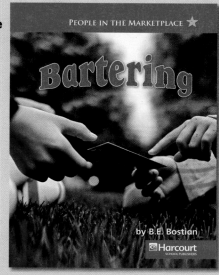

PEOPLE IN THE MARKETPLACE ★

Bartering

by B.E. Bostian

Harcourt
SCHOOL PUBLISHERS

BEFORE READING

Vocabulary Power Have children define the following words. Help them write one sentence for each word as it relates to the marketplace.

goods   trade   barter   value   online

DURING READING

Focus Skill **Categorize and Classify** Have children complete the graphic organizer to show that they understand how to categorize and classify information about the marketplace, as described in the Reader.

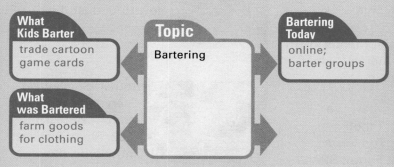

What Kids Barter	Topic	Bartering Today
trade cartoon game cards	Bartering	online; barter groups

What was Bartered
farm goods for clothing

AFTER READING

Critical Thinking Lead children in a discussion about why many people use money instead of bartering to get the things they want.

Write a Newspaper Ad Have children pretend they have something to barter. Have them write a newspaper advertisement describing what they have to barter and what they would like in exchange.

Readers' Theater
Every Student Is a Star

IT'S SHOWTIME!

Getting Started

★ Distribute the Big Idea activity sheet from your Readers' Theater.

★ Read through the script together. Make connections with unit contents.

★ Plan a performance using the **Prep ★ Practice ★ Perform** guidelines. Find ideas for props online.

Pressed for Time?

★ Perform a choral reading of the script with the whole class.

★ Assign parts for a one-time read-through.

★ Assign groups to read in your literacy center.

Read Along,

Read Aloud,

Reading Fun

BASIC

Carter, Don. **Send It!** Roaring Brook Press, 2005. Follow the week-long journey of a package from its sender to its recipient.

Cohn, Diana. **Dream Carver.** Chronicle Books LLC, 2002. A young Oaxacan boy dreams of exotic animals that he will one day carve, serving as an inspiration for readers to follow their dreams.

DiSalvo-Ryan, Dyanne. **Grandpa's Corner Store.** HarperCollins, 2000. Lucy and her neighbors work together to help her grandpa keep his store up and running.

Levitin, Sonia. **Boom Town.** Scholastic, 2004. The fictional characters capture the success of the entrepreneurial spirit during the California Gold Rush.

Stanley, Sanna. **Monkey for Sale.** Farrar, Straus, and Giroux, 2002. Two young girls are involved in a series of trades in order to purchase a monkey's freedom.

PROFICIENT

Berger, Melvin. **Round and Round the Money Goes: What Money Is and How We Use It.** Chelsea House, 1999. Take a look at the development of money from its start in the barter system to its modern forms of checks and credit cards.

Castañeda, Omar. **Abuela's Weave.** Lee and Low, 1995. A young Guatemalan girl and her grandmother weave some special creations, hoping to sell them at the market.

Cooper, Jason. **Around the World with Money.** Rourke Publishing, 2002. Look at different kinds of money used in many different countries, including the United States, Canada, Europe, Japan, and China.

Howard, Ginger. **A Basket of Bangles: How a Business Begins.** Millbrook Press, 2002. A young woman and four of her friends in Bangladesh change their lives by starting their own businesses.

Smothers, Ethel Footman. **The Hard-Times Jar.** Farrar, Straus and Giroux, 2003. Emma, a poor migrant worker, wants to save money for a book, but has to go to school instead, where she discovers a classroom library filled with books.

ADVANCED

Bernstein, Daryl. **Better Than a Lemonade Stand: Small Business Ideas for Kids.** Beyond Words, 2003. The 15-year-old author suggests a variety of unique ways that kids can earn money.

Godfrey, Neale S. **Why Money Was Invented.** Modern Curriculum Press, 2003. This simple introduction to money covers topic from budgeting and saving to give children real-life money skills.

Hall, Donald. **Ox-Cart Man.** Puffin, 1983. A classic book that tells the story of a nineteenth-century family that works together to earn a livelihood.

Hall, Margaret. **Your Allowance.** Heinemann Library, 2002. This helpful story shows kids how to budget their allowance.

Rotner, Shelley. **Everybody Works.** Millbrook Press, 2003. Photographs and words show people at work, celebrating the many ways people earn an income.

Additional books also are recommended at point of use throughout the unit. Note that information, while correct at time of publication, is subject to change.

For information about ordering these tradebooks, visit www.harcourtschool.com/ss1

Use these activities to help differentiate instruction. Each activity has been developed to address a different level or type of learner.

  ENGLISH LANGUAGE LEARNERS

20 minutes

Materials
- chart with dialogue
- table of items for buying and selling

BUY AND SELL **Have children use a rhyme to role-play the parts of producers and consumers.**

- Set up a marketplace by arranging goods for sale.
- Write a buying and selling dialogue for children to follow on chart paper.
- Review the names of the goods for sale.
- Invite pairs to take turns role-playing consumer and producer.
- The consumer should choose an item and start the dialogue. The producer should respond accordingly.

SPECIAL NEEDS

15 minutes

Materials
- magazines and catalogs
- art materials

PRODUCT PARADE **Have children hold a showcase of favorite products in the classroom marketplace.**

- Have children cut out or draw pictures of products that they use. Identify the materials each is made from or the place where it is grown or made.
- Have each child choose one product to display and describe.
- Ask each child to introduce their product. Suggest that they role-play as though they are the producer: *These berries were grown on my farm* or *This backpack was made in my factory.*
- Discuss with children why the product is important to consumers like themselves.

ADVANCED

40 minutes

Materials
- yellow paper
- art materials

AT YOUR SERVICE **Have children make a flyer to advertise a service.**

- Have children identify services that they can perform, such as rake leaves, walk dogs, or water plants.
- Have each child make a flyer advertising his or her service. The flyer should describe the service and how much it will cost.
- Encourage children to think of a catchy phrase that will help consumers remember their service.
- Put the flyers together to create classroom yellow pages.

MATHEMATICS CENTER

Cash Back

Have children work together to set up a classroom marketplace with items for sale. Children can price the items with tags or sticky notes. Organize the group into pairs, with one child acting as the seller and the other the consumer. Consumers use play money to buy items. Explain that both will count the money. First the consumer counts to the seller, then the seller counts again to verify the amount. Have children switch roles so that everyone has a chance to buy and sell.

SCIENCE CENTER

Product Safety

Discuss with children the importance of clear labeling for home products that might be hazardous. Read some examples of text from labels and consumer warnings from various products. Provide pictures or copies of labels that serve as warnings such as the skull and crossbones or the triangle with an exclamation mark inside. Invite children to create a graphic symbol and to write a short message designed to alert consumers to hazardous materials.

READING/LANGUAGE ARTS CENTER

Catalog Copy

Bring in a variety of catalogs for children to examine. Discuss the descriptive language that copywriters use to make goods sound appealing to consumers, listing adjectives and catchy phrases. Point out ways in which the copy urges consumers to buy certain items. Invite small groups to work together to create a classroom catalog of school supplies. Encourage each child to choose one school item and create a catalog entry for it, including an illustration and an irresistible description.

Drypack book bag
No one likes soggy paper. Do not be the last kid to get a Drypack book bag. Drypack will keep wild winter weather out. Get Drypack and stay dry.

ART CENTER

Sign Up

Discuss with children the importance of having an eye-catching sign to draw consumers into a business. Ask them to think about the signs around town that grab their attention. Children can work alone or with a partner to name a business and create a sign for it. Encourage them to use warm colors and bold lines that will attract consumers to their businesses.

The Assessment Program gives all learners many opportunities to show what they know and can do. It also provides ongoing information about each student's understanding of social studies.

 Online Assessment available at www.harcourtschool.com/ss1

OPTION 1 — UNIT TESTS
Unit 6

- **Unit Pretest,**
  Assessment Program, p. 45
- **Unit Review and Test Prep,** pp. 316–319

- **Unit Test,**
  Assessment Program, pp. 46–48

OPTION 2 — WRITING

- **Show What You Know,**
  Unit Writing Activity,
  Write an Ad, p. 320

- **Lesson Review,**
  Writing Activities, at ends of lessons

OPTION 3 — UNIT PROJECT

- **Show What You Know,**
  Unit Project,
  Class Fair, p. 320
- **Unit Project,**
  Performance Assessment, pp. 265P–265Q

- **Lesson Review,**
  Performance Activities, at ends of lessons

INFORMAL ASSESSMENT

- **Lesson Review,** at ends of lessons
- **Skills:**
  Practice, pp. 280, 291, 300, 306
  Apply, pp. 281, 291, 301, 307

- **Reading Social Studies,**
  Categorize and Classify, pp. 268–269
- **Literature Response Corner,** p. 275
- **Points of View, It's Your Turn,** pp. 292–293
- **Citizenship, Make It Relevant,** pp. 312–313

STUDENT SELF-EVALUATION

- **Reading Check Questions,** within lessons

- **Biography, Why Character Counts,** pp. 282–283
- **Map, Time Line, Graph, Diagram, and Illustration questions,** within lessons

OPTION 1 — PRETEST

Unit 6 Pretest (10 points each)

ANTICIPATION GUIDE

DIRECTIONS Read each statement, and circle Yes or No.

1. Some producers make things to sell. **(Yes)** No

2. Goods cannot be bought or sold. Yes **(No)**

3. A doctor provides a service. **(Yes)** No

4. When you buy something, you are a consumer. **(Yes)** No

5. You can count things on a bar graph. **(Yes)** No

6. An occupation is a job. **(Yes)** No

7. A budget keeps you from saving money. Yes **(No)**

8. <u>Scarce</u> means "more than enough." Yes **(No)**

9. People pay low prices when there is a lot of one product. **(Yes)** No

10. Countries trade goods with each other. **(Yes)** No

OPTION 1 — UNIT TEST

Unit 6 Test (6 points each)

SHORT ANSWER

DIRECTIONS Use the bar graph to answer the questions.

Books About Occupations

	0	1	2	3	4	5	6	7
nurse								
construction worker								
dentist								
veterinarian								
teacher								

1. How many occupations are shown on the chart? **5**

2. How many books were found about dentists? **3**

3. About which occupation were the most books found?

   construction worker

4. Were more books found about <u>nurses</u> or <u>veterinarians</u>?

   nurses

5. About which two occupations were the same number of

   books found? **dentists and teachers**

(continued)

OPTION 1 — UNIT TEST

Name _____ Date _____

MULTIPLE CHOICE (5 points each)

DIRECTIONS Select the letter of the best answer.

6. What does a producer do?

   (A) makes or sells goods and services
   B buys goods and services
   C builds factories
   D leads a country

7. What does a consumer do?

   A makes or sells goods and services
   (B) buys goods and services
   C builds factories
   D grows food

8. What do you call the money that people earn?

   A budget
   (B) income
   C trade
   D occupation

9. What happens to crops when there is not enough rain?

   A They turn green.
   B They get harvested.
   C They grow better.
   (D) They become scarce.

10. What do you call the exchanging of one thing to get another?

    A transportation
    (B) trade
    C services
    D manufacturing

(continued)

OPTION 1 — UNIT TEST

Name _____ Date _____

FILL IN THE BLANK (5 points each)

DIRECTIONS Write the word that completes each sentence.

marketplace	goods	wants	up	trade	services
factory		free enterprise			down

11. The role of producers is to provide goods and

    services .

12. **Goods** are products that can be bought or sold.

13. A person starting his or her own business is an example of

    free enterprise .

14. Things people would like to have are **wants** .

15. Machines that make goods are found in a **factory** .

16. When goods are scarce, the price goes **up** .

17. When there is a lot of a good, the price goes **down** .

18. A place where goods and services are bought and sold is a

    marketplace .

19. One country can **trade** goods with another country.

OPTION 2 — WRITING

RUBRIC

Name _____ Date _____

Unit 6 Writing Activity Guidelines

WRITE AN ADVERTISEMENT

Writing Prompt Write an ad for a product you want to sell. Use details to describe the item so others will want to buy it.

▶ **STEP 1** Talk about ads for products you have seen. Think about what the ads say and show.

▶ **STEP 2** Imagine that you have grown or made a product you want to sell. List some colorful words that describe it.
  - What is special about your product?
  - Why should consumers want to buy this item?

▶ **STEP 3** Use your list to write an ad to sell your product. Use persuasive language so that people will want to buy it.

▶ **STEP 4** Review your work to make sure you have used correct grammar, spelling, punctuation, and capitalization.

▶ **STEP 5** Make the changes. Then copy your ad neatly.

SCORE 4
- clearly states purpose of ad
- provides many descriptive item details
- shows a strong understanding of the roles of producer and consumer
- uses strong persuasive language
- contains few, if any, errors in grammar and punctuation

SCORE 3
- states purpose of ad
- provides some descriptive item details
- shows an understanding of the roles of producer and consumer
- uses some persuasive language
- contains some errors in grammar and punctuation

SCORE 2
- vaguely states purpose of ad
- provides few descriptive item details
- shows little understanding of the roles of producer and consumer
- uses little persuasive language
- contains many errors in grammar and punctuation

SCORE 1
- does not state purpose of ad
- provides no descriptive item details
- shows no understanding of the roles of producer and consumer
- does not use persuasive language
- contains serious errors in grammar and punctuation

OPTION 3 — PROJECT

RUBRIC

Name _____ Date _____

Unit 6 Project Guidelines

CLASS FAIR

Plan a class fair to sell goods and services.

▶ **STEP 1** With your class, make a list of goods and services you can provide. Think about the raw materials and resources you can use. Make plans to provide a variety of goods and services.

▶ **STEP 2** Together, decide where and when the fair will take place. Make a map that shows where each product or service will be sold.

▶ **STEP 3** Make a list of materials you will need to produce a product or offer a service. Prepare your goods or practice your service. Decide on a fair price. Practice your sales pitch.

▶ **STEP 4** Make a poster that advertises your product or service. Include the price.

▶ **STEP 5** Invite other classes to your class fair. After the fair, talk about why some goods and services sold better than others.

SCORE 4
- shows clear understanding of how limited resources affect producers and consumers
- creates interesting and persuasive ads
- understands fully the interdependence of producers and consumers
- shows clear planning and thorough organization

SCORE 3
- shows some understanding of how limited resources affect producers and consumers
- creates interesting ads that are somewhat persuasive
- understands the interdependence of producers and consumers
- shows planning and organization

SCORE 2
- shows little understanding of how limited resources affect producers and consumers
- creates ads that are somewhat interesting
- does not fully understand the interdependence of producers and consumers
- shows minimal planning and organization

SCORE 1
- shows no understanding of how limited resources affect producers and consumers
- creates ads that are not interesting or persuasive
- shows no understanding of the interdependence of producers and consumers
- shows no planning and organization

TAKE-HOME RUBRICS Copying masters of a student *Writing Rubric* and *Project Rubric* appear in the Assessment Program, pp. 50 and 52.
GROUP PERFORMANCE RUBRIC See Assessment Program, page x.

A Class Fair

Getting Started

Distribute the Unit 6 Project Guidelines provided on page 51 of the Assessment Program.

Introduce the unit project as you begin Unit 6. Have children develop the project components as they learn about people in the marketplace. Explain that a fair is a special event where people can sell goods and services to others. Ask children to think about things that they can sell at a class fair, including items brought from home, craft items they make themselves, and services they can provide. Encourage children to focus on what others might want to help them decide what they should produce for the fair.

The Big Idea

Work Producers and consumers depend on each other for the goods and services.

Project Management

Organize the class to work individually or in small groups depending on the goods or services they will offer for sale. Offer assistance and support as children carry out their ideas for creating and displaying goods and services.

Materials textbook, art supplies, butcher paper, copy paper, construction paper

Organizer Use the organizer as a sign-up sheet for producers to describe the details of their product. Have them use this information to generate an advertising flyer and determine where the fair should be held.

Goods or Services

Help children decide what goods they will produce or services they will provide for the fair. Suggestions include the following:

- craft items such as ornaments, covered boxes, decorated folders, book covers, wrapping paper, craft stick plant markers, painted tissue boxes, and decorated flower pots.
- recipes.
- items from home such as toys, games, trading cards, sporting goods.
- services such as pet care or yard work.

Allow class time for craft projects to be completed. Children with goods from home or those offering services can make posters or coupons to describe what they plan to offer.

Name	Good/Service	Materials	Display Space
Ben	dog walking	poster	wall
Rosa	pie recipe	index cards, markers, poster	table
Jeffrey	decorated boxes	shoe boxes, news-print, paint, glitter, ribbon, glue	table
Jeremy, Sally, Beth, Marco	carwash coupons	poster, bucket of carwash supplies, index cards, markers	floor
Mary and Anna	birdhouses	milk cartons, string, masking tape	table

Preparing for the Fair

When the craft projects and posters are complete, have children bring to school everything they need for the fair. Select children to create a flyer to announce the fair. Distribute the flyers locally and send them home to families. If money is to be exchanged, arrange for a pay station run by adult volunteers. Discuss how the fair should be set up so that goods are presented in an eye-catching way. Have children practice their sales pitches. Role-play so that children can anticipate the kinds of questions that consumers might ask them about their goods and services.

On the day of the fair, set up the booths in adequate space so that consumers can see what is for sale and move about comfortably.

Lesson Review Activities

You may wish to incorporate the following lesson review activities into the unit project.

- Lesson 1: **Make a Chart**, p. 279
- Lesson 5: **Draw Pictures**, p. 311

Assessment

For a project rubric, see Teacher Edition, p. 265O.

What to Look For

- Children determine goods and services to produce for the fair.
- Children advertise and set up the fair.
- Children provide information about their product and demonstrate effective sales techniques.
- Children analyze why certain goods and services sold more successfully than others.

Come to the
Grade 2 Fair
at Bailey School

Friday, April 9 from 1:30 to 3:00

We have what you need!

Goods!	Services!
recipes	dog walking
boxes	carwash
birdhouses	
seeds	

All proceeds go to the After-School Arts Program.

LESSON 1

Name _____ Date _____

Producers and Consumers

In each row, draw a picture to show what happens next. Then write <u>P</u> under the pictures of producers and <u>C</u> under the pictures of consumers.

❶ P   C

❷ P   C

❸ P   C

Use after reading Unit 6, Lesson 1, pages 276–279. **Homework and Practice Book ▪ 51**

SKILL PRACTICE

Name _____ Date _____

CHART AND GRAPH SKILLS
Pet Sitting

This bar graph shows how many hours the pet sitter works each day. Use the graph to answer the questions.

Pet Sitter's Hours

	0	1	2	3	4	5	6
Monday							
Tuesday							
Wednesday							
Thursday							
Friday							

❶ How many hours does the pet sitter work on Tuesday? __3__

❷ On which day does the pet sitter work the most hours?

_____ Wednesday _____

❸ On which days does the pet sitter work the same number

of hours? <u>Tuesday and Thursday</u>

❹ On which day do you think the pet sitter sees the fewest

pets? Why? <u>Friday. The pet sitter works only</u>

<u>two hours.</u>

52 ▪ **Homework and Practice Book** Use after reading Unit 6, Skill Lesson, pages 280–281.

LESSON 2

Name _____ Date _____

Saving, Sharing, Spending

This week you earned $10 for watering a neighbor's lawn and walking his dog. Your grandmother gave you $20 for your birthday. Answer the question. Then fill in the table.

How much money do you have in all? __$30__

What I Will Save	What I Will Share	What I Will Spend
Possible answers:		
• I will save __$10__.	• I will share __$10__.	• I will spend __$10__.
• I will put the money	• I will share the money with	• I will spend the money on
in a bank	people who	a new book
	need help	

Use after reading Unit 6, Lesson 2, pages 284–289. **Homework and Practice Book ▪ 53**

SKILL PRACTICE

Name _____ Date _____

CRITICAL THINKING SKILLS
Make a Choice When Buying

The products in each row cost about the same. Suppose that you can buy only one. Circle the product in each row that you would buy, and tell why.

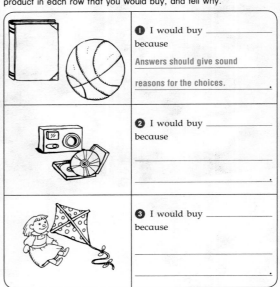

❶ I would buy _____ because

Answers should give sound

reasons for the choices.

❷ I would buy _____ because

❸ I would buy _____ because

54 ▪ **Homework and Practice Book** Use after reading Unit 6, Skill Lesson, pages 290–291.

LESSON 3

Name _____ Date _____

Tomatoes: From Vine to You

Complete the steps. Add words or pictures to show how fresh tomatoes become canned tomatoes.

Step 1: Possible answers are given. Drawing of a farmer in a field of tomatoes.  A farmer grows tomatoes.	Step 2: A truck brings the tomatoes to the factory.

Step 3: Drawing of a worker sorting big and little tomatoes. A worker sorts the tomatoes by size.	Step 4: Drawing of a worker putting cans into a cardboard box.  A worker packs canned tomatoes into boxes.	Step 5: 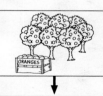 The boxes are loaded onto a truck.

Use after reading Unit 6, Lesson 3, pages 294–299. **Homework and Practice Book ▪ 55**

SKILL PRACTICE

Name _____ Date _____

CHART AND GRAPH SKILLS

From Beehive to Breakfast Table

① 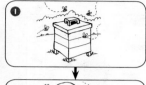   Write sentences to tell what is happening in the steps. The first one is done for you.

Bees make honey.

Possible answers:

②    A worker gathers the honey.

③    Honey is put in jars to sell.

④    Someone puts the honey on a muffin and eats it.

56 ▪ Homework and Practice Book Use after reading Unit 6, Skill Lesson, pages 300–301.

LESSON 4

Name _____ Date _____

A Lot or a Little

Draw a picture to show what could happen to make the oranges scarce. Write a sentence about your picture. Then answer the question.

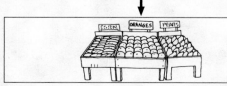

↓

Drawings will vary. Possible answers: The weather could be too cold for the oranges. The weather could be too dry for the oranges. Rain could make the ground too wet for the oranges to grow well.

↓

What will happen to the price of oranges if they become scarce?

The price of the oranges will go up.

Use after reading Unit 6, Lesson 4, pages 302–305. **Homework and Practice Book ▪ 57**

SKILL PRACTICE

Name _____ Date _____

STUDY SKILLS

Preview and Question

Read the paragraph. Then complete the K-W-L chart.

People may start a business to make money. Some businesses provide goods, such as food, clothing, shoes, or computers. Some provide services. Doctors, cooks, vets, and music teachers are examples of people who provide services. Children might start a business, too. Often, they do things for people in their neighborhood. When they get paid for their work, they can spend, share, or save the money they earn.

K-W-L Chart		
What I Know	**What I Want to Know**	**What I Learned**
Answers will vary. Children might say they could wash cars or walk dogs.	What kind of business could I start?	I could provide goods or services to people in my neighborhood.
Possible answer: I can spend it any way I want.	What are some choices I can make about the money I make?	Answers will vary. Children might say they can choose to spend, share, or save it.

58 ▪ Homework and Practice Book Use after reading Unit 6, Skill Lesson, pages 306–307.

LESSON 5

Name _____ Date _____

Partners in Trade

The map shows three countries and some products they trade. Use the map to answer the questions.

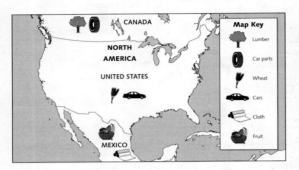

❶ Henry, in the United States, loves bananas. From which

country do bananas come? <u>Mexico</u>

❷ Jamie's mother, in Canada, wants to buy a car.

From where might her new car come? <u>United States</u>

❸ Carlos, in Mexico, wants to build a house. From which

country might the lumber come? <u>Canada</u>

Use after reading Unit 6, Lesson 5, pages 308–311. **Homework and Practice Book ■ 59**

STUDY GUIDE

Name _____ Date _____

Unit 6 Study Guide

Read the paragraph. Use the words in the Word Bank to fill in the blanks.

marketplace	occupation	consumers	goods
producers	factory	services	income	trade

People work at a job, or _____occupation_____, so

they can earn _____income_____ to buy things. Some

people make _____goods_____, or products that can

be bought and sold. They might work in a building called a

_____factory_____. Other people, such as dentists and

doctors, provide _____services_____. Both types of

workers are called _____producers_____. They sell their

goods or services to _____consumers_____. People go to

the _____marketplace_____ to find stores that sell things

that they want and need. There, people _____trade_____

money for goods or services they want.

60 ■ Homework and Practice Book   Use after reading Unit 6, pages 265–320.

UNIT 6 REVIEW AND TEST PREP

Name _____ Date _____

☆ Focus Skill — CATEGORIZE AND CLASSIFY
Reading Social Studies

Fill in the chart to categorize and classify information from the unit.

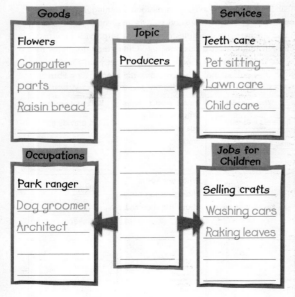

Use after reading Unit 6, pages 265–320.   **Homework and Practice Book ■ 61**

STATE AND COMMUNITY RESOURCES

Historical Societies

Museums

Parks

Guest Speakers

Discuss the Big Idea

Work **Producers and consumers depend on each other for goods and services.**

Discuss food, clothing, and other things that families use every day. Point out that even if people grow their own food or sew their own clothes, there are still other things that they must get from someone else. Explain that in this unit children will learn how people depend on each other for the things they want.

Make It Relevant Ask children where their families go to get the things they want.

Q **Where does the food you eat come from?**

A the grocery store; a farm

Access Prior Knowledge

Draw a concept map with the central circle marked *My Family*. Have children brainstorm the places they go and people they meet to help them get the things they want. Tell children that in this unit they will find out about the different jobs people do.

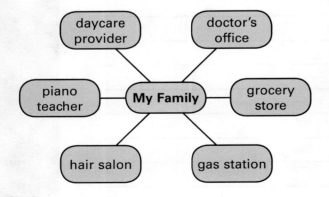

Unit 6 People in the Marketplace

Talk About **Work**

"I earned money to buy a gift for my brother."

Practice and Extend

Shopping Mall For shoppers wanting a variety of items, a shopping mall offers many choices in one convenient location. While some shops carry specialty goods, others provide services. Larger department stores serve as anchor stores for a mall and offer a large variety of goods and services in one location.

Talk About Children in the photographs across the bottom of the unit preview pages are participating in the free enterprise system by saving money and choosing things wisely.

"I think about the cost before I choose what I will buy."

"I use money I saved to buy what I want."

265

Discuss the Picture

Have children identify the location in the photograph as stores located within a mall. Discuss the different kinds of goods or services they can find in the stores that are shown.

Q How is a mall different from a downtown street with shops?

A A mall is convenient because many different kinds of shops are all in one location.

Discuss "Talk About"

Have volunteers read the quotations beside the photographs of the children. Discuss what the children have in common.

Q What are all the children talking about?

A All of them are talking about buying things.

Q How do the children decide what to buy?

A They decide what to buy based on how much money they have.

Have children work in pairs to ask and answer additional questions about either the shopping mall photograph or Talk About feature.

SCHOOL TO HOME

Use the Unit 6 SCHOOL TO HOME NEWSLETTER on pages S13–S14 to introduce the unit to family members and suggest activities they can do at home.

INTEGRATE THE CURRICULUM

READING/LANGUAGE ARTS Have children write a story about a trip to the mall. Tell them to include three stops in their shopping spree. Have them browse in one store, compare prices in one store, and buy a gift in the last store. Children can share their stories in a class "Mall Crawl."
Write a Story

MATHEMATICS Point out that anything can be used for money as long as everyone agrees that it has value. Give each child 20 paper clips and have children use the paper clips to "buy" school supplies from each other. Children can tag goods with prices and take turns buying and selling. Suggest children budget their paper clips to buy as much as possible. **Money**

OBJECTIVES

OBJECTIVES

- Use visuals to determine word meanings.

- Use words and visuals to preview the content of the unit.

RESOURCES

Picture Vocabulary Cards

Make Connections

Link Pictures with Words Have children read the word *consumer* and its definition. Write *consumer* on the board, and use it as the main cell of a web. Build the web by adding the other vocabulary words in the lesson. Help children describe how the consumer is linked to *producers, goods, services*, and the *marketplace*. Record their responses on the web.

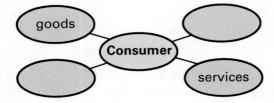

1 Visual Literacy: Pictures Have children look at the picture of the strawberry grower and read the vocabulary word *producer*. Then have them use the vocabulary word in a sentence about the picture.

Q Who is in the picture, and what is he doing?

A The picture shows a producer who grows strawberries.

2 Have children identify the goods being sold in the picture.

Q What other kinds of goods could people buy to use at the beach?

A Possible answers include sunblock lotion, towels, chairs, shades, and floats.

1

producer A person who grows, makes, or sells products. (page 276)

2

goods Things that can be bought and sold. (page 277)

266

Practice and Extend

ELL ENGLISH LANGUAGE LEARNERS

Frontloading Language: Work Use the following prompts to develop the academic language of work and the structures of categorizing and classifying.

(Beginning) Use the pictures to have children complete statements such as: *Examples of goods are ____, ____, and ____.* (strawberries, pails, milk)

(Intermediate) Have children complete this frame for each picture: *An example of a [vocabulary word] is ____.*

(Advanced) Invite children to use the pictures and definitions to complete this sentence frame: *A ____ is an example of a [vocabulary word] because ____.*

③

services Work done for others. (page 277)

④

marketplace Where people buy and sell goods and services. (page 304)

⑤

consumer A person who buys and uses goods and services. (page 279)

For more resources, go to
www.harcourtschool.com/ss1

267

③ Have children identify the worker in the picture for the word *services* as a painter and describe the service being provided.

Q Why does the painter provide this service?

A He provides a service to earn money.

④ Have children look at the picture for the word *marketplace* and identify the mall stores as an example of a marketplace. Invite children to discuss the goods they may buy at a marketplace. Point out that a marketplace does not have to be a mall.

Q What other stores in a marketplace do you use?

A Possible answers include supermarket, pharmacy, shoe store, and DVD rental store.

⑤ Have children read the definition of the word *consumer* and describe the action shown in the picture.

Q Who is the consumer in the picture? What is he buying?

A The consumer is the boy. He is buying a good, milk, from the vendor.

Q How do consumers and sellers come together at a marketplace?

A Sellers are at the marketplace to sell their goods or services, and buyers are there to get goods and services they want.

VOCABULARY POWER

Word Meanings Point out that the word *marketplace* is made up of two words: *market* + *place*. Point out that *supermarket* is another word made with *market*. Have children discuss both meanings and use the words in sentences. For example: *The consumer shopped for goods at the supermarket.*

INTERNET RESOURCES

For more resources, go to
www.harcourtschool.com/ss1

Categorize and Classify

- Use categories to classify information into groups.
- Interpret information from charts.

categorize p. 268   **classify** p. 268

Focus Skills Transparency 6; Categorize and Classify Graphic Organizer Write-On/Wipe-Off Card; Unit 6 Audiotext CD Collection

1 Introduce

1 Why It Matters Explain that some information can be grouped together. Each group is called a category. Putting information into categories shows how items are connected by their details. Write the following examples on the board:

- bear, cow, sheep, pig, wolf
- apple, banana, cabbage, lettuce
- chair, desk, dresser, sofa, stool

Discuss each list of words. For each group, help children determine a rule for classifying the items into the same category. For example, the rules for these categories might be *animals; healthful foods;* and *furniture.* Have children explain how the items in each group are alike.

Unit 6

Reading Social Studies

Focus Skill ★ Categorize and Classify

Why It Matters You can categorize and classify information to help you understand what you read.

Learn

When you categorize and classify, you sort things into groups.

2
- Decide what each group will be called.
- Place each thing in a group.

Read the paragraph below.

Categorize
Classify

Rob and Mom shopped at the Farmers' Market. They bought fresh food, plants, and toys. The foods they bought were peppers and cucumbers. Mom chose a yellow rosebush and daisies for the garden. Rob bought some toys—a wooden whistle and a puzzle.

When they finished shopping, Mom bought lemonade. Rob bought grape juice.

268

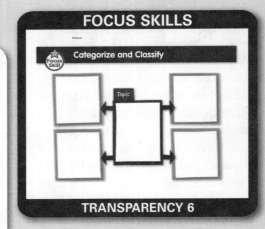

Practice and Extend

 READING/LANGUAGE ARTS Point out that categorizing information can help children make comparisons. Have children compare the following items: *boots, soccer shoes,* and *slippers.* Ask children to discuss the details of each shoe and determine other shoes that might also be placed in the same category. **Make Comparisons**

Categorize and Classify

Topic

TRANSPARENCY 6

Graphic Organizer Write-On/Wipe-Off Cards available

Practice

3

Food
peppers
_____

Topic
Shopping at the Farmers' Market

Plants
_____
_____

Toys
_____
_____

Drinks
_____
_____

Copy this chart to categorize and classify the things that Rob and Mom bought. Put them in four groups labeled Food, Plants, Toys, and Drinks.

Apply

As you read this unit, look for ways to categorize and classify information.

269

---

2 Teach

Learn

2 Discuss the definitions for *categorize* and *classify*. Then read aloud the paragraph on page 268. Invite children to list the items that were purchased. Have them consider details about each item, such as appearance and use, as they determine how to classify it.

Practice

3 **Visual Literacy: Chart** Use Focus Skill Transparency to copy the chart on page 269. Discuss the categories to help children complete the chart.

Q Which items are foods?

A peppers, cucumbers, lemonade, grape juice

Q Which items are not foods?

A rosebush, daisies, whistle, puzzle

ANSWERS: Food: cucumbers; Plants: rosebush, daisies; Toys: whistle, puzzle; Drinks: lemonade, grape juice

3 Close

Apply

Tell children that as they read the unit, they can classify information into categories. Remind them to use this strategy as they learn about producers and consumers and the goods and services they make or buy.

OBJECTIVES

- Recognize the importance of the supermarket to buyers in a community.
- Explain the process by which goods are delivered to markets.

RESOURCES

Unit 6 Audiotext CD Collection

Quick Summary

This excerpt is from *Supermarket* by Kathleen Krull (Holiday House, 2001).

This nonfiction story tells about a visit to the supermarket. It explores some of the places in the United States where food for the markets is grown. The story also describes how goods are transported.

Before Reading

Set the Purpose Discuss where children get the foods they eat. Explain that the supermarket is a place where foods from all over the country are sold. Explain that in this story, children will learn about producers, consumers, goods, and services. All of these things come together at the supermarket.

Have children make a word web, using the word *supermarket* in the center circle. Ask children to brainstorm items that they buy at the store. Add their responses to the web.

Start with a Story

SUPERMARKET

by Kathleen Krull
illustrated by Melanie Hope Greenberg

Shopping carts clang. ❶
Magic doors whiz open and shut.
Colors glow under bright white lights.
So many breakfasts, lunches, and dinners!
It's all at a special, necessary, very real place:
the supermarket.

270

Practice and Extend

BACKGROUND

About the Authors Kathleen Krull is a well-known author specializing in biographies. She uses her love of behind-the-scenes investigations to find out juicy details to share with her readers. Her subjects reflect her interests and her passions, including art and music.

REACH ALL LEARNERS

Leveled Practice Have children reread *Supermarket*.

(Basic) Have children name three foods they buy at the supermarket and tell in what part of the market they are found.

(Proficient) Ask children to tell where the foods they buy come from.

(Advanced) Have children draw a map of the supermarket where they shop.

According to surveys, shoppers decide in their first 8 seconds whether they feel comfortable in a store. The first thing they see helps them decide.

The doors don't really open by magic. When an electronic "eye" overhead "sees" you coming, it starts a motor to open the doors.

The supermarket is a whole world of its own. Where does all this crunchy, munchy, sweet, sour, fiery, frozen, fabulous food come from?

271

During Reading

1 Understand the Story Have children picture in their minds a supermarket they often visit. Ask them to volunteer some of the sights, sounds, and smells they experience there.

Q How do the displays, colors, and lighting create a mood in the supermarket?

A They make the supermarket seem inviting. They draw attention to certain products.

Q Why are the displays, colors, and lighting so important?

A Shoppers might buy more things if they like being in the store.

Visual Literacy: Illustration Have children discuss how the supermarket in the illustration is similar to stores they have visited. Discuss the features that make the store a place they want to be in, including friendly clerks and shoppers. Talk about how these features help the store sell more things.

 VOCABULARY POWER

Figurative Language Point out the vivid verbs that Kathleen Krull uses—*clang, whiz, rev up, zoom.* Explain the meaning of each verb. Discuss how vivid verbs make the writing more interesting and help the reader understand and appreciate the action. Invite children to use each of these vivid verbs in a sentence of their own.

INTEGRATE THE CURRICULUM

READING/LANGUAGE ARTS On page 271, point out the words that describe the word food—*crunchy, munchy, sweet, sour, fiery, frozen, fabulous.* Explain that these words are adjectives. Invite children to think of other words that describe the word *food.* Record their responses. **Adjectives**

HEALTH Provide children with various supermarket food ads. Ask pairs to plan a breakfast, lunch, or dinner, using the healthful food choices they find in the ads. Invite pairs to cut out the food choices and arrange them on a sheet of construction paper to make a poster. Remind them to give their poster a title and label each of the food choices. **Plan a Healthful Meal**

2 Understand the Story Discuss what farmers across the nation do to provide people with food. Have children find out what kinds of foods are grown in their state.

Q What do farmers need to grow crops?
A sunshine, soil, and water

3 Geography Have volunteers use an atlas to locate the places mentioned on page 272. Ask children to identify the capital cities and bordering states.

Q What does the map tell you about the places where crops are grown?
A Some things grow better in one place than in another.

Q Which state is famous for popcorn?
A Iowa

Happy Farms

Certain states are famous for certain foods: Iowa for popcorn, Vermont for maple syrup, Michigan for cereal, Wisconsin for cheese, Idaho for potatoes, Massachusetts for cranberries, Florida for oranges, California for grapes, Georgia for peaches and peanuts.

2 It all begins on farms. Our food comes from places with lots of sunshine, rich soil, and clean water. Farmers make decisions every day during the long months of growing.

272

Practice and Extend

VOCABULARY POWER

Compound Words Point out that the word *harvesttime* is a compound word: *harvest + time = harvesttime*. Challenge children to create more compound words using *time* (daytime, nighttime, anytime) or *times* (sometimes). Have children write the words as equations, or list the words and have children use them in sentences.

MAKE IT RELEVANT

At Home Encourage children to make a list of things they eat during the course of a week that are grown underground, grown on stems, or grown on trees. Have them make a three-column chart, labeled *Underground, On Stems,* and *On Trees*. Ask them to draw and label their findings for each category.

INTEGRATE THE CURRICULUM

SCIENCE Have children use Internet and library resources to find out interesting facts about plants, such as how they respond to light, why their roots grow down and stems grow up, and how touching or talking to plants affects them. Invite children to share their findings in a class discussion. **Characteristics of Plants**

4 At harvesttime, workers pick the fruits and vegetables. They pack everything neatly in boxes and load the boxes onto trucks.

Happy Farms

Picking fruits and vegetables can be painful, low-paying work. Cesar Chavez (1927-1993) became a hero for workers when he founded the National Farm Workers of America. **5**

273

4 **Understand the Story** Discuss the people required to get the food from the farm to the supermarket.

Q Who first gets the ripe crops ready for the market?

A The farmer and farmworkers harvest the crops. They package them for shipping.

Q How do the farmers and warehouses know what to send to each market?

A Workers at the market order the foods they want delivered.

Q Who takes the crops from the farm to the warehouses or the markets?

A Truck drivers move the crops on highways and roads.

5 **History** Explain that Cesar Chavez spent his life trying to improve safety for farmworkers. He helped raise wages and improve safety for the people who make sure that our food products get to market.

BACKGROUND

Cesar Chavez Cesar Chavez (1927-1993) was a Mexican American who devoted his life to improving working conditions for farmworkers. In 1994, President Clinton presented Chavez's family with the Presidential Medal of Freedom for Chavez's courage, leadership, sense of justice, and dedication to nonviolence.

ELL ENGLISH LANGUAGE LEARNERS

Use the illustrations on pages 272–273 to discuss the activities on a farm.

Beginning Ask questions such as *Who is putting vegetables in a box?* or *Who is loading boxes on a truck?* Have children point to the answer in the illustration.

Intermediate Identify a person in the illustration, and ask questions such as: *Is this worker carrying boxes or driving a truck?*

Who is the driver of the truck? Encourage children to answer in short sentences.

Advanced Invite children to write sentence strips that tell about actions such as: *The worker picks the vegetables. Another worker puts the vegetables in a box. A man carries the boxes to a truck.* Have children arrange the sentences in a sequence.

6 Understand the Story Have children discuss why truck drivers work at night. Mention that traffic is lighter at night. Also suggest that foods need to be stocked and ready at the supermarkets for shoppers to buy them during the day.

Visual Literacy: Illustration Have children identify the adjectives used to describe the trucks (small, big, gigantic) and match each adjective to one of the trucks in the illustration.

Q What is loaded in the big truck?

A watermelons

Q What is the company name on the small truck?

A Busy Bee Farms

Q What kinds of produce are painted on the side of the gigantic truck? What might this advertise?

A grapes, pears, apples, and other fruits; this shows that the farm might grow many different kinds of things

6 Small trucks, big trucks, gigantic trucks— all rev up their engines. Every night, drivers take off from farms or warehouses.

274

Practice and Extend

REACH ALL LEARNERS

Leveled Practice Have children create a supermarket shopping list.

(Basic) Have children list ingredients that are needed for a dish their family eats.

(Proficient) Ask children to create a list of ingredients for a meal and categorize them.

(Advanced) Invite children to make a menu for a full dinner and use it to create and categorize the shopping list.

VOCABULARY POWER

Synonyms Write *small* and *big*. Point out that these words are opposites, and show children examples, using classroom items. Explain that there are many synonyms for *small* that give clues to size, including *little* and *tiny*. Similar synonyms for *big* include *huge*, *enormous*, and *gigantic*. Have children use the words in sentences. Encourage them to choose a synonym that conveys an accurate size.

INTEGRATE THE CURRICULUM

READING/LANGUAGE ARTS Have children work together in small groups to create a chart showing how foods get from the farm to the table. Encourage children to use the text and illustrations on pages 272–274 to help them with each step. Ask children to use pictures and captions to fill in their charts.
Sequence

They zoom down the highway toward your town.

Response Corner

1 **Categorize and Classify** What kinds of things are found in a supermarket?

2 **Make It Relevant** What are some of the foods your family buys?

275

After Reading

Response Corner—Answers

1. **Categorize and Classify** Children should name different categories of items found in a supermarket, such as fruits, vegetables, meats, and breads.

2. **Make It Relevant** Have children name foods that their families buy on a regular basis.

✏ Write a Response

Have children write a story about going to the supermarket from the shopping cart's point of view. Use this story starter: *Carl the Cart was bored. It had been a slow day at the store. Then he saw Mrs. Lane coming right toward him. She had her wiggly little boy in her arms.*

For a writing response rubric, see Assessment Program, page xvi.

INDEPENDENT READING

Children may enjoy reading these books during the unit.
Additional books are listed on page 265J of this Teacher Edition.

César: ¡Sí Se Puede!/Yes, We Can! by Carmen T. Bernier-Grand (Marshall Cavendish, 2005). This book is a bilingual biography of Cesar Chavez.

Market! by Ted Lewin (Lothrop, Lee & Shepard, 1996). Six outdoor markets and the traders who buy and sell products in them are featured in this book.

Working Cotton by Shirley Ann Williams (Harcourt, 1992). Events in the daily life of migrant farmworkers in central California.

For information about ordering these trade books, visit **www.harcourtschool.com/ss1**

OBJECTIVES

- **Identify and explain the roles of a producer and a consumer.**

- **Describe how goods and services are related to a business.**

- **Recognize how producers are also consumers.**

VOCABULARY

producer p. 276 **business** p. 278

goods p. 277 **consumer** p. 279

services p. 277

CATEGORIZE AND CLASSIFY

pp. 268–269, 278, 279

RESOURCES

Homework and Practice Book, p. 51; Reading Support and Intervention, pp. 90–93; Success for English Learners, pp. 95–98; Vocabulary Transparency 6-1; Focus Skills Transparency 6; Categorize and Classify Graphic Organizer Write-On/Wipe-Off Card; Unit 6 Audiotext CD Collection; Internet Resources

---

1 Introduce

What to Know Ask a volunteer to read aloud the What to Know question. Explain that in this lesson, children will learn how people depend on one another for the things they need and want. Remind children to look for answers to the question as they read the lesson.

Build Background Invite children to describe their experiences running errands with family members. Discuss what types of businesses they have seen.

Lesson 1

Producers and Consumers

What to Know
How do producers and consumers depend on each other?

Vocabulary
producer
goods
services
business
consumer

Categorize and Classify

Christina and her family live in a community in which people have many kinds of jobs. Some workers grow or make products, and others sell products. A worker who grows, makes, or sells products is called a **producer**.

276

Practice and Extend

Express Path

When minutes count, look for the **EXPRESS PATH** to focus on the lesson's main ideas.

Quick Summary

This lesson explains the roles and interdependence of producers and consumers. It describes the kinds of goods and services that are provided and used.

Goods and Services

Products are also called goods. **Goods** are things that can be bought and sold. Christina's grandmother grows flowers to sell. Her dad makes parts that are used to make computers.

Producers also provide services. **Services** are work people do for others. Dr. Briggs takes care of Christina's teeth. Mr. West teaches her to play the cello.

Reading Check **How are goods and services alike?** Goods and services are both things that are bought and sold.

Goods

1

Services

277

2 Teach

Goods and Services

CONTENT FOCUS Producers are those people who provide goods and services.

Express Path

Have the class scan the section to find the meaning of the vocabulary terms. Then use the terms in sentences about the section.

1 Visual Literacy: Pictures Invite children to look at the pictures and identify jobs in Christina's community.

Q What goods or services does each producer provide?

A florist—flowers; factory worker—computer parts; dentist—healthy teeth; teacher—music lessons.

Economics Help children realize that people specialize in certain jobs, such as a dentist or teacher. Point out that these jobs require specific training or college programs. Ask children to brainstorm specialized jobs in their school, community, and state.

VOCABULARY

Vocabulary Transparency 6-1

MINI-GLOSSARY Read each term, and study its definition.
producer A person who grows, makes, or sells products. p. 276
goods Things that can be bought and sold. p. 277
services Work done for others. p. 277
business The making or selling of goods or services. p. 278
consumer A person who buys and uses goods and services. p. 279

WORD WORK Complete the activities below.

1. **producer**
WORD FAMILIES What is the root word of each of these words?

| production | producing | produced | **producer** |

produce

2. **goods, services**
CATEGORIZE VOCABULARY List three examples of each.
Goods
Possible answers: toys, food, clothes

Services
selling bread, cutting hair, teaching school

3. **business**
RELATED WORDS How are business and work related?
A business has people who work to make or sell goods
and services.

4. **consumer**
VOCABULARY CHART Show how consumers and producers go together.

| Producers make products. | → | Consumers buy products. |

TRANSPARENCY 6-1

READING SUPPORT/ INTERVENTION

For alternate teaching strategies, use pages 90–93 of Reading Support and Intervention to:

■ identify **phonemes**

■ practice **phonics**

■ reinforce **vocabulary**

■ build **text comprehension**

■ build **fluency**

Reading Support ▶ **and Intervention**

ELL ENGLISH LANGUAGE LEARNERS

For English Language Learners strategies to support this lesson, see Success for English Learners pages 95–98.

■ English-language development activities

■ background and concepts

■ vocabulary extension

Success for ▶ **English Learners**

Buying and Selling

CONTENT FOCUS Businesses make or sell goods or provide services for consumers to buy.

Express Path

Have pairs of children work together to find the answers to the Reading Check question.

2 Economics Invite children to share where their families shop in the community. Explain that another name for places where buyers and sellers come together is a *market*, such as a supermarket, school store, or online website that sells goods or services.

Q What are some goods and services that your family buys? Where do you buy them?

A Possible answers: food from a supermarket; books from the Internet; a dry cleaner to have clothes cleaned

Links Economics and Civics Discuss ways that workers in businesses benefit the community, such as by providing citizens with the goods and services they need, helping a community function, or providing jobs for other workers.

3 Economics Create a flowchart to show how producers and consumers depend on each other. Discuss the chart.

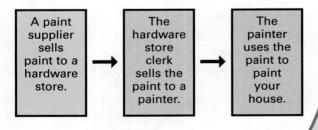

| A paint supplier sells paint to a hardware store. | → | The hardware store clerk sells the paint to a painter. | → | The painter uses the paint to paint your house. |

Buying and Selling

Christina and her mom go shopping downtown. Main Street has many businesses. A person who owns a **business** makes or sells goods or provides services.

2 Christina gets her hair cut at the salon. She and her mom buy sandals at the shoe store and raisin bread at the bakery. The salon, the shoe store, and the bakery are all businesses.

Hair Salon   Shoe Store   Bakery

278

Practice and Extend

READING SOCIAL STUDIES

Categorize and Classify Have children fill in a two-column chart that lists different kinds of goods in these categories: *Goods That Are Grown*, and *Goods That Are Made*.

▶ READING TRANSPARENCY

Use FOCUS SKILLS TRANSPARENCY 6.
Graphic Organizer Write-On/Wipe-Off Cards available

REACH ALL LEARNERS

Leveled Practice Discuss how producers and consumers are interdependent.

Basic Have children list producers and consumers in their school.

Proficient Ask children to draw pictures of producers and consumers interacting.

Advanced Have children write sentences to describe situations where producers and consumers interact.

Christina and her mom are consumers. A **consumer** is a person who buys goods or services. When consumers buy things, they provide money so producers can buy things. This makes producers consumers, too. The baker buys shoes. The shoe salesperson gets a haircut. The hairstylist buys bread.

Reading Check **Categorize and Classify**

How can a person be both a consumer and a producer? A producer makes or sells things and buys things as a consumer.

Summary Producers work to provide consumers with goods and services.

Review

① **What to Know** How do producers and consumers depend on each other?

② **Vocabulary** What is a **business** that provides goods in your community?

③ 🖍️ **Activity** Make a chart that shows goods and services you buy and use. Tell where you get them.

④ 🌟 **Categorize and Classify** When Christina got her hair cut, did she buy a good or a service?

279

HOMEWORK AND PRACTICE

Name _____ Date _____

Producers and Consumers

In each row, draw a picture to show what happens next. Then write P under the pictures of producers and C under the pictures of consumers.

page 51

---

3 Close

Summary

Have children read the summary and review the main points of the lesson.

- Consumers use goods and services that producers provide, and producers depend on consumers to buy their goods and services.
- Everyone is a consumer, and most people are producers.

Assess
REVIEW—Answers

1. **What to Know** Consumers are people who buy goods and services from producers. Producers are workers who grow, sell, or make products for consumers to buy.

2. **Vocabulary** Possible answer: A toy store is a **business** that provides goods in my community.

3. 🖍️ **Activity Assessment Guidelines** See Performance Rubric. This activity can be used with the Unit Project.

4. 🌟 **Categorize and Classify** She bought a service.

Use Focus Skills Transparency 6 or Categorize and Classify Graphic Organizer Write-On/Wipe-Off Card.

Read a Bar Graph

Why It Matters Some kinds of information are easier to find in a bar graph. A **bar graph** uses bars to show amounts or numbers of things.

Learn

1 A bar graph's title tells you the kind of information it shows. Each bar stands for a different group being counted. You read some bar graphs from left to right and others from bottom to top.

▋ Introduce

List the headings *Chicken, Pizza, Salad Bar,* and *Sandwiches* horizontally across the board. Tell children that these are foods that they sometimes have for lunch. Ask each child which of these foods is his or her favorite. As each child answers, draw a square above the heading on the board to make a bar graph. Then count the squares, and write the numbers at the top of each bar.

Why It Matters Explain that a bar graph makes it easy to see and understand information. Cover the bar graph except for the total numbers, and then uncover it. Point out that the total numbers provide information, but the bar graph helps you see right away which foods are most and least popular. The graph also makes it easy to compare the totals for each food.

2 Practice

1 How many dogs went to the Pet Palace on Tuesday?

2 On which day did the Pet Palace groom five dogs?

3 What were the two busiest days at the Pet Palace?

280

Practice and Extend

SOCIAL STUDIES SKILLS

Chart and Graph Skills
Read a Bar Graph

Dogs Groomed at the Pet Palace

		0	1	2	3	4	5	6	7
Sunday									
Monday									
Tuesday									
Wednesday									
Thursday									
Friday									
Saturday									

People We Know pages 280–281   Harcourt Social Studies   Social Studies Skills Transparency 6-1

TRANSPARENCY 6-1

INTEGRATE THE CURRICULUM

SCIENCE Display a variety of classroom objects that have different attributes in common, such as shape, color, size, or texture. Have children sort these objects and make a bar graph to compare those that share a certain attribute. Invite children to use the graph to ask and answer questions about the objects and their attributes. **Physical Attributes**

Dogs Groomed at the Pet Palace

	0	1	2	3	4	5	6	7
Sunday								
Monday								
Tuesday								
Wednesday								
Thursday								
Friday								
Saturday								

Apply

Make It Relevant Make a bar graph. Show different kinds of pets and the number of people you know who have each kind.

For online activities, go to
www.harcourtschool.com/ss1

281

Chart and Graph Skills

Learn

Economics Remind children that producers provide goods or services. Ask children if the Pet Palace provides goods or services. (services) Emphasize that producers are also consumers. The groomer is a consumer when she buys dog shampoo to do her job. She is also a consumer when she buys a new book or ticket to a movie.

1 Visual Literacy: Graph Explain that a bar graph uses rows or columns of squares or rectangles to create bars. Guide children to understand that the bar graph on page 281 is horizontal and reads from left to right, while the class graph made for lunch foods is vertical and reads from bottom to top.

Q How can you tell which days are the busiest at the Pet Palace?

A They have the most squares.

2 Practice

1. There were four dogs on Tuesday.
2. Five dogs were groomed on Thursday.
3. The busiest days were Monday and Saturday.

3 Close

Apply

Make It Relevant Children's bar graphs should include vertical or horizontal bars, numbers, and a title. The graphs should be easy to read.

INTERNET RESOURCES

For online activities, go to
www.harcourtschool.com/ss1

REACH ALL LEARNERS

Leveled Practice Have children create a bar graph.

Basic Have children make up data that shows pet food sold during one week.

Proficient Ask children to create a graph and title it.

Advanced Have children calculate total sales for the week.

HOMEWORK AND PRACTICE

Name _____ Date _____

CHART AND GRAPH SKILLS
Pet Sitting

This bar graph shows how many hours the pet sitter works each day. Use the graph to answer the questions.

Pet Sitter's Hours

	0	1	2	3	4	5	6
Monday							
Tuesday							
Wednesday							
Thursday							
Friday							

❶ How many hours does the pet sitter work on Tuesday? _3_

❷ On which day does the pet sitter work the most hours?
_____Wednesday_____

❸ On which days does the pet sitter work the same number of hours? _Tuesday and Thursday_

❹ On which day do you think the pet sitter sees the fewest pets? Why? _Friday. The pet sitter works only two hours._

page 52

OBJECTIVES

- Understand the importance of the actions and character of Wanda Montañez, and explain how she made a difference in others' lives.

RESOURCES

Unit 6 Audiotext CD Collection; Multimedia Biographies CD; Internet Resources; TimeLinks

Link to the Big Idea

Work Remind children that producers make things that consumers will want to buy. Wanda Montañez is a producer who makes clothes that people wear to show pride in their Hispanic culture.

Vocabulary Help Tell children that *Hispanic* describes a person who is from a Spanish-speaking country or culture.

Discuss the Biography

Economics Explain that producers want to make products that people will want to buy.

Q Why did Wanda Montañez think that people would buy her clothing?

A She knew other people wanted to show pride in their culture.

Biography

Trustworthiness

Respect
Responsibility
Fairness
Caring
Patriotism

Wanda Montañez

Born in Puerto Rico, Wanda Montañez is proud of her native country. When she moved to the United States, she went to many Puerto Rican festivals. She tried to find clothing she could wear to show pride in her Hispanic culture. She knew that others in the Hispanic community felt the same way she did.

Why Character Counts

Why is it important for a businesswoman like Wanda Montañez to be trustworthy?

Wanda Montañez started her own clothing company.

282

Practice and Extend

BACKGROUND

Wanda Montañez Salsa music serves as an inspiration for Montanez's clothing. Her clothing line, called Wepa Wear, uses bright primary colors along with words and phrases in Spanish. The word *wepa* is used in salsa music to show approval.

INTEGRATE THE CURRICULUM

LANGUAGES Invite any Spanish-speaking children to name Spanish words for articles of clothing. Have children design their own T-shirts with Spanish words in the design. Provide construction paper for the shirt designs. Have children cut out the shirts and display them on a miniature clothesline on the bulletin board. **Spanish**

Wanda Montañez designs clothing that shows Spanish words.

Wanda Montañez decided to create a line of clothing with Spanish words as part of the design. She gets ideas from Latin music and from listening to people talk. Wanda Montañez is helping others learn about her culture through her company's product.

GO ONLINE For more resources, go to **www.harcourtschool.com/ss1**

Time

| 1965 | | | | Present |
| Born | | | | |

1973 Moves to the United States from Puerto Rico

1986 Graduates from college

2003 Starts her clothing company

283

Visual Literacy: Pictures Have children compare the shirts in the photographs on page 283 with shirts they typically see or wear.

Q How do these shirts show Hispanic pride?

A The words on the shirts are printed in Spanish, and language is an important part of a culture.

Visual Literacy: Time Line Call attention to the time line on page 283. Point out that it only shows the year in which Wanda Montañez was born. Have children research the month and day of her birth.

TIMELINKS: Interactive Time Line

Have children add Wanda Montañez's birthdate to the one-year TimeLinks: Interactive Time Line.

Why Character Counts

Trustworthy businesspeople such as Wanda Montañez help customers feel they are being treated fairly. If consumers trust a businessperson, they are more likely to keep buying products from him or her.

GO ONLINE **INTERNET RESOURCES** For more resources, go to **www.harcourtschool.com/ss1**

ELL ENGLISH LANGUAGE LEARNERS

Have children draw pictures of cultural festivals that they know.

Beginning Have children name details in their pictures. Ask them to include single-word labels.

Intermediate Have pairs ask and answer simple questions about their pictures.

Advanced Have children write a caption for their picture and describe it to a classmate.

INTEGRATE THE CURRICULUM

VISUAL ARTS Invite children to design a product that shows pride in their own culture. Ask children to brainstorm school supplies, such as pencils, book covers, or backpacks, on which to show a word or symbol from their culture. Ask them to draw the item and show how its decoration would honor their cultural heritage. **Design a Product**

UNIT 6 ■ 283

Lesson 2

OBJECTIVES

- Understand people have many occupations.
- Recognize that people make choices about wants when spending money.

VOCABULARY

occupation p. 284
income p. 284
free enterprise p. 286
wants p. 288

CATEGORIZE AND CLASSIFY

pp. 268–269, 289

RESOURCES

Homework and Practice Book, p. 53; Reading Support and Intervention, pp. 94–97; Success for English Learners, pp. 99–102; Vocabulary Transparency 6-2; Focus Skills Transparency 6; Categorize and Classify Graphic Organizer Write-On/Wipe-Off Card; Unit 6 Audiotext CD Collection; Internet Resources

---

1 Introduce

What to Know Have a volunteer read the What to Know question. Point out that people buy goods or services and get paid to provide other goods or services. Remind children to look for answers to the question as they read the lesson.

Build Background Have children discuss jobs they do around their homes, such as taking out trash or raking leaves. Discuss jobs they do to earn money. Invite them to share jobs they would like to have as adults.

Lesson 2 Work and Income

 What to Know How do people get money to pay for goods and services?

Vocabulary
occupation
income
free enterprise
wants

 **Categorize and Classify**

Earning Money

People get paid for making or selling goods or for providing services. An **occupation** is a job a person works at to earn money. The money that people earn is called **income**.

park ranger

284

Practice and Extend

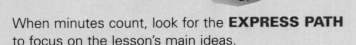
Express Path

When minutes count, look for the **EXPRESS PATH** to focus on the lesson's main ideas.

Quick Summary

This lesson discusses the work people do to earn money to pay for goods and services. It emphasizes the freedom people have to make choices about their occupations and how they spend their money.

People choose occupations in which they can do work they enjoy. Some may be good at singing or teaching. Others may enjoy building things or working with animals. Many people get special training for their jobs.

Reading Check **How do people choose their occupations?** People choose their occupations depending on what they enjoy or what they are good at.

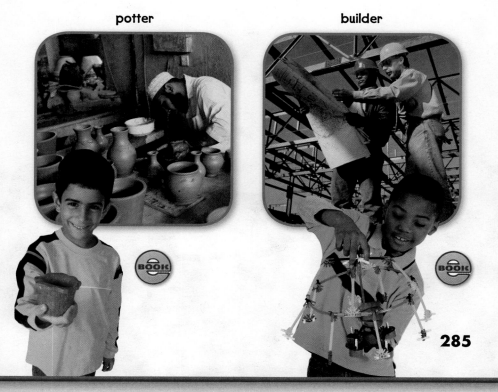

potter

builder

285

Earning Money

CONTENT FOCUS People get paid for the work they do.

Express Path

Ask children to scan the section to find ways people earn money.

① **Visual Literacy: Pictures** Discuss the pictures of occupations shown on pages 284–285. Elicit that the choices to do these occupations grew out of intrest and skill.

Q **What other reasons might these workers have for choosing their jobs.**

A the park ranger likes helping children; the potter feels satisfied by creating art; the builder enjoys improving the community

Interactive in the enhanced online student eBook

Point out that volunteer jobs are those people do without earning income. Volunteers do work without pay to help other people.

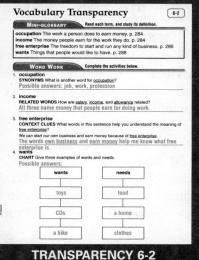

VOCABULARY

Vocabulary Transparency 6-2

MINI-GLOSSARY Read each term, and study its definition.

occupation The work a person does to earn money. p. 284
income The money people earn for the work they do. p. 284
free enterprise The freedom to start and run any kind of business. p. 286
wants Things that people would like to have. p. 288

WORD WORK Complete the activities below.

1. **occupation**
SYNONYMS What is another word for occupation?
Possible answers: job, work, profession

2. **income**
RELATED WORDS How are salary, income, and allowance related?
All three name money that people earn for doing work.

3. **free enterprise**
CONTEXT CLUES What words in this sentence help you understand the meaning of free enterprise?
We can start our own business and earn money because of free enterprise.
The words own business and earn money help me know what free enterprise is.

4. **wants**
CHART Give three examples of wants and needs.
Possible answers:

wants	needs
toys	food
CDs	a home
a bike	clothes

TRANSPARENCY 6-2

READING SUPPORT/ INTERVENTION

For alternate teaching strategies, use pages 94–97 of Reading Support and Intervention to:

- identify **phonemes**
- practice **phonics**
- reinforce **vocabulary**
- build **text comprehension**
- build **fluency**

Reading Support ▶ and Intervention

HARCOURT SOCIAL Studies People We Know

Reading Support and Intervention

ELL ENGLISH LANGUAGE LEARNERS

For English Language Learners strategies to support this lesson, see Success for English Learners pages 99–102.

- English-language development activities
- background and concepts
- vocabulary extension

Success for ▶ English Learners

HARCOURT SOCIAL Studies People We Know

Success for English Learners

Running a Business

CONTENT FOCUS People are free to start and run businesses and decide what to charge for the goods and services they provide.

Express Path

Ask children to examine the photographs and captions in this section. Then have them write a sentence describing the main idea.

2 Economics Explain that in a free enterprise system, people may start any kind of business they choose. Tell children that these are private businesses that offer goods and services for a profit. Explain that a profit is the difference between how much a business makes and the cost to run it.

Q What examples of free enterprise can you name?

A Possible answers: lemonade stands, garage sales, neighborhood and family-owned businesses

Link Economics and Government You may want to have children review the lesson on government services in Unit 1. Explain that both the government and private businesses provide us with goods and services we need. Point out that private business owners use the money they make from selling goods or services to run their business and make a profit. The government pays for the goods and services it provides with tax money.

Running a Business

Some people have ideas for businesses of their own. A person who likes to make a product might start a new business to sell that product. The freedom to start and run a business to make money is called **free enterprise**.

286

Practice and Extend

VOCABULARY POWER

Synonyms List on the board the following words: occupation, income, money, job. Ask: *Which two words name work people do?* (occupation, job) *Which two words name what people earn for doing a job?* (income, money). Encourage children to list other synonyms for each of these word pairs.

INTEGRATE THE CURRICULUM

MATHEMATICS Help children understand that a business needs to make a profit. Give children the following story problem to solve: *The materials to make each bracelet cost 75¢. If the children sell a bracelet for $1.50, how much profit will they make?* (75¢) Have children find the profits the children would make if they sold 5 or 10 bracelets. **Profit**

Children can take part in free enterprise. They can wash cars, rake leaves, care for pets, and sell things they make. These businesses are all forms of free enterprise. The children who do these jobs earn income.

Reading Check 🌟 **Categorize and Classify** What are some ways children can take part in free enterprise? Children can wash cars, rake leaves, care for pets, or sell things they make.

Children in History

❹

Annie Oakley

Annie Oakley's father died when she was very young. She had to learn to hunt animals for food. To earn money, she sold this food to other people in Cincinnati, Ohio. The income helped her family buy the things they needed. Later, Annie Oakley won many medals for her shooting skills.

287

BACKGROUND

Child Labor Laws In 1938, Congress passed the Fair Labor Standards Act, which included restrictions on child labor. This law was written to protect children from harsh or unsafe working conditions. Today, child labor laws limit children's work hours and promote children's health, safety, and education.

INTEGRATE THE CURRICULUM

READING/LANGUAGE ARTS Have children recite poems and rhymes that have to do with buying and selling, such as the following:

Cobbler, cobbler, mend my shoe,
Get it done by half past two.
Half past two is much too late!
Get it done by half past eight.
Stitch it up, and stitch it down,
And I'll give you a half a crown.

Use Rhyme and Rhythm

---

❸ Economics Explain that businesses can be family-owned, a government agency, a small business, or a large corporation. Point out that the children in the pictures are working as partnerships. A business can serve just a few consumers, a certain group of consumers, or even many consumers around the world.

Q **What are the advantages and disadvantages of running a business alone?**

A Possible answer: An advantage is you can decide what you want to do. A disadvantage is you would have to do all the work by yourself.

Q **What are the advantages and disadvantages of running a business with a partner or group?**

A Possible answer: An advantage is that everyone can share the work. A disadvantage is that everyone may not agree about what to do.

Children in History

Annie Oakley

❹ Tell children that Annie Oakley worked hard to learn hunting skills. Explain that Annie was nine years old when she began hunting to help support her family. Point out that she lived in the frontier area of Ohio at a time when children did not attend school regularly and hunting was a common way to get food.

Spending Money

CONTENT FOCUS People make choices about how to spend their income.

Express Path

Model for children how to turn the heading into a question, such as *How do people spend their money?* Then have pairs work together to write questions and answer them.

5 Economics Discuss the choices people make when spending money.

Q **What goods and services keep people safe and comfortable?**

A Possible answers: food, shelter, clothing, utilities, health care, transportation, day care

Q **What are examples of goods and services that people like to have?**

A Answers might include toys, sports equipment, recreational activities, vacations

Also discuss with children the benefits of saving money. Point out that people often work to save up for something special that they want. Elicit that people can save up to buy goods they would like to have, such as a new car, or services they want to use in the future, such as a college education.

Correct Misconceptions Explain to children that though we all have the same needs, we do not all have the same opportunities to meet our needs. Point out that for many people, basic needs such as food, clothing, and shelter are among their greatest wants.

Spending Money

People use their income to buy goods and services. They may also save some of it. They use their money to pay for wants. **Wants** are things that people would like to have. Pets, books, and new bicycles are wants. Some wants are needs. A home, food, and clothing are needs.

$ 15.80

288

Practice and Extend

People cannot buy everything they want. They have to make choices about what things are important to them. Most people first buy the goods and services that will keep them safe and comfortable. Then they buy other goods and services they would like to have.

⑤

Reading Check **How do people decide what goods and services to buy?**
People choose what goods and services are most important.

Summary People work so that they can earn income to buy goods and services.

Review

① **What to Know** How do people get money to pay for goods and services?

② **Vocabulary** What do people do with **income**?

③ ✎ **Write** Make a list of things you like to do. Choose one that you could do to earn income.

④ (Focus Skill) **Categorize and Classify** Write down the occupations of family members or adult friends. Circle the ones in which people make goods.

289

Summary

Have children read the summary and then restate the main points in their own words.

- People are free to choose their occupations.
- People earn income so that they can buy what they need and want.

Assess

REVIEW—Answers

1. **What to Know** People work at occupations to earn an income to pay for goods and services.

2. **Vocabulary** People use their **income** to buy goods and services. They may save some of it.

3. ✎ **Writing Assessment Guidelines** See Writing Rubric.

4. (Focus Skill) **Categorize and Classify** Discuss with children why the circled occupations provide goods and not services.

Use Focus Skills Transparency 6 or Categorize and Classify Graphic Organizer Write-On/Wipe-Off Card.

HOMEWORK AND PRACTICE

Name _____ Date _____

Saving, Sharing, Spending

This week you earned $10 for watering a neighbor's lawn and walking his dog. Your grandmother gave you $20 for your birthday. Answer the question. Then fill in the table.

How much money do you have in all? _$30_

What I Will Save	What I Will Share	What I Will Spend
Possible answers:		
· I will save _$10_	· I will share _$10_	· I will spend _$10_
· I will put the money	· I will share the money with	· I will spend the money on
in a bank	people who need help	a new book

page 53

ELL ENGLISH LANGUAGE LEARNERS

Have partners take turns answering questions about wants:
What can I buy that I can wear?
What can I buy that I can eat?
What can I buy that protects me?

Beginning Have children point to pictures in magazines.

Intermediate Ask children to give one-word answers.

Advanced Have children provide answers in complete sentences.

Critical Thinking Skills

OBJECTIVES

- Recognize that people do not always have enough money to buy everything they want.
- Understand the benefits and costs of making an economic choice.

VOCABULARY

budget p. 290   **bank** p. 290

RESOURCES

Homework and Practice Book, p. 54;
Social Studies Skills Transparency 6-2;
Unit 6 Audiotext CD Collection

❚ Introduce

Have children describe items for sale at a favorite store. Discuss how they make choices about the things they buy or the things they ask family members to buy for them. Have children share how the price of an item influences their choices. Invite them to share the benefits they might receive from a new purchase.

Why It Matters Point out that we may have unlimited wants but limited money. Explain that even people with a lot of money cannot buy everything they want. Money is a resource that we may not always have enough of. If we learn to make wise choices, then we will not waste our money.

Make a Choice When Buying

Why It Matters When you go shopping, you may see that some goods you want cost more money than you have. You must decide what you are willing to give up to get what you want.

Learn

1 A **budget** is a plan that shows how much money you have and how much money you spend. You can save money to buy something that costs a lot.

2 You can put the money you save in a bank. A **bank** is a business that keeps money safe. Money in a bank earns more money, called interest.

290

Practice and Extend

SOCIAL STUDIES SKILLS

Critical Thinking Skills

Make a Choice When Buying

❶ If you see the movie, what will you give up?

❷ If you decide to save for skates, what will you give up?

People We Know pages 290–291   Harcourt Social Studies   Social Studies Skills Transparency 6-2

TRANSPARENCY 6-2

INDEPENDENT READING

Invite children to read *Tight Times* by Barbara Shook Hazen (Viking, 1983). In this book, a young boy and his family must make careful decisions about what to buy during a time when money is scarce. Encourage children to discuss if they agree with his choices.

TIGHT TIMES
Barbara Shook Hazen
pictures by Trina Schart Hyman

Practice

Imagine that you have earned ten dollars. You want to see a movie. You also want to buy new skates. You will have to make a choice about spending or saving your money.

1 If you see the movie, what will you give up?

2 If you decide to save for skates, what will you give up?

3

Apply

Make It Relevant If you had ten dollars, would you spend the money right away or save it? Why?

291

Learn

1 Economics Explain to children that sticking to a budget means making hard decisions about what to buy. Tell them that when you make a choice, the choice that you do not choose is called the opportunity cost. Help children understand cost-benefit analysis by explaining that they should consider the opportunity cost when making choices.

Point out that some choices are "all or nothing"—an item is so expensive that we have no money left for other things.

Q What are some all-or-nothing choices you have made?

A Possible answers: to choose to have the TV on or off; to choose to have dessert or not

2 Economics Explain that money that is not used can be placed in a bank for safekeeping. Money earns interest when it is in a bank. Banks also loan money. If we borrow money from a bank, we pay interest for using it. Have children discuss ways they save money.

3 Practice

1. You will give up saving money for new skates.
2. You will give up seeing the movie.

Apply

Make It Relevant Invite children to justify spending or saving their money. If they choose to save their money, invite them to share the kinds of things for which they might save.

Critical Thinking Skills

REACH ALL LEARNERS

Leveled Practice Have children practice making a budget.

Basic Have children list income from weekly allowances or money earned and determine an item they would like to save for.

Proficient Have children list various expenses they will pay for during a week's time.

Advanced Have children use their weekly incomes to set up budgets for expenses.

HOMEWORK AND PRACTICE

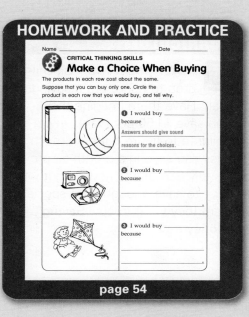

Name _____ Date _____

CRITICAL THINKING SKILLS
Make a Choice When Buying

The products in each row cost about the same. Suppose that you can buy only one. Circle the product in each row that you would buy, and tell why.

1 I would buy _____
because
Answers should give sound reasons for the choices.

2 I would buy _____
because

3 I would buy _____
because

page 54

Points of View

OBJECTIVES

- Compare and contrast children's daily lives to those of others.
- Explore different points of view about how individuals spend their money.

RESOURCES

Unit 6 Audiotext CD Collection

Link to the Big Idea

Work Explain to children that people work to earn money. People earn money to pay for things they want, and their spending habits differ depending on their age and responsibilities. People also save money and give money to charities in order to help others. Sometimes knowing what other people do with their money can help us make good decisions about how we use our own money.

Vocabulary Help Review with children that a *budget* is a plan for how money is to be saved and spent.

Discuss the Points of View

Economics Read aloud the Sidewalk Reporter's question. Have volunteers read aloud the answers. Discuss reasons that a person might feel it is important to save money.

Q Which responses are about saving money?

A Rick is saving to get himself a dirt bike, and Carlos sets aside a little each week. Mr. Johnson saves the rest after he pays bills.

The Sidewalk Reporter asks:

"How do you make sure that you spend your money wisely?"

Carlos

"I put $25 in a jar to spend each week on extras."

Rick

"I'm saving for a dirt bike, so I don't spend a penny of what I earn."

View from the Past

The First Bank

After the American Revolution, each state still used its own kind of money. Leaders started a bank in Philadelphia that would create one form of money for the United States.

292

Practice and Extend

INTEGRATE THE CURRICULUM

MATHEMATICS Ask children to figure out a savings plan. Have them imagine they can save $1.50 per week. Invite children to figure out how much they can save in a month (approximately $6.00) and how long it will take to save enough for a special item they want to buy. **Saving Money**

BACKGROUND

The First Bank On December 12, 1791, the United States government opened the Bank of the United States in Philadelphia, Pennsylvania. Commonly referred to as the "First" Bank of the United States, it was set up to serve merchants, politicians, landowners, and most importantly, the government of the United States.

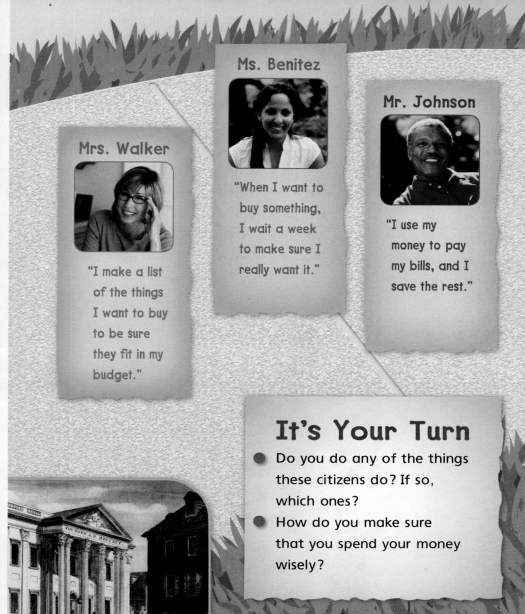

Mrs. Walker

"I make a list of the things I want to buy to be sure they fit in my budget."

Ms. Benitez

"When I want to buy something, I wait a week to make sure I really want it."

Mr. Johnson

"I use my money to pay my bills, and I save the rest."

It's Your Turn

- Do you do any of the things these citizens do? If so, which ones?
- How do you make sure that you spend your money wisely?

293

View from the Past

History Read aloud the information about the First Bank. Refer children to the map of the first thirteen states on page 189 in Unit 4. Explain that after the American Revolution these states set up their own banks and issued their own paper money. In 1791, the U. S. government decided to set up the Bank of the United States. This bank then issued money that was the same for all the states.

Q Why would buying and selling be harder if each state had its own kind of money?

A Possible answers: Buyers and sellers might not think the money was real; The money might be worth different amounts.

It's Your Turn–Answers

Ask children to read the questions and discuss their spending habits. Take a survey of how children save money. Discuss their strategies. Invite children to brainstorm ways they can better save the money they earn.

- Possible answers can include making lists, waiting before buying, and saving money.
- Possible answer: I decide if I really want what I am going to buy before I spend my money.

OBJECTIVES

- Understand how raw materials and resources are used to make a product.
- Identify the steps in a production process.
- Recognize that products are shipped to and sold at markets.

VOCABULARY

raw material p. 295
factory p. 296
human resources p. 296
capital resources p. 297

 CATEGORIZE AND CLASSIFY

pp. 268–269, 299

RESOURCES

Homework and Practice Book, p. 55; Reading Support and Intervention, pp. 98–101; Success for English Learners, pp. 103–106; Vocabulary Transparency 6-3; Focus Skills Transparency 6; Categorize and Classify Graphic Organizer Write-On/Wipe-Off Card; Unit 6 Audiotext CD Collection; Internet Resources

Introduce

What to Know Invite children to read aloud the What to Know question. Explain that raw materials are also called natural resources. Remind children to look for answers to the question as they read the lesson.

Build Background Ask children to recall when they assembled something. Invite them to discuss what was most difficult and to describe how someone else was able to help them.

Lesson **3**

From Factory to You

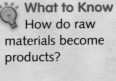 **What to Know** How do raw materials become products?

Vocabulary
raw material
factory
human resources
capital resources

 Focus Skill Categorize and Classify

Daniel wanted a new baseball bat for his birthday. His grandfather took him to the Louisville Slugger Museum and Bat Factory in Louisville, Kentucky. Together they learned how wooden bats are made.

Louisville Slugger Museum in Louisville, Kentucky

294

Practice and Extend

 *Express Path*

When minutes count, look for the **EXPRESS PATH** to focus on the lesson's main ideas.

Quick Summary

This lesson explains the process by which raw materials become goods. Human resources and capital resources are a needed part of this process.

A Bat's Beginning

The making of a bat begins in a forest of trees. Trees are **raw materials**, or natural resources used to make a product.

First, the trees are cut into many long sections. Next, the wood is dried. Then, the wood is shipped to the places where the bats are made.

Reading Check What raw material is used to make a baseball bat? Trees are used to make a baseball bat.

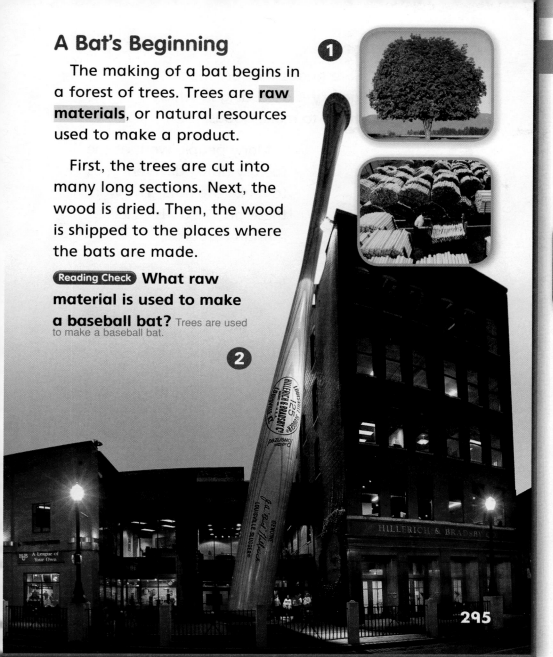

295

A Bat's Beginning

CONTENT FOCUS Goods, such as a baseball bat, come from raw materials.

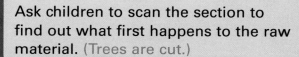

Express Path

Ask children to scan the section to find out what first happens to the raw material. (Trees are cut.)

1 Economics Point out that trees are a natural resource. Help children brainstorm other natural resources that might be used as raw materials, such as plants or water. Then point out that a natural resource is often used to make a variety of products. Invite children to name other products that are made from wood.

2 Visual Literacy: Pictures Direct childen to study the pictures on page 295. Ask children to speculate why it appears that a bat is leaning against a building. (publicity, landmark) Explain that this is the Louisville Slugger Museum, and it is also a factory where bats are made.

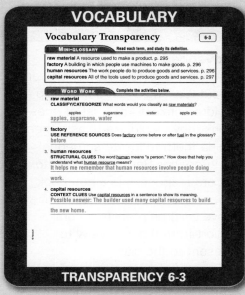
READING SUPPORT/ INTERVENTION

For alternate teaching strategies, use pages 98–101 of Reading Support and Intervention to:

- identify **phonemes**
- practice **phonics**
- reinforce **vocabulary**
- build **text comprehension**
- build **fluency**

HARCOURT SOCIAL Studies People We Know
Reading Support and Intervention

Reading Support ▶ and Intervention

ELL ENGLISH LANGUAGE LEARNERS

For English Language Learners strategies to support this lesson, see Success for English Learners pages 103–106.

- English-language development activities
- background and concepts
- vocabulary extension

HARCOURT SOCIAL Studies People We Know
Success for English Learners

Success for ▶ English Learners

At the Factory

CONTENT FOCUS Human resources and capital resources combine to produce goods.

Express Path

Have the class scan the section to find the meaning of the vocabulary terms. Then use the terms in sentences about the section.

3 **Economics** Ask children to share what they know about people who have factory jobs. Have them describe the many kinds of jobs people do in a factory. Point out that the work people do at any job is called *human resources*. Explain that human resources include work related to

- service
- training
- creating new ideas
- developing new designs with research
- health, strength, talents, education, and skills people use

At the Factory

Baseball bats are goods that are made in factories. A **factory** is a building in which people use machines to make goods.

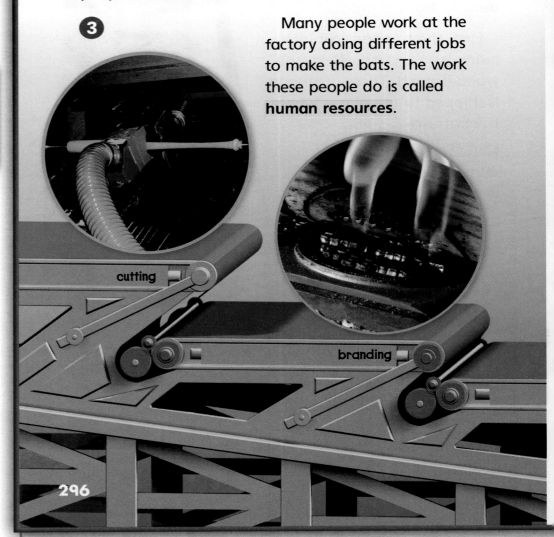

3 Many people work at the factory doing different jobs to make the bats. The work these people do is called **human resources**.

cutting

branding

296

Practice and Extend

VOCABULARY POWER

Word Web Have children brainstorm examples of human resources. Write *human resources* in the center of a web. Remind children that *human* means related to people. Ask children to fill in the web with skills and qualities that people bring to their work, such as strong arms for lifting, a college degree, or creative new ideas to improve goods.

REACH ALL LEARNERS

Advanced Direct children to interview a factory worker to learn about working in a factory. Help children brainstorm a list of questions they would like to ask. Then guide them to locate someone to interview. Remind children to record responses in a notebook or on tape (permission asked first). Have children prepare an oral report from the interview to present to the class.

All of the tools used to produce a good are called **capital resources**. At the factory, the wood is first placed in a machine that cuts it into a bat shape. After the bats are cut, they are branded. A worker burns the name of the company onto the bat. Then the bats are sanded and stained a certain color. Last, the bats are packaged. They are ready to be sold.

Reading Check How is the wood changed when it is made into a bat at the factory?
The wood is cut, branded, sanded, and stained.

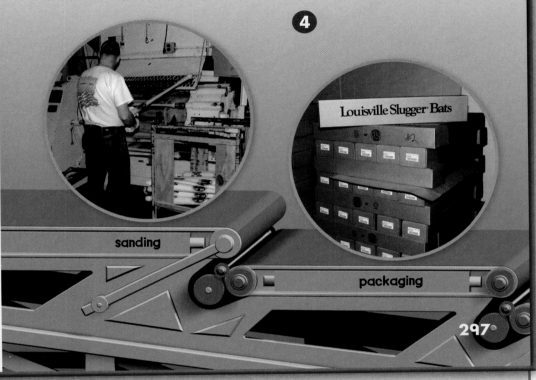
sanding
packaging
Louisville Slugger Bats
297

4 **Visual Literacy: Pictures** Have children identify the capital resources shown in the pictures on pages 296–297, such as the cutting machine or the packaging. Explain that there are many capital resources used to produce goods, including tools, buildings, equipment, land, and roads.

Q What other capital resources do you think are used to make bats?

A Possible answers: computers, branding tools, sandpaper, stains and brushes

Link Economics and Geography
Have children brainstorm a list of products that are unique to their state. Encourage children to identify the natural, human, and capital resources needed to produce them.

Q Why do you think these products are only produced in your state?

A Possible answers: the raw materials may only be available here; the company is only located here; tourists want to buy these products as souvenirs.

ELL ENGLISH LANGUAGE LEARNERS

Have children recognize and identify human resources and capital resources.

Beginning Ask children to locate *human resources* and *capital resources* in the lesson. Direct them to point to pictures that are examples of each word.

Intermediate Help children locate several examples of human and capital resources in the lesson. Help children write examples on index cards. Have them sort the cards into separate piles for each type of resource. Encourage them to shuffle the cards and repeat the sorting activity.

Advanced Ask children to define *human resource* and *capital resource*. Invite them to locate and name examples of each resource in the lesson.

MAKE IT RELEVANT

At School Have small groups research the raw materials, human resources, and capital resources needed to produce a classroom item. Help children choose a school item, such as writing paper or a desk. Ask children to research online and book sources for information. Direct them to make a poster display that includes pictures, captions, and brief descriptions of the resources. If possible, display the poster near the item.

To the Market

CONTENT FOCUS Goods are moved to markets in order to be sold.

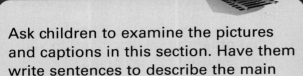 **Express Path**

Ask children to examine the pictures and captions in this section. Have them write sentences to describe the main idea.

5 **Visual Literacy: Picture** Have children scan the picture on page 298. Ask them: *How are the bats being moved to the market?* Discuss reasons that other forms of transportation might be used. Remind children that the work done by people loading and driving the truck are human resources, while the truck is a capital resource.

6 **Economics** Point out that the money a company earns for selling a product is not all profit. Explain that much of the money is used to produce more goods.

Q **What kinds of things do you think the money a company earns is used for?**

A Possible answers: to buy raw materials; to pay workers; to pay for capital resources

To the Market

The bats are finally ready for markets where people will buy them. The bats are moved to markets in many ways. Trucks or trains may deliver the bats to places around the United States. Airplanes may be used to take the bats to places around the world.

5

298

Practice and Extend

INTEGRATE THE CURRICULUM

 HEALTH Have children show safe lifting techniques. Explain that workers must lift heavy boxes correctly when loading goods on trucks, planes, or ships to avoid injury. Encourage children to research online for safety information. Ask children to create a safety sign with illustrations of correct lifting procedures to display in the classroom. **Safety**

REACH ALL LEARNERS

Leveled Practice Discuss how finished goods get to the market.

Basic Help children cut out magazine pictures of ways goods are transported to market.

Proficient Have children create a poster showing finished goods and a way to move them.

Advanced Guide children to label pictures with a description of the goods, means of transportation, and a likely market.

At a sporting goods store, Daniel and his grandfather find the bat they want to buy. The money they pay for the bat will be used to make more bats. **6**

Reading Check **Categorize and Classify**

How are goods, such as bats, taken to markets? They are taken to markets by trucks, trains, or airplanes.

Summary Human and capital resources are used to change raw materials into products to be sold.

Review

1. **What to Know** How do raw materials become products?

2. **Vocabulary** How does a company use its **capital resources**?

3. **Activity** Choose a raw material that comes from your community or state. Make a poster to show the things that can be made from it.

4. **Categorize and Classify** What is the difference between a capital resource and a human resource?

299

Chart and Graph Skills

Read a Flowchart

OBJECTIVES

■ Describe the purpose of a flowchart.

■ Interpret data on a flowchart.

VOCABULARY

flowchart p. 300

RESOURCES

Homework and Practice Book, p. 56; Social Studies Skills Transparency 6-3; Activity Pattern A13; Unit 6 Audiotext CD Collection; Internet Resources

Introduce

Hold up a picture of a wheat field and a picture of a loaf of bread. Ask children to tell how they think wheat from the field ends up in a loaf of bread from the store.

Why It Matters Tell children that a flowchart shows through text and pictures the steps involved in doing something. Remind them to follow the arrows that lead from one step to the next as they read a flowchart. Showing steps in order this way makes the process easier to understand.

Why It Matters A flowchart shows the steps needed to make or do something. You can use a flowchart to show the steps workers follow to make a product.

Learn

1 The title of the flowchart tells what it is about. Each picture has a sentence that tells about the step. The arrows show the order of the steps.

3 Practice

1 What does the flowchart on the next page show?

2 What is the first step?

3 What happens after the bats are made at the factory?

300

Practice and Extend

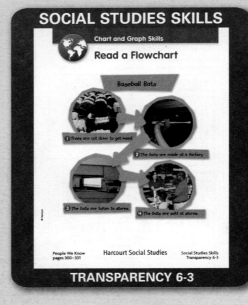
INTEGRATE THE CURRICULUM

MUSIC Provide children with copies of a popular song with sequence lyrics, such as "Polly Put the Kettle On," "There's a Hole in My Bucket", or "Peanut Butter and Jelly." Discuss the step-by-step pattern in the song you choose. Then assign children parts to sing, making sure they sequence the steps correctly. **Song Patterns**

Baseball Bats

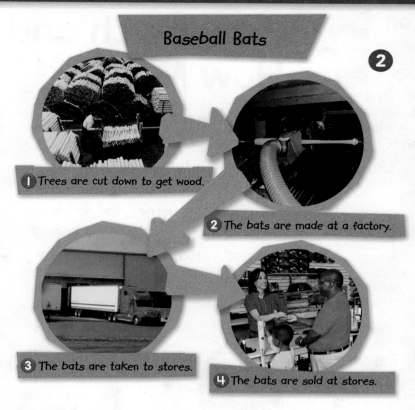

❷

1. Trees are cut down to get wood.

2. The bats are made at a factory.

3. The bats are taken to stores.

4. The bats are sold at stores.

Apply

Make It Relevant Make a flowchart showing the steps for something you do everyday.

 For online activities, go to **www.harcourtschool.com/ss1**

301

Chart and Graph Skills

Learn

❶ Have children find the word *flowchart*. Invite children to explain and give examples of things that flow, such as rivers. Guide children to see that a flowchart flows from one step to another in order.

❷ **Visual Literacy: Chart** Point out parts of the flowchart on page 301. Explain that the title tells what the flowchart shows. Discuss how arrows lead from one step to the next. Stress that the steps are arranged in order.

❸ Practice

1. The flowchart shows the order of steps used to make and sell baseball bats.
2. The trees are cut down to get wood for the bats.
3. The bats are taken to stores.

Apply

Make It Relevant The flowchart should contain multiple steps. Arrows should connect the steps in chronological order.

Invite children to think of another process they do everyday, and have them write six steps for it. Provide each child with a copy of Activity Pattern A13. Have children illustrate each step in a square. Then direct them to cut around the book, tape together the two parts at the tab, and fold along the lines. Lastly, have children draw a cover for their book.

GO **INTERNET RESOURCES**
For online activities, go to
www.harcourtschool.com/hss

REACH ALL LEARNERS

Leveled Practice Have children create a school day flowchart.

Basic Ask children to list in order four activities they do during the school day.

Proficient Direct children to draw and label a picture to explain each school day activity on the list.

Advanced Ask children to write a sentence to describe each picture.

HOMEWORK AND PRACTICE

Name _____ Date _____

CHART AND GRAPH SKILLS
From Beehive to Breakfast Table

Write sentences to tell what is happening in the steps. The first one is done for you.

Bees make honey.
Possible answers:

2. A worker gathers the honey.

3. Honey is put in jars to sell.

4. Someone puts the honey on a muffin and eats it.

PAGE 56

Lesson 4

PAGES 302–305

OBJECTIVES

- **Understand the concepts of scarcity.**
- **Understand that prices go up or down based on supply and demand.**

VOCABULARY

scarce p. 303   **marketplace** p. 304

CATEGORIZE AND CLASSIFY

pp. 268–269, 305

RESOURCES

Homework and Practice Book, p. 57; Reading Support and Intervention, pp. 102–105; Success for English Learners, pp. 107–110; Vocabulary Transparency 6-4; Focus Skills Transparency 6; Categorize and Classify Graphic Organizer Write-On/Wipe-Off Card; Unit 6 Audiotext CD Collection; Internet Resources

---

1   Introduce

What to Know Read aloud the What to Know question. Explain that even though stores have many things for consumers to buy, producers cannot always make enough goods for all the people who want them. Ask children to look for reasons why we produce more of one good and less of another as they read the lesson.

Build Background Have children recall goods that have been in high demand, such as toys or collector cards. Discuss what happens in the marketplace when there is not enough of a good for people to buy.

Lesson 4

What to Know
Why do we make, sell, and buy more of some things than others?

Vocabulary
scarce
marketplace

Categorize and Classify

How Much and How Many?

Producing Goods

Grace lives in New Jersey. Her family grows blueberries for products such as blueberry muffins. For good blueberries, the soil must be rich. There must also be enough sun and water, and the blueberry bushes must be healthy.

Blueberry bushes in New Jersey

302

Practice and Extend

Express Path

When minutes count, look for the **EXPRESS PATH** to focus on the lesson's main ideas.

Quick Summary

This lesson explains factors that can cause scarcity and how scarcity relates to pricing in the marketplace.

Farmers who grow blueberries can face problems. Without enough water, the berries can dry out in the hot summer sun. Too much rain can harm the blueberries, too. Cold weather can freeze the berries.

drought

If any of these things happen, blueberries will be scarce. When something is **scarce**, there is not enough of it to meet everyone's wants.

flood

Reading Check **What problems do farmers who grow blueberries face?** Too little water, too much rain, and cold weather can harm blueberries.

1

303

2 **Teach**

Producing Goods

CONTENT FOCUS Many factors affect the amount of a resource available for making products.

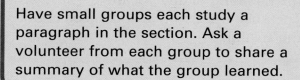

Express Path

Have small groups each study a paragraph in the section. Ask a volunteer from each group to share a summary of what the group learned.

1 **Visual Literacy: Pictures** Have children look at the pictures and use them to discuss how some weather conditions might make blueberries scarce. Point out that crops from other areas of the United States and other countries can also have problems as a result of poor weather conditions.

Q **How might some weather conditions affect the goods or natural resources of a place?**

A Possible answer: Bad weather may destroy natural resources. This would make goods produced from these resources cost more.

VOCABULARY

Vocabulary Transparency 6-4

MINI-GLOSSARY Read each term, and study its definition.

scarce Hard to find because there is not much of it. p. 303
marketplace A place where goods and services are bought and sold. p. 304

WORD WORK Complete the activities below.

1. **scarce**
USE REFERENCE SOURCES Does *scarce* come before or after *smell* in the dictionary?
before

2. **scarce**
CONTEXT CLUES Use the word *scarce* in a sentence that shows its meaning.
Possible answer: Some rare dog breeds are scarce.

3. **marketplace**
STRUCTURAL CLUES How do the two words in *marketplace* help you remember its meaning?
Market and place help me remember that a marketplace is a place where a market is located.

TRANSPARENCY 6-4

READING SUPPORT/ INTERVENTION

For alternate teaching strategies, use pages 102–105 of Reading Support and Intervention to:

- identify **phonemes**
- practice **phonics**
- reinforce **vocabulary**
- build **text comprehension**
- build **fluency**

Reading Support ▶ and Intervention

HARCOURT SOCIAL Studies People We Know
Reading Support and Intervention

ELL **ENGLISH LANGUAGE LEARNERS**

For English Language Learners strategies to support this lesson, see Success for English Learners pages 107–110.

- English-language development activities
- background and concepts
- vocabulary extension

Success for ▶ English Learners

HARCOURT SOCIAL Studies People We Know
Success for English Learners

High and Low Prices

CONTENT FOCUS Prices go up and down in the marketplace depending on the supply of products and the number of people who want to buy them.

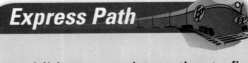
Express Path

Have children scan the section to find the meaning of any vocabulary terms. Then use the terms in sentences about the section.

Correct Misconceptions Explain to children that both *market* and *marketplace* refer to where buyers and sellers come together. Point out that a market can also be a place, such as a grocery store or supermarket.

2 Economics Define *supply* as the amount available and *demand* as the number of people who want something. Invite children to find the examples of these on page 304. (*Supply* is many or not many blueberries to sell; *demand* is many people or not many people who want to buy.) Point out that prices go up and down based on supply and demand.

Q What happens to the price of a good if the supply is scarce?

A The price will go up.

Link Economics and Geography Discuss how the seasons affect prices.

- When a fruit or vegetable is out of season, its price goes up, because it is shipped from far away or is grown in greenhouses.

- Products used during certain times of the year cost less off-season. For example, swim suits cost less in winter, and coats cost less in summer.

High and Low Prices

In the marketplace, the price of goods can go up and down. The **marketplace** is where goods and services are bought and sold. A price is what people pay when they buy a good or service. If there are not many blueberries and many people want to buy them, the price will go up. If there are many blueberries, or if not many people want them, the price will go down.

Whole Blueberry Pie $8

Blueberry Muffins $1 each

304

Practice and Extend

VOCABULARY POWER

Compound Words Point out that the word *marketplace* is made up of two words, *market* and *place*. Elicit that knowing what the two words mean can help children define the compound word as "a place where things are bought and sold." Encourage children to locate and define other compound words in the lesson, such as *blueberries* and *everyone*.

REACH ALL LEARNERS

Leveled Practice Discuss factors that cause scarcity and how scarcity affects goods.

Basic Name things that can be bad for a blueberry harvest.

Proficient Explain what can happen in the marketplace if blueberries are scarce.

Advanced Explain how a dry, hot summer can affect a consumer who wants to buy blueberry muffins.

Sometimes goods are scarce because there are few raw materials to make them. Other times, the raw materials cost too much. Goods can also be scarce if they take a long time to make. People have to pay more money to buy things that are scarce.

Reading Check **Why might the price of something go up?**
The price of something may go up if there is not enough if it or if many people want it.

Summary When there is a lot of a product, people will pay less. When a product is scarce, they will pay more.

Review

① **What to Know** Why do we make, sell, and buy more of some things than others?

② **Vocabulary** What will happen to the cost of blueberry muffins if blueberries are **scarce**?

③ **Write** Imagine that you are a farmer. Write about something that has caused your crop to fail.

④ **Categorize and Classify** Look around your classroom. Make a list of things that are made from the same raw material.

305

---

3 Close

Summary

Have children read the summary and then restate the lesson's key points.

- If there are plenty of goods, the price stays low. People pay more for goods that are scarce.

- Goods can be scarce if there are few raw materials to make them, or if they take a long time to make.

Assess

REVIEW—Answers

1. **What to Know** We make, sell, and buy things based on raw materials and goods that are available. This determines how much is produced and what price people will pay for the goods.

2. **Vocabulary** If blueberries are **scarce**, the price of the muffins will go up.

3. **Assessment Guidelines** See Writing Rubric.

4. **Categorize and Classify** Lists should show an understanding of how one raw material is used for many goods.

Use Focus Skills Transparency 6 or Categorize and Classify Graphic Organizer Write-On/Wipe-Off Card.

WRITING RUBRIC

Score 4
- clearly explains cause
- includes accurate details of effect on crop

Score 3
- adequately explains cause
- includes fairly accurate details of effect on crop

Score 2
- somewhat explains cause
- includes somewhat accurate details of effect on crop

Score 1
- does not explain cause
- does not include accurate details of effect on crop

HOMEWORK AND PRACTICE

Name _____ Date _____

A Lot or a Little

Draw a picture to show what could happen to make the oranges scarce. Write a sentence about your picture. Then answer the question.

Drawings will vary. Possible answers: The weather could be too cold for the oranges. The weather could be too dry for the oranges. Rain could make the ground too wet for the oranges to grow well.

What will happen to the price of oranges if they become scarce?
The price of the oranges will go up.

page 57

BACKGROUND

New Blueberry Plants
Elizabeth White grew up in New Jersey, living and working on her parent's cranberry farm. In 1911, she began working with Frederick Coville to develop ways to farm blueberry plants. White solicited help from local residents to find the best wild blueberry bushes so she could take cuttings and create new blueberry varieties. She and Coville produced the first commercial blueberry crop in 1916.

Study Skills

Preview and Question

OBJECTIVES

- **Use a K-W-L chart to preview a passage and set a purpose for reading.**

- **Record data and information in a K-W-L chart.**

RESOURCES

Homework and Practice Book, p. 58; Social Studies Skills Transparency 6-4; Unit 6 Audiotext CD Collection

Why It Matters New ideas are easier to understand when you read to answer questions.

Learn

① A K-W-L chart helps you record important facts before and after you read. The K-W-L chart on the next page shows what Marco knows about scarce goods. Copy the chart.

② Practice

Read the paragraph. Then add new facts to the K-W-L chart.

Sometimes a country does not have enough of a product for all of its citizens. When this happens, the country can import the product. To import a product means to get it from another country. Countries can also import the resources needed to make the product.

306

I. Introduce

Discuss with children the kinds of information they would need to include in a report about growing blueberries. Ask children to share what they already know about growing blueberries or other plants. Point out that they may already know some details, but need to learn if their ideas are correct. They will also have to learn new information for a report as well.

Why It Matters Explain to children that the process of learning is finding out new information and adding it to what we already know. Tell children that a K-W-L chart is a way to organize what they already know and pinpoint what they still need to find out about a topic. Point out that they can set a purpose for reading by deciding ahead of time what they would like to learn. A K-W-L chart also helps them remember facts and ideas after they have read.

Practice and Extend

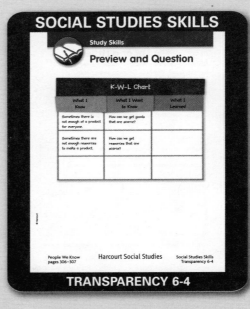

SOCIAL STUDIES SKILLS

MAKE IT RELEVANT

In Your State Ask children to organize information for a vacation destination. Provide books, travel magazines, or online sources with information about their state. Guide small groups to choose a place and create a K-W-L chart about the place. Point out that on a real vacation, they would complete the *L* column after visiting the location. Have the children share their charts with the class.

K-W-L Chart

What I Know	What I Want to Know	What I Learned
Sometimes there is not enough of a product for everyone.	How can we get goods that are scarce?	
Sometimes there are not enough resources to make a product.	How can we get resources that are scarce?	

Apply

Make It Relevant Make a K-W-L chart to show what you know and want to know about countries getting goods from one another. As you read the next lesson, add facts to show what you have learned.

1 Visual Literacy: Chart After children have copied the K-W-L chart, help them brainstorm what they know about scarcity and add it to the *K* column in Marco's chart. Point out that *K* stands for *know*. Ask children what they would like to learn about scarcity. Have them add their responses to the *W* column.

2 Practice

Read aloud the directions in the Practice section. Have children take turns reading the paragraph aloud. Work with children to add facts about scarcity to the *L* column in their charts.

Q Would you use a bar graph to organize the information from the paragraph on page 306? Why or why not?

A Children may note that a bar graph would not work as well because this paragraph is not about comparing several people or things.

3 Close

Apply

Make It Relevant The K-W-L chart should include at least two facts in the first column based on information from the previous lesson. The questions in the second column should directly relate to each fact. After reading the next lesson, children should complete the K-W-L chart with new facts that answer the questions.

REACH ALL LEARNERS

Leveled Practice Have children complete a K-W-L chart for a short current events article.

Basic Work as a group to complete a K-W-L chart for the article.

Proficient Invite children to compare and revise their charts.

Advanced Invite children to share information they added to the *L* column and explain why they chose to add this information.

HOMEWORK AND PRACTICE

Name _____ Date _____

STUDY SKILLS
Preview and Question

Read the paragraph. Then complete the K-W-L chart.

People may start a business to make money. Some businesses provide goods, such as food, clothing, shoes, or computers. Some provide services. Doctors, cooks, vets, and music teachers are examples of people who provide services. Children might start a business, too. Often, they do things for people in their neighborhood. When they get paid for their work, they can spend, share, or save the money they earn.

K-W-L Chart		
What I Know	**What I Want to Know**	**What I Learned**
Answers will vary. Children might say they could wash cars or walk dogs.	What kind of business could I start?	I could provide goods or services to people in my neighborhood.
Possible answer: I can spend it any way I want.	What are some choices I can make about the money I make?	Answers will vary. Children might say they can choose to spend, share, or save it.

page 58

OBJECTIVES

- Define and identify barter and the use of money as types of trade.
- Understand reasons why using money is considered a more efficient means of buying and selling.
- Understand the concept of trade with other countries.

VOCABULARY

barter p. 308   **trade** p. 309

CATEGORIZE AND CLASSIFY

pp. 268–269, 311

RESOURCES

Homework and Practice Book, p. 59; Reading Support and Intervention, pp. 106–109; Success for English Learners, pp. 111–114; Vocabulary Transparency 6-5; Focus Skills Transparency 6; Categorize and Classify Graphic Organizer Write-On/Wipe-Off Card; Activity Pattern A14; Unit 6 Audiotext CD Collection; Internet Resources

Introduce

What to Know Have a volunteer read aloud the What to Know question. Explain that people have always had needs they couldn't meet and extra items they couldn't use, and they looked for ways to solve this problem. Remind children to look for answers to the question as they read the lesson.

Build Background Organize the class into groups. Provide each group with a single good—pencils, paper, paper clips, and erasers. Have groups make trades with each other. Invite children to recall times they traded with friends.

Lesson

Barter and Trade

What to Know How does trade help people meet their needs?

Vocabulary
barter
trade

 Categorize and Classify

In the past, people would exchange their goods or services with others to get things they needed. They would barter with each other. To **barter** is to exchange things without using money.

Bartering long ago

308

Practice and Extend

Express Path

When minutes count, look for the **EXPRESS PATH** to focus on the lesson's main ideas.

Quick Summary

This lesson explains how and why people use bartering and money to get what they need. People barter by trading the extra things they have or use money in exchange for things they need. Individuals, as well as other countries, trade with each other.

Using Money

It can be hard to find people to barter with for the goods and services you need when you need them. Over time, people began to use money to buy and sell their goods and services. The buyer and seller agree on a fair price for a good or service.

Barter and money are both used to make a trade. A **trade** is the exchange of one thing for another.

Reading Check What can people use to make trades with each other? They can barter and use money.

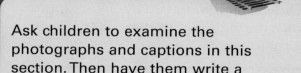

Money now has different forms.

People using money today

309

Using Money

CONTENT FOCUS People barter and use money to get the goods and services they need.

Express Path

Ask children to examine the photographs and captions in this section. Then have them write a sentence that describes the main idea.

Correct Misconceptions Children might think bartering only took place long ago. Explain that people still barter today. For example, a child may trade a baseball card to a friend for a toy.

1 Economics Explain that money is the most common medium used for trading goods and services. Have children study the pictures. Explain how credit cards, debit cards, and checks represent money transferred from one account to another. Discuss the convenience of carrying cards instead of cash.

Q **What types of coins and bills do we use in this country?**

A Possible answers: penny; nickel; dime; quarter; one-dollar bill

---

VOCABULARY

Vocabulary Transparency 6-5

MINI-GLOSSARY Read each term, and study its definition.

barter To exchange something without using money. p. 308
trade The exchange of one thing for another. p. 309

WORD WORK Complete the activities below.

1. **barter**
CLASSIFY/CATEGORIZE Would you classify barter under purchase or trade?
trade

2. **trade**
WORD FAMILIES Trade, trader, trading, and trades all have the same root word. Write it.
trade

3. **trade**
SYNONYMS Think of words that mean about the same thing as trade. Add them to the chart.
Possible answers:

```
        exchange
trade   swap
        barter
```

TRANSPARENCY 6-5

READING SUPPORT/ INTERVENTION

For alternate teaching strategies, use pages 106–109 of Reading Support and Intervention to:

- identify **phonemes**
- practice **phonics**
- reinforce **vocabulary**
- build **text comprehension**
- build **fluency**

Reading Support ▶ and Intervention

ELL ENGLISH LANGUAGE LEARNERS

For English Language Learners strategies to support this lesson, see Success for English Learners pages 111–114.

- English-language development activities
- background and concepts
- vocabulary extension

Success for ▶ English Learners

Trading with Other Countries

CONTENT FOCUS Countries trade with each other to get goods and services the citizens need.

Express Path

Direct children to use the illustrations as a springboard to discuss the main idea of the section.

2 **Link Economics and Geography**
Point out that we trade what people in other countries want for the things we want. Elicit that people in other countries can supply us with certain items.

Q Why might we need to trade with another country to get a certain item?

A Possible answer: The item may not be available here.

3 **Visual Literacy: Diagram**
Distribute copies of Activity Pattern A14. Have children look at the diagram on page 311. Ask them to identify products in their homes that come from one or more of the countries shown. Direct them to check labels on items or ask family members to help them identify each item's country of origin. Invite children to use the Activity Pattern to make a table of these goods, showing which country the items came from.

Interactive in the enhanced online student eBook

Trading with Other Countries

The people of a country cannot always provide all the goods and services that citizens want. These people can trade with **2** people in other countries to get raw materials, goods, or services. To get those, they may give other raw materials, goods, services, or money.

Reading Check **Why do the people of a country trade with people of another country?** To get goods and services the people of a country do not have enough of.

Products come into and go out of this port in New Jersey.

310

Practice and Extend

INTEGRATE THE CURRICULUM

MATHEMATICS On the board, write the names for various denominations of U.S. coins and paper money. Pass around play-money examples of each denomination. Have children practice using the terminology in sentences that describe amounts. For example; *Five pennies is the same as one nickel. Two nickels equal one dime. Four quarters and one dollar are the same amount.*
Monetary Units

REACH ALL LEARNERS

Leveled Practice Discuss trade with other countries.

Basic Ask children to name an item that we might trade with another country.

Proficient Invite children to draw and label pictures of items countries might trade.

Advanced Have children look at labels or tags on classroom items to find where they were made. Direct them to list the countries.

3 📖 Trade with the United States

From Germany

From Japan

From Mexico

To Germany

To Japan

To Mexico

What is a product that the United States gets from another country?

Summary People can trade raw materials, goods, services, or money with one another.

Review

1. **What to Know** How does trade help people meet their needs?

2. **Vocabulary** What do you do when you **barter**?

3. 🖌 **Activity** Draw pictures and write labels that show goods you would be willing to trade.

4. ⭐(Focus Skill) **Categorize and Classify** Make a list of goods and services you and your classmates could use to barter. Circle the services.

311

---

3 Close

Summary

Have children read the lesson summary and review the lesson's key points.

- Bartering or using money are ways people get things they need.
- People of a country will trade goods and services with people in other countries.

Assess

REVIEW—Answers

1. **What to Know** People trade something that they have enough of to get something that they need.

2. **Vocabulary** When you **barter,** you trade a good or service with someone for another good or service.

3. 🖌 **Activity Assessment Guidelines** See Performance Rubric. This activity can be used with the Unit Project.

4. ⭐(Focus Skill) **Categorize and Classify** Children should list goods and services they can easily provide. Children should demonstrate an understanding of the difference between goods and services.

Use Focus Skills Transparency 6 or Categorize and Classify Graphic Organizer Write-On/Wipe-Off Card.

HOMEWORK AND PRACTICE

Name _____ Date _____

Partners in Trade

The map shows three countries and some products they trade. Use the map to answer the questions.

CANADA

Map Key

Lumber

Car parts

Wheat

NORTH AMERICA

UNITED STATES

Cars

Cloth

Fruit

MEXICO

1. Henry, in the United States, loves bananas. From which country do bananas come? <u>Mexico</u>

2. Jamie's mother, in Canada, wants to buy a car. From where might her new car come? <u>United States</u>

3. Carlos, in Mexico, wants to build a house. From which country might the lumber come? <u>Canada</u>

page 59

REACH ALL LEARNERS

Advanced Point out that other countries use different forms of money. Encourage children to use reference sources to research and find pictures of different kinds of foreign currency. Invite them to share their findings with the class.

OBJECTIVES

- Understand that countries help each other in times of need.

- Recognize ways young citizens can make a difference in the lives of others.

RESOURCES

Unit 6 Audiotext CD Collection

💡 Link to the Big Idea

Work People work to earn money to buy the things they need and want. People also do work to help others without getting paid. Helping each other in times of need is a way for citizens to work for the democratic value of the common good.

Vocabulary Help Remind children that a *volunteer* is a person who does work without getting paid. Discuss the kinds of work volunteers do. Have children speculate on the reasons why people choose to volunteer.

Focus On: Democratic Values

Visual Literacy: Pictures Have children describe what they see in the photographs.

Q How were the citizens of many Asian countries affected by the big waves?

A Their homes, schools, and businesses were damaged or destroyed.

★ Citizenship ★

Countries Help Each Other

You have learned that countries trade with each other to get goods and services. Now read about how countries help each other in times of need.

When an earthquake caused powerful ocean waves to hit countries in Asia, many people lost their homes, schools, and businesses. Students at Pleasant Ridge Elementary School in Saline, Michigan, wanted to help. They decided to collect spare change. They raised more than two thousand dollars!

Children all over the United States worked to help people in Asia.

312

Practice and Extend

BACKGROUND

International Red Cross In 1859, Henry Dunant, a young Swiss man, saw the suffering caused by a battle in Italy. Wounded soldiers needed medical attention, so Dunant asked local people to help tend to their wounds and feed the men. Later Dunant urged the creation of national relief societies to care for people during times of war and disaster. The International Red Cross was formed in 1864.

INDEPENDENT READING

Encourage children to read *Clara Barton* by Christy Devillier (Buddy Books, 2004). This book tells the life story of Clara Barton, a nurse who began the American Red Cross.

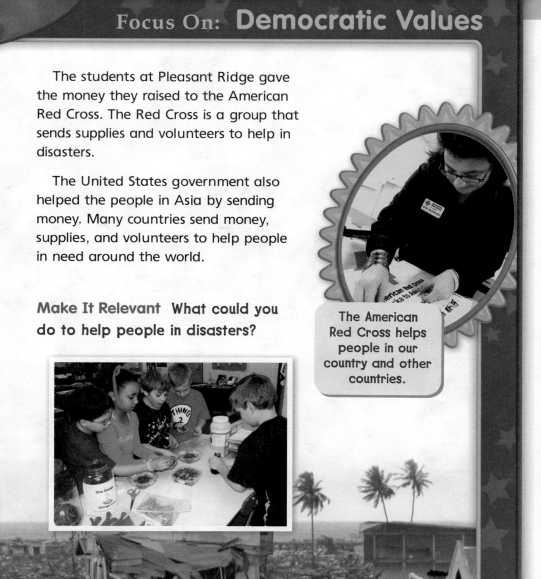

The students at Pleasant Ridge gave the money they raised to the American Red Cross. The Red Cross is a group that sends supplies and volunteers to help in disasters.

The United States government also helped the people in Asia by sending money. Many countries send money, supplies, and volunteers to help people in need around the world.

Make It Relevant What could you do to help people in disasters?

The American Red Cross helps people in our country and other countries.

Geography Have children look at a world map. Ask them to locate Michigan on the map. Then have them find the countries affected by the big ocean waves—Sri Lanka, Thailand, and India.

Q How did the students at Pleasant Ridge Elementary help people so far away?

A They collected spare change. The students raised two thousand dollars and donated it to the Red Cross. The Red Cross used the money to help the people in these faraway countries.

Make It Relevant

Have children read and discuss the question. Point out current problems and needs in other countries. Encourage children to think of ways that they could help people in need in other countries. Suggest they think of ways to help other than giving money, such as donating certain types of supplies.

💡 Link to the Big Idea

Work Point out to children that people depend on each other for goods and services. People who create goods and services are called producers, and people who use them are called consumers. Challenge children to name some producers in their community.

Preview the Games

Marketplace In this game, children are asked to look at the picture and answer the questions. The picture shows people buying and selling products and services in a marketplace. Prompt children with questions such as:

Q What are some of the goods being sold?

A Possible answers: t-shirts, sandwiches, lemonade, plants

Q What are some of the services being offered?

A Possible answers: face painting, dog washing

ANSWERS: The woman is selling produce and the man is selling pizza; The girl washing dogs is offering a service.

Practice and Extend

🖩 **MATHEMATICS** Have children imagine that they are offering the dog washing service like the girl in the Marketplace game. Ask them to pretend that they charge $1 per dog wash. If they wash five dogs that day, how much money have they made? **Making Money**

Leveled Practice Have children identify what some of the people in the marketplace are doing.

Basic Have children look at each section and name whether the person is a producer or consumer.

Proficient Ask children to name the specific job of each person in the picture.

Advanced Have children write a short paragraph about one person's role in the marketplace.

Look at the picture.

What goods do these people sell?

Who is offering a service?

Online Adventures GO ONLINE

Play an online shopping game with Eco. You will help him spend money wisely at a shop, a restaurant, and an arcade. Play now, at **www.harcourtschool.com/ss1**

315

Online Adventures Before children begin playing, explain that in this game they will be shopping using a budget. Review the opportunity costs involved in making good choices when spending and saving money. Tell children that Help Buttons in the game will refer them to pages in their textbook if they need additional information.

GO ONLINE **INTERNET RESOURCES**

For more resources, go to
www.harcourtschool.com/ss1

Share the Fun

At School Have children work in small groups to draw their own Marketplace games. Help them create a game similar to this activity based on the ideas of goods and services. When children are finished, ask them to share their games with classmates.

At Home Invite children to have their parents or guardians help them come up with other examples of producers. Encourage children to make a list of the different producers they come up with. Have children share their findings with classmates.

MAKE IT RELEVANT

In Your Community Encourage children to find ways in which they themselves are either producers or consumers. Have them think about when they are at home, when they go shopping, and what they do on weekends. Ask them to make a list, and have them share it with the class.

The Big Idea

Work Ask a volunteer to read aloud the Big Idea. Invite children to share something they learned in this unit about producers and consumers.

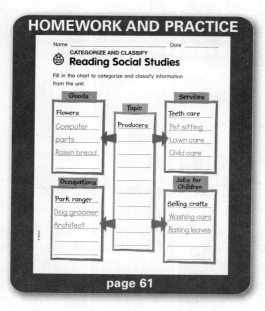

page 61

Reading Social Studies

 Categorize and Classify You may wish to have children review Reading Social Studies at the beginning of the unit. Charts should classify information about producers, including goods, services, occupations, and jobs for children.

Review and Test Prep

 The Big Idea

Work Producers and consumers depend on each other for goods and services.

Categorize and Classify

Copy and fill in the chart to categorize and classify what you learned about the goods and services producers provide.

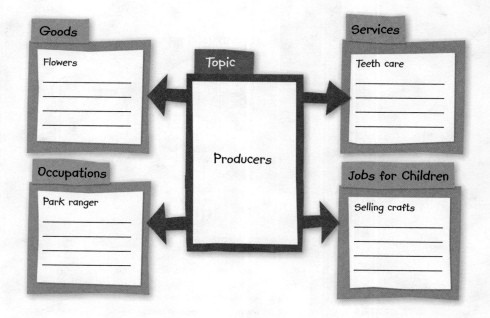

316

Vocabulary

Match the word to its meaning.

Word Bank

producer
(p. 276)

goods
(p. 277)

services
(p. 277)

consumer
(p. 279)

marketplace
(p. 304)

❶ things that can be bought and sold

❷ work done for others

❸ a place where goods are sold

❹ a person who buys goods and services

❺ a worker who grows, makes, or sells goods

Facts and Main Ideas

❻ What do we call the job a person does to earn money?

❼ Why do people earn income?

❽ What happens in a factory?

❾ What do you call all the tools used to produce a good?

    A human resources   **C** services

    B raw materials   **D** capital resources

❿ Which means to exchange something without using money?

    A barter   **C** consumer

    B occupation   **D** free enterprise

317

Vocabulary

1. goods

2. services

3. marketplace

4. consumer

5. producer

Facts and Main Ideas

6. The job a person does to earn money is an occupation.

7. People earn income to buy goods and services that they need and want.

8. At a factory, people use machines to make goods.

9. D, capital resources

10. A, barter

Critical Thinking

11. Possible answers: We would have fewer goods. Prices for some goods might cost more. There are some goods we could not have.

12. Make It Relevant Possible answers: We would have to spend most of our time making things. We would have fewer goods that we want.

Skills

13. June Bicycle Sales

14. 5 bicycles

15. Week 3

16. Week 1

⑪ What would happen if the United States could not trade with other countries?

⑫ **Make It Relevant** How would your life be different if your family had to produce all of the goods it wanted?

Skills

⑬ What is the title of this bar graph?

⑭ How many bicycles were sold in Week 2?

⑮ Which week had the most sales?

⑯ Which week had the fewest sales?

318

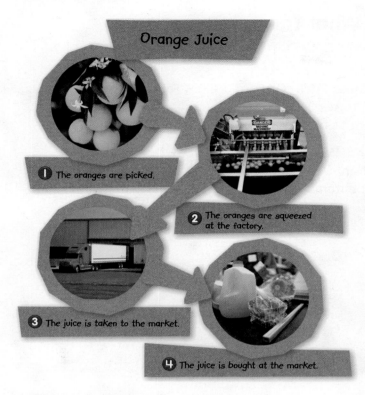

Orange Juice

1 The oranges are picked.

2 The oranges are squeezed at the factory.

3 The juice is taken to the market.

4 The juice is bought at the market.

17 What does this flowchart show?

18 What is the first step?

19 What happens after the oranges are squeezed?

20 What happens after the juice is taken to the market?

319

Skills

17. It shows the steps in producing orange juice.

18. The oranges are picked.

19. The juice is taken to the market.

20. It is bought at the market.

ASSESSMENT

Use the UNIT 6 Test on pages 46–48 of the Assessment Program.

Show What You Know

Unit Writing Activity

Create a Sales Pitch Discuss ads that children have seen that entice them to buy a product. Ask children to imagine they have an item to sell. Suggest they brainstorm descriptive words and describe special features about the product.

Write an Ad Suggest that children use their descriptive language to write an advertisement that will grab buyers' attention. Remind children to be persuasive and convincing. Have them look through magazines and newspaper ads for ideas.

You may wish to distribute the Unit 6 Writing Activity Guidelines on page 49 of the Assessment Program.

For a scoring rubric, see this Teacher Edition, page 265O.

Unit Project

Class Fair Before children begin, discuss the types of goods and services they plan to sell. List their ideas, and map out the display space children will need for each item. Have children use computer graphics and clip art to create a flyer. Provide art materials for posters that will advertise their goods and services. Use the posters to designate the area where each good or service will be sold.

You may wish to distribute the Unit 6 Project Guidelines on page 51 of the Assessment Program.

For a scoring rubric, see this Teacher Edition, page 265O.

> **LEVELED READERS**
>
> Use the LEVELED READERS for Unit 6.

Activities

Show What You Know

Unit Writing Activity

Create a Sales Pitch Think of something to sell. Why would others want to buy it?

Write an Ad Write an ad to sell your item. Use details to describe the item.

Unit Project

Class Fair Plan a class fair.

- Provide goods or services.
- Create ads and flyers.
- Sell your goods or services at the class fair.
- Think about why some items sold better than others.

Read More

Delivery by Anastasia Suen

From Corn to Cereal by Roberta Basel

The Story of Money by Betsy Maestro

GO ONLINE For more resources, go to www.harcourtschool.com/ss1

320

Read More

After the children's study of work and the marketplace, encourage independent reading with these books or books of your choice. Additional books are listed on page 265J of this Teacher Edition.

Basic *Delivery* by Anastasia Suen (Puffin, 2001). Children explore the many different things that are delivered to people.

Proficient *From Corn to Cereal* by Roberta Basel (Capstone Press, 2005). Children learn about food production, distribution, and consumption.

Advanced *The Story of Money* by Betsy Maestro (Houghton Mifflin, 1993). Children follow the history of money in its various forms from long ago to today.

SUMMATIVE TEST

Units 4–6

Summative Test

FILL IN THE BLANK (5 points each)

DIRECTIONS Write the word that completes each sentence.

trade	consumer	colony
immigrant	changes	invention

❶ When something becomes different, it ___changes___.

❷ A place that is ruled by another country is called a ___colony___.

❸ A person who comes from another place to live in a country is called an ___immigrant___.

❹ The lightbulb is an ___invention___ made by Thomas Edison.

❺ A ___consumer___ is a person who buys and uses goods and services.

❻ Countries ___trade___ with each other by exchanging one thing for another.

(continued)

Units 4–6 Summative Test   Assessment Program ■ **53**

SUMMATIVE TEST

Name _____ Date _____

MULTIPLE CHOICE (5 points each)

DIRECTIONS Select the letter of the best answer.

❼ What is the time yet to come?

  A past   **C** present
  Ⓑ future   **D** change

❽ Which of these is a place that is ruled by another country?

  Ⓐ colony   **C** memorial
  B landmark   **D** settler

❾ Which of these shows you the order in which things happen?

  A budget   **C** picture graph
  B diagram   Ⓓ time line

❿ Which word describes different ideas and ways of living?

  A history   Ⓒ diversity
  B tradition   **D** immigrant

⓫ Which of these helps you measure time?

  A diagram   Ⓒ calendar
  B bar graph   **D** product map

(continued)

54 ■ Assessment Program   Units 4–6 Summative Test

SUMMATIVE TEST

Name _____ Date _____

MULTIPLE CHOICE (5 points each)

DIRECTIONS Select the letter of the best answer.

⓬ What does Ieoh Ming Pei design?

  A pictures   **C** clothes
  Ⓑ buildings   **D** books

⓭ What do you call someone who provides goods or services?

  Ⓐ producer   **C** consumer
  B volunteer   **D** scientist

⓮ Where are raw materials made into products?

  A marketplace   Ⓒ factory
  B landmark   **D** office

⓯ Where do products from a factory go?

  A to a landmark   **C** to a farm
  B to a producer   Ⓓ to a marketplace

⓰ What do countries trade with each other?

  Ⓐ goods and services   **C** occupations
  B climate   **D** banks

(continued)

Units 4–6 Summative Test   Assessment Program ■ **55**

SUMMATIVE TEST

Name _____ Date _____

SHORT ANSWER (5 points each)

DIRECTIONS Use the flowchart to answer the questions.

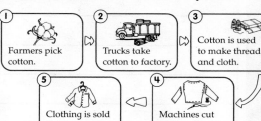

1. Farmers pick cotton.
2. Trucks take cotton to factory.
3. Cotton is used to make thread and cloth.
4. Machines cut and sew cloth.
5. Clothing is sold in stores.

⓱ What does the flowchart show about cotton?

  Cotton can be used to make clothing.

⓲ How does the cotton get to the factory?

  Trucks take it there.

⓳ What happens after the cotton is made into cloth?

  The cloth is cut and sewn into clothes.

⓴ What is the last step?

  The cotton clothes are sold in stores.

56 ■ Assessment Program   Units 4–6 Summative Test

NOTES

NOTES

For Your Reference

R1

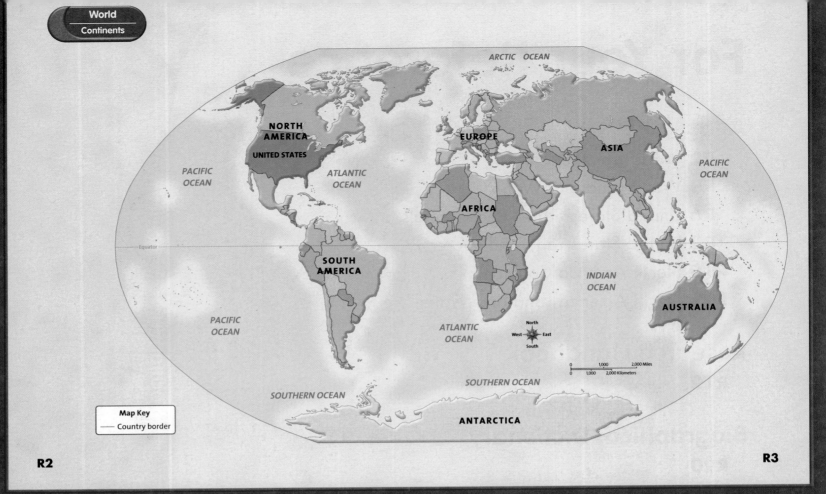

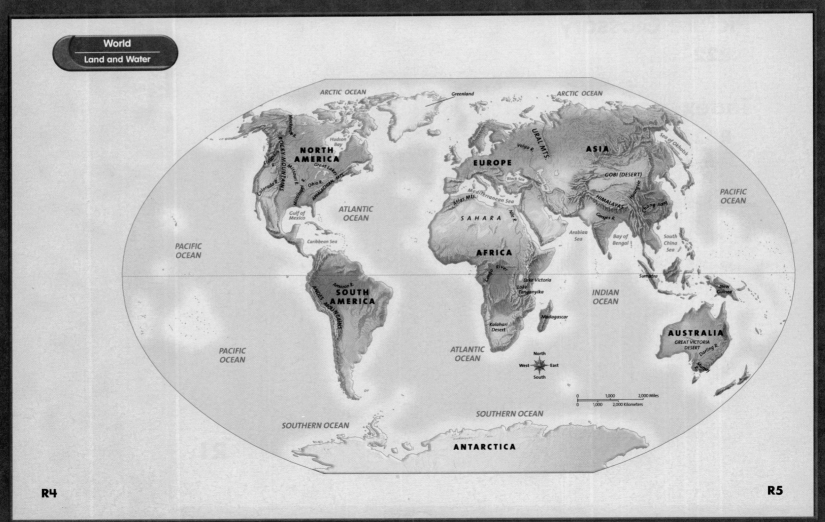

United States — States and Capitals

RUSSIA · ARCTIC OCEAN · Alaska (AK) · Juneau · CANADA · Bering Sea · PACIFIC OCEAN · 250 · 500 Miles · 0 · 250 · 500 Kilometers

Honolulu · Hawaii (HI) · PACIFIC OCEAN · 0 · 100 · 200 Miles · 0 · 100 · 200 Kilometers

CANADA

Washington (WA) · Olympia
Oregon (OR) · Salem
Montana (MT) · Helena
Boise · Idaho (ID)
Wyoming (WY)
North Dakota (ND) · Bismarck
Minnesota (MN) · St. Paul
Lake Superior
CANADA
Maine (ME)
Augusta · Vermont (VT) · Montpelier · New Hampshire (NH) · Concord · Boston
Lake Huron · Michigan (MI) · Lansing
Wisconsin (WI) · Madison
Pierre · South Dakota (SD)
Sacramento · Carson City · Nevada (NV) · California (CA)
Salt Lake City · Cheyenne · Great Salt Lake
Nebraska (NE) · Lincoln
Iowa (IA) · Des Moines
Lake Michigan · Lake Ontario · Lake Erie
New York (NY) · Albany · Massachusetts (MA) · Providence · Rhode Island (RI) · Connecticut (CT) · Hartford
Utah (UT) · Denver · Colorado (CO)
Illinois (IL) · Springfield · Indiana (IN) · Indianapolis · Ohio (OH) · Columbus
Pennsylvania (PA) · Harrisburg · Trenton · New Jersey (NJ)
Annapolis · Dover · Delaware (DE) · Washington D.C. · Maryland (MD)
Topeka · Kansas (KS) · Missouri (MO) · Jefferson City
West Virginia (WV) · Charleston · Frankfort · Kentucky (KY) · Richmond · Virginia (VA)
Arizona (AZ) · Phoenix · Santa Fe · New Mexico (NM)
Oklahoma (OK) · Oklahoma City
Arkansas (AR) · Little Rock
Nashville · Tennessee (TN) · Raleigh · North Carolina (NC) · Columbia · South Carolina (SC)
Atlanta · Georgia (GA)
PACIFIC OCEAN
Texas (TX) · Austin
Mississippi (MS) · Jackson · Alabama (AL) · Montgomery
Louisiana (LA) · Baton Rouge
Tallahassee · Florida (FL)
ATLANTIC OCEAN
MEXICO
North · West · East · South
250 · 500 Miles · 0 · 250 · 500 Kilometers
Gulf of Mexico
BAHAMAS
CUBA

R6

R7

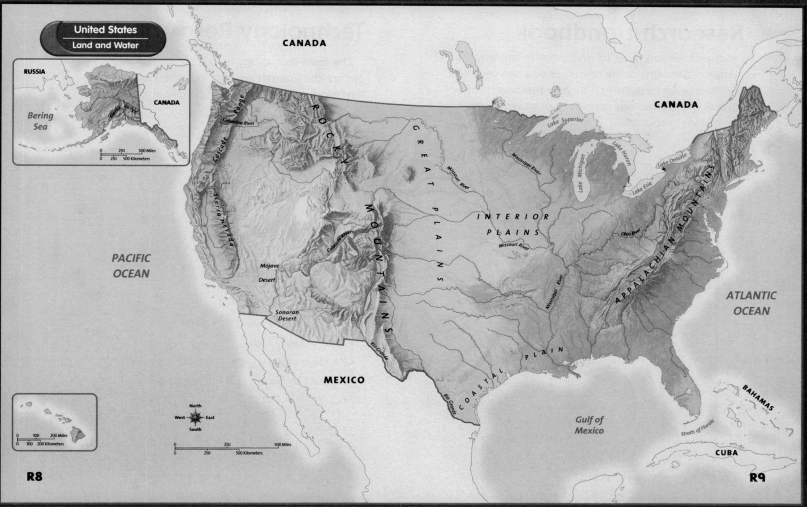

United States — Land and Water

RUSSIA · Bering Sea · CANADA · Denali (Mt.) · 250 · 500 Miles · 0 · 250 · 500 Kilometers

CANADA

Cascade Range · Columbia River · Sierra Nevada · Mojave Desert · Sonoran Desert · Rio Grande · Colorado River · ROCKY MOUNTAINS · GREAT PLAINS · Missouri River · Lake Superior · Mississippi River · INTERIOR PLAINS · Missouri River · Ohio River · Mississippi River · Lake Michigan · Lake Huron · Lake Ontario · Lake Erie · APPALACHIAN MOUNTAINS

PACIFIC OCEAN

COASTAL PLAIN · Rio Grande

MEXICO

ATLANTIC OCEAN

North · West · East · South
250 · 500 Miles · 0 · 250 · 500 Kilometers

Gulf of Mexico

BAHAMAS · Straits of Florida · CUBA

0 · 100 · 200 Miles · 0 · 100 · 200 Kilometers

R8

R9

R6–R9

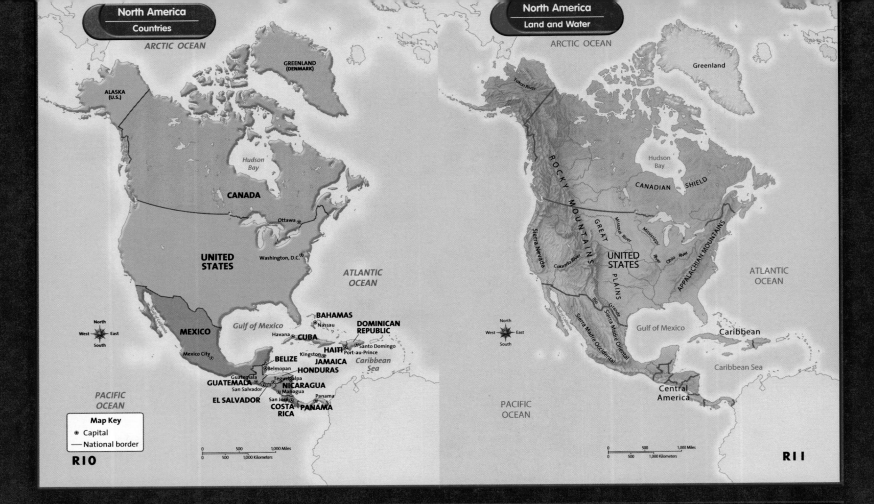

North America — Countries

ARCTIC OCEAN

GREENLAND (DENMARK)

ALASKA (U.S.)

Hudson Bay

CANADA

Ottawa ⊛

UNITED STATES

Washington, D.C. ⊛

ATLANTIC OCEAN

MEXICO

Gulf of Mexico

BAHAMAS
⊛ Nassau

DOMINICAN REPUBLIC

Havana ⊛ CUBA

Santo Domingo ⊛

Mexico City ⊛

HAITI
Port-au-Prince ⊛

Kingston ⊛

Caribbean Sea

BELIZE

JAMAICA

Belmopan ⊛

HONDURAS

Guatemala ⊛ Tegucigalpa ⊛

GUATEMALA

NICARAGUA

San Salvador ⊛ ⊛ Managua

EL SALVADOR

San José ⊛

Panama ⊛

COSTA RICA

PANAMA

PACIFIC OCEAN

Map Key
⊛ Capital
— National border

0   500   1,000 Miles
0   500   1,000 Kilometers

R10

North America — Land and Water

ARCTIC OCEAN

Greenland

Yukon River

Hudson Bay

ROCKY MOUNTAINS

CANADIAN SHIELD

Sierra Nevada

Missouri River

Mississippi River

GREAT PLAINS

Ohio River

APPALACHIAN MOUNTAINS

Colorado River

UNITED STATES

ATLANTIC OCEAN

Sierra Madre Occidental

Rio Grande

Sierra Madre Oriental

Gulf of Mexico

Caribbean

Caribbean Sea

Central America

PACIFIC OCEAN

0   500   1,000 Miles
0   500   1,000 Kilometers

R11

Research Handbook

Sometimes you need to find more information on a topic. There are many resources you can use. You can find some information in your textbook. Other sources are technology resources, print resources, and community resources.

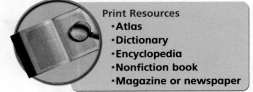

Technology Resources
• Internet
• Computer disk
• Television or radio

Print Resources
• Atlas
• Dictionary
• Encyclopedia
• Nonfiction book
• Magazine or newspaper

Community Resources
• Teacher
• Museum curator
• Community leader
• Older citizen

R12

Technology Resources

The main technology resources you can use are the Internet and computer disks. Television and radio can also be good sources of information.

Using the Internet

Information on the Internet is always changing. Be sure to use a site you can trust.

Finding Information

• Use a mouse and a keyboard to search for information.
• With help from a teacher, parent, or older child, find the source you want to search.
• Type in key words.
• Read carefully and take notes.
• If your computer is connected to a printer, you can print out a paper copy.

R13

Print Resources

Books in libraries are placed in a special order. Each book has a call number. The call number tells you where to look for the book.

Some print resources, such as encyclopedias, magazines, and newspapers are kept together in a separate place. Librarians can help you find what you need.

Atlas

An atlas is a book of maps. Some atlases show the same place at different times.

Dictionary

A dictionary gives the correct spelling of words. It also tells you their definitions or what they mean. Words in a dictionary are listed in alphabetical order. Guide words at the tops of the pages help you find the word you are looking for.

Guide Words

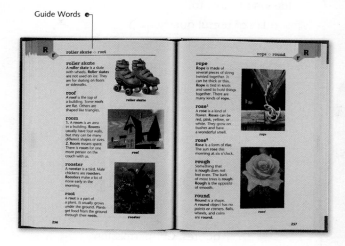

Encyclopedia

An encyclopedia is a book or set of books that gives information about many different topics. The topics are listed in alphabetical order. An encyclopedia is a good source to use when beginning your research.

You can also find encyclopedias on the Internet. These encyclopedias might have sound and video clips.

Nonfiction Books

A nonfiction book gives facts about real people, places, and things. Nonfiction books in the library are grouped by subject. Each subject has a different call number. Look in a card file or computer catalog to find a call number. You can look for titles, authors, or subjects.

Magazines and Newspapers

Magazines and newspapers are printed by the day, week, or month. They are good sources of the latest information. Many libraries have a guide that lists articles by subject. Two guides are the Children's Magazine Guide and the Readers' Guide to Periodical Literature.

Community Resources

Often, people in your community can give you information you need. Before you talk to anyone, always ask a teacher or a parent for permission.

Listening to Find Information

Before
- Decide who to talk to.
- Make a list of useful questions.

During
- Be polite.
- Speak clearly and loudly.
- Listen carefully. You may think of other questions you want to ask.
- Take notes to help you remember ideas.
- Write down or tape record the person's exact words for quotes. Get permission to use the quotes.
- Later, write a thank-you letter.

Writing to Get Information

You can also write to people in your community to gather information. Keep these ideas in mind as you write:

- Write neatly or use a computer.
- Say who you are and why you are writing.
- Carefully check your spelling and punctuation.
- If you are mailing the letter, put in an addressed, stamped envelope for the person to send you an answer.
- Thank the person.

Biographical Dictionary

The Biographical Dictionary lists many of the important people in this book. They are listed in alphabetical (ABC) order by last name. After each name are the birth and death dates. If the person is still alive, only the birth year is given. The page number tells where the main discussion of each person starts. See the Index for other page references.

Anthony, Susan B. (1820–1906) Women's rights leader. She helped get women the same rights that men have. p. 30

Anyokah Daughter of Sequoyah. When she was six years old, she helped her father create a writing system for the Cherokee people. p. 16

Armstrong, Neil (1930–) American astronaut. He was the first person to walk on the moon. p. 201

Banneker, Benjamin (1731–1806) African American scientist and writer. He helped plan the streets of Washington, D.C. p. 72

Bunyan, Paul A lumberjack of huge size and strength in American legends. His footprints are said to have created Minnesota's 10,000 lakes. p. 201

Carson, Rachel (1907–1964) American writer. Her books told people how to take better care of nature. p. 122

Carver, George W. (1864–1943) African American scientist. He worked on ways to make farming better. p. 255

Chapman, John (1774–1835) American pioneer known as Johnny Appleseed. He planted apple trees in large parts of Ohio, Indiana, and Illinois. p. 201

Edison, Thomas (1847–1931) American inventor. He invented the lightbulb and many other things. p. 254

Estefan, Gloria (1957–) Latin-American singer and songwriter. She shares her Cuban culture through her music. p. 257

George III of England (1738–1820) English King. He was against the colonists' fight for independence. p. 186

Gutenberg, Johannes (c. 1400–1468) German metalworker and inventor. He invented the printing press and movable type. p. 144

Henry, John African American railroad worker in American legends. He is said to have raced against a steam hammer and won. p. 201

Jefferson, Thomas (1743–1862) The third President of the United States. He helped write the Declaration of Independence. p. 190

King, Dr. Martin Luther, Jr. (1929–1968) African American civil rights leader. He received the Nobel Peace Prize for working to change unfair laws. p. 208

Lincoln, Abraham (1809–1865) The 16th President of the United States. He was President during the Civil War. He helped make it against the law to own slaves. p. 199

Montañez, Wanda (1964–) American businesswoman. Her clothing designs honor her Hispanic heritage. p. 282

Oakley, Annie (1860–1926) American entertainer. She was very skilled in shooting and showed that women could do many things. p. 287

Obama, Barack (1961–) The 44th President of the United States. p. 35

Parks, Rosa (1913–2005) African American civil rights leader. She refused to give up her seat on a bus to a white man. p. 215

Pei, Ieoh Ming (1917–) Asian American architect. He designs interesting buildings, such as the John F. Kennedy Presidential Library in Boston, Massachusetts. p. 256

Pitcher, Molly (1744–1832) Hero of the American Revolution. She carried water to the soldiers during the war. p. 188

Revere, Paul (1735–1818) Hero of the American Revolution. He warned the colonists in Massachusetts that the British soldiers were coming. p. 190

Roosevelt, Franklin D. (1882–1945) The 32nd President of the United States. He was President during World War II and worked for world peace. p. 35

Ross, Betsy (1752–1836) American seamstress. In American legends, she sewed the first American flag. p. 201

Salem, Peter (1750–1816) African American soldier. He fought in the Battle of Bunker Hill against the British. p. 188

Tan, Amy (1952–) Asian American writer. Her stories about the Chinese culture are read all over the world. p. 244

Truth, Sojourner (1797–1883) African American slave. She helped end slavery and worked for women's right to vote. p. 200

Tubman, Harriett (1820–1913) African American slave. She helped guide slaves to freedom on the Underground Railroad. p. 200

Tutankhamen (c. 1343–1323 B.C.) Egyptian Pharaoh. He became the Pharaoh when he was ten years old. p. 27

Washington, George (1732–1799) First President of the United States. He is known as "The Father of Our Country." p. 191

Picture Glossary

The Picture Glossary has important words and their definitions. They are listed in alphabetical (ABC) order. The pictures help you understand the meanings of the words. The page number at the end tells where the word is first used.

A

absolute location
The exact location of a place. The **absolute location** of the post office is 394 Oak Street. (page 67)

bank
A business that looks after people's money. People put money in the **bank** to keep it safe. (page 290)

B

ballot
A list of all the choices for voting. The voter marked her choice on the **ballot**. (page 28)

bar graph
A graph that uses bars to show how many or how much. This **bar graph** shows the money saved each month. (page 280)

barter
To exchange something without using money. People can **barter** instead of using money. (page 308)

business
The making or selling of goods or services. My parents have their own **business** selling flowers. (page 278)

border
A line on a map that shows where a state or country ends. The red line shows the **border** between Texas and Mexico. (page 46)

C

calendar
A chart that keeps track of the days in a week, month, or year. A **calendar** shows that there are seven days in a week. (page 250)

budget
A plan that shows how much money you have and how much money you spend. I make a **budget** every month. (page 290)

capital
A city in which a state's or country's government meets and works. Washington, D.C., is the **capital** of the United States. (page 33)

R22

R23

---

capital resources
All of the tools used to produce goods and services. A factory machine is a **capital resource**. (page 297)

citizen
A person who lives in and belongs to a community. Nick is a **citizen** of the United States. (page 8)

colony
A place that is ruled by another country. Virginia was the first English **colony** in North America. (page 180)

compass rose
The symbol on a map that shows directions. The **compass rose** shows directions. (page 94)

cardinal directions
The main directions of north, south, east, and west. The **cardinal directions** help you find places on a map. (page 90)

city
A very large town. There are many tall buildings in my **city**. (page 111)

communication
The sharing of ideas and information. The firefighter uses a radio for **communication** with other firefighters. (page 140)

conflict
What happens when people have different points of view on what to do or how to do it. There was a **conflict** about the rules of the game. (page 242)

change
What happens when something becomes different. In fall, some leaves **change** color. (page 174)

climate
The kind of weather a place has over a long time. The rain forest has a very wet **climate**. (page 86)

community
A group of people who live or work together. It is also the place where people live. My family has lived in our **community** for many years. (page 8)

Congress
The group of citizens chosen to make decisions for our country. **Congress** votes on new laws. (page 34)

R24

R25

consequence
Something that happens because of what a person does. The **consequence** of wearing muddy shoes is a dirty floor. (page 12)

consumer
A person who buys and uses goods and services. This **consumer** is buying fruit for a snack. (page 279)

country
An area of land with its own people and laws. We are proud of our **country**, the United States of America. (page 111)

D

diagram
A picture that shows the parts of something. The **diagram** helped me put my toy together. (page 176)

conservation
The saving of resources to make them last longer. **Conservation** of electricity is a good idea. (page 118)

continent
One of the seven main land areas on Earth. We live on the **continent** of North America. (page 110)

culture
A group's way of life. Music and dance are parts of my **culture**. (page 226)

diversity
Different ideas and ways of living. Many cultures bring **diversity** to our country. (page 240)

Constitution
A written set of rules that the government must follow. Our **Constitution** says that every adult citizen has the right to vote. (page 37)

council
A group of citizens chosen to make decisions for all the people. The **council** is discussing where to build the playground. (page 42)

custom
A group's way of doing something. One Hawaiian **custom** is to give flowers to visitors. (page 246)

E

election
A time when people vote for their leaders. The **election** to choose the President is held in November. (page 25)

R26

R27

---

environment
All of the things around us. We need to take care of our **environment**. (page 132)

factory
A building in which people use machines to make goods. Many people work at the **factory**. (page 296)

freedom
The right of people to make their own choices. Americans have the **freedom** to vote. (page 186)

future
The time yet to come. She studies hard to prepare for the **future**. (page 173)

equator
An imaginary line that divides Earth into northern and southern halves. Most of South America is south of the **equator**. (page 90)

fiction
Stories that may seem real, but in which some of the information is made up. The story of Little Red Riding Hood is **fiction**. (page 206)

free enterprise
The freedom to start and run any kind of business. **Free enterprise** helps these children earn money. (page 286)

G

geography
The study of Earth and its people. **Geography** teaches us about Earth and the people on it. (page 18)

F

fact
A piece of information that is true. It is a **fact** that humans have walked on the moon. (page 206)

flowchart
A chart that shows the steps needed to make or do something. The **flowchart** shows how to make a picture frame. (page 300)

fuel
A resource, such as oil, that can be burned for heat or energy. Gasoline is a **fuel** used in cars. (page 117)

globe
A model of Earth. We can find countries on our classroom **globe**. (page 110)

R28

R29

R26-R29

goods
Things that can be bought and sold. This store sells many kinds of **goods**. (page 277)

governor
The leader of a state's government. Every state has a **governor**. (page 26)

heritage
The traditions and values passed on by the people who lived before us. My grandmother teaches me about my **heritage**. (page 196)

human resources
The work people do to produce goods and services. This worker provides a **human resource** for his company. (page 296)

government
The group of citizens that runs a community, state, or country. Our **government** needs strong leaders. (page 18)

gulf
A large body of ocean water that is partly surrounded by land. The **Gulf** of Mexico is between Mexico and the United States. (page 80)

hero
A person who has done something brave or important. This **hero** saved someone's life. (page 200)

I

immigrant
A person who comes from another place to live in a country. My great-grandfather was an Irish **immigrant**. (page 236)

government service
A service that a government provides for citizens. Police officers provide a **government service**. (page 20)

H

hemisphere
Half of Earth. The northern **hemisphere** is north of the equator. (page 91)

history
The study of things that happened in the past. The **history** of our country is interesting. (page 178)

income
The money people earn for the work they do. Miguel will use his **income** to buy lemonade. (page 284)

independence
The freedom of people to choose their own government. George Washington fought for **independence**. (page 187)

island
A landform with water all around it. Deep blue water surrounds the **island**. (page 79)

landmark
A feature that makes a location special. The Alamo is a Texas **landmark**. (page 197)

legend
A story passed down through history. People in a **legend** do heroic things, but some of these actions are made up. (page 201)

intermediate directions
The directions in between the cardinal directions. Northeast is an **intermediate direction**. (page 94)

J

judge
The leader of a court. The **judge** listened to both sides of the case. (page 19)

language
The words or signs that people use to communicate. Some people use sign **language** to communicate. (page 227)

legislature
A group of citizens chosen to make decisions for a state. The **legislature** will decide if a new park is needed. (page 43)

invention
A new product that has not been made before. The lightbulb was Thomas Edison's **invention**. (page 254)

L

landform
A kind of land with a special shape, such as a mountain, hill, or plain. A mountain is a large **landform**. (page 76)

law
A rule that people in a community must follow. A speed limit **law** keeps people safe. (page 11)

location
The place where something is. The map will help you find your **location**. (page 66)

PICTURE GLOSSARY

map
A drawing that shows where places are. Can you find a lake on this **map**? (page 110)

map symbol
A small picture or shape on a map that stands for a real thing. This **map symbol** stands for a mountain. (page 113)

mayor
The leader of a city or town government. The **mayor** makes important decisions for our community. (page 26)

nonfiction
Stories that contain only facts. Newspaper stories are **nonfiction**. (page 206)

map grid
A set of lines that divide a map into columns and rows of squares. The star is at square C-3 on the **map grid**. (page 70)

map title
The title of a map. The **map title** tells what the map shows. (page 113)

memorial
Something people create to remember a person or an event. This **memorial** reminds us of a brave American. (page 198)

occupation
The work a person does to earn money. My dad's **occupation** is being a doctor. (page 284)

map key
The part of a map that shows what the symbols mean. Look for the symbol of the bridge in the **map key**. (page 46)

marketplace
A place where goods and services are bought and sold. This **marketplace** has many stores. (page 304)

natural resource
Something found in nature that people can use. Oil is a **natural resource**. (page 114)

ocean
A very large body of salty water. Ships sail across the **ocean**. (page 110)

past
The time before now. In the **past**, people used horses for transportation. (page 172)

pole
A point on Earth farthest from the equator. The North **Pole** is the point farthest north on a globe. (page 91)

problem
Something that is difficult to solve or hard to understand. The leaking pipe is a **problem** that we must deal with. (page 14)

product map
A map that shows where products are made or found. This **product map** shows where corn is grown in Michigan. (page 136)

peninsula
A landform that has water on only three sides. Part of Florida is a **peninsula**. (page 79)

present
The time right now. Today is the **present**. (page 173)

producer
A person who grows, makes or sells products. This **producer** grows fruit to sell. (page 276)

raw material
A resource used to make a product. Wood is a **raw material** used to make furniture. (page 295)

picture graph
A graph that uses pictures to stand for numbers of things. The **picture graph** shows that the most people chose baseball. (page 120)

President
The leader of the United States government. Barack Obama is the 44th **President** of the United States. (page 26)

product
Something that is made by nature or by people. Applesauce is a **product** made from apples. (page 136)

region
An area of land with the same features. We live in a mountain **region**. (page 82)

relative location
A description of a place that tells what it is near. The **relative location** of my house is next to the park. (page 66)

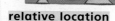
route
A way to go from one place to another. The **route** shown on this map is easy to follow. (page 142)

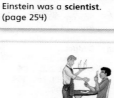
scientist
A person who observes things and makes discoveries. Albert Einstein was a **scientist**. (page 254)

solution
A way to solve a problem. The **solution** to the leaky pipe problem is to replace the pipe. (page 14)

responsibility
Something that a person should take care of or do. It is my **responsibility** to take these glasses I found to the store manager. (page 10)

rural
An area in the country, usually far from a city. This **rural** area is very peaceful. (page 126)

services
Work done for others. We paid the waiter for his **services**. (page 277)

source
A place something comes from. An encyclopedia is a good **source** of information. (page 184)

right
A freedom. Freedom of speech is one **right** we have as American citizens. (page 9)

S

scarce
Hard to find because there is not much of it. When money is **scarce**, George cannot buy candy. (page 303)

settler
One of the first people to make a home in a new place. The **settler** worked hard to farm the land. (page 180)

 Ohio
state
A part of a country. Ohio is one **state** of the fifty states in our country. (page 111)

suburb
A community near a large city. This **suburb** is about ten miles from the city. (page 128)

tax
Money paid to the government and used to pay for services. The **tax** we pay at the store helps pay for building roads. (page 21)

trade
The exchange of one thing for another. Is this a fair **trade**? (page 309)

U
urban
In, of, or like a city. They live in an **urban** area. (page 128)

Supreme Court
The court that decides on laws for the United States. The **Supreme Court** hears the most important cases. (page 36)

technology
The use of new objects and ideas in everyday life. Computers are a useful **technology**. (page 134)

tradition
Something that is passed on from older family members to children. Wearing kilts is a Scottish **tradition**. (page 246)

V

vote
A choice that gets counted. Every person's **vote** is important in an election. (page 28)

T

table
A chart that shows information in rows and columns. A **table** can be used to compare things. (page 88)

time line
A line that tells when things happened. This **time line** shows holidays. (page 192)

transportation
The moving of goods and people from place to place. Buses and airplanes are both used for **transportation**. (page 139)

W
wants
Things that people would like to have. I have more **wants** than I can afford. (page 288)

Index

The index tells where information about people, places, and events in this book can be found. The entries are listed in alphabetical order. Each entry tells the page or pages where you can find the topic.

For permission to reprint copyrighted material, grateful acknowledgment is made to the following sources:

Alfred Publishing, on behalf of Abilene Music: Lyrics from "What a Wonderful World" by George David Weiss and Bob Thiele. Lyrics copyright © 1967 by Range Road Music Inc., Quartet Music Inc., and Abilene Music, Inc. Lyrics copyright renewed and assigned to Range Road Music Inc., Quartet Music Inc., and Abilene Music. International copyright secured.

Atheneum Books for Young Readers, an imprint of Simon & Schuster Children's Publishing Division: Illustrations by Ashley Bryan from *What a Wonderful World* by George David Weiss and Bob Thiele. Illustrations copyright © 1995 by Ashley Bryan.

Candlewick Press, Inc.: Cover illustration by Peter H. Reynolds from *Judy Moody Declares Independence* by Megan McDonald. Illustration copyright © 2005 by Peter H. Reynolds.

Capstone Press: Cover photograph from *From Corn to Cereal* by Roberta Basel. Photograph © 2003 by Capstone Press.

Clarion Books/Houghton Mifflin Company: Cover illustration by Giulio Maestro from *The Story of Money* by Betsy Maestro. Ilustration copyright © 1993 by Giulio Maestro.

Dorling Kindersley Limited, London: From *The Random House Children's Encyclopedia.* Text copyright © 1991 by Dorling Kindersley Ltd. Originally published under the title *The Dorling Kindersley Children's Illustrated Encyclopedia,* 1991.

Dutton Children's Books, A Division of Penguin Young Readers Group, A Member of Penguin Group (USA) Inc., 345 Hudson St., New York, NY 10014: Cover illustration by Jennie Maizels from *The Amazing Pop-Up Geography Book* by Kate Petty. Illustration copyright © 2000 by Jennie Maizels.

Phyllis Fogelman Books, A Division of Penguin Young Readers Group, A Member of Penguin Group (USA) Inc., 345 Hudson St., New York, NY 10014: Cover illustration by Karin Littlewood from *The Color of Home* by Mary Hoffman. Illustration copyright © 2002 by Karin Littlewood.

Harcourt, Inc.: The Tortilla Factory by Gary Paulsen, illustrated by Ruth Wright Paulsen. Text copyright © 1995 by Gary Paulsen; illustrations copyright © 1995 by Ruth Wright Paulsen.

Heinemann Library, a division of Reed Elsevier Inc., Chicago, Illinois: From Lives and Times: Harriet Tubman by Emma Lynch. Copyright © 2005 by Heinemann Library.

Holiday House, Inc.: From *Supermarket* by Kathleen Krull, illustrated by Melanie Hope Greenberg. Text copyright © 2001 by Kathleen Krull; illustrations copyright © 2001 by Melanie Hope Greenberg. Cover illustration from *The Great Trash Bash* by Loreen Leedy. Illustration copyright © 1991 by Loreen Leedy. Cover illustration from *Betsy Ross* by Alexandra Wallner. Illustration copyright © 1994 by Alexandra Wallner.

Henry Holt and Company, LLC: Cover illustration from *Anansi the Spider* by Gerald McDermott. Illustration copyright © 1972 by Landmark Production, Incorporated.

Houghton Mifflin Company: Cover illustration by Lois and Louis Darling from *Silent Spring* by Rachel Carson. Illustration copyright © 1962 by Lois and Louis Darling.

Ideals Children's Books, www.idealspublications.com: Cover illustration by Robert Quackenbush from *The World in Your Hands* by Melvin and Gilda Berger. Illustration copyright © 1993 by Robert Quackenbush. Discovery Readers ™ Series, Ideals Children's Books.

Barbara S. Kouts, on behalf of Joseph Bruchac: "How the Prairie Became Ocean" from *Four Ancestors: Stories, Songs, and Poems from Native North America* by Joseph Bruchac. Text copyright © 1996 by Joseph Bruchac.

Lee & Low Books, Inc., New York, NY 10016: Cover illustration by Michelle Chang from *Goldfish and Chrysanthemums* by Andrea Cheng. Illustration copyright © 2003 by Michelle Chang.

Hal Leonard Corporation, on behalf of Quartet Music Inc.: Lyrics from "What a Wonderful World" by George David Weiss and Bob Thiele. Lyrics copyright © 1967 by Range Road Music Inc., Quartet Music Inc., and Abilene Music, Inc. Lyrics copyright renewed and assigned to Range Road Music Inc., Quartet Music Inc., and Abilene Music. International copyright secured.

Puffin Books, A Division of Penguin Group, A Member of Penguin Group (USA) Inc., 345 Hudson St., New York, NY 10014: Cover illustration by Wade Zahares from *Delivery* by Anastasia Suen. Illustration copyright © 1999 by Wade Zahares.

Random House Children's Books, a division of Random House, Inc.: Cover illustration from *The Cat in the Hat* by Dr. Seuss. ™ & copyright © 1957, renewed 1985 by Dr. Seuss Enterprises, L.P.

Range Road Music Inc: Lyrics from "What a Wonderful World" by George David Weiss and Bob Thiele. Lyrics copyright © 1967 by Range Road Music Inc., Quartet Music Inc., and Abilene Music, Inc. Lyrics copyright renewed and assigned to Range Road Music Inc., Quartet Music Inc., and Abilene Music. International copyright secured.

Reader's Digest Children's Books: Cover illustration by David Wenzel from *Way To Go!: Finding Your Way with a Compass* by Sharon Sharth. Illustration copyright © 2000 by Reader's Digest Children's Publishing, Inc.

Salish Kootenai College Press: Cover illustration by Debbie Joseph Finely from *How Marten Got His Spots and other Kootenai Indian Stories* by Kootenai Culture Committee, Confederated Salish and Kootenai Tribes. Illustration copyright © 1978 and 1981 by Kootenai Culture Committee, Confederated Salish and Kootenai Tribes.

Scholastic Inc.: From *Paul Bunyan and his Blue Ox* by Patsy Jensen, illustrated by Jean Pidgeon. Copyright © 1994 by Troll Associates. Cover illustration by Bert Dodson from *If You Were At...The First Thanksgiving* by Anne Kamma. Illustration copyright ©2001 by Scholastic Inc.

Sleeping Bear Press™: Cover illustration by Victor Juhasz from *D is for Democracy: A Citizen's Alphabet* by Elissa Grodin. Illustration copyright © 2003 by Victor Juhasz.

The Watts Publishing Group Limited, 96 Leonard Street, London EC2A 4XD: When I Was Young by James Dunbar, illustrated by Martin Remphry. Text copyright © 1998 by James Dunbar; illustrations copyright © 1998 by Martin Remphry. Originally published in the UK by Franklin Watts, a division of The Watts Publishing Group Limited, 1999.

Holiday Activities

At appropriate times of the year, the holiday backgrounds and activities provided in this section can be used to introduce or reinforce concepts related to important holidays. The holiday activities explore a variety of individual and community celebrations. They can prompt discussion of the similarities and differences in the traditions and cultures found in the United States.

Contents

Labor Day

Labor Day

LABOR DAY is a special day to honor workers for the contributions they have made to our community. Labor Day is celebrated on the first Monday in September. Most people do not have to work on this day. Many people watch parades, go on picnics, attend sports events, or join in recreational activities that they enjoy.

- The first Labor Day holiday was celebrated on Tuesday, September 5, 1882, in New York City.
- President Grover Cleveland signed a bill in 1894 to make Labor Day a national holiday.
- Children have a "job" to do, too—it is to go to school.
- Workers in Puerto Rico, Canada, Australia, and many parts of Europe celebrate Labor Day, too.

Career Day

On Labor Day, we celebrate the people who work hard in our community. Have children invite their parents into the classroom to have a career day. Invite guest speakers to talk about their jobs and how they help the community. Request that they bring visuals or props or wear the uniform they wear while working.

- Provide construction paper, markers, and crayons so children can make their own invitations to a parent or adult friend.

- Have children generate a list of all of the jobs they learned about from their guest speakers. Ask children to write about the job they felt was most interesting.

It's a Parade!

When Labor Day was first observed, it was proposed that there should be a parade that exhibited the labor organizations in the community, followed by a festival for workers and their families.

Have children organize a parade. First, brainstorm a list of community workers that they would like to feature in their parade, such as police officers, firefighters, teachers, construction workers, doctors, etc. Encourage children to choose a community worker that they would like to dress up as in the parade.

- Give children a variety of art materials or dress-up items to make their uniforms or work clothes.

- Supply children with classroom instruments or make instruments to use in the parade.

- Parade around the hallway. Arrange time with other teachers so children can talk about their costumes and the job they would like to do when they grow up.

Railroad Songs

Railroad builders were a group of people who worked hard in their communities. When people were making the railroad that extends across our country, they often sang songs to help them pass the time. Sing "I've Been Working on the Railroad" with children. Encourage children to make up their own verse to the song, based on a job they would like to do.

> *I've been working in the airport*
> *All the livelong day;*
> *I've been working in the airport*
> *Just to help folks find their way.*

Columbus Day

Christopher Columbus

Christopher Columbus was an Italian explorer. During his lifetime, many people thought that the world was flat, but Christopher Columbus believed that the world was round.

Columbus set sail in 1492 to prove his ideas about the world and to look for an easier route for sailors who were trading spices with Spain. He sailed on the flagship *Santa María*. He also brought two other ships with him, the *Niña* and the *Pinta*. Columbus and his crew eventually landed on an island in the Caribbean. Instead of finding a new trade route, Columbus discovered a new continent that lay between Europe and Asia. This continent was North America.

Four hundred years later, people in the United States decided to name a holiday in Columbus's honor. COLUMBUS DAY is a national holiday that is celebrated on the second Monday in October.

Ship Sculptures

Tell children that there is a monument in New York City dedicated to Christopher Columbus. If possible, show a picture of the monument. Explain that monuments are sculptures that are built to remember famous people and events. Provide modeling clay or dough so children can create their own monuments to Christopher Columbus. Suggest that children make models of the ships that Columbus sailed with—the *Niña*, the *Pinta*, and the *Santa María*. Show children pictures of the ships to use as guides.

Read a Compass

Explain that a caravel is a sailing ship like the ones used by Columbus on his first voyage. It was a wooden ship with tall masts and many sails. The shape of the boat was different from that of modern ships. But sailors on the caravels used compasses, just as crews of modern ships do, to help determine directions. Columbus and his men probably relied on a small compass.

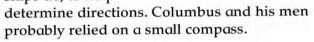

Provide a hand-held compass and invite children to identify directions of objects in the classroom. Help them familiarize themselves with the compass first.

1. Find north, south, east, and west on the face of the compass.

2. Turn the compass in any direction, and then hold it still. The needle will always come to rest pointing north.

3. Walk south, east, and west, using the compass to identify the direction.

Track the Path

Show children a globe of Earth. Tell children that they are going to try to guess the path that Christopher Columbus took to find new land. Remind children that Columbus began in Spain and went west through the Atlantic Ocean, landing on an island in the Caribbean.

Show children Spain on the map, and then show them the Bahamas. Let volunteers show different paths Christopher Columbus could have taken.

Veterans Day

Veterans Day

VETERANS DAY is observed on November 11 to honor all veterans. This holiday began after World War I ended. Americans wanted to give thanks for peace. They also wanted to thank the veterans for their patriotism and their willingness to serve their country. The holiday was called Armistice Day.

After World War II and the Korean War, Americans realized that the name of the holiday should change to recognize all veterans from all wars. The name was then changed to Veterans Day.

On Veterans Day, Americans take time to rest and relax with their families. They also take time to think about all the veterans, living and dead, who served our country.

- A veteran is a person who served in the Army, Navy, Marines, Coast Guard, or Air Force. Not all veterans served in wartime.

- This holiday is also celebrated in France, the United Kingdom, and Canada. In Great Britain, it is called Remembrance Sunday, and in Canada it is called Remembrance Day.

Wave the Flag

The American flag has been a symbol of patriotism and love of country for most Americans. When veterans came home from war, they were greeted with people waving the American flag in celebration of peace.

Make a class American flag. Draw an outline of the flag on bulletin board paper. Ask children to paint the blue box and the red and white stripes. After the paint is dry, have children use white chalk to draw fifty stars inside the blue box.

Military Graph

Remind children that there are five branches in the military: the Army, the Navy, the Marines, the Coast Guard, and the Air Force. Talk to children about the emphasis of each branch. Explain that the Army protects the land, the Navy protects the water, the Marines protect both the land and the water, the Coast Guard patrols the coast, and the Air Force patrols the air.

Ask children whether a member of their family is a veteran or is now a member of a military branch, or whether they know someone who is. Have children write the branch of service of the person, if they know it. If not, invite children to choose one. Create a class graph of the information, writing children's names above the branch of service.

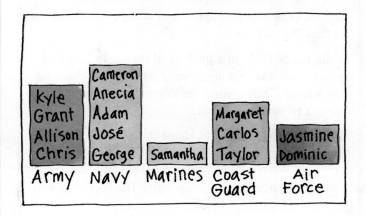

Someone Special

Explain to children that on Veterans Day, most Americans stop at 11:00 A.M. to take a moment of silence remembering those Americans who fought for peace.

Have children take a moment of silence to think about a person who they believe has done something important for the community. Then invite children to write and draw about that person. Be sure children include in their writing why that person should be recognized.

Compile children's writing to make a class book titled "Special People." As you share the book, invite each author to read his or her page.

Thanksgiving

THANKSGIVING DAY is a holiday that gives people time to give thanks, enjoy family gatherings, and join in holiday meals. Thanksgiving takes place on the fourth Thursday of each November.

In 1620, the Pilgrims sailed from England in search of a place where they could worship as they wished. They sailed from Plymouth, England, on a ship called the *Mayflower*.

Once the Pilgrims arrived near Cape Cod in Massachusetts, they started a settlement, which they named Plymouth. The settlers had to clear the land, build houses, and plant crops. It was a very difficult year, and during the first winter, half of the settlers died.

In the fall of 1621, as a gesture of thanks to God and to celebrate the first successful harvest, the Pilgrims had a feast. They invited the Wampanoag Indians to join the three-day festival.

- Turkey is the traditional Thanksgiving food. People at the 1621 Thanksgiving celebration ate wild turkey, fish, corn, fruit, and vegetables.

- President Abraham Lincoln made Thanksgiving a national holiday in 1863.

Popcorn

Explain to children that the Pilgrims did not know about corn when they landed in Plymouth. Corn was not grown in England, where they came from. The Indians introduced them to corn, showing them how to grow it and how to cook it. Tell children that the Pilgrim children may have had popcorn at the first Thanksgiving. Explain to children that corn kernels were dried out first. Then they were placed over the fire, where they began to pop.

Use a popcorn maker to pop popcorn. Have children generate a list of foods that contain corn.

Make a Scarecrow

Explain to children that farmers have been using scarecrows for many years. Scarecrows keep away crows that like to eat the vegetables in gardens. If crows and other small animals are kept to a minimum, the harvest will be better.

Make a scarecrow with children.

1. Stuff a small brown paper bag as the head of the scarecrow. Draw facial features.

2. Cut the shape of a scarecrow's body out of craft paper. Trace and cut the shape again to create the back. Ask children to decorate the body pieces.

3. Staple the body pieces together and stuff them with newspaper. Attach the scarecrow's head.

4. Attach the scarecrow to a post so it can stand.

Friendship Bracelet

The first Thanksgiving was held, not only to give thanks for a bountiful harvest, but to celebrate the help of and friendship with the neighboring Native Americans. Have children make a friendship bracelet to give to a friend who has helped them.

1. String colored beads on a piece of yarn to make a bracelet.

2. Have children exchange the bracelet with a friend in the classroom who has been helpful in some way.

3. Children may want to make other bracelets for friends not in their class.

Hanukkah

Hanukkah

Every year, between the end of November and the end of December, Jewish people celebrate HANUKKAH. Hanukkah is a celebration of the victory of the Maccabees over the Syrians.

Over 2,300 years ago, Judea, which is now called Israel, was taken over by the Syrians. The Syrians wanted all the people of the land to worship the Greek gods as they did. Judas Maccabeus and his brothers refused to worship these gods and went to war with the Syrians. After three years of fighting, the Syrians finally left Judea and the Maccabees reclaimed the Jerusalem Temple.

The Maccabees cleaned the Temple and lit an eternal light. They were concerned, however, that there was only enough oil to keep the lamp burning for one day. Miraculously, the oil burned for eight days, the time it took to bring in a fresh supply of oil.

Today people celebrate eight nights of Hanukkah to remember the victory and the miracle of the oil.

- A candle is lit for each of the eight nights that the oil burned.

- In America, families celebrate Hanukkah by giving and receiving gifts, decorating their houses, entertaining family and friends, eating special foods, playing a dreidel game, and lighting the menorah.

Create Gift Bags

During Hanukkah, families exchange gifts on each of the eight nights. Have children make a gift bag for a Hanukkah gift. Place a small paper bag in a shoebox. Dip a marble in paint, place it in the shoebox, and have children roll the marble on the paper bag to create a design. Allow children to dip other marbles in other colors and add to the design. When the bag is dry, encourage children to use black paint to add symbols of Hanukkah, such as the Star of David or a menorah.

Play the Dreidel Game

You will need:
- Dreidels
- Tokens or colored cubes

Explain to children that the dreidel game is a very popular game among Jewish children. The dreidel is a four-sided top with a Hebrew letter on each side. The letters mean "A Great Miracle Happened There." In Israel the symbols are different and mean "A Great Miracle Happened Here."

Organize children in groups of three or four to play a dreidel game. Place 30 tokens in the center of each group. Direct players to take turns spinning the dreidel and following the directions indicated by the symbols. At the end of the playing period, the player with the most tokens is declared the winner.

NUN—Nothing happens and the next player spins the dreidel.

GIMEL—The player takes all of the tokens in the pot.

HEY—The player takes half of the tokens in the pot.

SHIN—The player must put one token into the pot.

Dance the Hora

Learn a traditional dance called the Hora. Join hands to form a circle. Follow these steps as you dance to recorded music from Israel. Each step should take two beats.

Step 1 Step to the left with left foot.

Step 2 Cross right foot behind left foot.

Step 3 Step to the left with left foot.

Step 4 Hop on left foot and kick right foot in front of you.

Step 5 Hop on right foot and kick left foot in front of you.

Repeat these steps over and over again until the music stops.

Christmas

Christmas

CHRISTMAS is probably the most celebrated holiday around the world. People in countries such as Australia, Canada, England, Finland, France, Germany, Greece, Italy, Mexico, Norway, Sweden, and Ukraine celebrate Christmas.

Christmas is a religious holiday honoring the birth of Jesus. Christmas customs vary from family to family and are based on traditions of ancestors from other countries.

In the United States many Christians go to church on Christmas Eve for a special ceremony to welcome the day when Christ was born. On Christmas morning some children hurry to see if Santa Claus has left them gifts. In many homes families and friends come together for holiday meals and to exchange gifts.

- For nine days before Christmas, people in Mexico celebrate *las posadas*. They join in a search for a safe place for the infant Jesus. According to the custom, they are turned down every night except the last night, Christmas.

- In France some people burn a log in the fireplace from Christmas Eve until New Year's Day. According to ancient tradition, it ensures good luck for the new year's harvest.

- Italians call Christmas *Il Natale*, which means "the birthday."

Christmas Greetings

Tell children that there are many different ways to say Merry Christmas. Teach children the following greetings from other countries:

Italy - Buone Natale!

Sweden - God Jul!

Mexico - Feliz Navidad!

France - Joyeux Noel!

¡Feliz Navidad!

Make Piñatas

Tell children that in Mexico, as a part of the Christmas celebration, people make piñatas for the children. Piñatas are papier-mâché objects filled with candy and coins. Children take turns trying to break the object using a large stick. Once the object is broken, children scramble to collect the candy and coins.

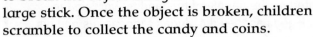

Let each child make a *piñata*.

1. Give each child a blown-up balloon.

2. Tear newspaper into strips about an inch wide.

3. Combine equal amounts of flour and water to make a paste. Place the newspaper strips in the paste. Wrap the wet strips around the balloon, completely covering the surface. Children may mold and add ears, noses, and other features to make animal faces.

4. Let the papier-mâché dry thoroughly. Then pop the balloon and have children paint the piñata.

5. Cut an opening in the bottom of the piñata and place a few pieces of candy in it. Tape the opening closed so the candy doesn't fall out.

Christmas Carols

Explain to children that Christmas caroling is a tradition that began in England. People walked around their neighborhood singing Christmas carols in hopes of a gift. Today the tradition continues in England and in the United States. Sing a variety of Christmas songs with children, such as "Jingle Bells," "Rudolph, the Red-Nosed Reindeer," and "Santa Claus Is Coming to Town." Let children sing the songs for other classrooms as if they were caroling.

Kwanzaa

Kwanzaa

KWANZAA is a nonreligious holiday that is celebrated by many African Americans. This holiday is celebrated for seven days, December 26–January 1. It was created in 1966 by Dr. Ron Karenga as a way to strengthen unity within African American families and their community. The festival was first observed to celebrate the first fruits of the winter season.

For seven nights, families gather, light a candle, and talk about one of the seven principles of Kwanzaa. Celebrations also include songs and dances, African drums, storytelling, poetry reading, and a large traditional meal.

- The seven principles celebrated during Kwanzaa are *unity, self-determination, collective work and responsibility, cooperative economics, purpose, creativity,* and *faith.*

- On the last day of Kwanzaa, many families gather for a feast called *karamu.*

Class Book

Explain to children that on the first night of Kwanzaa, African American families celebrate the principle of *umoja* (oo•MOH•jah), which means unity. Families talk about how to maintain unity in the family and in the community.

Make a class book about family traditions. *What are some things your family does together?* Ask children to draw a picture and write about a tradition that their family enjoys. Collate the pages and create a class book called "Family Traditions."

Kwanzaa Placemat

The *mkeka,* a placemat, is another symbol of Kwanzaa that represents tradition. The placemat is usually made of straw. It is placed on the table each night. The *kinara* (a seven-branched candlestick) is placed at the center of the mat, and then the mat is decorated with ears of corn (one for each child in the family) and other vegetables.

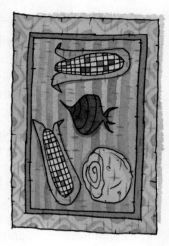

Have children make their own placemats.

1. Fold beige or yellow construction paper in half. Cut slits about 1 inch apart, starting at the folded edge and cutting up to about 2 inches from the edge of the paper.

2. Weave strips of paper into the cut construction paper. Begin each row in opposition (first one under, second over, and so on). Repeat to fill.

3. Cut fringes along the side edges. You may want to laminate the placemats for durability.

4. Have children cut out pictures of corn and other vegetables to place on the mat for decoration.

Colors of Kwanzaa

The colors of Kwanzaa are black, red, and green. Explain that many families decorate their homes with these colors during Kwanzaa. Let children decorate the classroom with black, red, and green-streamers in honor of the class Kwanzaa discussion.

Storytelling Drum

Music and storytelling are important parts of Kwanzaa celebrations. Let children see and touch different types of African drums (or make drums from empty coffee cans). Have children make up stories about happiness, danger, rest, storms, or celebrations. As they tell their stories, have them experiment with different rhythms that set the mood for the events in the story.

New Year's Around the World

New Year's

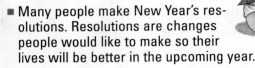

NEW YEAR'S DAY may be the oldest of all holidays. In the United States, it is celebrated on January 1. This holiday is a day to remember the past and look forward to the upcoming year.

- Many people make New Year's resolutions. Resolutions are changes people would like to make so their lives will be better in the upcoming year.

- The traditional New Year's song is "Auld Lang Syne," which means "good old days." Many people count down to midnight on New Year's Eve and sing this song to bring in the new year.

The CHINESE NEW YEAR is the longest and most important festival in China. The Chinese New Year begins on the first day of the first month of the lunar year and ends with the Lantern Festival on the 15th day of the lunar year.

- Families traditionally buy and wear new clothes, clean their homes, have family feasts, and—most importantly—pay off all debts.

- On New Year's Eve, children get to stay up as long as possible. It is believed that the longer they stay up, the longer their parents will live.

TET is the Vietnamese New Year. *Tet* means "the first morning of the first day of the new year." In many ways, it is similar to the Chinese New Year. Tet falls between the last ten days of January and the middle of February.

- Homes are cleaned to rid them of bad fortune. People resolve differences between family and friends.

- The color red symbolizes good luck and appears everywhere: on clothing, in homes, and in festive decorations.

Good-Luck Foods

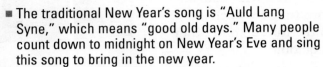

On New Year's Day, many people like to eat foods that they believe will bring them good luck. Explain to children that some people believe that foods shaped like a ring will bring them good luck because they symbolize "coming full circle." Invite children to brainstorm a list of foods they think are "lucky." Have children make a mural to show pictures of their good-luck foods.

Lucky Red Envelopes

As a part of both the Chinese and Vietnamese New Year celebrations, friends and relatives receive and give red envelopes. These red envelopes contain "lucky money" or other treats. Many believe that these filled envelopes are symbols that mean the upcoming year will be prosperous.

Have children make their own red envelopes to give as gifts. Show them how to fold, glue, and decorate red paper to make an envelope. Then ask children to draw and color play money. On the back of the bill, have children write a message of good cheer before placing it inside the envelope. Let them exchange their envelopes with classmates.

Dragon Dance

Explain to children that both Tet and Chinese New Year have celebrations that feature firecrackers and parades. The parades feature a dragon that winds its way through the crowds.

Have children create a paper dragon for their own New Year's dragon dance. Divide the class into small groups. Provide each group with a cardboard box, crepe paper, and craft materials. Explain that the box, held upside down, will be the dragon's head. Ask them to decorate the box with art materials to make a dragon's face. Then have each group attach a length of crepe paper to the back of the dragon's head. This will form the dragon's body and be carried by the other members of the group. Invite groups to attach streamers and other decorations to the sides of the dragon's body. To perform the dragon dance, have groups stand in a straight line, with one child holding the "head" of the dragon over his or her own, and the rest of the children behind, carrying the body over their heads. Have groups dip and sway to mimic a dragon's movements as they move about the room.

Dr. Martin Luther King, Jr.

On the third Monday in January, Americans observe DR. MARTIN LUTHER KING, JR., DAY. King worked hard for freedom, equality, and dignity of all races and peoples. He helped bring about change with nonviolent actions.

While King was a minister in Montgomery, Alabama, an African American woman was arrested because she refused to give her seat on the bus to a white man. King organized the Montgomery bus boycott. He led the African Americans in Montgomery to boycott the bus system until it was fair for everyone, regardless of color. It took 382 days for a law to be passed that made the bus policy equal for all riders.

King continued to speak against the poor treatment of African American people. He organized a historic march to the White House. At the Lincoln Memorial he gave a famous speech calling for freedom for all.

- On April 4, 1968, King was assassinated. Today we celebrate his birthday by remembering his work for equal opportunity.

- Many communities celebrate Dr. Martin Luther King, Jr., Day with picnics, parades, and marches.

Handprint Rainbow

Make a handprint rainbow with children. Provide construction paper of rainbow colors. Have children choose a color, and then have them trace and cut out four handprints. Create a class rainbow using everyone's handprints.

Discuss how working together helped the class make a beautiful rainbow. Explain that Dr. Martin Luther King, Jr., felt that teamwork helped solve many problems.

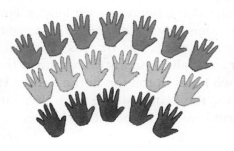

Team Building

Use the following activities to develop teamwork in the classroom.

Building Structures Divide the class into teams of three or four children. Provide children with toothpicks and miniature marshmallows. Challenge them to work together to build a structure using the toothpicks and marshmallows.

Creating Silly Animals Divide children into three teams. Ask the first team to draw a picture of an animal's head on craft paper. Tell the second team to draw a picture of an animal's body. At the same time have the third team draw a picture of animal legs and feet. Explain to the teams that they should work together to decide which animal they are going to draw and that everyone in the group needs to participate. Once everyone is finished, put the head, body, and legs and feet together to see the funny animal the entire class created.

Fair Play

In 1964, Dr. Martin Luther King, Jr., won a Nobel Peace Prize for his work to get equal treatment for all people. Explain that King wanted to create a world in which everyone would be treated fairly and would obey the same rules. Ask children what they think the words *fair* and *unfair* mean.

Invite children to act out scenes that show ways of solving problems peacefully. You may want to present scenarios such as the following:

- In the middle of a game on the playground, an older boy takes your soccer ball.

- A girl you know cuts in line in front of you at lunch.

- Your classmates say you run too slowly and they don't want you on their team.

Valentine's Day

VALENTINE'S DAY is celebrated every February 14. Candy, flowers, cards, and gifts are exchanged between loved ones in the name of St. Valentine. Nobody really knows when Valentine's Day first started. It contains parts of both Christian and Roman traditions.

There are three different saints that the Catholic Church recognizes by the name St. Valentine. One legend tells the story of a priest that lived in Rome. The Emperor Claudius decided that single men made better soldiers than those with wives and families, so he told his soldiers they could not marry. Valentine thought this was unfair and he continued to marry young couples in secret. When the emperor found out, he put Valentine in jail.

Another legend claims that Valentine sent the first "valentine" greeting himself. While in prison, Valentine fell in love with a young girl, his jailor's daughter. She visited him often to keep him company. Before he died, he sent her a letter which he signed "From your Valentine." This expression is still used today.

Puzzling Messages

Cut out several large hearts from pink or red posterboard. Have children work in pairs to write a Valentine's message such as *You are kind to others* or *You are a special person.* Ask pairs to draw designs around the message to decorate the heart. Then, have children cut zigzag or curved lines to make the heart into a puzzle. Place each heart puzzle in an envelope. Put all the envelopes into a bag. Invite pairs to select a puzzle and put it together to discover the message.

Coupons for Kindness

Explain to children that being kind to others shows we care about them. Invite children to make coupon books for family members or loved ones. Staple wide strips of drawing paper between a construction paper cover to make a booklet and give one to each child. Ask children to write *Kindness Coupons* on the cover. On each page, ask children to name a job or task they can do to show kindness. For example, for a brother or sister they may write: *You can borrow my paint set for one day.* For a parent, they might write: *Dear Mom, This is good for one big hug.* Have children present the coupon books to their families.

Magic Messages

Provide children with a heart shape cut from white construction paper. Have them use a white crayon to write a "secret message" on the heart. Explain that they will have to press hard. Encourage them to print simple messages such as *People love you* or *You are great.* Collect the hearts and redistribute them to children. Provide children with newspaper, red paint, and paintbrushes. Have children place the heart on the newsprint and brush over it with the red paint. The secret message will then appear.

Tugging Heart Strings

Discuss with children the people who help them each day. List their ideas on the board. Provide children with several paper heart cutouts and a length of yarn. Have groups write a thought of appreciation on a heart to each helper. For example, they might say *I like it when the librarian helps me find a book* or *The bus driver is nice because he waits for me.* Collect hearts according to the helper. Punch two holes at the top of the hearts. Have children string the hearts on the yarn. Present these heart strings to the helpers they honor.

Presidents' Day

Every third Monday in February, Americans honor their Presidents, among them George Washington and Abraham Lincoln. This national holiday is called PRESIDENTS' DAY.

George Washington was born on February 22. He was the first President of the United States and he is called the Father of Our Country. George Washington is remembered as being a peacemaker and a war hero. He also defended the Constitution and the Bill of Rights.

- President Washington is the only American President after whom a state has been named. Washington, D.C., the capital of the United States, is also named after him.

Abraham Lincoln was born on February 12. He was the sixteenth President of the United States. President Lincoln is remembered for freeing the slaves when he signed the Emancipation Proclamation. He also delivered one of the nation's most famous speeches, called the Gettysburg Address.

- Americans celebrate Presidents' Day in February because both of these great Presidents were born in February.

Money Details

Share a one-dollar bill and a five-dollar bill with children. Point out George Washington's face on the one-dollar bill and Abraham Lincoln's face on the five-dollar bill. Continue discussing details on the bills.

Children can design new bills. Have them plan and then draw a bill that features the current President of the United States. The face of the bill should include a picture of the President. The back may show a monument to the President or another symbol of the country.

President for a Day

Explain to children that the President has a very important job to do. It is the President's responsibility to make sure everyone in the United States is treated fairly and is safe. It is also the President's job to keep our nation at peace with other nations.

Invite children to pretend that they have to spend the day being the President of the United States. Invite them to make a President's diary entry by drawing a picture with a caption to show something they did for the nation during the day. Encourage children to use specific examples such as *I proclaimed a new holiday. I signed a bill today. I signed a peace treaty today.* Compile the entries into a single diary, and place it in the classroom library for others to enjoy. Encourage children to compare their activities as President with those of their classmates.

Hoecakes

You will need:

2 cups self-rising cornmeal
2 eggs
1 tablespoon sugar
2 tablespoons butter
3/4 cup milk
1/3 cup water
1/4 cup vegetable oil

Explain that George Washington usually ate hoecakes for breakfast. Hoecakes are a type of bread made with cornmeal. During Washington's time they were baked in a fireplace on the blade of a hoe.

Make hoecakes with children. Let them measure and mix the ingredients. Then have an adult pour the mixture onto a griddle and cook until brown and crispy. You may want to top the hoecakes with syrup, butter, or fruit. (Note: Be sure to check for allergies before letting children taste any foods.)

St. Patrick's Day

ST. PATRICK'S DAY is celebrated every March 17. Some people celebrate this holiday in honor of St. Patrick, the patron saint of Ireland. Irish families traditionally attend church in the morning and celebrate in the afternoon.

St. Patrick's Day activities allow many people to celebrate their Irish heritage and our country's connections to Ireland. People partake in customs such as eating corned beef and cabbage, wearing green-colored clothing, and displaying shamrocks. The city of Chicago even dyes the Chicago River green for the day!

St. Patrick's Day has been celebrated in the United States since 1737. That year, an Irish group in Boston held the first St. Patrick's Day parade. Today, more than 100 U.S. cities hold their own parades. The one held in New York City is the largest and most famous.

Leprechaun Hat Pencil Holders

In advance, have children bring in small clean soup or vegetable cans. Be sure each child has his or her own can. Have children wrap the outside of the can with green construction paper. Provide precut circles that are roughly an inch wider in diameter than the cans. Show children how to put glue on the bottom edge of the can and set it on the center of the circle to form a hat brim. Have them glue a strip of yellow paper around the bottom of the can to form a hat band. Invite them to decorate the outside of the "hat" with shamrocks and other symbols. Have them use their hats to hold pencils.

Make a Blarney Stone

Explain to children that in Ireland there is a very famous stone called a Blarney Stone. Legend has it that if you kiss the Blarney Stone, you will become a gifted speaker. Have children make "blarney stones" from smooth river rocks. Ask children to paint their stone a color they think will bring them good luck. Then have them paint a face on the stone. On a strip of paper smaller than the stone, ask each child to write what the stone will bring such as good luck, artistic talent, math talent, riches, or good health. After the paint on their stone has dried, have children glue the paper strip to the bottom. Arrange the stones in a display. Invite children to take turns reading their fortunes from the bottoms of the stones.

Lucky Shamrocks

Cut out large shamrock shapes from green construction paper. Give a shamrock to each child. Ask children to write their name on the stem of the shamrock. Then invite them to think of three things to complete this sentence frame: *I am lucky because* _____. Have them write a sentence on each leaf of the shamrock, telling three different ways that they are lucky. Display the shamrocks on a bulletin board.

Irish Treasure Hunt

Have children draw and cut out pictures of rainbows, pots of gold, shamrocks, and leprechauns from small squares of card stock. Collect the pictures once they are completed. Hide the pictures in various places in the classroom or on the playground. Then tell children they are going on a treasure hunt. Divide the class into groups of three or four. Allow children a certain amount of time to find as many of the pictures as they can. Bring the class together and ask them to count the number of pictures they have of each object (you may want to have some extra pictures in case a group finds very few on their own). Invite groups to use the pictures to assemble a picture graph.

Cesar Chavez Day

CESAR CHAVEZ DAY is an official holiday in many states. It honors the memory of the Latino labor leader Cesar Chavez. The purpose of this holiday is to promote service to the community. Cesar Chavez Day is celebrated on the Monday or Friday closest to March 31, his birthday.

On Cesar Chavez Day of Service and Learning, thousands of children from kindergarten to grade 12 participate in service projects that honor Chavez's life and work. Adults participate in beautification projects, programs to harvest fields of excess crops, park clean-ups, and community health fairs.

- Through the formation of the United Farm Workers of America, Chavez founded and led the first successful farm workers union in United States history.

- Cesar Chavez received the highest civilian awards from both the United States and Mexico: the Presidential Medal of Freedom and the Aguila Azteca.

I Make My School Beautiful

Take children on a walk around the school grounds. Have them notice places that look untidy or areas that are not attractive. Once back in the classroom, discuss some of these problem areas. Then invite children to work in small groups to come up with a plan to beautify one area of their school. Have them draw pictures that illustrate an idea they have to make it more attractive. Ask them to add a sentence that describes their idea.

Where Do They Come From?

Have children name some of their favorite fruits and vegetables as you list them on the board. Then help children research where these fruits and vegetables are grown. Invite children to use a large outline map of the United States to locate states that grow certain fruits and vegetables. Ask children to draw a symbol to locate the fruit or vegetable on the map.

Fairness Posters

Explain to children that Cesar Chavez worked hard to teach people in the community about the hardships faced by migrant workers. Point out that one way he did this was by displaying posters throughout the community. Discuss with children why it is important that everyone is treated fairly. Invite children to work in pairs to make a poster that advertises fairness. Ask them to write a sentence on the poster that tells something that people can do to treat others fairly. For example, they might say *Be polite; Talk to people with respect;* or *Pay workers what they deserve to be paid.* Have children draw a picture that illustrates their sentence.

"Helping Others" Accordion Book

Give each child a long strip of drawing paper. Demonstrate how to accordion-fold the paper five times to make a small book. Ask children to title the cover *Helping Others.* On the pages, have children copy these words: *I help my family; I help my school; I help my friends; I help my community;* and *I help my world.* Ask children to draw a picture on the page to show how they help each subject.

Cinco de Mayo

CINCO DE MAYO, which means "the fifth of May" in Spanish, is a national holiday in Mexico. It is also celebrated by Mexican Americans to honor the defenders of Mexican freedom.

On May 5, 1862, French troops invaded and attacked the city of Puebla, Mexico. The Mexican troops were made up of a group of untrained commoners. The French troops were greater in number and well trained. The Mexican army fought hard and defeated the French army. This victory was very important to the Mexican people because they won against all odds; this inspired a great amount of patriotism in the people. People celebrate Cinco de Mayo with fiestas, parades, mariachi music, and piñatas.

- Each May 5 in Puebla, Mexico, a mock battle is staged to remember and celebrate the victory over the French army in the Battle of Puebla.

Flag of Mexico

Show children Mexico on the map. There are many people in the United States who are of Mexican descent. These people or their relatives were born in Mexico and moved to the United States.

Look at and talk about the colors and images on a flag of Mexico. Have children make a Mexican flag of their own design. Divide the flag into three vertical lines. Paint the first column green, the second white, and the third red. Have them paint a coat-of-arms symbol in the center of the flag.

Make Maracas

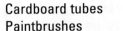

You will need:

Cardboard tubes	Paint
Paintbrushes	Glitter (optional)
Stickers (optional)	Rice or beans
Wax paper	Rubber bands

Remind children that in the United States, Mexican Americans celebrate Cinco de Mayo with songs and lively dances. One instrument that is used during celebrations is the maraca.

Make maracas with children.

1. Have children decorate cardboard tubes with paint, glitter, and stickers.

2. Cover one end of the tube with wax paper and then wrap the end tightly with a rubber band. Place a handful of rice or beans inside the tube. Then cover the opposite end.

3. Play Mexican music and have children shake their maracas to the rhythm of the music.

Native American Kickball

Explain to children that this game is played by the Tarahumara Indians in Mexico.

Organize children into two teams. Set up an obstacle course on the playground. Have children kick the ball through places such as the following: under the slide, over a chair, and through a tunnel. Ask the two teams to play as if they were in a relay. The first team to have its players kick the ball through the obstacle course wins.

Memorial Day

MEMORIAL DAY is a holiday set aside to remember and honor those who gave their lives for the United States. The holiday originated during the Civil War. It was called Decoration Day because it was customary for people to decorate the graves of the war dead. In 1971 Congress declared Memorial Day to be a national holiday that is to be celebrated on the last Monday in May.

- On Memorial Day, there is a memorial service at Arlington National Cemetery. A small American flag is placed on each grave. The President or Vice President of the United States lays a wreath at the Tomb of the Unknowns and gives a speech.

- Today Americans honor those who gave their lives in battle, as well as family members and friends whom they wish to remember.

Giving Thanks

Remind children that many people died in wars. Explain to them that these people should be honored because they were fighting for our country. The veterans wanted to make sure that this country was a place where people could live a safe and peaceful life. Ask children to name family members or friends who served in recent wars.

Ask children to make a thank-you card for one of the veterans who died in a war. Have them write in the cards why Memorial Day is an important holiday. If possible, send the cards to the families of the deceased veterans.

Make A Wreath

Explain to children that the Tomb of the Unknowns is a site where people can go to grieve for loved ones who never returned from a war. For different reasons, sometimes a person is not found after a war is over.

Every year the President or the Vice President places a wreath on the tomb on Memorial Day. Make a wreath with children.

1. Provide five sheets of red, white, or blue tissue paper to each child. Ask children to place the pieces of tissue paper on top of each other. Then have them fold the paper like a fan.

2. Give each child a chenille stem to wrap tightly around the center of the folded tissue paper.

3. Pull each piece of tissue paper to the center. Mold to create a flower.

4. Attach the flowers to a cardboard ring.

Sing a Song

Tell children that soldiers often end the day with the playing of the song "Taps." It is usually played on a trumpet or bugle. Sing the song for children and ask them to draw pictures of the image the song evokes. Then sing the song together. Invite children to use horns, kazoos, and other classroom instruments to accompany the song.

Taps

Day is done, gone the sun, from the lake,

from the hills, from the sky.

All is well, safely rest, God is nigh.

Independence Day

INDEPENDENCE DAY is a national holiday that commemorates the adoption of the Declaration of Independence on July 4, 1776. This holiday is the birthday of the United States of America.

Once there were only 13 colonies. People in the colonies were upset because they had to pay taxes to England. However, they could not vote or have any say in the English government.

In June 1776, the people decided to write a formal declaration of independence from England. Thomas Jefferson was in charge of writing it. On July 4, the Declaration of Independence was approved.

Today Americans celebrate the nation's birthday by displaying and wearing red, white, and blue. People also have picnics, have parades with marching bands, go to the beaches, have barbecues, and watch fireworks.

- The Declaration of Independence was adopted on July 4, 1776, but it was not actually signed until August 2 of that year.

- The 56 men who signed the Declaration of Independence did not use the kind of pen we use today. They dipped a turkey feather, or quill, into an inkwell and used the tip to write on the document.

Patriotic Songs

Set out red, white, and blue streamers and American flags. Invite children to wave them to the rhythm of patriotic music such as "You're a Grand Old Flag," "America," or "Stars and Stripes Forever."

Flag Etiquette

Explain to children that there are certain rules that people should follow when waving or displaying the American flag. Model the appropriate handling of the flag with a small flag. Explain some of the flag rules.

1. The flag should not touch the ground.

2. The flag should only be displayed from sunrise to sunset unless the flag is illuminated.

3. The flag can only be displayed vertically or horizontally.

4. When the American flag is displayed with flags from cities or states, it should be higher than those flags.

5. When the American flag is displayed with flags of other countries, during peacetime, the flags should all be at the same level.

Talk about proper flag etiquette. Ask: *Why do you think there are rules about hanging the American flag?* Discuss how the flag should be treated with respect.

Give children a small flag to place on their desks for the day. Make sure children hang or display their flags appropriately.

The Stars on the Flag

Explain to children that the stars on the flag represent the number of states included in the United States. Talk about how many stars are on the present-day flag.

Tell children that Betsy Ross may have made the first American flag. She placed only 13 stars, though, because there were only 13 colonies at that time. Show children pictures of the present-day flag and the first flag so they can compare the similarities and differences.

Then provide red, white, and blue construction paper and invite children to make models of each flag.

Activity Patterns

The reproducible patterns in this section are for use with instruction in designated lesson plans. You may also want to use the patterns to create other activities appropriate for children in your class.

Contents

Puzzle

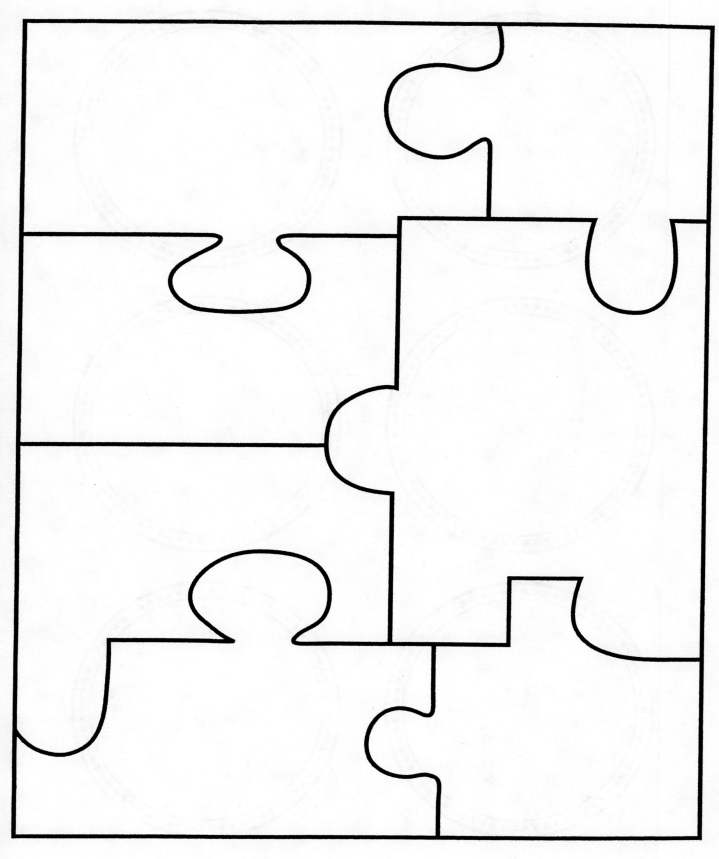

Chain

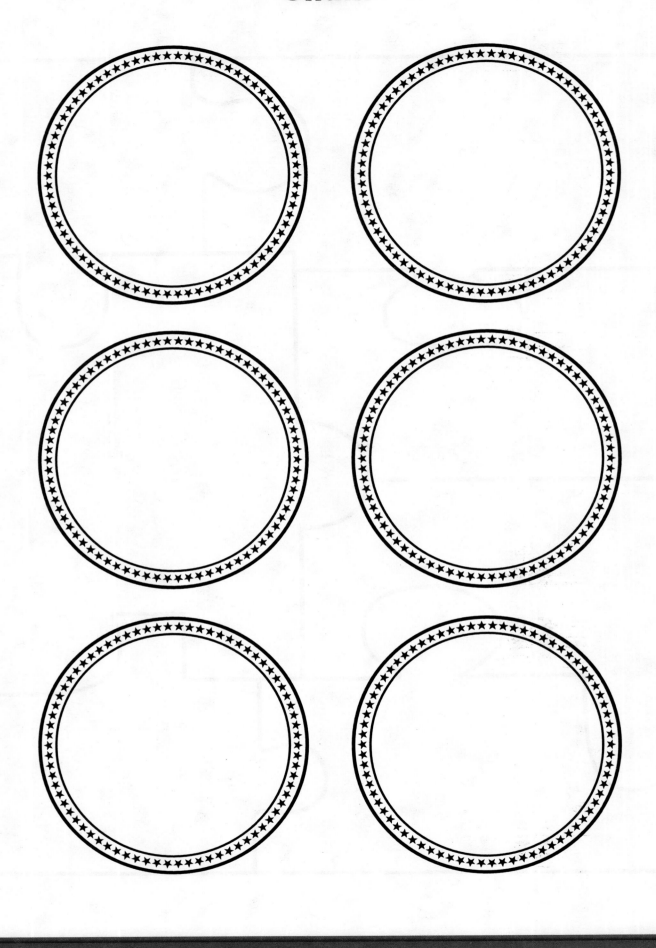

Design a T-Shirt

© Harcourt

Cube

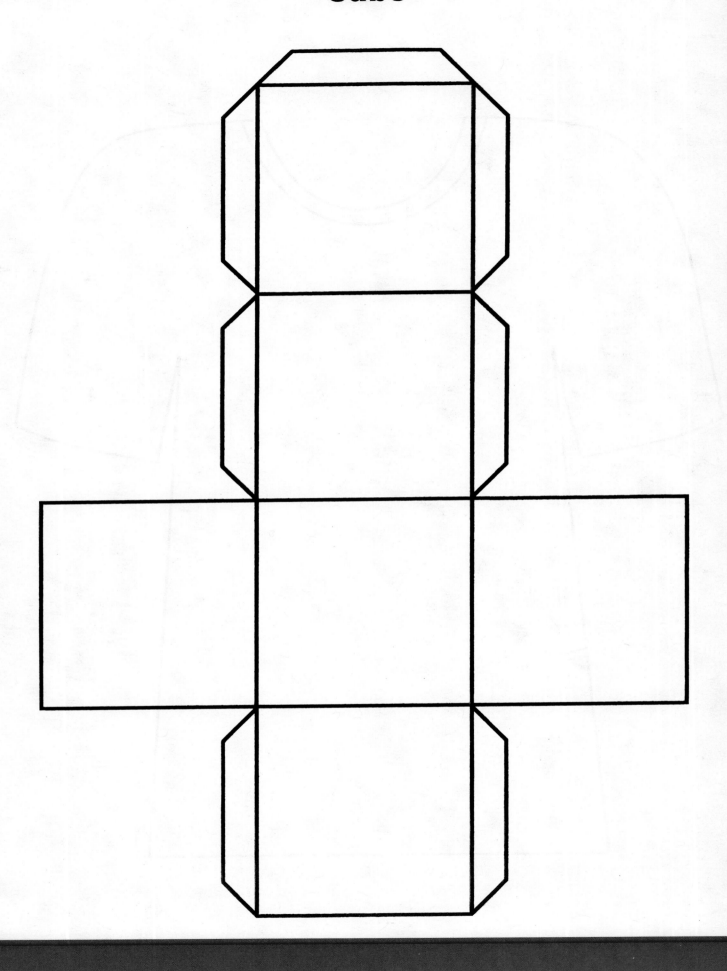

© Harcourt

Filmstrip

Picture Graph

Title _____

© Harcourt

Storyboard

In the News

Travel Passport

Name _____

Date of Birth _____

_____
Month   Day   Year

Place of Birth

_____

_____
State   Country

_____
Signature

PASSPORT

United States of America

─────────────────────────────── ✂

Name _____

Date of Birth _____

_____
Month   Day   Year

Place of Birth

_____

_____
State   Country

_____
Signature

PASSPORT

United States of America

Calendar

Month _____

Accordion Book

Tape

Tape

Product Table

	(utensils)	(shirt)	(television)

School to Home Newsletters

These school to home newsletters offer a link between students' study of social studies and students' family members. There is one newsletter, available in English and Spanish, for each unit. The newsletters include family activities as well as books to read.

Contents

School to Home

Harcourt Social Studies • People We Know • Unit 1

Newsletter

Governing the People

💡 The Big Idea

Government A government makes laws to help people be safe and get along.

Books To Read

Meet My Grandmother: She's a United States Senator by Lisa Tucker McElroy, Eileen Feinstein Mariano. Millbrook Press, Inc., 2000.

Shh! We're Writing the Constitution by Jean Fritz. Putnam Juvenile, 1998.

How States Make Laws by Suzanne LeVert. Marshall Cavendish, Inc., 2004.

© Harcourt

What to Know

Your child is about to begin studying how people govern themselves. In this first unit, Governing the People, the following essential questions will be discussed:

- How can citizens be responsible in their community?
- How does government help people?
- Why do we need leaders?
- How does our country's government work?
- What are the jobs of our community and state governments?

Home Activities

- Invite your child to imagine that the two of you are the mayors of your community. List what you would do to make your community a better place to live. Then help your child read the list to other family members and have them vote for the idea they like best. You may even want to write a letter to the real mayor to tell him or her about your idea.

- Talk with your child about voting. Then make a family decision, such as what to have for dinner or what to do this weekend, by voting. Relate this experience to voting on community issues and state issues, and voting for the President of the United States.

- Share news stories with your child about problems and conflicts between neighbors in your community or between nearby communities. Discuss how they resolved their differences. Did government officials help solve the problems? Were any laws broken or any new laws created? Compare these situations to the ways that different countries try to solve problems and conflicts.

Ideas to Discuss

- Why do people need governments? What would happen if people did not obey the laws that governments make?

- What do good citizens do? What rights and responsibilities do children have as citizens? How could you help others in your community?

- What government job do you think you would like to have? Why? What would you want to do if you were elected?

Ballots

GO ONLINE **For more resources, go to** www.harcourtschool.com/ss1

Carta para la casa

Boletín

El gobierno las personas

💡 **La gran idea**

Gobierno Un gobierno es el órgano que hace las leyes para que las personas vivan seguras y en paz.

Libros

Meet My Grandmother: She's a United States Senator
por Lisa Tucker McElroy, Eileen Feinstein Mariano. Millbrook Press, Inc., 2000.

Shh! We're Writing the Constitution
por Jean Fritz. Putnam Juvenile, 1998.

How States Make Laws
por Suzanne LeVert. Marshall Cavendish, Inc., 2004.

¿Para aprender?

Su hijo va a comenzar a estudiar cómo las personas se gobiernan a sí mismas. En esta primera unidad, *Governing the People* (El gobierno y las personas), se estudiará n las siguientes preguntas clave:

- ¿Cómo los ciudadanos pueden ser responsables en sus comunidades?
- ¿De qué manera el gobierno ayuda a las personas?
- ¿Por qué necesitamos líderes?
- ¿Cómo funciona el gobierno de nuestro país?
- ¿Cuá les son las responsabilidades de nuestros gobiernos estatales y municipales?

Actividades para la casa

- Anime a su hijo a imaginarse que ambos son alcaldes de su comunidad. Hagan una lista de lo que les gustaría hacer para que su comunidad fuera un mejor lugar para vivir. Luego, ayude a su hijo a leer la lista a otros miembros de la familia y votar por lo que má s les guste. Quizá s quieran escribir una carta al verdadero alcalde sobre su idea.

- Hable con su hijo sobre el voto. Luego, tomen una decisión familiar, como qué cenar o qué hacer el fin de semana, y voten.

Relacione esta experiencia con la votación por los problemas de la comunidad y del estado, y la votación por el presidente de Estados Unidos.

- Hable con su hijo sobre los problemas y conflictos entre vecinos de su comunidad o entre comunidades cercanas. Comenten cómo ellos resolvieron sus problemas. ¿Ayudaron los funcionarios gubernamentales a resolver los problemas? ¿Se infringió alguna ley o se crearon nuevas leyes? Comparen estas situaciones con las diferentes formas en que los países tratan de resolver los problemas y conflictos.

Ideas para comentar

- ¿Por qué las personas necesitan gobiernos? ¿Qué sucedería si las personas no obedecieran las leyes que hace el gobierno?

- ¿Qué hacen los buenos ciudadanos? ¿Qué derechos y responsabilidades tienen los niños como ciudadanos? ¿Cómo podrías ayudar a los demá s en tu comunidad?

- ¿Qué cargo del gobierno crees que te gustaría tener? ¿Por qué? ¿Qué te gustaría hacer si te eligieran?

© Harcourt

Visite www.harcourtschool.com/ss1 para hallar más recursos en Internet.

School to Home

Newsletter

The World Around Us
💡 The Big Idea

The Land Maps help us learn about the different kinds of land, water, and places around us.

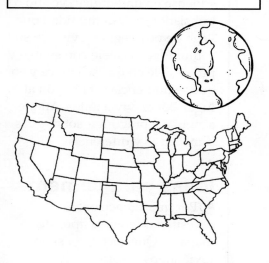

Books To Read

River Story
by Meredith Hooper. Candlewick Press, 2000.

Mountain Town
by Bonnie Geisert. Houghton Mifflin Company, 2000.

There's a Map in My Lap!: All About Maps
by Tish Rabe. Random House Children's, 2002.

What to Know

Your child is about to begin studying maps. In this second unit, The World Around Us, the following essential questions will be discussed:

■ How do maps help people find locations?

■ What countries and land-forms make up North America?

■ Why are seasons and climate different in different regions?

■ How are regions around the world different?

Home Activities

■ With your child, pretend that you are a river. Pantomime and talk about how the river looks, sounds, feels, and smells. Then take turns describing where your river starts, what it passes by, and where it ends. Tape-record or write about your imaginary journey, and share it with family members or your child's class at school.

■ Go to a library to look at a globe or a map of Earth with your child. Together, identify North America, the United States of America, bodies of water such as oceans, lakes, and major rivers, and at least two other countries. Make a list of everything your child finds on the globe or map.

■ Think of a family member, neighbor, or community worker who has come to live in your community from another region. Visit him or her with your child, and talk about how this region is alike and different from where this person lived before. Encourage your child to ask questions about these similarities and differences.

Ideas to Discuss

■ Why do people need different kinds of maps? What would happen if we did not have maps?

■ How are peninsulas different from islands? How are lakes different from rivers?

■ What is the climate like where you live? How does your climate affect how you live?

© Harcourt

GO ONLINE **For more resources, go to** www.harcourtschool.com/ss1

Carta para la casa

Boletín

El mundo que nos rodea

☼ La gran idea

La tierra Los mapas nos ayudan a aprender sobre los tipos de tierra, masas de agua y lugares que nos rodean.

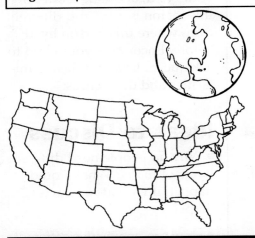

Libros

River Story
    por Meredith Hooper. Candlewick Press, 2000.

Mountain Town
    por Bonnie Geisert. Houghton Mifflin Company, 2000.

There's a Map in my Lap!: All About Maps
    por Tish Rabe. Random House Children's, 2002.

¿Para aprender?

Su hijo va a comenzar a estudiar los mapas. En esta segunda unidad, *The World Around Us* (El mundo que nos rodea), se estudiarán las siguientes preguntas clave:

■ ¿De qué manera ayudan los mapas a las personas a encontrar lugares?

■ ¿Qué países y accidentes geográficos forman América del Norte?

■ ¿Por qué las estaciones y el clima son diferentes en cada región?

■ ¿En qué se diferencian las regiones del mundo?

Actividades para la casa

■ Con su hijo, imagínense que son un río. Represéntenlo y comenten cómo se ve, suena, siente y huele el río. Luego, túrnense para describir dónde comienza, por dónde pasa y dónde termina. Escriban sobre su viaje imaginario o grábenlo y compártanlo con los miembros de su familia o con los compañeros de clase de su hijo.

■ Vaya con su hijo a una biblioteca para buscar un globo terráqueo o un mapa de la Tierra. Juntos, identifiquen América del Norte, Estados Unidos de América, las masas de agua, como los océanos, lagos y

ríos principales y, por lo menos, dos países más. Hagan una lista de todo lo que su hijo halle en el mapa o en el globo terráqueo.

■ Piense en un familiar, vecino o trabajador de la comunidad que llegó de otra región y vive en su comunidad. Visítelo con su hijo y pregúntele en qué se parece y en qué se diferencia esta región al lugar donde vivía antes. Anime a su hijo a preguntar sobre estas semejanzas y diferencias.

Ideas para comentar

■ ¿Por qué las personas necesitan diferentes tipos de mapas? ¿Qué sucedería si no tuviéramos mapas?

■ ¿En qué se diferencian las penínsulas de las islas? ¿En qué se diferencian los lagos de los ríos?

■ ¿Cómo es el clima en la región donde vives? ¿Cómo influye en tu vida el clima de tu región?

© Harcourt

Visite www.harcourtschool.com/ss1 **para hallar más recursos en Internet.**

School to Home

Newsletter

Using Our Resources

☼ **The Big Idea**

Resources People use the land and its resources to help them live.

Books To Read

Why Should I Save Energy? by Gen Green. Barron's Educational Series, Inc., 2005.

Supermarket by Kathleen Krull. Holiday House, Inc., 2001.

The Rusty, Trusty Tractor by Joy Cowley. Boyds Mills Press, 2000.

© Harcourt

What to Know

Your child is about to begin studying how people use the land and its resources. In this third unit, Using Our Resources, the following essential questions will be discussed:

■ What natural resources do people use? How do they use them?

■ What are some of the reasons people choose to live in a place?

■ How do people change their environment?

■ How have transportation and communication changed over time?

Home Activities

■ Have your child choose an item that can be recycled, such as a milk carton, can, or bottle. Together, turn it into something "new." For example, make a pencil holder from a can or a bird feeder from a milk jug. Invite your child to decorate the item. Then talk together about how to use recycled items to make simple gifts.

■ Play a search and match game with your child at the grocery store. Choose a farm crop item that is in its natural or original form, such as an apple or a bouquet of flowers. Then challenge your child to find processed and packaged products that include this item. You might locate a can of apple pie filling or a jar of apple-sauce, or some skin lotions that are flower scented.

■ Look around your house with your child for technology that family members use to make life easier. Talk about how it is used, who uses it, and if it really does make it easier or faster to do something. You might talk about a new electronic toy or a microwave or a digital watch. Encourage your child to think of new machines or tools that he or she would like to invent to improve life at home.

Ideas to Discuss

■ In what ways are natural resources important to us?

■ How can we care for our natural resources? What can we do at home?

■ How do new tools and machines help us? Does new technology always make our lives easier?

GO ONLINE

For more resources, go to <u>www.harcourtschool.com/ss1</u>

Carta para la casa

Usamos nuestros recursos

 La gran idea

Recursos Las personas usan la tierra y sus recursos para vivir.

Libros

Why Should I Save Energy?
por Gen Green. Barron's Educational Series, Inc., 2005.

Supermarket
por Kathleen Krull. Holiday House, Inc., 2001.

The Rusty, Trusty Tractor
por Joy Cowley. Boyds Mills Press, 2000.

¿Para aprender?

Su hijo va a comenzar a estudiar cómo las personas usan la tierra y sus recursos. En esta tercera unidad, *Using Our Resources* (Usamos nuestros recursos), se estudiarán las siguientes preguntas clave:

- ¿Qué recursos naturales usan las personas? ¿De qué manera los usan?

- ¿Por qué las personas eligen vivir en un lugar determinado?

- ¿De qué manera las personas cambian su medio ambiente?

- ¿Qué cambios se han producido en las comunicaciones y en los medios de transporte a través del tiempo?

Actividades para la casa

- Deje que su hijo elija un objeto que se pueda reciclar, como un cartón de leche, una lata o una botella. Juntos, conviértanlo en algo "nuevo". Por ejemplo, hagan un portalápices con una lata o un comedero de pájaros con un pote de leche. Anime a su hijo a decorar el objeto. Luego, comenten cómo usar los objetos que se reciclan para hacer regalos sencillos.

- En el supermercado, juegue con su hijo a un juego de buscar y emparejar. Elijan un producto que se cultive en una granja y que esté en su estado original o natural, como una manzana o un ramo de flores. Luego, anime a su hijo a hallar productos procesados y empacados que incluyan este producto. Quizás puedan encontrar una lata de relleno para tarta de manzana o un frasco de compota de manzana, o lociones para la piel con fragancia de flores.

- Con su hijo, busquen en su casa la tecnología que usan miembros de la familia para facilitar sus vidas. Comenten cómo se usa, quiénes la usan y si en realidad facilita o agiliza una tarea. Quizás quiera hablar sobre un nuevo juguete electrónico, un horno microondas o un reloj digital. Anime a su hijo a pensar en nuevas maquinarias o herramientas que le gustaría inventar para mejorar la vida en el hogar.

Ideas para comentar

- ¿De qué manera son importantes los recursos naturales para nosotros?

- ¿De qué manera podemos cuidar de los recursos naturales? ¿Qué podemos hacer en nuestra casa?

- ¿Cómo nos ayudan las herramientas y maquinarias nuevas? ¿La nueva tecnología nos facilita nuestras vidas siempre?

© Harcourt

 Visite www.harcourtschool.com/ss1 **para hallar más recursos en Internet.**

School to Home

People Long Ago
☀ The Big Idea

History History is the story of how people and places change over time.

Books To Read

Happy Birthday, America
  by Mary Pope Osborne.
  Roaring Brook Press, 2005.

What Was It Like Before Electricity?
  by Paul Bennett. Steck-Vaughn, 1995.

When Lightning Comes in a Jar
  by Patricia Polacco.
  Philomel, 2002.

© Harcourt

What to Know

Your child is about to begin studying people in the past and present. In this fourth unit, People Long Ago, the following essential questions will be discussed:

■ How do people and places change over time?

■ What do we know about the people who lived in North America long ago?

■ How did our country get its independence?

■ How do we honor our American heritage?

■ How do we honor people and events in our country's history?

Home Activities

■ Share your family history with your child by looking at photographs and family heirlooms. Discuss customs, beliefs, and traditions that have been passed down in your family. Visit the library or use the Internet to research the country or countries your ancestors came from.

■ With your child, create a time line of historical events in your family, such as births, graduations, and holiday celebrations. Your child might like to illustrate some of the events on the time line. Have him or her put the pictures in the correct order and then tell family members about each event.

Ideas to Discuss

■ What are some ways people learn about their past?

■ How does knowing about the past help our family today?

■ Why do you think it is important for grandparents to pass down their family history to their children and grandchildren?

Carta para la casa

Las personas del pasado

 La gran idea

Historia La historia es el relato de cómo las personas y los lugares cambian con el tiempo.

Libros

Happy Birthday America
   por Mary Pope Osborne.
   Roaring Brook Press, 2005.

What Was It Like Before Electricity?
   por Paul Bennett. Steck-Vaughn, 1995.

When Lightning Comes in a Jar
   por Patricia Polacco.
   Philomel, 2002.

¿Para aprender?

Su hijo va a comenzar a estudiar los pueblos del pasado y del presente. En esta cuarta unidad, *People Long Ago* (Las personas del pasado), se estudiarán las siguientes preguntas clave:

- ¿Cómo han cambiado las personas y los lugares a través del tiempo?
- ¿Qué sabemos acerca de las personas que vivieron en América del Norte hace mucho tiempo?
- ¿Cómo obtuvo nuestro país su independencia?
- ¿De qué manera honramos nuestra herencia norteamericana?
- ¿De qué maneras honramos a las personas y sucesos de nuestra historia?

Actividades para la casa

- Comparta la historia de su familia con su hijo observando fotografías y objetos antiguos de la familia. Comenten las costumbres, creencias y tradiciones que han pasado de generación en generación. Visiten la biblioteca o usen Internet para investigar el país o países del que provienen sus antepasados.

- Con su hijo, hagan una línea cronológica de sucesos históricos en su familia, como nacimientos, graduaciones y celebraciones de días festivos. Quizás su hijo quiera dibujar algunos de los sucesos. Pídale que coloque los dibujos en el orden correcto y que luego cuente a sus familiares cada suceso.

Ideas para comentar

- ¿Cuáles son algunas maneras en que las personas aprenden sobre su pasado?

- ¿Cómo el conocer nuestro pasado ayuda a nuestra familia hoy en día?

- ¿Por qué creen que es importante que los abuelos pasen sus tradiciones a sus hijos y a sus nietos?

© Harcourt

Visite www.harcourtschool.com/ss1 **para hallar más recursos en Internet.**

School to Home

A World of Many People

☀ The Big Idea

Culture Our country is made up of many different people and cultures.

Books To Read

We All Sing with the Same Voice
by J. Philip Miller and Sheppard M. Green. HarperCollins, 2005.

Zora Hurston and the Chinaberry Tree
by William Miller. Lee & Low Books, 1996.

Lord of the Cranes
by Kerstin Chen. North-South, 2002.

What to Know

Your child is about to begin studying people and their cultures. In this fifth unit, A World of Many People, the following essential questions will be discussed:

- What is culture?
- Why is the United States a country of many cultures?
- How are families different? How are they alike?
- Who are some Americans who have made a difference in our lives?

Home Activities

- Take your child to the grocery store. Spend some time in the aisle where ethnic foods are displayed, and talk about the countries where these foods are popular. Let your child choose an inexpensive food item to try at home. As you prepare and eat the food together, talk about how it is the same as or different from foods your child likes.

- Check in your local library or newspaper about upcoming celebrations that honor other cultures. Choose one and plan to attend it with your child. Later, have your child draw some of the images he or she remembers from the celebration.

- Look at this month's calendar with your child. Take turns asking each other questions about the information on the calendar. For example, *Which month does the calendar show? How many days are in this month? What is today's date?*

Ideas to Discuss

- What basic needs do all people have, no matter where they live?

- What are some ways people learn about their culture?

- Why would a person from another country want to come to the United States to live?

For more resources, go to www.harcourtschool.com/ss1

© Harcourt

Carta para la casa

Boletín

Un mundo de muchas personas

 La gran idea

Cultura Nuestro país está formado por muchas personas y culturas diferentes.

Libros

We All Sing with the Same Voice
por J. Philip Miller and Sheppard M. Green. HarperCollins, 2005.

Zora Hurston and the Chinaberry Tree
por William Miller. Lee & Low Books, 1996.

Lord of the Cranes
por Kerstin Chen. North-South, 2002.

¿Para aprender?

Su hijo va a comenzar a estudiar los pueblos y sus culturas. En esta quinta unidad, *A World of Many People,* (Un mundo de muchas personas), se estudiarán las siguientes preguntas clave:

- ¿Qué es la cultura?
- ¿Por qué Estados Unidos es un país de muchas culturas?
- ¿En qué se diferencian las familias? ¿En qué se parecen?
- ¿Qué estadounidenses han dejado un impacto en nuestras vidas?

Actividades para la casa

■ Lleve a su hijo al supermercado. Pasen un rato en el pasillo donde se exhiben los alimentos étnicos y hablen de los países donde estos alimentos son populares. Deje que su hijo elija un alimento barato para probarlo en la casa. A medida que prepara el alimento y comen juntos, hablen de las semejanzas y diferencias entre ese alimento y los alimentos que le gustan a su hijo.

■ Investiguen en la biblioteca o en los periódicos locales cualquier celebración que esté por realizarse en la que se honren otras culturas. Elija una y planee asistir con su hijo. Después, pídale que dibuje algunas de las imágenes que recuerda de la celebración.

■ Con su hijo, observen el calendario de este mes. Túrnense preguntándose la información del calendario. Por ejemplo, *¿Qué mes muestra el calendario? ¿Cuántos días tiene el mes? ¿Qué fecha es hoy?*

Ideas para comentar

■ ¿Qué necesidades básicas tienen las personas sin importar dónde viven?

■ Cuáles son algunas de las maneras en que las personas aprenden sobre su cultura?

■ ¿Por qué una persona de otro país quisiera venir a América a vivir?

© Harcourt

 Visite www.harcourtschool.com/ss1 **para hallar más recursos en Internet.**

School to Home

People in the Marketplace

 The Big Idea

Work Producers and consumers depend on each other for goods and services.

Books To Read

Crackers
   by Becky Bloom. Orchard Books, 2001.

The Kids' Money Book
   by Jamie Kyle McGillian. Sterling Publishing Company, Incorporated, 2004.

Earning Money (Let's See, Economics)
   by Natalie M. Rosinsky. Compass Point Books, 2003.

© Harcourt

What to Know

Your child is about to begin studying how people work to earn and spend money and how your child is a part of our economy. In this sixth unit, People in the Marketplace, the following essential questions will be discussed:

- How do producers and consumers depend on each other?

- How do people get money to pay for goods and services?

- How do raw materials become products?

- Why do we make, sell, and buy more of some things than others?

- How does trade help people meet their needs?

Home Activities

- Take a walk with your child around your neighborhood or another part of your community. Together, list the shops and other businesses your family uses. Keep a list for a week of places in the neighborhood, such as the post office, the cleaners, or the market, that your family visits. Talk about the goods or services that your family purchases from each business.

- Help your child start saving money. The savings can be kept in a "piggy bank" or in an actual bank savings account. Suggest that your child choose something he or she wants to buy as a goal for saving.

- Gather three or four of your child's favorite items, such as clothing, food, and a toy. Invite your child to guess where each item was made. Then check labels, boxes, and tags to find out. If possible, locate the countries of origin on a map or a globe. Have your child make a list of the different places where the goods came from.

Ideas to Discuss

- What is the difference between goods and services?

- Many family members have jobs away from home. How are these jobs different from their jobs at home?

- What are some goods that are made in countries other than the United States?

GO ONLINE **For more resources, go to** www.harcourtschool.com/ss1

Carta para la casa

Boletín

Las personas en el mercado

 La gran idea

Trabajo Productores y consumidores dependen unos de otros para satisfacer la demanda de bienes y servicios.

Libros

Crackers
por Becky Bloom. Orchard Books, 2001.

The Kids' Money Book
por Jamie Kyle McGillian. Sterling Publishing Company, Incorporated, 2004.

Earning Money (Let's See, Economics)
por Natalie M. Rosinsky. Compass Point Books, 2003.

¿Para aprender?

Su hijo va a comenzar a estudiar cómo las personas trabajan para ganar y gastar el dinero, y cómo él forma parte de nuestra economía. En esta sexta unidad, *People in the Marketplace* (Las personas en el mercado), se estudiarán las siguientes preguntas clave:

- ¿De qué manera dependen unos de otros los productores y consumidores?

- ¿Cómo obtienen las personas el dinero para pagar por los bienes y servicios?

- ¿De qué manera la materia prima se convierte en producto?

- ¿Por qué fabricamos, vendemos y compramos algunos productos más que otros?

- ¿De qué manera el comercio ayuda a las personas a satisfacer sus necesidades?

Actividades para la casa

- Dé un paseo con su hijo por el vecindario u otra parte de su comunidad. Juntos, hagan una lista de las tiendas y otros negocios que use su familia. Durante una semana, anoten los lugares que visite su familia en su vecindario, como el correo, la tintorería o el supermercado. Hablen sobre los bienes que su familia compra o los servicios que usa en cada negocio.

- Ayude a su hijo a comenzar a ahorrar dinero. Los ahorros los puede poner en una alcancía o en una cuenta de ahorros bancaria. Sugiérale que elija algo que quisiera comprar como una meta para el ahorro.

- Junte tres o cuatro de los objetos favoritos de su hijo, como ropa, alimentos y un juguete. Anímelo a que adivine dónde se fabricó cada uno. Luego, revise los rótulos, las cajas y las etiquetas para descubrirlo. Si es posible, ubique en un mapa o en un globo terráqueo los países de origen. Pida a su hijo que haga una lista de los diferentes lugares de donde provienen los productos.

Ideas para comentar

- ¿Cuál es la diferencia entre bienes y servicios?

- Muchos miembros de la familia tienen trabajos lejos de la casa; ¿en qué se diferencian estos trabajos de los caseros?

- ¿Cuáles son algunos productos que se fabrican fuera de Estados Unidos?

© Harcourt

Visite <u>www.harcourtschool.com/ss1</u> **para hallar más recursos en Internet.**

Index

Bibliography
CONFIRMED AND CURRENT RESEARCH

HISTORY AND HISTORICAL THINKING LITERATURE

Ashby, R., Lee, P., and Dickinson, A. (1997). How Children Explain the Why of History: The Chata Research Project on Teaching History. *Social Education, 61* (1), 17–21.

Barton, K. (1996). Narrative Simplifications in Elementary Students' Historical Thinking. *Advances in Research on Teaching, 6,* 51–83.

Barton, K. (1997a). History—It Can Be Elementary: An Overview of Elementary Students' Understanding of History. *Social Education, 61* (1), 13–16.

Berson, M.J. (2004). "Digital Images: Capturing America's Past with the Technology of Today. *Social Education.* 68 (3).

Blake, D. W. (1981). Observing Children Learning History. *The History Teacher, 14,* 533–549.

Booth, M. (1980). A Modern World History Course and the Thinking of Adolescent Pupils. *Educational Review, 32,* 245–257.

Downey, M., and Levstik, L. (1991). Teaching and Learning History. In Shaver, J. P. (Ed.), *Handbook on Research in Social Studies Teaching and Learning.* New York: Macmillan.

Foster, S. (1999). Using Historical Empathy to Excite Students About the Study of History: Can You Empathize with Neville Chamberlain? *The Social Studies* (January/February), 18–24.

Garcia, J., and Michaelis, J. (2001). *Social Studies for Children: A Guide to Basic Instruction.* Needham Heights, MA: Allyn & Bacon.

Levstik, L. S., and Barton, K. C. (1997). *Doing History: Investigating with Children in Elementary and Middle Schools.* Mahwah, NJ: Lawrence Erlbaum Associates.

McDiarmid, G. W. (1994). Understanding History for Teaching: A Study of the Historical Understanding of Prospective Teachers. In Carretero, M., and Voss, J. F. (Eds.), *Cognitive and Instructional Processes in History and the Social Sciences,* 159–185. Hillsdale, NJ: Erlbaum.

National Center for History in the Schools (1996). *National History Standards.* Los Angeles.

National Council for the Social Studies (NCSS) (1994). *Expectations of Excellence: Curriculum Standards for the Social Studies.* Washington, D.C.

National Council for the Social Studies (NCSS) (2004). *Powerful Teaching and Learning in the Social Studies* [online]. Available: http://www.ncss.org/standards/positions/powerful.html

Porter, P. H. (2005) Writing in the Content Areas: Warm-up, Build Muscle and Win the Championship. *Social Studies Review.* 44 (2).

Seixas, P. (1996). Conceptualizing the Growth of Historical Understanding. In Olson, D. R., and Torrance, N. (Eds.), *The Handbook of Education and Human Development: New Models of Learning, Teaching, and Schooling,* 765–783. Cambridge: Blackwell Publishers.

Seixas, P. (1997). Mapping the Terrain of Historical Significance. *Social Education, 61* (1), 22–27.

Seixas, P. (1998). Student Teachers Thinking Historically. *Theory and Research in Social Education, 26* (3), 310–341.

Symcox, L. (2002). *Whose History? The Struggle for National Standards in American Classrooms.* New York: Teachers College Press.

VanSledright, B. A. (1996). Closing the Gap Between School and Disciplinary History? *Advance in Research on Teaching, 6,* 257–289.

VanSledright, B. A. (2002). *In Search of America's Past: Learning to Read History in Elementary School.* New York: Teachers College Press.

Wilson, S., and Wineburg, S. S. (1988). Peering at History Through Different Lenses: The Role of Disciplinary Perspectives in Teaching History. *Teachers College Record, 89* (4), 525–539.

Wineburg, S. S. (1991a) On the Reading of Historical Texts: Notes on the Breach Between School and Academy. *American Educational Research Journal, 28* (3), 495–519.

Wineburg, S. S. (1991b). Historical Problem Solving: A Study of the Cognitive Process Used in the Evaluation of Documentary and Pictorial Evidence. *Journal of Educational Psychology, 83,* 73–87.

Yeager, E. A., and Davis, O. L., Jr. (1996). Classroom Teachers' Thinking About Historical Texts: An Exploratory Study. *Theory and Research in Social Education, 24,* 146–166.

Yeager, E. A., and Wilson, E. K. (1997). Teaching Historical Thinking in the Social Studies Methods Course: A Case Study. *The Social Studies,* May/June, 121–126.

Zarnowski, M. (2003). *History Makers: A Questioning Approach to Reading and Writing Biographies.* Portsmouth, NH: Heinemann.

Zinn, H. (1997). *A People's History of the United States.* New York: New Press.

INTEGRATION OF LITERATURE

Lamme, L. L. (1994). Stories from Our Past: Making History Come Alive for Children. *Social Education 58* (3), 159–164.

National Council for the Social Studies (NCSS) (2004). *Notable Trade Books for Young People* [online]. Available: http://www.socialstudies.org/resources/notable/

Porter, P. H. (1995). A Story Well Told: Children's Literature and the Social Studies. *Social Studies and the Young Learner* (November/December), 8 (2).

MULTICULTURAL APPROACHES

Parker, W. C. (2005). *Social Studies in Elementary Education* (12th ed.). Upper Saddle River, NJ: Pearson.

Rényi, J., and Lubeck, D. R. (1994). A Response to the NCSS Guidelines on Multicultural Education. *Social Education 58* (1), 4–6.

PRIMARY SOURCES

Barton, K. C. (1997). I Just Kinda Know: Elementary Students' Ideas About Historical Evidence. *Theory and Research in Social Education, 25* (4), 407–430.

Trofanenko, B. (2002). Images of History in Middle-Grade Social Studies Trade Books. *New Advocate, 15* (2), 129–132.

Wineburg, S. S. (2001). *Historical Thinking and Other Unnatural Acts: Charting the Future of Teaching the Past.* Philadelphia, PA: Temple University Press.

READING EXPOSITORY TEXT

Blachowicz, C., and Ogle, D. (2001). *Reading Comprehension: Strategies for Independent Learners.* New York: Guilford.

Dickson, S., Simmons, D., and Kameenii, E. (1996). *Text Organization and Its Relation to Reading Comprehension: A Synthesis of the Research.* Oregon: University of Oregon. [online]. Available: http://idea.uoregon.edu/~ncite/documents/techrep/tech17.html

Duke, N., and Bennett-Armistead, V. (2003). *Reading & Writing Informational Text in the Primary Grades: Research-Based Practices.* New York: Scholastic, Inc.

Farstrup, A., and Samuels, S. (Eds.), (2002). *What Research Has to Say About Reading Instruction.* Newark, NJ: International Reading Association.

SOCIAL PARTICIPATION

Sunal, C. S., and Haas, M. E. (2005). *Social Studies for the Elementary and Middle Grades: A Constructivist Approach* (2nd ed.). Boston, MA: Pearson.

Tornery-Purta, J., Schwille, J., and Amado, J. (1999). *Civic Education Across Countries: Twenty-Four National Case Studies from the IEA Civic Education Project.* Amsterdam, Netherlands: IEA.

SOCIAL STUDIES AND CROSS-CURRICULUM CONNECTIONS

Parker, W. C. (2005). *Social Studies in Elementary Education* (12th ed.). Upper Saddle River, NJ: Pearson.

USE OF GRAPHIC ORGANIZERS

Howard, J. (2001). Graphic Representations as Tools for Decision Making. *Social Education, 65* (4), 220–223.